To the mestizo and Indian people who struggle daily to improve the quality of life and social justice in our beloved, but long-suffering country of Mexico

—*Manuel Aguilar-Moreno*

On August 13th of 1521, heroically defended by Cuauhtemoc, the City of Tlatelolco fell in the hands of Hernán Cortés. It was not a triumph neither a defeat, but the painful birth of the Mexican people.

—*Memorial inscription in the Plaza of the
Three Cultures, Tlatelolco, Mexico City*

HANDBOOK
TO LIFE IN THE
AZTEC WORLD

MANUEL AGUILAR-MORENO

California State University, Los Angeles

OXFORD
UNIVERSITY PRESS

OXFORD

UNIVERSITY PRESS

Oxford University Press, Inc., publishes works that further
Oxford University's objective of excellence
in research, scholarship, and education.

Oxford New York
Auckland Cape Town Dar es Salaam Hong Kong Karachi
Kuala Lumpur Madrid Melbourne Mexico City Nairobi
New Delhi Shanghai Taipei Toronto

With offices in
Argentina Austria Brazil Chile Czech Republic France Greece
Guatemala Hungary Italy Japan Poland Portugal Singapore
South Korea Switzerland Thailand Turkey Ukraine Vietnam

First published by Facts On File, Inc., 2006

First issued as an Oxford University Press paperback, 2007
198 Madison Avenue, New York, NY 10016
www.oup.com

Oxford is a registered trademark of Oxford University Press

Library of Congress Cataloging-in-Publication Data
Aguilar-Moreno, Manuel.
Handbook to life in the Aztec world / Manuel Aguilar-Moreno.
p. cm.
Originally published: New York : Facts on File, 2006.
Includes bibliographical references and index.
ISBN 978-0-19-533083-0 (pbk.)
1. Aztecs—History. 2. Aztecs—Social life and customs.
3. Aztecs—Antiquities. 4. Mexico—Antiquities. I. Title.
F1219.73.A35 2007
972—dc22
2007004316

1 3 5 7 9 8 6 4 2
Printed in the United States of America
on acid-free paper

CONTENTS

LIST OF ILLUSTRATIONS

LIST OF MAPS

LIST OF TABLES

FOREWORD

This remarkable handbook by Manuel Aguilar-Moreno introduces us to a cultural awakening that we have been privileged to witness over the past two decades. Our knowledge of the Aztec civilization has changed dramatically. Once perceived as a ruthless "tribe" seemingly obsessed with bloodshed, the Aztec are now seen as no more or less brutal than any other imperial civilization in their efforts to "bring the war home." Every time I look upon the famous colossal monument known as the Aztec Calendar, I try to imagine what the rituals following Aztec military campaigns must have been like and how the thousands of people who participated in these events reassured themselves that their investment in supplying food, making weapons and equipment, and committing the lives of their children would grant them the benefits of conquest that their emperors had guaranteed.

All over the world, at different points in time, heads of state have had to devise astounding dramas and public spectacles to foster public trust in their military policies. We are fascinated by Roman triumphs, yet although their victories were more important for ambitious politicians than the battlefields where the fighting took place, we conveniently forget or ignore that those who marched in captivity to celebrate the glory were condemned to brutal deaths by the thousands in the Coliseum. The Aztec were no different. Warfare, sacrifice, and the promotion of agricultural fertility were inextricably linked

to religious ideology. Aztec songs and stories describe four great ages of the past, each destroyed by some catastrophe wrought by vengeful gods. The fifth and present world only came into being through the self-sacrifice of a hero who was transformed into the Sun. But the Sun refused to move across the sky without a gift from humankind to equal his own sacrifice. War was thereby waged to feed the Sun his holy food and therefore perpetuate life on Earth. The Aztec used no term like *human sacrifice*. For them it was *nextlaualli*, the sacred debt payment to the gods. For the soldiers, participation in these rituals was a means of publicly displaying their prowess, gaining rewards from the emperor's own hand, and announcing their promotion in society. But these executions worked just effectively as a grim reminder for foreign dignitaries, lest they ever consider war against the empire.

Even the name *Aztec* is debated by scholars. The word is not really indigenous, though it does have a cultural basis. It was first proposed by a European, the explorer-naturalist Alexander von Humboldt and later popularized by William H. Prescott in his 1843 publication *The History of the Conquest of Mexico*. *Aztec* is simply an eponym derived from *Aztlan*, meaning "place of the white heron," a legendary homeland of seven desert tribes collectively called Chichimecs who miraculously emerged from caves located at the heart of a sacred mountain far to the north of the Valley of Mexico. They enjoyed a peaceful existence hunting and fishing until they were divinely inspired to fulfill a destiny of conquest by their gods. They journeyed until one day they witnessed a tree being ripped asunder by a bolt of lightning. The seventh and last tribe to emerge from the mountain, the Mexica, took the event as a sign that they were to divide and follow their own destiny. They continued to wander for many more years, sometimes hunting and sometimes settling down to farm, but never remaining in any one place for very long. After the collapse of Tula, the capital of a Toltec state that dominated central Mexico from the ninth to the 13th centuries, they decided to move south to Lake Tetzcoco (Texcoco).

Impoverished and without allies, the Mexica were soon subjected to attacks by local Toltec warlords, who forced them to retreat to an island where they witnessed a miraculous vision of prophecy: an eagle perched on a cactus growing from solid rock. It was the long-awaited sign for Tenochtitlan, their final destination. Having little to offer other than their reputation as fearsome warriors, the Mexica had no other choice than to hire themselves out as mercenaries to rival Toltec factions. Eventually they were able to affect the balance of power in the region to such a degree that they were granted royal marriages. The Mexica, now the most powerful of the seven original Aztec tribes, incorporated their former rivals, and together they conquered an empire. Eventually they gave their name to the nation of Mexico, while their city of Tenochtitlan became what we know today as Mexico City. Historians still apply the term *Aztec* to the archaeological culture that dominated the Basin of Mexico but recognize that the people themselves were highly diversified ethnically.

Tenochtitlan was officially founded in 1325, but it would be more than a century before the city rose to its height as an imperial capital. Between 1372 and 1428 three successive Mexica emperors—Acamapichtli, Huitzilihuitl, and Chimalpopoca—served as the vassals of a despotic Tepanec lord named Tezozomoc of Azcapotzalco. Sharing in the spoils of victory, they each succeeded in expanding the Mexica domain south and east along the lake. However, when Tezozomoc died in 1427, his son Maxtla seized power and had Chimalpopoca assassinated. The Mexica quickly appointed Chimalpopoca's uncle, a war captain named Itzcoatl, as

tlatoani, or ruler. Itzcoatl allied himself with Nezahualcoyotl, the deposed heir to the throne of Tetzcoco, the Acolhua kingdom lying on the eastern shore of the lake. Together the two kings attacked Azcapotzalco. The siege lasted more than 100 days and only concluded when Maxtla relinquished his throne and retreated into exile. Itzcoatl and Nezahualcoyotl then rewarded the Tepanec lords who had aided them in overthrowing the tyrant. The three cities of Tenochtitlan, Tetzcoco, and Tlacopan formed the Triple Alliance and the Aztec Empire.

Itzcoatl died in 1440 and was succeeded by his nephew Motecuhzoma Ilhuicamina. Motecuhzoma I, as he was later known, charted the course for Aztec expansionism for the remainder of the 15th century; he was succeeded by his son Axayacatl in 1468. As a prince, Axayacatl had proven himself a capable military commander, and now he sought to capitalize on the conquests of his illustrious father by surrounding entirely the kingdom of Tlaxcala to the east and expanding imperial control over the Mixtecs and Zapotecs of Oaxaca to the south. By 1481, Axayacatl had died. He was succeeded by Tizoc, who ruled briefly but ineffectually. In 1486, the throne passed to Tizoc's younger brother, Ahuitzotl, who proved himself to be an outstanding military commander. Ahuitzotl reorganized the army and soon regained much of the territory lost under the previous administration. He then initiated a program of long-distance campaigning on an unprecedented scale. The empire reached its apogee under Ahuitzotl, dominating possibly as many as 25 million people throughout the Mexican highlands. Ahuitzotl in turn was succeeded by the doomed Motecuhzoma II, who suffered the Spanish invasion under Hernán Cortés.

In 1519, a band of 250 Spanish adventurers stood above Lake Tetzcoco and gazed upon Tenochtitlan. The Spaniards were dumbfounded, and many of the soldiers wondered if what they were looking upon wasn't a dream. The more worldly veterans of Italian wars compared the city to Venice but were no less astonished to find such a metropolis on the other side of the world. At the invitation of the emperor Motecuhzoma, Cortés led his men across the great Tlalpan causeway into Tenochtitlan. He later described much of what he saw in his letters to the Holy Roman Emperor, Charles V. Cortés marveled at the broad boulevards and canals, the temples dedicated to countless gods, as well as the magnificent residences of the lords and priests who resided with the emperor and attended his court. There was a central market where thousands of people sold everything from gold, silver, gems, shells, and feathers to unhewn stone, adobe bricks, and timber. Each street was devoted to a particular commodity, from clay pottery to dyed textiles, and a special court of judges enforced strict rules of transaction. All manner of foods were bartered: dogs, rabbits, deer, turkeys, quail, and every sort of vegetable and fruit.

Although Tenochtitlan was founded on a small island located off the western shore of Lake Tetzcoco, the landmass was artificially expanded to cover more than five square miles. The city was divided into four districts. Each district was composed of neighborhood wards of land-owning families called *calpulli*, an Aztec term meaning "house groups." Most of the *calpulli* were inhabited by farmers who cultivated bountiful crops of corn, beans, and squash with an ingenious system of raised fields called *chinampas*, while others were occupied by skilled craftspeople. Six major canals ran through the metropolis with many smaller canals that crisscrossed the entire city allowing one to travel virtually anywhere by boat, the principal means of economic transportation to the island. Scholars estimate that between 200,000 and 250,000 people lived in Tenochtitlan in 1500, more than four times the population of London at that time.

There were also three major causeways that ran from the mainland into the city. These were spanned with drawbridges that when taken up, sealed off the city. Freshwater was transported by a system of aqueducts of which the main construction ran from a spring on a mountain called Chapultepec on a promontory to the west. Even though the four districts had temples dedicated to the principal Aztec gods, all were overshadowed by the Great Temple, a human-made mountain constructed within the central precinct and topped by dual shrines dedicated to the Toltec storm god Tlaloc and the Chichimec war god Huitzilopochtli. The surrounding precinct itself was a city within a city, consisting of more than 1,200 square meters (nearly 4,000 square feet) of temples, public buildings, palaces, and plazas enclosed by a defensive bastion called the *coatepantli*, or "serpent wall," so named after the scores of carved stone snake heads that ornamented its exterior.

After the complete destruction of the pre-Columbian city during the siege of 1521, all knowledge of Tenochtitlan's central religious precinct remained largely conjectural. The belief that the Great Temple might lie below Mexico City's Zócalo (central square) was seemingly confirmed in 1790 with the unearthing of the monolithic sculptures known as the Aztec Calendar (or Sun Stone) and the statue of Coatlicue, the legendary mother of Huitzilopochtli. Colonial writings and diagrams appeared to indicate that the base of the Great Temple was approximately 300 feet square with four to five stepped levels rising to as much as 180 feet in height. Staircases were constructed on the west side that ended before two shrines constructed at the summit. However, it would be only systematic archaeological excavation that could either confirm or deny what the Spanish invaders had actually witnessed.

On February 21, 1978, Mexico City electrical workers were excavating a trench six feet below street level to the northwest of the main cathedral when they encountered a monolithic carved stone block. Archaeologists were immediately called to the scene to salvage what turned out to be an 11-foot stone disk carved with a relief in human form. Recognizing the golden bells on the figure's cheeks, salvage archaeologists identified the image as a goddess known as Coyolxauhqui, or She Who Is Adorned with Bells. According to a legend recorded by the colonial Spanish friar and ethnographer Bernardino de Sahagún, there once lived an old woman named Coatlicue, or Lady Serpent Skirt, together with her daughter, Coyolxauhqui, and her 400 sons at Coatepec, meaning "snake mountain." One day as Coatlicue was attending to her chores, she gathered up a mysterious ball of feathers and placed them in the sash of her belt. Miraculously, she found herself with child, but when Coyolxauhqui saw what had happened to her mother, she was enraged and shrieked, "My brothers, she has dishonored us! Who is the cause of what is in her womb? We must kill this wicked one who is with child!"

Coatlicue was frightened, but Huitzilopochtli, who was in her womb, called to her, "Have no fear, mother, for I know what to do." The 400 sons went forth. Each wielded his weapon, and Coyolxauhqui led them. At last they scaled the heights of Coatepec.

At this point there are many variations to the story, but it appears that when Coyolxauhqui and her 400 brothers reached the summit of Coatepec, they immediately killed Coatlicue. Then Huitzilopochtli was born in full array with his shield and spear-thrower. At once he pierced Coyolxauhqui with a spear and then struck off her head. Her body twisted and turned as it fell to the ground below Snake Mountain. Huitzilopochtli next took on the 400 brothers in equal measure and slew each of them in kind.

Careful examination of the Coyolxauhqui stone led the director of excavations of Mexico's National Institute of Anthropology and History (INAH), Eduardo Matos Moctezuma, to conclude that the monument was "in situ," meaning it had never been seen by the Spaniards much less smashed and reburied like so many other carvings. Remembering that Coyolxauhqui's body was said to have come to rest at the foot of the mountain, the archaeologists began to surmise that Coatepec, which is to say its incarnation as the Great Temple itself, might be located very nearby. It was not long before the archaeologists discovered parts of a grand staircase and then the massive stone serpent heads, literally signifying Coatepec, surrounding the base of the pyramid itself. The Great Temple had been found by decoding a 1,000-year-old legend.

Since 1978 the INAH has carried out nearly continuous excavations, uncovering no less than six separate building episodes of the Great Temple as well as numerous smaller temples and palaces of the surrounding precinct. Excavations carried out by Leonardo López Luján and his associates have unearthed more than 120 caches of priceless objects buried as offerings from vassal states within the matrix of the Great Temple itself. Extending excavation north to the point of even tunneling under Mexico City streets, archaeologists have found an incredible new structure called the House of the Eagles, named for stone and ceramic statuary portraying the heraldic raptor. This latest discovery has yielded even greater art treasures. Perhaps the most dramatic finds are the frightening life-size images that Mexican archaeologists identify as Mictlante-cuhtli, god of the underworld. López Luján and his associates have noted the appearance of similar figures in codices where they are being drenched in

offerings of blood. Applying new archaeometric techniques to identify microscopic traces of organic material, the archaeologists detected extremely high concentrations of albumin and other substances pertaining to blood on the floors surrounding the pedestals on which the statues once stood, further testament to the historical veracity of the ancient pictographic narratives. One of the most remarkable finds has been the recent recovery of a stone box that had been hermetically sealed with a layer of plaster. Inside were found the remains of an entire wardrobe, headdress, and mask for a priest of the temple of Tlaloc, the ancient Toltec god of rain and fertility whose shrine stood next to that of Huitzilopochtli at the summit of the Great Temple pyramid. Despite the lavish depictions of Aztec ritual clothing in the codices, none had ever been known to survive the fires of Spanish evangelistic fervor—until now. The discovery provided our first glimpse at the perishable artifacts for which Aztec pomp and ceremony was so famous.

The most dramatic changes to our perception of the Aztec have come with a critical reappraisal of the histories of the conquest itself. Spanish accounts traditionally portrayed the defeat of the Aztec Empire as a brilliant military achievement with Cortés's vastly outnumbered but better-armed troops defeating hordes of superstitious savages; however the reality of the events is far more complex and much more fascinating. During the first year and a half of the conflict, the Spaniards rarely numbered more than 300 and frequently campaigned with fewer than 150. Their steel weapons may have had an impact initially, but they soon ran out of gunpowder and by 1520 had eaten their horses. So what really accounted for their incredible achievement? The fact is that the Spaniards owed their success not so much to superior arms, training, and leadership as to Aztec political factionalism and disease.

Deconstructing the myth of the conquest, scholars have now demonstrated that in nearly all their battles, the Spaniards were fighting together with Indian allied armies numbering in the tens of thousands. Initially these troops were drawn from disaffected states lying to the east and west of the Basin of Mexico, especially Tlaxcala, but by 1521 even the Acolhua of Tetzcoco, cofounders with the Mexica of the empire, had appointed a new government that clearly saw greater opportunity in the defeat of their former allies. To what extent the Spaniards were conscious of strategy in coalition building and to what extent they were actually being manipulated by Indian politicians is unknown. Further aiding the Spanish conquest was disease. Prior to the arrival of the Europeans, smallpox and typhus were unknown in Mexico, and there was no understanding by either the Europeans or the Indians that disease was caused by contagious viruses. Before long, however, successive epidemics raged through the Indian population, each time taking away as many as 25, 50, and sometimes even 75 percent of the inhabitants of a city-state. By summer 1521, smallpox in particular created a situation that allowed Cortés to assume the role of a kind of "king-maker," appointing new governments among his allies, as the leaders of the old regimes loyal to the Mexica succumbed. On August 13, 1521, Cortés defeated Tenochtitlan at the head of an allied Indian army estimated by some historians at between 150,000 and 200,000 men, but only after what historians consider to be the longest continuous battle ever waged in the annals of military history.

—John M. D. Pohl, Ph.D.
Peter Jay Sharp Curator
and Lecturer in the
Art of the Ancient Americas
Princeton University

ACKNOWLEDGMENTS

I would like to extend special thanks to the many people who with their unconditional support made it possible for me to author this work. First, I want to thank my graduate students and research assistants at California State University, Los Angeles. I can truly say that without their help this project would not have been possible. They are Catherine Girod, Itzcoatl Xochipilli (†), Alejandro Castilla, Steven Trujillo, Annelys Pérez, Laura Odermatt, Dania Herrera, Gabriela Torres, Cindy Urrutia, María Ramos, Gabriel Vázquez, Fonda Portales, Dianna Santillano, Shankari Patel, Ricardo García (CSU Fullerton), and Rubio González (CSU Fullerton).

I am grateful to Dr. John M. D. Pohl, curator and lecturer of pre-Columbian art at the Princeton University Museum, for honoring me with the meaningful foreword to this book. His continuous advice and friendship have been very important in the development of my academic career.

Special thanks to Fonda Portales, who with great energy, enthusiasm, and excellence undertook the titanic task of editing the whole manuscript. She was of critical help in maintaining my mental sanity.

A warm acknowledgment to Annelys Pérez, Dianna Santillano, Marcelle Davis, Sina Samart, Edna Ortiz-Flores, Luis Ramírez, and Cynthia MacMullin for their technical support and suggestions in some of the chapters.

My gratitude to Fernando González y González for his magnificent and artistic photographs of the Aztec sites and monuments. His important and valuable collaboration is a true act of faith and friendship, going back to childhood.

My appreciation to Fonda Portales, Lluvia Arras, María Ramos, Karla López, Richard D. Perry, Annelys Pérez, Marc Seahmer, and Mario Dávila for their excellent drawings that accompany this book.

Thanks to Dr. Kim Eherenman, Dr. Michael Smith, and Dr. Miguel León-Portilla for their translations to English of some Nahuatl Poems.

Special recognition to Claudia Schaab, Melissa Cullen-DuPont, Katy Barnhart, and the editorial staff of Facts On File for their enlightening support and orientation during the writing process of the book.

I want to thank the Instituto Nacional de Antropología e Historia and the Museo Nacional de Antropología for their support and availability with diverse aspects of this work.

I wish to thank my friends and colleagues Dr. Karl Butzer, Dr. Linda Schele (†), Dr. Soeren Wichman, Dr. Alfonso Lacadena, Dr. Karl Taube, Prof. Rhonda Taube, Dr. Michael Coe, Prof. Felipe Solís, Dr. Miguel León-Portilla, Dr. Henry B. Nicholson, Dr. Enrique Florescano, Dr. Alfredo López Austin, Dr. Leonardo López Luján, Dr. James Brady, Dr. Michael Smith, Dr. María Teresa Uriarte, Dr. John Bierhorst, Dr. Ross Hassig, Dr. Mary Ellen Miller, Dr. John Pohl, Dr. Nikolai Grübe, Prof. Otto Schöndube, Dr. Guillermo de la

† Deceased

Peña, Dr. Enrique Krauze, Dr. Magdiel Castillo, Dr. Mauricio Tenorio, Dr. Bill Fisher, Dr. Carlos Rincón, Dr. Blas Castellón, Dr. Jeffrey Parsons, Dr. William Sanders, Dr. Kirsten Tripplett, Prof. Juan Miró, Dr. Kent Reilly, Dr. Virginia Fields, Dr. Julia Guernsey-Kappelman, Dr. Bruce Love, Dr. Perla Petrich, Dr. Norberto González Crespo, Dr. Silvia Garza Tarazona, Dr. Willy Minkes, Dr. Sebastian Van Doesburg, Dr. Megan O'Neil, Prof. Susana Ramírez-Urrea, Dr. José María Muriá, Dr. Christopher Donnan, Dr. Richard Leventhal, Dr. Wendy Ashmore, Dr. Robert Sharer, Dr. Michael Blake, Dr. Michael Mathes, Dr. Davíd Carrasco, Dr. David Stuart, Dr. Stephen Houston, Dr. Michel Graulich, Dr. Carlos Vélez-Ibáñez, Dr. Rafael Moreno Villa, Prof. Edward Forde, Dr. Abbás Daneshvari, Drs. Marilyn and Giorgio Buccellati, Dr. Kim Eherenman, Dr. Iris Engstrand, Dr. Carl Jubran, Prof. Víctor Cuéllar, Prof. Rubén Arroyo, Dr. Denise Dupont, Dr. Carl Selkin, Dr. Eloise Quiñones-Keber, Dr. Eduardo Douglas, Eduardo Torres, Dr. Marc Zender, Dr. Luis Enrique Garay, Dr. Joaquín Moreno Villa, Dr. Héctor Moreno Villa, Dr. Juan Lozano, and Dr. Amado González Mendoza for sharing with me their knowledge, their avant-garde view of life, and their friendship.

To my parents, Manuel and Aurora; my siblings, Yoya, Nany, Ricardo, Luis, and Luz Elena; my young nephew Diego (Tlamatini); and my young niece Ana Sofía (Xochiquetzal), I thank you for your affection and support and for always believing in me.

Finally, I want to acknowledge my many former students at the Instituto de Ciencias and ITESO University in Guadalajara, Mexico; Saint Peter's Prep in Jersey City, New Jersey; University of Texas at Austin; University of San Diego, California; Semester at Sea program of the University of Pittsburgh; and California State University, Los Angeles, for sharing with me wonderful experiences and insights during the classes and the cultural trips throughout diverse parts of Mexico and the world.

INTRODUCTION

Proud of itself
is the city of Mexico-Tenochtitlan.
Here no one fears to die in war.
This is our glory.
This is Your Command,
oh Giver of Life!
Have this in mind, oh princes,
do not forget it.
Who would conquer Tenochtitlan?
Who could shake the foundation of heaven?

From *Cantares Mexicanos*,
a 16th-century collection of
Nahuatl poems

In 1507, when the Aztec celebrated once more their New Fire ceremony atop of the Hill of the Star, nobody could have imagined that their civilization would be destroyed just a few years later by the Spanish army that came from an outside world. The military clash brought steel blades against *maquahuitl* (wooden swords with obsidian blades), guns against arrows and spear-throwers (atlatls), iron helmets against feather headdresses. Palaces, pyramids, canals on the lakes, priests, kings, and sacred books—all were vanquished by the conquest. How was this possible?

Although the Aztec had numerical superiority over the Spaniards, the Spaniards possessed a technological superiority. In addition, throughout the course of the conflict, the European invaders gained thousands of indigenous allies who wanted to rid themselves of Aztec oppression. The Spaniards and Aztecs were not really fighting the same kind of war. The two groups fought with different weapons and had completely opposing concepts of war. The Aztec strategy was not to defeat enemies by ruining their cities or massacring their population. They took captives for sacrifices to their gods, and they benefited by exacting tribute from the dominated peoples. Their conception of war was rooted in rituals, conventions, negotiations, and rules. On the other hand, the Spaniards utilized the characteristics of total war: the ambush, the deceit, and the trickery. They approached their Aztec enemies with words of apparent peace and then suddenly attacked and massacred them. In battle, instead of taking captives, the Spanish killed as many warriors as they could. In the end, they annihilated the Aztec Empire, and without negotiations, they incorporated the defeated peoples into the Spanish Empire by destroying their gods and their beliefs, abolishing their political institutions, humiliating their authorities, and, finally, submitting the Aztec into slavery.

The Aztec were unable to decipher the mechanisms of the total warfare of the Spaniards, and the repressive policies that the Aztec had had with subjugated Indian groups proved to be fatal. The Tlaxcaltecas, Huexotzincas, Cholultecas, and their former allies the Tetzcocans allied with the Spaniards and created a formidable army that eventually succeeded in vanquishing the Aztecs. The warfare system brought by Spain to America, completely incomprehensible to the Aztec people, was a precedent of modern warfare: an efficient, atrocious, and destructive mechanism of systematic extermination, serving to obscure political and economic ambitions.

For the Prussian general Karl Von Clausewitz, war is the continuation of politics. War can also be considered as a window that reflects a civilization in its critical moments, when its most fundamental tendencies are visible. It is a moment when human beings show themselves nakedly and express all of the good or all of the evil that they are capable of creating. In this sense, the wartime behavior of and between the Spaniards and Aztecs during the conquest is powerfully revealing.

The Aztec civilization, the last of the Mesoamerican cultures that grew out of the achievements of its predecessors—the Olmec, Maya, Teotihuacanos, Zapotec, and Toltec—was still being isolated from the rest of the world and could not resist an attack from a force that came from the outside. It was a strange and tragic end, one that would be equivalent to the armies of today facing an invasion from outer space!

The objective of this book is to present to the modern reader an overview of the life and civilization of the Aztec. The first chapter of the book introduces the Mesoamerican cultures, offers a general glimpse of Aztec archaeology, and provides an account of the main historical primary sources. Chapter 2 presents the creations myths and the stories of the great migration of the Aztec, as well as a summary of the main events in their history. Chapter 3 deals with the Mesoamerican geography and the concept of sacred space in the Valley of Mexico. Chapter 4 elucidates several aspects of Aztec society and government, expounding on political and social hierarchies and institutions. Chapter 5 discusses warfare and its implications for Aztec society. Chapter 6 studies religion, cosmology, and mythology. Chapter 7 presents Aztec funerary beliefs and customs. Chapters 8, 9, and 10 each explore the creative endeavors of the Aztec people: Chapter 8 deals with the main artistic traditions, including stone sculpture and lapidary and feather work; chapter 9 covers the architecture of Tenochtitlan and other Aztec cities; and chapter 10 analyzes the diverse literary styles, the codices, and their writing system. Chapter 11 discusses the scientific innovations of the Aztec—mathematics, astronomy, and calendars. Chapter 12 reviews the diverse aspects of economy, industry, and trade, including descriptions of *chinampa* agriculture, the use of water, markets, and other elements of Aztec prosperity. Chapter 13 gives a glimpse into the daily life of the Aztec, elaborating on the roles of women, shamanism and medicine, education, games, attire, food, and music, among other aspects. And finally, chapter 14 presents the Spanish conquest and the transculturation process that eventually created the mestizo people of present-day Mexico and its Indian-Christian traditions.

The research for this book was based on primary sources written in the 16th century, both by Indians and Spaniards. Among the colonial sources consulted were the chronicles of the ladino Indian historians (individuals of mixed Indian and Spanish blood who were fully bilingual and bicultural), such as Hernando Alvarado Tezozomoc, Chimalpahin Quauhtlehuanitzin, Diego Muñoz Camargo, and Fernando de Alva Ixtlixochitl. Other sources studied were the works of the Spanish chroniclers, such as Hernán Cortés, Bernal Díaz del Castillo, Bernardino de Sahagún, Motolinia, Diego Durán, and Juan de Torquemada, among many others. The orthography used by these authors for the names of Aztec personages and sites has been utilized. In addition, a great amount of archaeological, anthropological, and art historical books written by modern scholars was consulted, and their investigations have been very beneficial for this present work.

It is important to make a clarification about the use of certain terms. The word *Aztec* refers to all those groups that migrated from Aztlan to the Valley of Mexico. One of those groups was the Mexica, who eventually would become the dominant culture in central Mexico. For this reason, some historians have used the name *Aztec* to refer to the Mexica, whereas other scholars, such as Alfredo López Austin, refuse to use the word *Aztec* in reference to the Mexica. In this work the word *Mexica* will be used for the inhabitants of the great city of Tenochtitlan, the creators of the so-called Aztec Empire. The word *Aztec* will be used as a generic name to refer to the group of cultures that inhabited the Valley of Mexico, such as the Tepanec of Tlacopan (Tacuba) and *Azcapotzalco*, the Acolhua of

Tetzcoco, the Chalca of Chalco, the Toltec of Colhuacan, and so on. It is possible that the term *Aztec* will, in some instances, include the Mexica people because it reflects a shared cosmovision and a common set of social and political practices. When a more precise term is needed, *Mexica* or *Mexica-Aztec* will be used to emphasize the reference to that particular people, as well as the general Aztec culture.

The objective in writing this book was to continue the search for an understanding of Aztec civilization and to discuss the main aspects of the culture in a format that would allow the reader to appreciate and admire the achievements of that long-gone, magnificent civilization. The Aztec historian Hernando Alvarado Tezozomoc wrote in the 16th century about keeping the historical memory of the Aztec people:

> Thus they have come to tell it *[history]*,
> thus they have come to record it in their
>   narration,
> and for us they have painted it in their codices,

the ancient men, the ancient women.
Thus in the future
never will it perish, never will it be forgotten,
always we will treasure it . . .
we who carry their blood and their color,
we will tell it, we will pass it on
to those who do not yet live, who are yet to be
    born,
the children of the Mexicans, the children of
    the Tenochcans (1975: 4–5).

Modern-day archaeologist Michael Smith asserts that the history of the Aztecs is fully alive and will not be forgotten (2003: 293). It lives in the painted codices, in the Spanish and Indian chronicles, in the ruins of Aztec houses and temples, in their impressive stone sculpture, and in the studies of scholars. But more important, the Aztec history lives in the Mexican people of today, those who live in the Valley of Mexico, and those who are proud to keep the symbol of the foundation of Tenochtitlan in their national flag.

GUIDE TO PRONUNCIATION AND SPELLING OF NAHUATL TERMS

The Nahuatl language, spoken among the Aztec and among many present-day indigenous groups, was phonetically transcribed in the Roman alphabet by Spaniards during the 16th century. Nahuatl words usually have the stress on the penultimate (second to last) syllable. In modern times, names of places or towns are often pronounced with the rules of Spanish language, even writing the stress mark on the last syllable, for example in *Tenochtitlán* and *Teotihuacán*. But in this book all words will follow the rules of the Nahuatl language, including such names of cities; therefore, they appear without the Spanish-accent mark and should be pronounced with the stress on the penultimate syllable: TenochTItlan and TeotiHUAcan.

VOWELS ARE PRONOUNCED AS IN SPANISH:

a	as "ah" in f*a*r	C*a*lmec*a*c
e	as "ay" in *a*ce	T*e*petl
i	as "ee" in d*ee*p	C*i*ntl*i*
o	as "oh" in t*o*te	Te*o*tl
u	as "oo" in r*u*le	T*u*la

CONSONANTS ARE PRONOUNCED AS IN ENGLISH *EXCEPT* FOR THE FOLLOWING:

x	as "sh" in *sh*ell	Me*x*ica, *X*ochimilco
z	as "s" in *s*uit	A*z*tec, A*z*capotzalco
hu	as "w" in *w*aste, *w*eed	*Hu*ehuetl, A*hu*itzotl
ll	as in fu*ll*y	O*ll*in, Ca*ll*i
que, qui	as "kay" or "kee" in *c*ase, *k*eep	*Que*tzalcoatl, tian*qui*ztli
cu	as "kw" in *qu*asar, *qu*ery	Coatli*cu*e, *Cu*icatl
tl	as in T*l*ingit	*tl*atoani, tecpa*tl*
tz	as in pre*tz*el	*tz*ompantli, *tz*itzimime

1

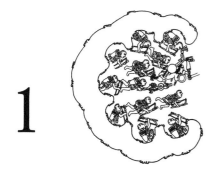

MESOAMERICAN CIVILIZATIONS AND AZTEC ARCHAEOLOGY

The archaeology of Mesoamerica has revealed a long and rich cultural history, from the small butchering sites of Upper Paleolithic hunter-gatherers to the large, well-populated city-states present at the time of European contact. Following is a synopsis of the cultural evolution of this area, as well as a brief history of the archaeological research about the Aztecs and a synopsis of the historical resources written by some of the first Spaniards to arrive in Mesoamerica. Although archaeology is often a science of deduction, the Aztec are well known through ethnographic data collected by the first Spaniards who encountered this highly advanced society, and several researchers have corroborated the archaeological and historical records.

The dates herein are approximations because different researchers have somewhat varying opinions (although the advent of radiocarbon dating in about 1950 has aided in producing chronologies that are more precise), and because continued research calls for the revision of former conclusions. The major periods—Preclassic, Classic, and Postclassic—are further reduced into separate phases and subphases. For the sake of brevity, some of these phases have only been touched upon, and others have been omitted. This synthesis includes only major known cultures of pre-Columbian Mesoamerica.

While some village sites dependent on seafood developed along the coast in the absence of agriculture, the development of agriculture led to small settlements showing the first manifestations of urbanization, which in turn led to large and powerful cities comparable to those in the Old World. Although cultural evolution is usually the result of a dominant society of higher complexity over one of lesser complexity, simple societies can develop into more complex societies in the absence of a highly complex society. Such was the case in Mesoamerica.

Mesoamerica saw the rise of four large and powerful unifying cultures before the Spanish conquest. These were the Olmec, the Teotihuacanos, the Toltec, and the Aztec. While the Maya never developed into an empire, their culture, which is still present today, reached a vast area. Each of these cultures was influential throughout Mesoamerica, not only in its own time but for centuries later.

THE AREA OF MESOAMERICA

Anthropologist Paul Kirchhoff first used the term *Mesoamerica* (Greek for "Middle America") to describe the constricted land area in Mexico and Central America with a shared cultural unity. The northern boundary of the area lies in central Mexico, at the southern edge of the Chihuahua desert; the area extends south and east to contain southern Mexico, including the Yucatán Peninsula, Guatemala, Belize, El Salvador, and parts of Honduras, Nicaragua, and the northern part of Costa Rica (see map 1).

The physical environment ranges from arid desert to hot and humid jungle. This diversity in climate results in a great variety of available food, both plants and animals, as well as a multiplicity of materials for building shelters, making cloth, and trading for exotic goods from other areas.

Temperatures vary considerably in Mesoamerica. The area north of the Tropic of Cancer has relatively hot summers and cold winters, whereas the area south of the Tropic of Cancer has less temperature variation. Rainfall also fluctuates greatly throughout the region. The northern reaches of Mesoamerica, at the southern end of the Chihuahua-Zacatecas Desert, may only get a few centimeters of rain per year, while the Gulf Coast area may get several meters. The rainy season typically lasts from May through October, September being the rainiest month. March usually produces the least amount of rainfall.

The shared cultural features of Mesoamerica were mostly confined to this particular area, although possible Mesoamerican influence can be seen in the U.S. Southwest at sites such as Snaketown in Arizona, as well as at Cahokia, in what is now East St. Louis. Common features throughout Mesoamerica included a calendar, hieroglyphic writing, books of bark paper and deer skin, knowledge of astronomy, a ball game played with a solid rubber ball on a special court, large markets with trade ports, the use of chocolate beans as money, human

CHRONOLOGICAL CHART OF MESOAMERICA

PERIODS & DATES			CENTRAL MEXICO	GULF COAST	OAXACA	WEST MEXICO	MAYA AREA
POSTCLASSIC	LATE	1521	Spanish Conquest 1519–1521				
			Aztec *Tenochtitlan* *Tlaxcala*	**Aztec** **Totonac** **Huastec**	**Mixtec** *Mitla* *Yagul*	**Tarascan**	*Tayasal (Itzá)* *Santa Rita* *Tulum* *Mixco Viejo* *Iximché* *Utatlan* *Mayapán*
	EARLY	1200	**Toltec** *Tula* **Chichimec**				**Toltec Maya** *Chichén Itzá*
CLASSIC	LATE	900	*Xochicalco* *Cacaxtla*		**Zapotec** *Monte Albán*		**Classic Maya** *Labná Uxmal* *Puuc & Central Yucatán* *Hochob Becan* *Yaxchilán* *Palenque* *Tikal* **Pacific Coast** *Cotzumalhuapa*
	EARLY	600	**Teotihuacan**	**Classic Veracruz** *Remojadas* *El Tajín* *Cerro de las Messas*		*Ixtlán del Río*	*Copán* *Dzibilchaltún* *Cerros* *Kaminaljuyú*
PRECLASSIC	LATE	200 C.E. B.C.E.	*Cuicuilco*	**Olmec** *Tres Zapotes*		*Teuchitlán* *Chupícuaro* *Colima*	*Escuintla* *Izapa* *Abaj Takalik*
	EARLY	300 700 1500	*Tlatilco*	*La Venta* *San Lorenzo*	**Danzantes Culture** *Dainzú*	*Xochipala* *Capacha*	*Ocos*

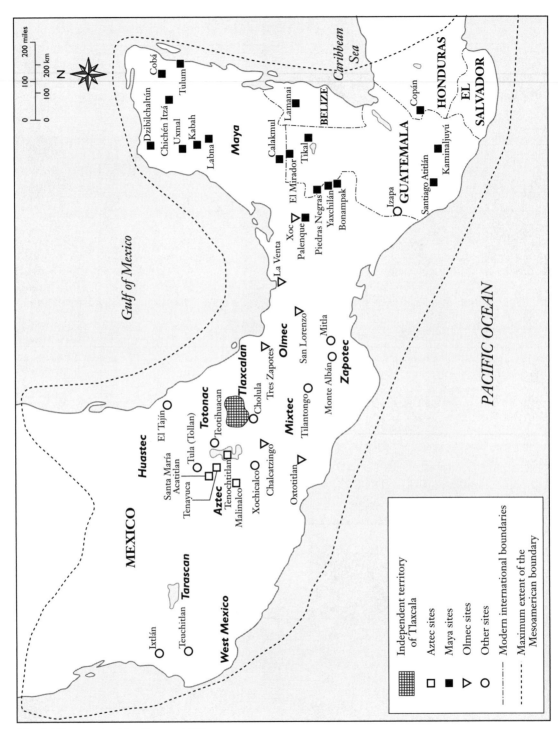

Map 1 Mesoamerica (after Pasztory 1983)

sacrifice, confession and penance by drawing blood, and a very complex pantheon.

THE PEOPLE OF MESOAMERICA

Prehistoric Period

During the Wisconsin Glaciation period at the end of the Pleistocene era (approximately 50,000 to 10,000 B.C.E.), the ocean waters were frozen into ice, lowering the sea level and exposing the Bering land bridge, a strip of land approximately 600 miles (1,000 km) wide that connected Siberia and Alaska. It is a widely held belief in anthropology that hunters on the Asian continent migrated to North America across this land bridge. The exact date of the migration and whether the migration occurred in one or several waves are still open to scientific debate because any archaeological sites located along the Pacific coast are now obscured beneath hundreds of feet of ocean water. What is known, however, is that these hunter-gatherers spread south across the North American continent, including what is now Mexico, eventually reaching Tierra del Fuego at the southern tip of South America. All of the human skeletal material recovered from this period indicates that these early hunters descended from the Mongolians of Asia and were ancestral to the American Indians. There is no evidence in North America of earlier hominid species, such as Neanderthals or *Homo erectus.*

HUNTER-GATHERERS

The earliest humans to occupy Mesoamerica were hunter-gatherers who lived in small bands that moved from place to place in search of food. These nomadic hunter-gatherers did not establish towns or villages during this period, but they often returned to favorite areas year after year. Although these people have been referred to as big-game hunters, anything that was edible was gathered and eaten.

Animal remains uncovered at habitation sites reveal that many different types of animals were exploited, including large animals such as mammoths and mastodons, as well as small animals, snails, snakes, and marine animals.

As the climate became warmer and drier in the early Holocene era (our current era, which started in approximately 10,000 B.C.E.), many large animal species, such as the mastodon, mammoth, horse, camel, giant bison, ground sloth, and dire wolf, became extinct, and large areas of the New World were transformed into deserts. Wild plant foods became a more important part of the hunter-gatherer diet as meat became more scarce.

The Archaic Period

THE AGE OF DOMESTICATION

The next period, known as the Archaic period, is referred to by scholars as the era of incipient cultivation, during which domesticated plant foods were still not as important as wild plants and animals. The term *domestication* can be defined as evolution directed by the interference of humans as opposed to evolution directed by natural selection. It refers to the human manipulation of planting seeds. Radiocarbon dating (also called carbon-14 or RC dating) shows that domestication of plants began in approximately 6000 B.C.E. At this time, humans realized that seeds could be planted in a cleared area and left to grow and that larger seeds would produce larger plants.

Although people still relied mostly on hunting and gathering, chili peppers, avocados and squash began to be cultivated. Archaeologist Richard Mac-Neish has estimated that approximately 5 percent of the diet came from cultivated plants during the Archaic period. Formal agriculture was still unknown, but plots of ground were cleared close to favored hunting and gathering areas, seeds were planted, and the gardens were left to grow with little or no tending. When the families or bands returned to the area on the seasonal round, the gardens were ready for reaping. This human interference resulted in slightly larger plants than those collected from the wild, an effort that maximized the crop's yield for a less demanding amount of work.

The domestication of plants in Mesoamerica led to semi-sedentary villages. Larger bands, consisting of several families, settled into these sites, and perhaps only separated and moved out to hunt and gather during the dry seasons. The few village sites found are larger than the campsites of the nomadic hunter-gatherers of the Glaciation period. This early agricultural period lasted from 5000 B.C.E. until 3400 B.C.E. Along with the crops previously mentioned, bottle gourds, crookneck squash, and beans began to be cultivated. The shift toward a domesticated agriculture necessitated more durable tools. True manos and metates (millstones used to grind maize and seeds) were developed during this period, as well as more delicate blades, end-scrapers, and choppers, used for cutting and chopping plant foods. As villages became established, the first evidence of complex burials appears.

RISING SETTLEMENTS

Some time around 3400 B.C.E., approaching the end of the Archaic period, permanent settlements began to appear, although caves were still used by hunters. Two bean varieties were added to the list of domesticated crops, and corn was greatly improved. Pumpkins may also have been domesticated during this period, and cotton was commonly harvested. Dogs became a favored food, and the earliest Mesoamerican dog remains are found in sites dating to this period. Storage pits allowed for a sedentary lifestyle; however, analysis of coprolite (fossilized excrement) has determined that the diet still consisted of about 70 percent wild plants and animals. Trapping or collecting small game animals such as foxes, skunks, turtles, lizards, and birds replaced the hunting of larger game such as deer and peccaries. As a result, the tool assemblage changed during this period, from large projectile points to snares, net bags, long obsidian blades, stone bowls, and oval metates.

The final stage of the Archaic period saw the introduction of crude pottery around 2300 B.C.E. The presence of pottery is one of the main indicators of a fully sedentary society, as a more reliable food supply would allow for some people to spend time on specialized crafts and more durable items

1.1 This model in Mexico City's Museum of Anthropology includes manos and metates, Aztec instruments to grind maize and seeds. (Fernando González y González)

could be utilized. During this period, agriculture accounted for 35 to 40 percent of a villager's diet. Although some people still lived nomadically, many lived in small pit-house villages.

Preclassic, or Formative, Period

The Preclassic period, also called the Formative period, saw yet another increase in sedentary villages, both in frequency and in size. As people became more capable of producing their own food, they could settle into one spot year-round. Both effective farming and the abundance of ceramics characterize the Preclassic phase. The beginning of the Preclassic period has been arbitrarily set at 1800 B.C.E., with the appearance of pottery in abundance. Although hunting, gathering, and fishing were still the primary economic activities, farming based on maize, beans, and squash had progressed to the point where permanent villages had sprung up throughout Mesoamerica. The more reliable food supply offered by farming resulted in a much larger population and a more sedentary lifestyle. Small permanent villages grew into large urban areas, with permanent housing, markets, and religious centers.

CHIAPA DE CORZO

One of the earliest known permanent settlements from the Preclassic period is found at Chiapa de Corzo, in the Grijalva Depression of Chiapas in southern Mexico. During the Middle Preclassic period, around 700 B.C.E., the planned architectural arrangements that later became common throughout Mesoamerica had begun. At this time, Chiapa de Corzo was the principal chiefdom in Chiapas and may have evolved into a kingdom by the Late Preclassic, when the palace was constructed and the temple was enlarged. The people of Chiapa de Corzo were primarily farmers and potters. Maize was processed on well-worn metates, and the pottery technique was advanced and sophisticated.

Rain cults developed during the Early Preclassic in areas as far north as the U.S. Southwest to the southern frontier of high culture in Central America. Uncontrollable weather patterns, such as droughts and floods, made the rain deity the oldest and most important in the pantheon. In Mesoamerica at this time, the rain deity was related to the cult of the jaguar in the tropical lowlands of Veracruz and Tabasco. The rain deity was called by different names in different parts of Mesoamerica and later came to be associated with other gods, such as agricultural deities and war deities.

The Middle Preclassic period witnessed a great increase in population and the establishment of permanent settlements. These large settlements show signs of being the first urban areas in the New World. Archaeologist Gordon Childe identified 10 criteria used to distinguish urban civilizations from simpler societies: large, dense settlements; territorially based states rather than kinship groups; capital wealth gathered from taxes and tribute; monumental public works; a class-stratified society; full-time craft specialists; long-distance trade of luxury items; representational art (including portraiture); writing; and a true or exact science. These criteria are all found at sites dating to the Preclassic period, as are innovations in land use and the control of water for irrigation. As competition for resources increased, as a growing population demanded more food supplies from land and water resources, society became more stratified. The physical environment of Mesoamerica favored certain areas that were ideal for the birth of a class-based society.

THE OLMEC

Childe's criteria are fully manifested in the coastal plains of the northern end of the Isthmus of Tehuantepec, in southern Veracruz, and adjacent Tabasco. The remains found in this area are Olmec, a culture named after a small, historically known people called the Olmeca who inhabited the area much later. The Preclassic discoveries are thought to represent the ancestors of this historical Olmeca group, or Olmeca-Xicallanca, and are therefore referred to as the "archaeological Olmecs" in an attempt to clarify the use of the same name for two different peoples who lived in the same area at different times. What these people actually called themselves is a mystery, as is where they came from. The Aztec spoke of an ancient government in a legendary land called Tamoanchan, located on the Gulf Coast. Tamoanchan is not a Nahuatl (the language of the Aztec) name, but rather comes from the Mayan language. Since the Olmec heartland is virtually surrounded by Mayan-speaking peoples, it has been hypothesized that the Olmec were also a Mayan-speaking people. However, recent linguistic research suggests that the Olmec spoke a form of the Mixe-Zoquean language, from which the Maya borrowed many of their words, especially for high-status items. Although the origins of the Olmec are unknown at this time, the Olmec contributions to Mesoamerican culture are significant, including a style of art that spread throughout Mesoamerica and perhaps the first great religious or ceremonial organization. For these contributions, their culture is referred to as the "Mother Culture of Mesoamerica."

San Lorenzo   San Lorenzo is the earliest known urban settlement in Mesoamerica. First excavated in 1945 by Matthew Stirling, San Lorenzo is located approximately 36 miles (60 kilometers) from the Gulf Coast along the Coatzacoalcos River in Veracruz and is believed to date from 1500 to 400 B.C.E., with its peak between 1150 and 900 B.C.E. It may have been the largest center of civilization in Preclassic Mesoamerica. The first three phases at San Lorenzo, dating from 1500 to 1150 B.C.E., are considered to be pre-Olmec. What began as a small farming village, part of the widespread early farming culture influenced by the Pacific Coast, later became the largest settlement of its time in Mesoamerica.

Modest construction began after 1350 B.C.E., but after 1250 B.C.E., the Olmec quarried basalt 42 miles (70 kilometers) away in the Tuxtla Mountains. They floated giant boulders of basalt out to sea and moved them up the Coatzacoalcos River on rafts. These basalt boulders were used in monumental carvings. During the earliest phase at San Lorenzo, ceramic items were also being produced. The ceramic complex known as the Olmec, characterized by small solid and large hollow figurines, appeared about 1150 B.C.E. The Olmec also made pots and dishes decorated with the simple motifs seen on larger sculptures.

During the Middle Preclassic period, large-scale architecture appeared at San Lorenzo in the form of a large, earth platform that rose above the fertile floodplains of the rivers to a height of about 150 feet (45 meters). The platform, located atop a natural plateau above the rivers and measuring 1,200 meters by 750 meters (3,960 feet by 2,475 feet), was constructed of fill brought up from below in baskets. Many mounds, rectangular courts, and pyramids were built on top of it. Although basalt boulders were imported for use in other monuments, none were used in erecting this monument. Rather the platform and the individual structures were built of locally available sedimentary rock, colored clay, and soil. This platform is thought to be the first large-scale modification of the physical environment in Mesoamerica and was apparently used for civic-religious functions rather than for agricultural use. This example of a public works project was among the first of what would develop into the Olmec culture. The amount of work required to build the plat-

form and to carve the massive monuments indicates that there was a stratified society in place, with a ruling class to direct the work of laborers belonging to lower classes.

The most famous archaeological finds related to the Olmec are the colossal heads, carved of imported basalt. Each represents a human head, with no elements of supernatural features, and they are thought to be portraits of Olmec rulers. These heads are as large as three meters (10 feet) in height and weigh as much as several tons. Each carving wears a helmet similar to that used in the ball game played throughout Mesoamerica and may indicate the origins of the game.

Although obsidian sourcing indicates a large long-distance trade network, the developments at San Lorenzo are considered to be indigenous to the area and not the result of external sources migrating into the area.

From 1150 to 900 B.C.E., changes occurred in the material culture. Stone monuments became more abundant, and more-complex iconographic motifs began to appear on ceramics. Ceramic figurines appeared in greater numbers and varieties, including those depicting ball players.

Sometime during the 11th century B.C.E., many of the stone monuments were deliberately destroyed, removed from their platform and then buried in the surrounding ravines. Why this occurred is unknown, but San Lorenzo was abandoned in approximately 1000 B.C.E. Scholars discuss two theories for the destruction of the stone monuments: One possibility suggests a foreign invasion, and the other proposes a ritual "killing" of the monuments to prevent their power from being usurped by enemies.

La Venta   Current data indicate that there was a power shift from San Lorenzo to La Venta after 900 B.C.E.; however, this is only a tenuous interpretation, as there is little data from other Olmec sites. La Venta, located on an island in a coastal swamp in the modern-day state of Tabasco, was originally thought to be a ceremonial center where people from outlying areas would meet for ritual celebrations or to market. However, further archaeological research conducted from 1985 to 1988 by Rebecca González Lauck and William Rust revealed a large cosmopolitan center with residential areas and an outlying

1.2 Olmec colossal head from San Lorenzo, Veracruz (Getty Images)

population occupying small "islands" on high land along the rivers.

The oldest known pyramid in North America is located at La Venta and is thought to be a representation of a volcanic cone in the Tuxtla Mountains, about 40 miles away. This earthen mound towers 32 meters (105.6 feet). Like the Olmec at San Lorenzo, the La Venta Olmec quarried basalt from the Tuxtla Mountains for use in their colossal heads and other sculptures. It was once thought that the Olmec revered those mountains as sacred and therefore built the pyramid as a monument dedicated to that place. Recent excavations at the site have revealed that the pyramid is actually rectangular with stepped sides and inset corners. Because pyramids often contain elaborate tombs, it is now thought that the structure at La Venta may be an extension of the ancient idea of the burial mound or monument. As this particular pyramid has yet to be excavated, it is still unknown whether this is the case.

Although La Venta suffered a violent end around 400–300 B.C.E., as shown by the destruction of many of its monuments, it remained a cult center. Offerings of Late Preclassic ceramics and a Spanish olive jar from the early colonial period were found at the site. Archaeologists Philip Drucker and Robert Heizer believe that offerings may have been made there in modern times.

Tres Zapotes and the Origins of Early Writing
Tres Zapotes lies about 96 miles (160 kilometers) northwest of La Venta, in the low hills above the basin formed by the Papaloapan and San Juan Rivers. It consists of approximately 50 earth mounds spread over a distance of roughly two miles (3.2 kilometers); there is little evidence to indicate a ranked hierarchy among the architectural groupings. While Tres Zapotes was occupied at the same time as La Venta, it reached its peak during the Late Preclassic period.

There is evidence, though weak, that associates the beginnings of writing in Mexico with the settlement at Tres Zapotes. This evidence consists of jade artifacts that are now in public and private collections. Because their provenance is unknown, they do not constitute conclusive evidence; however, they are carved in the Olmec style and are incised with hieroglyphs that appear to be ancestral to Mayan glyphs. This early Mesoamerican writing is associated with the calendar. Historical events such as births, marriages, conquests, and deaths are put into a chronological framework, and one of the main functions of this early writing appears to be the legitimization of ascension to the throne.

If writing indeed began at Tres Zapotes, it may have joined an early dating system. One of the oldest dated monuments in the New World was found at Tres Zapotes. Known as Stela C, it is a basalt monument with a were-jaguar (one of the important symbols of Olmec society) on one side and a Long Count date corresponding to September 3, 32 B.C.E., of the Gregorian calendar on the other. (The Long Count is a calendrical computation system, originally developed by the Maya that establishes a starting, or "Zero," date and from there counts the days elapsed.) Another artifact, a duck-billed winged figure with human features known as the Tuxtla Figurine, has a Long Count date corresponding to

March 14, 162 C.E. As both of these artifacts were found in the Olmec heartland, it is possible that it was the Olmec who invented the Long Count dating system and possibly developed the astronomical observations for which the Maya have been credited. However, another artifact with a Long Count date of December 8, 36 B.C.E., was found outside the Olmec heartland. As it predates Stela C by four years, it is still unknown exactly when and where the Long Count Calendar was developed.

The Origins of Mesoamerican Iconography: The Were-Jaguar and Other Animal Motifs While San Lorenzo, La Venta, and Tres Zapotes do not encompass the entire Olmec world, they are of great importance. The iconography associated with Mesoamerican religion is first found at these three sites.

One of the religious symbols found is the were-jaguar, a hybrid of jaguar and human. The Olmec apparently believed that in the distant past a woman cohabitated with a jaguar, and together they produced a line of were-jaguars who became the founding rulers of the Olmec civilization. These creatures are represented in Olmec art with features such as a plump infant would have, except that they also possess snarling mouths, toothless gums or long fangs, and claws. Their heads are cleft, divided in such a way as to remind the viewer of the place where corn emerges from the ground, and they are always depicted as sexless. Although Miguel Covarrubias, an artist and archaeologist, felt that all of the rain gods found throughout Mesoamerica could be derived from the were-jaguar, a greenstone figure found outside Las Limas, Veracruz, contradicts that hypothesis. This figure is of an adolescent boy holding a were-jaguar in his arms. Incised on both shoulders and both knees are the profile heads of four different gods, each having distinctive features but all featuring cleft heads. This adolescent figure led to research that indicated that the Olmec worshipped a variety of gods, not all of which had the features of the were-jaguar.

Other common Mesoamerican icons found in Olmec art are animals such as the crocodile, eagle, and shark. A bearded face, a supernatural being often thought to be a rain god, and a feathered serpent are also common. Often, the serpent is shown with a man sitting inside its gaping mouth, which probably represents a cave. It would be tempting to interpret these symbols as having the same meaning as they did at the time of the Spanish conquest, but to do so would be merely speculation and requires a careful iconographic analysis.

The Mother Culture of Mesoamerica As mentioned above, the Olmec were apparently responsible for what would later become trans-Mesoamerican art styles and religious beliefs, hence giving the Olmec culture the distinction of being the Mother Culture of Mesoamerica. Olmec cultural traits emanated from San Lorenzo, La Venta, and Tres Zapotes, and then traveled from the heartland in southern Veracruz and Tabasco into all other areas of Mesoamerica, as far as the west coast of Guerrero and south into El Salvador. Whether this diffusion of influence occurred because of a ruling empire, a common set of religious beliefs, or through a vast trade network or colonization remains unknown.

Classic Period

The Classic period spanned from 200 to 900 C.E. It was characterized by remarkable cultural development. Some scholars have referred to it as Mesoamerica's Golden Age. Great advancements took place in astronomy, mathematics, calendrics, art, architecture, urbanization, writing, ceramics, and religious ceremonies.

THE ZAPOTEC

Around 1000 B.C.E., power moved from the Olmec heartland to the Valley of Oaxaca, which was (and still is) occupied by the Zapotec people. Located in the southern highlands of Mexico, the Valley of Oaxaca is a Y-shaped drainage basin with an area of approximately 1,500 square miles (2,500 square kilometers) and consists of three zones—an alluvial plain, a gently sloped piedmont, and a steep mountain area, with agriculture almost exclusively confined to the lower two areas.

Monte Albán The Zapotec capital, Monte Albán, is a magnificent example of engineering. The ceremonial center marked by stone-faced pyramids is located atop a high, steep ridge about 1,320 feet (400 meters) above the valley floor. Construction of the pyramids had begun by 750 B.C.E. It has been estimated that by 200 B.C.E., the population at Monte Albán was 10,000–17,000. Once again, it is unknown where these people originally came from or why the area developed as it did. It has been proposed that the area developed because of a competition for environmental resources, because of a commercial need for a trade route post, and because of a need for a defensible location. However, archaeologists William Sanders and Deborah Nichols argue against these possibilities, noting that the population was well below carrying capacity during the Preclassic period and that the elevated location is too inconvenient to facilitate trade. Sanders and Nichols instead suggest that either a group of farmers colonized the valley from outside or agriculture developed from a local hunter-gathering population. These arguments are based on the amount of arable land available, as well as the availability of water for irrigation in the lower zones. Rainfall in the valley is moderate, making the control of water extremely important for crop survival. Whatever the reasons for its development, Monte Albán was a large urban area that survived until the Spanish conquest.

Besides having been the capital of the Oaxacan Zapotec, Monte Albán is also significant for its contribution to the Mesoamerican calendar. The Mesoamerican calendar appeared during the late Middle Preclassic, and it is clear that the historic Mesoamericans relied on two calendars—a 260-day ritual calendar and a 365-day solar calendar. Every 52 years, the first day of the ritual calendar coincided with the first day of the solar calendar. A stela found at Monte Albán has been interpreted as the 260-day ritual calendar, the first to suggest that the masses were organized by a schedule of rituals. It is interesting to note that the Long Count dating system found at Tres Zapotes, which would be highly used by the Maya later, is absent at Monte Albán.

THE MAYA

As early as 2000 B.C.E., the Maya lived in small fishing villages; they later developed large settlements. The area occupied by the Maya consists of the modern Mexican states of Yucatán, Quintana Roo, Campeche, Chiapas, and Tabasco, as well as Belize, Guatemala, western Honduras, and El Salvador. The heartland of Classic Maya civilization lay in the northern lowlands of Guatemala and extended into what is now Belize. Millions of Maya still occupy this area, with many of them still living according to traditional Maya practices and beliefs and speaking Mayan languages (at the time of conquest, the Spaniards recorded 31 Mayan languages). Although Maya civilization flourished for thousands of years, there was never a single Maya empire. Instead, several smaller states developed. Despite this, there was a cultural unity throughout the Maya region, as demonstrated in the artistic and architectural styles, rituals, and elite goods.

While the written language of the Maya was initially thought to be indecipherable, art historians, linguists, archaeologists, and epigraphers (those who study ancient written languages) working since the 1950s have been able to decipher the majority of hieroglyphic texts. These texts reveal a long history of war and dominance by secular rulers. The Mayan languages are significantly different from other languages of Mesoamerica and vary among one another in the same way that European Romance languages vary. This similarity to European languages indicates a fairly recent origin, an extensive interaction, or both.

Although the Maya culture began to develop during the Early Preclassic period, it was during the Late Preclassic that many of the cultural markers began to appear. The most notable of these is the architecture demonstrated in massive ceremonial buildings and palaces, as well as the development of complex communities. (For more details about Maya culture, see the *Handbook to Life in the Ancient Maya World* in this same series.)

THE TEOTIHUACANOS

The Classic period was a time of remarkable developments in Mesoamerica. Up until this time, populations were greatest at the southern end of the Valley of Mexico. It was during the Early Classic period that the Valley of Teotihuacan experienced a rapid population growth with a correlating decline of population throughout the Valley of Mexico that lasted the 500 to 600 years of Teotihuacan dominance. During this time the peoples of Mesoamerica built large cities comparable to those in other parts of the world. Archaeologist William Sanders has estimated that by the end of the Early Classic period, despite the population decline due to the popularity of Teotihuacan, the population of the Valley of Mexico was still 40 times greater than during the Middle Preclassic.

Ideas that began during the Preclassic period reached their full development during the Classic. For instance, writing may have become utilized throughout most Mesoamerican regions, and the pantheon of gods and goddesses that the Olmec had created multiplied and became collectively shared throughout Mesoamerica. Human sacrifice also became more common and widespread throughout the Gulf region.

The City of Teotihuacan While the Valley of Mexico had been occupied for many millennia, major settlements had not appeared in the area, and cultural developments lagged behind those of the Olmec and other earlier societies until the Classic period. Despite a lack of metal tools and beasts of burden, the people of the Classic period were able to build large cities, the greatest one being Teotihuacan. In 600 C.E., Teotihuacan was the sixth largest city in the world. Teotihuacan is located in a small valley approximately 27 miles (45 kilometers) northeast of present-day Mexico City. It is in a high (7,425 feet [2,250 meters] above mean sea level), relatively flat basin and is environmentally suitable for the cultivation of maize and beans, as well as other crops. However, the tracts suitable for canal irrigation are few and localized.

It is still not known where these people, known simply as the Teotihuacanos, came from, nor how they called themselves. The name of the city comes from the Aztec and means "place of the gods." Most of the population likely came from other settlements in the Valley of Mexico, as well as other areas. The population of Tlaxcala, located east of Teotihuacan, decreased as the population of Teotihuacan increased. The Tlaxcalans had been erecting buildings in the *talud-tablero* style (consisting of a sloped wall with a horizontal panel above) since about 300 B.C.E., and this architectural style became one of the distinguishing features of Teotihuacan. It is unlikely

that Teotihuacan gained control without warfare, and sites dated from just prior to or during the early stages of development are in defensible locations. While warfare may have originally been symbolic (as with the later Aztec), it was probably quite real at the onset of Teotihuacan society.

Despite the mystery surrounding Teotihuacano origins, there is evidence that suggests the reasons they chose this area for their great city. The first settlement lies approximately a half mile west of the Temple of the Moon. It does not seem that water was the reason for selecting this location; better springs were located to the southwest. The attraction to this site appears to have been its proximity to a group of caves. Caves play an important role in Mesoamerican religion and mythology. Pre-Columbian Mesoamericans believed that caves were the source for humankind's origin, and for the Sun and Moon's origin as well. It was also believed that caves provided access to the Underworld and to the womb of the Earth and are therefore symbols of the earth's fertility. The decision to settle this location, then, was probably guided by religious beliefs; Teotihuacan was considered to be a sacred center by people across Mesoamerica. An extensive network of caves runs in a southeasterly direction under the Pyramids of the Sun and Moon. Directly under the Pyramid of the Sun is a lava tube that runs more than 100 meters and ends in four chambers. Interestingly, use of this cave predates the construction of the pyramid, and the cave remained a cult center after the decline of the city. There are no natural springs located in this cave (which would have made it exceptionally sacred), and so U-shaped drains were installed to channel water inside. The cavernous space is roofed with basalt slabs, and the walls are plastered in mud.

Architectural Dominance The city, covering more than 12 square miles (20 square kilometers), is architecturally dominated by two large pyramids, the Pyramid of the Moon and the Pyramid of the Sun; a wide street known as the Avenue of the Dead, which runs north to south; and the Temple of Quetzalcoatl, the centerpiece of the Ciudadela (Citadel). More than 100 other temples, shrines, altars, and smaller temple mounds dot the city plan. At first thought to be about a mile long, the Avenue of the

Dead actually runs for almost three miles (five kilometers) southward from the Pyramid of the Moon. The Pyramid of the Sun, the Pyramid of the Moon, the Ciudadela, residences for the elite, and smaller pyramids and platforms are all located along the first mile of the avenue and may have contributed to the initial belief that the avenue only ran that length. An east-west trending road crosses the Avenue of the Dead at the Ciudadela. Also located at the city are more than 2,000 apartment compounds, a sign that Teotihuacan supported a substantial population.

Many people from Mesoamerica would have been attracted to the marketplace, and this increase in migration and trade would have led to problems regarding social control. Sacred symbols, as well as the sacredness of the site itself, would have provided the basis for social control. It appears that Teotihuacan was the first place in Mesoamerica to turn the agricultural fertility cult into a state religion.

Stone Monuments Carved stone monuments are less common at Teotihuacan than at earlier settlements. A few stone statues exist, one of which is a water goddess, predecessor to the later Aztec goddess Chalchiuhtlicue, found in the plaza of the Pyramid of the Moon. Another is a composite stela thought to be a field marker for the ball game played throughout Mesoamerica. If this is the case, it is the earliest evidence for the ball game in the Valley of Mexico.

A Different Method of Writing The writing system at Teotihuacan differed from the inscription systems in other parts of Mesoamerica. Rather than a fully developed written language, there appears to be a well-developed protolanguage. There are few linear texts, making discovery and interpretation difficult. Anthropologist James Langley began to look at Teotihuacan art from a different perspective and searched for patterns of abstract decorations and motifs. He found them in the costumes, ornaments, attributes of figures, and representations of the natural world. He referred to these repetitive designs as notational signs. Because the spoken language at Teotihuacan is still unknown, it is difficult to attain a complete understanding of the written language. Archaeologist Karl Taube, more recently, has provided further analysis about the nature of Teotihuacan's writing.

A City with Influence There is clear evidence of trade between the Teotihuacanos and Maya. It was during this period that the Maya began using the military imagery of Teotihuacan, and the first large-scale Maya territorial war may have occurred during the late fourth century. Yet the decline of Teotihuacan began after 500 C.E. with the disintegration of commercial ties with northwestern Mexico and the Guatemalan highlands. A century later, the only outside relationship Teotihuacan had was with El Tajín in Veracruz.

The City's Decline From 650 until 750 C.E., the city still prospered but no new construction appeared. During this period, ceramic figurines became larger and represented deities or elites and warriors, and murals became more secular and began to portray rulers.

In approximately 750 C.E., a large fire, deliberately set, destroyed the political and religious center of the city. The destruction selectively targeted temples, pyramids, and public buildings. Monuments were looted, sculptures were shattered, and divine effigies were destroyed. More than a mile (two kilometers) of architecture was demolished, smashed, and burned—such severe devastation would have required a large task force and probably took several days or even weeks. It is still unknown who was responsible for the mass destruction, but speculation leans toward local residents or close outsiders (possibly including Tolteca-Chichimeca groups) who may have grown tired of the ruling dynasty. Available data indicate that the destruction was relatively bloodless, indicating that it may have occurred during a time of internal conflict. Another indication of internal conflict is that, although the center of the city met with almost total destruction, the outlying areas were left standing. Archaeologist René Millon believes that for Teotihuacan to have been destroyed with such violence, the state government must have been nearly impotent. Although a population of about 40,000 remained after its fall, Teotihuacan was never again the capital of a regional state.

The ritual destruction of monuments dates back at least to the Olmec. In fact, in Teotihuacan, the

Temple of Quetztalcoatl had been the subject of ritual destruction at an earlier date and was afterward rebuilt in front of and on top of what had been destroyed. The magnitude of the destruction at Teotihuacan sets it apart. While the form of destruction was ritual, its purpose appears to have been political.

TLAXCALA

While Teotihuacan was the largest settlement during the Classic period, it did not exist in isolation, and many contemporary cities thrived as well. As mentioned above, the *talud-tablero* architectural style found at Teotihuacan came from the Tlaxcala area. This area began developing several hundred years before Teotihuacan, and its florescence was manifested in more than 25 civic-ceremonial centers. The trade route between the Valley of Mexico and the southern lowlands, known as the Teotihuacan Corridor, was established well before the development of Teotihuacan, and Tlaxcala was a gateway that probably served as a distribution center. Although Teotihuacan dominated the Valley of Mexico, its influence in Tlaxcala was concentrated in the northern part of that state, with very little influence present in other sites such as Cholula in the modern state of Puebla.

CACAXTLA

Cacaxtla, probably dating to the Preclassic period, is famous for its murals. In 1975, looters discovered the murals in several buildings spread throughout the city, and they reported their find to local priests, who in turn notified the INAH. Controlled excavations ensued, during which five different phases of construction were identified. Offerings at the site consist of more than 200 bones, most of which belong to children, including unborn infants. They had been sacrificed by cremation, mutilation, and dismemberment, and the bone fragments found suggest that they were also sacrificed by having their skulls crushed. The skeletons of 10 children, each accompanied by a dog, were found in one of the passageways. Ethnographic data from the Aztec indicate that children were sacrificed during the Tlaloc festival and upon completion of a temple or building; this may also have been the case at Cacaxtla.

The murals at Cacaxtla are Mayan in style, with human figures depicted more realistically than the more geometric figures of Teotihuacan. The Maya God L, the lord of merchants, is depicted in a mural in the Venus Temple. Writing found at Cacaxtla is not Mayan, however. It is a hybrid of Teotihuacan and Oaxacan scripts, as well as unique innovative elements, and was used to identify key figures. Although the art style at Cacaxtla indicates Mayan presence, there is little other cultural material to support it, and the Mayan traits were probably imported by an intermediate group, such as the Olmeca-Xicallanca, whose homeland was adjacent to the Mayan area. Lying 15 miles (25 kilometers) northeast of Cholula, Cacaxtla was referred to by Diego Muñoz Camargo, an early Spanish chronicler, as the seat and fortress of the Olmeca-Xicallanca.

During the Epiclassic period, from 650 to 900 C.E., several smaller cities competed for the power that had disintegrated with the fall of Teotihuacan. New political and trade alliances were formed, and a new artistic style developed. Foreigners, likely from the Gulf Coast lowlands and Yucatán Peninsula, arrived in the Valley of Mexico and its surrounding highlands. As in Cacaxtla's case, the connection between these peoples and the Maya has been observed in the archaeological record.

CANTONA

The city of Cantona, located in the modern state of Puebla, was occupied during the Classic period and was second in size to Teotihuacan, but sometime during the early Epiclassic period, housing compounds appeared. Unlike the compounds found at Teotihuacan, these were groups of house mounds that were sealed off except for one point of access. Access to the sacred architecture was carefully controlled through walkways and gates. Archaeologists have thus far located 24 I-shaped ball courts and believe that 18 of these were in use at one time. A large amount of carved stone and sculpture has been found there, much of it characterized by a revealed Mayan influence and detailed phallic representations.

Eventually, the entire site was fortified, and a dense population grew. The city remained fortified until about 1000 C.E., when it was abandoned. Although considered to be an important site, less than 1 percent of the site surface has been investigated, and there is very little literature available on archaeological work conducted there.

EL TAJÍN

El Tajín, in northern Veracruz, is another important Epiclassic site. There are at least 17 ball courts and an elite center present in ruins. The site was named by the modern Totonac, who believe that 12 old men, the lords of the thunderstorm (the rain god), live in the ruins there.

First occupied during the Classic period and closely allied with Teotihuacan, El Tajín was quite extensive and covered an area of approximately 146 acres, with other ruins scattered over several thousand acres. Sometime during the seventh or early eighth century, El Tajín began its systematic conquest of other sites in the region, and evidence of Classic culture is found in the fill (the soil that falls in between structures, essentially burying them) of Epiclassic buildings. El Tajín was ultimately destroyed by fire around 1000 C.E.

At the center of El Tajín lies the Pyramid of the Niches. Small by Mesoamerican standards (only about 60 feet [18 meters] high), the pyramid is a four-sided structure built in the *talud-tablero* style and is characterized by six tiers rising to an upper sanctuary and carved stone blocks facing each tier. Each tier has 365 niches carved into the facades. This form of architecture is a signature mark of El Tajín and appears at other sites influenced by or conquered by El Tajín. The largest palatial complex at the site is the Building of the Columns, with narrative scenes depicting ceremonial life carved on the columns. A complex system of drains, canals, and storage tanks was developed to divert water for storage and runoff.

The iconography of Classic-period Veracruz is distinct from that of other areas, with human sacrifice being the most important theme. One relief carving at El Tajín, in the South Ball Court, shows a ritual scene complete with human sacrifice. The scene depicts a ball player on the ball court, fully regaled in athletic clothing, being sacrificed; the Death God rising from a vase of pulque behind him prepares to receive the sacrifice. A common icon associated with human sacrifice is the vampire bat, which would have been attracted to blood spilled during a sacrifice or bloodletting ritual. Art historian Michael Kampen postulates that the presence of the feasting vampire bats may have been interpreted as a sign that the gods accepted the sacrificial offerings. The vulture is another recurrent motif in the art at El Tajín and probably represented the gods' acceptance of the blood offerings as well.

LA QUEMADA

The northwestern Mesoamerican frontier, bordered by the modern states of Durango, Zacatecas, and Sinaloa, did not see any large cities until the Epiclassic period. La Quemada, which flourished from 500 to 900 C.E. and was located in the Malpaso Valley approximately 30 miles (50 kilometers) southeast of modern Zacatecas, lies in ruins. Its location on a hilltop offered a defensible position. Walls built for defensive purposes have been found, and it seems that most of the population lived behind these walls. While neither the calendar nor an extensive writing system was present at La Quemada, the Mesoamerican ideology was expressed in architectural structures, ceramic decorations, iconographic depictions, and sacrificial practices. The large quantity of disarticulated bones found at La Quemada and at other population centers in the area indicates that warfare and possibly human sacrifice played major roles in these civilizations. Several indicators suggests this. The *tzompantli* (skull rack) was a major architectural innovation of La Quemada and was subsequently used to exhibit trophy heads from sacrificial victims. Other innovations of La Quemada were the colonnaded hall, usually with a sunken patio, and the steep-sided pyramid. The colonnaded hall, an I-shaped ball court, and the steep-sided pyramid are all connected by a raised causeway, similar to the causeways found in the Yucatec area. At one time, the academic community considered La Quemada to be a station along the "turquoise road" from Chaco Canyon, in the present-day U.S. Southwest, to Tula in central

Mexico. However, archaeologist Ben Nelson's research indicates that the rise of La Quemada predated those societies. As with other settlements in pre-Columbian Mexico, La Quemada was burned and abandoned around 900 C.E., but modern radiocarbon testing indicates that the site was possibly used as a shrine after its abandonment.

ALTA VISTA

Alta Vista, also known as Chalchihuites, approximately 105 miles (175 kilometers) northwest of La Quemada, also dates to the Epiclassic period. The site is located in an area with a great deal of mineral deposits, including malachite, jadeite, hematite, chert, and flint. These deposits were mined extensively beginning in the Late Preclassic, with an expansion after 400 C.E. Teotihuacan controlled Alta Vista, and the mined mineral products were taken to the capital city for processing. Alta Vista's cultural peak occurred about 800–850 C.E., during which time the central temple was remodeled into a pyramid. In about 900 C.E., parts of the city were burned, and much of the population emigrated.

The Postclassic Period

The Postclassic period spanned from 900 to 1521 C.E. It was characterized by change produced by migrations and militarism. The majority of the cultures of the Classic period collapsed, and new groups such as the Toltecs and the Aztecs emerged.

THE TOLTEC

Although no cities the likes of Teotihuacan developed during the Epiclassic, the influence of that great city continued through that period and into the next. The power vacuum created by the fall of Teotihuacan was filled by the Toltec of Tula in the Postclassic period. Tula apparently was not an empire; however, it was the largest city in Mesoamerica at that time. The Toltec influenced much of Mesoamerica, as well as much of northern Mexico, parts of the Guatemalan highlands, and most of the Yucatán Peninsula. Later central Mexican cultures and Mayan dynasties did not fail to claim descent from the Toltec.

Tula   Lying 36 miles (60 kilometers) northwest of Teotihuacan, in the present-day state of Hidalgo, Tula was originally settled in the Late Preclassic period as a center for mining lime to be used in building the large city. The provincial center, Chingu, was located about six miles (10 kilometers) east of Tula and was composed of a large plaza and numerous residential compounds. As Teotihuacan began its greatest expansion, ties with Tula were cut. Many people stayed in the region, however, making their living by farming in the lower terrain, which provided the best soil.

Tula was an ethnically diverse city comprised of peoples from different backgrounds, including the Nonoalca (originally from the lowlands), the Olmeca-Xicallanca (who came from the Puebla-Tlaxcala area, but probably originated in the Gulf lowlands), the Mixtec, and the Chichimec, who came from the northwest. Many of the people at Tula were great artists and craftspeople, and the name *Toltec* comes from the Nahuatl word referring to a skilled craftsperson or artisan. After the fall of both La Quemada and Alta Vista in the north, innovations such as the skull rack and colonnaded hall from those cities appeared in Tula, indicating migration or cultural diffusion from the north. Central Mexicans referred to all of these peoples from the north as the Chichimec. As these were urban-dwelling peoples known to be obsidian and flint workers, turquoise artists, and feather workers, the founding of Tula by the Chichimec is a logical, though not definite, conclusion. The Aztec claim that the Toltec were great artists is evident in the shell and stone mosaics, metal and turquoise ornaments, and plumbate ceramics—the first true glazed ceramics in the Western Hemisphere, which were produced along the Pacific coastal plain near the modern Mexican-Guatemalan border. These wares were probably commissioned by the Toltec.

During the first half of the 10th century, Tula experienced an expansion into urbanism. The city covered nearly eight square miles (13 square kilometers), and the peak population has been estimated at 30,000 to 60,000 people. The residents of the major settlement at Tula, known as Tula Grande, did not produce food, but were craftspeople, tradespeople, and religious leaders. However, the residents of the outlying areas did more than produce food; they mined lime and also produced manos, metates, and chert tools.

The Cult of Quetzalcoatl   The major occupation of the site was during the Tollan phase, from 950 to 1150 C.E. Tula Grande was the only major civic-religious center during this phase. This period coincides with the life of a prestigious and wise ruler known as Quetzalcoatl, whose identity was conflated with the god Feathered Serpent and, in time, became deified. This cultural hero was credited with bringing his people the greatest developments and splendors in the arts, sciences, written words, and all elements of civilization. He came to be considered a man-god by other cultures, as well, a symbol of the glory of the Toltec, wisdom, and the power of mediation between heaven and earth.

The Art of Sacrifice   Representations of the gods are rare at Tula, whose carvings depict mostly images of military power. Toltec iconography reflects a strong warrior aristocracy, as in the famous Atlantes. There are several images of the eagle vessel, used to receive human hearts, as well as the *tzompantli*, or skull rack, used to display human heads. One actual *tzompantli* was discovered east of Ball Court II with fragments of human skulls scattered over the surface of the ball court. These skulls were probably trophies from the losers of the ball games.

Impending Doom   According to the Aztec, the end of Toltec dominance came after a series of droughts, which caused factional conflicts between the Toltec-Chichimec and Nonoalca. In 1156 or 1168 C.E., the last Toltec ruler, Huemac, moved the capital to Chapultepec. Some Toltec-Chichimec stayed at Tula for another 15 years before moving south as far as Cholula. On the way, they subjugated all they encountered. Archaeological evidence shows that Tula saw a violent end, with ceremonial halls burned to the ground and the Serpent Wall, a 40-meter- (132-foot-) long wall painted with friezes depicting serpents eating humans, toppled. This came at a time when the Chichimec were pushing south, and it may have been they who caused the downfall of Tula.

1.3 The Atlantes of Tula stand on top of the Temple of Tlahuizcalpantecuhtli. (Manuel Aguilar-Moreno)

THE MAYA-TOLTEC OF CHICHÉN ITZÁ

Beginning in about 850 C.E., the Maya center of Chichén Itzá began to rise in power. Chichén Itzá dominated most, if not all, of the northern Yucatán until its fall from power in about 1200 C.E. By the early 16th century, there were 16 Maya political centers in the northern Yucatán, each dominated by temples, palaces for the nobility, and houses for the wealthy. Also in the early 16th century, the highlands of Guatemala had Maya kingdoms, most notably the Quiché and Cakchiquel kingdoms, whose rulers claimed descent from the Toltec. These highland kingdoms were quickly conquered by the Spanish armies and their Indian allies in the mid-1520s, while the Maya of northern Yucatán were able to resist Spanish domination until the 1540s. Many of the isolated Maya centers remained independent for much longer, but by the end of the 17th century, the entire Maya region was under direct or indirect Spanish control.

THE ZAPOTEC OF MITLA

Tula was not the only state to develop during the Early Postclassic. Mitla, about 24 miles (40 kilometers) southwest of Oaxaca City, was the center of Zapotec civilization. Mitla was a Nahuatl word for the land of the dead; the Zapotec called it Liobaa, the Place of Rest. Mitla is not well known archaeologically, but it is thought to have developed about 1200 C.E. Although it is not one of the grandest cities in Mesoamerica, Mitla's architecture is exceptional. The site consists of five architectural groupings, including three Postclassic palaces and two Classic-period temple complexes, which were reused in the Postclassic period. House mounds spotted the suburban areas up and down the Río Grande de Mitla, and farmers occupied the surrounding areas. The Spanish priest Francisco de Burgoa visited the site in the 17th century and was told about a vast underground chamber where Zapotec kings and nobles, as well as heroes killed in battle, were buried. Burgoa claimed to have found the passage leading to it but was so horrified he left the passage and sealed it up. The location of the chamber has yet to be found.

THE MIXTEC

The Mixtec occupied an area in western and northern Oaxaca known as the Mixteca, which consists of three separate subareas: the Mixteca Baja in western and northwestern Oaxaca, the Mixteca Alta to the east of the Mixteca Baja, and the Mixteca de la Costa in the lowlands of Oaxaca along the Pacific coast. Rather than integrating into one large kingdom, the Mixtec organized themselves into multiple kingdoms, each with an independent lord; the Mixtec did not develop large cities.

Because of an immeasurable demand for a small amount of arable land, the Mixtec resorted to endemic warfare and political alliance to expand their kingdoms. By approximately 1350 C.E., the Mixtec had infiltrated the Valley of Oaxaca through warfare and through strategic marriage. Often, if a Mixtec leader subdued a town by force, he would fortify his leadership by marrying into the local royalty. By the time of Spanish contact, the Mixtec occupied most of the Zapotec sites. This proved to be a fortunate establishment of unions. By uniting with the Zapotec, the Mixtec were able to avoid defeat by the Aztec.

The Mixtec were excellent artists, and many magnificent artifacts have been recovered from their tombs. Four Mixtec codices currently exist that survived the Spanish conquest. These codices are deerskin books and cover a time span beginning around 940 C.E. They depict historical events, including births, marriages, deaths, and military conflicts. The Mixtec were known in Mesoamerica for their artistic abilities, and the Mixtec artistic influence can be seen as far north as Cholula, which resulted in the Mixteca-Puebla style, as well as far to the south.

THE AZTEC

The Aztec, who called themselves Mexica, derived their name from a semi-mythical place called Aztlan (the Land of White Herons or the Place of Whiteness), a legendary island in a lake in western or northwestern Mexico. The actual location of Aztlan has been debated for centuries, by the Aztec themselves and by modern scholars. Lakes in Michoacán, Jalisco, Guanajuato, and Nayarit have all been considered. Archaeologist Ignacio Bernal describes the Aztec homeland as "A succession of very small, rather prosperous valleys surrounded by large areas of nearby desert" (1980: n.p.). In the early 12th century, the Aztec, a group of Nahuatl-speaking people, began migrating from Aztlan toward central Mexico, stopping at Chicomoztoc (Seven Caves) on the way. Here, the seven tribes that made up the Aztec rose up and became one. At some point during their migration, a second group, the Mexica, joined the Aztec. In this sense, the Aztec include all the peoples who migrated to the Valley of Mexico from Aztlan. The Mexica were the particular people who founded Tenochtitlan, but the publication of historian William Prescott's *History of the Conquest of Mexico* in 1843 popularized the term *Aztec* when Prescott used the name to refer to all Nahuatl speakers in the region. Since then scholars and the general public have erroneously used the terms *Mexica* and *Aztec* as synonyms.

Huitzilopochtli, the war deity, is said to have given the Mexica their name. Although of obscure origins, the name may have come from *Mexitl*, a secret name for Huitzilopochtli. The name *Aztec* is also applied to the members of the Triple Alliance, the Mexica and their allies from Tetzcoco and Tlacopan. As a united force, three groups became the dominant political and military power in central Mesoamerica, only dislocated by the Spanish conquest. Because cultures worldwide have similar stories of origin, they are usually not to be taken literally but are rather intended to justify rule by an elite lineage. However, in the case of the Aztec, it has been argued that their migration accounts are historical rather mythological. Archaeologist Michael Smith gives two reasons for this. First, the accounts are presented in a historical context, rather than as a part of the Aztec mythology. Second, the Nahuatl language is not native to central Mexico; it was brought there from the north during the last centuries before Spanish contact. This reflects an actual migration from the north.

By the time the Mexica arrived in the Valley of Mexico, sometime during the early 14th century, various groups occupied the area, and the Mexica, not wanted by anyone, moved from one place to another until they were finally allowed to settle in Colhuacan, where they worked as serfs for the landowners. When a young Colhua princess was given as a bride to the Mexica chief in 1313 C.E. and then sacrificed in the hope that she would become a war goddess, the people of Colhuacan expelled the Mexica. The Mexica then wandered through the Valley of Mexico until they reached the islands on the swampy western shore of the Lake of the Moon, where they could replicate Aztlan. They split into two groups: One group settled in Tenochtitlan, named for their chief Tenoch (in Nahuatl, the name is derivative of *tetl*, meaning "rock," *nochtli*, meaning "cactus," and the suffix *tlan*, indicating location); the other group settled in Tlaltelolco, just north of Tenochtitlan. The Mexica were later known as the Tenochcas, referring to Tenochtitlan. As the lake was drained, the islands became geographically united with two separate governments. In 1367, the Mexica began working as mercenaries for the Tepanec king Tezozomoc of Azcapotzalco, also located on the lake. The cities of the Valley of Mexico fell under the power of this joint force. In 1375, Acamapichtli, the first Mexica ruler, came to power, and as a consequence, the era of Mexica superiority began. The origins and migration of the Aztec will be further discussed in chapter 2.

Brief History of Aztec Archaeology

Early Expeditions

According to anthropologist José Luis Lorenzo, referring to the history of archaeology in the years after the conquest in his 1998 book (cowritten with Lorena Mirambell and Jaime Litvak King), if archaeological expeditions occurred in the Spanish colonies during the 16th century, they would have been carried out by private parties with the permission of the Spanish crown; the tombs of chiefs would have been excavated in return for one-fifth of the gold, silver, and precious stones found. These early expeditions would have amounted to little more than looting sanctioned by the royalty of Spain. But in 1759, Charles III initiated the first true archaeological work in the Americas. This work focused mainly on excavating sculpture and architecture, rather than on uncovering settlements as whole entities; however, this move opened up Spanish America to further study by European naturalists.

1.4 Illustration of Coatlicue based on drawings presented in a 1792 publication by Antonio de León y Gama (Lluvia Arras)

Urban Archaeology

In 1790, during the installation of water pipes under Mexico City, important Aztec sculptures such as the Sun Stone, or so-called Aztec Calendar, and a monumental statue of the Earth goddess Coatlicue were found under the pavement of the Zócalo, the main plaza in the center of Mexico City. These finds were significant in the evolution of a new nationalism that would include the Indians of Mesoamerica. Historian Antonio de León y Gama wrote about the Aztec works found and stressed that the Aztec were not irrational or simpleminded, but were in fact superior artisans. The Sun Stone was displayed in the cathedral, and the statue of Coatlicue was sent to the Royal and Pon-

tifical University of Mexico. Other artifacts were displayed at the university as well in what became the first exhibition of pre-Hispanic art in Mexico. As a result, the National Museum was founded at the university in 1825.

ADVENTURERS AS ARCHAEOLOGISTS

From its inception, the museum displayed objects recovered through archaeology, although most of these artifacts were not recovered from their original contexts. In 1827, the Mexican government of President Guadalupe Victoria, declared that, under Article 41 of the Maritime and Border Customs Duty Schedule, the export of Mexican monuments and antiquities was prohibited, further contributing to a sense of Mexican nationalism. Also around this time, a loose group of businessmen and adventurers appeared in Mexico. Among them were John L. Stephens and Desiré Charnay. These men wished to show the world that Mesoamerican cities comparable to those of Egypt, Greece, and Rome had existed in the New World prior to European contact. Taking into account theoretical and technological disadvantages, Stephens's and Charnay's work was so well done for their time that it is useful even today.

UNCOVERING TENOCHTITLAN

In 1897, archaeologist Arthur Noll published "Tenochtitlan: Its Site Identified." In this report, Noll described landmarks present at that time and identified the limits of the town of Tenochtitlan at the time of first Spanish contact—a town he referred to as an "Indian pueblo." While Noll did not excavate the settlement at that time, he described artifacts that were unearthed during previous excavations, noting that neither the conquistadores nor the iconoclastic prelate Fray Juan de Zumárraga, in an attempt to remove pagan reminders of native religion from the sight of the natives, would have moved such massive stone monuments far from their original places. This observation proved significant because it would affirm Noll's descriptions of the approximate original location of the artifacts. These descriptions would be vital in locating the original site of Tenochtitlan.

Three years later, in 1900, under the direction of Leopoldo Batres, an ex-militiaman and amateur archaeologist, more archaeological remains of Tenochtitlan were found during the excavation of a trench under the Calle de las Escalerillas (present-day Guatemala Street) in Mexico City. These findings are described in *Archaeological Explorations on Escalerillas Street*. President Porfirio Díaz had named Batres as inspector general of archaeological monuments after Batres had worked in Teotihuacan starting in the 1880s. Although Batres's finds in Teotihuacan were impressive, his work was highly criticized by professional archaeologists because of his reckless excavation methods. In 1910, Díaz was removed from power, and Batres lost his post.

Incorporating Indian Values

What began with the uncovering of the Sun Stone and the Coatlicue statue continued when the end of Diaz's dictatorship brought about changes in the way the past and present Indians were perceived. The armies of the Mexican Revolution were made up almost entirely of peasants, who were mainly Indians. Their struggle brought about an awareness of the social injustices inflicted upon Mexico's indigenous peoples, including those Indians who were first conquered by the Spaniards. This in turn brought about a need to incorporate the unaccounted-for pre-Hispanic Indians into Mexican history. And so, in 1910, the International School of Archaeology and Ethnology was formed by an agreement with France, Germany, and the United States. The school's development was influenced by the ideas of American anthropologist Franz Boas, who felt that the field was still underdeveloped in the United States. Hence, Mexicans at the school studied under some of the best archaeologists, anthropologists, and ethnographers of their time.

MANUEL GAMIO

Manuel Gamio, who studied under Boas at Columbia University in New York, was among the first to conduct research for the International School. In 1911 and 1912, under the direction of Boas and anthropologist Edward Seler, Gamio conducted investigations in San Miguel Amantla near Azcapotzalco and pioneered the use of modern archaeological techniques in Mexico. Gamio was also the first to apply theories of anthropology to archaeology in Mesoamerica. His work there established the Archaic, Classic and Postclassic time line in that area. His work in 1913 in Mexico City's Zócalo area revealed the southwest corner of the Great Temple of Tenochtitlan. Throughout his career, Gamio served as general inspector of archaeology in Mexico and later as the director of the International School of Archaeology and Ethnohistory. He worked for several years in the Teotihuacan Valley, the final product of which was the three-volume *La población del valle de Teotihuacan*. After that publication, Gamio left the field of archaeology to devote himself to working to solve the social problems of the Indians of Mexico.

GEORGE VAILLANT

A contemporary of Gamio, the American archaeologist George Vaillant also worked extensively in the Valley of Mexico. In 1927, he was hired by the American Museum of Natural History in New York and began working at Preclassic period (Formative) sites in Mesoamerica. He published several reports and presented a chronology of the Preclassic period. Vaillant was the first Mesoamerican archaeologist to use stratigraphic techniques to apply relative dates to archaeological data. (Stratigraphy indicates the layers of soil uncovered during an excavation. Objects found in lower layers are assumed to be older than objects found in layers closer to the natural surface.) During the 1930s, Vaillant and his wife conducted excavations at Classic and Postclassic sites and, in 1938, published a paper that correlated archaeological evidence to the information cited in historical Aztec sources. Although Vaillant did not make any remarkable Aztec discoveries (his work focused on smaller items, such as ceramics, that better reflected daily life than did the great architecture), his work is among the most important in Mesoamerica. His chronology of Aztec ceramics is still used today. In 1941, he published *Aztecs of Mexico*, a synthesis of Aztec archaeology up to that point. It was a great loss to Mesoamerican archaeology when, in 1945, Vaillant, at the height of his career, committed suicide.

Instituto Nacional de Antropología e Historia

ALFONSO CASO

Throughout the 1930s and '40s, the Mexican government fervently joined the archaeological community. In 1938, the first government-supported agency, the Instituto Nacional de Antropología e Historia (INAH), was founded by the Mexican archaeologist Alfonso Caso under the Ministry of Education. (In 1932, Alfonso Caso had discovered the treasure in Tomb 7 at Monte Albán.) The INAH became responsible for anthropological, archaeological, and historical research, educational activities, the administration and restoration of archaeological and artistic monuments, and the publication of reports and

articles, as it still is to this day. In 1942, the National Museum of Archaeology, Ethnography and History, the Office of Pre-Hispanic Monuments, and the Office of Colonial Monuments were brought under the auspices of the INAH. And in 1948, the Instituto Nacional Indigenista (INI) was formed, under the directorship of Caso. The INI still works closely today with the INAH in programs to study the history and traditions of Mexico's indigenous peoples.

With Vaillant's publication of "A Correlation of Archaeological and Historical Sequences in the Valley of Mexico," the first archaeological report to consider not only the archaeological data derived from excavation but also the written records of the Aztec, a new field developed. In it, these two primary sources were compared in order to understand more fully both sources. This marriage of archaeology, anthropology, and history is known as ethnohistory, and despite the establishment of the International School of Archaeology and Ethnology, ethnohistorical methods were not widely exercised in Mesoamerican scholarship until the 1970s. In most cases, the historic record was consulted only after archaeological investigations had been conducted, and the historic record was consulted in order to verify the archaeological findings. However, a German team of researchers, led by Paul Kirchhoff, reversed this antiquated methodology, as demonstrated through Kirchhoff's published works. They consulted the written record first and then performed archaeological research to confirm the written history.

IGNACIO BERNAL

Caso, 40 years before, and Mexican archaeologist Ignacio Bernal were exceptions, using ethnohistorical methodology in their work. Bernal worked extensively in Oaxaca from 1942 to 1953 and defined the Monte Albán I, II, and III periods. He later worked in the Olmec area, published work about the Toltec and the Aztec, and afterward directed the National Museum of Anthropology, which opened in 1964. The museum was set up not to display great works of art but to portray everyday life. Bernal's work made it possible for the public to learn a great deal about indigenous Mexican cultures, both living and long gone.

By the 1960s and '70s, ethnohistorical methods were so widespread, archaeologist Ronald Spores reports, that there were at least 100 researchers in Latin America utilizing the methodology to elucidate archaeological records. The use of ethnohistory continues to be vital to research today.

SURVEY WORK

Extensive survey work began in the Valley of Mexico in the 1960s, affirming another modern trend in Mesoamerican archaeology. The first major survey, directed by archaeologists William Sanders, Jeffrey Parsons, and Robert Santley from 1963 to 1973, focused on the Valley of Mexico as a whole rather than on a single site. The purpose of the survey was to study the relationship of many sites within the entire region. Large areas of land were examined intensively in order to locate the remains of different settlements. As of 1974, the data collected were not significant enough to explain the cultural changes within the study area; however, Sanders, Parsons, and Santley were able to define eight to 10 different phases, settlement sizes, complex architectural monuments, and site locations in relation to major natural and cultural features. This survey led to further research in settlement systems, in which a large area is studied in order to determine the relationships of smaller sites within the area.

ARCHAEOLOGICAL LEGISLATION

A federal law passed in 1972 provides that all archaeological artifacts found in Mexico are part of a national heritage and that any lands containing archaeological remains become national property. This legislation, which has its advantages and disadvantages, resulted in the Mexican government's complete control of archaeology in Mexico. This means that all archaeological excavations, including emergency excavations resulting from development, must have a permit from the INAH, guaranteeing that the government participates for the benefit of national interest. Unfortunately, this also means that the archaeologists of the INAH must forgo personal projects that address the problems of national archaeology. Although there has been substantial government support of archaeology and anthropology, it leans toward the use of research that furthers the interests of the government (for example, revenue generated by tourism to archaeological sites).

An example of the effect of the 1972 legislation is provided by the 1978 case of Coyolxauhqui, a relief carving of the eldest daughter of Coatlicue, which was unearthed during construction excavation. Because of the national interest in the carving, the extensive excavation called for a halt on construction, the removal of many modern and colonial buildings, and the subsequent excavation of the Great Temple under the direction of archaeologist Eduardo Matos Moctezuma. In this project participated also the noted archaeologists Leonardo López Luján and Francisco Hinojosa among many others. The excavation took place from 1978 to 1982 and resulted in the publication of *The Great Temple of the Aztecs: Treasures of Tenochtitlan* in 1988 by Matos Moctezuma. This book offers a brief analysis of each of the seven construction stages of the temple (although the first stage lies under the water table and so was not excavated), as well as a catalog of the artifacts and human and animal remains found there.

MODERN AZTEC ARCHAEOLOGISTS

Aztec archaeological research continues to this day. In recent times there have been several archaeologists of the INAH working at Aztec sites and conducting research related to the Aztec history. Among them, besides Matos Moctezuma, can be mentioned Francisco González Rul, Felipe Solís, López Luján, Hinojosa, Roberto García Moll, María Teresa García, Enrique Méndez, Beatriz Zúñiga Bárcena, María Olivia Torres, José Hernández Rivero, Carlos González, Bertina Olmedo, Laura Ledesma, Giselle Canto, Jorge Angulo, Carlos Barreto, Lorena Mirambell, Hortensia de Vega Nova, Norberto González Crespo, Silvia Garza de González, Mari Carmen Serra Puche, Linda Manzanilla, Bárbara Konieczna, Salvador Guilliem Arroyo, and Raúl Arana.

In addition to these foreign and Mexican archaeologists, Michael Smith from the United States has worked and is still working extensively in the area once occupied and controlled by the Aztec. His work includes but is not limited to research on the Aztec migration from Aztlan, the development of cotton-spinning technology, and the Aztec Empire. His book, *The Aztecs*, is an excellent source of information for Aztec scholars and the general audience.

The above information on Aztec archaeology is by no means exhaustive but is intended to provide a general idea of the archaeological research that has been conducted in the Valley of Mexico, as well as Mesoamerica as a whole, over the past 125 years. For the sake of brevity, many archaeologists have not been mentioned here but are nonetheless greatly appreciated for their contributions to understanding Aztec civilization.

MAIN HISTORICAL PRIMARY SOURCES ABOUT THE AZTEC

In their zeal to convert the Aztecs to Catholicism, the Spaniards had much of the Aztec written history destroyed; however, several friars collected and recorded information from Aztec informants, and some of the conquistadores recorded their own experiences of New Spain. The Franciscan friars were concerned with gathering information from the Aztecs for the purpose of understanding their religion in order to prevent the Aztecs from reverting back to pagan idolatry after converting to Catholicism. The contribution of these historical documents to the modern understanding of the Aztec cannot be overstated.

Fray Bernardino de Sahagún

Among the first Spaniards to collect anthropological and historical information from the Aztecs was Fray Bernardino de Sahagún, a Franciscan monk. Sahagún was born in 1499; he arrived in New Spain in 1529. He quickly learned the Nahuatl language and, realizing that Aztec history was disappearing

with the extermination of the older generation, began to interview the Aztec elders living at Tepeapulco, near Mexico City, as well as four youths who served as interpreters. From 1547 until 1569, Sahagún compiled his work into the 12-volume *General History of the Things of New Spain*. This compendium, known as the *Florentine Codex*, describes the natural history of New Spain, the Aztec gods, the rituals and sacrifices, and the divinations and omens involved in the indigenous cosmology, astrology, and theology. It also provides an account of the daily life of the Aztec people themselves, including the history of the Aztec rulers, the business of the merchants and artisans, and the medicinal practices of Aztec physicians. The most distressing aspect of the *Florentine Codex* to the Spaniards was the description of the conquest of Mexico from the Aztec point of view. Because of its pro-Indian narrative, the Spanish Inquisition suppressed Sahagún's work for 300 years and delayed its impact on Mexican culture until modern times. Nevertheless, modern-day scholars such as Michael Smith consider this work to be the most comprehensive and methodical firsthand account of the Aztec.

Toribio de Benavente (Motolinia)

Toribio de Benavente was also among the first Franciscans to reach New Spain. He was born in Benavente, Spain, at the end of the 15th century and changed his name, according to custom, from Paredes to Benavente. As a Franciscan friar, he took a vow of poverty. When the Indians of Tlaxcala first saw him in his tattered robe, they repeated the word *motolinia*, meaning "poor." As this was the first Nahuatl word he learned, he changed his name to Motolinia so as not to forget it. Motolinia wrote about the Indians' religious conversion, the Indian customs, and the Franciscan missionary endeavor. Motolinia's ethnographic work resulted in three books: *De moribus indorum*, the *Historia de los indios de Nueva España*, and *Memoriales*. He was so loved by the Indians that at his burial in 1568, the crowd of Mexicans had to be restrained from cutting pieces of his habit as relics.

Diego Durán

Another friar invaluable in recording Aztec history was Diego Durán. Born in Seville, Spain, in 1537, Durán traveled to New Spain as a child. He entered the Dominican Order in 1556 and was commissioned to study the religion and customs of the Aztec. His work, which included interviews with informants of all ages and social classes, as well as studies of native manuscripts, also resulted in three works, written between 1574 and 1579: *Book of the Gods and Rites, The Ancient Calendar,* and the *History of the Indies of New Spain.* These books provide a wealth of information on both preconquest and colonial history in Mexico, and each has been imperative to archaeological research. These books remained overlooked in the National Library of Madrid until José Fernando Ramírez, a Mexican scholar, discovered them in the 1850s.

Fray Juan de Torquemada

Fray Juan de Torquemada belonged to a subsequent wave in the evangelization of New Spain. He left Spain as an officer but later became a Franciscan monk. He studied Aztec history, language, and antiquities and later became a professor and superior at the College of Santiago de Tlatelolco. After collecting information from the Aztec for 20 years, he published *Monarquía indiana* in 1615. This work is considered to be truthful and impartial, despite Torquemada's leanings toward the church.

Carlos de Sigüenza y Góngora

Another Aztec historian was Carlos de Sigüenza y Góngora, born in 1645 in Mexico City, where he studied mathematics and astronomy under his father and then entered the Order of the Jesuits in 1660. He was expelled from the Jesuit College in Tepotzotlan in 1667 and the next year began to collect manuscripts and to study Aztec history with the intention of writing a history of ancient Mexico. Unfortunately, he died in 1700, before publication,

and his collection of manuscripts was lost; however, even though his works were never published, Sigüenza y Góngora's story is significant as it reveals the transculturation process that had evolved since the first friars came into contact with the Aztecs.

Hernán Cortés

As stated previously, several of the conquistadores wrote of their experiences in New Spain as well. Among them was Hernán Cortés, the leader of the conquest who led troops into Tenochtitlan and gathered Indian allies along the way. Cortés's *Letters from Mexico* is a compilation of five letters sent to Emperor Charles V in Spain, describing his experiences in New Spain. Cortés tells Charles that after landing on the Mexican coast on April 22, 1519, he learned of a kingdom in the interior, Tenochtitlan, powerfully ruled by Motecuhzoma. He became determined to reach the kingdom and convince the leader to acknowledge the superiority of Queen Juana and her son Charles, the rulers of Castile.

Despite his receiving messages from Motecuhzoma insisting that the intruder leave, Cortés and his army continued their journey toward the Valley of Mexico, and eventually, on November 8, 1519, Cortés entered Tenochtitlan. Motecuhzoma greeted Cortés and his men and offered them hospitality in the palace; Cortés responded by taking Motecuhzoma prisoner. This betrayal was the beginning of the defeat of the Aztec, though they resisted with great strength.

Bernal Díaz del Castillo

One of Cortés's men, Bernal Díaz del Castillo, also recorded his experiences of the conquest in his book *The True History of the Conquest of New Spain.* The first two chapters describe Díaz's role in two previous expeditions to the Mexican coast, one led by Francisco Hernández de Córdova, in 1517, and another led by Juan de Grijalva in 1518. The following chapters are dedicated to his descriptions of the conquest, to his observations of the Indian culture, and to his testimony of the politics involved in the near-expulsion of Cortés, who would have been replaced by weaker leaders who would have been content to make a few modest settlements on the coast. Although Díaz was more than 70 years old when he started to write his account, his memory of events was still quite clear. One of his objectives in writing *The True History of the Conquest of New Spain* was to correct what he felt were the errors of others who had written before him. In this, Díaz provides a valuable service to all historians.

Other Chroniclers

Including those already mentioned, there is an extensive list of chroniclers who wrote about Aztec history and civilization during the 16th century. Some of these individuals and their works are Gerónimo Mendieta, *Historia eclesiástica indiana*; Hernando Alvarado Tezozomoc, *Crónica mexicana*; Domingo Chimalpahin, *Relaciones originales de Chalco Amequemecan*; Fernando de Alva Ixtlixochitl, *Obras históricas*; Juan Bautista Pomar, *Relación de Texcoco*; and Alonso de Zorita, *Breve y sumaria relación de los señores de la Nueva España*. Several codices also provide in conjunction with the chronicles a plethora of essential information. They include the *Codex Borbonicus*, the *Codex Magliabecchiano*, the *Codex Mendoza*, the *Codex Azcatitlan*, the *Codex Telleriano-Remensis*, and the *Codex Aubin*.

It should be noted that these early chronicles should be read with caution as they are written by Spanish hands. The friars saw and wrote about Indian culture through a Catholic and Spanish lens, and Cortés and his fellow conquistadores wrote at least in part in an attempt to justify their actions to the Spanish royalty. Their texts are biased. With this said, they do, however, provide an excellent source of pre-Columbian history and the history of the conquest of the Aztec.

READING

The Area of Mesoamerica

Coe and Koontz 2002, Weaver 1993: Mexico from the earliest hunter-gatherers through to the Aztec.

The People of Mesoamerica

Marcus 1992: Mesoamerican writing; Pohl 1999, Adams 1991: Mesoamerican cultures; Millon 1981: Teotihuacan.

The Aztec

Aveni, Calnek, and Hartung 1988, Matos Moctezuma 1988: the Aztec Great Temple; Cortés 1986, Díaz del Castillo 1963: conquest of Mexico; Smith 2003, Soustelle 1979, Davies 1982: Aztec civilization.

Brief History of Aztec Archaeology

Gruzinski 1992, Fagan 1985, Fagan 1997, Townsend 2000, Smith 2003, Weaver 1993: Aztec civilization and archaeology.

Main Historical Primary Sources about the Aztec

Sahagún 1951–69, Motolinia 1971, Durán 1994, Torquemada 1980, Cortés 1986, Díaz del Castillo 1963, Alvarado Tezozomoc 1975, Chimalpahin 1997, Alva Ixtlilxochitl 1975–77: principal chroniclers.

2

EVOLUTION OF AZTEC CIVILIZATION

ORIGINS AND THE GREAT MIGRATION

In 1521, the last Aztec emperor, Cuauhtemoc, was defeated by the Spanish army, assembled and led by Captain Hernán Cortés. The Aztec Empire was conquered in the interest of the Spanish monarchs and under the sponsorship of Christianity, and the Christian faith was imposed upon the Mesoamericans as part of their path to cosmic salvation in exchange for their political autonomy. Despite the destruction and death caused by the conquest, this milestone in history gave room for positive cultural exchange among the Mesoamericans and the Spaniards. In addition, it allowed the opportunity for devoted historians and human rights activists such as Fray Bernardino de Sahagún, Fray Toribio de Benavente (Motolinia), and Fray Diego Durán, among other colonial scholars, to accurately document and preserve Aztec history and culture. Thanks to the efforts of these colonial historians, the Aztec civilization remains the best historically documented pre-Columbian society of the Americas. The origins of the Aztec civilization, however, remain obscure.

Aztlan

The Aztec arrived in the Valley of Mexico in 1325 C.E. The Mexica people (one of the Aztec tribes) knew that the Valley of Mexico had been inhabited previously by multiple Mesoamerican cultures that arrived hundreds of years before the Aztec-Mexica established their empire and built the city of Tenochtitlan. According to Durán, the Aztec originally migrated from the island of Aztlan, hence the name *Aztec*, which means "people of Aztlan." The Mexica tribe was the last of the Aztec tribes to abandon the island by celestial command. *Aztec* was a self-denominating name that was later adopted by the Mexica upon their arrival in the Valley of Mexico. The word *Aztlan* has two possible translations. The first and most common translation is "place of whiteness"; the second is "place of the herons." Either translation has a strong connotation to the color white as either a symbolic or an implied distinction of its geographical location. Aztlan was surrounded by water and mist, and by divine instruction, the Aztec created the city of Tenochtitlan as an attempt to re-create Aztlan in the Valley of Mexico.

FACT OR FICTION?

Many archaeologists and scholars still debate whether the island of Aztlan ever existed or if it is

2.1 An image of Aztlan, the place of origin of the Aztec, from the Codex Boturini *(Fernando González y González)*

only a mythological place that symbolizes Aztec historical creation. Even in the midst of debate, archaeologists and scholars have attempted to locate geographically Aztlan, but to this day they can only speculate that the southwestern area of the United States, the northwest part of Mexico, or the western area of Mexico are the best possible locations from which the Mexica originally departed. Perhaps the most unfortunate event that eradicated concrete evidence of the accurate location of Aztlan was the destruction of ancient manuscripts around 1428 C.E. by order of the king Itzcoatl, who believed it would be more beneficial for his subjects not to know the truth about their past. Many decades later Durán wrote in his reports about the desperate attempt by the following king Motecuhzoma I to recover the history of the Mexica by congregating warriors and wise men to be sent on an expedition to locate the mythical island of Aztlan. It is believed the expedition was successful in finding a place that was or at least offered identical characteristics unique to Aztlan. Regrettably, the accounts by Durán were written shortly after the conquest of Tenochtitlan and before an accurate mapping of the American continent was made; therefore, he could not give a specific location of where this place was situated.

The myth of the Aztec origin from Aztlan shows the strong belief in the concept of a sacred landscape, in which indigenous people attached special significance to geographic features. This appears to have been of central importance to Mesoamerican cultures from the earliest times. Mountains, large rocks, caves, springs, rivers, trees, roads, particular features along the edge of the sea, or landmarks with a strange or unique form were identified with mythological events in the remote past, creation stories of the world and of human beings, heroic deeds of ancestors, or places inhabited by powerful spirits or deities. This ideology explained the origin of the world and celebrated the central and special place of one's group in the natural order.

AN ALTERNATE PERSPECTIVE

In the same way as Durán, the anonymous indigenous codex *Historia de los mexicanos por sus pinturas* mentions an island called Aztlan that was surrounded by a lake. On one of the shores was a mountain named Colhuacatepec or Colhuacan, which means "twisted hill," that contained a cluster of seven caves known collectively as Chicomoztoc. This place was conceived as the archetypal homeland or place of creation and origin of the Chichimec people. The same document says that in this place, located northwest of New Spain, the god Camaxtle hit a rock with his baton, and from it emerged 400 Chichimecs, whose name means "hunters" or "dogs." All of the important 16th-century chronicles, both indigenous and Spanish, make reference to this place and present pictorial representations in some of the codices.

Durán considered Aztlan, Colhuacan, and Chicomoztoc to be different names for the same place of origin located to the north of New Spain, near Florida. The last seven Chichimec (Nahua) tribes that populated the Valley of Mexico were the Xochimilca, Chalca, Tepaneca, Colhua, Tlahuica, Tlaxcalteca, and Mexica, and they all came from the same place of origin.

Chicomoztoc

The *Historia tolteca-chichimeca* and the *Map of Cuauh tinchan No. 2* recount and illustrate a different story of the exodus from Chicomoztoc (see figure 2.2). In these sources, it was a group of seven earlier Chichimec peoples who settled in the Valleys of Cholula and Puebla and who emerged from the caves; they were the Cuauhtinchantlaca, Totomiuaque, Acolchichimeca, Tzauhcteca, Zacateca, Malpantlaca, and the Texcalteca. The *Map of Cuauhtinchan No. 2* illustrates the significance of the act of leaving the cave as a metaphor for the act of creation by conducting the New Fire ceremony. This ritual portrayed the exit of human beings from the womb of the Earth as the start of time. The same document also mentions that in Chicomoztoc the Chichimec performed penance for four days, fasting and letting their blood. These rituals may have been understood to have produced altered states of consciousness or hypnotical trances because Chimalpahin refers to Chicomoztoc as Quinehuayan, or the place where one is possessed.

Another ritual performed in Chicomoztoc was the perforation of the nasal septum by which Chichimec chiefs became *tlatoque*. This symbolized the conversion of the nomadic Chichimec into the civilized Toltec. Thus, in this case the caves played a

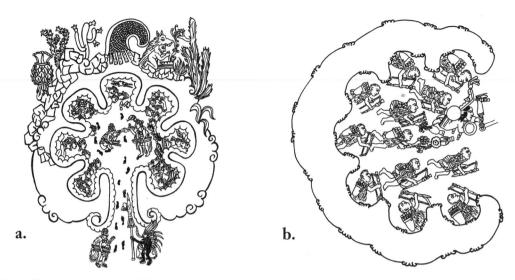

2.2 a) Chicomoztoc, the place of the seven caves, in the Historia tolteca-chichimeca; *b) Chicomoztoc in the* Map of Cuauhtinchan No. 2 (Mario Dávila)

role as places of transformation and legitimization of the lineages and genealogies of the groups that held power.

SEARCHING FOR CHICOMOZTOC

Chimalpahin describes the mysterious place as Chicomoztoc Tzotzompa Quinehuayan, where there are seven holes in the rock. It is a place of fright, filled with *tzihuactli* (thorny plant), *necuámitl* (wild maguey or agave), *teocomitl* (biznaga cactus), *xihuallacatl* (large green squashes), *zacatl* (grass), and parched places.

The chronicles motivated historians to search for the location of Chicomoztoc. Sahagún places it in Cerro Coliuhquitepetl, on the territorial boundary between the Mexica and the Michuaca (Tarascans of Michoacán). Paul Kirchoff locates it in Cerro Culiacán, near the town of San Isidro Culiacán in the state of Guanajuato. Wigberto Jiménez Moreno places it in the Tula-Xilotepec region in the state of Hidalgo, while Alfredo Chavero locates it in the region of the present city of Culiacán in the state of Sinaloa. Both Fray Juan de Torquemada and Francisco Xavier Clavijero identified it with the ruins of La Quemada in the state of Zacatecas. Some folk-

loristic traditions place it on Mexcaltitan Island in Nayarit or Lake Pátzcuaro in Michoacán. But most modern authorities tend to consider Chicomoztoc as a mythical rather than an actual place.

Chicomoztoc represents the idea of the emergence of human beings from cavities in the body of the Earth. Aztec shamans and sorcerers then applied this idea in their incantations to the human body where the seven openings are referred to as seven caves. As time passed, the guardians of the Mesoamerican tradition preserved their sense of identity and origin by recreating Chicomoztoc at their sites, either by taking advantage of natural caves or by excavating them. In this sense, all the chroniclers and historians are correct, because many Chicomoztocs existed in all parts of Mesoamerica.

This idea was confirmed in 2000 when archaeologist James Brady, and several other colleagues, including the author of this text, studied an artificial group of seven caves aligned in an escarpment in the site of Acatzingo Viejo, in the state of Puebla. Unfortunately, the seventh cave was destroyed about seven years ago by the construction of a road that leads to a PEMEX (the national oil company) installation; however, ethnographic data have confirmed the existence of the now lost cave.

The fact that there were once seven caves at Acatzingo Viejo immediately suggests a relationship with Chicomoztoc. Perhaps the best-known representation of Chicomoztoc is that found in the *Historia tolteca-chichimeca* with its seven internal chambers. It should be noted that within the indigenous sources there is no consensus on the physical form. In some ethnohistoric documents, the mythical place is portrayed as a linear arrangement of seven discrete caves. The linear arrangement in the *Codex Vaticanus A* and the *Atlas of Durán* closely resembles the arrangement noted at Acatzingo Viejo.

The alignment of seven caves can therefore be interpreted as a re-creation of Chicomoztoc, the mythical place of origin. Cave complexes have a clear relationship with the foundation of towns and were ritual hearts of the community that legitimized the very settlement. Thus, the seven caves symbolize the establishment of the settlement and the origin of a new ruling dynasty.

Just as pyramids are artificial re-creations of the primordial mountain, the Chicomoztocs of Mesoamerica can be an artificial representation of the cave from which humans emerged. Taken together, the two constructions became a powerful statement that a town, as is the case of Acatzingo Viejo, had been built at the very center of the cosmos because the primordial mountain and the place of human creation both define the spot. The importance of centering sites in sacred landscapes is a well-recognized Mesoamerican preoccupation. The cave complex also represents the generative womb of the Earth that is at the same time the guardian of the natural forces such as wind and water. And so the holiness of the complex made it an appropriate landmark around which to build a temple. The mountain/cave symbol comes to represent the very basis of Mesoamerican ethnic identity. As noted, this deep relationship between people and the mythic Chicomoztoc was so deep that people were identified with the cave itself throughout Mesoamerica.

Migration from Chicomoztoc

Historical data collected from colonial accounts reveal that the story of the great migration of the Aztec begins with the departure of the seven tribes from the seven caves out of which they emerged.

According to Durán, the exodus was part of a celestial command that instructed all tribes to abandon the caves and emerge into the light to explore the world outside, to find places of pleasant weather and agricultural abundance, to walk the earth, and to establish cities that would host their tribes and honor the gods. The tribes slowly departed from the caves; some groups left together, and others waited for an unusual situation or phenomenon to interpret as a celestial sign in order to leave. This passive and lengthy abandonment of Aztlan/Chicomoztoc allows room to speculate that besides agricultural or climatic reasons that forced the massive migration, it could have been also motivated by philosophical or religious beliefs.

In the year 820 C.E., tribes of Chichimec affiliation began to abandon the seven caves. The seven tribes were the Xochimilca, the Chalca, the Tepanec, the Colhua, the Tlahuica, the Tlaxcalteca, and the Mexica. The Mexica by command of their god, who had promised them a paradisiacal land full of richness, stayed behind in the caves for another 302 years after the first tribe originally departed from the seven caves.

THE XOCHIMILCAS AND THE CHALCAS

The seven tribes eventually arrived at the Valley of Mexico and established cities and territories. The

2.3 Chicomoztoc, as depicted a) in Codex Vaticanus A *and b) in the* Atlas of Durán (Mario Dávila)

first to arrive were the Xochimilcas, who traveled around the lake Tetzcoco in the Valley of Mexico until they encountered a hospitable place to found their villages. The lords of the Xochimilcas extended their nation and founded the towns of Tochimilco, Tetela, Hueyapan, Tlamimilolpan, Xumiltepec, Tlacotepec, Zacualpan, Totolapan, Tepoztlan, and Chimalhuacan. The second to arrive were the Chalcas, who established their lordships next to the Xochimilcas and lived peacefully as neighbors. They founded the village of Tlalmanalco, and from there they ruled over other villages such as Cuaxochpan, Ayotzinco, Chalco, and Atenco, but because of their small population, the Chalcas remained an appendix to the Xochimilcas.

THE TEPANECAS AND OTHERS

Following the Chalcas, the Tepanecas arrived at the shores of Lake Tetzcoco and took ownership of the area of Tlacopan (Tacuba), establishing the village of Azcapotzalco where the nobles ruled and controlled their small district of villages, among them Tacubaya, Coyoacan, Tlalnepantla, and Tenayuca. Shortly after, three more of the seven tribes arrived and also established their territories and founded small cities. Upon the arrival of the six tribes at the Valley of Mexico, population heavily increased, and the lords and nobles established a governmental scheme similar to Europe's feudal system to maximize the development of urbanization and to render the villages more habitable and open for mercantilism. This was how the Valley of Mexico was divided among multiple ethnic groups.

THE MEXICA

In the year 1122 C.E. the last tribe of Aztlan, the Mexica, left the seven caves in search of the Promised Land. It is believed that during this time, the Mexica adopted this particular name to denominate their tribe and also to honor their high priest Mexitl, who led the massive exodus ordered by their supreme deity, Huitzilopochtli. Huitzilopochtli favored the Mexica above the others of the original seven tribes, and for the Mexica he had reserved a land of pure richness and exuberance that would surpass any they had seen in Aztlan. Huitzilopochtli, later identified as a god of war, communicated directly with his high priests via dreams and profound trances, bestowing on them omens, prophecies, and navigational tools to arrive at their promised land and avoid dangerous situations. Huitzilopochtli at times could be kind and generous with the Mexica; he allowed them to establish towns and small villages throughout the long journey of their migration. He would designate the locations in which towns could be edified so that the earth would be fertile and water abundant. Then the Mexica would rest for periods of 10 to 20 years in these towns, geographically protected from enemies and other menacing threats so that the chosen tribe would have time to replenish its strength and increase its numbers before resuming the migration. In addition, these towns would serve as sanctuary for the old, the sick, and the weak when they were granted permission by Huitzilopochtli to abandon the migration. They would remain in these towns to honor their supreme god.

FINDING A PLACE TO SETTLE

On the long journey toward the Valley of Mexico, the Mexica circled the lands of the Chichimec. The Chichimec were looked down upon and considered uncivilized and inferior when compared to other, more sophisticated cultures of Mesoamerica such as the Toltec, Mixtec, Totonac, and Mexica. The Chichimec were nomads and lived in poorly established seasonal settlements. Their nomadic lifestyle prevented them from developing an agricultural system. Their diet consisted of herbs, worms and snakes, and wild game such as white rabbits, deer, and birds. The Chichimec did not develop a communal society and often moved in family packs rather than as a tribe. Some Chichimec tribes had migrated to the Valley of Mexico and through contact with other groups there became civilized. The Mexica, in fact, were a Chichimec tribe, but as they became powerful and civilized, they looked down on other Chichimec, especially those who stayed in the deserts of the north and remained nomadic.

These nomads in the vicinity of the Valley of Mexico did not look kindly upon the new Mexica settlers, but the Chichimec's nomadic lifestyle played a crucial role in their avoiding any major territorial dispute with the Mexica. The Chichimec did not possess a sophisticated culture, and they had no religion or cult. This particular lack of highly developed civilization forced them to steer clear of direct confrontation with the Mexica and move their seasonal camps deeper inside the forest away from the new settlers.

Patzcuaro   These new lands that once belonged to the Chichimec became one of the most important villages founded by the Mexica. They founded the town of Patzcuaro, in the modern state of Michoacán, and stayed there for a few years. The town was built next to the great lagoon of the same name. At first glance, the lagoon closely resembled their homeland of Aztlan and caused confusion among tribe members, who at some point believed they had arrived at their destination. In Patzcuaro, the Mexica cultivated corn and chilies to offer to their god during rituals and to use them as part of their diet to sustain their local population. The beauty of the lagoon of Patzcuaro allured even the most loyal high priests, and they conducted elaborate rituals to consult Huitzilopochtli and ask if he would allow them to remain in Patzcuaro. The divine response was unenthusiastic; however, the high priests asked permission to allow a small group of people to remain in Patzcuaro. To this petition Huitzilopochtli responded very benevolently and told his high priests that they should remain alert, and when a group of people of various ages entered the lagoon to bathe, they should hide their cloths and immediately abandon the town. The Mexica did so; they abandoned Patzcuaro while some members of their tribe bathed. When the unsuspecting villagers emerged from the lagoon, they found themselves naked and abandoned. Not knowing where to go, they stayed in Patzcuaro. These deserted men, women, and children later became an autonomous tribe known as the Tarascans, direct descendants of the Mexica.

Malinalco   In another stage of the migration, a powerful woman named Malinalxochitl rose among the nobles of the tribe. She was a sister of Huitzilopochtli and a powerful sorceress who knew all sorts of magical crafts and incantations. Due to her divine blood and her knowledge of powerful arts, she became feared by all members of the Me-

xica tribe. Very secure in her bewitching arts, she often challenged the authorities of the high priests and on many occasions even the authority of the lord Huitzilopochtli. Malinalxochitl's powerful spells became an affliction for the Mexica leaders. A cult in her honor arose among certain members of the tribe, and she protected them in exchange for their complete loyalty. To those who opposed or defied her, she would often bring sudden and painful death by commanding wild beasts and poisonous snakes, scorpions, and spiders to poison her victims.

Desperate, the high priests invoked the help of Huitzilopochtli to aid the Mexica in getting rid of the powerful sorceress. Huitzilopochtli talked to them and communicated that he had heard their lamentations and pain, but that they needed to be strong and to remember that only through him could the Mexica become lords of all the wealth, gold, silver, precious stones, and colorful feathers that would be waiting for them upon their arrival to their final destination. He also warned the leaders of the tribe not to fall under the trickery of the wicked sorceress' spells that she was using to allure some members of the tribe; again he emphasized that only through the bravery of their hearts and the hard work of their hands could the Mexica obtain such riches. Finally, Huitzilopochtli instructed the Mexica to leave the village while Malinalxochitl and her followers slept and not to worry about her evil spells. Huitzilopochtli would prevent Malinalxochitl from following their trail the next morning and shield them against her hex. Then the Mexica left in the middle of the night and headed toward Tula, where Huitzilopochtli guided the tribe to the top of a hill known as Coatepec.

Upon daybreak the powerful sorceress Malinalxochitl woke up to find herself and her followers deserted by the tribe and unable to follow them. Then, enraged and cursing them with vile words, she migrated to a location deep within the heavy forest and established a town known as Malinalco. In this town she found refuge along with her followers, and before her departure, she taught its entire population the powerful arts of magic and sorcery. Hence the inhabitants of this town even today are acknowledged as powerful wizards and witches who practice all sorts of spell crafts.

Mount Coatepec Upon the arrival of the Mexica to Mt. Coatepec in the land of Tollan, they encountered small bands of Chichimec and members of the Otomí tribe, who were upset about the invasion of their land without being first consulted for permission. Not heeding the tribes' anger, the Mexica promptly set up camp and began to build an altar in honor of their faithful god. Huitzilopochtli advised his loyal priests to direct his tribe down the hill to the area of the meadows, where the Mexica would divert the waters of the nearby river to create a dam and to block purposely all possible areas from which the water could escape. This is perhaps the first artificial lagoon or lake recorded in Mesoamerican history. The lake was promptly blessed with the arrival of wild ducks, herons, humming birds, a wide array of fish, frogs, and aquatic flora, which transformed the lake into a paradisiacal location. The land of Tollan became another temporal sanctuary for the Mexica to pause, gather their strength, and increase their number.

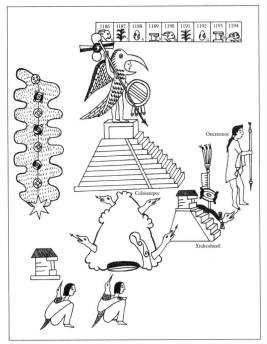

2.4 History of the birth of Huitzilopochtli at Coatepec, from the Codex Azcatitlan *(Lluvia Arras)*

There in Coatepec, Huitzilopochtli established a ball court and a *tzompantli* (skull rack). Some members of the tribe became accustomed to the relaxation they enjoyed on this land, and they grew lazy and fond of a sedentary lifestyle until one day they no longer honored and feared their lord Huitzilopochtli. They rebelled and tried to convince the priests to finalize their migration and take ownership of the land known as Tollan. Upon this rebellious attitude, Huitzilopochtli's anger was awakened, and he decided to destroy their temporal sanctuary and forsake those who had defied his will. One night while the Mexica quietly slept, the sacred hill of Tzompanco was hit by lightning and a macabre thunder was heard throughout the entire area of Coatepec and Tollan. It is said that the angry god came down from the sky mercilessly striking all those who had rebelled against his divine orders and tried to obstruct his will. The next morning, the Mexica woke up to find the bodies of those forsaken by Huitzilopochtli brutally mutilated with their chests cut open and their hearts ripped away.

Scholars believe that this story serve as a mythological account to explain an actual event—a bloody war between two particular groups striving for the supreme leadership of the tribe. In addition, scholars also believe that this event became the birth of the sanguineous cult to the god Huitzilopochtli, in which the high priests would offer human sacrifices and extract human hearts for the god to sustain his appetite and to appease his anger. (See chapter 6 for the myth of the birth of Huitzilopochtli and the death of Coyolxauhqui.)

The next morning after the massacre, the priests were instructed by Huitzilopochtli to destroy the artificial lake, to remove the dam, and to drain out all the water to restore the meadows to their original form. Once this task was completed, the Mexica were instructed to evacuate the area without further delay or risk once again the fury of their lord.

Chapultepec In the year 1168 C.E., the Mexica left the area of Coatepec and were ordered to go to the area of Tequixquiac, where they rested for a few years. Later they resumed their migration to the area of Xaltocan, where they were again instructed to plant corn and chilies to help them sustain their population. They also built fences and perishable walls to protect their tribe from outsiders. After a few years, the Mexica continued their search for the Promised Land. They traveled to many areas, where they encountered increasing hostility of the lords of already-established tribes. They moved from Ecatepec to Tulpetlac, Azcapotzalco to Tacuba and Coyoacan until they finally arrived in about 1285 C.E. to the area on Lake Tetzcoco known as Chapultepec, an important source of water.

On this occasion, the Mexica faced powerful adversaries, who, unlike the Chichimec, had established sophisticated civilizations, feudal systems of government, and ownership of the land. Constantly feeling unwelcome, the Mexica priests invoked once again the wisdom of their god Huitzilopochtli, who told them to wait for an opportunity to conquer the land and to wait for his signal to strike their enemies. In the meantime, they were to establish themselves at Chapultepec and to construct solid walls to protect their village, maintain vigilance day and night, and guard their women and children. Huitzilopochtli then, for the first time ever, gave the Mexica instructions to elect a warrior as a leader to protect the tribe against enemy forces of the two neighboring nations. They elected a captain named Huitzilihuitl, who diverted much of the energy of the community to craft arrows, bows, clubs, spears, and sharp stones that could be used as piercing projectiles. In the accounts of Durán, this appears to be the first indication of the Mexica's evolution from a religious and agricultural civilization into a militarily aggressive society.

Their stay in the area of Chapultepec was not very pleasant. According to indigenous accounts, Copil, a direct descendant of Malinalxochitl, craved to avenge his mother's honor. He traveled to the neighboring kingdoms instigating fear of and hatred for the Mexica. Under his prodding, the lords and kings disliked the Mexica tribe, and Copil's intrigues turned the situation hostile and violent. Copil devised to ambush Huitzilopochtli and his tribe: Copil and his people secretly waited for the Mexica at the foothill of a lagoon known as Tepetzinco to deliver the final blow and finally avenge his mother, but Huitzilopochtli already had outguessed Copil's intentions and directed the Mexica to move in the opposite direction around the lagoon and surprise Copil's army. Upon ambushing and capturing Copil's forces, Huitzilopochtli ordered that while the captives were alive to cut open their chests, rip out their beating hearts, and hold them up to the Sun as a sacrificial offering.

Once again the Mexica had been protected by their god and delivered from danger. Unfortunately, Copil's death did not change the political situation for the Mexica. The other tribes had been harboring a great amount of hatred and remained extremely hostile, to the point that Mexica men, women, and children alike had to be instructed in how to build and employ all sorts of weaponry to defend their tribe. War kept erupting, but it was to the kingdom of the Chalcas that the Mexica lost their war leader when he was captured and later killed. Even with their success, the Chalcas grew fearful of the determination and the bravery of the Mexica tribe. Though the Chalcas outnumbered the Mexica, Chalca forces had been severely damaged and reduced by the small number of Mexica. After their last confrontation, the Chalcas swallowed their pride and abandoned their violent efforts and terminated a war that depleted both groups.

Colhuacan   To avoid further bloodshed, the Mexica deserted the area of Chapultepec and moved to the area of Colhuacan (a prestigious Toltec enclave). There, before entering the unknown territory, Huitzilopochtli spoke to his priests and advised them to send an emissary to the king of Colhuacan to ask permission to establish camp on his territory. He also advised them this time to act with diplomacy, to avoid war at any cost, and to accept whatever land they were offered, even if it was not fertile. The messenger of the Mexica was pleasantly greeted by Achitometl, the king of Colhuacan. The lord of Colhuacan did not turn away the Mexica but rather offered them a section of a land known as Tizapan that remained uninhabited due to the hostility of its environment.

Tizapan   The soil was barren and poisonous animals aggressively defending their territory against human invasion overpopulated the land. Still, the Mexica followed the orders of their protector, enduring all the adversities of nature, and planted their civilization in Tizapan. Eventually the hostile area became more habitable, and the Mexica planted their corn and began to establish trade with their neighboring town. People from Colhuacan eventually began to intermingle more and more with the refugee tribe. As time went by, Mexica families began to strengthen their alliances by marrying into noble Colhuacan families to obtain political power. Their political situation was relaxed and even familiar, and their daily life staggered in routine and mundane tasks as the Mexica came to a point of peace and harmony with their neighbors. This situation awoke the impatience of Huitzilopochtli, the god of fire and war, for he saw his people submerged in an endless, mediocre daily life. Once again he spoke to his priests via dreams to warn them that the time had arrived for the Mexica to rise in war and claim complete dominion of the land. He proclaimed that more than ever, they were closer to their final destination. Huitzilopochtli advised the priests to elaborate a plan to surprise the Colhuas.

The Mexica sent an emissary to ask for the hand of King Achitometl's daughter to be crowned as the Mexica's new queen and bride of Huitzilopochtli. King Achitometl agreed to the union. The maiden was then taken to the Temple of Huitzilopochtli and killed as a sacrificial offering. Later a great feast was offered, to which King Achitometl and his court were invited. Upon completing their banquet, the high priest emerged in a ceremony dressed with the remains of the torn up skin of the King Achitometl's daughter. This spectacle enraged the king, and he ordered his court to avenge his daughter by shedding the blood of the Mexica. He commanded every single citizen to come out and battle. They outnumbered the Mexica and pushed them into the lake. Eventually the diminished population was forced to flee to Acatzintitlan, a group of swampy islands surrounded by reeds.

The last war left the Mexica tribe in a state of confusion and desperation. The Mexica population had been diminished, and they now felt desolate. One more time, the priests invoked the wisdom of their god for guidance. Huitzilopochtli then told the priest to speak with his people, for now they were ready to go to the Promised Land.

Tenochtitlan From Acatzintitlan, the Mexica continued their migration in the lake area until they arrived at nearby Mixiuhtlan, which means "place of birth." There, they found a beautiful section of the lake with crystal clear water. The trees, the plants, and the flowers were all white, and not a single leaf was colored green. From the waters emerged white fish, frogs, and aquatic snakes. Birds flying and landing around the lake displayed an elegant white plumage; everything was in perfect balance and harmony, just as they had heard it was many generations ago in their native Aztlan.

According to the verbal accounts collected by Durán, this precise moment represented a celebration of pure joy and hopefulness; these people who had suffered so much at the hands of destiny had finally arrived at their final destination. Men, women, children, farmers, nobles, and the priests without distinction of rank or gender all came together to celebrate this day in which the prophecy became fulfilled.

The same night, Huitzilopochtli gave his priests a final prophecy and specific instructions on how to locate the exact area to start building their promised city. In dreams he came and ordered them to look for the heart of his nephew Copil, the same heart that he had torn away from his chest. Huitzilopochtli said to the Mexica that when he had hurled the heart of his nephew, it landed on top of a rock, and on that rock Copil's blood gave birth to an enormous nopal cactus. On top of the cactus, they would find an eagle nesting and devouring a serpent. The eagle's nest would be covered with the most beautiful feathers, the colorful feathers of all the birds it had already devoured. And on top of that nest they would build their city and name it Tenochtitlan. The name *Tenochtitlan* comes from the Nahuatl words *tetl* (rock), *nochtli* (cactus), and *tlan* (a suffix indicating location) and means "place of the cactus on the rock." At last, the long journey of the Mexica ended, and in 1325 C.E. they were finally ordered to establish roots and claim ownership of the area.

MEXICA-AZTEC HISTORY

The history of the Mexica in the Valley of Mexico began in the year of 1318 C.E., when their long migration from Aztlan ended and they built the city of Tenochtitlan. This is the precise moment when this seminomadic tribe entered the Valley of Mexico to eventually rise as one of the most powerful empires of pre-Columbian America. It was around this time that the Mexica became identified and known as the Aztec, or "people of Aztlan." The Mexica apparently did not call themselves Aztec; they maintained the denominational name of Mexica or Colhua-Mexica to establish their historical link to the ancient Toltec civilization and to emphasize their noble lineage.

Settling a City

Upon entering this new location, the Mexica knew that this white paradisiacal land that they had found at the shores of Lake Tetzcoco now belonged to them by order of their god. The Mexica searched around the lake's shores for the eagle's nest they had heard about in prophesy; finally someone discovered the exact representation of the sign described to the high priest in his dream but in the middle of the lake: the majestic eagle resting on top of a nopal growing from a huge rock. The Mexica pushed their canoes into the water and navigated to the center of the lake to set the first stone and build an altar to their sun god Huitzilopochtli. This was described in the accounts of Fray Diego Durán as a very significant and emotional moment in Aztec history. Every single member of the community, men, women, and children, kneeled in prayer and thanked their divine benefactor for finalizing their long journey and giving them a place to call home.

The next day Cuauhtlequetzqui, the highest priest of Huitzilopochtli, ordered everyone to be ready by dawn to start cutting trees and wood to build an altar, to give thanks for the god's protection and to continue in his favor. But even in their joy, the Mexica had other issues to face. The land designated by Huitzilopochtli layed within the bordering parameters of the kingdoms of Azcapotzalco and Tetzcoco, and the Mexica did not possess the military capacity nor the financial enterprise to exercise any form of political or militant pressure over the neighboring kingdoms. They fully understood that they were placed in the middle of two stronger kingdoms and any factor triggering war would obliterate their small civilization. For a small period of time,

2.5 *Foundation of Tenochtitlan, from the* Codex Mendoza *(Manuel Aguilar-Moreno)*

the Mexica became hunters, food gatherers, and agriculturalists. Later on they designated days of travel to neighboring towns to sell and trade raw materials in exchange for manufactured goods or other forms of raw materials not available to them. This brought the unpleasant attention of the inhabitants of the neighboring towns, especially from the people of Azcapotzalco, who immediately complained to their king to enforce some form of taxation on the Mexica. King Tezozomoc, ruler of Azcapotzalco, made decrees, which heavily taxed the Mexica for using the land and for conducting business within the territories of his kingdom. The Mexica sent diplomats to persuade the king to lessen his harsh policies, but the committee only angered him. The king instead implemented even heavier taxation laws upon the Mexica. The Mexica knew that military action was not an option and that any form of retaliation would completely wipe them out; they were in a precarious position and obligingly, though only temporarily, accepted the heavy penalties.

Establishing a Government

These events called for a drastic reevaluation of Mexica-Aztec politics. The Mexica-Aztec tribe

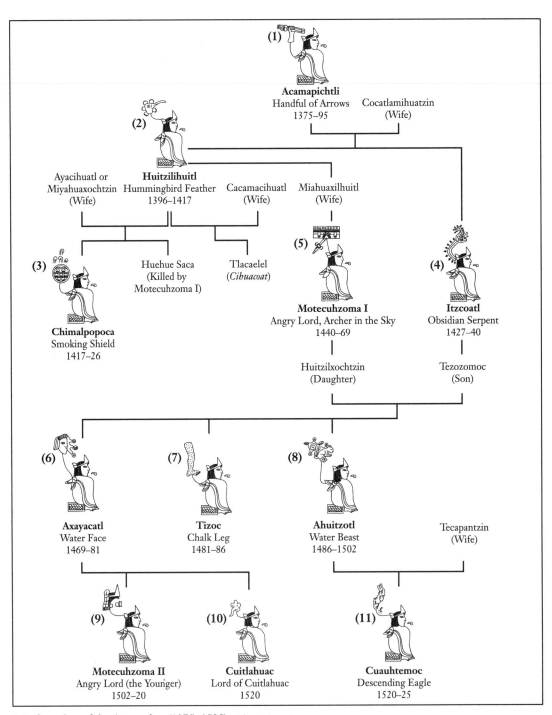

(1)

Acamapichtli
Handful of Arrows
1375–95

Cocatlamihuatzin
(Wife)

(2)

Ayacihuatl or
Miyahuaxochtzin
(Wife)

Huitzilihuitl
Hummingbird Feather
1396–1417

Cacamacihuatl
(Wife)

Miahuaxilhuitl
(Wife)

(5)

(3)

Huehue Saca
(Killed by
Motecuhzoma I)

Tlacaelel
(*Cihuacoat*)

Chimalpopoca
Smoking Shield
1417–26

Motecuhzoma I
Angry Lord, Archer in the Sky
1440–69

(4)

Itzcoatl
Obsidian Serpent
1427–40

Huitzilxochtzin
(Daughter)

Tezozomoc
(Son)

(6)

(7)

(8)

Axayacatl
Water Face
1469–81

Tizoc
Chalk Leg
1481–86

Ahuitzotl
Water Beast
1486–1502

Tecapantzin
(Wife)

(9)

(10)

(11)

Motecuhzoma II
Angry Lord (the Younger)
1502–20

Cuitlahuac
Lord of Cuitlahuac
1520

Cuauhtemoc
Descending Eagle
1520–25

2.6 Genealogy of the Aztec rulers (1375–1525) (Lluvia Arras)

needed to evolve into a more complex and sophisticated political power. The wise men and the priests decided to begin to expand into a kingdom. Mexica-Aztec nobles began to make political alliances with the neighboring towns and kingdoms through marriages. Then the elder and wise men decided that it was time to hand over the power to a king to expand their kingdom. They had to select a strong monarch who would be the embodiment of Huitzilopochtli on earth.

KING ACAMAPICHTLI

The search began by tracing the lineage of all Aztec nobles in hopes of finding an individual who unified all the qualities of a great king. One day they heard news about Opochtzin, a high-ranking official of noble and Mexica lineage who had married into a noble family of Colhuacan, taking Atotoztli for his wife. Together they had Acamapichtli, a strong youth famous for his courage and good looks. To the Mexica-Aztec, Acamapichtli had the most excellent training to be king. It was then that Acamapichtli married the noble lady Ilancueitl to reinforce a political alliance with the lords of Colhuacan. After their marriage, the new rulers were brought to Lake Tetzcoco and crowned as the first king and queen of Aztec in 1375 C.E.

Acamapichtli ruled his kingdom effectively, and during his years in power, the city of Tenochtitlan began its construction. Buildings, residential areas, temples, parks, canals, and streets were created. The kingdom became more organized and enjoyed a certain period of peace and growth. King Acamapichtli had established his kingdom, but Ilancueitl had failed to produce an heir to the throne. This brought concern to the council of wise men, for they saw great misfortune for the kingdom if Acamapichtli should die without leaving a trained prince to occupy his throne. They all agreed that the king should take several wives from the local nobles. Each member of the council then gave him a young daughter as a wife to produce heirs to the throne. From these unions, Acamapichtli sired several children: Cuatlecoatl, Tlacahuepan, Tlatolzaca, Epcoatl Ihuiltemoc, and Tlacacochtoc. With Cocatlamihuatzin, the daughter of Cuauhtloquezqui, the highest priest of Huitzilopochtli, he

sired Huitzilihuitl, who became the most important of all the princes favored among the people. In addition, Acamapichtli had an illegitimate son named Itzcoatl with a Tepanec woman from Azcapotzalco; this son would later be venerated for his brave character, charismatic personality, and aptitude for leadership that allowed him to become king of his land. Itzcoatl was adopted by Cocatlamihuatzin and that is the reason why the native historian Chimalpahin considered him as her son.

Acamapichtli ruled for a period of 20 years, until 1395. Knowing that his death was approaching, King Acamapichtli called his council of wise men to give them his final instructions. He apologized for not being able to free the city from the domination of the king of Azcapotzalco. He did not appoint an heir because he wanted to have a democratic election. He specially requested that the entire city should choose their new king out of all possible seven princes he had fathered. In addition, he gave specific orders to have all his surviving wives well taken care of, and at the end of his speech, the first king of the Aztec, Acamapichtli, died at the age of 70. Unlike the later Aztec kings, Acamapichtli's burial was simple, almost average. He was not buried in a majestic tomb with gold tributes and a massive sacrifice of slaves. At the end of his reign, the Mexica-Aztec kingdom was extremely impoverished, and even the king had hardly anything to eat.

Political Expansion
KING HUITZILIHUITL

Unlike many other world monarchies, the Aztec monarchy consulted public opinion to elect their next ruler. The council met, and they all agreed that since each member had given Acamapichtli one daughter, the future king would be related through blood with one of the members, thereby ensuring the council's position and its importance in making political decisions. It was then in the year of 1396 that the elders convoked a massive congregation, with all the inhabitants asking them to elect their new king. All four sectors of the city of Tenochtitlan were called to vote: Moyotlan, Zoquiapan (or Teopan), Atzacoalco, and Cuepopan. The people, after paying honors to Huitzilopochtli and after hearing the passionate speeches of their priests and elders, claimed prince Huitzilihuitl as their new king and ruler of the Mexica-Aztec.

Huitzilihuitl's contribution to the kingdom was mainly in the political arena. The Mexica-Aztec remained a subcolony to the grand lord of Azcapotzalco, and taxation was extremely high, preventing the Mexica-Aztec from progressing and obtaining financial freedom. The council then proposed to have Huitzilihuitl ask for one of the daughters of the king of Azcapotzalco in order to establish a political alliance, to decrease taxation laws, to grant autonomy to the lands they inhabited, and to gain a degree of political independence. The council sent two elders to the king of Azcapotzalco to ask for one of his daughters in marriage. King Tezozomoc accepted the proposal and was pleased to send one of his daughters, Ayaucihuatl, as a consort and queen of the Aztecs. However, this decision did not please most nobles in King Tezozomoc's court, for they recognized the political and economical interests behind the marriage proposal and the multiple concessions the Mexica-Aztec were aiming to obtain. Nevertheless, the Aztec king, Huitzilihuitl, married Princess Ayaucihuatl. (An alternate source to Durán's, written by Chimalpahin, varies on the following events and parts of Aztec genealogy.)

Shortly after the union, she gave birth to Prince Chimalpopoca, whose name means "ring, or shield, of smoke." A great feast was celebrated in honor of the newborn prince, and all the nobles from Azcapotzalco were invited. During the celebration, it is said that the queen took the opportunity to ask her father to reform the laws, eliminate taxation, and grant complete autonomy to the Aztecs. From ancient readings, it appears that King Tezozomoc agreed to his daughter's petition, but these concessions made other powerful families from Azcapotzalco grow angry with envy, and they pressed the king to sustain all original policies. King Tezozomoc opted to maintain peace and please both sides on some level. He eliminated some of the taxes, yet sustained the most important ones that benefited the noble families of Azcapotzalco. Great honors were bestowed upon Queen Ayaucihuatl; she was beloved by the Aztec, and 13 years after her ascension, her people suffered and mourned her

death with great pain. Two years later, King Huitzilihuitl died, barely into his 30s, leaving the young prince Chimalpopoca as his heir to the throne.

KING CHIMALPOPOCA

Chimalpopoca followed the same politics as his father after becoming king of the Aztec in 1417, and he maintained a strong relationship with his maternal grandfather, King Tezozomoc. The young king hardly played any important role in the game of politics; he was inexperienced and an orphan without parental advice, completely subjugated to interests of the council. On the other hand, his grandfather loved him and wished to help him. Noticing his great affection, the council took advantage and often requested favors and avoided paying tribute to the lords of Azcapotzalco. The situation shifted from bad to critical when King Chimalpopoca made a request for access to the clean water from Chapultepec and to have the people of Azcapotzalco donate free labor, clay, and building materials to construct an aqueduct to bring this water to Tenochtitlan. The king of Azcapotzalco did not like the request; he observed that the Aztec, through the council, were constantly asking for favors and paying little in taxes. All the same, the king took the request to his council to ask for approval.

The council of Azcapotzalco, which was already extremely upset with the special favors granted to the Aztec monarch, took it as an opportunity to retaliate and call war against the Aztec. Under the claim that the relative newcomers had taken possession of their land without paying any form of tribute to their kingdom, the council of Azcapotzalco ruled that war was inevitable and that the Aztec tribe needed to be eliminated. King Tezozomoc, unable to contain the council members, begged them to spare his grandson and only to send him to exile. The council replied that his grandson was only associated to the kingdom of Azcapotzalco via a mother-son relationship; therefore, his true loyalty would remain connected to his father's interests only. They predicted that King Chimalpopoca would be loyal to the Aztec and not to the lords of Azcapotzalco. Upon hearing the final verdict, the old king Tezozomoc died of anguish. It remains uncertain what exactly happened, but the original strategy of open war was eliminated. Chimalpopoca's enemy opted to enter the palace secretly and murder Chimalpopoca and his only son while they slept, making sure no other prince would ascend to the throne and become king.

KING ITZCOATL

The murder of the royal family left the Aztec in a state of panic. Without strong leadership, their small kingdom was constantly under the menace of becoming eradicated. Conditions called for a leader who would give the Mexica-Aztec kingdom hope of survival against the dominion of the enemy kingdoms within the vicinity. The Aztec sought out military leadership. They needed a strong warrior king to protect the land and lead them into battle if necessary. It was then that the council traced the line of descendants of their great second king, Huitzilihuitl. Among all of Huitzilihuitl's line of descendants, only his brother Itzcoatl, the illegitimate son produced by King Acamapichtli and a Tepanec woman, met all the necessary qualifications. Without further delay, in the year of 1426, Itzcoatl ascended to the throne. The festivity of his ascension was quickly eclipsed by the level of tension and hostility between the Aztec and the Tepanec lords of Azcapotzalco. The Mexica-Aztec tried to evade war, and as a last gesture of good faith, they sent Itzcoatl's nephew Tlacaelel as a messenger advocating for peace. Maxtla, the new king of Azcapotzalco, did not want to persuade his advisers to opt for a peaceful coexistence between the two kingdoms and replied by simply saying that war was inevitable.

At that moment, the new king of the Mexica-Aztec showed his true power; he and Tlacaelel gave an emotional speech that exalted the masses and led their people to battle. The Mexica-Aztec of Tenochtitlan allied with Tetzcoco and Tlacopan (a dissident Tepanec town) to form the Triple Alliance, a strong military-political-economic coalition that would give origin to what became the Aztec Empire. The long tyranny of the Tepanec of Azcapotzalco had created hatred among its subjects. Tetzcoco, a tributary town of the Mexica, and the rebellious Tepanec of Tlacopan therefore risked their destinies to unite with the Mexica in a desperate war for liberation. The Mexica-Aztec and their allies fought fanatically and quickly overpowered their enemy. Only hours after the battle had begun, the Tepanecs started to retreat to their land. King Itzcoatl followed his enemy and invaded the city of Azcapotzalco, mercilessly killing the majority of the population; then he ordered the city to be burned down and the temples and royal treasures to be looted. When the battle ended, not much remained of the Tepanecs or of the city of Azcapotzalco. For the Aztec, this victory represented a significant passage through which they gained autonomy, ownership of their enemy's land, and a new warlike lifestyle. Political treaties now took a backseat; under the leadership of their new king, the Aztec began to spread fear and war, establishing colonies outside their original dominions. In the same fashion as the Tepanecs, the Coyoacans and Xochimilcas were defeated and annexed into the expanding Aztec kingdom.

In the year 1440, and after 14 years in power, the great warrior king Itzcoatl quietly died, afflicted by disease. Under his regime, the Aztec defeated the Tepanec of Azcapotzalco and freed their land from the Tepanec's oppressively strong fist. In addition, the Aztec expanded their territory and colonized neighboring tribes. Consequently, King Itzcoatl's funeral was a majestic display of wealth and formalities that lasted 80 consecutive days.

Military Expansion
KING MOTECUHZOMA I ILHUICAMINA

After Itzcoatl's death, his nephew Motecuhzoma Ilhuicamina (also known as Motecuhzoma I or Motecuhzoma the Elder) was elected as the new king. The new king ended the period of mourning, and after he was crowned, he invited his people to celebrate and to enjoy some of the new riches they had obtained from their recent conquests. This is perhaps one of the first times that the entire kingdom saw tangible riches distributed among the nobles and the commoners alike.

Another important event during Motecuhzoma Ilhuicamina's coronation was the visit of King Nezahualcoyotl, the ruler of Tetzcoco. There was a mutual friendship between the kings; they both came from similar backgrounds and were distant cousins. After the magnificent banquet celebrated in honor of the great kings, Nezahualcoyotl spoke privately with his cousin Motecuhzoma Ilhuicamina. He revealed that his main interest was to keep peace between the two kingdoms, especially since Nezahualcoyotl's land was not in such a fortunate situation as the land of the Aztec. In Tetzcoco, there was strife, hunger, and manifold casualty due to constant battles waged to defend their small kingdom against invaders. The Aztec king replied in a friendly manner and assured his cousin that there was no need for concern, that he would maintain perpetual peace with the people of Tetzcoco and that their kingdoms would work together to improve their defenses.

It appears that King Motecuhzoma I easily convinced the council to maintain peace with the people of Tetzcoco, but a simulated war against Tetzcoco was acted out to intimidate other towns and to mark Aztec superiority to the people from Tetzcoco. Upon concluding the simulation of war, the two kingdoms rejoiced and came together to celebrate. This well-structured plan enabled the two kingdoms to develop a symbiotic relationship. The small kingdom of Tetzcoco became an independent kingdom attached to the fast growing Mexica-Aztec kingdom. Unlike other lands conquered and subjugated to slavery, Nezahualcoyotl's territory and its inhabitants, having entered into the Triple Alliance, enjoyed freedom and rights. This methodology of politics rendered the Aztec culture as a very powerful and sophisticated one, which quickly developed a sharp political perspective.

After the "victory" of the lands of Tetzcoco, King Motecuhzoma I ordered the halt of all military activities and began the construction of a temple dedicated to Huitzilopochtli. During the next 12 years, military activity was reduced, and the Aztec king called upon all his newly colonized territories to provide materials, labor, and tributes to the great temple. Shortly after the decree, materials and labor started to arrive from the newly subjugated tribes—Azcapotzalco, Coyoacan, Xochimilco, Cuitlahuac, and Mizquic—as well as from Colhuacan, Tlacopan, and Tetzcoco. The 12-year peace and construction phase came to an abrupt stop when the masters of construction demanded larger bricks of stone to carve sculptures to adorn Huitzilopochtli's temple.

None of the Aztec land, including the newly conquered colonies, had the stone resources. It was necessary to travel abroad to import the stone, among other materials, to serve for ornamentation. King Motecuhzoma I decided to send an emissary to the nearby nation of the Chalcas to demand labor and material from their territories. Their leader, Lord Cuateotl, bitterly replied that his nation would not obey nor respond kindly to the demands made by the lords of Tenochtitlan. He reminded the Aztec king that the nation of the Chalcas was a free state and had no obligation to provide or pay tribute to Tenochtitlan or its gods. In addition, as a final warning, he closed his message by assuring the Aztec king that the Chalca were ready to engage in a bloody battle to ensure their freedom and defend their borders if necessary. King Motecuhzoma I interpreted the Chalca approach as a lack of diplomacy and as a great insult perpetrated against himself and his people. Immediately after receiving the message, he gave orders to destroy the Chalca and their city, temples, and gods, and to loot their treasure to pay for the completion of the sacred temple.

The Aztec then went to battle; they met with a brave and well-prepared adversary. Battles became ruthless, but the Chalcas appeared to be losing ground to the Aztec warriors when the Chalcas asked for five days of rest owing to religious duty. The annual festivity to honor their god Camaxtle was upon them, and they had taken an oath to conduct festivities in which Aztec blood would be the highest offering to their patron deity.

It is not quite clear why the Aztec respected the Chalca petition, but without further action, the Aztec went back to their resting camps and allowed for five days of peace to pass before returning to the battleground. Word of the events arrived to the Aztec king, and he too made the promise to honor Huitzilopochtli with festivities of blood if his divinity would lead the Aztec to victory.

At the end of the five days, the Aztec and Chalca met once more in battle. This time the war had become a sacred crusade in which, according to the two nations, even their gods would clash against each other on the battlefield. The battle concluded with the annihilation of the Chalcas when the Aztec troops cornered them in the hill known as Cocotitlan. There the Chalcas begged for mercy and for another rest period, but this time the Aztec denied it and imprisoned all the survivors. Upon the troops' return, King Motecuhzoma I greeted and honored his warriors with wealth and high honors. The prisoners then were sacrificed in honor of Huitzilopochtli; it is said that a huge bonfire was made and that the prisoners slowly burned while the priests ripped their breasts open and tore out their hearts. As for the territory of the Chalcas, it was confiscated, and their citizens became subjugated to the laws of the Aztec and their colonies.

Under Motecuhzoma I, the Aztec treasury multiplied, marking the beginning of the military power of the Aztec. The nobles gained power, wealth, territory, and slaves. Previously colonized lands remained loyal, living under fear of the powerful city of Tenochtitlan. Soon after, other tribes followed the same fate as the Chalcas and the ones before. Amequemecan, Tepepula, the Huastecs, Xochpan, Tzincoac, and Coaixtlahuaca soon fell and became subject to Aztec taxations.

Besides his military interest, King Motecuhzoma I emphasized the importance of Aztec history and sent multiple expeditions in search of Aztlan, the Aztec place of origin. Although expedition leaders were never sure if they found the real seven caves of Chicomoztoc, Motecuhzoma felt confident that he had recovered Aztec history and had given his people a sense of pride and identity. Throughout his reign, Motecuhzoma I also established his name in history. He was beloved by his people and feared by his enemies, and under his leadership, the Aztec kingdom became an empire. By the time of his death in 1469, after almost 30 years in power, Motecuhzoma I left a legacy of wealth, land, and grandeur no other Aztec king before him had accomplished.

KING AXAYACATL

The Aztec council members, in agreement with Lord Nezahualcoyotl of Tetzcoco, elected the sixth king. They chose a young man, son of Motecuhzoma, by the name of Axayacatl, who had a very good relationship with the many members of the council and was a distant nephew of Nezahualcoyotl. The new king was given an expanding empire that had accumulated riches and military power, but Axayacatl was never able to surpass his father's legacy. His regency was remembered as a combination of major conquest (as in the Valley of Toluca), some minor campaigns, and shameful military defeat (against the Tarascans). At the same time, however, his reign was distracted by intrigue and conspiracy by his enemies. For example, five years after his ascension to the throne, the noblemen of the Mexica city of Tlatelolco plotted to take hostage the city of Tenochtitlan, destroy the council of the elders, and emancipate Tlatelolco, with the ultimate goal of making it the new capital of the kingdom.

The ruler Moquihuixtli was the principal conspirator of this plot. He agitated his people, made idle promises, and claimed that the war god would grace them with victory. Axayacatl responded by going to war against the Tlatelolco province and massacring the rebels. The small town had no effective line of defense against the armies sent from Tenochtitlan. The city was seized, and Moquihuixtli was killed at the local temple of Huitzilopochtli, and his body was thrown to the bottom of the stairway. King Axayacatl was merciful with the lives of the women and children and the men who had not taken part in the rebellion, but the citizens of Tlatelolco were severely punished: They lost their Mexica citizenship, were lowered to the ranks of slaves, and were forced to pay high taxes to any other colonized territory.

In order to restore his reputation and to recover the respect and admiration of his people, King Axayacatl decided to wage war against the Tarascans and claimed the land of Michoacan as the newest annex to the Aztec kingdom. Unfortunately, Axayacatl did not enjoy the same success as his father had had acquiring land; Axayacatl's army of 24,000 men was nearly annihilated by the Tarascans, who were also formidable warriors. His vain dream of incorporating the land of Michoacan into his empire proved to be catastrophic. Most of King Axayacatl's military campaigns that followed met similar disappointing results, and at his time of death in 1481, his kingdom faced multiple upheavals and conspiracies that threatened Aztec stability.

KING TIZOC

The seventh king, Tizoc, rose to the throne in the same year as the funeral of his predecessor. Tizoc, who was Axayacatl's brother, was one of the youngest Aztec kings. Not properly trained as a warrior, much less as a monarch, he was often riddled with doubt. He is considered to be a very minor character in Aztec history. According to the writings of Durán, the emperor's system of government was heavily criticized because of his lack of courage. He showed no interest in expanding Aztec territory, he did not increase the empire's wealth, and under his leadership, all military activity became passive. The only significant achievement attributed to Tizoc was his interest in finishing the construction of the temple of Huitzilopochtli. King Tizoc died five years after his coronation. Due to his lack of character and his passiveness, it is believed that his death was part of a military conspiracy in which he was poisoned.

KING AHUITZOTL

After the death of their seventh king, the Aztec looked for a candidate who would be the exact opposite of Tizoc. They desired a young warrior full of vitality and strong military interest. The council decided to choose the youngest son of their fifth king, Motecuhzoma. However, this time, many nobles were hesitant about the election, for the past monarchs Axayacatl and Tizoc, also direct descendants of the great Motecuhzoma I, had failed to bring glory to the Aztec or to surpass the golden age of their father. With great controversy, in the year 1486, King Ahuitzotl, Motecuhzoma I's last son, ascended to the throne. The eighth monarch of the Aztec quickly came to enjoy the support of his military comrades, as he showed genuine interest in developing new martial strategies and greatly favored the military class. Although Ahuitzotl undertook war campaigns, he was best remembered for concluding, after eight kings and endless struggles, the construction of the Great Temple dedicated to Huitzilopochtli, their supreme deity.

King Ahuitzotl invited all the people that inhabited his vast lands to celebrate; every noble, warrior, commoner, and slave was commanded to attend the festivities that would represent the culmination of Aztec supremacy over the Valley of Mexico. There was no distinction of class, gender, or ethnicity. Tenochtitlan erupted with people, and it is said that from an aerial view, the city resembled a gigantic ant colony.

The ceremony began with the placement of the four most powerful lords of the Aztec Empire at the top of the pyramid, each one situated at a cardinal point. King Ahuitzotl stood next to the statue of Huitzilopochtli; beside him stood the ruler of Tetzcoco, Lord Nezahualpilli; the ruler of Tlacopan; and the king's adviser (*cihuacoatl*), Tlacaelel. The drums began to play at early dawn, and the first sacrifice took place. Lines of slaves and prisoners awaited as each lord conducted the sacrificial offering. One prisoner after the next was sacrificed from dawn to dusk for four continuous days; the temple of Huitzilopochtli poured a river of blood that emanated from the four cardinal points. It is said that 80,400 people were sacrificed during the four days, but this was probably an exaggeration. People at the footsteps of the temple waited for the blood to come down, then they collected it in small containers and spread it over their houses, temples, and municipal courts, as well as their faces, as a blessing. Tenochtitlan was covered in blood, and on the fifth day after the sacrificial ceremony had ended, the king honored the bravest warriors and lords by covering them with riches of gold and new weaponry.

Unlike the previous monarch, King Ahuitzotl worked hard to expand the Aztec Empire. During his government, he fought against multiple city-states and annexed them to Tenochtitlan. He engaged in war with the cities of Izhuatlan, Miahuatlan, Tehuantepec, and Amaxtlan and obtained great wealth. He colonized lands extending as far south as Guatemala. Because the newly acquired lands required protection and military domination, Ahuitzotl declared that all freeborn males of the age of 18 and up should be trained as warriors in order to reinforce the army and secure Tenochtitlan's economic interests. Additionally, Ahuitzotl devoted a great amount of effort to properly urbanizing the capital and populating cities such as Alahuiztlan and Oztoman, which he later used as military centers.

In the year 1502, upon return from a war fought in the area of Oaxaca, King Ahuitzotl was very ill. It is unknown what disease afflicted him, but in less than a year he lost his strength and became thin and brittle. He died accidentally that same year, during the inauguration of an aqueduct in Tenochtitlan. With his death, the empire suffered a great loss, for he was loved by his people, respected by the council, and admired by his military men. Under his government, the Aztec prospered, and their cities were modernized.

Aztec Civilization Reaches Its Zenith

MOTECUHZOMA II XOCOYOTZIN

In the year 1502, the Aztec elected Motecuhzoma Xocoyotzin (also known as Motecuhzoma II or Motecuhzoma the Younger) as their 10th monarch. He was the son of King Axayacatl, and he was strongly favored among many elders because he combined military and leadership qualities; in addition, he descended from a high-ranking noble house with strong prestige and power. Upon ascending to the throne, King Motecuhzoma II set in motion innovative policies that dissolved conventional political perceptions of the Aztec Empire. He saw the council of the elders as an outdated institution that needed reorganization to keep the empire alive. One of his first decrees was to establish a court of young apprentices who would serve the young king both in the military and intellectual fields.

The candidates were selected from the most influential and noble families of the Aztec Empire. Motecuhzoma II required that all candidates be male, between the ages of 10 and 12, and the legitimate child of two noble parents. He wanted young disciples so as to mold them more easily to his own ideology. The young boys were brought to the palace and raised to serve the royal family. Although their noble blood guaranteed them privileges and an elevated social status, they were warned always to be truthful and loyal to their king. The most insipid violations of trust and loyalty were grounds for immediate execution. Motecuhzoma II's clever strategy was created to protect him against conspiracy and treason, which had destroyed previous monarchs. Ironically, Motecuhzoma's demise was lurking

beyond the land of his empire. His official crowning ceremony took place in 1502, the same year the Spaniards arrived at the island of Cuba and began to colonize the Americas.

From 1503 to 1520, the Aztec Empire suffered a period of tumultuous upheavals; colonized territories struggled to gain their independence and, in most cases, were brutally subdued. Motecuhzoma II focused his attention on maintaining the unity of the Aztec Empire in response to these rebellions against Tenochtitlan and its monarch. Political policies created by the Aztec had curtailed tributary colonies' ability to prosper; their wealth was sent to Tenochtitlan, yet they had little or no political role in governmental issues. Different indigenous groups demanded autonomy and the elimination of taxation. This threat to Aztec supremacy forced the king to rule with an iron fist: Motecuhzoma II inflicted the most horrific capital penalties to those who defied his authority; torture, destitution, enslavement, and death were among the most severe forms. The 10th king of the Aztec made sure that his authority was respected and that no one who opposed him would go without punishment. In addition, he would also leave destitute the traitor's family and direct descendants by confiscating their possessions and land and by condemning them to slavery for life. On the other hand, Motecuhzoma II benevolently rewarded loyalty to both Aztec and colonized lands. When town and local rulers were loyal to his crown, they received sponsorship to build temples, schools, and palaces, and on many occasions their taxes were significantly reduced. His politics assured that those loyal to him could live peaceful lives and those who rebelled would earn a painful and cruel death.

The towns of Quetzaltepec and Tototepec serve as an example of Motecuhzoma's brutality. The inhabitants had become convinced by local leaders that a magnificent opportunity had arisen, positioning the towns to rise against Tenochtitlan and intimidate the new king. They built walls and trenches and blocked all roads and entrances to their towns. In addition, they refused to pay their taxes and claimed total independence from the Aztec Empire. Taking advantage of their geographical location, the two towns established military bases to ambush Aztec troops as they approached, while the Quetzalli

River protected the other side of their towns. They therefore believed themselves to be safe from enemy intrusion and left only a few warriors to protect the location. Historical records note that Quetzaltepec and Tototepec were agricultural societies, militarily inferior to Tenochtitlan. Nevertheless, these two cities, probably driven to their limit by Aztec oppression, decided to take a chance and gamble their peace to obtain their freedom. Motecuhzoma II and his troops arrived at the outskirts of the cities, and in a final gesture of good faith, the king sent messengers asking for immediate surrender of the troops and demanding only the heads of the leaders of the rebellion. In exchange, he would spare the cities, and no further penalties would be applied. Quetzaltepec and Tototepec refused the peace treaty and, as a final gesture of defiance, killed Motecuhzoma's messengers and disposed of their bodies in the river. King Motecuhzoma then gave the order to invade and burn down the cities and to kill every adult male, without mercy.

The Aztec troops displayed a mastery of military strategy. Motecuhzoma's army of 400,000 men razed the two towns of Quetzaltepec and Tototepec. The king formed several brigades of warriors, allowing all of his men time to eat and rest. While one brigade stormed Quetzaltepec and Tototepec, the other brigades rested. With this method, the attacks continued in a nonstop loop, and by the end of the first day of fighting, the cities had been breached. Meanwhile, other Aztec troops approached the Quetzalli River, quickly crossed it in canoes, and took control of the area. Motecuhzoma's tactics assured the Aztec a quick and bloody victory. The cities were completely destroyed, and the main conspirators were captured and taken to Tenochtitlan to be sacrificed in honor of Huitzilopochtli. Although he expected many people to die during the battle, Motecuhzoma gave specific instructions to his soldiers that they should not harm any women or children, whom he saw as victims caught up in the conspiracy of their towns' avaricious leaders.

Wars continued during the first years of Motecuhzoma's ascension to the throne. Shortly after Quetzaltepec and Tototepec, other important groups rose to overthrow the monarch, among them the Huexotzincas, Cholultecas, Tliliuhquitepecas, and Tlaxcaltecas, who followed similar fates. Fray Diego Durán depicts King Motecuhzoma II in his early years as a strong military figure who always took command of his armies to impart fear among the neighboring kingdoms.

During times of peace, Motecuhzoma would allow his army to relax, but for fear that the warriors would become passive, he would often call upon neighboring rival cities to participate in a *xochiyaoyotl*, or flower war. These events can be loosely interpreted as tournaments in which the war's consequences were real and the prisoners captured were sacrificed to local deities as trophies, but also in which no communal destruction took place and the participating cities' mutual feelings of hostility were kept between each other. In Aztec society, warriors gladly went to war but even more during the *xochiyaoyotl* because it was thought that warriors who died during these tournaments would have a pleasant death and would be taken to the same heaven or paradise in which Huitzilopochtli resided. These tournaments were used as battlefield-training sessions, and they provided prisoners of war who were sacrificed to the gods in order to gain favors.

A Prophetic Friend The Aztec Empire finally reached its plateau sometime during the rule of Motecuhzoma II. One day the monarch received a visit from his good and much older friend, King Nezahualpilli, lord of Tetzcoco. He arrived to warn him about an omen he had seen in the sky. He predicted that a more powerful kingdom would rise and destroy the Aztec Empire, that Motecuhzoma's cities would be torn down, his wealth stolen, and his land invaded. Nezahualpilli's apocalyptic vision came in conjunction with the appearance of a comet in the sky that foretold great catastrophes. Motecuhzoma summoned his astrologers, sorcerers, wizards, and healers to interpret the apparition of the comet in the night sky. Unfortunately, none of them had seen it or paid attention to the celestial event. The monarch, in shock and anger, sent all these men to be executed and their families disposed of and enslaved as the ultimate penalty for not fulfilling their responsibility as guardians of the celestial bodies. Once again, King Motecuhzoma consulted his good friend King Nezahualpilli, who only repeated the same prophecy. Motecuhzoma wept all night, and perhaps for the first time, he felt helpless and afraid. It is speculated that from this moment on, he became paranoid, and any unusual behavior or event triggered a deep-held anxiety to which he always reacted violently. After the last meeting between the two kings, the Aztec Empire began to slowly collapse.

Spanish Contact

A few years after King Nezahualpilli prophesied the arrival of the Spaniards, news arrived at Tenochtitlan about a floating mountain that had been seen passing along the empire's shores. Motecuhzoma II decided to send two of his most loyal men on a secret mission to investigate the phenomenon. Teuctlamacazqui and Cuitlalpitoc ventured out to the coast of Mexico. Upon their return, they described to the king a huge mountain with clouds floating on top of the ocean. Pale men with long beards and helmets occasionally emerged from the interior of the mountain. The Aztec scouts had seen a Spanish warship, which they described as a mountain, the ship's spinnakers (sails), which they equated with clouds, and the armor-clad Spaniards aboard the ship. Motecuhzoma paid the scouts well for their service and ordered them to keep the information a secret on penalty of death.

Immediately the king summoned his new set of priests, wizards, and diviners to predict who these pale men were. After the priests conducted multiple rituals and entered into trances, they arrived at the conclusion that these men were the direct descendants of the fair-skinned god Quetzalcoatl (Feathered Serpent), who had been exiled by other deities in a distant past. Quetzalcoatl, a peaceful god who taught humans how to harvest the earth, left Tula one day on a raft of snakes heading east promising to come back one day. (Over the years, the Toltec man-god Quetzalcoatl had become a full-fledged god in the Mesoamerican pantheon.) The description given to the priests by the two witnesses led them to believe that these men were Quetzalcoatl's descendants and had arrived to reinstall the peaceful teachings of the feathered serpent, long forgotten by the followers of the blood cult to Huitzilopochtli. This proved to be a fatal assumption in the history of the Aztec that brought devastation to their empire three years later when Hernán Cortés and the Spaniards disembarked in Veracruz.

When the conquistadores landed on the coast of the modern state of Veracruz, King Motecuhzoma II sent a commission of men to greet them and to take them directly to the city of Tenochtitlan. By this time, Motecuhzoma had become extremely paranoid. After the multiple prophecies about the destruction of Tenochtitlan, he became increasingly insecure, irrational, and in many cases, hysterical; he even considered hiding himself and his court inside a cave in order to remain safe from the approaching destruction. The Spaniards arrive in Tenochtitlan and were received with the highest of honors. The king and the nobles invited the foreigners to take residency in the imperial palace; Hernán Cortés, the captain of the expedition, gladly accepted. Clear communication was possible with the aid of the Spaniards' interpreter, Malintzin (La Malinche), or Doña Marina, an Indian woman who had learned to speak several languages, among them Nahuatl and Spanish. Malinche later became Cortés's mistress.

Historical accounts written by Durán described a meeting between the Spaniards and the Aztec king in which Motecuhzoma II offered Cortés a large amount of gold in exchange for Cortés's promise to return to his motherland and never set foot in Mexico again. Cortés refused the offer under the excuse that he was there to claim the land for his majesty King Charles V of Spain and to bring the teachings of Christianity to the natives of the land. After a long talk, Motecuhzoma and his court of men were made prisoners and secluded in their own palace under the pretense that they were going to be instructed in the Christian faith. In reality, the Spaniards were not interested in teaching religion, but rather in looting all the wealth from the palace, especially gold.

The Spanish Conquest

KING CUITLAHUAC

Tenochtitlan suddenly found itself under the control of the foreigners; the city's population was confused by the surprising events and their emotionally unstable king. Small groups began to plot the murder of

Cortés and the Spaniards. The council of elders, disapproving of the forced cooperation of Motecuhzoma with the Spaniards, decided to elect Cuitlahuac as the new king; however, Cuitlahuac, a patriotic warrior, lasted only about two months in his position because he died of smallpox, a disease to which the Indians did not have immunity. (Brought from the Old World by Europeans, smallpox decimated the native population of Mesoamerica and eventually became the main cause of indigenous deaths throughout the Americas.)

With Cuitlahuac dead, the conspirators waited for the annual festival known as Toxcatl, the official ceremony dedicated to the gods Tezcatlipoca and Huitzilopochtli. During this festival, while the Spaniards were distracted, the conspirators planned to murder them. It is unclear how Cortés uncovered the plot, but it is clear that he suspected a rebellion. He decided to pretend that he was unaware of the plot against him and his men and allowed the celebration to take place.

Cortés, however, needed to leave Tenochtitlan to stop a Spanish army that had been sent from Cuba to arrest him under charges that he was not loyal to the Spanish Crown. He left Pedro de Alvarado in command of the city. In Cortés's absence, while 10,000 unarmed Aztec noblemen were gathered for the celebration of Toxcatl in the courtyard of the main plaza at Tenochtitlan, Alvarado ordered 40 of his men to block all four exits from the courtyard and to murder all the Aztec nobles. Surprised by the attack, the nobles tried to escape, but they found themselves defenseless. The Aztec community, in a state of confusion, tried to defend itself, but its failure to organize a military defense spontaneously pushed it to defeat. In order to pacify the frenzy of the mob, Cortés, who had just returned, took Motecuhzoma to the top of a tall building where he forced him to command his people to surrender. Because of Motecuhzoma's mediocre speech and his acceptance of defeat, the Aztecs turned against him and threw stones and arrows at him, calling him a coward and a traitor. From that moment on, Motecuhzoma II was stripped of his crown and title by both the Aztecs and the Spaniards. Motecuhzoma met his death after the attack. The Spanish chronicles say that he died as a consequence of wounds produced by the stoning, but Indian accounts affirm that he was murdered by the Spaniards, stabbed five times while he slept. Because Motecuhzoma had lost the respect of his subjects and the interest of the Spaniards, no one took an active interest in setting the record straight. The exact nature of his death remains a mystery to this day.

KING CUAUHTEMOC

The crumbling Aztec Empire dispensed of the protocol and the rituals they had used in the past. The Aztec selected a new king to lead them into battle against the Spaniards. King Cuauhtemoc was elected in 1520 immediately after the unexpected death of Cuitlahuac. The son of the great king Ahuitzotl, he was a young warrior whose fighter spirit and devotion verged on fanaticism. Admired and loved by his people, the brave Cuauhtemoc led his troops against the Spanish invaders and created strongholds in the areas of Tenayuca, Cuauhtlalpan, Tula, and Tulantzinco. Under the direction of Cuauhtemoc, the Aztec might have completely defeated Cortés and his 500 men had the new king ascended to the throne earlier. The Aztec, for example, inflicted a painful defeat on the Spaniards known as the Noche Triste (Sorrowful Night). They lost the majority of their army and the rest retreated to Tetzcoco, where later they planned the siege of Tenochtitlan. But the Spaniards had already taken possession of important cities and had made powerful alliances with the enemies of the Aztec. The indigenous tribes of the Tlaxcaltecas, Xochimilcas, Huexotzincas, Chalcas, and Tetzcocanos united with Cortés in the war against the Aztec. These alliances were the key element in the destruction of Tenochtitlan and the Aztec Empire. By 1521, Cortés, marquis of the Valley of Oaxaca, conquered the Aztec and annexed the land of Mexico as a colony of King Charles V and his Catholic kingdom of Spain.

The last Aztec king, Cuauhtemoc, ruled for a short three-year period. After capturing Cuauhtemoc, the Spaniards tortured him in order to obtain the secret location where he kept the imperial treasures. It is uncertain that such treasures ever existed; they may have been a product of popular accounts by the natives, or they may have been a fiction created by the ambition of the Spaniards. But King Cuauhtemoc never confessed or betrayed his people.

Fearful that the Aztec would rise again against the Spaniards to rescue their monarch, Cortés took Cuauhtemoc with him on an expedition to Las Hibueras (Honduras), and there, under the charges of a possible conspiracy, sentenced the Aztec king to death by hanging. Cuauhtemoc was hanged from a tree, and his body was buried in secret place (supposedly along the border of Guatemala and Honduras) to prevent loyal followers of Cuauhtemoc from building a shrine.

In 1949, under the altar of the church in the town of Ixcateopan, Guerrero, archaeologists found what they believed to be the remains of Cuauhtemoc. The discovery created a controversy burdened with nationalistic and ethnic reactions, and a subsequent interdisciplinary research study demonstrated that the skeleton recovered was not that of Cuauhtemoc. However, traditional stories prevailed, and an exhibit of the bones remains in Ixcateopan today. More important, the people of the town are convinced that they have the tomb of the last Aztec king.

Not much is known about the last king of the Mexica, as little was written about him prior to the Aztec-Spanish war. History shows him to be a brave warrior and a loyal king, which earned him timeless admiration from both his people and his enemies.

After the conquest, in 1524, the first monastic orders arrived in Mexico and millions of native peoples were baptized under the Christian faith. This marked the end of the Aztec civilization and the beginning of 300 years of Spanish colonization.

READING

Origins and the Great Migration

Limón Olvera 1990, Durán 1994, Motolinia 1971, Aguilar and Brady 2004, Sahagún 1951–69, Arroyo Gaytán 1997, Manzanilla and López Luján 1993, Torquemada 1980, *Codex Boturini* 1944, *Codex Chimalpopoca* 1986, Alvarado Tezozomoc 1975: Aztlan, Chicomoztoc, and Colhuacan.

Mexica-Aztec History

Clendinnen 1991, Durán 1994, *Codex Azcatitlan* 1949, Davies 1982, *Codex Boturini* 1944, Sahagún 1951–69, Torquemada 1980, Clavijero 1978, Chimalpahin Quauhtlehuanitzin 1997, Alvarado Tezozomoc 1975, Díaz del Castillo 1963, Alva Ixtlixochitl 1975–77: Aztec historical events.

3

GEOGRAPHY OF
THE AZTEC WORLD

THE CONCEPT OF SACRED LANDSCAPE

It is said that the nomads of the northern steppes of Mexico (the Chichimec who included the Mexica) essentially had an astral religious view. Yet when they later migrated into the central valleys of Mexico, where peoples lived in a developed agricultural setting, they adopted agrarian gods related to the Earth (rain and corn) and combined them with those of the Sun, sky, and stars. In essence, as these two religious ideas (astral and agrarian) integrated, the Sun and the rain became the two great forces that came to rule the Aztec world and became the gods of two dominant societies. The warriors worshipped the sun god Huitzilopochtli, while the civilian population worshipped Tlaloc, the rain god. Both gods shared the highest place in the temple of their city.

This belief in the cosmological duality of sky and earth reveals the numerous aspects of nature that the Aztec either deified or held as extremely sacred. Among the most important of these were the Sun, the mountains, the Earth, the caves, the wind, and especially water in the form of rain, lakes, and rivers. All of these forces in one way or another provided sustenance and were depended upon for survival. Thus, life-giving natural forces were not only deified but permeated every aspect of Aztec daily life. The forces of nature were holy because they provided life. The combination of earth and water symbolized fertility itself, and most living things were thought to spring ultimately from the Earth. Caves played a major role in this respect as the metaphorical uterus of the Earth. According to the *Histoyre du Mechique* (a manuscript attributed to Fray Andrés de Olmos), Cinteotl, the maize god, was born in a cave and emerged to the surface of the mountains and fields to bring food to human beings. In keeping with this concept, religious and spiritual symbolism was incorporated into everyday living.

Urban Planning and the Cardinal Points

One example of this concept of the landscape being sacred can be seen in the location of Aztec cities and how they were established, planned, and built. The Aztec had a primary belief that the four directions of north, south, east, and west represented the four elements of the sun, the earth, the wind, and the rain. The Sun was the most important natural force because it rose in the east and set in the west. As the Sun ran along this dominant east-west axis, it also determined standards of survival by telling the people when to plant crops, when to harvest, and when the dry and wet seasons would occur. This sacred life-giving movement of the Sun was held in such high regard that even buildings and streets were placed in an east-west direction in honor of the forces that brought sustenance. This combination of agriculture and religion in the community resulted in visible expressions of religious and aesthetic forces coming together and becoming a part of the everyday life of the people. Thus the religious worship of the natural elements of everyday life brought the Aztec community into a direct spiritual contact with these primary elements of sun, sky, clouds, rain, wind, earth, water, and mountains.

TENOCHTITLAN

Other concrete manifestations and examples of these natural-religious expressions of sacred landscape are seen in the urban planning of Tenochtitlan, the Aztec capital. The Aztec assimilated and expounded upon these concepts of sacred landscape from the area predecessors of Teotihuacan and Tula. The Teotihuacanos and Toltecs also built their cities in lines of east-west and north-south directions oriented toward the rising of the Sun in the east and its setting in the west. These precedents enhanced the Aztec religious creation stories of one of their gods being born as the Sun and the birth of the people from their primordial mother, who is manifested in the female Earth.

Early Mexica-Aztec history and mythology preserve the story of a people originally coming from a place called Aztlan in the north and eventually migrating to Tenochtitlan in the central valley of Mexico. During this migration, the wandering Mexica are said to have stopped for a time at the sacred mountain Colhuacan, which contained the caves of Chicomoztoc (Seven Caves). In this story, the mountain acts as a source of life, where water is found in abundance, and the caves represent the womb of the Earth giving birth to humanity. In the next stage of the journey, the Mexica stopped at another mountain they named Coatepec, where they participated in rites of regeneration and rededication. It was there where the story of the birth of the god Huitzilopochtli began. Centuries later at Tenochtitlan, the Aztec would build a great pyramid with Huitzilopochtli's shrine on top, commemorating a mythic mountaintop battle between Huitzilopochtli and his siblings (see chapters 2, 6, and 9). Thus the ideas of sacred mountain, mother earth, the birth of the people, and the battle of the god Huitzilopochtli would all be manifested and commemorated in the building of a similar human-made mountain shrine, the Great Temple, in their capital of Tenochtitlan.

The Aztec word for city was *altepetl* (water mountain or water-producing mountain), further illuminating the link between the Sun, water, mountains, and Earth and the Aztec's historical myths and religious beliefs, and their incorporation into daily life. It must be noted that these stories have long prior histories in Mesoamerica and that the Aztec-Mexica probably took these versions and adapted them from earlier Classic Maya, Zapotec, and Toltec histories from as early as 950 C.E.

The Natural Elements

THE FERTILE EARTH

The Aztec use of sacrificial human blood is another example of the land being held as sacred. Human blood was the primary ritual fertilizing agent, ensuring the rising of the Sun, regeneration of the Earth's planting cycle, and ensuring the arrival of water for crops and seasonal changes. In Aztec religious mythology as stated earlier, the mountains were the heart of the Earth from which the Earth's life force, which governed all aspects of life, came. The mountains gave food and sustenance. As their gods had once offered their own blood as a sacrifice to sustain these natural life-giving forces, the Aztec, too, were obligated to do the same. Thus the religious aspects of buildings, state governance, war, social customs, and any other activity were tied to religious rituals of sacred land, natural forces, and sacrificial offerings. Furthermore, the Aztec buildings and temples themselves later symbolized a validation of Aztec rule, certified by the sacred Earth itself through religious sacrificial rites and rituals (see chapters 6 and 9).

As the idea of obtaining food from the land developed, the notion of belonging to the land and its interaction between humankind and nature grew. This idea became of such profound importance to the Aztec that they created a cyclical calendar of festivals performed in various sacred cities and natural locations. These religious rituals, in combination with the natural landscape, symbolized the regularity of seasons and the fertility of crops and animals. It also validated the status and functions of the religious leaders and secular rulers. Therefore, political legitimacy, religion and its rituals, food, shelter, and clothing all derived validity from the sacred landscape and natural forces. The Earth was viewed as the giver of life and the ultimate recipient of all that grows and moves on the surface. The Earth also was seen to have regenerative powers and was identified with procreation and agricultural fertility.

WATER

Overall, the Aztec had a metaphysical worldview, and the physical environment had wills and personalities. During the late 15th century, when the ruler Ahuitzotl inaugurated a new aqueduct bringing water into Tenochtitlan, priests dressed up as the female water deity Chalchiuhtlicue, or Jade-Skirt, and welcomed the water by burning incense, presenting turquoise, and sacrificing quail. In this ritual, the deity, priest, and natural element became equivalent and inseparable in action and thought. Water (in all of its manifestations), like the Sun and the Earth, was a life-giving force to be worshipped and honored in the various rituals throughout everyday life. Water and its sources were an extremely important resource for the Aztec, who valued cleanliness. Bathing and washing clothes was common practice. Another common practice was the use of steam baths (*temazcalli*), which were used for both physical and spiritual cleansing. It is said that the ritual steam bath was so important to the Aztec that almost every household had access to one.

The Symbolism of Human-made Architecture

The structure of sacred geography melded together topographical features and human-made symbols, allowing for religious communication among the

3.1 View of Mt. Tlaloc, with the temple of Ehecatl in the foreground, located in Huexotla, Mexico State (Fernando González y González)

people who embodied the social order, the natural forces, Aztec deities, and ancestral heroes.

TENOCHTITLAN

The great urban pyramid at Tenochtitlan was a principal icon of sacred geography designed to manifest the inherent power of things seen and unseen in the natural environment. By incorporating a combination of human-made architecture and sculpture with the sacredness of the landscape (in essence copying it), and through the use of religious rituals, the Aztec were able to reenact continually their creation myths that involved all of the natural elements, thereby invoking spiritual connection and material blessing from their gods.

MT. TLALOC

Another example of the joining of the natural and the artificial was at the temple on Mt. Tlaloc, located about three miles east of Tetzcoco and Huexotla, where an annual royal pilgrimage occurred every April or May, at the height of the dry season. Ascension of the mountain takes about six hours. There at the top, a ceremony was performed to call forth rain from within the mountain. It was commonly believed that water from streams and lakes, rain from the mountaintops, and clouds originated in the mountains. For this reason, the Aztec connected the mountains with water. This pilgrimage, which culminated with the Aztec king walking through a womblike enclosure in the temple atop Mt. Tlaloc, was a fertilizing mission to a sacred place where the underworld met the sky and where energy could be recycled between the social and natural orders. The Aztec rulers themselves would become active agents performing essential roles in the change of seasons by honoring the rain god Tlaloc with sacred regalia, food, and human blood. In this ritual, the Aztec ruler and priests, by fertilizing the god and mountain with these offerings, ensured in the weeks to come that the first clouds of the rainy season that formed around the mountain would eventually become dark thunderstorms blown down by the god Quetzalcoatl onto the valley, bringing the renewing life-giving rain for the growth of crops. The Aztec were so meticulous in their manner of incorporating religion and nature that a line of sight can be plotted from the Great Temple of Tenochtitlan to a notch between Mt. Tlaloc and its neighbor, Mt. Tlalocto, where the Sun rises on equinoctial days. This implies the intricate and complex overall cosmological and architectural planning of these temples with the seasons and the Sun.

Honoring Sacred Landscapes

To the Aztec, the Earth was the center of life: It gave birth to all life (such as people, crops, and animals) and also took life away. Thus the sanctity of the Earth lay in both its creative and destructive forces that reside in caves symbolizing the cavities of its womb. In time, everything that emerged from the Earth returned back to it.

FESTIVALS

The Aztec had a great number and variety of rituals and festivals celebrating the cyclical forces of nature. Huey Tozoztli was celebrated at the height of the dry season, consecrating the dried seed corn to prepare it for the coming planting. It was followed by the festival of Huey Tecuilhuitl, which took place in the middle of the rainy season and honored the first tender shoots of maize that appeared in the growing period. That last of the corn festivals was Ochpaniztli, which signaled the harvest time and the coming of the dry season. Many ceremonies featured honoring both maize and earth deities together.

ART AND ARCHITECTURE

The Aztec carved many stone monuments (along with buildings) that were either placed facing the mountains or at the foot or top of the mountains, many times facing east to the rising Sun. These monuments commemorated the daily appearance of the Sun and its provision of heat, light, and the eternal renewal of the seasons, and further reveal how Aztec daily life was inextricably combined with celebrating religious festivals that honored their gods and nature. The same was true of other forms of buildings, architecture, and art.

STONE DISK OF COYOLXAUHQUI

If the rituals and sacrifices could not be performed at the sacred mountains (because they were either too

far or too inconvenient to reach), then the rituals were performed at the human-made altars and pyramids of a city. One of the most striking examples of combining a sacred myth with the natural landscape is the carved stone disk of Coyolxauhqui, which lay at the foot of the stairs of Huitzilopochtli's pyramid temple in Tenochtitlan. The 3.5-meter (10-foot) disk is a carving that illustrates the story of how the warrior-god Huitzilopochtli protected his mother by fighting, killing, and decapitating his jealous sister Coyolxauhqui at the top of Mt. Coatepec. As the disk commemorated this battle and victory on Mt. Coatepec, the Great Temple was also called Mt. Coatepec. The disk honored this sacred myth and mountain, as did the reenactments of the myth in ritual ceremonies performed on this man-made mountain. The Great Temple provided a focus that united religion, architecture, and nature.

In this same way, all the urban pyramids, shrines, and artwork combined sacred religious myths together with natural forces and displayed the eternal power of the natural environment. Additionally, these material examples of sacred landscape strengthened religious beliefs and emphasized the Aztec sense of obligation to return the food and energy that society had taken from the Sun, sky, Earth, and water. It was a way of keeping the natural cycles of rebirth, renewal, and rejuvenation intact (see chapter 8).

GREAT PYRAMID AT TENOCHTITLAN

The Aztec history and economy were also legitimized and validated by the land and ritual sites reaffirming their existence as far back as the primordial beginnings of time. In actuality, the Great Temple at Tenochtitlan had two temples that represented two sacred mountains. The first temple commemorated the myth of the god Huitzilopochtli, which validated Aztec history and the Aztec right to rule and to make war. The second temple was built to honor the god Tlaloc, who was the god of the mountain of sustenance; representing water, rebirth, and the life-giving forces of wind, sky, and rain. In addition, the Great Temple stood as a symbol of the cosmic process in motion since the creation of time. It was the cosmic symbol and embodiment of a mythical event, a symbol and memorial of achievements and rulers that provided an explanation of the land and history, thereby giving the Aztec a sense of identity in the natural world. In essence, they conducted almost all aspects of their lives in step with the cyclic rhythms of the seasons, which gave them a sense of rightness and a conviction of how to live their lives.

The dry season, for example, was a time for war, whereas the beginning of the rainy season was a time for cultivation. All of their religious rituals, ceremonies, commemorative monuments, buildings, and pyramids not only incorporated their sense of the natural forces, the landscape, and themselves as all living and affecting one another as one but also legitimized Aztec conquests. Nature and religion gave them the right to claim land and people, validating the state government as an integral part of the cosmic order; they also provided security in establishing a sense of being. The Aztec believed that the natural forces of the world and humanity were dependent on each other, and this reciprocity was responsible for their past, their present, and their future.

The Aztec may have worked out complex chronological systems in an attempt to understand such natural phenomena as the seasons and the movement of the stars. Nature was also used as a way to understand their past, foresee the future, and regulate their religious rites and put them in their proper sequence and order according to the natural time frame of the seasons.

THE VALLEY OF MEXICO: THE LAND, THE LAKE, AND NATURAL RESOURCES

Geographical Environment

Most people will agree that certain environments facilitated the development of great civilizations.

One such environment was the Valley of Mexico. This valley provided the elements necessary for humans to settle, ponder, and create. Although the Valley of Mexico lacked a large river, it had many necessary factors for civilization such as freshwater, fertile land, game, and some natural barriers. Although most of the water has by now been drained from the valley, during the time of the Aztec Empire (1428–1521), the landscape resembled a water-filled bowl, with the five lakes surrounded by mountains and active volcanoes. This physical geography provided the raw materials for the Mexica to build the Aztec Empire.

The Aztec were the last Native American civilization to live in the Valley of Mexico, and most of the landscape still bears the ancient Nahuatl (Aztec) names. The landscape is dominated by three large snowcapped volcanoes: Popocatepetl (Smoking Mountain), Iztaccihuatl (White Woman), and Mt. Tlaloc (Rain God). The southern end contains a volcanic escarpment called the Ajusco, which continues on the west. These mountains served as a natural barrier that limited the number of people who arrived at the fertile basin.

LAKES

The Valley of Mexico had five interconnected lakes that covered the central basin (see map 2). These lakes were Lake Zumpango, Lake Xaltocan, Lake Tetzcoco, Lake Xochimilco, and Lake Chalco. They were created thousands of years ago when the Valley of Mexico was a true valley whose rivers first flowed from the south to form Lake Chalco and Xochimilco, which then flowed north through a broad channel into the slightly lower and salty water of Lake Tetzcoco. The water then continued to flow farther north to connect and form Lake Zumpango and Lake Xaltocan. The freshwater aspect of Lake Chalco and Lake Xochimilco, which contrasted with the undrinkable water of Lake Tetzcoco, played an important part in Aztec society and culture because during the rainy season, these lakes had a tendency to overflow and threaten the livelihood of people in the larger central basin.

In the 1200s, the cluster of southwestern islands in Lake Tetzcoco that would become the city of Tenochtitlan teemed with wildlife. These islands

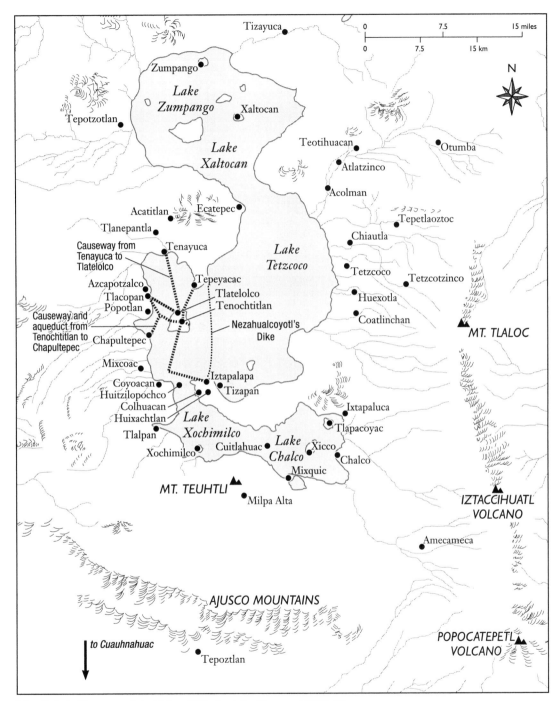

Map 2 Lake Tetzcoco and the Valley of Mexico (after Townsend 2000: 27)

were surrounded by marshes, willow groves, reed beds, and nopal cacti growing on upturned rocks. This plant life in turn fed an abundant aquatic life that attracted a variety of waterfowl, such as eagles, herons, ducks, and cranes.

THE VALLEY BEFORE THE AZTEC

The valley saw different civilizations flourish long before Tenochtitlan was established. Teotihuacan, for example, dominated the Valley of Mexico between 200 and 600 C.E., and it was one of the largest cities in the world. However, around the year 700 C.E., Teotihuacan was burned to the ground, and most of its inhabitants disappeared. Did they die? Migrate? No one knows for sure. Some scholars believe that the city's collapse led to a population decline in the surrounding area. But this fertile area could not remain underpopulated for long, and about 100 years after the fall of Teotihuacan, a new group of nomadic people who spoke Nahuatl began to arrive on the shores of the five lakes. Other scholars think that there were Chichimec-nomadic groups who arrived during the last years of Teotihuacan. They settled down as subjects of the great city and learned its highly advanced customs and traditions. In a certain moment they played a role in the destruction of Teotihuacan and birth of Tollan (Tula) and the Toltec civilization.

These Nahuatl speakers commanded a language that had never been spoken in central Mexico. According to their legends, they arrived in waves of tribes and over time intermarried with the settled inhabitants of the Valley of Mexico. Their offspring resettled many ancient towns and created numerous new ones during the main period of migrations (800–1200 C.E.). Azcapotzalco, a town that occupied the western shore of Lake Tetzcoco and had prospered alongside Teotihuacan, continued being an important center. Two small towns named Xaltocan and Zumpango developed on islands among marshes and shallow lakes in the north. Continuing waves of Nahuatl tribes led to other polities such as Colhuacan, Tlalpan, Xochimilco, Mixquic, and Chalco, which sprung up in and around Lake Chalco and Lake Xochimilco to the Southeast. The people made this area economically stable because they used the plentiful summer rains and freshwater springs to create hillside farming terraces and develop *chinampa* agriculture (shallow marshlake farming).

Watering Systems

CHINAMPAS

The southern area of the lakes had been highly developed over the centuries. Today, one may hire a flat-bottomed canoe and drift through the quiet narrow canals of the "floating gardens of Xochimilco," but these are only a fragment of the surviving *chinampa* system that once covered miles of lakebed terrain. During the days of the Aztec Empire, the *chinampa* farming zone on Lake Xochimilco produced at least half of the food for Tenochtitlan, which may have had as many as 200,000 inhabitants people upon the arrival of the Spaniards in 1519. However, as early as the 1450s, Tenochtitlan's population already exceeded 150,000 people, and the Tenochcas were continually in need of new tracts of land in order to feed themselves. They accomplished this by conquering most of the cities in the valley and using the conquered people to build, perfect, and expand agricultural terraces, aqueducts, and *chinampa* fields. All aspects of maintenance, from irrigation to fertilization, were tightly controlled and regulated, with a high regard for reusing all of the materials at their disposal. (In fact, the Aztec were so concerned about not letting anything go to waste, that the *chinampa* gardens were even fertilized with human excrement collected in canoes from Tenochtitlan and then transported to the fields.) For more information about *chinampas*, see chapter 12.

NATURAL SPRINGS

Located in Lake Tetzcoco, basically a large, salty lake, Tenochtitlan was always in search of sources of freshwater. Although the Aztec took over and expanded the *chinampa* system in Lakes Xochimilco and Chalco to feed themselves, they had to look for other new sources of freshwater. Studies and archaeological evidence show that the Aztec were able to build a sophisticated drainage system of dams, sluice gates, and canals in order to control the water supply to their huge tracts of floating farms. These measures helped avoid flooding in the rainy season while maintaining moisture during the dry season to ensure that plentiful harvests could occur year round.

Though aqueducts were also built to bring freshwater into the city, the Tenochca had a continual problem about water. During the rainy season the valley was prone to flooding by violent storms, which would then drain very slowly, and during the dry season, there was a problem of not having enough water to drink as evaporation tended to lower the water level. During the 1400s, the lake around Tenochtitlan was already quite shallow, so there was a great fear that especially during times of drought, the lake might dry up. These worries were heightened soon after Tenochtitlan allied itself with Tetzcoco and Tlacopan (ca. 1428); in the dry season, the Aztec had a difficult time supplying the city with drinking water from the springs on the island.

AQUEDUCTS

The birth of the empire (through the Triple Alliance) probably led to large population growth, yet the water of the lake itself was too salty for drinking. The only solution was to bring in freshwater from the springs that flowed on the mainland. At first, the Aztec brought this water in their canoes, but as this was an inadequate method of transporting water, Motecuhzoma I had built an aqueduct more than three miles (five kilometers) long and about five feet (1.5 meters) wide to bring water from the springs of Chapultepec. This remarkable work of engineering was made following the design of King Nezahualcoyotl of Tetzcoco. A second aqueduct was later built from the southern city of Coyoacan to provide water for the ever-growing Tenochtitlan. Nezahualcoyotl of Tetzcoco also started numerous water projects to bring freshwater to towns and cities in his area of the empire. Among the best preserved are the channels that brought water from springs below Mt. Tlaloc and Santa Catarina del Monte to the town of Tetzcotzingo (see chapter 9). Yet even with the aqueducts, the people were still dependent on seasonal rain to water the vast terrace systems and new farmlands in the foothills. Once again, as the population in the central valley

increased, it is probable that the population eventually exceeded the food production made available through rainfall agriculture. Thus as more aqueduct systems were employed, the rivers were diverted in the northwest to create dams and streambeds for even larger fields suitable for farming.

In addition to the *chinampa* farms and the irrigation needed to produce crops on the islands and the mainland, the lakes of the valley also contained extensive reed beds, which provided another almost inexhaustible source of prime material. The Aztec learned to use fibers from not only the reed plant but also palm leaves, cane slats, cacti, and notably the long broad leaves of the aloe plant to make all kinds of items, such as baskets, seats, mats, stools, and small low tables. The *petlatl* (fine and coarse reed mats) was as much an object of everyday life as the overstuffed recliner is today. (The *petlatl* [petate] is still widely used at present.) In fact, the reed mat became an important symbol of Aztec kingship.

The Spanish writer and soldier Bernal Díaz del Castillo, who took part in the conquest of Mexico, likened the many cities built on the lakes to those of the legendary medieval tales of Amadis of Gaul. Today, most of the lakes are drained and modern Mexico City's towers and buildings command the center of the valley. This city, one of the largest on earth, covers about a third of the entire central valley, and only a very small portion of the lakes remains. Thus, the Tenochca developed the physical environment of the Valley of Mexico into an empire that first the Spaniards and, later, Chilangos (a sardonic nickname given to people who live in Mexico City) have transformed into the hectic capital of modern Mexico.

THE ISLAND CITY OF TENOCHTITLAN

Centuries ago, the Aztec founded their island capital in a breathtaking site known as the Valley of Mexico. Today the site is not ideal. Mexico City sits on a fault line in an unstable lake bed surrounded by mountains and active volcanoes that trap smog. Nevertheless, 23 million people (one out of five Mexicans) continue to live in the city. Why? They live there because they are held by traditions of power that hark back hundreds of years.

Origins

Tenochtitlan, the capital of the Aztec Empire, stood on the site of modern Mexico City. These are not different cities. Tenochtitlan is the foundation and the cultural base for Mexico City. The story of Tenochtitlan begins in the early 1300s when a tribe known as the Mexica, a Chichimec subgroup arrived in the Valley of Mexico. But by the time of their arrival, most of the Valley of Mexico appeared to be taken. The north was controlled by the Otomí, the west by the Tepaneca, the east by the Acolhua, and the south by the Xochimilca, the Colhua, and the Chalca. The Mexica, however, followed a vision spoken to them by their god Huitzilopochtli, who told them to settle where the mighty eagle sat upon the nopal (prickly pear) cactus devouring a snake. The Mexica saw this sight on a small island located in the center of Lake Tetzcoco. In 1325, they built their city upon that island and named it Tenochtitlan (the place of the nopal that grows on the rock). A second city named Tlatelolco was built around the same time a few hundred meters north on an adjoining island by dissident Mexica, the Tlatelolco, who would become great traders.

The twin islands upon which Tenochtitlan and Tlatelolco were built did not at first sight appear to have the resources needed for the growth of an empire. There were meager agricultural prospects and a lack of building materials. Furthermore, Tenochtitlan and Tlatelolco were surrounded by cities that were generally hostile. However, the Mexica were very close to the practices of their hunter-gathering ancestors, and they were thus able to make use of the positive features of the islands. If at first they could not farm, the many forms of available, edible aquatic life, snakes, fish, and birds allowed hunting, and other types of produce such as frogs, crustaceans, insect eggs, and lake algae allowed a type of gathering. As the Mexica were surrounded by hostile neighbors,

Tenochtitlan came to specialize in war. Surrounding enemies were easily reached via the lake, which allowed large numbers of soldiers and materials to be moved by canoe. Tlatelolco, on the other hand, took advantage of its proximity to other people to develop trade with the Colhua, Chalca, Xochimilca, and Mixquica to the south, the Acolhua in the east, and the Tepanec in the west. The traders of Tlatelolco became so successful that their market became the largest in Mesoamerica. Therefore, after only a few decades, the Mexica of Tlatelolco and Tenochtitlan began to make their influence felt as "traders and raiders."

Initially, the Tenochca were vassals of the more powerful city of Azcapotzalco, but they eventually allied themselves with Tetzcoco and Tlacopan to conquer Azcapotzalco in 1428. The Triple Alliance was the beginning of the Aztec Empire because it brought together three important tribes from the Chichimec migrations: the Mexica of Tenochtitlan, the Acolhua of Tetzcoco, and the Tepaneca of Tlacopan.

City Layout

People often compare the island city of Tenochtitlan with Europe's Venice, but the urban traditions of the Aztecs were based on Mesoamerican concepts. Mexica *pipiltin* (nobles), *macehualtin* (commoners), and *pochtecah* (traders) learned about their nomadic Chichimec and civilized Toltec ancestors in public schools. They learned that the Tenochca and other Nahuatl-speakers used the name *altepetl* (water-mountain) for "city" because a city was a copy of the natural environment. Since they believed that the landscape was bound by the four cardinal directions, they divided their cities into four quarters, and they raised a two-temple pyramid at the heart of each city. This pyramid represented the womb of the pregnant Earth reaching out to the heavens, and the two temples represented the belief that the universe was ruled by a force that had a male and a female aspect. Therefore, duality and the four directions were an integral part of the institutions, plan, and architecture of Tenochtitlan and later Mexico City.

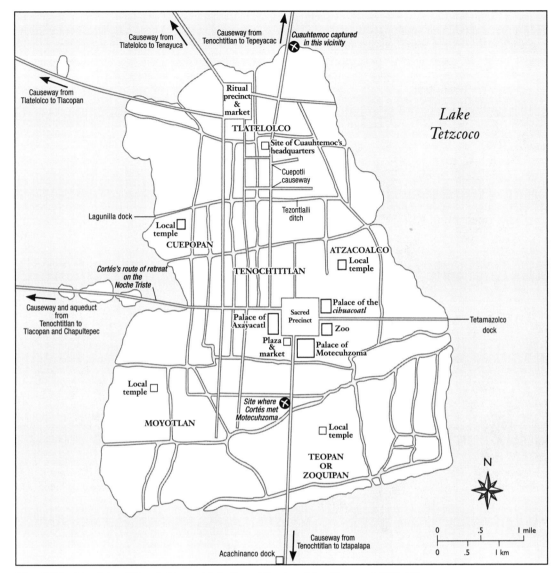

Map 3 The island city of Tenochtitlan, with its Sacred Precinct (after Townsend 2000: 29)

Government

The *altepetl* (city) of Tenochtitlan was ruled by the *tlatoani* (speaker, or "he who speaks") and the *cihua-coatl* (woman-serpent). This dual leadership reflected the Aztec belief that every institution, from families to cities, should be represented by the male and female force that governed the universe. The *tlatoani*, by speaking for the city and controlling the military forces, represented the father who worked outside harvesting, trading, and fighting. The *cihuacoatl* pro-vided for the internal rule of the city just as a mother directed the activities of the home. Eventually, as in Rome, the growth of the Aztec Empire led to a change in government, and the office of *tlatoani* become kinglike. The first of these independent kings was Itzcoatl (1427–44); he was chosen by a council of four people because he was related to the last *tlatoani* and had military experience. Subsequent leaders were chosen for the same reasons.

Tenochtitlan, like most Aztec cities, had four *campan* (quarters), and it is possible that at one time the council that selected the *tlatoani* had represented each quarter of the city. There is some evidence of this from the Huichol and Cora, Chichimec tribes who never migrated south to the Valley of Mexico. These two tribes, from the present-day states of Jalisco and Nayarit, continue to organize their towns and villages into four quarters (A, B, C, and D). Every year the elders from each quarter choose two people from one quarter to rule for a year. They always choose in the same order, so if in 1900 the rulers came from the A quarter, then in 1901 the elders would choose someone from the B quarter, and so on. Furthermore, the historian James Lockhart discovered Spanish records written after the conquest that show evidence of a rotational system in indigenous institutions at Chalco and Tenochtitlan.

Social Identities

People in the Aztec world defined themselves by their *altepetl*, so the people of Tenochtitlan saw

3.2 View of the city of Tenochtitlan-Tlatelolco, with its causeways and bridges. Detail of a mural by Diego Rivera, National Palace, Mexico City (Fernando González y González)

themselves as Tenochca. There was however a smaller unit of organization called the *calpulli* (big house) that represented a clan and a neighborhood. Usually, the *calpulli* was made up of a group of *macehualtin* (commoner) families led by *pipiltin* (nobles). According to laws passed by Motecuhzoma II, each *calpulli* had to have a school (*telpochcalli*). The *calpulli* also served as the basis for the squadrons of the Aztec army, for maintaining small temples to the god of the *calpulli*, and for other such needs of everyday life (see chapters 4 and 5).

Becoming a Center of Trade

In 1474, the Tenochca ruler Axayacatl captured Tlatelolco (see chapters 2 and 5). This event affected every *altepetl* and *calpulli* in the Aztec Empire because the union of these two cities made the site of Tenochtitlan-Tlatelolco the economic and political center of the Valley of Mexico. Tlatelolco was a trade city whose *pochtecah* (merchants) had over time created the largest market in Mesoamerica, in large part owing to three characteristics, identified by architectural historian Wolfgang Braunfels common among waterfront cities such as Tlatelolco and Venice: Ships can dock in front of homes, people from the trade city have an impulse to acquire possessions or colonies, and the city is entered at the center. Tenochtitlan, meanwhile, was the city of warriors. The drive to conquer came from that city. Each Aztec ruler began his reign with a campaign to bring prisoners for sacrifice at the great temple. The conquest of Axayatctl led, therefore, to the concentration of trade and tribute in Tenochtitlan-Tlatelolco. This city for all intents and purposes became the capital of the Aztec Empire.

Tenochtitlan-Tlatelolco resembled a spider web. This city, situated in the western part of Lake Tetzcoco, was connected to the mainland by five great causeways (*calzadas*) to Tlacopan, Chapultepec, Tenayuca, Iztapalapa, and Tepeyac. Three of these causeways led to the heart of the city and the Sacred Precinct of Tenochtitlan. The city was divided into four *campan*, which were organized into smaller equal plots (*calpulli*) marked off by canals and streets. The central precinct of Tlatelolco with its famous marketplace was in the north, connected to the causeway to Tlacopan. Many of the streets that were crossed by water also had bridges that could easily be removed. These main causeways also acted as dikes, which were easy to build due to the shallowness of the lake. Yet here and there, the causeways were broken to let the water flow under wooden bridges, because it was dangerous to bottle up the currents of the lake. This dense grid of walkways, narrow canals, and causeways also provided routes for foot traffic and canoes, which were needed because the Aztec had no wheeled vehicles.

Architecture

The architecture of the city was dominated by bright colors and triangular shapes. Aztec architecture consisted of open square areas and raised quadrangular platforms forming hollow squares within regular geometrical shapes. Additionally, all of the ceremonial buildings, platforms, and stairways were symmetrically arranged to provide a visual hierarchy oriented to Aztec religious beliefs founded in the four directions. Pyramids and plazas were built along a line showing a dominant east-west axis. Their construction also symbolized and echoed sacred beliefs in the elements of earth, wind, fire, and water; for example, pyramids for Ehecatl (the wind) tended to be circular to allow the god to circle around his temple (see chapter 9).

The Sacred Precinct

The Sacred Precinct was the most important ceremonial center in Tenochtitlan, and today many of its ruins lie beneath downtown Mexico City. The Sacred Precinct measured approximately 182 meters (600 feet) east to west and 160 meters (528 feet) north to south. Within its wall were wide-open spaces and pyramids with multi-colored shrines. The wall had gates to the north, south, and west that led to the great causeways of Tacuba, Iztapalapa, and Tepeyac. In addition, there was a gate to the east that led to the Tetamazolco dock. The Great Temple was the highest building, with two shrines atop: a red painted shrine to Huitzilopochtli and a blue painted shrine to Tlaloc. It commanded the eastern half of the Sacred Precinct and was neighbored by a *tzompantli* (skull rack). The round temple pyramid of Quetzalcoatl rose roughly in the center. The western half contained the *calmecac* (school for the nobles), the ball court, and the Temple of the Sun. The Sacred Precinct represented the fusion of Toltec and Chichimec beliefs that was integral to Aztec religion: Inside the walls, a priest who entered from the western entrance would walk by the *tzompantli*, adjoining ball court, and circular pyramid of Quetzalcoatl, all of Toltec origin, on his way to the Great Temple with its twin shrines to the Chichimec solar god Huitzilopochtli and the pre-Toltec rain god Tlaloc. These buildings symbolized the past and the present, the Toltec and the Chichimec heritage of the Aztec.

The area just outside the walls of the Sacred Precinct held buildings needed for the everyday running of the city, such as palaces, houses of dignitaries, and the marketplace. The house of the *cihuacoatl* and the royal zoo stood along the eastern wall. The Palace of Axayacatl bordered the western wall, and the southern gate led to the imperial palace of Motecuhzoma II (the site occupied by the modern National Palace). These two palaces housed the *tlatoani*, his wife, family, and many of the bureaucrats needed to run the city. Archaeology at other Aztec sites reveals that surrounding houses were probably the homes of the paper makers and ink makers, who provided these tools needed by the rulers. This main square was also the site of one of Mesoamerica's largest markets, second only to Tlatelolco's market. Tenochtitlan's marketplace was very orderly but also crowded with people.

Market of Tlatelolco

The center of Tlatelolco was the economic center of the united city Tenochtitlan-Tlatelolco, and it had two halves. The western half contained the main pyramid of Tlatelolco, which is the current site of the Plaza of the Three Cultures. The eastern side had the marketplace of Tlatelolco, which was the largest in the American continent (see chapter 9). Cortés reported that as many as 60,000 people exchanged goods in this market. In shape, it resembled a modern-day open-air market (*tianguis*) in Mexico or a swap-meet in the United States. The selling of merchandise was organized into specific areas and then by rows. Items ranged from basic necessities, such as corn and tomatoes, to exotic goods, such as feathers and bolts of the finest cloth. Nearby judges heard complaints of cheating and stealing and issued harsh sentences. The Aztec did not use coins or paper money. Instead they bartered and used cacao (cocoa beans), cotton cloaks, and gold-filled feather quills for money (see chapter 12).

Residential Homes

Most Aztec homes in Tenochtitlan were rectangular houses built of adobe walls and thatched roofs. Simple homes might have only one building with one doorway, but larger homes had several buildings whose doors opened around a central courtyard. The size of the house depended on whether *pipiltin* or *macehualtin* lived there. An important Aztec city for evidence about families and living arrangements is Quauhchichinollan because census documents for this city from the 1540s have survived. The English version of the census for Quauhchichinollan, by S. L. Cline, reveals joint families and nuclear families living side by side, but the joint family was more common. It included a father, a mother, children, and other relatives. The houses of *pipiltin* were sometimes raised platforms and colored with vibrant colors, but these homes followed the same basic design of buildings arranged around a central courtyard.

Effects of the Conquest

In 1521, the Aztec Empire came crashing down. An alliance of Spaniards and mostly Tlaxcalans conquered the great city of Tenochtitlan-Tlatelolco. The leader Hernán Cortés then built a new city on top of the Aztec capital. Eventually, this new city received the name of Mexico. A few Spaniards might have concerned themselves with the purity of their blood, but the majority of the population in Mexico City soon became mixed. The descendants of the Aztec, knowing that they had had a dual Chichimec-Toltec heritage, over time accepted that their heritage had become both indigenous and Spanish.

The site that embodies this acceptance of *mestizaje* (mixed blood) is Mexico-Tenochtitlan. In Mexico City, three places of worship represent the concept of the duality of *mestizaje*. At the corner of Guatemala and Argentina Streets stand the remains of the Great Temple of Tenochtitlan and its shrines to Tlaloc and Huitzilopochtli. To the north is the Plaza of the Three Cultures with its Tlatelolco pyramid and a Spanish church on top. And in the neighborhood of Tepeyac is located the modern basilica of Our Lady of Guadalupe. These three buildings prove that the belief in duality or *mestizaje* will remain as long as Mexico exists. However, Mexico City must give up some of its power. The centralization of the Aztec Empire did not end with the Spanish conquest. Today, trade and tribute (taxes) still flow from the provinces to the capital, but not enough money is given in return, even as Mexicans flock north to the United States. As long as Mexico City retains its great centralized power, Mexicans from other cities will continue to migrate north, and eventually, they will develop a new *mestizaje* based on a Mexican and American heritage.

CITY-STATES AND NEIGHBORING PEOPLES

The Valley of Mexico has been the stage for a thousand dramas. Long ago, a teenager hid himself as warriors from Azcapotzalco approached his father. This teenager was named Nezahualcoyotl, and in the following moments, he witnessed what no one should ever see: The people approached his father, the ruler of Tetzcoco, and stabbed him to death (c. 1412 C.E.). Nezahualcoyotl survived and fled. Though heartbroken, he grew into a respected leader, and in time he brought an army from Tlaxcala and Huexotzinco into the Valley of Mexico to seek justice. More than a hundred years later (in 1519), strangers with "smoking trumpets" (gunpowder weapons) arrived in the area controlled by Tlaxcala. They were Spaniards led by Cortés and his translator, a native woman named Malintzin (La Malinche). Cortés defeated the Tlaxcalans and made them his allies. The Spaniards and the Tlaxcalans marched to the Valley of Mexico, and for the second time, an army of Tlaxcalans battled in the Valley of Mexico. Nezahualcoyotl and Cortés both took advantage of the political situation in the Valley of Mexico and beyond. Both allied themselves with the Tlaxcalans because their lives depended on it. Studying the tribes that made up the Aztec Empire can explain the factors that led to the march of the Tlaxcalans.

The Heritage of Teotihuacan

People had lived in the Valley of Mexico for thousands of years. In 1418, the Valley of Mexico was controlled mostly by Nahuatl-speaking tribes who believed that they had a dual Chichimec-Toltec heritage. For them, human time began with Teotihuacan, the city of the gods.

They were wrong. Teotihuacan was a huge and prosperous city, but it was built by humans who had already been living in the Valley of Mexico. Teotihuacan dominated the Valley of Mexico from the first to the eighth century C.E., and its great works of art, monuments, and pyramids prove that indeed Teotihuacan controlled other city-states. Goods from this great city traveled as far away as modern New Mexico to the north and modern El Salvador to the south, and their beliefs in the Feather Serpent (Quetzalcoatl) and goggle-eyed Tlaloc continued up to the arrival of Cortés. There were also the ruins of Toltec Tula, dating from the 10th to the mid-12th centuries, located about 60 miles to the northwest of Tenochtitlan. Tula became a center of mythic significance, in part because of its historical achievements that grew in the legends of the people who would become the Aztec.

The Chichimec

The Nahuatl-speaking Chichimec from the north began arriving in the Valley of Mexico around 800 C.E. in waves. During the 10th century, some Chichimec groups arrived and allied themselves with the Nonoalca to create Tula and the Toltec Empire. Other Chichimec groups continued arriving, and by around 1200, they probably contributed to the fall of the Toltec.

There were primarily four major migrant Chichimec groups who wandered into the central valley of Mexico. The first group established cities such as Tlaxcala, Tenayuca, Huexotla and Chalco; the second were the Tepanec, who would eventually settle on the western side of Lake Tetzcoco at Azcapotzalco; the third were the Acolhua, who would take over the unoccupied lands of the eastern basin, with Tetzcoco as their capital; the fourth would be the Mexica-Aztec, who built Tenochtitlan and Tlatelolco on the remaining uninhabited islands on the lake.

Around 1371, Tenochtitlan became a subordinate to the expanding Tepanec city-state of Azcapotzalco, the first society to rise to empire status since the fall of Tula 300 years before. Yet in time, the Tepanec allowed the Mexica to conquer their own *chinampa* settlements. The Mexica executed many campaigns in the Xochimilco area, approximately 10 miles south of Tenochtitlan.

As time passed, the Mexica continued joining the Tepanec in other campaigns and expeditions as far south as Cuernavaca, west into the Toluca valley, and even into the old Toltec lands that lay in the northwest. The Mexical also aided the Tepanec in their war with Chalco at the southwestern end of the lakeshore and in campaigns and conquests against Xaltocan. Again the Mexica were awarded with significant tracts of land. Intermarriage between the ruling class of the two peoples further strengthened the Mexica position in an empire that eventually reached as far as Cuauhtinchan in the valley of Puebla.

At the time of Nezahualcoyotl's birth (1402), the Otomí people controlled the north shores of the central lakes, but the rest of the valley was controlled by Chichimec tribes. The Tepanec controlled the west, the Acolhua ruled the east, and the Chalca, Xochimilca, Colhua, and Mixquic ruled in the south. Other city states such as Tlaxcala, Huexotzinco, and Cholula were outside the Valley of Mexico to the east. Tezozomoc, leader of the Tepanec, coveted the Acolhua city-states. In fact, the Acolhua and the Tepanec did not need to fight because Tezozomoc's granddaughter was married to the Acolhua ruler, Ixtlilxochitl, and was the mother of Prince Nezahualcoyotl, but since ambition does not respect family, Tezozomoc declared war on the Acolhua.

This war lasted several years. Ixtlilxochitl came close to victory, but Tezozomoc sent warriors to murder Ixtlilxochitl. They succeeded and Nezahualcoyotl escaped to Tenochtitlan, where his uncles Itzcoatl, Motecuhzoma, and Tlacaelel lived, and then traveled to Tlaxcala and Huexotzinco to gather support. Tezozomoc was now the most powerful ruler of the Valley of Mexico.

Nothing happened while Tezozomoc lived, but when he died in 1427, pandemonium set in. Maxtla, a son of Tezozomoc, murdered his brother and seized the Tepanec throne. Itzcoatl became the *tlatoani* of Tenochtitlan. The next year a combined army of Mexicas, Acolhuas, Tlaxcalans, and Huexotzincas attacked Azcapotzalco for 112 days. According to legend. Nezahualcoyotl slew Maxtla, and Azcapotzalco fell. Afterward, the Huexotzincas and Tlaxcalans went home. The Mexica of Tenochtitlan, the Acolhua of Tetzcoco, and the dissident Tepanec of Tlacopan, meanwhile, had formed the alliance that began the Aztec Empire.

The Aztec Empire

The Aztec Empire began with an alliance among the city-states of Tenochtitlan, Tetzcoco, and Tlacopan. This alliance allowed the Aztec to increase their manpower, and under the able leadership of Itzcoatl and Nezahualcoyotl, the empire grew by conquering, first Azcapotzalco, then the rich agricultural city-states of Xochimilco and Chalco. The Aztec went on to conquer the other cities of the valley, including Colhuacan, Tlalpan, Milpa Alta, Mixquic, Xicco, Tlapacoyac, Ixtapaluca, Cuitlahuac, and Huixachtlan. Ironically, only Tlaxcala resisted Aztec armies.

Over time and through prolonged contact, the Aztec inherited, selected, and adapted various religious, economic, and social forms from a succession of the earlier peoples. For example, each Chichimec tribe held in high regard and even incorporated many of the religious myths and practices from Teotihuacan. The great works of art, monuments, and pyramids were respected and even viewed as sacred. In addition, the ruins of the Great Tollan (place of the reeds), from which the name Tula derives, became a center of mythic significance. The people of Tetzcoco claimed a close affinity to the Toltec because their first *tlatoani* Xolotl had married a Toltec princess. Later, the Aztec claimed and absorbed the cultures and religions of both of these past empires to establish their own validity and authority.

From both cities, the Aztec not only incorporated their images and ideas of construction and art but also adapted their sacred mythologies. For example, the Aztec derived a creation story about the birth of the Sun, which broke the primeval setting of silence and darkness of the world. Tula also provided the fable of the ruler-builder-priest-god Topiltzin-Quetzalcoatl and his struggle for power and rivalry with the shamanic wizard Tezcatlipoca. These sacred mythologies allowed the Aztec to accept practices of animal and human sacrifice. Furthermore, the ideology of empire was justified by Teotihuacan and Tula.

Time passed, and by 1519, only Tlaxcala opposed the Aztec, who controlled most of central Mexico. But hope was running out for the Tlaxcalans until the Spaniards, led by Hernán Cortés and guided by Malinche, arrived from the east. Did the Tlaxcalans believe that Cortés was Quetzalcoatl? It is not known, but once again, the Tlaxcalans allied themselves with someone (the Spaniards) who brought war to the Valley of Mexico. The Tlaxcalans were a great asset. Their Chichimec-Toltec heritage made them strong. They had archers and warriors as good as any in the Aztec Empire. The war lasted two years, and when it was over, the Aztec Empire was shattered. Most of the Aztec city-states, including Tetzcoco, eventually united themselves with the Spaniards, and Tenochtitlan finally fell on August 13, 1521.

In the end, many cities joined the Spaniards because of the overwhelming and despotic rule of the Aztec. For years, they had suffered military threat, economic and political oppression, and humiliation. Among these were the Tlaxcalans, the town of Tepeaca, the Huexotzincas, and the Chololans, an old ally of the Aztecs' who wanted their own independence. Eventually, even Tetzcoco lent her support to the Spanish, letting the Spanish use their eastern shore as a harbor for their boats and ships to attack Tenochtitlan. So, the Aztec were conquered not just by the Spanish but by many surrounding indigenous allies led by the Tlaxcalans.

LINGUISTIC HISTORY AND DISTRIBUTION OF THE NAHUA PEOPLES

The Aztec peoples spoke languages that have been classified as Nahuatl, and today this language continues to be used by more than 1 million speakers in Mexico and Central America. People commonly believe that Nahuatl is a dialect, but that assumption is incorrect. Nahuatl is a language. Dialects are varieties of a single language, whereas languages cannot be understood by a speaker of another language. For example, a Spanish speaker cannot understand Nahuatl or Russian, but he or she can understand Mexican Spanish and Castilian Spanish. Furthermore, Nahuatl and Spanish belong to different groups of languages that are known as language families. Today, because of the comparative method, we know that Spanish belongs to the Indo-European family and Nahuatl belongs to the Uto-Aztecan family. The comparative method is a procedure in which cognates (words from different languages with similar pronunciation and meaning) are compared. For example, the Spanish *uno*, French *une*, and Latin *unus* are Indo-European cognates for the word "one." In the comparative method, scholars take these cognates apart sound by sound and discover patterns that help them determine relationships. These can then be illustrated by a family tree. (The table on page 69 shows a partial family tree for Indo-European languages.)

Today, most Nahuatl speakers occupy an area from central Mexico to El Salvador, but they originated elsewhere. Their histories proclaim that they came from a place called Aztlan (see chapter 2). Linguist Catherine Fowler, in 1983, convincingly showed that the homeland of Uto-Aztecan-speaking groups was in an area centered in Arizona and includes parts of New Mexico, Sonora, Chihuahua, Nevada, and California. This is a large area far from central Mexico. At this point, however, it is impossible for scholars to link the mythical Aztlan to the homeland of Uto-Aztecan languages. After all, there are many speakers of other Uto-Aztecan languages such as the Hopi, Comanche, Tarahumara, Cora, and Huichol who have never lived within the Aztec Empire. Therefore, two things are needed to present the history of Nahuatl: the comparative method and Aztec legends.

Scholastic Explanation of the Origins of Nahuatl

The comparative method depends on two principles: that cognates are related and that sound change

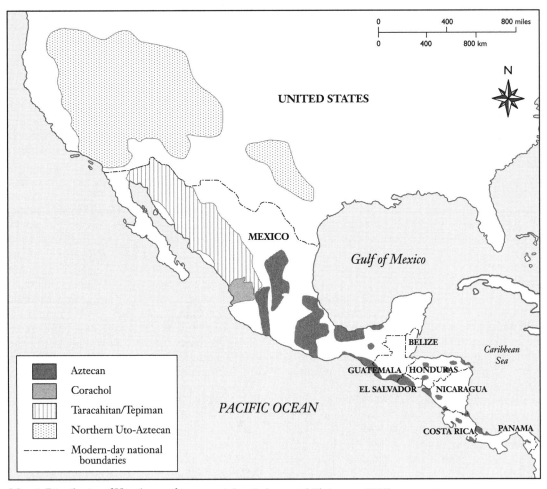

Map 4 Distribution of Uto-Aztecan languages (after Beekman and Christensen 2003)

FAMILY TREE OF INDO-EUROPEAN LANGUAGES

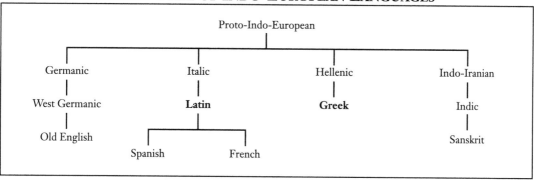

is not random. Language families are similar to human families. A mother language, such as Latin, gives birth to daughter languages, such as Spanish and French. The table below shows some cognates in the Uto-Aztecan family. Among the member languages of Hopi, Tubalatulabal, Tarahumara, Cora, Central Nahuatl, Pochutla Nahuatl, and Pipil Nahuatl, the cognates for "screech owl" are probably clearest: in Hopi, *tokori;* Tubalatulabal, *tukluluh;* Tarahumara, *tutuguri;* Cora, *tukuruu;* Central Nahuatl, *tekolootl;* Pochutla, *tekolo't;* and Pipil, *tekuluut.* They share the sounds *t, k,* or *g* and *e, o,* or *u.* It is easy for the consonant *k* to change to *g* (pronounce *ago* and *ako* and see how similar these words are); this is a regular sound change. It is even easier for vowels to change, and that is why these cognates have *e, o,* or *u* in similar positions.

In the table below, there is a clear pattern; the first consonant in the cognates for "water" and "three" changes from *p* ➔ *b* ➔ *h* or *w* ➔ nothing.

This and other sound changes lead to the language tree shown in the table on page 70. In it, Tubalatulabal, Hopi, and Southern Uto-Aztecan (SUA) are three branches (among others not presented here) of the Uto-Aztecan family. As the table indicates, at some time in the past the SUA branch broke off. This means that SUA speakers lost contact with the speakers of Hopi and Tubalatulabal. If these patterns are an indication of migrations, then SUA clans traveled south into northern Mexico, southwest through the hills of Nayarit and Jalisco, and southeast into the Valley of Mexico until they reached the Atlantic Ocean and Central America. Northern Mexico peoples spoke Sonoran branch dialects, which included Yaqui, Tarahumara, and Tepehuan. Nayarit and Jalisco spoke the closely related Cora and Huichol. Central Mexico spoke Central Nahuatl; Pochutla, a town in Oaxaca, spoke Pochutla Nahuatl, and Central America spoke Pipil Nahuatl.

COGNATES OF UTO-AZTECAN LANGUAGES

	Hopi	Tubalatulabal	Tarahumara	Cora	Central Nahuatl	Pochutla Nahuatl	Pipil Nahuatl
Pine	Loqo	woho-	okoko	huku	okotl	okot	ukut
Water	**p**aa-	**p**aa-	**b**a'wi	hah	aatl	at	aat
Screech owl	Tokori	Tukluluh	tutuguri	tukuruu	tekolootl	tekolo't	tekuluut
Louse	Ati	- - -	te, teke	ate	atemitl	ato'mi	atimet
Three	**p**aayom	Paay	**b**aikia	**w**aika	yeeyi	ey om	yey

FAMILY TREE OF UTO-AZTECAN LANGUAGES

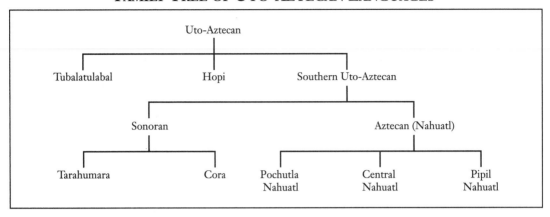

Many linguists have grouped Nahuatl (or Aztecan) into three branches: Pochutla Nahuatl, Pipil Nahuatl, and Central Nahuatl. These are basically groupings of dialects of Nahuatl, but whereas Central Nahuatl has many surviving dialects, Pipil and Pochutla Nahuatl are almost extinct. The table below shows cognates for the three groups.

Pipil and Central Nahuatl are for the most part identical. Pochutla varies more, as in the examples for "grass" and "cane," where it has an *e* instead of the *a* in Central Nahuatl and Pipil. Based on evidence regarding sound change, linguists have concluded that Pochutla was the first dialect to split off. Then, at a later time, Central Nahuatl and Pipil split. It is impossible to say when in time these splits occurred, because time is difficult to estimate in the comparative method. We can turn to Aztec legends, however, for a chronology.

NAHUATL (OR AZTECAN) DIALECT GROUPS

	Central Nahuatl	Pochutla Nahuatl	Pipil Nahuatl
Cane or reed	aakatl	Aket	Aakat
Eye	ish	ishtotolu't	ish
Heavy	etiik	Eti	Etik
Grass	sakatl	Skeet	Sakat

Aztec Legends on the Origins of Nahuatl

Nahuatl-speaking tribes first began to arrive in the Valley of Mexico around 800 C.E., but we do not know which dialect they spoke. These tribes eventually came to be known as the Chichimec, and one branch of the Chichimec, together with the Nonoalca, created the Toltec civilization (950–1200) that ruled central Mexico from the city of Tula. There appear to have been many conflicts between the Nonoalca and the Chichimec. One of these conflicts was preserved in the myth of Topiltzin-Quetzalcoatl. During the 10th century, Quetzalcoatl (Feathered Serpent) ruled Tula. He was considered a wise ruler, but his pacifism angered some people. One day an enemy from a warlike faction tricked Quetzalcoatl into getting exiled. A dejected Quetzalcoatl gathered his followers, left Tula, and traveled east until he reached the sea, where he boarded a snake raft and disappeared from Toltec records. Maya writing and images continued the story, and they record that in 989 C.E., foreigners led by a chief named Kukulkan (Feathered Serpent) conquered Chichén Itzá.

In another story, the Nicoya people led by two chiefs fled to modern Nicaragua to escape Olmeca-Xicallanca oppression. Their name Nicoya (or Nicoyotl) can be translated as "I am a wild dog." Therefore, it is probable that these people saw themselves as Chichimec. The Nicoya spoke Pipil, or a very similar dialect.

After the fall of the Toltec (c. 1200), the migrations of the Chichimec into the Valley of Mexico continued. Groups such as the Tlahuica, Chalca, Acolhua, Tepanec, and Mexica arrived and created a new civilization of city-states. Eventually, the Mexica, the Acolhua, and the Tepanec from Tlacopan allied themselves and created the Aztec Empire. The people of the Aztec Empire spoke a dialect from the Central Nahuatl group that scholars call Classical Nahuatl.

Conclusion

The comparative method and Aztec legends help explain the history of Nahuatl, one of many languages making up the Southern Uto-Aztecan branch of the Uto-Aztecan family. Nahuatl speakers eventually developed three dialect groups: Pochutla, Pipil, and Central Nahuatl. Pochutla might have been the language of the Toltec but that cannot be proven. Pipil was the language found in Central America. Classical Nahuatl, one of the dialects of Central Nahuatl, became the language of the Aztec Empire. Eventually, the Aztec Empire fell, but its descendants use dialects of Central Nahuatl to this day. This language is common in the Mexican states of Veracruz (314,121 speakers), Puebla (399,324), Tlaxcala (24,728), Hidalgo (205,079), San Luis Potosí (131,363), Guerrero (130,550), the State of Mexico (39,823), Mexico City (28,309), Morelos (18,974), and Oaxaca (9,158). In other words, more than 1.3 million people continue to use the melodic language of the Aztec Empire.

READING

The Concept of Sacred Landscape

Townsend 2000, Soustelle 1979: sacred geography; Townsend 2000, Smith 2003: Mt. Tlaloc; Gruzinski 1992, Durán 1967, *Codex Boturini* 1944, Sahagún 1951–69: myths and rituals; Soustelle 1979: water.

The Valley of Mexico: The Land, the Lake, and Natural Resources

Escalante 2002, García Quintana and Romero Galván 1978, Sanders, Parsons, and Santley 1978: hydraulic problems and works in the Valley of Mexico; Palerm 1973: Lake Tetzcoco; Townsend 2000, Soustelle 1979, Sahagún 1951–69: the Valley of Mexico.

The Island City of Tenochtitlan

Coe and Koontz 2002, Smith 2003, Townsend 2000: the foundation of Tenochtitlan and Tlatelolco; Lockhart 1992, Townsend 2000, Smith 2003: Aztec urban traditions; Hassig 1988, Hinton 1972, Smith 2003: kings and commoners; Braunfels 1988, Hassig 1988, Smith 2003: the union of Tenochtitlan and Tlatelolco; Smith 2003, Townsend 2000: architecture; Coe and Koontz 2002, Matos Moctezuma 1980, Smith 2003, Thomas 1993, Townsend 2000, Tsouras 1996: the central precincts of Tenochtitlan and Tlatelolco; Smith 2003, Cline 1993: the homes of Aztec commoners and nobles.

City-States and Neighboring Peoples

Davies 1980, León-Portilla (*The Broken Spears*) 1992, Tsouras 1996: the death of a king; Davies 1980, Tsouras 1996; importance of Tlaxcala; Smith 2003: city-states and tribes; Davies 1980, Hassig 1988, Tsouras 1996: rise of Tezozomoc.

Linguistic History and Distribution of the Nahua Peoples

Campbell 2001: comparative method, cognates, and Indo-European family tree; Fowler 1983:

Uto-Aztecan homeland; Boas 1917, Campbell and Langacker 1978, Silver and Miller 1997: cognates of Uto-Aztecan; Campbell 1985, Silver and Miller 1997: Uto-Aztecan family tree; Campbell 1997: Southern Uto-Aztecan clan migrations; Campbell 1985, Silver and Miller 1997: Nahuatl dialect groups; Coe and Koontz 2002, Nicholson 2001: Quetzalcoatl myth; Campbell 1985: Nicoya legend.

4

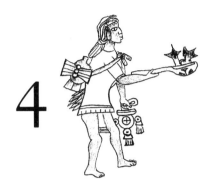

SOCIETY AND GOVERNMENT

Social Structure and Class Hierarchy

The social structure of the Aztec was divided into two classes of free individuals who had the rank of citizens, determined by birth: the nobles (*pipiltin*; singular, *pilli*) and the commoners (*macehualtin*; singular, *macehualli*). Within this structure were different levels. The hierarchy of the nobles in descending order was the *tlatoani* (plural, *tlatoque*; the king/ruler), the *cihuacoatl* (second-in-command and ruler over internal affairs), the *Quetzalcoatl totec tlamacazqui* and the *Quetzalcoatl tlaloc tlamacazqui* (two supreme priests), the *tetecuhtin* (singular, *tecuhtli*; the high lords), and the *pipiltin*, or the rest of the nobles.

Pipiltin

The highest-ranking *tlatoani* was the Aztec emperor and ruler of Tenochtitlan (*huey tlatoani*) who was also a member of the Triple Alliance (together with the cities of Tlacopan and Tetzcoco). Other *tlatoque* ruled over smaller cities and towns. Each of the *tetecuhtin* controlled a smaller area called a *calpulli* (neighborhood).

Priests, or *tlamacazqui*, came from both noble and peasant backgrounds, but only the men of noble birth could become the high priests *Quetzalcoatl totec tlamacazqui* and *Quetzalcoatl tlaloc tlamacazqui*. *Quetzalcoatl totec tlamacazqui* was associated with the cult of Huitzilopochtli, the war god, while *Quetzalcoatl tlaloc tlamacazqui* was associated with Tlaloc, the rain god.

Despite these specific social distinctions, there were in a sense only two levels in the Aztec social structure—noble and non-noble. In Nahuatl, the word *pilli* means "child." A person could only be considered a *pilli* if he or she was a child or a descendant of a king. The status of the *pilli* was transmitted through male and female lineages alike. Even if only one parent was a *pilli*, the child would be of the status of a *pilli*. Similarly, if a child's father was the *tlatoani*, the child still would be of the status of a *pilli*.

Members of the nobility enjoyed certain privileges. They lived in impressive houses with many servants and possessed expensive luxuries such as fine food, elegant clothes, works of art, and rich jewelry. Among Aztec men, only the *pipiltin* were allowed to be polygamous, because they alone could afford many wives. The *Crónica Mexicayotl* lists 22 children of Axayacatl, 20 of Ahuitzotl, and 19 of Motecuhzoma. Tlacaelel, the *cihuacoatl*, had five children with his principal wife, then a son or daughter by each of his 12 secondary wives.

Another privilege that the nobles received was tribute from the *macehualtin* in the form of personal services, food, and labor. This arrangement facilitated the building and maintenance of temples, palaces, and other public places in Tenochtitlan and elsewhere.

Furthering the nobility's standing was the privilege to enter their children in the *calmecac* (school of higher education) to be trained in the military arts, religion, law, history, the calendar, oral literature, and writing. Girls of noble heritage also attended the *calmecac*, but they learned skills such as how to direct servants in household tasks, how to weave cotton textiles, and other concerns of the home. The purpose of the nobility was to serve the ruler, another aspect of the *calmecac* education, and they were given jobs as ambassadors, tax collectors, provincial governors, teachers, scribes, judges, priests, and army generals.

Macehualtin

The Nahuatl word *macehual*, in a general sense, means "commoner." The *macehualtin* included merchants, artisans, peasant farmers, and the rest of the free citizens who were not of noble birth. For the Aztec, the commoners were the backbone of society; they worked the fields, sold and traded goods, and gathered tribute to give to the *tlatoani* as a tax. Those taxes would then go back to the community to maintain activities and services.

Macehualtin had to work for and serve the nobility. They worked on noble lands and at palaces and were required to go to war if they were called. All *macehualtin* belonged to a *calpulli* and possessed land that at their death was inherited by their descendants.

The *macehualli* children went to school just as the *pilli* children did; however, rather than receiving instruction at the *calmecac*, the commoners attended the *telpochcalli* (youth house). If a child was exceptionally gifted, he would be allowed to attend the *calmecac*. At the *telpochcalli*, the boys learned how to become warriors, and the girls, good housekeepers. The children also learned the basics of their ancestral history and religion.

Within this group was its own hierarchy, for the *pochteca* (merchants) and master craftsmen outranked any peasant farmer. Nevertheless, these groups could accumulate great wealth through their trade but were never considered nobles, because they usually did not have a royal blood heritage.

Below the commoners in social rank were the *mayeque* (landless serfs) and then the *tlacotin* (slaves). The *mayeque*, a kind of subclass of the *macehualtin*, were not part of a *calpulli* because they were bound to the land of the nobles they served, although they were free individuals. The *tlacotin* were also bound to a master's land but for different reasons. One became a slave as a result of being punished for a crime, usually theft, as a result of acquiring a gambling debt, or by being captured in war. Also, during times of famine or hardship, people sold their children into slavery, but individuals could buy back their freedom if situations improved. So slaves were bound to a master only as long as their debt was to be paid. The master was required to feed and clothe the slave, and the slave was required to work without pay. Slaves could marry whomever they chose, and the children of slaves were born free. (For more information about slavery, see chapter 13.)

TLATOANI

The *tlatoani* (he who speaks) was the king of a city-state, and he owned or controlled the land within that city-state. All rulers of *altepetl* (town) communi-

4.1 *A tlatoani seated on his* icpalli, *based on the* Codex Mendoza *(Maria Ramos)*

ties held the title of *tlatoani*, regardless of how large or small their population was. The *tlatoque* of Tenochtitlan believed they were superior to the *tlatoque* of neighboring communities. Over time the Tenochtitlan *tlatoque* conquered many towns and ruled a vast area.

In painted manuscripts, the *tlatoani* is depicted sitting on an elevated platform or chair (*icpalli*) wearing a pointed crown. This platform or throne was reserved especially for the king and was covered with one or both of the ancient Mesoamerican symbols of royalty, a reed mat or a jaguar pelt.

To the Mexica-Aztec, the correct lineage was important for legitimate rulership. Upon their arrival in the Valley of Mexico, the Mexica sought alliance with the royal line of Colhuacan in order to link themselves with the Toltec heritage. A princess from Colhuacan was all that the Mexica needed to validate their rulership. Legitimate rulership was achieved through the marriage of a Colhuacan princess and Acamapichtli, the son of a Mexica nobleman. Each local Aztec city-state dynasty could therefore trace its ancestry back to Tula, although some histories may be fictional due to a person's desire to be in power.

Duties of the *Tlatoani*

The good ruler was a protector of his subjects who carried them in his arms and united them. He ruled by taking responsibilities and assuming civic burdens. Metaphorically, he carried his subjects in his cape, and so when he governed, he was obeyed.

A *tlatoani* owned or controlled land within the city-state and received tribute from his subjects, both commoners and subordinate lords. He oversaw the marketplace and the temples. As the military leader, he organized campaigns into battle and oversaw the defense of the city-state. He also resolved judicial matters that could not be resolved through the normal process in the lower courts.

According to Fray Bernardino Sahagún, the ruler was responsible for taking care of cities that had been destroyed during warfare, events related to death, and natural disasters, such as famine and plague. Within the city walls, he tended to the maintenance of the markets and the ball courts, sanitation, the upkeep of city roads and monuments, the supervision of the *patolli* games (a popular board game played with beans as dice) throughout the city, and the security of the citizens. He was obligated to attend and participate in all religious ceremonies, making sure that all rituals were conducted properly, including the offering of copal (a resin that was burned) to the gods. Politically and militarily, the Aztec emperor (*huey tlatoani*) was in charge of installing subordinate province and city rulers (other *tlatoque*) and lords and assembling the seasoned warriors for battle.

The Process of Becoming a *Huey Tlatoani*

When an emperor died, a brother or a son of the previous ruler usually succeeded to the office, but sometimes a nephew or grandson was elected. A high council of *tetecuhtin*, lords who were male relatives of the deceased ruler, selected the next *huey tlatoani*. The *cihuacoatl* also could declare his choice as next *tlatoani*. There was one important condition to becoming a *huey tlatoani*: One must first be a *tlacateccatl*. The *tlacateccatl* was a position on the supreme military council made up of four brothers or relatives of the *tlatoani*. The *tlacateccatl*, together with the *tlacochcalcatl*, were the highest military commanders holding the offices of *otontin* (Otomies) and *cuauhchiqueh* (shorn ones). Only the most courageous battlefield veterans would be allowed to enter these two offices.

The *huey tlatoani*, besides being an experienced warrior, acted as the mouthpiece for the god Huitzilopochtli, and as such, he sponsored religious celebrations and led many of the state rituals. The *huey tlatoani*'s sacred position was seen as the god Tezcatlipoca's choosing. Tezcatlipoca (Smoking Mirror, or Obsidian Mirror) was associated with the notion of destiny or fate. He had omnipotent universal power and was the supernatural basis for political authority. In conjunction with governing political authority, he was the deity to whom the most lengthy and reverent prayers in the rites of kingship were directed.

When a man was chosen to be the new *huey tlatoani*, he underwent ceremonies and activities to transform himself into being worthy to speak with the voice of the gods Tezcatlipoca and Huitzilopochtli. Those ceremonies were performed during the inaugural period, which lasted a few days.

The Inaugural Ceremony of the *Huey Tlatoani*

According to archaeologist Richard Townsend, the inaugural ceremony of the supreme ruler of the Aztec Empire (*huey tlatoani*), the *tlatoani* of Tenochtitlan, was completed in a sequence of four phases: (1) the separation and retreat; (2) the investiture and coronation; (3) the coronation war; and (4) the confirmation.

SEPARATION AND RETREAT

The rulers of Tetzcoco and Tlacopan (cities that were part of the Triple Alliance) led the new *tlatoani* of Tenochtitlan, who was wearing only a loincloth, to the base of the stairway of the Great Temple. Feigning weakness, as a sign of humility, the new *tlatoani* was supported by two other noblemen on his climb to Huitzilopochtli's shrine. Once he was at the top of the temple, he was dressed in a dark green cape with skull and crossbone designs. He burned incense at the shrine and then descended the stairs, moving deliberately slowly and solemnly while the crowds were silent. He then entered the Tlacochcalco (military headquarters and armory in the central precinct of Tenochtitlan) with other nobles to begin the four-day, four-night retreat with fasting and penitential observances. Every noon and midnight, the soon-to-be ruler, accompanied by the others, silently revisited the Huitzilopochtli shrine, where incense was burned and a bloodletting ceremony was performed. The new *tlatoani* offered drops of his royal blood from his pricked calves, arms, and earlobes. During this period, speech was only directed toward Tezcatlipoca, addressed as "lord of the near and the nigh," "wind," or "night."

INVESTITURE AND CORONATION

The new ruler's return to society had a more commanding mood. He departed from the Tlacochcalco with the nobles and entered one of the royal palaces. Within the palace, nobles and the *tlatoani* of Tetzcoco dressed Tenochtitlan's ruler in the regalia of the state—a sign and first step of the new ruler's command. As Tenochtitlan was part of the Triple Alliance with Tetzcoco and Tlacopan, the *tlatoani* of Tetzcoco took a crown of green stones, all worked in gold, and placed it upon the new ruler's head. He then pierced the septum of his nose and inserted a green emerald as thick as a quill pen, after which he inserted two round emerald earplugs in gold settings in the new ruler's ears. On his arms, from elbow to shoulder, two brilliant gold bracelets were placed. On his ankles, anklets of dangling gold bells were tied. The Tetzcocan king then shod him with elegantly gilded, jaguar-skin sandals and dressed him with a gilded and painted mantle of very thin and shiny henequen-like fiber similar to cotton. And finally, a waistband made of the same henequen-like fiber was placed around him. The Tetzcocan king then took him by the hand and led him to a throne, the *cuauhicpalli*, meaning "eagle seat" or "jaguar seat." This seat, similar to the *icpalli*, was decorated with eagle feathers and jaguar hides. The nobles and

the new *tlatoani* then made many speeches of encouragement and admonishment.

Once he was crowned, dressed, and seated, the *tlatoani* of Tenochtitlan was carried on an eagle and jaguar throne fixed to a litter to go to the Great Temple. On top of the pyramid at Huitzilopochtli's shrine, he was given a jaguar's claw for sacrificial bloodletting from his ears and legs. More admonishments, prayers, and sermons were given while quail was sacrificed to the deity.

The procession then descended the pyramid to go to a place described as the location of an eagle vessel or sun stone. The *tlatoani* offered more drops of his royal blood from his arms and legs and sacrificed another quail. Another covenant was thereby made to confirm his rule at the center of the world in the present sun, or era, of creation.

The *tlatoani* was then carried in the litter to a building known as the Coateocalli (house of foreign gods). In the Coateocalli, the religious objects and paraphernalia of conquered foreign nations were kept. Here, he again offered blood sacrifices to affirm his obligation to attend to the cycle of religious festivals.

The final destination for the new ruler to gain ritualistically the right to rule was the earth temple known as Yopico. The inner chamber, which symbolizes a cave, had a sunken receptacle in the floor for offerings during the springtime planting festivals of Tlacaxipehualiztli and Tozoztontli. This was a place for ritual communication with the Earth. There, in the sunken receptacle, the *tlatoani* once again offered incense, his blood, and a quail as sacrifice—a gesture to the Earth that he would govern justly. This endeavor marked the final transfer of power for him to become officially the new *tlatoani*. As he emerged from that inner chamber, the *tlatoani* was then symbolically reborn into his new social role as *huey tlatoani*.

The *huey tlatoani* was then returned to the palace and seated for the ceremony of speeches, which marked the end of the investiture and coronation segment of the inaugural process. The speeches that the *tlatoani*, elders, nobles, and chiefs gave were memorized and part of the collective memory of the society. The order in which they spoke was determined by ritual. First, the *tlatoani* spoke, and two speakers from the audience followed with their speeches. Then the *tlatoani* spoke again, followed by another speaker from the audience, who gave his speech. Finally, the *tlatoani* spoke for the last time and then two quick epilogues from the audience were given.

At the beginning of this ceremony of speeches, the *tlatoani* accepted the position with his memorized speech of about 1,000 words. The formal delivery was based on its content and stylistic repetition of metaphor. The *tlatoani* spoke humbly that he was a commoner, a laborer, and in his lifetime, he had been in excrement and in filth. The audience speakers who stood up to give a speech were either great priests, great noblemen, or other great dignitaries. The first audience member spoke about 1,000 words. He elaborately welcomed the new *tlatoani*, talked about the demise of the last one, and advised and cautioned the rest of the people about the rulership of the new *tlatoani*. Another audience member spoke about 600 words. He offered the new *tlatoani* goodwill and wishes. His speech was more light hearted.

When the *tlatoani* spoke for the second time, he gave a speech of about 400 words, and he talked about his unworthiness and promised to bow to the assessments or duties of his audience. A third audience speaker then warned of an uncertain future and told the *tlatoani* to rest.

The *tlatoani* then gave the last and longest (about 2,200 words) of his speeches. He invoked the power of his lord. He admitted he might be in error but "perhaps for a while, for a day, I shall dream, I shall see in dreams. Perhaps for a while I shall be able to support the bundle, the carrying frame of our great-grandfathers" (Durán 1967: 2, 301). The speech predominantly dealt with the issues of the time, the evils of drinking and smoking. He told a story of a nobleman's fall through drinking. And so he reminded the audience of the fragility of humans.

Then the last audience member spoke, and his speech concluded the inauguration. He told the *tlatoani* that the audience had heard and loved his speech. He said that the *tlatoani* "may be in the excrement, in the refuse, but that Tloque Nahuaque, the ever-present and ever-near, takes someone from there. He washes and bathes him. The lord who is ever-present and ever-near will desire that he will carry the load, he will bear the burden, he will reign. He will also direct and guide. The audience member speaker then told the rest of the audience to do their work, to perform their duties of life and give support to the lord who is ever-present and ever-near, who presides over the night and the wind" (Sahagún 1951–69: 10, 47–85).

At the end of the inaugural speeches, the *huey tlatoani* became the incarnation of the lord Tezcatlipoca and was the god's tool. The *tlatoani* was thus able to dictate the law and establish authority to punish offenders.

THE CORONATION WAR

To prove his leadership in battle, the *huey tlatoani* needed to go to battle to win tribute and to capture prisoners for sacrifice in the final ceremony of confirmation. Prisoners that had been taken captive during the coronation war were sacrificed during the following confirmation feast.

CONFIRMATION

Allies and enemies alike of the Aztec, administrative officials, and important rulers were invited to an inauguration feast hosted by the *huey tlatoani*. They all were required to give gifts. The gifts they brought included cloth and clothing, jewelry, bundles of feathers, loads of corn and cacao, baskets of fruit, flocks of turkeys, deer, quail, and fish of many kinds. The *tlatoque* of Tetzcoco and Tlacopan began a dance in the patio of the palace; nearly 2,000 assembled nobles, chieftains, and high-ranking warriors joined in. Singers and musicians playing on a great *huehuetl* drum set the rhythm. At just the opportune moment, the new *tlatoani* made his dramatic arrival to the social event. Prisoners that had been taken captive during the coronation war were then sacrificed as a sign to Huitzilopochtli that the *tlatoani*'s main purpose was war.

Another purpose of the confirmation ceremony was for the *huey tlatoani* to distribute the insignia of rank to the Tetzcoco and Tlacopan kings on the first day and then to the rest of the public when he returned to his throne. Those who received gifts and emblems of authority were all high officials, including nobles, warriors, and priests, as well as elders from the *calpultin* wards of Tenochtitlan, provincial governors, tax collectors, and chieftains. Originally, the confirmation ceremony's purpose was to validate the ruler's authority, but by the end of the 15th century, the ceremony showed the absolute power of the *huey tlatoani* and the Mexica elites within the Aztec Empire. The distribution of insignia of rank during the confirmation ceremony proved that the Aztec nobility throughout the empire was superior to all.

From the death of the former ruler to the sacrifice of the coronation war prisoners, the whole process was a ritualistic transfer of power from the old *tlatoani* to the new one. The new *tlatoani* of Tenochtitlan was then officially prescribed as the new ruler to govern the Aztec Empire.

The Eleven *Tlatoque* of Tenochtitlan

Although a *tlatoani* by definition ruled over a given town, the *tlatoque* of Tenochtitlan over time conquered many towns and ruled a vast area covering central and southern Mexico. The following is a list of *tlatoque* of Tenochtitlan. (For the lineage of the Tenochtitlan *tlatoque*, see figure 2.6.)

1. Acamapichtli   1375–95
2. Huitzilihuitl   1395–1417
3. Chimalpopoca   1417–26
4. Itzcoatl   1427–40
5. Motecuhzoma I Ilhuicamina   1440–69
6. Axayacatl   1469–81
7. Tizoc   1481–86
8. Ahuitzotl   1486–1502
9. Motecuhzoma II Xocoyotzin   1502–20
10. Cuitlahuac   1520
11. Cuauhtemoc   1520–25

ACAMAPICHTLI (HANDFUL OF ARROWS), 1375–1395

According to the Spanish chronicler Diego Durán, Acamapichtli's father, Opochtzin, was a high-ranking Mexica and his mother, Atototzli, was the daughter of one of the four Colhua kings. (At the time there were four simultaneous dynasties at Col-

huacan.) With a direct line of royalty on his mother's side, especially being connected to the royal line of Colhuacan, which was also tied to the royal line of Tula, Acamapichtli had the right to become the ruler of the Mexica. He was named ruler of Tenochtitlan in the year 1375.

His first wife, Illancueitl, could not have children, so Acamapichtli was given more wives so that he could produce offspring who could potentially become noblemen and rulers of Tenochtitlan. Cuauhtloquezqui gave his daughter Cocatlamihuatzin to Acamapichtli. From this union came Huitzilihuitl, who became the next *tlatoani* of Tenochtitlan. Acamapichtli had a son, Itzcoatl, with a Tepanec woman, and he eventually became the fourth *tlatoani* of Tenochtitlan.

HUITZILIHUITL (HUMMINGBIRD FEATHER), 1395–1417

Tenochtitlan expanded during Huitzilihuitl's reign. People from all over the valley moved into the city, and powerful dynasties were united through marriage alliances. Huitzilihuitl married many princesses from several of the more powerful central Mexican dynasties, including the Tepanec of Azcapotzalco. Huitzilihuitl petitioned the Tepanec ruler Tezozomoc for his daughter, and some scholars say it was through this marriage that Chimalpopoca, the next *tlatoani*, was born. Another chronicler, Chimalpahin, writes that Huitzilihuitl married Miyahuaxochtzin, who came from Tiliuhcan Tlacopan. From this wife came two sons, Chimalpopoca and Huehue Saca, a *tlacateccatl*, but Huitzilihuitl's wife died young, so he then turned to the Cuauhnahuac dynasty for another wife. It was known abroad that the Cuauhnahuac *tlatoani* was a great sorcerer who protected his daughter from male admirers through the use of magic. The *tlatoani* refused Huitzilihuitl's request, saying that his daughter was accustomed to living a luxurious lifestyle that she would not have at Tenochtitlan. The legend says that Huitzilihuitl's response came to him in a dream: He shot a hollow arrow filled with precious jewels into the Cuauhnahuac palace, and it fell at the feet of the princess. After finding the jewels, the couple was soon wed. This marriage established the first Mexica-Aztec alliance with a state outside the Valley of Mexico. The son of this

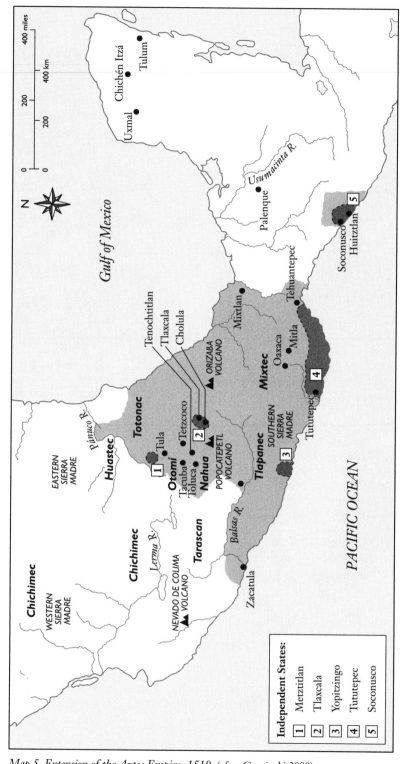

Map 5 Extension of the Aztec Empire, 1519 (after Gruzinski 2000)

union, Motecuhzoma I Ilhuicamina, would later be one of the great Mexica kings.

Huitzilihuitl led many military campaigns, but the conquered towns became subjects to the Tepanec in Azcapotzalco, not to the Mexica in Tenochtitlan.

CHIMALPOPOCA (SMOKING SHIELD), 1417–1426

Under Chimalpopoca's rule, the Mexica helped the Tepanec with a rival that was gaining momentum— the Acolhua of Tetzcoco, in the eastern valley. A new Acolhua king, Ixtlilxochitl, challenged Tezozomoc and caused a war to break out. With Chimalpopoca's help, Ixtlilxochitl was killed, and victory went to the Tepanec. As a reward to the Mexica, Tezozomoc granted the city-state of Tetzcoco as a tributary subject.

When Tezozomoc died in 1426, the Mexica supported Tezozomoc's chosen heir, Tayauh; however, Tayauh's brother Maxtla usurped the throne. Chimalpopoca died under suspicious circumstances, probably assassinated by orders of Maxtla.

ITZCOATL (OBSIDIAN SERPENT), 1427–1440

Itzcoatl was the younger brother of Huitzilihuitl and the illegitimate child of Acamapichtli: As *tlatoani*, Itzcoatl created an advisory office called the *cihuacoatl* to which he appointed Tlacaelel, his nephew.

More significantly, early in Itzcoatl's reign, in 1428, the leaders of Tenochtitlan, Tetzcoco, and Tlacopan formally established the Triple Alliance after the dramatic victory over Azcapotzalco. Their first task was to secure the Valley of Mexico. Itzcoatl conquered the south-shore towns of Lake Xochimilco: Coyoacan (an old Tepanec town), Xochimilco, and then Cuitlahuac. These towns were the bread basket of the region. The *chinampas* in the freshwater lakes of Chalco and Xochimilco produced a large supply of produce for tribute foodstuffs. The Triple Alliance, however, was unable to conquer the neighboring city-state of Tlaxcala or the Tarascan region. Eventually Tenochtitlan gained more control over the other two city-states of the Triple Alliance, and more

tribute goods such as jade, gold, rubber, food, and slaves fell into the hands of the Mexica nobility.

MOTECUHZOMA I ILHUICAMINA (ANGRY LORD, ARCHER OF THE SKY), 1440–1469

The fifth *tlatoani* was Motecuhzoma I. The impressive Great Temple of Tenochtitlan, underwent construction during his reign. Motecuhzoma I politically consolidated the Valley of Mexico by taking steps to reduce the threat of rebellions among subject city-states: Rulers who could be manipulated easily into following the command of the Mexica were appointed, new administrative positions were established, and the tribute system was enforced more stringently.

He also expanded the empire beyond the Valley of Mexico by joining military forces with Nezahualcoyotl of Tetzcoco. The Mexica and Acolhua together were partners to reconquer Cuauhnahuac, then the rest of Morelos, the Gulf Coast area, and the modern state of Oaxaca. Because conquering and war were so vital to Motecuhzoma's administration, it seems appropriate that he created a new title, the *cuauhpilli* (eagle lord), awarded to the most successful soldiers in the army.

AXAYACATL (WATER FACE), 1469–1481

Axayacatl was selected as the next *tlatoani* of Tenochtitlan. He consolidated conquests and reconquered city-states. Three major battles occurred during the reign: Two were victorious (over Tlatelolco and Toluca); the other was a defeat (against the Tarascans).

Before Tenochtitlan got involved, there already was a war between Colhuacan and its ruler, Xilomantzin, and Tlatelolco and its ruler, Moquihuixtli. Then Axayacatl became embroiled when his older sister, Chalchiuhnenetzin, who was married to Moquihuixtli, complained that her husband mistreated her and had acquired a concubine whom she did not like. Axayacatl had found an excuse to attack Tlatelolco. When the war was turning against Moquihuixtli and the Tlatelolca, Axayacatl ordered that Xilomantzin, the ruler of Colhuacan, be killed, thereby debilitating the possibility of an alliance between the two states. The result was a very humiliating defeat for Tlatelolco and the death of its ruler Moquihuixtli. Axayacatl then installed a military governor to rule Tlatelolco in place of the formerly independent *tlatoani*.

TIZOC (CHALK LEG), 1481–1486

Axayacatl's youngest brother, Tizoc, was a very poor military leader and a weak ruler; consequently, he added little new territory to the empire. In fact, he began his administration with a defeat during his coronation war against the Otomies of Metztitlan. To compensate for his lack of success, he commissioned the Tizoc stone, a sculpture that depicts him conquering many towns. Most of the towns on that stone were actually conquered by his predecessors, so the monument stands as an object of political propaganda. His term in office was short. It appears that he was assassinated with poison by a military conspiracy.

AHUITZOTL (WATER BEAST), 1486–1502

Ahuitzotl, another younger brother of Axayacatl, succeeded Tizoc. Shortly after Ahuitzotl's coronation, the Great Temple was completed with much celebration.

Ahuitzotl expanded the empire by bringing the Valley of Oaxaca and the Soconusco Coast of southern Mexico into the empire. Economically, these regions were vital; they were an important source of tropical lowland products such as cacao and feathers. Ahuitzotl also established client states and outposts along the Tarascan border, and he sent colonists from the Valley of Mexico to settle a fortress at Oztoma along the southern part of the Tarascan frontier.

Ahuitzotl's prosperity as a result of newly acquired territorial expansion caused him to have more power over the other two *tlatoani* in the Triple Alliance. Officially the empire was still run by the Triple Alliance, but Ahuitzotl accumulated more power and took over more of the duties of running the empire. Under his reign, the title of *tlatoani* became *huey tlatoani*, or *huehuetlatoani* (supreme king).

MOTECUHZOMA II XOCOYOTZIN (ANGRY LORD), 1502–1520

Motecuhzoma II Xocoyotzin was an experienced general in many of Ahuitzotl's wars of conquest, but his style of leadership was completely opposite of Ahuitzotl's. Reserving all important military and government positions for members of the Mexica hereditary nobility, he eliminated the status of *cuauhpilli* (eagle lord) introduced by his great-grandfather Motecuhzoma I, which praised the most successful soldiers in the army, and he also killed many of Ahuitzotl's officials. Motecuhzoma II also consolidated the conquered lands of Ahuitzotl and controlled them through terror. He continued the long-standing war with Tlaxcala but was never able to defeat them. The Aztec Empire did manage to surround the Tlaxcalan area, however, and reduce its commerce with the outside world.

Meeting of Hernán Cortés In 1519, Motecuhzoma II Xocoyotzin, flanked by the ruler of Tlacopan, Tetlepanquetzatzin, and the ruler of Tetzcoco, Cacamatzin, met the Spanish captain Hernán Cortés in Tenochtitlan. He invited the Spaniards to stay at the Palace of Axayacatl. The god Huitzilopochtli had told Motecuhzoma through the priests that the Spaniards were to remain there as friends, and they received gifts from Motecuhzoma daily. But the Spaniard's fears of being ambushed and trapped inside the palace haunted them. Officers of Cortés lobbied to entice Motecuhzoma out of his palace into the quarters of the Spaniards and hold him there to ensure their safety. Cortés agreed to the plan after learning of a battle between the Aztec and the Spaniards' allies the Totonac. Some of the Totonac, six Spaniards, and a horse died in the battle, which started when they refused to give tribute to Aztec warriors. This event confirmed to Cortés that the Spaniards were no longer perceived as victorious men but were subject to defeat.

Cortés and his soldiers took Motecuhzoma prisoner but allowed the *tlatoani* to continue leading his people from inside the palace and fulfilling all of his duties, such as collecting tribute and settling disputes. When Motecuhzoma heard of a plan to free him, he reminded his people that Huitzilopochtli had told them that they should give their pledge to the king of Spain, Charles V. He said that if he was in captivity, it was because Huitzilopochtli had willed it.

"Peaceful" ties between the Aztec and the Spaniards were broken, however, when the Spaniards insisted that the human sacrifices in Aztec rituals come to an end. Many times the Spaniards had asked him to put a stop to them, but this time they offered to replace the existing gods on top of the pyramid with the Christian icon of Saint Mary and a cross. If Motecuhzoma would not allow this, Cortés's people would pull down the gods themselves. Motecuhzoma conferred with his priests and Huitzilopochtli and then agreed to have the altar of Mary and the cross set opposite that of the god Huitzilopochtli. From the moment the altar and cross were set next to Huitzilopochtli on top of the temple, the gods Huitzilopochtli and Tezcatlipoca told the priests that the Spaniards must leave the country or be killed.

Death of Motecuhzoma II The Spaniards did stay, and many battles followed. The god Huitzilopochtli promised victory to the Aztec and so the fighting continued. Motecuhzoma, meanwhile, had lost the support of his troubled warriors, who no longer considered him a ruler who could lead them to victory.

According to the chronicler Bernal Díaz del Castillo, Motecuhzoma, while in captivity, went with guards to a battlement of the roof to persuade his people to no longer fight with the Spaniards. Four of the chiefs approached and talked with Motecuhzoma with tears in their eyes, lamenting his and his children's misfortune by being captured. They notified him that they had found a ruler to replace him and would continue the war because they had vowed to the gods to fight until every enemy was killed. They then asked for his forgiveness and consoled him by telling him that they prayed to Huitzilopochtli and Tezcatlipoca for his safe return to his people. Before another word was spoken, a shower of arrows and darts fell near Motecuhzoma. Three stones hit the ruler: one on the head, another on the arm, and another on the leg. While Motecuhzoma had been talking with the chiefs, the Spanish guards had withdrawn, leaving the *tlatoani* unprotected. He was carried back to his apartment

but refused to be treated medically for his wounds, and as a consequence, he died. An Indian account, however, claims he was strangled by the Spaniards. Motecuhzoma died in 1520 having ruled 19 years.

CUITLAHUAC (LORD OF CUITLAHUAC), 1520

Cuitlahuac reigned for only 80 days, falling victim, along with thousands of other Aztec, to smallpox, a highly infectious disease marked by a high fever, bodily aches, and skin lesions. The Spaniards were immune to the disease, but those native to the American continent had never been exposed to the deadly virus. During his brief time in power, Cuitlahuac battled with the Spaniards, ordering attacks on them and the Tlaxcalans.

Either during Cuitlahuac's rule or shortly after, the Tetzcocan officially became allies to the Spaniards and helped them on the battlefield, as well as housing soldiers on their land. Coanacotzin, the ruler of Tetzcoco, made the agreement but died shortly thereafter of disease. His successor was a young, brave warrior by the name of Ixtlilxochitl, who was later baptized under the name Hernán Cortés.

CUAUHTEMOC (DESCENDING EAGLE), 1520–1525

Under Cuitlahuac's successor, Cuauhtemoc, fighting continued between the Aztec and their allies and Hernán Cortés and his Indian allies from Tlaxcala, Cholula, Huexotzingo, Tetzcoco, Chalco, and Tlalmanalco. But the Spaniards' allies were not loyal for very long: Although some towns still supported the Spaniards, most refused to help them after a time. Success in the battles see-sawed between the Aztecs and Spaniards. Many Aztec, meanwhile, died of starvation, disease, and lack of freshwater, but Cuauhtemoc and the Aztec warriors tried to fool the enemy, partaking of feasts to show they were strong and well supplied.

Cortés knew, however, that the Aztec did not have any more supplies of food or water and hoped to use the situation to his advantage. Amid the warfare of the three-month siege of Tenochtitlan (May–August 1521), Cortés sent a message to

Cuauhtemoc by way of some Aztec prisoners: He demanded that Cuauhtemoc surrender. Cortés told Cuauhtemoc that the king of Spain, Charles V, did not want the city of Tenochtitlan destroyed. If Cuauhtemoc would surrender, Cortés promised that he would pardon all that was in the past. Cuauhtemoc sent the prisoners back to Cortés with no response other than to leave Mexico at once. He then ordered a meeting with all of his chieftains, captains, and priests so they could discuss the matter. Their final decision was to continue fighting. The Aztec were victorious for a time, but the Spaniards and Tlaxcalans ultimately succeeded.

The End of the Last *Tlatoani*   During the siege, Cortés sent a Tetzcocan chieftain prisoner to Cuauhtemoc with food and another message to surrender. In the message Cortés reiterated that Cuauhtemoc would be respected as the ruler of his territory. Cuauhtemoc's councilors advised that he should work toward peace but not to give a response for three days so that the priests could consult with the gods as to what they should do. Cuauhtemoc ordered bridges to be repaired, canals deepened, and fresh supplies of arms given to the warriors. In the meantime, the messengers relayed the message to Cortés that Cuauhtemoc needed three more days for deliberation. Cortés fed the messengers well, and as a gesture of gratitude, Cuauhtemoc gave Cortés mantles with another message that he would meet with him as soon as he was ready.

Cuauhtemoc did not believe Cortés's promise that he would be allowed to rule over Tenochtitlan because of the circumstances attributed to Motecuhzoma's death and because of the heinous acts that the conquistadores had committed against the rest of the Aztec people. Cuauhtemoc and his warriors attacked the Spaniards; Cortés advanced into the city as a counterattack. Cuauhtemoc, seeing the city under siege, wanted peace but would still not meet with Cortés because he was afraid that he would perish in the same manner as Motecuhzoma.

Fighting desisted for several days while Cortés waited for a response from Cuauhtemoc. Every night many of the Aztecs came to the Spaniards' camp for food, and for this reason, Cortés withheld

from attacking. But with no response from Cuauhtemoc, Cortés ordered Captain Gonzalo de Sandoval to invade the part of the city where Cuauhtemoc was taking refuge. After much destruction, Cuauhtemoc fled, in a company of 50 canoes, with his wife, his family, his captains, other women, and his property of gold and jewels. Sandoval saw him fleeing and ordered a halt to the siege. He sent Captain García Holguín to follow Cuauhtemoc but not to hurt him. Bluffing, García Holguín and his soldiers pretended to make preparations to shoot him with their muskets and crossbows. It worked. Cuauhtemoc stopped, notified them that he was the king of the city, and told them not to disturb his belongings, his wife, or his family. Only then would he surrender to Cortés. Cuauhtemoc was captured on August 13, 1521.

Holguín and Sandoval led Cuauhtemoc to Cortés with great delight. Cuauhtemoc surrendered to Cortés, saying that he had done his duty to defend his city but could do no more. He was now a prisoner and wished to die by Cortés's dagger. Cortés told Cuauhtemoc that he considered him very brave for defending his city so well and that he should rule over his provinces and Mexico just as before. Cortés also expressed his regret that Cuauhtemoc had not made peace before the city had been destroyed and so many people had died. Cuauhtemoc's wife, family, chieftains, and belongings were then restored to him, and they went to Coyoacan as a severe rain and thunderstorm fell upon them.

Palaces of the *Tlatoque*

Just outside the Sacred Precinct of Tenochtitlan were the palaces of the great rulers. The Palace of Axayacatl was on the southwest side of the ritual precinct. Next to it was the old Palace of Motecuhzoma I. The new Palace of Motecuhzoma II was on the southeast end along the causeway to Ixtapalapa. Today, the National Palace of Mexico stands in its place.

Palaces were the place of residence and work for the *pipiltin* and the *tlatoani*. Whatever the noble's occupation, the palace had many offices and was the place for most of the dealings with the people. At the time of the Spanish conquest, hundreds of people,

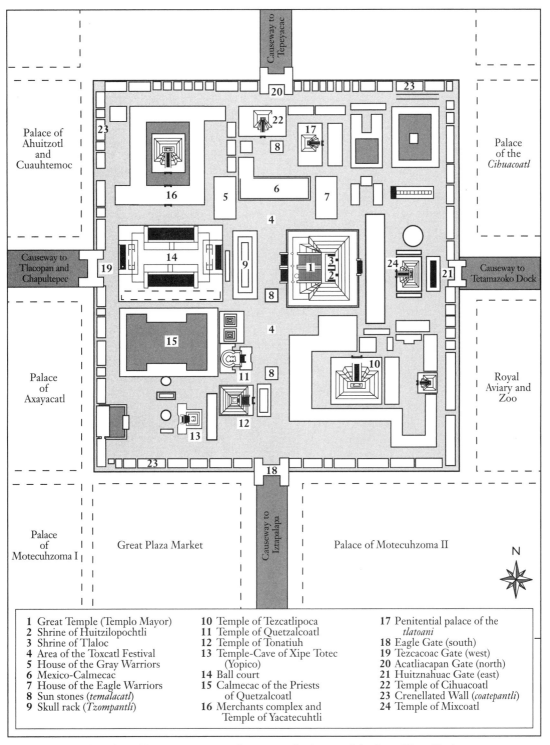

Map 6 *Tenochtitlan's Sacred Precinct, its surrounding imperial palaces, and the Great Plaza Market* (after Tsouras 1996)

The image contains the following labels:

Causeway to Tepeyacac

Palace of Ahuitzotl and Cuauhtemoc

Palace of the *Cihuacoatl*

Causeway to Tlacopan and Chapultepec

Causeway to Tetamazoko Dock

Palace of Axayacatl

Royal Aviary and Zoo

Palace of Motecuhzoma I

Great Plaza Market

Causeway to Iztapalapa

Palace of Motecuhzoma II

N

1 Great Temple (Templo Mayor)
2 Shrine of Huitzilopochtli
3 Shrine of Tlaloc
4 Area of the Toxcatl Festival
5 House of the Gray Warriors
6 Mexico-Calmecac
7 House of the Eagle Warriors
8 Sun stones (*temalacatl*)
9 Skull rack (*Tzompantli*)

10 Temple of Tezcatlipoca
11 Temple of Quetzalcoatl
12 Temple of Tonatiuh
13 Temple-Cave of Xipe Totec (Yopico)
14 Ball court
15 Calmecac of the Priests of Quetzalcoatl
16 Merchants complex and Temple of Yacatecuhtli

17 Penitential palace of the *tlatoani*
18 Eagle Gate (south)
19 Tezcacoac Gate (west)
20 Acatliacapan Gate (north)
21 Huitznahuac Gate (east)
22 Temple of Cihuacoatl
23 Crenellated Wall (*coatepantli*)
24 Temple of Mixcoatl

nobles and their servants, could be seen bustling amid these grand palaces.

MOTECUHZOMA II XOCOYOTZIN'S PALACE

Motecuhzoma II Xocoyotzin's royal palace was used for habitation as well as for governmental purposes. The palace contained courthouses, warriors' council chambers, tribute storage rooms, rooms for bureaucratic officials and visiting dignitaries, a library, an aviary, a zoo, and various courtyards, gardens, and ponds. The palace was accessible either from the street or by boat.

The sovereign's apartments were on the second floor, as were rooms for the kings of the allied cities of Tetzcoco and Tlacopan. Much of the ground floor was used for various official functions. One part housed the supreme civil and criminal courts and also the special tribunal that judged dignitaries accused of crimes or serious misdemeanors. The *achcauhcalli* was the place for the officials of second rank who carried out the judicial orders. Another section contained the room for the council of war, which was attended by the chief military commanders. Other rooms on the ground floor were the *pe-*

tlacalco (public treasury), where maize, beans, grain, and other foodstuff as well as clothes and all kinds of merchandise were stored, and the hall of the *calpixque*, where the officials responsible for the tax collection worked. Other parts of the palace were used as prisons, either for prisoners of war or for ordinary criminals. Also in the palace was the Tlacxitlan, the high court, where all of the complaints of the *macehualtin* were heard and judged by the rulers, princes, and high judges. At the Teccalli or Teccalco, commoners and vassals could also petition their complaints to judges and noblemen. At the Tecpilcalli, noblemen, brave warriors, valiant men, and the wise in war were sentenced by the ruler to be stoned before the people.

AXAYACATL'S PALACE

The eastern front of the Palace of Axayacatl looked to the precinct of the Great Temple. A causeway from Tlacopan ran alongside the palace to come out in the western precinct of the temple. At the time of the conquest, the Spaniards stayed at this palace when they first arrived to Tenochtitlan.

CIHUACOATL

The *cihuacoatl* (woman serpent), named after the goddess Cihuacoatl, was second in command to the *huey tlatoani*. He was a kind of prime minister who looked after the day-to-day duties of the Aztec Empire. He handled official finances, organized military campaigns and appointed commanders, determined rewards for warriors, and served as supreme judge. Some of the duties between the *tlatoani* and *cihuacoatl* overlapped, such as on ritual matters or when the *tlatoani* was absent. When the *tlatoani* left on military campaigns, the *cihuacoatl* moved into the palace and acted as ruler in his absence. And so the duties of the *cihuacoatl* lay mainly within the confines of the city, while the *tlatoani*'s powers operated on a social sphere.

The goddess Cihuacoatl that inspired this position was associated with the Earth, agricultural

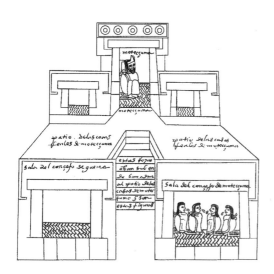

4.2 Palace of Motecuhzoma II, including his offices, as rendered in the Codex Mendoza *(Maria Ramos)*

fields and crops, and childbirth, when women were likened to warriors. Thus, the link of the *cihuacoatl* with the goddess lies in his religious obligations to priestly agricultural matters of the female wet season. During religious festivals such as Huey Tecuilhuitl and Tititl, festivals devoted to the Earth and its vegetation, the *cihuacoatl* and various attendants impersonated the deity Cihuacoatl.

Certain privileges accompanied the *cihuacoatl* office, but the position was not important in any city other than Tenochtitlan. The *cihuacoatl* received a considerable amount of the tribute from conquered cities, although the honors paid to him were second to the *huey tlatoani*'s. Only the *cihuacoatl* did not need to take off his shoes in the *tlatoani*'s presence. The *cihuacoatl*, along with a high council of *tetecuhtin* nobles made up of the male relatives of the deceased ruler, was also instrumental in choosing the next *tlatoani* of Tenochtitlan.

Itzcoatl, the fourth *tlatoani* of Tenochtitlan, created the advisory office of *cihuacoatl* to help in the affairs of the ruler. As in the position of *tlatoani*, only nobility could hold the office of the *cihuacoatl*. Tenochtitlan's first *cihuacoatl* was Tlacaelel, one of the most brilliant and wise politicians of Aztec history, contributing significantly to the grandeur of the empire. The Mexican novelist Antonio Velasco Piña called him "the Aztec among the Aztecs" (2001:378). Tlacaelel was a son of Huitzilihuitl (second *tlatoani* of Tenochtitlan) and the half brother of Chimalpopoca and Motecuzohma I. Tlacaelel was born in 1398 and became *cihuacoatl* in 1427. He died in 1487, having lived 89 years and been *cihuacoatl* for 60 years. He knew eight of the great rulers of Tenochtitlan and served as *cihuacoatl* under five of them; Itzcoatl, Motecuhzoma I Ilhuicamina, Axayacatl, Tizoc, and Ahuitzotl.

After Tlacaelel died, his legitimate son Tlilpotoncatzin took office during the reign of Ahuizotl. In 1503, Tlilpotoncatzin died, and Tlacaeleltzin Xocoyotl, the son of a nobleman in Tenochtitlan, took office. He died in 1520, and the fourth *cihuacoatl* of Tenochtitlan became Matlatzincatzin, who was installed along with Cuitlahuac as the 10th *tlatoani*. The last *cihuacoatl* to hold office was Tlacotzin in 1524, who was baptized with the new name of Don Juan Velásquez Tlacotzin after the Spanish conquest.

4.3 A portrait of the cihuacoatl *Tlacaelel* (Maria Ramos, after León-Portilla 1987: 47)

PRIESTS

Structure of the Priesthood

The structure of the priesthood was very much like the structure of Aztec society. The top rung of the priesthood was reserved for the *tlatoani*, for in Aztec society, religion and state were not separated. The priestly offices below the *tlatoani* followed this hierarchy: the Quetzalcoatl Totec Tlamacazqui and Quetzalcoatl Tlaloc Tlamacazqui, the Mexicatl Teohuatzin, the Huitznahua Teohuatzin and Tecpan Teohuatzin, students from the *calmecac*, and applicants for the priesthood (*tlamacazton*).

The level of ascension in the priesthood was first the novice priest, then the offering priest (*tlamacazqui* or *alfaqui*), then the fire priest (*tlenamacac*), and finally the Quetzalcoatl, or high, priest. All priestly attendants were assisted by *calmecac* students and priestly aspirants.

4.4 *Types of priests, as depicted in the* Codex Mendoza: *a) a senior priest* (tlamacazqui) *offering incense; b) a* tlamacazqui *of the* calmecac; *c) a novice priest receiving physical punishment from a senior priest; d) a* tlamacazqui *sweeping the temple* (Maria Ramos)

Becoming a Priest

Children destined to the priesthood were raised by their mother and father, or nursemaid, until the age of 10, 12, or 13. They were then delivered to the *calmecac* to learn how to be a fire priest, an offering priest, or a warrior. Most of the children who went to the *calmecac* schools came from the higher class. Only the gifted commoner child was allowed into the *calmecac*.

When children entered the *calmecac*, they were taught things of ritualistic importance such as music, dance, how to address the deities, and ritual performances. They also learned the count of days, the book of dreams, and the book of years, as well as the

gods' songs that were inscribed in books. Good rhetoric or orations were essential to the *calmecac* curriculum because those who did not speak well or greet others well were punished by drawing blood from them with maguey spines.

Types of Priests
QUETZALCOATL

Each of the two highest priests presided over the shrines on top of the Great Temple. These priests, equal in position, were named the Quetzalcoatl Totec Tlamacazqui (the plumed serpent, priest of our lord) and the Quetzalcoatl Tlaloc Tlamacazqui (the plumed serpent, priest of Tlaloc). The different cult responsibilities alternated according to the dry and rainy seasons. The Quetzalcoatl Totec Tlamacazqui was dedicated to Huitzilopochtli, and Quetzalcoatl Tlaloc Tlamacazqui was dedicated to Tlaloc, the god of rain. (The word *Totec* was an old cult name from a time before the Aztec came to the Valley of Mexico.) *Tlamacazqui*, meaning "priest" or "giver of things," further distinguished them in their rank.

In theory, lineage was not considered in the appointment of these offices, but in practice, many of the high priests were of noble origin. To be elected to the high priest office, the priest had to have led an exemplary life of righteousness and had a pure, good, and compassionate heart. The priest could not have been vindictive but must have esteemed, embraced, and wept for others. He must have been devout and god-fearing. The *tlatoani*, the great judges, and all other rulers elected him to be called Quetzalcoatl, and he was then named to be either the priest of Huitzilopochtli or Tlaloc. These priests were the only ones allowed to marry and have a family of their own, but they lived moderately as they followed a specialized way of life.

MEXICATL TEOHUATZIN

The Mexicatl Teohuatzin was seen as the general commander and overseer of rituals. He was also the superintendent of the *calmecac*.

HUITZNAHUA TEOHUATZIN AND TECPAN TEOHUATZIN

The Huitznahua Teohuatzin and the Tecpan Teohuatzin assisted the Mexicatl Teohuatzin in governing the rest of the priestly orders. The Huitznahua Teohuatzin was mainly concerned with ritual matters, and the Tecpan Teohuatzin attended to questions related to education. These priests held responsibility over certain temples and performed administrative duties on the *teopantlalli* (temple lands). They supervised the selection of deity impersonators who wore the sacred masks and other regalia in public performances and processions; sometimes they wore the masks and costumes themselves. They also attended to the communal festivals and worship activities pertaining to the cults of their temple deity.

TLENAMACAC

Fire priests, or *tlenamacac* (fire seller), were responsible for human sacrifices. Though other priests assisted in the sacrifice, only the fire priests could use the flint knife for the extraction of the heart from the sacrificed victim. In preparing for the human sacrifice, the fire priest and the other priests would strip the captive. The victim was given wine to drink and was lightly beaten. Sometimes the captive fought against the sacrifice, especially if he was a chieftain; if the captive was not a chieftain, he laid his back on the round sacrificial stone and allowed the priest to slash open his breast, seize his heart, and raise it toward where the sun came forth. After the victim had been sacrificed, the priests danced, each one grasping the head of the captive in his hand.

The *tlenamacac* also performed the New Fire ceremony that occurred every 52 years. Also called Toxiuhmolpilia, or "binding of the years," this ceremony ensured the rebirth of the Sun and the movement of the cosmos for another 52 years. The priests brought ritually prepared bundles of wood that represented the previous 52 years for a fire on top of the sacred mountain Huixachtlan (thorn-tree place), or the Hill of the Star. Those flames created the New Fire and the new cosmic era.

Like all Aztec rituals, the New Fire ceremony followed a prescribed procession. All the people in the town looked at the Hill of the Star and carefully watched the movements of the stars, particularly the Tianquiztli, meaning "marketplace," the group that we call Pleiades. Seeing that the heavens did not stop moving, the *tlenamacac* took a warrior as a sacrifice. They opened his chest with a flint knife, took out his heart, and threw it in a fire that was started in the chest cavity of the warrior as the entire town watched. The townspeople then cut their ears and flung the blood in the direction of the fire on the mountain. This New Fire then was taken down the mountain and carried to Huitzilopochtli's temple on top of the Great Temple in Tenochtitlan. Fire priests as well as other messengers took the fire back to the cities so that people could place it in their homes.

TLAMACAZTEQUIHUAQUE

The Lords of the Sun, or *tlamacaztequihuaque* (warrior priests), carried the effigies of deities in the vanguard of Aztec armies during war campaigns. They captured enemies and made appropriate sacrifices in the battlefield. It was their duty to take the lead in the war campaign as they were always a day's distance ahead of the brave and seasoned warriors. They also solved disputes among warriors about captives; for instance, if no one had witnessed the taking of a particular captive and several warriors claimed him, the Lord of the Sun decided between them and settled the quarrel (see chapter 5).

CIHUATLAMACAZQUE

Women priests called *cihuatlamacazque* taught the girls who went to the all-girl *calmecac* or *telpochcalli* school. These priests were the personification of earth-mother cult deities and maize goddesses. Aside from instruction, the women priests also directed the rituals of some festivals dedicated to fertility goddesses, although they were not allowed to officiate in the sacrifices.

TLAMATINI

A highly esteemed teacher-priest was called a *tlamatini* (wise man; plural, *tlamatinime*). The wise man was an exemplary person. He possessed writings and owned books. He represented tradition and the road and as such was the leader of men, a bearer of responsibility, a physician, a counselor, a philosopher, a poet-writer, a companion, and a guide. A good wise man was a trustworthy person, an instructor worthy of confidence, deserving of credibility and faith. A *tlamatini* was very knowledgeable in all aspects of life and in the dealings of the land of the dead.

OCELOQUACUILLI AND NAHUALLI

Oceloquacuilli (jaguar priests) were the priests of Great Nahualpilli, a god of the Huastecs who was the Chief of Magicians, the Great Sorcerer, and the Great Nahual. When the Aztecs invaded the Huastecs, they took the idol of Nahualpilli and placed him in Tenochtitlan to perform his magic.

The priests of Great Nahualpilli were called not only *oceloquacuilli* but also *nahualli*, or *nahual*, indicating their role as wise men, sorcerers, and magicians. The *nahualli* was given power and wisdom as a reward for his fasting, being locked in the temple, and remaining celibate. Some of the characteristics of the role of the *nahualli* were very similar to those of the sadhus or gurus, the holy men of India. In Mesoamerican thinking, the *nahualli* had three main functions: As the *tlaciuhqui*, he was to bring rain; as the *tecuitlazqui*, to remove the freeze and hail from the fields; and as the *tlacatecolotl*, to transform into an owl (or another animal) and provoke evil and disease.

The *nahualli* could be supernaturally transported to Tlalocan (place of abundance of water and sustenance) where he worked to bring rain and fertility to the Earth. The *nahualli* controlled the amount of rain that fell from the sky and with it the resulting good or bad harvests, and he demanded the sacrifice of blood as a symbol of rain. The *nahualli* transformed himself into animals such as the jaguar, dog, turkey, owl, and even into a ghost woman, and in this form, he punished rebellious members of the community with famine, disease, or death. However, at the same time, he risked suffering personally any actions taken against him in his animal form: The *nahualli* typically worked by night, and if he was captured as an animal, he would die with the arrival of dawn. The *nahualli* had very exuberant and messy hair, carried a golden shield, and wore blood red sandals. *Nahualli* were born under the sign Ce Quiahuitl (One Rain).

The word *nahua*, from which the word *nahual* derives, means "wisdom" but also carries, according to historian and linguist Angel María Garibay, connotations of deceit, prestige, disguise, and dissembling (1971). These other meanings gave the *nahualli* an air of mystery in Aztec society. In general, the transfiguration of the *nahualli* caused damage to those around him.

TETONALMACANI

When a baby was born in Aztec society, he or she received a name taken from the *tonalamatl* (a divinatory book of the Sun or destiny) and in this way was mystically joined to the divinity. That name, which became part of the personality of the individual, was his or her *tonalli*, or *tonal*, his fortune or destiny.

A *tonalli* could become diseased from *espanto* or *susto*, or in the Nahuatl language, *tetonalcahualiztli* (loss of the tonalli). This happened when an individual offended the protective divinities or spirits of things and places. It could also happen when a person received a strong blow to the body or when a person received an intense psychological impact, such as a strong attack of anger or a serious scare. To cure the individual, in such cases, a priest called a *tetonalmacani* (he who cures the tonalli) made an offering to Tonatiuh (the sun god) and performed a magical treatment or cleansing on the patient.

Priest Activities

Priests led a chaste, pure life of moderation. They were god-fearing, and as such they were not to lie nor be proud nor look upon women. The 16th-century Catholic chronicler Sahagún emphasized that in no way was there filth or vice among the priests. If a priest sinned and drank pulque (an alcoholic beverage) or was lustful, no mercy was shown: He was strangled, burned alive, or shot with arrows. If a priest sinned lightly, others drew blood from his ears, flanks, and thighs with maguey spines or a sharpened bone.

Priests had three main duties: performing rituals, administrating and caretaking, and educating others. During rituals, they offered their own blood as a sacrifice, gave food to the gods, and burned incense (copal). The object used to burn copal in the offerings and during sacrifices was an incense burner, similar in appearance to a frying pan. The long, straight, hollow handle of the incense burner often represented serpents. During these performance rituals, priests were also responsible for keeping the sacred fires burning in large braziers, playing music, and making many offerings to the gods.

As part of their duties of administration and caretaking, priests managed the construction, personnel, and provisions of the temples. Sweeping was done daily so that the temple grounds and the gods were properly taken care of.

The third priestly duty was education. Priests took charge of the *calmecac*, supervised the *tlamacazton* (novices, young initiates) and lay personnel, and cared for the sacred books. They taught others about the gods, rituals, calendar, and astronomy.

In order to serve their deities within their daily rituals, priests were more devoted to prayer and performances of penance than the rest of the Aztec people. They prayed three times during the day and once at night. Novice priests gathered wood to keep watch at night and carried the logs on their backs. After finishing a day of work, they saw to their godly obligations of doing penance. For penance, at night they cut maguey spines to place them in the forest, desert, or near the water. For this venture, no more than one person at a time went. The priests first bathed and then went naked carrying shell trumpets, incense ladles, a bag full of incense, and pine torches. At places where the maguey spines were placed, the trumpet was then blown. The younger priests went a half league while those who performed great penances went two leagues.

At midnight the principal priests bathed themselves in water. Also at midnight, when the night was divided in half, everyone arose and prayed. If a person did not wake up, the others gathered together to draw blood from his ears, breasts, thighs, and calves.

All observed the rite of fasting, but at different intervals. At midday the small boys ate and then called *atamalqualo* when it was time for fasting. They would not eat again until the next day at midday. At midnight others ate and then would not eat again until the next midnight. No chili or salt was eaten, nor did they drink water. If anyone ate even a little bit, the fast was broken.

Bernal Díaz del Castillo described the priests as wearing black cloaks, similar to cassocks, and long gowns reaching to their feet. Some had hoods, like those worn by canons, and others had smaller hoods, like those of the Dominicans. The priests wore their hair very long, down to the waist, and some wore it down to the ankles. Their hair was covered with blood and so matted together that it could not be separated. He also noted that their ears were cut to pieces by way of penance, and their fingernails were very long. According to Díaz they stank like sulfur and decaying flesh. It was said that these priests were very pious and led good lives.

TECUHTLI

Tecuhtli means "dignitary" or "lord" and was a title given to a noble who was elected or was appointed by the *tlatoani* to oversee the people in a given area. *Tetecuhtin* always came from among the *pipiltin*. The person holding the *tecuhtli* title could be an agricultural landowner, a judge, or a military commander. The *tecuhtli* landowner represented his people before the higher authorities. He was to speak for the people under his care and to defend them against excessive taxation or any infringement on their land. The *tecuhtli* legal officer judged lawsuits, and the *tecuhtli* military commander led the group that he was required to furnish in war.

After death, the title of *tecuhtli* did not necessarily pass down to one's descendants automatically. In the early days of the Aztec Empire, the next elected *tecuhtli* had to be a nobleman but could have been a close or distant relative or of no relation at all. Although the *tlatoani* had the power to designate a new *tecuhtli*, the nobles in the *teccalli* (lord house) made the final decision about who became the next *tecuhtli* to rule over them. (During the time of Motecuhzoma II, the election was more of a presentation in which the ruler appointed the name of his choice to be the next *tecuhtli*.) Election to the position of *tecuhtli* depended on the capacity of the candidate and in one's outside connections.

To gain higher status, whether a person was a *pilli* (noble) or a *macehualli* (commoner), one had to earn it. The *tecuhtli* was a man of importance. His name carried the respectful termination of *-tzin*, such as Axayacatzin or Ahuitzotzin. He had distinguishing clothes and jewels. He lived in a *teccalli* that was maintained by the townspeople or villagers, who owed him tribute of wood, water, and domestic service. Unlike the *tecuhtli* title, the land estates belonging to the *tecuhtli* were transmitted to his heirs, at which point they became *pillalli* (land belonging to the *pipiltin*), despite the fact that there was a law that land was to be communal. The sons of dignitaries were then allowed inherited revenues as well as the opportunity to be preferred in the higher social circle.

Those who aspired to the office of *tecuhtli* did not desire wealth as did the rest of the Aztec people; they were more concerned with an honorable reputation. Wealth was not pursued, although it came as a result of increasing power and official expenses. The *tecuhtli* and his family did not pay taxes, but the commoners paid tribute to him as well as to the *tlatoani*.

Place of Residence of the *Tetecuhtin*

Ultimately, all land was owned by the *tlatoani*, but to the *tetecuhtin* the *tlatoani* granted estates called *teccalli* (lord house) for ruling over the people. The *tecuhtli*'s palace was located either in the same *calpulli* (neighborhood or district) as the rest of the commoners or just outside it, among other nobles. In addition, land was set aside for him. The revenue from this land was the *tecuhtli*'s own income on top of the foodstuff, clothing, and provisions the *tlatoani* allowed him. In return, the *tecuhtli* would be obliged to present himself before the king whenever he was called for.

The *tecalli* was very elaborate. Bernal Díaz del Castillo described a *tecuhtli*'s palace in Iztapalapa that he saw as the Spaniards marched to Tenochtitlan. It was very large and built with the best stone. The roof timbers were made of cedar and other sweet-smelling woods. The rooms were very big, and the patios were covered with cotton awnings. The garden contained a variety of plants, flowers, including roses, fruit trees, and a pool of water. Also a boat had access to this orchard from the lake Tetzcoco.

CALPULLI

A *calpulli* was a group of families who lived near one another. *Calpulli*, in urban settings, comprised neighborhoods. In our modern categories, a *calpulli* can be understood as a district, quarter, or neighborhood of a town. In some *calpulli*, residents belonged to one profession, while in others, there was a mixture of farmers, craftsmen, and traders. The craftsmen *calpulli* could consist of feather workers, goldsmiths, precious-stone workers, or other artisans. For the most part, the *macehualtin* were grouped within a *calpulli*.

The city of Tenochtitlan was divided into four *campan* (territorial divisions organized according to the cardinal points), and each *campan* was composed of several *calpulli*. In rural areas, some of the *calpulli* wards were a territory spread out over a great area, while others were clustered together to form rural towns. A small *calpulli* could consist of a cluster of 10 to 20 houses, while a larger *calpulli* could be composed of several wards under a common *tecuhtli*. Those serving the local lord lived in the *teccalli* (lord house). Urban wards generally consisted of noble dwellings while those who lived in the rural wards were peasants.

All *calpulli* wards contained a temple to which the members of the community dedicated themselves. The temple was administered by a priest, or *quacuilli*, who played a role equivalent to the parish priests of today. The citizens worked and maintained plots to support themselves. A *telpochcalli* (commoner's school) existed in each *calpulli*. The distinguished and outstanding warriors of the *calpulli* were responsible for educating the students in martial arts at this school. The young men who trained at the *telpochcalli* were then responsible for the upkeep of the school, and they provided daily fuel and provisions, made repairs to the building, and cultivated a field for the support of the school.

The Aztec identified themselves according to their *calpulli* or community. They did not consider themselves as a culture or as a collective whole. Each *calpulli* and, in a larger sense, each *altepetl* (town) had its own history with its own identity. People from Tenochtitlan would therefore have identified themselves as Tenochca; those from Xochimilco, as Xochimilca; and so on.

Although the *calpulli* was ultimately run by the *tlatoani* via the elected or appointed *tecuhtli*, members of the *calpulli* elected a *calpullec* (headman) to distribute lands to them according to need. The *calpullec*'s job was to maintain census maps of the *calpulli*. The maps showed all vacant and occupied lots of land in the *calpulli*. Through these maps, a current record was kept of all people who should be paying tribute to the state. At the death of a *calpulli*

member, the name glyph that represented the head of the household was erased and was replaced by his successor. The *calpullec* was not necessarily from the noble class, but he had to have held the office of elder. Members of the *calpulli* were responsible for cultivating land for the *calpullec* so that he could perform his job full time. He was required to meet with the members of the *calpulli* to discuss their needs, and he had to report daily to the chief tribute collector (*calpixque*) to receive orders.

In the eastern Nahua area of present-day Puebla and Tlaxcala, nobles headed large *teccalli*. Commoners were attached to them by obligations of service and tribute. In the Valley of Mexico, Morelos, and the Toluca area, members of a *calpulli* were under the jurisdiction of a noble, and the local commoners were required to pay tribute to him. The nobles owned land apart from the *calpulli* in which some peasants were considered dependent on their lord to work these lands. Within the conquered areas of the empire, the members of the equivalent of the *calpulli* were also required to provide services for the local ruler and the Aztec administrator.

Both the *teccalli* and the *calpulli* were territorial units, but not much is understood about their full organization. In the *calpulli*, land was distributed among the members for their use. If new land opened up, or if an existing plot was left abandoned, the *calpulli* council would reallocate the land. Land was not usually sold, rather it was passed down to heirs; however, some *calpulli* lands were privately owned by certain commoners and could be sold. But ultimately, the land remained under the general jurisdiction of the *calpulli* and the *altepetl* (city-state).

HOUSEHOLD

The Aztec Home

Most of the *macehualtin* houses were made of sun-dried brick and were L-shaped with one story. The number of rooms increased with the family's wealth, but the most modest homes had one main room.

The entrance opened up to a patio in the center, while the side facing the street was closed for privacy. The average house had a kitchen, a room where the entire family slept, and two altars. One altar was located near where they slept, and the other was located near the door. The kitchen was a separate building in the courtyard; the *temazcalli* (steambath) was also built separately from the house. Immediate families and their extended families occupied these houses.

Whether an elaborate or modest home, furnishings were simple and sparse. *Petlatl* (mats), *petlacalli* (chests), and a few seats woven out of reeds or rushes provided the furniture in both the rich and poor Aztec houses. Both a great lord and a commoner slept on mats, although some might have a bed curtain over them, which was the case when the Spaniards stayed in Axayacatl's palace. During the daytime, in both private houses and the courts, the same *petlatl* used for sleeping became a seat, set on a mound of earth or on a wood platform. A more evolved chair, an *icpalli* was a legless seat made of wood or wickerwork with a back slightly higher than the sitter's head. One would sit on the *icpalli* cross-legged on the ground and lean backward a little. This chair was common among the people but only the emperor's *icpalli* could be covered with cloth or skins and adorned with gold.

A family's storage box or chest where clothes, pieces of cloth, and jewels were kept was called a *petlacalli*. (This same word also identified the state treasure and formed part of the name of the official, the *petlacalcatl*, in charge of the finances of the empire.) The household *petlacalli* was only a covered basket with easy access. A very strict law against theft kept people from stealing. Other chests found in the house contained their gods (small and large), small stones and flints, and books of paper made from the bark of a tree that contained the signs and dates of past events.

In the middle of every house lay the hearth and the image of Huehueteotl, the old god of fire. The hearth consisted of three stones on which sat the pots, and between the stones, logs were burned. The mystical power of the fire god was within the stones, and it was believed that anyone who offended the fire by walking on the hearthstones would die.

Household Populations

The average number of individuals in a household in Tenochtitlan cannot be known for sure, but authorities such as anthropologist Jacques Soustelle suggest that four to seven people lived under the same roof (1979: 9). This estimate is suggested to be modest, because servants also lived within the same dwelling; however, supposing that the average number of people to a household was seven, there were 80,000 to 100,000 households within Tenochtitlan and Tlatelolco, bringing the population to above 500,000 but below 1 million. Other scholars disagree with these calculations, and now, ethnohistorian Edward Calnek's suggestion that 200,000 individuals populated Tenochtitlan is widely accepted.

Family Relationships

Aztec families were closely knit and supportive of each other. Parents, grandparents, and neighbors helped rear the children in the neighborhood. Aunts and uncles also helped raise and support the upbringing of children. If a member of a family refused to help guard the family children, they were considered bad people by other society members.

Ideally, the family was expected to behave properly, to work industriously, and to treat one another and the elders with respect. Elders played an important role in Aztec ceremonies, and though strict laws prohibited the rest of society from being drunk in public, the elderly were allowed to drink alcoholic beverages in excess.

Roles of Men and Women

FATHER

According to Fray Bernardino Sahagún, one's father was the source of lineage. The man was the head of the family. If he had more than one wife, he was to treat all of them as equals. The father was to store up wealth for himself and for his family, and he was to take care of his assets responsibly. He regulated family life, distributed his wealth with care, and established order in the home.

MOTHER

Sahagún writes that a woman's greatest duty was as a mother. She was to be sincere, vigilant, and an energetic worker. He further describes the ideal Aztec woman as an attentive teacher, willing to serve others and be mindful of their welfare. He emphasizes that she was to be careful, thrifty, and constantly at work.

CHILDREN

Children, especially newborns, were called precious stones or feathers of the precious quetzal bird, and they were believed to be gifts from the gods. A legitimate child was born to a man and wife who had been properly married; this usually meant the first marriage that underwent the appropriate marriage rites (see chapter 13 for more information). A good son was expected to be obedient, humble, gracious, grateful, and reverent. He was also expected to follow his parents' characters and way of life. A good daughter was required to be obedient, honest, intelligent, discreet, of good memory, respectful, prudent, modest, and chaste. When a child was orphaned, his or her uncle and aunt provided support.

READING

Social Structure and Class Hierarchy

Boone 1994, Day 1992, Soustelle 1979: privileges of nobles, commoners; Edmonson 1974: lineage, commoners, social structure.

Tlatoani

Blythin 1990, Durán 1967: inaugural speeches; Carrasco and Matos Moctezuma 1992: *tlatoani* defined; Sahagún 1951–69: *tlatoani* traits; Smith 2003,

Townsend 2000, Sahagún 1951–69: appearance, duties, requirements, inaugural process of a *tlatoani*.

The Eleven *Tlatoque* of Tenochtitlan

Chimalpahin Quauhtlehuanitzin 1997: lineage; Day 1992, Díaz del Castillo 1963, Smith 2003, Townsend 2000: details of life of *tlatoani*; Díaz del Castillo 1963: death of Motecuhzoma; Horcasitas 1979: meaning of *tlatoque* names; Townsend 2000: dates of Tenochtitlan *tlatoque* rule.

Palaces of the *Tlatoque*

Matos Moctezuma and Solís Olguín 2002, Soustelle 1979: Motecuhzoma II's palace; Sahagún 1951–69: list of rooms in palace; Townsend 2000: location of palaces; Carrasco and Matos Moctezuma 1992, Soustelle 1979: Axayacatl's palace.

Cihuacoatl

Berdan 1982: duties of *cihuacoatl*, Tlacaelel; Chimalpahin Quauhtlehuanitzin 1997: lineage of *cihuacoatl*; Offner 1983, Soustelle 1979: *cihuacoatl* duties, social structure; Alvarado Tezozomoc 1975, Velasco Piña 2001: Tlacaelel; Townsend 2000: hierarchy of nobles.

Priests

Prescott 2000: Quetzalcoatl priest, women priests; Sahagún 1951–69: priests' studies and duties; Carrasco and Matos Moctezuma 1992, Smith 2003: sacrifice priests; Townsend 2000: structure of priesthood and duties.

Tecuhtli

Berdan 1982: definition of *tecuhtli*; Smith 2003: land rites; Lockhart 1992, Soustelle 1979: duties, rites, and palace of *tecuhtli*.

Calpulli

Berdan 1982, Boone 1994, Soustelle 1979, Smith 2003: *calpulli*, *tecuhtli*; Carrasco and Matos Moctezuma 1992: community; Boone 1994: *calpullec*.

Household

Day 1992, Sahagún 1951–69, Soustelle 1979: family relationships, commoner house; Díaz del Castillo 1963, Soustelle 1979: contents of house; Calnek 1976: population.

5

WARFARE

The Aztec engaged in warfare for a variety of reasons. Primarily, they sought to gain domination over territories for economic and political reasons. Their ultimate goal was to conquer city-states in order to force them to pay tribute. Secondarily, they sought to gain religious favors, and warfare allowed them to take captives and use them for sacrifice. In fact, most of the victims sacrificed to the Aztec gods were captured during battle.

The themes of warfare and battle were dominant in Aztec culture. An Aztec male's identity was defined by his success in warfare. Even in female identity, warfare was important; childbirth was compared to combat, and women who died in childbirth were equated to warriors. Male education at the *telpochcalli* schools emphasized military skills and values, and the main aim of the *telpochcalli* curriculum was to create warriors.

Although social status in Aztec society was largely predetermined by family lineage, warfare provided a means to climbing the social ladder. Young warriors elevated their social status by taking captives in battle, and more important, they secured that status for their descendants.

A great amount of what is known about Aztec warfare is a result of the fact that they were the culture that clashed with the Spanish army. Spanish priests and conquistadores wrote down what they witnessed at the time of the conquest, and the Aztecs themselves, being very prolific, also wrote and displayed their culture through literature and art.

TRAINING

At the time of his birth, a young male's destiny was predetermined not only by his gender but also by the day on which he was born. The date of his birth would determine what kind of warrior he would become; for example, those born on the day *matlactli cuauhtli* (10 Eagle) were destined to be good soldiers. They would have strength and courage, spur others to valor, hurl themselves against their foes, smash their ranks, and put terror into their hearts. For all males, military service was mandatory, and it

was the job of these warriors to maintain the great military empire that Tenochtitlan had become in the 15th century.

For a male born to a common family, his primary education, between the ages of three and 15, was given by his parents. They taught him about his *calpulli* and the role he would play in serving it. A youth's early years would be spent performing physical labor that would strengthen his body and included carrying wood, water, or supplies and food purchased in the marketplace at the center of the city. By the age of seven he would be trained to manage his family's boats and to fish on Lake Tetzcoco.

A very important element in his preparation to becoming a warrior was food rationing. This was determined by age: At the age of three, he was given only a half cake of maize per meal; by age five, he was given a full cake; and by the age of 12, he was given a cake and half. Only during ritual feasts was the youth allowed to consume more. The principal reason for this was to instill discipline in the future warrior, as it was expected that in times of battle he would have to march for days without food. Indolence was not tolerated, and punishments included beatings and stings with agave thorns (see chapter 13).

There were two types of schools that offered military training: the *calmecac* and the *telpochcalli*. Most commoners attended the *telpochcalli* because it provided the most direct route to becoming a warrior.

Calmecac

The *calmecac* trained the Aztec political and military elite, principally the sons of the upper nobility, but also some lower nobility and commoners who were to become priests. Because the objective of the *calmecac* was to train priests, most of the education focused on the intellectual aspects of Aztec life, though military training was also included.

The *calmecac*s were attached to the temples, and the one in Tenochtitlan was located in the main ceremonial complex and was dedicated to the god Quetzalcoatl. It is uncertain at what age the young males entered the *calmecac*. The king's sons apparently entered the temple at the age of five and were raised there until they were old enough to go to war.

Those entering between the ages of six to 13 were usually the sons of lower nobility. One thing is certain: Training in the *calmecac* began earlier than that in the *telpochcalli*.

Training in the *calmecac* was rigorous. It not only covered that which was taught at the *telpochcalli* but also focused on the intellectual aspects of Aztec life. Among the subjects the youths were taught were reading and writing, songs, the calendar, the book of dreams, and the book of years. The youths were expected to arise at midnight and pray to the gods. Domestic chores were also part of the curriculum, and tasks included preparation of their own food, sweeping before dawn, and gathering wood to tend the fire (see chapter 13). At the age of 15, the warrior aspect of their education began with their first instruction in the use of weapons.

One important difference between the sons of nobles and warriors, and the sons of commoners was the expectation placed on their accomplishments. It was believed that the sons of nobles and warriors were more inclined to the warrior's life than other boys were, and these youths, whether trained in the *telpochcalli* or the *calmecac*, received military instruction in the house of the eagle and jaguar military orders. (For more on the *calmecac*, see chapter 13.)

Telpochcalli

Each of the city wards (*calpulli*) had at least one *telpochcalli*. Youths between the age of 15 and 20 received an extensive military education at the *telpochcalli*. By the year 1519, an average of 489 youths between the ages of 15 and 20 received their education at the *telpochcalli* in Tenochtitlan. Here the young men learned to be courageous and to serve the gods of the Earth (Tlaltecuhtli) and the Sun (Tonatiuh), although the divinity to whom the institution was dedicated was Tezcatlipoca. Tezcatlipoca, was believed to manifest the most commendable values of a soldier. Among the god's traits were confidence and courage.

Upon arrival at the school, a male youth was brought before the *telpochtlato*, the ruler of the school, and the sacred image of Tezcatlipoca. There, the *telpochtlato* said:

Here our lord has placed him. Here you understand, you are notified that our lord has given a jewel, a precious feather, a child has arrived. In your laps, in the cradle of your arms we place him. And now we dedicate him to the lord, shadow, wind, Tezcatlipoca and pray that he will sustain him. We leave him to become a young warrior. He will live here in the house of penance where the eagle warrior and the jaguar warrior are born (Sahagún 1950–69: 3, 51–53).

In comparison to the *calmecac*, the intellectual training at the *telpochcalli* was less rigorous, and the staff of the *telpochcalli* consisted of accomplished veteran soldiers, rather than priests, who trained the youths in military skills. The youths were taught discipline by realizing domestic chores. These included sweeping the house, cleaning, building walls, and farming. The youths were also expected to work with teams of other boys in public works as a means to facilitate cooperation and strengthen a sense of civic duty; these teams collaborated particularly in the cleaning and repair of the aqueducts, canals, and

5.1 Male students arrive at the telpochcalli *for military training, from the* Florentine Codex *(Lluvia Arras)*

causeways that criss-crossed the city and provided vital links for transportation. Other exercises included training in martial arts and transporting large pieces of firewood and branches from the forests to the city to heat and decorate the school. Hauling firewood was an important physical activity because it built up strength, and over time the number of pieces of firewood that the youth carried on his back increased. This would help the youths later in battle when they would be expected to carry shields, food, and military supplies and weapons across vast distances of open battlefields filled with enemy warriors.

Ritual was also a very important part of their day. At sunset, the youths bathed and painted their bodies black and dressed in mesh capes and neckbands. After the sun had set, they ignited fires and sang and danced until after midnight, when they retired to the *telpochcalli* to sleep.

The young men were not allowed much entertainment. Aztec society prohibited drunkenness, which was punished by public beating and at times even by death by hanging. Alcohol was hence completely forbidden to *telpochcalli* youth. The only enjoyment a youth could hope for was to keep a mistress, yet this was only possible if he could afford one. Because the primary objective of the school was to create warriors, the youth's day was expected to involve backbreaking labor, as this would help prepare him for war. All meals were eaten at home, after which the young men were required to return to the *telpochcalli*. The only forms of "recreation" were singing and dancing in the evenings and exercise, all of which enabled the *telpochcalli* youth to bond with the other boys of the *calpulli* spiritually while they improved their agility and coordination. These two skills would become essential in both hand-to-hand combat and troop movement. The content of the songs the youths sang was also important because it involved the exploits of the gods, cultural heroes, or warriors of the *calpulli* who had accomplished great feats of heroism.

It was common for the *telpochcalli* masters to be only slightly older than the students themselves. Among the duties of the masters was to watch and observe the new boys to determine who was physically fit and who showed respect and good judg-

ment. This often was achieved by intimidating the youths with insults and physical bullying. This method of training was seen as essential in determining who would thrive in the life and death situations of real combat. Rewards for endurance included the prospect of eventually becoming a master of youths, and the possibility of becoming a *telpochtlato* later in life. The *telpochtlato* were responsible for training an entire generation of seasoned warriors who were essential to the survival of the empire.

War captains (*yaotequihuaque*) were primarily entrusted with training the youths in matters of war. These veteran warriors taught the young men to handle weapons, including shooting arrows from a bow, throwing darts with an atlatl (spear-thrower), and holding a shield and a *maquahuitl* (a kind of saw-sword carved of wood and affixed with an edge of sharp obsidian razor blades). Youths were taken on as apprentices to carry supplies and arms for the instructing warrior when he went to war. At first they assisted by carrying baggage and arms for soldiers; later the novices carried their own arms. Eventually, they would be allowed to participate fully in battle and to attempt to capture enemy prisoners for sacrifice.

Prior to full participation in battle, the youths were introduced to combat situations in a variety of manners. Their first combat training was symbolical and took place in the principal religious festivals held annually. These festivals were held in Tenochtitlan's main ceremonial center in front of the Great Temple (see chapter 6). The festivals were held to celebrate the planting season and the conclusion of war season, and included dancing, singing, and feasting. The most important events to the warriors were the staged battles. Featured in these gladiatorial battles were high-ranking enemies captured during the previous campaign season; here, these warriors would fight for their lives against heavily armed opponents.

Also encouraged among the students were mock battles between the youths of both the *telpochcalli* and *calmecac*. These would be held as competitions in which participants were rewarded with food and gifts. It was during these mock battles that the veteran warriors of different ranks and specializations

5.2 A veteran soldier accompanied by two novice soldiers, in the Codex Mendoza (John Pohl)

would teach the boys to handle basic weapons such as slings, bows, arrows, and spears. The most promising students would be advanced to train in the use of the *maquahuitl* and shield.

At the age of 20, those youths who wanted to become warriors went to war, but before the novice could go to war, he had to have a sponsor to accompany him. The youth's parents achieved this by approaching veteran warriors with food, drink, and gifts in order to entice the best sponsor for their son. The nobility's greater ability to pay doubtless resulted in their sons' being watched over by better and more experienced warriors, and their success rate in battle was predictably higher than for the commoner youths, who could not afford the best teachers. The warriors took great care of the youths in the wars, and they showed the youths how to take captives once the tide of the battle had turned in the Aztec's favor.

Taking a captive unaided in a youth's first battle was very impressive. If he had assistance (up to five others), a decision was made about who had actually taken the captive. The captive was then distributed among those helping in the following manner: The

actual captor took the body and the right thigh; the second who had helped him received the left thigh; the third took the right upper arm; the fourth took the left upper arm; the fifth took the right forearm; and the sixth took the left forearm. Then the tuft of hair growing from the captor's nape was cut. If the captor had required the help of others to take a prisoner, his hair was shorn on the left side of his head, with the right side left long, reaching the bottom of his ear. Thus the youth was honored, but he was also told to take another captive unassisted to prove that he was a man.

A youth who failed to take a captive after going to war three or four times was called a *cuexpalchicacpol*, or "youth with a baby's lock," meaning that he still possessed the tuft of hair at the nape of his neck. (A warrior's hair was styled in accordance with his rank; therefore, his hairstyle was a symbol of distinction. The most common were the top knot [*temillotl*] and the shorn head with a center crest and two side tufts.) Thus shamed, he redoubled his efforts to take a captive. If he failed to take one unassisted, his head was pasted with feathers. One who took no captives at all, even with assistance, had the crown of his head shaved, and he would never achieve martial fame. However, this was a consideration only for those youths aspiring to a military career. The bulk of the army was made up of commoners who were sent into battle as auxiliaries and had little hope of achieving martial fame in any case.

Because the *telpochcalli*'s main goal was to prepare the Aztec youths for war, the school's instructor demanded the youths' total attention, great physical effort, bravery, and the ability to withstand intense pain. This was not taken lightly by the trainers or indeed by wider society, since the well-being of the entire empire depended on the training of these future warriors. The *telpochcalli* was expected to produce powerful and courageous warriors. As a result, those who deviated from the training were gravely chastised. One source depicts a teacher beating the head of his student with a firebrand because he left school to live with a prostitute. This discipline was applied not only to the students but also to the teachers, and punishment often involved the taking of valued possessions. Adornments and valued lip pendants were removed, and in order to humiliate the individual publicly, his warrior hairstyle was cut off.

MILITARY RANKS AND ORDERS

The three major avenues for social advancement in Aztec society were commerce, the priesthood, and a distinguished military career. In order to advance socially in the military, the warrior had to demonstrate great feats of military prowess, which were generally measured by the number of captives taken in battle (see figure 5.3). Although slaying enemies was important, the true indicator of a successful campaign was the taking of captives for sacrifice. The quality of the captive was also important because some enemies were considered more difficult to capture than others were. Achieving rank therefore depended on the quality as well as the quantity of the captives.

Most of the Aztec army was composed of troops of commoners (*yaoquizqueh;* singular, *yaoquizqui*) without military distinction. Although historical accounts place considerable emphasis on the elite warriors, the possibility of military advancement through one's deeds and abilities was possible, but social class was the primary influence on the success of a military career. Sons of nobility always had the best opportunity to have not only better military training but also the best ranking positions due to the status of their fathers. Military ranking was intimately tied to the overall social structure of Aztec society, and social ranking was tied to political offices, the latter defining rights and requiring the holder to have a specified status. The hierarchy in the military was as follows:

Huey tlatoani (commander in chief of the army)
Cihuacoatl (prime minister and second in command)
Supreme Council of War (group of four *tetecuhtin* with high military ranks)
Xiquipilli (regiment, or battalion, consisting of groups of 8,000 men divided in units of 400)

There were also ranks of authority equivalent to general, colonel, and captain.

The *telpochcalli* youth's first battle was of extreme importance because it was his opportunity for advancement in rank. If he had been brave in battle, he would be named *tiachcauh* (master of youths). Once he was considered valiant and thought to have reached manhood, he was named *telpochtlahto*. Each *telpochcalli* had a *telpochtlato, tiachcauh*, or *telpochtequihua* (military instructor). If the youth captured four enemies, he could advance to the rank of *tequihua* (plural, *tequihuaqueh*), and later he could reach a variety of higher ranks, such as *tlacochcalcatl* (general), *tlacateccatl* (commanding general), or *cuauhtlahtoh* (chief), or perhaps become a *topileh* (one who has owned a staff), a constable.

The commander in chief was the *huey tlatoani*, also called *tlacatecuhtli* (lord of the men or warriors), and often led the army into battle himself. He was at the apex of Aztec society, and by the 15th century, the position equaled that of emperor. The emperor's most trusted adviser was the *cihuacotl*, who outranked other advisers. Following the *tlatoani* and the *cihuacoatl* was the Supreme Council of War, which was composed of four main officers:

the *tlacateccatl* (he who commands the warriors), the highest commanding general; the *tlacochcalcatl* (man of the house of darts), an army general in charge of the arsenal; the *etzhuahuancatl* (person from Etzhuahuanco, the place where one has scratched with blood), a prestigious warrior; and the *tlillancalqui* (keeper of the dark house, or dweller of Tlillan, the place of blackness). Only the highest nobility were allowed to hold these four offices. The emperor's heirs held the highest office of the *tlacateccatl*, while the remaining offices were given to his brothers or close relatives. Courageous warriors and members of the emperor's council held additional offices and titles. Those titles granted to valiant warriors did not strictly allocate rank but were honors given for performance in battle.

Other military ranks included the *achcacauhtin*, who were in charge of declaring war or subduing rebelling provinces. These positions were usually held by courageous warriors, but the title signified that the *achcacauhtin* were a type of judicial officer who oversaw arms, doctrine, and training.

The elder warriors, the *cuauhhuehuetqueh* (eagle elders; singular, *cuauhhuehueh*), also held an important place in the military hierarchy. Although they were no longer allowed to fight in battle, they played a significant role in the campaigns. Their responsibilities included organizing the troops and camps and informing the wives of warriors slain in battle.

In addition to individual ranks, the Aztec army was organized into hierarchical units. The smallest tactical unit consisted of four or five soldiers under the command of a veteran. These units were grouped into squads of perhaps 20 men, and larger units of 100, 200, and 400 men, each with their own commanders. Reflecting Aztec social structure, these units were drawn from and organized by *calpulli* with the intention of creating cohesive social, as well as military, units. Beneath ward levels, each unit marched separately under its own battle standard. Above ward levels, the army was organized by city with its own banner (allied cities followed the same general organization), and the entire army then marched under the standard of the king. Most veteran soldiers were dispersed throughout the army, but the military orders also operated as separate units. The typical size of an army was a regiment or battalion called a *xiquipilli*, which contained 8,000 men, with larger forces being composed of multiples or fractions of this number.

Otontin and *Cuauhchicqueh* Orders

The orders of the *otontin* (Otomies; singular, *otomitl*) and the *cuauhchicqueh* (shorn ones; singular, *cuauhchic*) were the highest military orders. Capturing five or six enemies qualified a warrior entrance to the *otontin* order, and he was given a *tlahuizmatlatopilli* or *xopilli*, an emblem symbolic of heroism. He also carried a *maquahuitl* and a shield decorated with a design of four crescents, and he was allowed to wear his hair bound in a tassel with a red ribbon.

In order to enter the *cuauhchicqueh* order, warriors had to take many captives and perform more than 20 brave deeds. The *cuauhchicqueh* order was of higher status than the *otontin* order and included in its membership many high-ranking commanders, such as the *tlacateccatl*, the *tlacochcalcatl*, and the *cuauhnochtecuhtli* (eagle prickly-pear lord). Certain characteristics were particular to this order. For example, their heads were entirely shaved except for a piece of hair braided with a red ribbon above the left ear. They would also paint half of their heads blue and the other half red or yellow. The attire would include a loincloth and an open-weave mantle of maguey fiber.

Both of these military orders had their own house in the emperor's palace, and within these quarters, nobility and commoners were separated. The Supreme Council of War congregated to debate military matters in the *cuauhcalli*, the house of the eagle and jaguar military orders. The emperor presided over these meetings. Apparently, the *cuauhchicqueh* warriors also met in the *cuauhcalli*, although they did not play a role in decisions of the state. The highest of the several warrior orders was that of the nobles (*otontin* and *cuauhchicqueh*), followed by the eagle and jaguar warriors. There were other less known orders like the coyote, bear, and skull warriors.

Eagle and Jaguar Warriors

As anthropologist Ross Hassig has pointed out, seasoned warriors also belonged to the military orders customarily referred to as eagles (*cuacuauhtin*) and jaguars (*ocelomeh*). Theoretically there was no difference between these two groups, and they were therefore sometimes called the *cuauhtlocelotl* (eagle-jaguar warriors). These variant terms probably signified differences in the attire of the individual

a.

b.

c.

d.

e.

f.

5.3 Depictions of Aztec warriors from the Codex Mendoza: *a) an otomitl, b) a cuauhchic, c) a warrior with one captive, d) a warrior with two captives, e) a warrior with four captives, f) a tlacateccatl (Fonda Portales)*

5.4 The remains of the cuauhcalli *(House of the Eagle and Jaguar Warriors), next to the Templo Mayor (Great Temple) in Mexico City* (Fernando González y González)

warriors rather than internal distinctions drawn by the orders themselves. Those admitted to either order had to be *tequihuaqueh*, but they could have been students from either the *calmecac* or the *telpochcali.*

Although these orders where composed largely of nobility, this was not the only qualification. Military ability was greatly commended, and a warrior could join the order if they had captured more than four enemies. Thus, commoners were admitted if they could achieve elevation to the *cuauhpipiltin* (noble eagle warrior) rank. However, hereditary nobles always had the advantage because of the superior training they received as youths, the social rank of their fathers, and their connection to superior veteran warriors.

The emperor granted a variety of rights to the warriors who advanced to the eagle and jaguar orders because of ability and achievement. These privileges included the right to wear otherwise proscribed jewelry and daily military attire, to dress in cotton and wear sandals in the royal palace, to eat human flesh and drink *octli* (pulque) in public, to keep concubines, and to dine in the Royal Palaces. Yet there remained a distinction between the distinguished commoners who became *cuacuauhtin* and *ocelomeh* and the meritocratic hereditary nobles, who received greater privileges. For example, the nobleman's full-body war suit (*tlahuiztli*) was made of animal skins, unlike the feathered one worn by the commoners. Regardless of this distinction, the commoners who became *cuauhpipiltin* were still assured

5.5 Terra-cotta image of an eagle warrior found in the cuauhcalli, *Museum of the Templo Mayor, Mexico City* (Fernando González y González)

that their male offspring were eligible for noble treatment, which included warrior training in the *calmecac.*

MILITARY INTELLIGENCE

Two of the most crucial aspects of Mesoamerican warfare were espionage and communication. Espionage allowed leaders to keep abreast of political and military events, while communication allowed them to establish and maintain political initiatives and ties and to direct armies in the field. Because the empire was held together by Aztec action, or threat of action, rather than by structural reorganization, communications and intelligence concerning both foreign and internal areas were vital. To gather information and convey messages, both formal and informal, four institutions were used: merchants traveling throughout Mesoamerica, formal ambassadors, messengers, and spies.

Merchants

The *pochtecah* (merchants; singular, *pochtecatl*) were long-distance traders of a variety of goods throughout a vast geographical area that included not only the Aztec Empire but also independent regions with no allegiance to Tenochtitlan. The information that merchants brought back from within and outside the empire was specific and involved general assessments of the local political climate based on the way they had been received.

Gathering this information for the Aztec Empire was incidental to their primary trading duties, although at times they were given specific orders. The *tlatoani* Ahuitzotl, for instance, ordered merchants to use trade as an excuse to spy on the lands of Anahuac (the name given to Mesoamerica by the Aztecs). Disguise was an important element of a merchant's spy tactics when entering hostile areas beyond the Aztec Empire. Sometimes they disguised themselves as natives of other areas by cutting their hair in the style of the locals and learning their language. This was essential because discovery of their deception would have resulted in death.

The killing of a merchant was considered just cause to declare war. Oftentimes the merchant would provoke war because he would demand trade or request materials for some domestic or religious purpose. Independent cities had very little choice but to either kill or expel the merchant or to become subjects to Tenochtitlan.

In their travels, merchants journeyed with shields and swords, prepared for battle if necessary. If they were successful in confrontations, they were rewarded by the emperor in the same manner a warrior would be. If they were openly attacked, the emperor quickly sent warriors to their aid.

As the empire expanded, the importance of merchant military intelligence increased. The farther away a conquered land lay, the more important it became to know what was going on at all times. The Aztec required advance knowledge in order to be able to subdue planned rebellions, invasions, or hostile actions. Hence, the *pochtecah* were held in high esteem, and when they were attacked or murdered, retaliation was deemed necessary. It was not so much the merchant's life that mattered as much as the information he was supplied.

Ambassadors

Official ambassadors were a more formal means of contact and intelligence. They were received in peace even by enemy cities. Usually these ambassadors were sent to independent cities to ask them to become tributaries to Tenochtitlan. The refusal of such a request would make the area a candidate for conquest, and if the ambassador was killed, his death would definitely result in war.

Messengers

According to anthropologist Ross Hassig, a system of messengers was utilized by the Aztec to convey information within the empire and to sustain contact with faraway cities and armies in the field. This messenger system functioned by having relays of men stationed about five miles (8.4 kilometers) apart along the main roads. These messengers were responsible for transmitting a variety of correspondence. For instance, if the emperor died, news of his death would be dispatched from Tenochtitlan to the rest of the empire by sending messengers, although the main responsibility of these couriers was to convey political messages to and from the Aztec emperor. This system was mostly utilized in times of war when word was sent out to inform allied kings about rebelling provinces, to instruct allies to mobilize men for a war, and to advise tributary towns along the army's line of march of its imminent arrival and of its dietary needs.

Spies

Once war was declared, formal spies were sent out for tactical intelligence. Before troops were mobilized, the spies (*quimichtin*, literally, "mice"; singular, *quimichin*) were sent out in disguise, dressed like the enemy and speaking their language in order to scrutinize the enemy's fortifications, army, and preparations. Their job was also to identify traitors of the enemy and to pay them to obtain information. At this point, maps were made of the foreign territory, and obstacles, such as rivers, were marked.

Being a spy was a dangerous occupation because if one were discovered, it meant death and the enslavement of one's family. Thus, spies were greatly compensated with gifts such as land for their perilous work.

WOMEN AND WAR

Women's roles in the war effort were secondary, although their lives were greatly affected and influenced by many aspects of warfare. Women could not be warriors, but when necessary, they defended their families, homes, and men to the point of death.

There exists at least one graphic chronicle of women acting as warriors in order to defend their community. Diego Durán, the Dominican priest who conducted research immediately after the conquest of Tenochtitlan, wrote that during the Spanish siege of Tenochtitlan, the Aztec were on the offensive, but Cuauhtemoc lacked the men and strength to defend himself and the city. Many of his people had died because so many of his allies had abandoned him and had fled the city, as well as owing to hunger. Cuauhtemoc, nevertheless, decided not to show cowardice in the face of the Spanish and pretended that he did not lack warriors. The last Aztec *tlatoani* asked all women to ascend to the flat roofs of their houses, where they made insulting gestures at the Spaniards.

When Cortés saw the great number of people on the rooftops and filling the streets of the city, he

5.6 Women defending their community, in the Atlas of Durán *(Lluvia Arras)*

feared that he would not be able to conquer Tenochtitlan without causing harm to his army and allies. Nonetheless, he urged the Chalcas and the Tetzcocans to take courage and all the Spanish men to return to the combat. At this time they realized that the warriors who stood on the roofs were women. They sent word to Cortés about this and then began to ridicule and insult the enemy and attack and kill many of them. In the end, the Spaniards, greatly aided by their Indian allies, vanquished the Aztec and made the courageous king Cuauhtemoc flee.

This was probably not the first time women were used as the last defense of the community. But the greatest impact warfare had on women was widowhood. Women and their children were constantly left without husbands and fathers. Many of the funeral rites held in the *altepetl* for warriors killed in battle or sacrifice would address the widows of the warriors. The *tlatoani* would encourage women not to let sadness overwhelm them and to take courage and show love for those who died fighting for their empire.

As a sign of mourning, Aztec women carried the cloaks of their dead husbands in procession. They wore their hair loose, and they would clap their hands to the beating of the drums. They wept bitterly, and at times they danced, bowing their heads toward the earth. At other times, they danced leaning backward. The sons of the dead men also were present, and they wore their father's cloaks, carrying on their backs small boxes containing their father's lip, ear and nose plugs, and other jewelry. Emotions in such processions would escalate to such proportions that the entire community would be filled with fear and trembling.

As a consequence of war, women faced another fearful experience—capture. When any community was defeated, the priests and warriors moved in to take booty and to organize a regular tribute payment. Women were often part of immediate and long-term tribute payments to victorious communities. When the Aztec were victors, they would take captive women, children, and warriors and tie them together with cords drawn through the perforations in their noses. Or, as in the case when the Aztec defeated the Huastecs, the maidens and daughters of Huastecs who had been seized and the children who did not yet have their noses or ears perforated were forced into wooden yokes, which hung around their throats. They were all tied together this way. As in all wars, women were killed alongside their men and children, especially when enemies resisted Aztec forces or vice versa.

UNIFORMS AND WEAPONS

Uniforms

Valiant deeds in battle were rewarded with great honors, arms, and insignia. These rewards were given to both nobles and commoners alike. Once a youth had captured a warrior, he would begin to move up in rank. Not only did he receive honored titles, he would also receive clothing that reflected his rank and distinguished him from other warriors. The title he earned and the decorations adorning his new clothing depended on how many prisoners he had captured.

When a youth captured one captive without assistance, he would become a leading youth (*telpochyahqui*) and was given the title *tlamani* (captor). The young man would be presented to the emperor, and in his presence, the youth would have his face painted with red ochre and his temples anointed with yellow ochre by the emperor's *calpixque* (tribute collectors). At this point the emperor would present the youth with the warrior's garb to be worn in peacetime. There are different accounts pertaining to the clothing. According to the friar Sahagún, the young warrior was granted an orange cape with a striped border and scorpion design. He was also given two *maxtlatl* (loincloths), one that was carmine-colored with long ends, and the other that was many colored. According to the *Codex Mendoza*, the young warrior was granted a mantle with a flower design, called a *tiyahcauhtlatquitl*, or the "brave man's equipment" (see figure 5.3).

When a warrior took two captives, he was once again taken to the emperor's palace and given a mantle with red trim. He was awarded a uniform consisting of a body suit called the *tlahuiztli*, a tall conical cap called a *copilli*, and a *chimalli* (shield) marked with black designs, described as hawk scratches. The *tlahuiztli* was made of sewn cotton, a luxurious material. Red, yellow, blue, or green feathers were meticulously stitched to the cloth in the workshops of conquered city-states and sent to Tenochtitlan each year as tribute. In addition to the battle suit, the emperor rewarded these soldiers with a distinctive cape called a *tilmatli* that allowed them to display their rank when off-duty. The loincloth, or *maxtlatl*, they were given was handwoven and embroidered by the soldier's own wife and mother. The method of wrapping the cloth around the body and tying the ends at the front was a distinctive fashion for Aztec men. The knot was then passed through an opening in the *tlahuitztli*. Sandals were woven with thick grass soles to which were stitched a cotton strip to support the ankle and ties (see figure 5.3).

When a warrior took three captives, he was given a lavishly worked garment called an *ehecaila-cacozcatl*, or "wind-twisted jewel mantle," and an insignia in the shape of a butterfly called a *tlepapalotlahuiztli*, which had an accompanying red-and-white feather tunic. At this point, the deserving warrior was given the title *tiachcauh* (leader of youths), and he would dwell in the *telpochcalli* to teach the youth about war.

When a warrior took four captives, he was presented with the *ocelototec* war garment (a Jaguar style *tlahuiztli*, with a helmet adorned with feathers), a mantle of two stripes of black and orange with a border, and the emperor allowed the warrior's hair to be cut like that of a *tequihua* (veteran warrior). The warrior was also granted one of the titles of the veteran warrior: *mexihcatl tequihua, tolnahuacatl tequihua*, or *cihuatecpanecatl tequihua*. The title of *tequihua* distinguished these warriors from the rest and indicated that they had been presented with honor, weaponry, and special insignia (see figure 5.3).

The way a warrior was treated after he took more than four captives also varied according to the reputation of the enemies he had captured. Of course, this was not constant throughout Aztec history, and it varied among the groups they encountered and the resistance their enemies exerted. For example, at the time of the Spanish conquest, the Huastecs and other coastal groups were not highly thought of, and when one Aztec warrior captured even 10 of these enemy warriors, he was not given any more accolades. He would simply be known as *yaotequihua* (veteran warrior and leader of the youths). However, if a warrior's fifth captive was from Atlixco, Huexotzinco, or Tliliuhquitepec, he received notable esteem and was named *cuauhyacatl* (great captain). The emperor gave him numerous gifts: a blue labret (lip ornament), a headband with two tufts of eagle feathers and ornamented with silver flint knives, leather earplugs, a bright red net cape, a diagonally divided two-colored cape, and a leather cape.

To take a sixth captive from Atlixco or Huexotzinco was considered an impressive achievement, and the captor was given further gifts: a long yellow labret, a headband ornamented with two tufts of eagle feathers and with gold flint knives, a cape with several possible designs such as a serpent mask or earthen vessel or a jaguar cape with a red border, a loincloth with long ends and either the eagle claw or marketplace design, and black sandals with red or orange leather thongs. The warrior in this position earned the titles of *tlacochcalcatl* (general) or *tlacateccatl* (commanding general) for this great accomplishment (see figures 5.3 and 5.12).

Award ceremonies for the warriors took place during the feast of Tlacaxipehualiztli (Flaying of

Men), held during the second of the 18 months of the solar calendar. Veteran warriors received four pieces of black cloth, and the *telpochyahqui* (leaders of youths) were given capes. This type of clothing was more than just a necessity or a vanity item; it was a significant marker of martial and social status.

The importance given to certain garments was key in identifying a warrior's status and accomplishment. Undistinguished commoner warriors were forbidden to wear the fabric and attire of the accomplished warriors; they were allowed to wear only a maguey-fiber mantle that bore no distinctive designs or fine embroidery, and they were not allowed to use sandals. Other social regulations included the length of the mantle, which could not reach below the knee, unless it was concealing war wounds on the individual's legs. And novices could not wear any insignia awarded for courageous deeds when they entered battle for the first time. This applied to both commoners and nobles.

Undistinguished warriors wore only body paint and a loincloth during war; novices wore maguey-fiber clothing for their initial battle. Body armor made of quilted cotton was only worn by military leaders. The attire of courageous warriors and war leaders was more ornamented and included neckbands of shells or gold, netted capes of twisted maguey fiber, and leather corselets. They also painted their faces with black stripes. Only nobles were allowed to wear lip plugs, earplugs, and nose-plugs of gold and precious stones. Although courageous warriors and military leaders could also wear plugs, they were made of ordinary materials such as wood or bone.

Only the emperor and great lords wore armbands, anklets, and headbands of gold. In times of peace, the emperor wore a blue and white mantle, called a *xiuhtilmatli*. (It was a crime punishable by death for anyone else to wear this garment.) Other objects reserved for the emperor were jeweled ornaments, a helmet, and an insignia called a *cuauhchiahtli*. The emperor also wore two plume tassels (*ananacaztli*), which were placed on the side of the royal insignia crest.

It is important to point out that such distinctions were worn more as status symbols and performed no protective duties. Items such as armbands were worn only occasionally in battle.

Insignia

To honor military accomplishments, individual markings were given to warriors. Markings came in an array of forms and included helmets and crests of various sorts, shields, and other attire. These marking could hold a variety of meanings. They indicated the general rank one held in the military, but they could also be highly individualistic. Social standing often affected what type of markings warriors received, but this was not the sole criterion to receive such merits. Even emperors who had not accomplished particular exploits lacked some of the distinctive insignia.

Insignia were so significant that they were stored with the royal tribute and were only worn on designated occasions. The emperor of Tenochtitlan was the only one allowed to award them, and they were given on special and auspicious days and during special feasts.

There were exceptions to these rules, however. In times of major battles, insignias were awarded to brave warriors and nobles before a campaign and also to other allied emperors and their brave and noble warriors. Weapons, scenes of great deeds in the past, gods, and previous emperors, as well as more abstract designs, were represented on insignia.

Insignias were usually received as tribute but were also made by the feather workers of Tenochtitlan. Many of them were also captured in war and were given to the emperor so he could then award them to deserving warriors. These types of insignias usually represented participation in certain battles.

If warriors performed poorly during battle, the emperor had the right to deprive warriors of certain insignia honoring their military achievements. Insignia were not hereditary because they signified an individual's achievements, and so insignia were buried or cremated with a warrior when he died.

Thus, status attained in war was marked by the honors one received, the way one's hair was worn, the jewelry one was entitled to wear, the clothing one wore in peace, and the arms, armor, and insignia worn in war. Status was displayed by both commoners and nobles, although in different ways, and what could be worn and by whom changed during the course of Aztec history.

Body Paint

Throughout Mesoamerica the practice of using body paint was essential in battle. The Maya, Tlaxcaltec, Huastec, and Aztec all used body paints in warfare. Among the Aztec, the application of specific face paint was an indication of martial success. When a warrior attained a captive, his face was painted yellow and red. Courageous warriors (*tiyahcauhtin*) painted their bodies black and painted their face with black stripes on which they sprinkled iron pyrite (*apetztli*). The use of body paint was also utilized by the military orders; for example, the *cuauhchicqueh* had half of their heads painted blue and the other half red or yellow to signify their status in the order. Face and body paints were used in much the same fashion as the insignia presented for valorous deeds.

Weapons

What is written about Mesoamerican arms comes from 16th- and 17th-century accounts. There is a substantial amount of discussion on Aztec weapons, and various depictions of weaponry exist in different codices, in sculpture, and in paintings. There are also preserved examples in museums. As anthropologists Ross Hassig and John Pohl have indicated, however, the picture is incomplete. One finds a repetition of the most important weapons in historical sources, while other weapons receive minimal mention in only a few scattered documents. This suggests that other, less commonly known arms may be forgotten.

OFFENSIVE WEAPONS

The most common division of arms was that between offensive and defensive weapons. Offensive weapons were used to attack the enemy by projected force. These weapons included bows and arrows, darts and atlatls (spear-throwers), spears, slings, *maquahuitls* (wooden saw-swords), and clubs (see figure 5.7). Defensive weapons were worn as protection and included body armor, helmets, and shields. The Aztec's main offensive arms can be divided into projectile weapons and shock weapons.

Projectile Weapons Projectile weaponry was designed to strike the enemy from long distances. They included atlatls, bows, and slings. The atlatl was a spear-thrower used to project darts. This device allowed the user to throw an object with greater force and for longer distances than a spear could be thrown by hand. Certain accounts credited the god Opochtli with creating the atlatl, while others give credit to the Aztec for inventing it during their early years in the Basin of Mexico. Archaeological studies, however, have shown that the atlatl predates the Aztec and is depicted in murals at Teotihuacan, the Classic-period site of El Tajín, and the sculptures of the *atlantes* of Tula.

The atlatl was the Mesoamerican weapon most associated with the gods, and they are often depicted carrying it. The craftsmanship on many of these spear-throwers was ornately and artistically executed. For example, Cortés received an atlatl with a turquoise head in the form of a serpent from Motecuhzoma II. Other decorations included human figures, symbols in low relief, and gold ornaments. It is speculated that these types of ornate spear-throwers were probably only used on ritual or ceremonial occasions. Extant atlatls are approximately 0.6 meters (2 feet) in length and 35–37 millimeters (1.5 inches) in width at the upper end, tapering to 19–25 millimeters (0.7–1 inch) at the lower end. The dart is placed against a hook at the upper end in a 5–10 millimeter (0.2–0.4 inch) groove for its bed. Other examples have two grooves, which may indicate that they were intended for throwing two darts simultaneously. Attached to the sides of the atlatls are finger grips, which either come in the shape of actual holes in the device or pegs extending from the sides. In either shape, the finger grips are usually positioned about a third of the way from the lower end. There are, however, some examples that do not indicate the existence of finger grips.

Darts were used with the atlatl. They were made out of oak with feathered butts and came in several varieties. The majority of extant examples are single-pointed, and many were fire-hardened. Others have obsidian, fishbone, copper, or flint points. Certain examples are barbed, others are two-pronged, and still others are three-pronged. Fire-hardened darts were known as *tlacochtli*, or

5.7 *Aztec weaponry and equipment: atlatls, or spear-throwers (a1 and a2); a bow (b1), arrow (b2), and quiver (b3); a* maquahuitl *(c); a* tepoztopilli, *or long spear (d); and shields (e1, e2, and e3)* (Lluvia Arras, after Pohl 2001: 37)

tlatzontectli. The three-pronged darts were called *minacachalli* and were often used to hunt aquatic birds.

Sahagún states in his writings that the darts were made during the feast of Quecholli, but this account probably refers only to the normal resupply of darts for the armory. Assertions that atlatl darts were carried in a quiver appear to be incorrect, and the usage in battle attests to it. According to Spanish sources, the darts were highly effective, and they could pierce any armor and still inflict a deadly wound. Especially dangerous were the barbed darts because the point

had to be cut out from the wound rather than simply being pulled out.

No extensive amount of quantitative data exists about the effectiveness of the pre-Columbian Mesoamerican atlatl. Data from other parts of the world show exceptional accuracy and force for up to 46 meters (150 feet); experimental tests put the range at more than 55 meters (180 feet), with an extreme in one test of 74 meters (243 feet) by an inexperienced thrower. The atlatl was highly accurate and gave greater range of motion than the unaided spear, with 60 percent more thrust. The penetrating power of atlatl-propelled darts was greater than arrows thrown at the same distance.

Despite the superior thrust of the atlatl, bows (*tlahuitolli*) were major weapons in pre-Columbian Mesoamerica. They measured up to 1.5 meters (5 feet) long and were made from animal sinew or deerskin thong bowstrings. War arrows (*yaomime*) had a variety of points: barbed, blunt, and single pointed, made of obsidian, flint, or fishbone.

Archers kept arrows in quivers (*mixiquipilli*) during battle. The number of arrows kept in a quiver is uncertain, but some data suggest around 20 per quiver. In depictions archers are shown with a single quiver. Contrary to Huastec claims and unlike the arrows of Indian groups elsewhere, Aztec arrows were not poisoned. Fire arrows (*tlemime*) were used against buildings.

Many bows and arrows were given as tribute throughout the Aztec Empire. During the feast of Quecholli, when ordinary war supplies were made, the Aztec crafted arrows. They gathered reeds to use for shafts, which they straightened over fires and smoothed. Next, they cut the reeds to equal sizes and bound the ends with maguey fiber so they would not split. Finally, they glued the points to the shafts with pine pitch, and the arrows were fletched. It was important to make the arrows uniform to give greater accuracy to the archers. The best bows were made of hickory and ash wood with strings made from rawhide or animal tendons.

The conquistador Bernal Díaz del Castillo reported the fatal effect of the Indians' archery skills. He wrote that the people of Cimaltan could shoot an arrow through a double thickness of well-quilted cotton armor. The archers of Teohuacan (Tehuacan) were famous for their ability to shoot two or three arrows at a time as skillfully as most could shoot one. Sufficient quantitative data regarding how far a bow could shoot an arrow is lacking, but according to tests performed with North American Indian bows, the typical range for an arrow to travel was about 90–180 meters (300–600 feet), varying with the size and pull of the bow and the weight of the arrow. Aztec arrows' stone points weighed as much as steel points. The obsidian points made a superior weapon that was remarkable for the finely cut glasslike edges, the serrated edges of the points, and the con-

ical shape, all of which helped the arrow penetrate animal tissue.

Díaz del Castillo's admiration for the Indians' use of bows, lances, and the *maquahuitl* was surpassed only by their use of the sling stone, which he claimed was far more damaging. Maguey-fiber slings (*tematlatl*) were used to fling stones at the enemy. A furious hail of stones could severely wound even the most armored of Spanish soldiers. Slings were so effective that slingers and archers usually served together because they complemented each other in the battlefield.

The stones used as ammunition were not collected during battle but rather were shaped and stored in advance. They were also sent to Tenochtitlan as tribute. Comparative data indicate that slings had a range in excess of 200 meters (660 feet) with randomly selected stones in Mesoamerica but exceeded 400 meters (1,320 feet) with lead pellets in ancient Greece; slingers in the imperial Roman army could pierce chain mail at 500 paces (approximately 2,500 feet). As with arrows, standardizing the shapes and sizes of stones increased velocity, distance, and accuracy.

Shock Weapons Shock weapons were used in hand-to-hand combat to cut, crush, and puncture the enemy. These weapons were often the ones that determined the outcome of battles. Among the Aztec, these weapons included thrusting spears, swords, and clubs.

Descriptions of Aztec thrusting spears (*tepoztopilli*) claim that they were longer than those of the Spanish and had a total length of between 1.67 and 2.2 meters (5.5 and 7.2 feet). According to 16th-century accounts, they cut better than the Spanish knives. They had a diamond-shaped head with a cutting surface of stone blades that was 31 centimeters (1 foot) wide and sharp enough for the Indians to use them to shave their heads. The length of the blade indicates that they were used to slash and not simply to thrust, which would have been as easily achieved with a simple point. While the *tepoztopilli* was effective for thrusting and slashing, as well as for parrying, at a distance, it was less effective if the enemy closed in, although the blades on the rearward portion of the head permitted an effective backward

5.8 The maquahuitl was a wooden sword with obsidian blades along its edges. (Lluvia Arras, after Pohl 2001: 21)

pull. Apparently one pierced Díaz del Castillo and it went through his metal armor only to be stopped by the thick underpadding of cotton.

Surviving examples of Aztec thrusting spears are not known, although there are numerous 16th-century illustrations. There was one example that survived in the Royal Armory in Madrid, but it was destroyed in the great fire of 1884. A mislabeled print of this weapon does exist.

The use of thrusting lances and other thrusting spears in Mesoamerica greatly predates the Aztec. The weapons were present among the Preclassic-period Olmec, at Teotihuacan, and among the Classic-period Maya.

Another basic shock weapon was the Aztec sword known as the *maquahuitl.* There was at least two varieties of this sword—one-handed and two-handed. They were constructed from wood, usually oak, and were 76–102 millimeters (3–4 inches) wide and a little more than a meter (3.5 feet) long. Obsidian or flint blades were glued into grooves along the edge. The shapes, indicated by drawings, included rectangular, oval-shaped, and pointed designs. The glue used was both bitumen and "turtle dung glue." Certain *maquahuitl*s had thongs through which the user could put his hand to secure the weapon in battle.

Descriptions of the two-handed variety indicate that they were about 10 cm (4 inches) wide and as tall as a man. The *maquahuitl* was bladed on both sides and could be used in a powerful downward slash or to inflict a sharp backhand cut. According to the conquistadores, these swords were able to cut the head from a horse with a single blow, better than those of the Spanish. They also described their clever construction in that the blades could be neither pulled out nor broken.

Examples of the *maquahuitl* are not known to have survived, but there are numerous depictions of it in various 16th-century drawings. Like the thrusting spear, the one example in Madrid's Royal Armory was destroyed by the fire in 1884. A mislabeled print also remains: In it, the stone blades of the *maquahuitl* are closely set, forming a virtually continuous cutting edge. Other drawings indicate that they were sometimes discontinuous, forming a gapped, possibly serrated edge.

Various types of clubs were also used in Mesoamerican warfare. Some were made of wood alone, but others called *huitzauhqui* had stone blades. The *cuauhololli* (wooden mace) was made of hard wood and had a spherical ball at the end. The *cuauhololli* was a crusher and was effective in a downward blow but considerably less in an upward blow. The *macuahuitzoctli* was another type of club that had a knob of wood protruding from each of its four sides and a pointed tip. These relatively unspecialized clubs were fairly widespread.

DEFENSIVE WEAPONS

Aztec defensive weapons included shields, helmets, and various types of body armor used for protection. Aztec military shields (*yaochimalli*) came in a variety of designs and materials (see figure 5.7). Many were made of hide or plaited palm leaves. A description made by a conquistador describes a shield called the *otlachimalli* as being made of a strong woven cane with heavy double cotton backing. Earlier accounts describe shields of split bamboo woven together with maguey fiber, reinforced with bamboo as thick as a man's arm and then covered with feathers.

Cuauhchimalli shields were made of wood. Others were made with a feather facing over which was laid beaten copper. Some shields had such innovative designs that they rolled up when they were not needed in fighting and could be unrolled to cover the body from head to toe. Shields were covered with painted hide, feathers, and gold and silver foil ornamentation. There was variation in the feather ornamentation by color, type, and design, according to the owner's status, merit, and so forth. The shields used by the Aztec were round, although square or rectangular examples are found through the Classic and early Postclassic periods in the Maya area, Gulf coast, and at Cacaxtlan (present-day Cacaxtla, Tlaxcala).

Hernán Cortés sent the king of Spain an Aztec shield made of wood and leather that had brass bells attached to the rim and a gold boss with the figure of Huitzilopochtli. The handle had carvings of four heads—a puma, a jaguar, an eagle, and a vulture. According to the account of the "Anonymous Conqueror," the majority of shields sent to Spain were of the type used in dances and ceremonies (*mahuizzoh chimalli*) and not the sturdy war shields. One shield examined by the historian and diplomat Peter Martyr d'Anghiera in Spain was made of stout reeds covered with gold, and the back was lined with a jaguar skin. The lower part of the shield was decorated with a feather fringe that hung down more than a *palma* (21 centimeters, or 8.2 inches). The hanging border of feathers was a common feature, and though apparently fragile, it afforded additional protection to the user's legs. This type of feather fringes could easily stop a spent projectile and deflect others. This is a feature that predates the Aztec and is depicted in murals at the Classic site of Cacaxtlan, at Teotihuacan, and among the Classic Maya. These shields were prob-

ably intended primarily for protection against projectiles and not against clubs or swords.

Tenochtitlan's feather workers produced many shields, but the Aztec also received a variety of shields as part of their tribute. Examples of tribute shields included ones covered with fine, many-colored feather work and gold, depicting weapons, gods, emperors, and scenes of great deeds in the past. These shields were created from fire-hardened sticks so strong and heavy that it is reported that not even a sword could damage them. According to the conquistadores, a crossbow could shoot through them but not a bow.

The two feather shields in the Württembergisches Landesmuseum in Stuttgart, Germany, are 0.71 and 0.75 meter (28 and 30 inches) in diameter, respectively, and have 3-millimeter (0.12-inch) foundations of wood strips bound together by fine interwoven cords. Four round sticks, 12 millimeters (0.47 inches) in diameter, cross the shields horizontally, and to these sticks and the leather patch on each shield are attached two leather handles. The outer surfaces of the shields are covered with thick parchment, covered with feathers glued to the surface.

Quilted cotton armor (*ichcahuipilli*) was a customary component of battle garb in Mesoamerica (see figure 5.10). This garment was made of unspun cotton firmly sewn between two layers of cloth and stitched to a leather border. The thickness of the *ichcahuipilli* (one and a half or two fingers) allowed neither an arrow nor an atlatl dart to penetrate it. It came in several styles: a type of jacket that tied at the back, a sleeveless jacket that tied in the front, a sleeveless pullover that hugged the body and reached to the top of the thigh, and a sleeveless pullover that flared and reached the mid-thigh. As with their other weaponry, the Aztec received some cotton armor in tribute.

The *tlahuiztli* war suit consisted of long sleeves and leggings, thereby covering not only the torso but also the arms and legs (see figure 5.9). The *tlahuiztli* contained no padding but was worn over the cotton armor and closed in the back. Different types existed, and 12 are recorded as having been received as tribute. Although most resembled animal skins, the suits of noble warriors were constructed of feathers sewn to a backing fabric. The *tlahuiztli* suits of animal skins were only worn by meritocratic nobles.

Both of these types of suits offered some type of protection on the limbs from projectiles, whereas the *ichcahuipilli* protected the torso. The suits of higher status were known for their fine feather work. This suit offered more than just vanity because the slick surface of feathers may have provided superior protection than animal skins. Depending on the backing, these suits were probably also lighter and cooler. *Tlahuiztli* suits apparently predated the Aztec; a jaguar suit worn by a warrior is depicted at the Classic-period site El Tajín.

Feather tunics called *ehuatl* were used by war leaders over their cotton armor. This attire was not as common as the *tlahuiztli* suit and was used primarily in the areas east of Tenochtitlan, stretching from Tetzcoco to Tlaxcallan. The tunic was made of cloth over which feathers were set in rows. On the border were hung feathers, and it resisted lances, arrows, and even swords. The *ehuatl* lacked sleeves and leggings and thus was inferior to the *tlahuiztli* suits for protection (see figure 5.10). The continuing usage of this garment may have been due to divine affiliations, since many gods bearing arms are depicted wearing these types of garments. Such examples are found in murals at Teotihuacan and in carvings at early Postclassic Chichén Itzá. Certain warriors of higher nobility also wore other types of body armor. Among these were armbands (*matemecatl*) and skin greaves (*cotzehuatl*) of wood, bark, or very thin gold, both covered with leathers and feathers. There were also wristlets (*matzopetztli*). These items had very little protective value and were worn with the *ehuatl*.

Construction of helmets varied, as some were made of wood and bone and highly decorated with feathers. Others were made of the head of wild animals—wolves, jaguars, and pumas—supported over a frame of wood or quilted cotton. The wearer would gaze out from the animal's opened jaw.

Also incorporated into the garb of the warrior was a wide breechcloth (*maxtlatl*) that covered their

5.9 *a) An eagle helmet and* tlahuiztli, *from the* Lienzo de Tlaxcala; *b) a jaguar helmet and c) a coyote helmet and their respective* tlahuiztli, *from the* Codex Mendoza *(Fonda Portales)*

5.10 *Two types of body armor: a) the* ichcahuipilli, *consisting of quilted cotton, and b) the* ehuatl, *a feather tunic worn over the* ichcahuipilli (Fonda Portales, after Pohl 2001: 26–27)

thighs. Over this was often worn a hip-cloth. Some warriors also wore sandals (*cactli*).

NONMARTIAL WEAPONS

Several other weapons served little or no martial function in Postclassic central Mexico. The blowgun (*tlacalhuazcuahuitl*), for example, was primarily used to hunt birds and was not a military weapon. Clay pellets were blown and propelled through a hollow tube. Pellets ranging from 8.5 to 34 millimeters (0.3–1.3 inches), averaging 14.7 millimeters (0.6 inch) were found at the Classic site of Teotihuacan, indicating that they were used in a blowgun of 1.5 to 1.7 meters (5–5.5 feet) in length.

Chronicle accounts do not mention the axe (*tlateconi*) in a military context, but it is often found illustrated in the codices under martial context. Axes were intimidating but were unlikely weapons, since commoners would have been very skilled in their use. In codices one finds people or gods wearing war garb (the *ehuatl*) and carrying axes.

Knives are very seldom referred to as weapons of war. The *tecpatl* was a large flint knife used mainly for sacrificial purposes; it was sometimes also called an *ixcuahuac*. A general term for knife was *itztli* (literally, "obsidian" or "obsidian fragment"), which also encompassed razors, lancets, and so forth. Knives

were carried in battle, but their major use in war-related events seems to have been in sacrificing captives and other victims.

Illustrations of Uniforms According to Rank

TLATOANI

According to Fray Bernardino Sahagún's descriptions, the Aztec emperor wore an *ehuatl* decorated with red feathers over an *ichcahuipilli*. The skirt was made of pieces of leather to protect the legs and was decorated with quetzal feathers. He also wore bracelets and

5.11 *Uniforms of a) the* tlatoani, *from the* Codex Ixtlilxochitl, *and b) the* pochtecah, *from the* Florentine Codex (Fonda Portales)

5.12 *Uniforms of Mexica warriors, as depicted in the* Codex Mendoza: *a) the* tlacateccatl, *b) the* tlacochcalcatl, *c) the* huitznahuatl, *and d) the* ticocyahuacatl (Fonda Portales)

anklets made of gold. The *copilli* (crown), encrusted with turquoise, was exclusive to the emperor and select nobles of high rank. On his back appeared the imperial Aztec emblem (see figure 5.11).

TLACATECCATL

This distinguish warrior wore the banners of general on his back. His facial paint and shield were characteristic of the gods of death. He used a long-sleeved *ehuatl* and painted leather skirt and wore the *quetzalteopamitl* (national Mexica standard), made of gold and quetzal feathers (see figures 5.12 and 5.3).

POCHTECAH

The uniform of the interregional tradesmen, spies, and ambassadors consisted of luxurious clothing, including a *maxtlatl*, a *tilmatli* (cape), and elaborate jewelry (see figure 5.11).

OCELOPILLI

The *tlahuiztli* with helmet and jaguar marks were reserved for jaguar warriors who captured four enemies. These were also used by the members of the elite order of jaguar gentlemen. Jaguar warriors used the *ichcahuipilli* underneath the *tlahuiztli*, and out of an opening in the forehead came a knot of the *maxtlatl* (see figures 5.9 and 8.32). The *ocelopilli* would use a *maquahuitl* and shield, both finely decorated with feathers and gold.

YAOTELPOCHTLI

When the army was on the move, the novice soldiers (*yaotelpochtli*) and the slaves transported all the army's equipment. The various arms, clothes, and military implements would be tied to a piece of wood, which would then be carried on their back (see figure 5.2).

YAOTEQUIHUAQUE OTONTIN

This captain used a green *tlahuiztli*, which characterized his status as captor of five enemies. The captains and other high officials would wear ornaments constructed of bark paper, cloth, and feathers attached to their backs by leather straps in a manner that would not detract from the agility and mobility of the warrior. These banners, or standards (*cuachpantli*), served to indicate the position of military units and coordinate the movements in the battlefield (see figure 5.12).

CUAUHCHIC

The *cuauhchicqueh* were elite combat troops used to provoke attacks, complete difficult missions, and give strategic assistance during combat. They did not pretend to have hierarchical status and were honored to be frontline combatants. Their hairstyle consisted of a shaved head save for a crest down the middle and two side tufts, and they used a yellow *tlahuiztli* and a paper emblem painted in flag form attached to their backs. (Figure 5.3 shows a *cuauhchic*; his shield has the decorative motif of the spiral fret [*xicalcoliuhqui*].)

TLAMACAZTEQUIHUA

This *tlahuiztli* of the warrior priest was black and white to represent a starry night. The hat was conical, its form taken from a Huastec design, probably commemorating the conquest of these people by the Aztec. (The uniform in figure 5.13 corresponds to a warrior priest who has captured four enemies.)

YAOQUIZQUEH

The clothing of a Mexica warrior consisted simply of a *maxtlatl* and *ichcahuipilli*, accompanied by the *maquahuitl* as a defensive weapon (see figure 5.3c). (Figure 5.13 shows a warrior who has captured one enemy soldier.)

a.　　　　　**b.**

5.13 Uniforms of a) a warrior priest and b) a Mexica warrior (Fonda Portales, after Pohl 1991: 31)

Battle Tactics and Strategies

The Aztec were not usually concerned with positional war, or war for the possession of a defined battlefield area unless it served some particular purpose. Their goal was to maneuver the enemy into situations of entrapment, and this demanded perfect coordination and timing.

The primary battle tactic that the Aztec utilized called for the majority of soldiers to form a succession of long lines and charge against the enemy. Victory would be realized when the army surrounded and entrapped the enemy and penetrated the center of the enemy's formation. Leaders called out line movements by using drums and shells. Once formation was ready, a group of archers and slingers launched a storm of projectiles against the enemy line. Immediately after the projectiles began to fly the *cuauhchicqueh*, serving as shock troops, were sent in to break the enemy line and initiate hand-to-hand confrontation. The *cuauhchicqueh* consisted of elite soldiers and were known for being very brave. During battle they would scream their battle cry, *atl-tlachinolli*, which means "water-burned thing," a metaphor for blood and fire, the products of war. After the *cuauhchicqueh* came the veteran warriors, who where magnificent to behold and very brave, according to descriptions made by Spanish soldiers.

Once both lines came into contact, the outcome of the battle depended on the strength and ability of each individual. Because the use of the *maquahuitl* required great physical effort, the men would take shifts every 15 minutes to maintain a strong front line. The more experienced warriors were in the front line, while the young and inexperienced went behind as relief, all the while learning the art of war from the veterans.

The battles lasted many hours and were very bloody, and given the nature of the *maquahuitl*, many combatants were left maimed. During the arduous struggle of hand-to-hand combat between the frontline men, the soldiers behind the Aztec front line badgered the enemy with the *tepoztopilli*, a type of lance with an obsidian point.

Times of Attacks

Battles usually began in the morning, typically at dawn. Although the enemy expected dawn attacks, it was common place to call surprise attacks. If during the day the battle was not won, both armies would disengage shortly before sunset. Night attacks were rare because the dark made it almost impossible to control large-scale movements and troops. Among Mesoamerican groups such as the Mixtec, Zapotec, and Otomí, however, small-scale night raiding was common. For the Aztec, night attacks were only undertaken against nearby and familiar targets and never during distant campaigns. In short, they used the tactic only where difficulties of control and communication were minimized and they were confident of a relatively easy victory.

Signals

The first order of business was to raise a system of battlefield signals. This was achieved by establishing a command post on an adjacent hill with a direct sight line to the army. Signals were sent by relay. Runners were spaced at four-kilometer (two-and-a-half-mile) intervals.

Smoke was effective for communicating at longer distances between the *xiquipilli* (troops), as were polished iron pyrite mirrors from which the Sun's rays could be flashed as messages. To warn other camps and cities of war or that an army was approaching, smoke signals were the general means of communication. Signals also initiated prearranged coordinated attacks. This involved an exceptional level of coordinated planning and control of troop movements.

During tactical communications, a frontal attack was usually signaled by a diversity of noisemaking devices. These included drums and trumpets but could also be the voices of the warriors in the form of shouts and whistles. This was common in times of victory. Usually the Aztec leader, either the emperor or a general, signaled the attack with a conch-shell trumpet. Other devices were also used; for example, the *tlatoani* of Tetzcoco used a small drum to signal his troops. Retreat was also signaled by the same sound. For times when the troops were too far apart to hear the leader's signal, fire would be used in coordinating attacks.

The effective use of sound devices for signaling an army's advance did not deter the individual warriors from also making noise. It was common for warriors of each unit to enter battle shouting the name of their town and beating their shields with their swords. To avoid chaos, the tall *cuachpantli* standards could serve as a visual guide to troops in the melee. Unit leaders wore the standards as they led their troops into battle (see figure 5.12). The standard was so important that if the bearer was killed or the *cuachpantli* was taken, the whole unit would be thrown into commotion. The Spanish thought that this happened because the Indians believed the loss of their standard was an evil omen. In reality this commotion was due to the fact that during battle verbal commands were nearly impossible to issue or hear; therefore, the standard was the towering sign indicating where and when the unit should advance and retreat. The standard enabled the individuals and groups to keep in touch with their main body.

Psychologically, the loss of the standard was a large blow to the rest of the unit, but this was only secondary to the loss of direction. The loss of the standard indicated that the warriors could not determine where their comrades were going, and this heightened the risk of being cut off and captured by the enemy. The agitation displayed by the army units had real tactical importance, as it meant total disruption of control and blinded the troops. The use of a standard may have been an Aztec invention, although similar standards were shown in earlier eras in pottery, murals, and sculptures.

Insulting the enemy was also commonplace at the beginning of battle. For this reason the *cuauhchicqueh* were fond of wearing their hair in tufts, much like professional clowns, and even acted out skits mimicking the enemy's weakness in their efforts to get them to break ranks. In Aztec society, the crudest gesture one could give another person was the exposure of one's genitals and buttocks. This was so popular and common that even women and children were encouraged to do so if the opportunity presented itself. Other provocative insults were threats of extreme torture and cannibalism.

The Order of Battle

According to anthropologist Ross Hassig, the considerable variety in the battle dress of the Aztec was a consequence of the insignia and distinctive attire granted to individuals to assert to their rank, class, past exploits, or membership in military orders. The social hierarchy also pertained to offensive weapons. All warriors usually carried shields, but use of the *ichcahuipilli* (cotton armor) was restricted to those warriors who had demonstrated skill, usually *tequihuaqueh* and members of military orders. Thus, commoners were more susceptible to injury, as their head and body were unprotected. Commoner warriors died in greater numbers in both projectile showers and in hand-to-hand combat.

The different weapons also conveyed distinct social implications. Projectile weapons were generally of lower status than shock weapons, for at least three reasons: 1) Projectile weapons such as slings and bows were associated with commoners because they were used for hunting and were the main arms of the Chichimec (nomadic peoples of the northern deserts); 2) shock weapons such as the *maquahuitl* or a staff weapon required vast training and practice, which were an indication of class; and 3) bows and slings were not as effective in combat as shock weapons, particularly against armored opponents. The only projectile weapon that was regarded highly was the atlatl for its association with the gods. The utilitarian use of this weapon as a hunting tool had been suspended because of its somewhat short range. On the other hand, in military combat it was useful for its great penetrating power, even against armored opponents.

In its entirety an elite warrior's battle attire consisted of body armor, a shield (often with protective feathers attached at the bottom), a helmet, and a *tlahuiztli* suit or an *ehuatl* tunic. When combat reached the hand-to-hand stage, warriors resorted to shock weapons such as the *maquahuitl*, a club, or a thrusting spear. Atlatls and darts were also used.

Novice warriors, both nobles and commoners, did not wear body armor, though they did have shields and wielded thrusting spears, clubs, and *maquahuitl*. The majority of Aztec troops, however, were non-specialists (mostly commoners) who acted as slingers and archers. These differences in armor and weaponry had a major effect on which troops were likely to be killed first.

Warfare in Mesoamerica was very structured and usually began with the firing of projectiles. All warriors, regardless of skill or rank, were ordered to start each battle by launching their projectile weapons. Such a large wave of fire could cause considerable damage.

As archers required both hands to shoot their arrows, they were not able to hold shields; therefore, archers were sometimes protected by other warriors or shieldsmen. Although the Aztec archer's rate of fire is not known precisely, it is estimated that they probably fired around six arrows per minute and therefore used up all their arrows in about three minutes. It is thought that stone slingers exhausted their supplies of ammunition even faster, as their rate of fire was higher than the archers'.

It is suggested by witnesses that the Aztec waited until they were within 50–60 meters (164–197 feet) of the enemy before they opened fire. This was for a variety of reasons. Firstly, the closer the target was, the more accurate the warriors would be in their aim. Secondly, it allowed short-range weapons such as the atlatl to be most effective. The shorter the range, the greater the penetration, and as this increased the likelihood of a fatal shot, it in turn reduced the number of projectiles needed to be carried into battle. By attacking at a short distance, the Aztec were able to maximize their firepower and successfully break up opposing formations or drive them from fixed positions.

Troops would fire until all their ammunition was used up. Just as the wave of fire was subsiding, the first ranks would close with the enemy, having taken advantage of the covering fire and prevented the exposure of troops who had run out of ammunition. It was during this time that the atlatl was most effective, as it lacked the range of the bows and slings but was very powerful at short range and was therefore able to break up enemy lines. These elite weapons were used only by soldiers advancing on their enemy; the atlatl was useless once hand-to-hand combat had begun because it was held in the right hand and meant that a warrior could not use a defensive weapon to parry blows. For this reason the atlatl was used only briefly during battle, and depictions show warriors carrying only four or five darts.

As the lines moved forward, the atlatls were switched for shock weapons. The archers and slingers would continue to fire until their weapons were exhausted, then they would most likely move to the back, before they became exposed to the enemy's shock weapons.

The most experienced warriors would be sent into hand-to-hand combat first with the intention of delivering a swift defeat. Sometimes the emperor would lead the warriors into battle, but usually the military orders came first. The first to advance were the warriors of the *cuauhchicqueh* order, who fought in pairs and were sworn to fight until death if necessary. They were deployed mainly as shock troops, but they could also operate as a rear guard if the army was forced to retreat and as reinforcements if anyone got into difficulty. The *cuauhchicqueh* were so fearless in battle that they had a reputation for being impossible to overrun once ordered to hold a position.

The *otontin* order followed the *cuauhchicqueh*, and after them came the veteran warriors, the *tequihuaqueh*, who were in charge of the first organized units. Each leader entered battle at the head of their respective units. As these units were made up of a mix of veteran and novice warriors, the veterans' duty was to support, teach, and protect the young warriors in combat. The Aztec emperor was known to enter battle with his entourage of generals surrounding him. This order of battle was then duplicated by the allied cities as they advanced in separate units behind the Aztec.

Order among the troops ensured survival on the battlefield. When a warrior was wounded or lost on the battlefield, his unit closed around him to protect him. Those who were found breaking ranks or disobeying a leader were beaten or killed. The movements of the warriors working together were strategic and planned. If troops moved in too quickly to charge an enemy, the cohesive front could be lost and the effectiveness of their army destroyed. For example, if the Aztec front turned back in cowardice or in surrender, the retreating troops would be forced into a collision with the reinforcements behind them, and the resulting confusion could leave them all open to defeat.

To maintain a solid front, armies tried to prevent themselves from being outflanked. Soldiers fought only those directly in front of them, and so long lines were formed to create troop cohesion and solidarity, as well as creating a line of defense that posed enemies directly in front of warrior. Hand-to-hand combat required each man to defend his own position. Battlefield tactics of course varied according to certain situations, but generally, the Aztec army tried to surround the enemy and attack it from all sides. Surrounding and flanking an enemy was a common practice. It placed more soldiers on the front line who could fight with fatal weaponry, and it cut off the enemy from further reinforcements. This kind of formation was especially effective against similar infantry styles; however, once this battle plan faced the horses of the Spaniards, Aztec troops were unequipped to withstand a cavalry charge.

To make battle formations more effective, individuals has to be very conscious of their own physical stances within the formation. Soldiers kept their weight balanced between their left, forward foot and their right foot, which would advance the body as the warrior threw a weapon of any kind. Once this forward motion was engaged, the soldier stepped back and raised his shield with his left foot forward to deflect any defensive blows. With this kind of position, enemies were only separated by about 2 meters (6 feet), the length of the arm extension and the weapon.

The battle was initiated by an attack of arrows, darts, and sling pellets from around 45 meters (50 yard) generally in a push to disrupt formations. The use of bowmen and slingers from conquered provinces was typical. Their job was to stand at the front line and instigate combat, after which they could withdraw to the back or retreat to the sides to inflict harassing fire. These frontline soldiers were dependent on their superior arms and broad, heavy shields to protect them from the barrage of enemy fire; however, these generally young novices would eventually become wounded. Other strategies had to be employed.

The next command in the battle was a charge. It is important to note that an Aztec war was a running war. The troops depended on their sheer inertia to try to smash through the enemy line; hence, downhill attacks were considered optimal as gravity served to compel soldiers forward. The subsequent impact of one force against another must have been horrific. Once troops on both sides had recovered from the impact, combatants would engage each other one on one so that they could swing their deadly weapons without hindrance. Because wielding the *maquahuitl* and shield demanded a tremendous amount of energy, men fought in 15-minute shifts throughout the battle in order to keep the center strong. Officers dutifully observed the situation for any signs of weakness in the enemy's formation as well as to direct reserves of veterans to fill gaps among their own formations as needed.

Occasionally the opposition was too strong to continue hand-to-hand combat, so the army would fall back just enough to allow the archers, slingers, and atlatl wielders to sue projectiles. The same tactic also supported orderly withdrawals in the face of superior forces. When the entire unit or army was forced back, it moved in the direction of its camp, where additional projectiles could be retrieved to turn the tide against opponents who did not have a fresh supply. The ability to conduct an orderly withdrawal was also necessary in a prolonged battle, as fighting did not generally continue at night.

The Aztec always left two generals in Tenochtitlan for the purpose of strategic reinforcement. Additional troops dispatched from Tenochtitlan were largely of use in relatively nearby battles, such as against Xaltocan or Xochimilco. But reinforcements were also sent directly from Tenochtitlan to distant campaigns of extended duration, in one case after 20 days of combat.

Ultimately, the Aztec preferred to surround their enemies and entrap them by double envelopment. This tactic could be dangerous, as it necessitated extending the flanks at the expense of maintaining a strong center. The Aztec offset the problem by ensuring that they always fought with superior numbers. A surrounded and frightened enemy would fight to death if they thought their lives were at stake. Aztec commanders therefore tried to induce controlled retreats along prescribed routes where panicked troops could be easily exposed to slaughter by reserves concealed in adjacent cornfields, trenches, foxholes, and even under piles of loose grass and leaves.

Ambushes

The ambush was among the most successful and skillfully executed of the Aztec tactical maneuvers. These were often simple attacks at strategic times and locations where the attacker had the most advantage, such as at narrow mountain passes or from seemingly deserted houses. The most spectacular ambushes, however, involved the use of a deceptive ruse in which the Aztec forces retreated, pretending that the enemy was winning the battle. If the hoax was executed convincingly, the enemy advanced to gain more advantage. But once the enemy had compromised its position, the Aztec turned on them with additional troops and either attacked them from behind or used troops to cut them off from their tactical and logistical supports.

One feint described many times in the historical accounts involved the use of foxholes and covers. During the war with Tehuantepec, King Axayacatl advanced at the front of his army. When the opponents attacked, he fell back to a place where his soldiers were hidden by straw, whereupon they attacked Tehuantepec's troops and won the battle. In another famous example, King Motecuhzoma I Ilhuicamina formed his units and attacked the Huastecs before feigning a retreat. This drew the Huastecs forward until 2,000 armed, Aztec *cuahuchicqueh* and *otontin* warriors, camouflaged with grass, rose to their feet and destroyed them. This same simple tactic was used in many other wars. In the war against Tollocan (Toluca), King Axayacatl and eight of his generals concealed themselves in straw-covered holes in the ground. Once the Aztec army had retreated past their location, they leapt out, killed the Tollocan lords, and routed the army. Political assassination before battle was not a significant factor in Mesoamerican warfare, but in battle the ruler was a legitimate target, since his death could shorten the battle and the war.

Conquest and Aftermath

The Aztec's initial objective was to force the enemy into submission and ultimately take control of the city under attack, but if the defending army failed to surrender and withdrew to the city, the battle was carried to the city itself. When this occurred, the Aztec resorted to burning temples and their associated buildings. Because politics and religion were unified, burning down a town's main temple was a devastating blow to the enemy and the ultimate sign of Aztec victory. Temples were usually the most venerated and heavily fortified sites within the city; burning them meant that the enemy had succeeded in penetrating and overcoming the strongest resistance. More pragmatically, the temple precincts also contained the city's armories, and burning them deprived the embattled army of their arms and war supplies. Burning the temples also meant that the local gods had been defeated, although their images were not necessarily destroyed. The Aztec often removed them, along with the local priests, to Tenochtitlan, where

Mazatlan

Ehecatzquapechco   Miquetlan

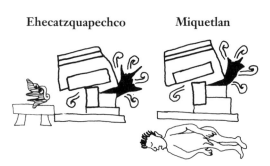

5.14 *The burning of a temple, as depicted in the* Codex Mendoza *(Fonda Portales)*

the gods were housed in the *coateocalli* temple in the Sacred Precinct.

Burning an entire city to the ground was not common but could be used as a last resort. Depending on the defeated town's willingness to negotiate, the city might be burned if it did not surrender once its main temple had been fired. When the Aztec defeated Coaixtlahuaca, for example, the people fled to a shelter in the nearby hills. The Aztec burned the temple but refrained from razing the city when its citizens promised to pay tribute. When the lords of Alahuiztlan refused to keep their word and become tributaries, the city was finally razed.

Burning the entire town was thus not an invariable consequence of defeat, although battles often led to this result when the clash was between major adversaries. But burning a town did not mean its complete and eternal obliteration; if a defeated town was burned, its inhabitants were expected to rebuild it. Thus, during the conquest of Tenochtitlan, the Aztec taunted the Spaniards and their allies by telling them to burn the city, because they knew that if the Spaniards won, the Aztec would be forced to rebuild it anyway, and if the Aztec won, they would force their enemies to rebuild it.

Fortifications

Hassig has found that though most urban settings were not fortified, specific battle plans anticipated encountering fortifications. When the Spaniards attacked Tenochtitlan, for example, they found that the Aztec had built walls, earthworks, and trenches. Temporary battlements in streets and atop houses were ubiquitous during the battle for Tenochtitlan. Even cities without a wall and great fortresses had fortified structures—usually the main temples and their enclosed precincts. When fortifications were encountered, different battle tactics and timing were involved.

In the war to conquer Oztoman, King Ahuitzotl's forces attacked the city, broke the wall and its fortress, and burned the temple. Motecuhzoma II Xocoyotzin's forces did the same in the war with Tecuhtepec. When the Aztec attacked Xochimilco, the people reportedly retreated behind a defensive

wall and wounded the attackers through holes constructed in the barrier. It is not clear whether these holes were loops through which arrows could be shot or whether they were holes to accommodate thrusting lances. Ingeniously, the Aztec solved this problem by using sticks and digging implements to tear down the wall, precipitating a Xochimilca surrender.

Another significant type of Mesoamerican fortification was the stronghold detached from its associated city. It was usually atop a hill, where the advantage of height and a difficult ascent provided a natural defense to supplement the structure's walls and battlements. Large stones were cleverly rolled down on attackers and provided an effective first line of defense.

While these fortified hilltop sites, such as the one atop the island of Tepelpolco near Tenochtitlan, did not protect their cities, they did serve two important purposes. First, they could be used as places of refuge in the event of attack. When residents fled to a detached fort near the town of Cuezcomaixtlahuacan, the Aztec army was foiled in its attempt to conquer them. And when the Spaniards and their allies attacked the Matlatzincas, their warriors fought the Spanish party while the women and children, with their belongings, fled to the nearby stronghold. When the battle grew even fiercer, the warriors also retreated to the fortress. Second, these shelters could house additional warriors. When Cortés attacked Cuauhquechollan (Huaquechula), warriors surprisingly emerged from the adjacent hilltop fort to fight the Spaniards. Unfortunately, these sites could be vulnerable to siege if they were not equipped with adequate supplies of food and water.

Sieges

One of the Aztec's main concerns in battle and in playing out a successful siege operation was to keep allies from helping those under attack. Accordingly, the Aztec dispatched army units to neighboring towns in the region to intimidate and thereby ensure that they did not aid the enemy.

If the war was not won on the open battlefield, the enemy could retreat behind fortifications. Under such conditions, unless the attackers gained entry through deceit or treason, the Aztec might simply withdraw in disappointed resignation. Barring this, the attacking army had three options in defeating the protective barriers: breaching the fortifications, scaling the walls, or laying siege to the target.

Unbreached fortifications could still be scaled, but this was uncommon. When the Aztec tried to conquer the six-walled fortress of Quetzaltepec, night scouts were sent to find a way to enter; they found none. As a result the Aztec constructed wooden ladders, used them to scale the walls, and successfully conquered the fortress. This same tactic was utilized during Cortés's absence from Tenochtitlan; the Aztecs attacked the Spaniards who had stayed in Tenochtitlan by scaling the walls of their fortress.

If neither breaching nor scaling the walls succeeded, then a siege was the last resort to overcoming the fortress. Aztec siege of a town in the Basin of Mexico was feasible because the Aztec could easily ferry supplies by canoe. But logistical constraints rendered sieges virtually impossible elsewhere. More than other tactics, sieges depended on factors other than the military skills mastered by the Aztec. Time, expense, and the presence of potentially hostile groups surrounding the target city affected siegecraft. Enemy resistance in the area could intensify, and the besieged city might be reinforced and resupplied while Aztec supplies dwindled. Moreover, the Aztec themselves could be attacked. So, instead of sending a small army capable of defeating a city by siege, the Aztec sent a large army to overwhelm it.

Large siege machines did not exist in Mesoamerica, and only the weapons normally used in combat were available to the attackers. Projectiles had harassment value in besieging fortifications, and atlatl darts and stones proved to be effective. Both could be lobbed over the walls of fortifications with telling effect, and burning arrows were used to set buildings afire.

Since extended sieges were usually not feasible, because of expense and taxation on ammunition resources, defensive fortifications could be rudimentary. Meant to house women and children when the city was under attack, and nobles who needed a rest from the strains of ongoing battle, strongholds could doubtless have been built to withstand sustained sieges, and their absence reflects the limitations of the attacking army. During this time they could still negotiate the terms of surrender from a better bargaining position than if they had suffered outright defeat.

Though fortifications in Mesoamerica were effective, they were infrequently used. First, the Aztec had already developed some countermeasures. Second, the cost of protecting the entire perimeter of the fortress would have been enormous, particularly for sprawling agricultural towns. Third, inhabitants were unlikely to be able to repulse a massed enemy at any given point along the walls. Fourth, the likelihood of betrayal seriously reduced the value of such protection, particularly considering the expense involved. But most important, the use of fortifications in Mesoamerica was not advantageous to the city's wider social networks. The city itself might be safe, but its fields and stores beyond the walls still vulnerable. Its smaller unfortified dependencies were also unprotected, and without these the city was lost anyway. Ultimately, lying in wait behind fortified walls did not allow the city to continue as the hub of an organized social system.

Captives of War

The first captives taken in combat were bound to sacrifice. This could take the form of *tlahuahuanaliztli* (gladiatorial sacrifice), in which the leg of the prisoner would be tied with a rope to the surface of a circular sacrificial stone (*temalacatl*), and the captive would battle against Aztec warriors better armed until he was defeated and then sacrificed. Another form of sacrifice was the *tlacamictiliztli* (heart extraction), in which the captive would be laid face up over a rectangular stones called a *techcatl* and held down by four priests. A fifth priest would open the chest cavity with an obsidian blade (*tecpatl*) and extract the heart, which was offered to the Sun and then placed in a *cuauhxicalli* (special receptacle for this function). In the excavations of the Great Temple of Tenochtitlan, a *techcatl* was found in the sanctuary of Huitzilopochtli. In yet another form of sacrifice the captive was tied to a wooden frame placed on the floor and was killed by the arrows of various warriors (for more on human sacrifice, see chapter 6).

PRINCIPAL AZTEC MILITARY CAMPAIGNS

Reasons for Fighting

According to Hassig, one reason that led to Aztec territorial expansion was their own unpredictable ecological situation. The island that the Mexica populated was located in the western portion of salty Lake Tetzcoco. This island was barren and could not supply the population with enough food. The unavailability of nearby land made agricultural intensification impossible. The solution for this dilemma was military expansion in order to conquer and extract tribute from more fertile lands. However, feeding the population was not the only reason for Mexica expansion. The wealth and power that the king and his nobles could attain also fueled the Mexica-Aztec thirst for battle.

Around this time, the royal lineage changed, and there was a shift from patrilineal patrimony to a system whereby the *tlatoani* was chosen from a small group of upper nobility based predominately on his ability. The nobles were particularly careful in their selection of a king because they knew that the more competent a ruler was, the more they in turn would prosper. The economic prosperity of everyone was threatened by an inadequate leader, particularly the prosperity of the nobility who depended on tribute from conquered lands as the Aztec Empire grew. Any sustained military failure undermined the Aztec's reputation and shrank an empire that relied heavily on the perception of Aztec power. This came with a corresponding reduction in tribute goods and lands, and as these flowed disproportionately to the nobility, failure struck directly at their interests and their support for the *huey tlatoani*. Inactivity or continued failure would threaten the ruler's position. Thus, the dual dynamics of social stratification and royal succession were major motivators of Aztec expansion and warfare.

The capital of Tenochtitlan faced no real threat from outsiders even though there were no special fortifications in place. This was a result of its island location. The Aztec were able to cross to the mainland by canoes and a series of causeways, but when threatened they were able to remove the wooden bridges that were built at intervals. Although the central part of the city was not formally fortified, it was enclosed by a wall as it contained the main arsenal, which was watched over day and night.

In fact, the magnitude of the empire and its large population were the main factors that protected the city much more than its location. In the early years of the Aztec Empire, Tenochtitlan was occasionally threatened by outsiders, but by the time of the Spanish arrival, it had become the largest city in the Valley of Mexico. As a consequence, there was no single city that had a large enough military force to threaten it. The empire's territory was so large that any enemy would find it hard to attract logistical assistance. Tenochtitlan's primary defense was not fortifications built of wood or stone, but its location and size joined together with an extensive buffer zone of tributary provinces.

Since the Aztec did not construct roads outside the main center of a town, they could not launch campaigns during the rainy season, from late May to September. The harvest followed; therefore, the campaign season was limited to the period between November and May when large armies could be assembled and provisioned after the agricultural season. The movement of Aztec armies was complicated by their large size. When marching on the trails connecting settlements, the Aztec army was confined to double files, each 8,000-man *xiquipilli* (battalion) stretching for more than seven miles, increasing an eight-hour march to 13 for the entire army. In order to ease the strain that a large campaign would cause, each *xiquipilli* began its march on a different day and often traveled to a common destination by different routes. Such campaigns would take vast amounts of time and supplies, and without resupplying, the Aztec army could only last about eight days.

Main Campaigns

Officially, Tenochtitlan was founded in 1325, but it would be more than a century before it reached the height of power as an imperial capital. Although vassals of the tyrannical lord Tezozomoc of Azcapotzalco, the Mexica *tlatoque* Acamapichtli, Huitzilihuitl, and Chimalpopoca were successful in expanding their own territory south and east along Lake Tetzcoco. When Tezozomoc died in 1427, his son Maxtla took power and had Chimalpopoca assassinated. The Aztec immediately elected Chimalpopoca's uncle, a war captain named Itzcoatl, as *tlatoani*. An alliance was quickly formed between Itzcoatl and the deposed heir to the throne of Tetzcoco, Lord Nezahualcoyotl, and they decided to attack Azcapotzalco. The duration of the siege was more than 100 days and ended when Maxtla fled into exile. The Tepanec lords of Tlacopan who aided Nezahualcoyotl in the overthrow of Maxtla were greatly rewarded. The three cities established the Aztec Empire through the Triple Alliance.

In 1440, Itzcoatl died and was succeeded by his nephew Motecuhzoma Ilhuicamina. The trend of Aztec expansionism for the remainder of the 15th century would be epitomized by Motecuhzoma I. As anthropologist John Pohl has pointed out, to the west of the Basin of Mexico were the fierce Tarascans, who dominated a rich trade in luxury goods that moved by seagoing rafts along the Pacific coast from South America to the Baja California Peninsula. To the south and east were wealthy confederacies dominated by the Zapotecs, Mixtecs, and Eastern Nahuas, the latter being kinsmen of the Aztec but nonetheless bitter rivals for the domination of the southern Mexican highlands. The *cihuacoatl* Tlacaelel advised Motecuhzoma I that in order to dominate these territories, he should first establish bases of operation on the peripheries of these more powerful states. The area that is present-day Morelos and Guerrero was the first focus of Motecuhzoma's campaigns, as from there, his armies could later initiate continuous attacks for months and even years at a time.

When he became *huey tlatoani*, Motecuhzoma I also ordered construction of the Great Temple dedicated to the Toltec rain god Tlaloc and the Aztec tribal hero-god Huitzilopochtli (see chapter 9).

To accomplish such a task he ordered that all the city-states of the Basin of Mexico contribute materials and labor, thereby proving their loyalty to Tenochtitlan. The city-state of Chalco, as ally to both the Mixtecs and the Eastern Nahua, refused. As a result the Chalcas were conquered in 1453, but instead of having a direct confrontation with the Eastern Nahuas of Tlaxcala, the Aztec decided to attack the Huastecs and Totonacs of the Atlantic Gulf coast. The use of various innovational strategies resulted in the Aztec's conquering much of northern Veracruz, and as a result, they attained an empire rich in tributes of exotic shell, cotton, cacao, gold, and the priceless feathers of tropical birds.

By 1458, the Mixtec kingdom of Coixtlahuaca (in present-day Oaxaca) also found itself under attack. This time the Aztec imperial army had marched 500 miles south from the Basin of Mexico in order to attack the enemy. Different accounts state that Motecuhzoma I Ilhuicamina organized the expedition to avenge the murder of 160 merchants by Coixtlahuaca's Lord Atonal. However, with 300,000 troops, the invasion force was clearly intended as more than simply a punitive expedition. By the time Atonal summoned the help of numerous other Mixtec kingdoms—including Teposcolula, Tilantongo, and Tlaxiaco as well as the Eastern Nahua city-states of Cholula, Huexotzinco, and Tlaxcala with which Coixtlahuaca was confederated—it was too late. The city-state of Coixtlahuaca was defeated before relief could arrive. Many of Atonal's men were captured and later sacrificed at the Great Temple of Tenochtitlan; Atonal, on the other hand, was assassinated by being garroted. This defeat astonished scores of city-states and kingdoms throughout Puebla and Oaxaca. This event marked the beginning of the end of an era of unparalleled independence and affluence throughout Mesoamerica.

In 1468, Motecuhzoma I was succeeded by his son Axayacatl, who had already proven himself a capable military commander by leading an expedition against the Zapotec of Tehuantepec. Now, as *huey tlatoani*, he sought to capitalize on the conquests of his illustrious father by entirely surrounding the kingdom of Tlaxcala and expanding imperial control over the Huastecs and Mixtec. According to Diego Durán, Axayacatl and his uncle Tlacaelel commissioned a new monument for Tenochtitlan's central religious precinct, a great round stone carved with the image of the Sun dedicated to war and the conquests of the empire—the so-called Aztec Calendar. As tradition dictated, they received aid in the form of materials and labor from Nezahualcoyotl of Tetzcoco, Totoquihuaztli of Tacuba, and the other Aztec city-states. In order to take captives for sacrifice at the inauguration of the stone, a war was proposed against the Tarascans.

The center of the Tarascan Empire was located in Michoacan, meaning "place of the fishes," where 1 million people were ruled by a hereditary lord whose capital was at Tzintzuntzan, on Lake Patzcuaro. The army of 20,000 men that Axayacatl had mobilized was half the size of the Tarascan army, but this did not discourage him from directing his troops to attack. The battle lasted through the day and well into the night. As the Sun rose the next morning, Axayacatl had lost the best of his shock troops and was forced to retreat to Tenochtitlan. By the time he reached the Aztec capital, less than a fifth of his army remained. As a result, the Sun Stone was not able to obtain its promised tribute of hearts and blood, and the defeat was a devastating blow to the empire. It was not long before several city-states began armed rebellion to try to take advantage of the chaotic situation. Axayacatl died in 1481 and was succeeded by Tizoc, whose rule was short lived and ineffectual. It was suspected that he was even assassinated by members of his own court.

The throne then passed to Tizoc's younger brother Ahuitzotl, in 1486, who proved to be an outstanding military commander. Among his accomplishments, the reorganization of the army helped him regain much of the territory lost under the former *tlatoque*. He then initiated a program of long-distance campaigning on an unprecedented scale. Bypassing the Tarascans, Ahuitzotl succeeded in conquering much of coastal Guerrero, gaining free access to the strategic trade routes along the Pacific coast through Acapulco. By the year 1497, he had reconquered much of Oaxaca and marched through Tehuantepec into Chiapas as far as the modern-day Guatemalan border. Realizing the danger of moving so far away from his supply sources, however, he decided to head back, only to

find, on his attempt to return, that he had been betrayed by the Zapotecs. In order to make peace, he agreed to marry one of the daughters of the Zapotec king Cocijoeza and to cede to the Zapotec governorship over the newly conquered province of Soconusco. Despite these setbacks, the empire reached its height under Ahuitzotl, controlling more than 25 million people throughout the Mexican highlands.

In 1502, Motecuhzoma II Xocoyotzin gained the throne. His goal was to expand to the south and east, attacking first the Mixtec coastal state of Tututepec and later sponsoring conquests to the east into Tabasco. By the time of the first sighting of Spanish ships off the Gulf coast, in 1517, Motecuhzoma II was even contemplating an invasion of the kingdoms of the Maya on the Yucatán Peninsula.

Mobilization of Troops and Supplies

The supplies needed to maintain the Aztec army came from two sources, the *calpulli*s and stores assembled by tributary kingdoms at designated points along the marching route. A majority of the food consumed by the young warriors was prepared by their own family or from a tax contribution from the marketplace vendors. The Aztec used this method specifically to cause as little impact as possible on the economies of the allied nations. Furthermore, there was to be an avoidance of any serious devastation to crops, or the men and women who grew them, by the army.

Despite the fact that a warrior's father might have been a craftsman, he was expected to do his share of the labor in the *calpulli*'s communal fields. In October, the harvest was reaped. The next step was to husk the maize and dry it, then grind it with manos and metates of stone by family compound. The pulverized meal was then moistened with water, shaped in 15-cm (six-inch) round flat cakes (tortillas), and toasted on a hot flat ceramic disk (*comalli*). Before the war season began in November, the warrior's mother, sisters, and wife were responsible for preparing a host of tortillas, beans, chili peppers, and other seasonings, as well as jerky of dried venison, peccary, and turkey. This would all be packed into a large basket to be carried by the *telpochcalli* youth who would assist the warrior during the coming campaign. After the warrior's departure, the family would go into withdrawal for four days, during which they would fast and pray to the gods for his safety. As part of penitential offerings, his father would perform auto-sacrifice. This involved piercing his tongue, ears, arms, and legs to draw blood that would be offered to the gods so they would bring his son back safely the following spring.

Porters called *tlamemehque* were responsible for transporting the bulk of provisions and equipment during the first long-distance campaigns undertaken by the Triple Alliance; for example, during the attacks of Coixtlahuaca in 1458, no fewer than 100,000 porters accompanied the troops, each carrying as much as 50 pounds in material. As more foreign kingdoms throughout southern and eastern Mexico were conquered, the empire obligated each territory to maintain permanent stores to be used by the army when traveling. This system enabled them to sustain large armies, and by 1500, the Aztec were able to maintain armies in the hundreds of thousands for years at a time if need be.

Mobilization of the Aztec army was done on the basis of units of 8,000 men, called *xiquipilli*. Each unit consisted of men from the 20 *calpulli* of Tenochtitlan. After mobilizing the *xiquipilli*, the *huey tlatoani* and his advisers had to decide the most effective way of moving them out of the city without disrupting the ordinary business of the city. The solution often was to move out the army over a period of several days; for example, during the march on Tututepec, the number of men involved was so massive that it would have been necessary to allocate different departure dates for each *xiquipilli*. When the troops were outside the borders of the city, they marched an average of 10 to 20 miles a day, depending on the gravity of the circumstances or the need to make a surprise attack.

Along the way, the Aztec army was joined by an equal amount of allied troops. As a result, no fewer than four different routes had to be taken to accommodate so many men. This probably explains the widely divergent pattern of battles recorded throughout southern Mexico during the course of a campaign. The Aztec army was divided into self-sufficient bodies of troops that moved in bulk along separate but parallel routes toward a predetermined destination. The tactical assumption was that each unit would be large enough to defend itself if attacked along the way by an opposing army until it could be joined by another. Once conflict began, the unit leader would send a runner to warn the rest of the army about the attack. The other units would then attempt to arrive at the battle scene within hours and attack the enemy's exposed flanks or rear. The fact that all Aztec armies were made up of light infantry enabled the units to move quickly when necessary, even in the most rugged terrain.

Massive troop movements of this scale could only be coordinated by well-trained officers; however, exactly how the chain of command actually functioned remains unknown. The commander in chief was the *huey tlatoani*, and during the early days of the empire, the emperor took a personal role in field combat. Second in command was the *cihuacoatl*, whose main responsibility was to rule Tenochtitlan in the absence of the emperor, but he could act as commander in chief on the battlefield as well. Under normal circumstances, direct responsibility for the army during a campaign rested with the Supreme Council of War, made up of four commanders. The distinct role of each commander included the organization of supply lines, the formulation of marching routes, and devising battlefield strategy and the directions for the actual attack. These plans were carried out for the Supreme Council by officers whose ranks were similar to those of major, colonel, captain, and so on.

Tenochtitlan's supply lines could only last for a certain period of time, especially on long-distance campaigns. As a result, the army had to count on stores supplied by tributary city-states. These stores would be situated along the marching routes. The Aztec Empire's expansion was tactical in that the empire wanted to acquire as much quality land as possible; therefore, it focused on the areas along commercial exchange routes. The Aztec would place leaders of defeated cities in high offices, but in order for them to keep their power, they would be forever indebted to the empire. They had to pay tribute, which greatly affected the population of the conquered land. In order to keep this system moving smoothly the Aztec eventually appointed tax collectors (*calpixque*) to the conquered kingdoms; a permanent garrison of Aztec troops would support each tax collector.

Following the conquest of Coixtlahuaca, the empire devised a number of ingenious strategies for dividing up the confederacies of Eastern Nahua, Mixtec, and Zapotec city-states. Initial tactics were ruthless. Under Motecuhzoma I, defeated populations were either sold into slavery or brutally executed before the Great Temple of Tenochtitlan. The loss of valued labor was then replaced by Aztec populations who instituted new governments modeled on local prototypes, as exemplified in Huaxyacac (Oaxaca City), where the colonists even appointed their own king. In other cases, the Aztec sought to maintain local political systems but subverted them by exploiting factional differences within royal families, especially among a king's offspring, who often disputed titles of inheritance and became embroiled in wars of succession that dissipated national cohesion. The Aztec became masters at spotting weakness in foreign kingdoms and selecting their own candidates to support as claimants. Pictographic documents from Coixtlahuaca, for example, indicate that following Atonal's death, an heir was appointed from a rival dynasty, while one of Atonal's wives was appointed tax collector. In extreme cases, those desperate enough to "bargain with the devil" might actually invite the Aztec army into their territory in order to settle a dispute. Other tactics to disrupt political institutions were more devious. Among the Eastern Nahuas, Mixtecs, Zapotecs, and their allies, royal marriages were often planned generations in advance. When the Aztec conquered any single member of a confederation, the *huey tlatoani* or a ranking noble sometimes demanded a marriage with a local woman of royal blood. Such acts not only bound the Aztec royal line to that of the defeated royalty but also disrupted predetermined marriage alliance patterns. No matter which strategy was employed, the goal was to expand continually a network of foreign kings who could best support any Aztec army that needed to move through their territory in the course of a campaign.

TRIBUTE

The Aztec relied on the tribute system as an important source of supplies for the army. Along their march, the army would demand food from allied and previously subjugated towns. Hassig has calculated, using Spanish sources, that each *xiquipilli* of 8,000 men consumed 7,600 kilograms (about 8.4 tons) of maize per day and that an eight-day resupply required more than 60,000 kilograms (about 66 tons) of maize (1988: 64). The tribute system therefore required very skillful planning. Each major town and its dependencies were obligated to grow food for the Aztec army. In order to have food ready for the army along the marching route, runners were sent two days prior to the army's departure to alert the leaders of the town to gather supplies. This was sufficient time for each local ruler to gather the maize from his far-off villages and have it ready when the Aztec army arrived. This in turn made the journey through the expanse of their empire quick and easy for the Aztec army.

The tributary system not only made it possible for the army to receive supplies through long campaigns. It also contributed to the wealth of the Aztec king and his nobles. The wealth of the empire was directly tied to the tribute collected from subjugated kingdoms and thus created complex links throughout Mesoamerica. As one can imagine, this type of system was difficult to maintain and manage. The Aztec did so through a variety of ties linking tributary centers to Tenochtitlan.

Although the Aztec exerted hegemonic control over tributaries and each state became politically dependent, the Aztec usually allowed the local ruler to stay in power so they would not have to deal with local administration. A potential problem with this system lay in that it did not shift the loyalty of the tributary population from their own ruler to the Aztec emperor. Along the same line, the Aztecs also did not change local economic relations, as Tenochtitlan needed the maintenance of healthy local economies in order for them to be able to pay their new tributary obligations. All the wealth that was siphoned off by imperial tribute became a local net loss; however, the tributary demands made by the Aztec activated local production and often expanded trade relationships to secure the goods required. Furthermore, for many tributaries, being connected to an Aztec-dominated trade network of rare and elite goods was financially beneficial.

The Aztec did not expect religious integration from their tributary lands. The state and its imperial aspirations were fully supported by the religious orthodoxy, but religious motivation was not a primary reason for war. The state did, however, exploit religious mandates to further its aims; for instance, there were times when the Aztec ruler mandated labor and materials from both tributary and independent towns to aid in the construction of temples to the gods. If a town failed to do so, war would be declared. The construction of such religious temples was decided by the king, not the priests or religious events, and independent towns who received such a mandate from the *tlatoani* tended to be in the direct line of Aztec expansion. This suggests that kings used religion to support their political agenda. Nonetheless, there exists no indication of forced religious conversion of conquered towns. No Aztec gods have been found beyond the Valley of Mexico, except where there were the occasional migrations of Aztec population. The ideological basis for Aztec expansion, therefore, did not lie in religion but in the economic benefits and social promotion that war presented to both commoners and noble soldiers.

Items

The Aztec conquered a group of bordering city-states and organized them into tributary provinces. They selected a prominent town to head each province, and these towns gave each province their name. Usually the selected town had been the capital of the most powerful city-state in the area, but at other times another town was chosen. Each province was assigned an annual triple quota by the Triple Alliance. This data was written in manuscripts stored in the imperial capitals. An example of such a manuscript exists in the second part of the *Codex Mendoza*, compiled in early colonial times. According to the *Codex*, in which each province is

detailed, the province of Coayxtlahuacan (Coixt-lahuaca), for example, located in the modern state of Oaxaca and populated by Mixtec speakers, paid an annual tribute of 4,000 textiles a year. Other tribute items paid annually were two feathered warrior costumes with shields, two strings of jade beads, 800 quetzal feathers, 40 bags of cochineal dye, 20 gourd bowls of gold dust, and one royal feather headpiece. An imperial tribute collector, or *calpixqui*, was responsible for supervising the assemblage and transport of these goods to Tenochtitlan.

The quantity and diversity of goods mentioned as imperial tribute in the *Codex Mendoza* is impressive. The most common items of tribute tended to be military, such as warrior costumes and shields. This tribute symbolized the military domination over the provinces. Also popular were luxury items such as tropical feathers, copal incense, paper, and liquidambar. Secondary items sent as tribute were foodstuffs, animal products, and building materials.

The tribute system was used to extract local specialties from each province. To illustrate, cochineal dye, made from an insect that inhabits the nopal (prickly pear cactus), was made in many towns in the Coayxtlahuacan region. As indicated by art historian Mario Dávila and archaeologist James Brady, the town of Tochtepec was required to deliver 16,000 rubber balls (*ulli*) to Tenochtitlan every year, to be used in the ball game and in some other ritual activities (2004: 40–41). Tribute towns in Morelos, meanwhile, sent bark paper as a principal item of tribute. Sometimes, however, the Aztec asked for goods that were not indigenous to the tributary towns. The tropical feathers and jade beads mandated from the towns of Coayxtlahuacan, for example, were not available in highland Oaxaca. To acquire these items, Coayxtlahuacan had to engage in trade with other areas. At first glimpse, it may seem that the Aztec did this so they would not have to go through the effort of acquiring goods from distant places; in reality, the Aztec received exotic goods such as these from merchants independent of the tribute system, so the Aztec probably did this to encourage commerce throughout the empire. Forcing people from provincial towns to engage in long-distance trade was part of the economic system of the Triple Alliance.

FLOWER WARS

In their move to conquer and expand the empire, the Aztec faced numerous powerful obstacles. Internal Aztec political dynamics emphasized success by conquering less formidable political entities, and the Aztec avoided difficult rivals unless they posed a particular threat and could not otherwise be conquered. Whereas a battle for a single city could be decisive, such was not the case for larger polities. The Aztec knew that large empires would meet impending threat at their borders; defeat would only apply to the loss of the immediate area while the enemy's army withdrew into the safety of its home territory.

Consequently, the Aztec chipped away at the peripheries of other empires rather than delivering decisive blows. The Aztec engaged these enemies in continual though intermittent combat in a long-term war of attrition that the Aztec were sure to win due to their outweighing number of troops. When the enemy was pinned down, the Aztec would then conquer adjacent areas of the empire and gradually encircle the city center. With this tactical maneuver, the empire's supply and communication lines were cut off, distancing it from the help of allies, and the empire was left defenseless and unable to retreat.

The Aztec attempted to dominate difficult enemies by holding flower wars (*xochiyaoyotl*). Ritualistic in nature, these battles were prearranged, fought with limited armies, and intended to make

5.15 The flower war was included in a mural by Diego Rivera, painted in the National Palace, Mexico City.
(Fernando González y González)

sacrificial prisoners more accessible. They also allowed veteran soldiers a formal opportunity to train younger soldiers, although this was a smaller justification for a much larger military purpose. Essentially, the flower wars served as an intimidation tactic. If the Aztec could successfully scare their opponents into believing that they were superior, the opponents might voluntarily surrender to the Aztec. If they were not successful, more battles, with more armies and more weapons, would follow. Over time, Aztec forces would surround enemies and isolate them from supplies and reinforcements. Unable to flee, the opponent would eventually be defeated.

The flower war was an effective method of imperial expansion because it was relatively inexpensive, not requiring the number of troops or supplies of a full war, and because it did not inhibit expansion elsewhere, as armies were not exhausted by the flower war's demands. Through the flower wars, the Aztec maintained their military prowess, intimidated their enemies, and kept their supplies from being depleted.

The institution of the *xochiyaoyotl* seems to have originated after the terrible famines that devastated central Mexico from 1450 to 1454, under Motecuhzoma I. These calamities led people to think that the gods were angry because there were few human sacrifices offered to nurture them. The rulers of the Triple Alliance and the lords of Tlaxcala, Huexotzinco, Cholula, and Atlixco mutually agreed to gather captives for sacrifice to the gods. As fighting was primarily a means to take prisoners, they arranged combats, and on the battlefield, the warriors tried to kill as few men as possible. As well as a political instrument, war was above all a religious rite.

Ethnohistorian Jacques Soustelle has suggested that the practice of flower wars was an important factor in the fall of Tenochtitlan because it fueled the rivalry with Tlaxcala, a formidable enemy of the Aztec Empire that later would join the Spaniards in the war of conquest (1979: 214). So, the Aztec world was destroyed both by internal conflicts that had to do with the subjugation of other indigenous groups and by external forces such as the unexpected appearance of the Spanish, their ideology, and their system of warfare, which the Aztec were unable to decipher.

READING

Training

Pohl 2001, Sahagún 1951–69: significance of warrior's date of birth; Pohl 2001: warrior's early years; Smith 2003: *telpochcalli* vs. *calmecac*, depending on social status; Hassig 1988, Sahagún 1951–69, Durán 1994: *calmecac*; Hassig 1992, Aguilar-Moreno ("Semblanza") 2002, Pohl 2001, Carrasco 1998, Sahagún 1951–69, Hassig 1988, Smith 2003: *telpochcalli*.

Military Ranks and Orders

Hassig 1988, Sahagún 1951–69: military ranks and social advancement; Aguilar-Moreno ("Semblanza") 2002: primary military hierarchy; Hassig 1988: description of military offices and ranks; Hassig 1988, Sahagún 1951–69: eagle and jaguar warriors; Hassig 1988, Durán 1994, Sahagún 1951–69: *otontin* and *cuachic* orders; Hassig 1988: military houses in the emperor's palace; Hassig 1992: hierarchical units; Hassig 1988, Sahagún 1951–69: merchants; Hassig 1988: ambassadors, messengers, and spies; Durán 1994, Carrasco 1998: women and war.

Uniforms and Arms

Hassig 1988, Berdan and Anawalt 1993, Sahagún 1951–69, Durán 1994: clothing and gifts given according to captured enemies and social status; Hassig 1988, Sahagún 1951–69, Durán 1994: insignia and body paint; Hassig 1988, Sahagún 1951–69, Durán 1994, Pohl 2001, Díaz del Castillo, 1963: offensive weapons, projectile weapons; Hassig 1988, Díaz del Castillo 1963: shock weapons; Hassig 1988: defensive weapons and nonmartial weapons.

Battle Tactics and Strategies

Pohl 2001, Aguilar-Moreno ("Semblanza") 2002: descriptions of primary battle tactics; Hassig 1988: times of attacks; Hassig 1988, Durán 1994, Díaz del Castillo 1963, Pohl 2001: signals; Pohl 2001: insults to initiate battle; Hassig 1988, Sahagún 1951–69, Durán 1995, Díaz del Castillo 1963, Pohl 2001: order of battle; Hassig 1988: ambushes; Hassig 1988, Díaz de Castillo, 1963: reinforcements and withdrawal; Hassig 1988, Durán 1994: conquest and aftermath; Hassig 1988: fortifications and sieges; Aguilar-Moreno ("Semblanza") 2002: captives of war.

Principal Aztec Military Campaigns

Pohl 2001: main military campaigns and conquests, supplies, and troop movements; Hassig 1992: main reasons for fighting.

Tribute

Hassig 1992: reasons why the Aztec employed a tribute system; Smith 2003, Berdan and Anawalt 1993: examples of types of tribute.

Flower Wars

Hassig 1992, Soustelle 1979: flower wars.

6

RELIGION, COSMOLOGY, AND MYTHOLOGY

STRUCTURE OF THE UNIVERSE

The Aztec devised a 260-day calendar that was used not only to organize time but also to define space, identify important days, and guide daily existence. It was also instrumental to Aztec mythology.

The calendar consisted of 20 day-names, each oriented toward a cardinal direction and moving continuously in a counterclockwise pattern (for details, see chapter 11). The calendar's dual function in practical daily matters and in spiritual matters embodied the important concept of duality in Aztec thought. The principle of duality, of joining oppositional forces together into a cohesive whole, permeated Aztec spirituality and society, both of which were interconnected.

Celestial Plane

The Aztec universe was layered and stratified, and celestially embodied the hierarchical values of the earthly realm. The celestial plane was composed of 13 different levels. It is probable that of these 13 levels, the "inferior skies" (those closer to Earth) were incorporated into the inhabitable Earth. According to the *Codex Vaticanus A (Codex Rios)* and the *Historia de los mexicanos por sus pinturas*, the 13 skies from top to bottom were the dwelling of Ometeotl (Omeyocan), the red sky, the yellow sky, the White sky, the sky of ice and rays, the blue-green sky of the wind, the black sky of the dust, the sky of stars of fire and smoke (stars, planets, and comets), the dwelling of Huixtocihuatl (salt or saltwater and birds), the dwelling of Tonatiuh (the Sun and the demonic female entities known as *tzitzimime*, the dwelling of Citlalicue (Milky Way), the dwelling of Tlaloc (rain) and Metztli (the Moon), and the inhabitable Earth (see figure 7.3).

Ometeotl—the Dual Divinity, or Lord of Duality—was the Aztec creator god and engendered both male and female qualities. Ometeotl dwelled in the 13th sky, the highest heaven, known as Omeyocan. From this great vantage point, Ometeotl was able to preside over the entire universe, including the Moon, the Sun, and the stars, all of which inhabited the lower skies.

The Terrestrial Plane

From Ometeotl the four Tezcatlipocas were born, each identified with a cardinal direction. Of the four, the Black Tezcatlipoca was the god Tezcatlipoca (Smoking Mirror); he was the most venerated and feared. Quetzalcoatl, or the white Tezcatlipoca, was the Black Tezcatlipoca's polar opposite, for Quetzalcoatl was a benevolent god and was associated with the color white and with the west. However, because of their dual natures, possessing both good and bad qualities, representing black and white, and life and death. Quetzalcoatl and the Black Tezcatlipoca were constantly engaged in a cosmic struggle, a struggle that would result in both the end and the beginning of worlds. The Earth and the universe were thus created from this cosmic struggle and would therefore comprise both benevolence and evil.

The terrestrial plane was thought of in terms of five cardinal directions: the east, north, south, west, and center, or *axis mundi*. Each direction had a particular god, symbol, and color and often had its own bird, plant, or tree. The east stood for the region of Tlapallan, symbolized with a reed as it was associated with Xipe Totec, the Red Tezcatlipoca, god of vegetation and renewal of nature. The Black Tezcatlipoca could be seen in the north ruling over Mictlampa, the region of the dead, symbolized by flint. The Blue Tezcatlipoca, also known as Huitzilopochtli, the god of the Sun and of war, corresponded to the south, the region of Huiztlampa, signified by the rabbit. The White Tezcatlipoca was commonly identified with the west, called Cihuatlampa, represented by the *calli*, or house. At the center of the Earth was the Great Temple of Tenochtitlan. Tenochtitlan corresponded to the concept of *cemanahuac*, the idea that the primordial homeland consisted of a tract of land (*tlalticpac*) surrounded by water. Tenochtitlan also resembled the original Aztec city of Aztlan, which had also been erected on land surrounded by water. Within Tenochtitlan was the ceremonial enclosure of the

Great Temple, with two altars of Huitzilopochtli and Tlaloc atop (see chapter 9).

The two most important celestial bodies were the Sun and the planet Venus, also known as the Morning Star, whose arrival was anticipated with fear. The gods of the Sun and Venus were invariably conceived as masculine, whereas the Moon and the Earth were both masculine and feminine.

Humans lived in Tlalticpac, which means "on the Earth." The Earth, in addition to being on the back of a marine monster, was also thought to be a gigantic toad, whose face formed the entrance to the underworld, and who devoured the dead.

The Underworld

According to the *Codex Vaticanus A*, the underworld was made up of nine layers, eight of which were underneath the Earth's surface. The nine layers were the inhabitable Earth, the passage of waters, the entrance to mountains, the hill of obsidian knives, the place of frozen winds, the place where the flags tremble, the place where people are flayed, the place where the hearts of people were devoured, and the place where the dead lie in perpetual darkness (see figure 7.3). The downward journey into the underworld was taken by the souls of the dead until they reached the ninth level, known as Mictlan Opochcalocan, and where they resided for eternity.

MAIN MYTHS

The Legend of the Suns

According to Aztec mythology and as evidenced in the Aztec Calendar (Sun Stone), before the present age there were four previous ages, or worlds. Each world had a name that corresponded to the calendar, as well as a deity and a race of people. Each world was also associated with one of the four elements: earth, water, fire, and wind. In addition to sharing the attributes of its corresponding element, the

demise of that world would be dictated by its ruling element.

The previous worlds, better known as "suns," were each created out of destruction. Each sun's demise was due to a natural catastrophe prompted by a fight between the two conflicting deities, Quetzalcoatl, representing life, fertility, and light, and the Black Tezcatlipoca, representing darkness and war. Each cataclysm was prescribed by the sun's ruling element and would bring an end to the world and death to all of its inhabitants.

Out of death and destruction, however, a new and better world was born, in which humanity lived in a more perfect stage than that of the previous suns. The four previous ages were the sun of *ocelotl* (jaguar) or earth, the air or wind sun, the fire sun, and the sun of water. Note that these are the suns of the four elements.

After the destruction of each world, the Black Tezcatlipoca and Quetzalcoatl were in charge of recovering the lost cosmic order together, with the winner of the argument of the previous age presiding over the next sun. All four Tezcatlipocas were engaged in the re-creation of the entire world and universe and its inhabitants.

The first sun, the world of the *ocelotl* or earth, was ruled by the Black Tezcatlipoca and was populated by giants. This sun ended as a result of Quetzalcoatl overpowering and defeating Tezcatlipoca by throwing him into the sea, whereupon Tezcatlipoca emerged as a jaguar. Other deadly jaguars also emerged, devouring the giants that roamed the Earth and thus ending the first sun. As a result of Quetzalcoatl's victory over Tezcatlipoca, he presided over the second sun, the wind sun. Tezcatlipoca returned to Earth to topple Quetzalcoatl and was victorious, bringing this sun to an end by a hurricane wind. The third sun, the sun of fire rain, was presided over by Tlaloc, the rain god. For the second time, Quetzalcoatl was responsible for ending another world, this one destroyed by fire that rained from the sky. The fourth sun was presided over by Chalchiuhtlicue, Tlaloc's sister. This sun of water was destroyed by a deluge, in which the resulting flood cleared out everything. As a result, the people of this previous world were turned into fish.

After the deluge that ended the fourth world, the present age, the sun of movement, came into existence. The fifth sun will conclude on a day called *nahui-ollin* (4 Movement), as a result of earthquakes.

sun god Tonatiuh, and Tecuciztecatl, who became the god of the Moon. The ancient city marks where the fifth sun was created.

Creation of the Fifth Sun in Teotihuacan

According to Mexica and Nahuatl tradition, the gods gathered in the dark at Teotihuacan, to plan the creation of the fifth sun. The arrogant god Tecuciztecatl volunteered himself to be the new Sun and bring light to the Earth. The gods agreed to this and asked Nanahuatzin, a modest god, to accompany the proud Tecuciztecatl.

After doing penance in the two hills erected especially for them, the two gods, dressed in their ritual regalia, were ready to sacrifice themselves by jumping into a ritual bonfire at Teotihuacan. Tecuciztecatl felt fear to jump into the bonfire, so the first god to sacrifice himself was Nanahuatzin, also known as the Proxy One, and who was dressed modestly, showing his humble nature. Bravely, he threw himself into the fire without hesitation. He then rose to the heavens, first appearing in the east as the Sun and a proud new god, now named Tonatiuh. Ashamed, Tecuciztecatl then jumped into the fire, rising to the heavens to become the Moon. However, so as not to usurp the brightness of the Sun, one of the gods threw a rabbit up at the Moon, thus dimming its brightness and forever emblazoning the rabbit's image on the Moon's face for future generations to witness.

To continue bathing the world with his solar rays, Tonatiuh demanded blood from the other gods in order to move along his course. Upon witnessing the bravery displayed by these two gods, the other gods agreed to sacrifice themselves and embraced death, thereby ensuring the Sun's radiance and movement across the sky. Quetzalcoatl began to pull the hearts from the gods with a sacrificial blade. Therefore, to ensure the Sun's movement, subsequent humans had to be sacrificed in order to thank and appease the deity Tonatiuh.

Consequently, Teotihuacan, whose Nahuatl name means "place where they become gods," is the site of the Pyramids of the Sun and the Moon, commemorating the gods Nanahuatzin, who became the

The First Human Beings and the Discovery of Maize

The fifth sun needed to be populated, as the people from the previous sun had been exterminated. Quetzalcoatl journeyed into the underworld, known as Mictlan, to retrieve the bones of the dead of the fourth sun from Mictlantecuhtli, Lord of the Land of the Dead, and his wife Mictlancihuatl. From those bones, Quetzalcoatl would re-create the human beings necessary to inhabit the new world.

Mictlantecuhtli agreed to release the bones to Quetzalcoatl under one condition: Quetzalcoatl had to sound a conch shell four times around Mictlan. This seemingly easy task was a trick; the conch that Mictlantecuhtli gave Quetzalcoatl was flawed—it did not have any holes—making it impossible for Quetzalcoatl to sound the conch. Quetzalcoatl, however, could not be fooled, and he ordered worms to burrow holes into the shell. Additionally, he had bees go inside the conch shell in order to produce a loud, resonating sound.

Seeing that Quetzalcoatl had met his condition, Mictlantecuhtli allowed Quetzalcoatl to take the bones, but before long, he had a change of heart. Mictlantecuhtli set a trap, and Quetzalcoatl fell into a deep pit. Being a deity, Quetzalcoatl was able to revive himself and escaped the underworld with the bones, which had broken in the fall.

Upon ascending to Earth from the underworld, Quetzalcoatl went to a place called Tamoanchan to grind the bones with the aid of the goddess Cihuacoatl, also known as the Woman Serpent and patron of fertility. To bring life to the bones, Quetzalcoatl and other deities drew blood from their male members and poured it over the bones. The bones were revived from the blood of the gods, and thus the first human beings of the fifth sun were created. Because the bones were broken on their way from the underworld, humans of the fifth sun are composed of many different sizes. The first human couple created were Cipactonal and Oxomoco.

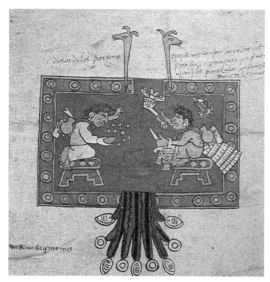

6.1 The first human couple, of the fifth sun, Oxomoco and Cipactonal, as depicted in the Codex Borbonicus (Manuel Aguilar-Moreno)

macehualtin, "the deserved ones." Humans, in return, were forced to be thankful to the gods for these benefits and were obligated to sustain the gods with maize and other Earth products. However, due to the dual nature of the Earth, the good things of the world were also threatened by the possibility of droughts and cataclysms that could bring destruction and death. The Aztec ensured the continued benevolence of the gods by appeasing them with continued propitiation rituals and human sacrifice.

The Origin of Pulque

Now that humans had food, a sun, and a moon, they needed something that would bring joy to their lives. The gods gathered and decided that the people of the fifth sun should be able to partake in

To feed the people, Quetzalcoatl transformed himself into an ant in order to be able to enter Mt. Tonacatepetl, also known as the Mountain of Sustenance, which contained the food for the new peoples. From the mountain, he gathered the grains of maize, which would become the main food source for the people of the fifth sun. However, in order for a ready supply to be continually available, the god Nanahuatzin was summoned to open up Mt. Tonacatepetl. With the help of the four Tlaloc gods, or gods of rain, Nanahuatzin succeeded in opening up the mountain and spilling the seeds and kernels, which became the food supply for the new people. Tlaloc is thus always associated with crops, as he is the main purveyor of rain and therefore also associated with fertility.

The sun god Tonatiuh and the rain god Tlaloc helped humans produce maize and flowers, which provided life and joy on Earth. Because the gods had volunteered to sacrifice themselves in order to activate the Sun and Moon, they maintained life in the universe. The gods, then, by means of their will, effort, and sacrifice, bestowed life to humans, and for that reason men and women were called

6.2 Mayahuel, goddess of the maguey and pulque, from the Codex Borbonicus *(Drawing by Lluvia Arras and Karla Lopez)*

something that would make them want to rejoice with music and dance. One night, Quetzalcoatl went to the goddess Mayahuel, the goddess of maguey (agave plant), and convinced her to descend to Earth with him.

Once on Earth, they bound themselves into a tree, each taking up a branch. When Mayahuel's grandmother woke up the next morning, she found that her granddaughter was missing. Enraged, the grandmother summoned the *tzitzimime*, the demonic female celestial entities, embodied as the stars above, and told them to go find Mayahuel. When they found the tree that was holding both Quetzalcoatl and Mayahuel, the tree split into two, dropping the branches to the ground. Recognizing the branch that hid Mayahuel, the grandmother proceeded to shred it, giving parts to the *tzitzimime* so that they could eat greedily and consume her. They did not touch Quetzalcoatl's branch, and once they left, he shape-shifted back to his usual form. In mourning, he proceeded to bury what was left of Mayahuel. It was from this humble grave that the first maguey plants sprang forth, and from the sap of this plant was made the alcoholic beverage pulque. Pulque was used in Aztec rituals and ceremonies, as well as in celebrations and festivals, and is still enjoyed today by contemporary Mexicans.

The Birth of Huitzilopochtli

Unlike most pre-Hispanic myths, which share many of the same characteristics, the myth of Huitzilopochtli is uniquely Aztec. Huitzilopochtli is therefore considered to be the cult god or the patron god of the Aztec. As a solar deity, Huitzilopochtli is closely related to and overlaps with Tonatiuh.

Huitzilopochtli's mother was Coatlicue, or She of the Serpent Skirt. Coatlicue, known for her devout nature and virtuous qualities, was at Mt. Coatepec one day, sweeping and tending to her penance, when she discovered a bundle of feathers on the ground. She decided to save them and placed them in her bosom. Without her realizing, the feathers impregnated her. Coyolxauhqui, Coatlicue's daughter, and her 400 brothers, collectively called the Centzon Huitznahua, became enraged when they saw that

their mother was pregnant. Prompted by Coyolxauhqui, and in an episode of pure anger and disgrace, they plotted to kill their own mother. Coatlicue, aware of her children's plants, was consoled and assured by her unborn son. Then, as Coyolxauhqui and the Centzon Huitznahua reached Coatepec to slay their mother, Coatlicue gave birth to Huitzilopochtli. In a move to save his mother, Huitzilopochtli, who was born fully armed, stabbed and beheaded Coyolxauhqui with his *xiuhcoatl*, or "turquoise serpent," a sharp weapon. Her body fell from Coatepec, and broke into pieces at the base of the mountain. He then proceeded to kill his half brothers, murdering nearly all of them with the exception of the few that got away and fled south.

It was believed that Huitzilopochtli was the Sun, and the Centzon Huitznahua constituted the stars, disappearing with the rising of the Sun. The Great Temple in the Aztec capital, Tenochtitlan, served as a monument to this myth. The pyramid's south side represented Coatepec, the Serpent Mountain, and it was there at the base that a huge round stone of Coyolxauhqui's dismembered body was excavated (see chapter 9). This massive carved stone served as a reminder of Huitzilopochtli's defeat of his enemies. Incidentally, it was at the Great Temple that many sacrifices took place, as if reenacting the slaying of Coyolxauhqui, for the sacrificed bodies, usually of captives or prisoners, were thrown down from the top of the pyramid, landing on the Coyolxauhqui stone. Like Tonatiuh, Huitzilopochtli required blood and hearts from sacrificed subjects in order to make his track across the heavens and assuring the Sun's appearance in the east every morning.

The Mythical Foundation of Tenochtitlan

The Aztec began as a tribe of people known as the Mexica or Mexitin, their name derived from their lord, Mexi. They left Chicomoztoc (the Seven Caves) located in the mythical land of Aztlan in 193 C.E. in search of their promised land. The migration was long and hard, lasting hundreds of years, and many settlements were founded en route. They were guided on their course by their patron god, Huitzilopochtli, who would communicate to his people and advise them along their course via the priests, who were mediators between the earthly and the celestial realms.

When the Aztec finally reached the Valley of Mexico in the 13th century, they knew that they were close to their promised land, but Huitzilopochtli warned them of hardships to be encountered in this already-settled land. He urged them to prepare themselves accordingly. This land was none other than the area once controlled by the great city of Teotihuacan and later by Tula, which had been settled for hundreds of years prior to the arrival of the Aztec to that region. There were still many settlements in the area that were remnants of those grand civilizations, and so following the advice of Huitzilopochtli, the Aztec fortified themselves and prepared for battle in Chapultepec. However, the Aztec and their patron god had other adversaries to contend with, namely Huitzilopochtli's nephew Copil, who was out to avenge his mother, Huitzilopochtli's sister Malinalxochitl (see chapter 2).

Huitzilopochtli had ordered that Malinalxochitl, who was once part of the caravan in search for the promised land, be left behind, for she had developed wicked and evil practices of witchcraft and could contaminate the rest of the caravan. Accordingly, Malinalxochitl and her flock were abandoned, left alone to fend for themselves.

Copil could not bear his mother's betrayal by his uncle, so he set out to search for Huitzilopochtli. He soon learned of Huitzilopochtli's arrival at Chapultepec in the Valley of Mexico. Once in the valley, Copil gained support from the surrounding towns by telling them of the atrocious and tyrannical ways of the Aztec, thus joining forces and gaining the military support necessary to overcome the Aztec. Certain of the Aztec defeat, Copil went to the hill called Tepetzinco, or Place of the Small Hill, to view the massacre from a good vantage point.

However, Huitzilopochtli could not be outwitted, as he was well aware of his nephew's plans. He therefore instructed his people to go to Tepetzinco, where hot springs ran at the base of the hill. Huitzilopochtli demanded that they slay Copil, pull out his heart, and bring it to him.

The priest, Cuauhtlequetzqui, carrying an image of Huitzilopochtli, led the delegation to Tepetzinco and proceeded to do as Huitzilopochtli instructed. Once the heart of Copil was presented to Huitzilopochtli, he instructed the priest to throw the heart into the center of the lake. The place where Copil's heart landed was called Tlacocomolco.

Despite this defeat, the peoples from the region still wanted the Aztec to be ousted from their territory and so began to wage war against them. The enemies, namely the Chalca, continued to surround Chapultepec Hill and attacked the Aztec. They succeeded in their attack and even managed to capture the Aztec leader, Huitzilihuitl. The survivors, who included women, children, and the elderly, sought asylum in a deserted town named Atlacuihuayan (Tacubaya). The Chalca did not find it necessary to follow the survivors, as they were few and disenfranchised.

After replenishing themselves, the defeated Aztecs rebuilt their forces, and upon Huitzilopochtli's request for them to be strong and proud, they went to their enemies at Colhuacan to ask for a place in which their wives and children could stay and live in peace. After much deliberation with his council, the king of Colhuacan granted the Aztec a site by the name of Tizapan, a most undesirable site, where snakes, reptiles, and other beasts resided. However, the Aztec took the offer and made that land theirs, taming the harsh environment and making do with what was given to them.

Later, the king of Colhuacan had his messengers report on the status of Tizapan. He was amazed to learn that the Aztec had cultivated the land, built a temple to Huitzilopochtli, and made the snakes and local reptiles a part of their diet. Impressed with the news he received from his messengers, the king granted the requests made by the Aztec that they be allowed to trade in Colhuacan and that they be able to intermarry with the people of Colhuacan.

This was not the promised land of the Aztec, however, and Huitzilopochtli requested, via the priests, that they leave this land in search for the true Aztec capital, adding that their departure must be a violent departure, not a peaceful one. Huitzilopochtli ordered his people to ask the king of Colhuacan, named Achitometl, for his daughter, so that she might serve Huitzilopochtli and become a goddess, to be called the Woman of Discord. The Aztec did as they were told by their god.

King Achitometl agreed to this honor, and after the pageantry that followed this transaction between the tribes, the young woman was taken to Tizapan. Once in Tizapan, she was proclaimed Tonantzin (Our Mother) by the Aztec and then sacrificed in the name of Huitzilopochtli. As was customary and part of Aztec ritual practices, after the young woman was sacrificed, her skin was flayed. Her flayed skin was worn by a "principal youth" who sat next to the Aztec deity. From that time on, she was both Huitzilopochtli's mother and bride and was worshipped by the Aztec.

King Achitometl was summoned and, not knowing that his daughter had been killed, accepted the invitation and attended the ceremony with other dignitaries of his town, bringing precious gifts in honor of his daughter, the new Aztec goddess, and the Aztec god Huitzilopochtli. When King Achitometl entered the dark temple, he commenced his offerings and other ceremonial rights. As he drew closer to the figures, with a torch light in his hand, he was able to discern what was before him, the youth wearing the flayed skin of his daughter and sitting next to their deity. Disgusted and filled with fright, the king left the temple and called on his people to bring an end to the Aztec.

The Aztec fought vigorously, and although they were pushed into the water by the opposition, they managed to flee to Iztapalapa. The Aztec were in a state of desolation. Huitzilopochtli tried to comfort his people who had suffered so much in search of their promised land. They were not far from it, so the Aztec continued moving from town to town, seeking refuge where they could.

One day as they roamed the waters, they saw signs that had been prophesied by the Aztec priests. One was a beautiful, white bald cypress (*ahuehuetl*), and from the base of the tree a spring flowed. This spring was surrounded by all white willows. All around the water were white reeds and rushes, and white frogs emerged, as well as white snakes and fish. The priests recognized all these signs as predicted by their god and rejoiced for they had found their promised land.

Soon after, Huitzilopochtli came to the priest named Cuauhtlequetzqui and told him Copil's heart, which was thrown into the lake as prescribed by him, had landed on a stone, and from that stone a nopal (prickly pear cactus) sprang. The nopal was so grand and magnificent that an eagle perched there daily, feeding from its plentiful fruits and enjoying the sun. It would be surrounded by beautiful and colorful feathers from the birds that the eagle fed on.

The priest relayed this message to the people, who responded with joy and enthusiasm. Once more they went to the spring where they had seen the wonderful revelations of their god but were surprised to find two streams instead of one, and instead of white, one stream was red and the other was blue. Seeing all this as good omens, the Aztec continued their search for the eagle perched on a nopal, which they soon beheld. The people bowed their heads to this sight in all humbleness, and the eagle did the same in turn. They had finally reached their promised land, and here they built Tenochtitlan.

On the Mexican flag today is an eagle proudly standing on a nopal, which grows from a stone. This symbolism speaks to the Aztec myth and to the Aztec's perseverance and spiritual belief system. Indeed, Tenochtitlan went on to be the capital of the Aztec Empire.

In pre-Hispanic imagery of this myth, the fruit that grows from the cactus is represented as human hearts, and in the eagle's beak is an *atl tlachinolli*, a symbol of fire and water that could have been mistaken for a snake by the colonists, for this is what appears in the eagle's beak on the modern-day flag.

THE AZTEC GODS

The Origin of the Gods

The Aztec religion was polytheistic (belief in many gods) and was therefore composed of a multitude of gods and goddesses. Every town, neighborhood, and family had a corresponding deity. Additionally, every deity was represented by any combination of animal, plant, and human traits. The Aztec gods embodied fundamental Aztec principles such as the concept of duality, the predilection for multiplicity (polytheism) over individuality (monotheism), and the important connection between the gods, humans, and the natural environment.

Although the Aztec religion was indeed very complex and can be described as polytheistic, there is also a certain tendency toward a theoretical monotheism (belief in a primordial single god). Aztec poets and philosophers, for example, bestowed many epithets on the primordial god Ometeotl, the Lord of Duality: Ipalnemoani, "the giver of life"; Tloque Nahuaque, "the one that is everywhere" or "the ever present"; Moyocoyani, "the one that acts by itself with absolute freedom" or "the one who invents himself."

Although the creator Ometeotl was also known as Tezcatlipoca, Tonatiuh, and Xiuhteuctli-Huehueteotl, it was understood that they all represented preeminent personifications of the supreme deity. The supreme deity was eternal but somewhat remote from the world and from human beings; therefore, other gods were sent to mediate in the affairs of men and women. These gods exhibited benevolent powers in many senses, but they were also subject to the limitations and imperfections of the earthly realm. They could be moved by a whim or through passion, be hurt or maimed, and could suffer debilitation and be subject to death.

The Mexica considered the supreme deity Ometeotl to be both the father (Ometecuhtli) and mother (Omecihuatl) of the other gods. Both fundamental beings were called Tonacatecuhtli and Tonacacihuatl, the Lord and Lady of Our Sustenance, deities that nourished humanity.

The Aztec religion was inclined to syncretism rather than proselytism. When the Aztec conquered other towns they did not impose their own gods onto the conquered nations but rather incorporated the gods of the peoples they conquered. Therefore we find a variety of gods who serve as patrons of sorcerers, nomadic hunters, soldiers, agriculturalists, fishermen, as well as gods from particular regions, inhabiting the tropical forests, the coasts of the Gulf of Mexico, the Pacific Ocean, and the central plateau.

The Nature of the Gods

The Aztec gods were anthropomorphic and related through the bonds of kinship. The numerous gods of the Aztec pantheon had complex hierarchies. Although the gods were immortal, and as such would exist into eternity, this did not prevent them from dying or returning to life an infinite number of times.

The gods had superhuman powers and resided in the different levels of heaven and the underworld, as well as inhabiting specific places on Earth. They could be called upon to manifest themselves instantaneously at many different sites. When the Aztec gods were summoned they could visit human beings in diverse ways, often appearing in dreams or through fantastic visions or disguised as *nahualtin* (singular, *nahualli*), or animal embodiments. These beings were generally zoomorphic and important to rituals and the auguries of Aztec divination. Nahua can be found in Aztec iconography depicted in the codices and chronicles with characteristics that allowed for their identification.

Although the gods were benevolent and provident in their relationship with humankind, they could also be frightful, arbitrary, and maleficent. They presided over special scopes of nature or aspects of human culture and could be adopted as protectors by an ethnic or socioeconomic group.

Organization of the Aztec Pantheon

In the official Aztec religion, 144 Nahuatl names corresponded to the gods. Of these names, 66 percent belong to deities considered masculine, and 34 percent, to deities of feminine gender. According to historian Rafael Tena, the important gods of the Aztec pantheon can be identified through three different, complementary methods: 1) the analysis of the functions of the gods, 2) the frequency whereupon they received an official cult, and 3) the presence of their respective temples within the ceremonial enclosure of Tenochtitlan (1993: 22–31).

THE FUNCTIONS OF THE GODS

Anthropologist Henry B. Nicholson in volume 10 of the *Handbook of Middle American Indians* (1971: 395–446) proposed distributing the Aztec gods into three groups consisting of 17 gods who ruled over similar functions and powers.

1. Creative and provident gods
   1. Ometeotl, the Dual Divinity or the Divine Pair: supreme deity
   2. Tezcatlipoca, Smoking Mirror: creative, omnipotent god
   3. Quetzalcoatl, the Feathered Serpent: creative and beneficial god
   4. Xiuhtecuhtli, Lord of the Year or Lord of the Turquoise: god of the fire
   5. Yacatecuhtli, Lord at the Vanguard: god of merchants and travelers

2. Gods of agricultural and human fertility and of pleasure
   6. Tlaloc, "the one that is made of earth": god of waters
   7. Ehecatl-Quetzalcoatl, Wind-Feathered Serpent: god of wind
   8. Xochipilli, the Flower Prince: god of the fertilizing sun and of joy
   9. Xipe Totec, Our Flayed Lord: god of the vegetation that must perish but is reborn
   10. Cinteotl, God of the Maize
   11. Metztli, Moon: deity of the Moon
   12. Teteoinnan, Mother of the Gods: universal mother goddess

3. Gods that conserve the energy of the world but require the nutriments of war and human sacrifices to replenish their power
   13. Tonatiuh, "the one that is illuminating": god of the Sun
   14. Huitzilopochtli, Hummingbird of the South: solar god of war, the tutelary god of the Mexica
   15. Mixcoatl, Cloud Serpent: god of the Milky Way
   16. Tlahuizcalpantecuhtli, Lord of the Dawn: god of the planet Venus
   17. Mictlantecuhtli, Lord of the Place of Dead: god of the underworld

THE GODS IN RITUALS

Each celebration of the *xiuhpohualli* (the solar year) had a corresponding god or gods worshipped in ritual. These celebrations include the following:

Atlcahualo, or Cuahuitlehua: Tlaloque
Tlacaxipehualiztli: Xipe Totec and Huitzilopochtli, Tlaloque
Tozoztontli, or Xochimanaloya: Tlaloque, Coatlicue
Huey Tozoztli: Cinteotl, Chicomecoatl, Chalchiuhtlicue, Tlaloque
Toxcatl: Tezcatlipoca and Huitzilopochtli
Etzalcualiztli: Tlaloque and Chalchiuhtlicue
Tecuilhuitontli: Huixtocihuatl, Xochipilli
Huey Tecuilhuitl: Xilonen and Cihuacoatl
Tlaxochimaco, or Miccailhuitontli: Tezcatlipoca and Huitzilopochtli, Mictlantecuhtli
Xocotlhuetzi, or Huey Miccailhuitl: Xiuhtecuhtli-Otontecuhtli, Yacatecuhtli, Mictlantecuhtli
Ochpaniztli: Teteoinnan-Toci, Tlazolteotl, Coatlicue, Cinteotl and Chicomecoatl
Teotleco: Tezcatlipoca and Huitzilopochtli, Huehueteotl, Yacatecuhtli
Tepeilhuitl, or Huey Pachtli: Tlaloc, Tlaloque, Tepictoton, Centozontotochtin, pulque gods, major mountains
Quecholli: Mixcoatl, Camaxtle, Huitzilopochtli, Coatlicue
Panquetzaliztli: Huitzilopochtli, Tezcatlipoca, Painal, Yacatecuhtli
Atemoztli: Tlaloque, Tepictoton mountains
Tititl: Ilamatecuhtli, Cihuacoatl, Tonantzin Yacatecuhtli
Izcalli, or Huauhquiltamalcualiztli: Xiuhtechtli, Tlaloc, Chalchiuhtlicue

Other celebrations of the *xiuhpohualli* were the Pillahuano (Xiuhtecuhtli), Atamalcualiztli (Cinteotl), and Toxiuhmolpilia, or New Fire ceremony (Xiuhtecuhtli, Huitzilopochtli).

Celebrations of the *tonalpohualli* (ritual lunar calendar) also worshipped particular gods. They include the following:

Nahui ollin, "4 Movement": Tonatiuh
Chicome-xochitl, "7 Flower": Chicomexochitl and Xochiquetzal
Ce-mazatl, "1 Deer": Cihuapipiltin

Ome-tochtli, "2 Rabbit": Ometochtli and Izquitecatl
Ce-acatl, "1 Cane": Quetzalcoatl
Ce-miquiztli, "1 Death": Tezcatlipoca
Ce-quiahuitl, "1 Rain": Cihuapipiltin
Ome-acatl, "2 Cane": Omeacatl
Ce-tecpatl, "1 Knife": Huitzilopochtli, Camaxtle
Ce-ozomatli, "1 Monkey": Cihuapipiltin
Ce-itzcuintli, "1 Dog": Xiuhtecuhtli
Ce-atl, "1 Water": Chalchiuhtlicue
Ce-calli, "1 House": Cihuapipiltin
Ce-cuauhtli, "1 Eagle": Cihuapipiltin

The most important Aztec gods based on their frequency in Aztec rituals were therefore Tlaloc (Tlaloque) and Chalchiuhtlicue, Xiuhtecuhtli-Huehueteotl-Otontecuhtli, Huitzilopochtli, Tezcatlipoca, Cinteotl and Chicomecoatl-Xilonen, Mixcoatl, Yacatecuhtli, Ometochtli, Xipe Totec, Tonatiuh, Cihuapipiltin, Teteoinnan-Toci, Tlazolteotl, Ilamatecuhtli-Cihuacoatl, Coatlicue, Quetzalcoatl, Mictlantecuhtli, Painal, Omeacatl, Huixtocihuatl, Xochipilli-Chicomexochitl, and Xochiquetzal.

THE TEMPLES OF THE GODS

According to the rank in importance of the sanctuaries within Tenochtitlan, it can be inferred that the main gods were Huitzilopochtli, Tlaloc, Tezcatlipoca, Quetzalcoatl, Tonatiuh, Cihuacoatl, Chicomecoatl, Xochiquetzal, Xipe Totec, Mixcoatl (Teotlalpan), and Xiuhtecuhtli-Otontecuhtli (Xococ). In daily practice the most popular gods were Ometeotl, Tezcatlipoca, Quetzalcoatl, Huitzilopochtli, Tlaloc, Xiuhtecuhtli, Tonatiuh, Cinteotl, Xipe Totec, Mixcoatl, Cihuacoatl, and Mictlantecuhtli.

The Aztec Pantheon

Ahuiateteo (Gods of Pleasure) Five different gods made up a group of deities called the Ahuiateteo, which was associated with the south. They represented the dangers and repercussions of excessive pleasure associated with drinking, gambling, and sex. The number five (*macuilli*) was incorporated into each god's name because the numeral five symbolized excess. Their names are Macuilcuetzpalin (5 Lizard), Macuilcozcacuauhtli (5 Vulture), Macuiltochtli (5 Rabbit), Macuilxochitl (5 Flower), and Macuilmalinalli (5 Grass).

Chalchiuhtlicue (She of the Jade Skirt) The water goddess of rivers, lakes, streams, and still water (see figure 10.2), she embodies the life-giving qualities of water and is kin to Tlaloc, the great rain god. They both rule over weather. As the goddess of water, she is associated with fertility and creation. She is therefore also the goddess of birth, playing an important role in Aztec birth rituals and ceremonies. Chalchiuhtlicue can also call forth the destructive aspect of water, as she did to destroy the previous world through a great flood.

Chicomecoatl (Seven Serpent) She is a maize goddess representing another aspect of Chalchiuhtlicue. When Chalchiuhtlicue is depicted with ears of maize in her hands or on her back she is known as Chicomecoatl, the goddess of food and produce (see figure 8.25). She is associated with sustenance in the form of food and drink.

Cihuacoatl (Snake Woman) She represents the creative power of the Earth and is also known as Our Mother (see figure 8.16). The power of the Earth to create life is Cihuacoatl's role as goddess of midwifery. She is also associated with the sweat bath. The power of Earth to destroy life is also Cihuacoatl's duty, and as all things that are born eventually die, she is often depicted as a skeletal hag. She can be quite fearsome when represented as a warrior bearing her shield and spear. Her qualities overlap with Teteoinnan, Toci, Tlazolteotl, and Ilamatecuhtli, and she is paired with Quilaztli. The name *cihuacoatl* was also the title of the secondary ruler (prime minister) in Tenochtitlan.

Cihuateteo (Women Gods) One of two groups of supernaturals who accompany the Sun on its passage from east to west, the Cihuateteo are female warriors, or women who have died in childbirth (see figure 8.27). They haunt the crossroads at night, can cause seizures and insanity in people, and are known to steal children. They also seduce men and cause them to commit adultery and other sexual transgressions.

Cinteotl (Centeotl; Maize God) According to the *Florentine Codex*, he is the son of the aged earth goddess Toci. Cinteotl can be identified by the vertical line on his face. His headdress has maize ears.

Coatlicue (She of the Serpent Skirt) Identified by her skirt made of snakes (see figure 8.14), Coatlicue is an earth goddess that embodies life and death. She is the mother of the Aztec patron god Huitzilopochtli, Coyolxauhqui, and the Centzon Huitznahua, or 400 Southerners. By extension, she is considered also the mother of the people, giver of fertility.

Coyolxauhqui (She of the Bells on the Cheeks) She is the older half sister of Huitzilopochtli and warrior daughter of Coatlicue. She is also a moon goddess. She is represented with bells made of metal. Her body was mutilated after she was decapitated by Huitzilopochtli on Mt. Coatepec (see figure 8.18).

Ehecatl (Lord of the Wind) Ehecatl announces the coming of the rain and is an avatar of Quetzalcoatl. He wears a mask in the shape of a duck beak, and diverse pieces of shell jewelry. He carries a cut conch pectoral called an *ehecailacacozcatl*.

Huehuecoyotl (Old Coyote) He is the god of dance, music, and carnality, and the patron deity of feather workers.

Huehueteotl (Old God) God of the hearth and the household and lord of fire. He is represented as an old figure with his legs crossed and his hands resting on the knees. Often he has some features of Tlaloc (see figure 8.26), expressing a link between the two deities. He holds in his head a huge brazier that was used for burning incense or even to produce fire.

Huitzilopochtli (Hummingbird of the Left, Hummingbird of the South) Supreme and patron deity of the Aztec, god of sun, fire, and war, he is the Blue Tezcatlipoca. He wears a blue-green hummingbird headdress and carries the *xiuhcoatl*, the fire serpent that is the weapon he uses to fight his enemies. He frequently is represented bearing on his back the

6.3 Huitzilopochtli, the war and sun god, as depicted in the Florentine Codex *(LLuvia Arras and Karla Lopez)*

anecuyotl, the head of a fantastic animal. He led the Mexica during part of their pilgrimage from Aztlan to the promise land of the Valley of Mexico and determined the place of the foundation of Tenochtitlan, their capital city. He was worshipped in the Great Temple of Tenochtitlan and was honored with massive human sacrifices throughout the year. The god Painal, an avatar of Huitzilopochtli, was associated with warfare and the ball game as a metaphor of war.

Huixtocihuatl (Goddess of Salt) Older sister of the Tlaloque (the attendants of the rain god). Her skirt had motifs of waves of water and jadeite. She was associated with the sea (salt water).

Ilamatecuhtli (Cihuacoatl, Citlalicue, Quilaztli; Aged Woman) Goddess of Earth, death, and the

Milky Way, Ilamatecuhtli wears a skirt with dangling shells known as a star skirt and is depicted with a fleshless mouth. She was worshipped in a temple called Tlillan (darkness). Her festival was Tititl, during which a female slave who impersonated her was sacrificed.

Itzpapalotl (Obsidian Butterfly) Earth goddess of war and sacrifice by obsidian knife, she is identified with the bat and the *tzitzimime* (star "demons" that devoured people during the solar eclipses). Itzpapalotl is a fearsome deity.

Itztlacoliuhqui-Ixquimilli (Curl Obsidian Knife) He is the deity of castigation, blindness, and stoning and also the god of frost, snow, and coldness.

Macuilxochiti (Five Flower) He is the principal god of the Ahuiateteo and the patron god of the palace folk as well as of games and gambling, especially the *patolli* game (see chapter 13). In addition, Macuilxochitl is the deity of the flowers and excessive pleasures. He punishes people by inflicting hemorrhoids and diseases of the genitals. He is closely associated and often overlapping with Xochipilli, the Flower Prince.

Mayahuel (Goddess of Maguey) As the maguey deity, she is associated with pulque. Mayahuel is depicted sometimes with attributes of the water goddess, including fertility and fecundity. She is most often represented as emerging from a flowering maguey plant (see figure 6.2). According to a myth, she was killed by the *tzitzimime*, and when Quetzalcoatl buried her bones, the first maguey sprouted. In other accounts, she is mentioned as "the woman of four hundred breasts," probably a reference to the sweet milky *aguamiel* (sap) of the maguey, which, when fermented, produces pulque.

Mictlantecuhtli (Lord of Mictlan) God of death and the underworld (Mictlan, or "place of the dead"), he is identified with gloom and darkness. He is frequently represented as a skeleton with bloody spots (see figures 7.1 and 8.35). He is married to Mictlancihuatl. Quetzalcoatl fought with Mictlantecuhtli to retrieve the bones of human beings of the previous era and create them again in the present

era, the fifth sun. This battle symbolized the constant interaction and duality between life and death.

Mictlancihuatl (Mictecacihuatl; Lady of Mictlan) Wife of Mictlantecuhtli, lord of the underworld, she was a goddess of death (see figure 7.1).

Mixcoatl (Cloud Serpent) God of hunting, Mixcoatl is the main god of the Otomies and Chichimec. He is identified with the Milky Way and the stars and is the Red Tezcatlipoca, also called Camaxtle in Tlaxcala. He is also identified with the souls of dead warriors that were sacrificed and ascended to the heavens as stars. He is painted with red and white stripes and wears a black mask. He has some associations to war and fire. According to myth, he is the father of the great god Quetzalcoatl and the Centzon Huitznahua, the 400 stars that fight with Huitzilopochtli in Coatepec (see chapter 9).

Ometeotl (God of Duality) Ometeotl rules over the highest heaven, Omeyocan, the 13th heaven, and the "place of duality." He is the primordial creation force. He embodies both male (Ometecuhtli) and female (Omecihuatl) characteristics and is also referred to as Tonacatecuhtli and Tonacacihuatl, the couple also known as Lord and Lady of Our Sustenance. Ometecuhtli and Omecihuatl form the ancestral couple who sent the souls of humans to be born on Earth. For this reason, they are linked to Oxomoco and Cipactonal, the aged divine first parents of humankind. Even though artistic representations of Ometeotl are not common, he is identified as a grandparent figure and depicted as an elder.

Ometochtli (Two Rabbit) Generic name of the gods of pulque and their associated priests. The most famous gods of pulque were Patecatl, the husband of pulque goddess Mayahuel, Tepoztecatl, Tomegauh, and Papaztac.

Quetzalcoatl (Feathered Serpent, Precious Serpent) As the wind god, it was believed that he sweeps the path for the rain gods so that they will produce rain. He is represented wearing his characteristic emblem, the *ehecailacacozcatl* (the jewel of the wind), a pectoral in the shape of a cut conch. He is one of four children of Ometeotl, the god of

6.4 Quetzalcoatl, the Feathered Serpent, god of wind and wisdom, in the Florentine Codex *(Lluvia Arras and Karla Lopez)*

creation. Quetzalcoatl is identified with creating heaven and earth and is associated with fertility, water, and life. He is also the planet Venus, worshipped as Tlahuizcalpantecuhtli (Lord of the Dawn). He is the White Tezcatlipoca, patron of priests and rulers. In later times, the image of the god was confused with the historical figure of Ce Acatl Topiltzin Quetzalcoatl, the king of the legendary city of Tollan (Tula), and there emerged the conception of the man-god. Quetzalcoatl was also associated with wisdom, arts, and philosophy.

Temazcalteci (Goddess of the *Temazcalli*) Temazcalteci is goddess of the steam bath (*temazcalli*), medicine, and herbs and patroness of those in the medical field, surgeons, and housewives. Her image was kept in bathrooms. Her name means "grandmother of the baths."

Tezcatlipoca (Smoking Mirror) God of rulers, warriors, and sorcerers, Tezcatlipoca is omnipresent and invisible (see figure 8.37). He is an embodiment of change through discord and conflict. Omnipotent god of fate and punitive justice, he often merges into Itztlacoliuhqui-Ixquimilli. He is a creator but also a destroyer, a provider of fortune as well as disaster. He is associated with the earth, and his companion spirit is the jaguar. He was called diverse names, among them Tepeyollotl (Heart of the Mountain), which was his jaguar aspect.

Tezcatlipoca appears in the codices with a smoking mirror on his head, and in other instances, the mirror substitutes for one of his feet. Sometimes a serpent emerges from that mirror in his foot. He is the Black Tezcatlipoca. One of his most popular avatars was Omeacatl (2 Reed), the patron of banquets. There was a nocturnal festival in his honor in which people had "communion" with his body made of corn dough in the shape of a bone.

Tezcatzoncatl (He of the Shining Hair) As patron god of wine or pulque, he is the protector of intoxicated individuals.

Tlahuizcalpantecuhtli (Lord of Dawn) Tlahuizcalpantecuhtli is one of the dual aspects of Quetzalcoatl, the other being Xolotl. He is a fierce deity, the personification of Venus, known as the Morning Star, whose arrival is met with fear. In certain seasons of the year, it was believed that the rays from the Morning Star could inflict severe damage to people, maize, and water.

Tlaloc (God of Rain and Lightning) Tlaloc has goggled eyes and large jaguar teeth and resides in mountain caves. He is a provider of sustenance and together with his consort Chalchiuhtlicue ruled the Tlaloque who were the multiple spirits of mountains and powerful environmental phenomena. Early beginnings of Tlaloc can be traced back to the central Mexico region in the first century B.C.E. At Teotihuacan he appears with maize, water, and lightning. In Aztec times he was so important that he had a special shrine on top of Mt. Tlaloc (see figure 3.1), and he shared the Great Temple of Tenochtitlan with Huitzilopochtli (see figure 8.36). His attendants were the Tlaloque, and they lived in the corners of the universe holding pots that contained the diverse types of rain. They produced thunder by hitting the pots; when they broke them, lightning bolts were produced. The Tlaloque were considered to be the multiple spirits of mountains and the natural phenomena.

Tlaltecuhtli (Earth Lord) Represented either as a god or goddess, Tlaltecuhtli's image is often carved on the bottom of Aztec sculptures and *cuauhxicalli* (the vessels in which the hearts of sacrificial subjects were contained), symbolizing their contact with the Earth (see figure 8.13). His image merges sometimes with aspects of Tlaloc and Mictlantecuhtli. According to a myth, Quetzalcoatl and Tezcatlipoca carried Tlaltecuhtli down from heaven and mutilated its body. They left one part of the body in the sky, and with the other they created the Earth.

Tlazolteotl (Filth Goddess) She is the goddess of purification and healing particularly of those ailments brought about by sexual excess and lust. Penitents perform confession and bloodletting procedures before an image of the goddess. In the codices she is portrayed with a black area around her mouth. Her cleansing role is manifested by a grass broom that she carries.

Toci (Teteoinnan, Tlalli Iyollo; Our Grandmother, Mother of the Gods, Heart of the Earth) An aged grandmother, she is an earth goddess and patron of midwives and healers. She is associated with the sweat bath and Temazcalteci and is also identified with Tlazolteotl. She was related to war and was called the Woman of Discord.

Tonacatecuhtli (Lord of Our Sustenance) He is a form of Ometeotl, the aged creator god. Tonacatecuhtli is linked to the miracle of procreation and in several scenes appears with couples making love.

Tonatiuh (Sun God) He is the god of the east, represented typically with the body painted in red and a large solar disk emitting rays. Tonatiuh is a fierce warlike god that requires the hearts of sacrificed prisoners. His attributes overlap with those of Huitzilopochtli.

Tzapotlan Tenan (Mother of Tzapotlan) She is the goddess of her birthplace, Tzapotlan. She is a

healer and the creator of *uxitl*, an oil used to cure many diseases, especially those related to the head, but also including the throat, feet, hands, face, and lips.

Tzitzimime (Star Demons) These demons of darkness are responsible for attacking the Sun during an eclipse. Female *tzitzimime* could also cause harm on Earth, devouring people. They produced a great deal of anxiety and fear among the Aztec population. Itzpapalotl was one of the most important.

Xipe Totec (Our Lord the Flayed One) Together with Mixcoatl, Xipe Totec is considered to be the Red Tezcatlipoca. He is the patron of goldsmiths and god of agricultural renewal, associated with spring and rebirth. Priests and warriors paid homage to him, wearing the flayed skin of a sacrificed person for about 20 days at a time. This was symbolic of rejuvenation, shedding the old skin for the new. Xipe Totec was the patron of gladiatorial sacrifice. As such, victims of the gladiatorial combat were

6.5 Xipe Totec, god of the renewal of vegetation, in the Codex Borbonicus (Lluvia Arras and Karla Lopez)

ities by inflicting them hemorrhoids and venereal diseases.

Xochiquetzal (Flower Quetzal) Goddess of the arts, passionate love, young female sexual power, flowers, and physical pleasure, she was patroness of weavers, presided over pregnancy and childbirth, and took care of young mothers. She was similar to Toci, Tlazolteotl, and the other mother goddesses in all respects but that she remained always young and beautiful. She is identified by a floral headband containing emerald quetzal feathers.

Xolotl (Dog God) He was the *nahualli* of Quetzalcoatl and accompanied him on his trip to the underworld to collect the bones of human beings. He is the double or twin of Quetzalcoatl, playing the role of evening star. He is depicted with physical deformities, is associated with dwarves and hunchbacks, and is the patron god of twins, who were considered monstrous and were feared.

Yacatecuhtli (Lord of the Big Nose, Lord at the Vanguard) Patron god and protector of merchants, especially of the rich *pochtecah* (long-distance traders), Yacatecuhtli used a walking staff that was considered very sacred and wore fine clothes. He had a special temple that was the residence of his priests and where the young *pochtecah* were trained. Yacatecuhtli, resembles in many aspects the Catholic saint Christopher, the patron and protector of travelers.

RITUALS

Priests

At the top of the religious hierarchy were the revered priests of Quetzalcoatl, Huitzilopochtli, and Tlaloc. In the *Florentine Codex*, Fray Bernardino Sahagún provided a list of 37 names corresponding to ministers, or *tlamacazque*, who performed many rituals and administrative functions that related to the religious cult. The Mexica also had their

6.6 Xiuhtecuhtli, god of fire, in the Florentine Codex (Lluvia Arras and Karla Lopez)

flayed and offered to the god during Tlacaxipehualiztli, the "flaying of men" festival.

Xiuhtecuhtli (Turquoise Lord) He is the god of fire and the patron of rulership and time. He is also known as Ixcozauhqui, Huehueteotl, and Cuezaltzin, which means "flame." He carries a *xiuhcoatl* (fire serpent) on his back. Xiuhtecuhtli was simultaneously feared because he created disastrous fires and revered for creating fires for warmth, cooking, and baths.

Xochipilli (Flower Prince) He is the patron god of the arts, dancing, painting, feasting, flowers, pleasure. He overlaps with the god of gambling, Macuilxochitl, as well as with Cinteotl, the maize god, because of his generative powers. Xochipilli punishes those who indulge in excessive sexual activ-

fortune-tellers, which they called *tonalpouhque*, or "readers of destiny," as well as healers, prestidigitators, illusionists, and shamans or wizards. (For more details about priests, see chapter 4.)

Ceremonies and Festivals

Religious rites were practiced throughout the cycle of the calendar festivals, which were closely associated with the seasons and agricultural production. All these rites, including human sacrifices, had the purpose of recovering the forces of the gods and securing their favors, so that life was maintained in the universe. (For more details about festivals and rituals, see chapters 11 and 13.)

RITUAL HUMAN SACRIFICE

One of the better-known Aztec rituals was the human sacrifice that they conducted in the name of their gods. The Aztec believed that in order for the Sun to rise in the east, they had to appease their gods by providing them with sacrificial blood. Although there are many misunderstandings in regards to Aztec sacrifices, it is important to bear in mind that all sacrifices were done within a spiritual and ritualistic context and not as a blood sport.

The souls of the people that were sacrificed to the sun gods, which were usually warriors, were secured a place in paradise. Still other sacrificial subjects were chosen for their fine characteristics, and they would in turn feel honored to be chosen, as it was a great privilege to be of the chosen few.

An example of a sacrifice was the annual festival of Toxcatl, dedicated to the god Tezcatlipoca. A fine youth was chosen to impersonate Tezcatlipoca on the day of the sacrifice. For a year before his sacrifice, the youth was given the best that life could offer. He was treated with great honor and respect and was given four beautiful mistresses, all this

because he was seen as the living manifestation of this god.

On the day of the sacrifice, there were ceremonies and rites performed. The youth was then laid on his back on a stone slab atop a temple, and with a sacrificial knife, the priest would stab the young man's chest, pulling out his heart and raising it so that the spectators could behold the still-throbbing young heart.

The appendix to the second book of the *Florentine Codex* presents 78 buildings dedicated to the gods within the Sacred Precinct of Tenochtitlan. In addition to temples, built on staggered platforms or pyramids, which they called *teocalli*, or "god houses," these ritual structures or monuments included the *temalacatl*, or (circular) "stone of the gladiatorial sacrifice"; *cuauhxicalli*, or "vase of the eagle" (a receptacle for the hearts of victims offered to the Sun); *tzompantli*, a "rack of skulls"; *tlachtli*, or "court for the ball game"; and sacred springs such as the *tozpalatl*.

Sacrifice in Context

To be able to comprehend human sacrifice as practiced by the Aztec, it is necessary to know their myths, related rituals, and belief system and how they perceived the universe and the cosmological realm.

The Aztec gods sacrificed themselves for life on Earth to exist, so the Aztec felt a great sense of debt to their gods for their sacrifice. The Aztec believed that they had to repay this great favor by providing the gods with the greatest gift and sacrifice of all, that of human life. Additionally, since the Aztec saw the universe to be interconnected—that is, they believed that the celestial realm and the earthly realm informed each other—the idea of appeasing the gods with human blood was not only due to a sense of debt but also because the sunrise and its ability to shine and bring warmth to the Earth was dependent on it. Indeed, the gods demanded this human blood from the Aztec people, for according to the Aztec belief systems, the sole purpose of the Mexica in this earthly realm was to ensure that the universe was kept alive via the blood of sacrificial subjects. The human sacrifices done in the name of their gods resulted in the continued existence of the Aztec world, and without them everything would cease to exist.

Deity Impersonators

To indulge the bloodthirsty deities, the Aztec needed people to sacrifice. The majority of the sacrificed subjects were warriors captured in battle. To be chosen to be sacrificed, however, was a great honor, as it would ensure life after death because the sacrificed would join the sun deity. In addition to sacrificing warrior-enemies, the Aztec also sacrificed persons who were chosen to represent a deity, usually slaves, and on very rare occasions elite persons were sacrificed. Those individuals impersonating a deity were known as *ixiptla*. Usually, warriors or young slaves were chosen to be *ixiptla*. This was a belief system composed of deep symbolism and meaning, as the young men were representing a deity, and the deity was in turn representing a natural celestial entity such as the Sun, the Moon, or the winds, and it was to these natural forces that the sacrifice of young slaves was hoped to appease the natural forces that brought about fertility and abundance to people.

As human sacrifices were done in a deeply religious and ritualistic context, most human sacrifices were performed on special festivals as prescribed by the 260-day calendar. On such occasions, there were celebrations in which various rituals and offerings were made to the gods, such as paper, flowers, or incense. Many of the main myths were reenacted, including the creation of the cosmos.

Other occasions that prompted human sacrifices would include wars or battles or natural phenomena or disasters, such as eclipses or flooding. Whatever the occasion, a series of pageantries and rites, some of which included dance, had to be performed before and after the sacrifice.

Examples of rituals that were done prior to the human sacrifices included maintaining a night vigil and a bath for the sacrificial subject, especially if an *ixiptla*. After the cleansing or ritual bath, the young god impersonator would be dressed like the deity he or she was representing and reenact events that were identified with that deity. Another pre–human sacrifice ritual included painting the victim white.

Types of Human Sacrifices

Depending on the type of sacrifice being performed, there were other, associated rituals, leading up to the death. Types of sacrifice included extraction of the heart, decapitation, dismemberment, drowning, or piercing by arrows, to name some examples. Instruments of choice included, but were not limited to, a *techcatl*, which was a sacrificial stone; a *cuauhxicalli*, a container to hold hearts; and a *tecpatl* (flint knife), which was used to stab the subject. Furthermore, as human sacrifices were religious practices, they all took place at holy sites such as the Great Temple in Tenochtitlan, a sacred mountainous landscape, or a ball court. As the largest temples belonged to the two most revered deities—Tlaloc, for his power over the rain, and Huitzilopochtli, for his power over the Sun—these deities accordingly received the most human sacrifices.

Among the most common types of human sacrifice practiced by the Aztec was the pulling of the heart from the subject's chest (*tlacamictiliztli*), the gladiatorial sacrifice (*tlahuahuanaliztli*), and decapitation. Other types included sacrifice by arrows (*tlacacaliztli*), burying the victim alive, strangulation, or burning the victim in a ritual fire. It was also common to combine types of sacrifices, such as the removal of the heart followed by a decapitation. The priests presided over sacrifices and other rituals as they were the earthly embodiments and/or mediators of a deity.

After the human sacrifices, another series of rituals would follow. These rituals were dictated by the occasion, the reason for the sacrifice, and the deity that the sacrifice was for. So, for example, if the human sacrifice was made in the name of Xipe Totec, the sacrificed person's skin would be flayed and then worn by a young male who would represent the god in the festivals and rituals that followed. Other postsacrifice rituals included eating the flesh of the sacrificed being, burying the body, severing the head and placing it on a *tzompantli*, and then tossing the body from the top of a pyramid, as in a sacrifice for Coyolxauhqui.

Festivals and Sacrifice

Since human sacrifices corresponded to special festival days, most of which were in honor of a deity and were included in the 18-month, 20-day calendar, each of these rituals had a name in Nahuatl.

1. Atlcahualo: The patron deities were Tlaloque and Ehecatl, and the victims were captives and children. This human sacrifice took place in the mountains Epcoatl, Pantitlan, Netotiloyan, and Chililico.
2. Tlacaxipehualiztli: The patron deities were Xipe Totec, Huitzilopochtli, and Tequizin-Mayahuel. The victims were warrior captives and god impersonators, usually slaves. The ritual consisted of extraction of the heart, and then the skin would be flayed and draped over a youth representing the deity. This sacrifice was conducted during the day in the Temple of Yopico.
3. Tozoztontli: The patron deities included Tlaloc-Chalchiuhtlicue and Coatlicue. This ritual was by extraction of the heart.

4. Huey Tozoztli: The patron deities included Cinteotl, Chicomecoatl, Quetzalcoatl, and Tlaloc. The ritual was conducted during sunrise and the middle of the day. The sacrificed included boys and girls and deity representatives.
5. Toxcatl: The patron deities included Huitzilopochtli, Tlacahuepan, Tezcatlipoca, and Cuexcotzin. Victims included warrior captives; sacrifice was by extraction of the heart. This ritual was held in Tlacochcalco.
6. Etzalcualitztli: The patron deities were Quetzalcoatl and Tlaloc. This sacrifice, extraction of the heart, was conducted at midnight at the shrine to Tlaloc in the Great Temple.
7. Tecuilhuitontli: The patron deities were Huixtocihuatl and Xochipilli. This sacrifice was conducted during the day at the Tlaloc shrine in the Great Temple and would be done by extraction of the heart.
8. Huey Tecuilhuitl: The patron deities included Xilonen, Quilaztli-Cihuacoatl, Chicomecoatl, and Ehecatl. These deities required four captive victims. This sacrifice was conducted one hour before sunrise and during the morning and would be done by extraction of the heart.
9. Tlaxochimaco: The patron deities were Huitzilopochtli, Tezcatlipoca, and Mictlantecuhtli,

6.7 *Types of human sacrifice: a)* tlacamictiliztli *(extraction of the heart), according to the* Codex Magliabecchi; *b) burning, from the* Atlas de Durán; *and c)* tlacacaliztli *(piercing with arrows), as shown in the* Historia tolteca-chichimeca (Lluvia Arras and Karla Lopez)

among others. The chosen victims were elderly.

10. Xocotl Huetzi: The patron deities included Ixcozauhqui, Xiuhtecuhtli, Chalmecacihuatl, Yacatecuhtli, and others. This ritual was done in the Tlacacouan temple.

11. Ochpaniztli: The patron deities were Chicomecoatl, Toci, Teteoinnan, and Chiconquiahuitl. Sacrificed subjects included deity representatives and captives. The type of sacrifice was decapitation and extraction of the heart.

12. Teotleco: This ritual was dedicated to all gods, but especially Xochiquetzal, and consisted of extracting the heart of captives. It was done in Teccalco.

13. Tepeilhuitl: The patron deities were Matlalcueye, Milnahuatl, and Tlaloc-Napatecuhtli. Victims included boys and two royal women. This ritual was done in Centzontotochtiniteopan during the day and night by heart extraction.

14. Quecholli: The patron deities included Mixcoatl-Tlamatzincatl, Izquitecatl, and Coatlicue. Type of sacrifice was extraction of the heart and decapitation. This ritual was done during the day in Coatlan, Mixcoatepan, and Tlamatzinco.

15. Panquetzaliztli: Huitzilopochtli was one of the patron deities. Victims were slaves and captives. Offerings included *tzoalli*, figures made of dough that contained ground amaranth, human blood, and honey. The sacrifice was done by heart extraction in the Great Temple's shrine to Huitzilopochtli.

16. Atemoztli: The patron deities included the Tlaloques, and the sacrifice was by decapitation.

17. Tititl: The patron deities included Yacatecuhtli, Ilamatecuhtli, and Tona-Cozcamiauh. The sacrifice was heart extraction followed by a decapitation. It took place at the Great Temple, Yacatecuhtli-Iteopan, Huitzilincuatec-Iteopan, and Tlaxico.

18. Izcalli: The patron deities included Ixcozauhqui-Xiuhtecuhtli, Nancotlaceuhqui, and Cihuatontli. Among the victims some were impersonators of the god Xiuhtecuhtli, and every four years the victims were women. This sacrifice was done at night at Tzonmolco.

Interpretations of the Meaning of the Human Sacrifice

Of Mesoamerican cultures, Aztec human sacrifices were the largest in quantity of victims. This is because the number of sacrifices performed by each village represented the power that a village yielded; therefore, the number of sacrifices performed by the Aztec, which ran in the thousands, both attested to and ensured their power and grandeur over the whole of Mesoamerica.

There has been much speculation as to why the sacrifices took place to begin with. One theory has to do with the fact that on very few occasions, the Aztec ritually consumed some of the flesh of those who were sacrificed. It has been suggested that mass sacrifices were conducted because there was a lack of meat and protein resources. This idea, however, fails to note that the persons who consumed the flesh ritualistically were but a very few and that the common people did not have access to this ritual. Other proposed ideas have been that sacrifices were a method of population control and that they were a way to neutralize the violence that existed within the Aztec community. All of these ideas are not without dispute and perhaps fail to understand this ritual within its own historical and mythological context.

It is safe to say that the Aztec practiced human sacrifice as a way to maintain the Earth's stasis, that is, to maintain the flow of life in the universe, to ensure afterlife to the sacrificed subjects, and to control and appease an uncertain and unstable environmental via their gods. In short, human sacrifices were done to appease the gods so that they would continue providing fertility and good things to Earth and ensure the Sun's rise and rotation, and the overall operation of the universe, and to show gratification to the gods for their own sacrifices to the human realm.

Even though human sacrifice has been practiced in almost the entire world, it is with the Aztec of Mesoamerica that this ritual practice was taken to new heights. When the Spaniards arrived to the New World, they were horrified at the sight of the priest covered with blood that had grown crusty from time and its related human sacrifice rituals.

Even in their own land Christians had fought to bring an end to small game sacrifices and the occasional human sacrifices practiced among heathens. By the time the conquistadores arrived to the New World, Christianity had proven triumphant in Europe in bringing pagan practices to an end as well as ending polytheism. Therefore, they were alarmed to find such practices in the New World and viewed the native population of the Americas as plagued by the same demons that had plagued the Greeks and Romans with their human sacrifices and pantheon of deities.

Additionally, they misinterpreted the Aztec belief system and so failed to understand the context in which these human sacrifice rituals were based. To the Christians, the sacrifice of Jesus Christ was the only sacrifice needed in order for humanity to redeem itself. With Jesus on the cross, sacrifices were no longer needed nor practiced in Christianity; therefore, the Aztec belief system had to be eradicated and replaced with Christian values. Only that way would the Indians have a chance to save themselves from their "demonic pagan" ways.

The Aztec were forced by the conquistadores and the subsequent Spanish colony to abandon their spirituality and convert to Catholicism. With the forced elimination of their rituals, including the most important to the Aztec, the human sacrifice ritual, the whole of the Aztec worldview was shattered: After all, it was human sacrifice that kept the Aztec world going and appeased their gods. The concept of the universe as dependent on the blood of the sacrificed victims thus came to end. The Aztec calendar was also abandoned, as were the myths, deities, and sacred sites. This belief system was in turn transplanted by a new worldview and spirituality, although it was not entirely European Catholicism. The church was not entirely successful in its conversion of the Mesoamerican Indians. Rather, an Indianized Catholicism developed that learned to see in the bloody and suffering images of Christ a continuity of their practices of human sacrifice (see chapter 14).

READING

Structure of the Universe

Taube 1994, Durán 1994, Sahagún 1951–69, Matos Moctezuma 1988, *Codex Vaticanus A*, *Historia de los mexicanos por sus pinturas:* the celestial and terrestrial planes, the underworld.

Main Myths

Codex Chimalpopoca: Legend of the Suns; Durán 1994: origin of pulque; *Codex Azcatitlan:* birth of Huitzilopochtli; Durán 1994, Alvarado Tezozomoc 1975, Sahagún 1951–69, *Codex Boturini:* foundation of Tenochtitlan.

The Aztec Gods

Caso 1981, León-Portilla 1963, 1970: origin of the gods; Florescano 1997, Tena 1993: nature of the gods; Taube 1994, Coe and Koontz 2002, Sahagún 1951–69, Durán 1994, Miller and Taube 1993, González Torres 1991, Nicholson 1971: Aztec pantheon.

Rituals

Sahagún 1951–69, *Codex Magliabecchi*, Motolinia 1971: diverse rituals and ceremonies.

Human Sacrifice

González Torres 1979, 2003, Miller and Taube 1993, Sahagún 1951–69, Durán 1994, Torquemada 1980, Smith 2003: concept and types of human sacrifice.

7

FUNERARY BELIEFS AND CUSTOMS

Abundant symbolism and mythology give meaning to the many questions about Aztec culture, including death. Recurring themes, such as duality, reciprocity, and inevitable change, permeated Aztec life and thought. Analyzing their beliefs about death clarify some of the motivations behind Aztec rituals and practices. Much like the modern world, the Aztec nation struggled with the same philosophical questions of human existence examined today. Deep within Aztec cosmology and philosophy was the belief that in order for there to be life there had to be death. The grandeur of the Aztec civilization was deeply rooted in this unique vision and integrated ideas about death as a necessary concession to the astral forces that gave them the privilege of life and existence.

Their agricultural lifestyle also ensured a special understanding of the relationship between Earth, humankind, and death. It validated the cycle of life and death in a very primal display of nature at work—the Sun rose and set every day; the Moon appeared and faded away according to its phases; and plant life died in the dry months only to be reborn in the rainy season more abundant and magnificent than before.

Other evidence of this unique Aztec conception is found in the more aesthetic aspects of Aztec culture, such as art and poetry. It also formed part of their medicinal practices. One Aztec manuscript has in its last chapter a description of the impending signs of death and remedies that might lessen the agony of dying. Nature also collaborated in revealing other aspects of death. Spanish friar Bernardino de Sahagún wrote of omens, or warning signs, provided by birds. Owls in particular were considered the messengers of the gods of death Mictlantecuhtli and Mictlantecihuatl, who were calling for those destined to inhabit their world, Mictlan. If an owl called out above an Aztec home or from a nearby tree, it was believed that someone there was going to die or become ill or that the family would face such a horrible peril that it might endanger all of their lives. If it was heard calling out two or three times, death was certain, especially if someone in that home was already ill.

What the Aztec achieved from this vantage point was a cosmological perspective that afforded them a way to give meaning and purpose to even the most tragic reality of the human existence—death. This perspective of life asserted that the gods had the power to both give and take life. This awareness provides the context for the study and analysis of Aztec concepts of death. It is evident in their collective consciousness and daily life, and it gives insight into their sacrificial practices. Ideas about death are clearly transmitted from a place of deep reverence for the universal energy that permitted their creation and survival. These concepts and beliefs might have appeared to be unintelligible and odd to Spanish explorers.

CREATION MYTHS AND CONCEPTS ABOUT DEATH

The Aztec's understanding of the dual nature of life rested in a variety of myths that authenticated their relationship with the gods and, in turn, with death; in fact, the Aztec accepted life and death as reciprocal counterparts essential to their survival. Their

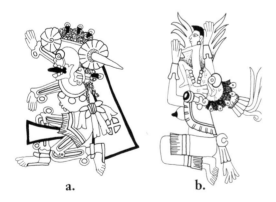

7.1 a) Mictlantecuhtli, the god of death, and b) Mictlancihuatl, the goddess of death and wife of Mictlantecuhtli, as depicted in the Codex Borbonicus (Fonda Portales)

creation myths shed light on Aztec beliefs concerning death.

Acutely aware of their mortality, the Aztec presented their convictions about the regeneration of life through death in such myths and spoke plainly of their indebtedness to the gods for their existence. According to the *Codex Chimalpopoca*, the base of the Mesoamerican people was the legend of the cosmogonic ages, or "suns," that have existed and perished in violent ways. During these epochs, the creator gods had engaged in great cosmic struggles that had established the existence of suns. Four previous suns emerged and disappeared at the hands of the gods: These were the ages of earth, air, water, and fire. The fifth in the series was the current age, that of the sun of movement (Nahui Ollin). It began as a result of a mysterious sacrifice of the gods, who created it with their blood and gave life to a new generation of human beings on Earth. This age also embodied the principle of destruction and death.

According to the myth, the human beings of the first sun were made of ash. The water finished with them, transforming them into fishes. The second generation of human beings was formed as giants. Despite their great physical size, this group was deficient and weak in nature. Indigenous texts say that when they fell down by accident, "they fell down forever." The giants were devoured by tigers. The human beings of the third sun were destroyed by fire, and the few survivors were turned into *guajolotes* (wild turkeys). The human beings that lived in the fourth sun were obliterated by strong winds and were turned into monkeys that lived in the mountains like "ape-men" (*tlacaozomatin*).

Each sun ended in a cataclysm, annihilating the previous peoples; however, even in this great tragedy, there is optimism and rebirth for the Aztec. Instead of repeating history—one that would be fatally identical to the previous one—the new cycle produced more evolved human beings. The fifth and current age, the sun of movement, had its origin in Teotihuacan and from there also came the grandeur of the Toltec with the wise prince Quetzalcoatl.

The *Codex Matritense* (included in Sahagún's *Primeros Memoriales*) explains the creation of the fifth sun with another myth about two gods that offered to throw themselves into a fire pit in order to be transformed into the Sun. One was the arrogant god Tecuciztecatl and the other was the humble god Nanahuatzin. When the time of the sacrifice came, Nanahuatzin threw himself into the fire without hesitation, transforming himself in the fifth sun, whereas Tecuciztecatl became fearful. He later entered the fire, and his destiny was to become the Moon. Once this sacrifice was completed, the diverse gods gathered at Teotihuacan waited for the Sun to rise. Quetzalcoatl and some others discovered it coming from the east. It was resplendent. A little later the Moon appeared, also from the east.

However, a problem remained: While both celestial bodies had appeared, neither moved. Understanding this as a sign of their fate, the gods freely accepted death, sacrificing themselves by and offering their own blood, or *chalchiuatl* (precious water) to generate movement of the Sun. With this collective action, they ensured the existence of the era of the fifth sun: As soon as the Sun began to move, days and nights marked their daily journey across the horizon. The privilege of life was therefore thanks to the self-sacrifice of the gods.

After the fifth sun was created in the divine fire of Teotihuacan, the ancient gods preoccupied themselves with the creation of a new species of human beings on the terrestrial plane. However, the task of creating a new generation of men and women required the use of the remains of human beings from previous ages. Quetzalcoatl, symbol of the wisdom of ancient Mexico, accepted the mission of creating these human beings, as well as providing food sources for them. To begin his work, Quetzalcoatl traveled to Mictlan, "the place of the dead," to rescue the "precious bones" of humans of previous ages in order to give life to a new era.

Mictlantecuhtli, lord of the underworld, initiated a series of difficulties to keep Quetzalcoatl from locating and taking possession of the human bones of past generations. But a determined Quetzalcoatl enlisted the aid of his double, or *nahualli*, and of the wild worms and bees, and succeeded in retrieving the bones. He took them to Tamoanchan (place of origin), where he ground the bones and placed them in a precious earthen dishpan. He gave them life with his own blood by piercing his penis in an act of self-sacrifice. In this myth, a new population appeared as a result of Quetzalcoatl's penitence or sacrifice. This is the reason that this group is called *"macehualtin,"* which in a more extended definition means "the deserved ones by the penitence."

These ancient myths would in later times strongly influence Aztec religion. The human beings of the fifth movement had received their life through the self-sacrifice of the gods; therefore, in an act of reciprocity, they would be compelled to offer their own blood to preserve the life of the Sun.

The Aztecs through experience and reflection discovered that all is susceptible to change and end. Both themes—the instability of nature and living things and their fatal end, which for man and woman means death—were the motifs that drove indigenous wise men to meditate and search for a deeper meaning and purpose to life and nature. These ideas about change and death, reinforced by the legend of the preceding worlds and the destruction of them by cataclysm, caused Nahua wise men to conceive of life as a kind of dream and understand Time (*cahuitl*) as "that, that Life is leaving to us" (León-Portilla 1970: 174).

The cultural impact of their beliefs about change, personal death, and demise of the world was so profound that the Aztec could be described as a people obsessed, fascinated, and tortured by the idea of unavoidable destruction. And yet, these same concerns inspired them to find a way to supersede instability and death. The Aztec committed to a mission to avoid the tragic ending of previous ages. They reasoned that if the gods had created humans with the blood of their sacrifice, then humans could offer their own blood and give strength to the life of the Sun, thereby maintaining the existence of this world, the fifth sun.

They came to regard their existence as the sole cosmic source of energy for the Sun. This warrior mysticism led the Aztec to believe that sacred war and sacrifice would preserve the life of the Sun and in this way forever connect death at war with the Giver of Life, identified as the Sun (Tonatiuh). The Aztec lived with the constant fear that the Sun would lose its strength and cease to rise. This feeling of hopelessness was especially prominent at the end of every 52-year cycle, when grand ceremonies were held to coax the Sun into reappearing.

FUNERARY PLACES OF DESTINATION

The Aztec vision of their physical universe, which included funerary destinations, was symbolized in the design of their ceremonial centers: An immense island divided in four quadrants or directions. Each direction contained a set of symbols (see figures 9.1 and 9.2). The east was the region of light (the sunrise), fertility, and life, symbolized by the color white. The north was the direction of darkness, coldness, and war. It was where the dead were buried and was the color black. In the west was the house of the Sun. The west represented birth and decay, the mystery of origin and end. It was the place of the color red. Finally, the south was the region of heat, fire, and tropical weather. It was the direction of the color blue.

Aztec conception of the afterlife is almost as extensive and diverse as their living world. As with most aspects of Aztec life, many factors contributed to determining one's destiny in life as well as in death. In as much as they could ascertain, most facets of Aztec life were strategically purposed and carefully planned. The date of a person's birth as marked by the Aztec calendar (see chapter 11) influenced many aspects of a person's life, for example. From it, Aztec wise men were able to determine personality characteristics, burden and fate, and other attributes of a person. With this same precision, the final destination of a person's soul was dictated by the manner in which the person died and, in some cases, by the person's occupation in life.

The bodies of the dead were returned to the interior of Mother Earth by either cremation or burial. Metaphorically, this meant that the Earth, represented by the great mother goddess Coatlicue, reclaimed the bodies of the dead of any kind into her womb. This same ascription was accorded to her masculine counterpart, the god Tlaltecuhtli, the monster of the Earth. The body or the ashes remained in the earth (soil), feeding Tlaltecuhtli and Coatlicue, but the soul of an individual traveled to a predetermined place, depending on the kind of death he or she experienced.

The journey into afterlife was an arduous voyage for some and a passage to eternal joy for others. Some of the Aztec dead still faced a myriad of travails in their journey to the underworld, while others were elevated to godlike status, and still others enjoyed a tranquil and blissful existence in the afterlife. Morality and lifestyle seemed to have little effect on the final resting place of an Aztec soul, which posed an ideological challenge for the Catholic chroniclers whose belief systems were bound to the idea that a person's behavior and attitude in life directly affected the quality of his or her afterlife. In the Catholic belief system, either a person would enjoy the glory and riches of heaven through honorable living or suffer eternally in the depths of hell. But for the Aztec, the form of death was the one and only deciding factor and was a frequent topic of discussion for Aztec thinkers who contemplated the passage of time and the inevitability of death with obsessive fervor.

According to the Spanish chroniclers Sahagún and Durán, there were four specific places where the soul could go: Chichihuacuauhco, Tonatiuh-Ilhuicac, Tlalocan, and Mictlan.

Chichihuacuauhco

Chichihuacuauhco, the Orchard of the Gods, literally means "in the wet-nurse tree." This paradise was also called Tonacacuauhtitlan. It received children whose innocence had been protected as a result of their early death. These infants had died while still nursing and therefore had not yet eaten directly from the earth, rendering them pure and untainted—that is, not indebted to the gods for the earthly riches they had not yet consumed.

The landscape of this place was abundant, with trees whose branches produced breasts that poured drops of milk to feed the little ones. There were two beliefs about the souls of this realm. The first held that the children would return to the world and repopulate it when the present race was destroyed. The second was that these souls would return to

7.2 *Chichihuacuauhco, the heaven of innocent dead babies with a tree with breasts to feed them, in the Codex Vaticanus A* (Lluvia Arras)

Earth through a woman's womb after an indeterminate period of time.

Tonatiuh-Ilhuicac

The souls of soldiers fallen at war and the souls of mothers who died during childbirth rested in Tonatiuh-Ilhuicac, the Heaven of the Sun. This was the home of the Sun and perhaps the most desirable ending to earthly existence because it was considered a place of honor. The souls that arrived here had the privilege of accompanying the Sun in its daily cycle. The soldiers went to the eastern realm and escorted the Sun as it rose through the morning sky. They spent their sunlit time in mock battles and war songs. It can be inferred from such a blissful conclusion that this place of rest was a great motivation for soldiers, for if they died at war, they would be "chosen" to live in the house of the Sun. It

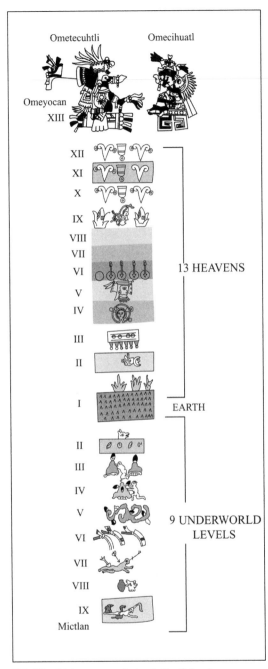

Ometecuhtli   Omecihuatl

Omeyocan
XIII

XII
XI
X
IX
VIII
VII
VI   13 HEAVENS
V
IV

III

II

I   EARTH

II
III
IV
V   9 UNDERWORLD
VI   LEVELS
VII
VIII
IX
Mictlan

7.3 The 13 heavens and nine hells of the Aztec universe, as presented in the Codex Vaticanus A (Lluvia Arras)

demonstrates the strong ideological interaction between religion and politics and allows for the Aztec ideal of immortality and reincarnation.

Women who died in childbirth also shared the privilege of inhabiting Tonatiuh-Ilhuicac because death during labor was considered death at battle with natural forces to bring new life into the living world (Tlalticpac). The souls of these women warriors went to the western realm, Cihuatlampa (the women's side), and joined the Sun in its nightly descent, carrying him on a mantle made of quetzal plumes. They marched before him, shouting with joy, fighting and praising him. They left him in the place where the Sun sets, where he was received by those of the underworld. These women became goddesses called the Cuihuateteo, "the divine women."

After four years of joy and happiness, these souls could inhabit clouds. The male warriors were changed into beautiful birds or butterflies that flew freely between heaven and Earth. The women became *cihuapipiltin* goddesses and returned to their earthly homes in search of their spinning and weaving instruments. On occasion they were made visible to their husbands.

Tlalocan

The paradise of the rain god, Tlaloc, received individuals specifically chosen by him. It is believed that any death related to water had his direct intervention. Death by drowning or lightning, dropsy, gout, lepers, mange, or tumors were indications that the person would rest in Tlalocan. This was also the place where children sacrificed to Tlaloc arrived. Those who came here became attendants of Tlaloc; they were called *ahuaque* and *ehecatotontin*, "masters of water" and "little winds."

The corpses of these individuals were not cremated but buried. This gesture represented a direct offering of human flesh to the gods that made vegetation and rain possible. These remains were thought of as seeds that lived and germinated deep within a sacred mountain, which in turn produced the water in the form of clouds, rivers, and winds to feed the earth.

7.4 Tlalocan, the paradise of the rain god Tlaloc, shown in the Tepantitla Mural, Teotihuacan (Drawing by Fonda Portales, after Gendrop 1988)

This paradise is represented in a constant state of summer with a lush garden of flowers, exuberant vegetation, and warm rain. Its inhabitants lived in blissful tranquility, free from fatigue, worries, and problems.

Mictlan

Deemed the underworld, Mictlan was physically understood as the underbelly of the Earth. It was a dark region reserved for the souls of everyone else, regardless of social class. It was a place of uncertainty and mystery. The souls of individuals who died of old age, any natural cause, or diseases, accidents, or circumstances not specified by the gods of the other three destinations inhabited this region.

Mictlan was the mansion of the god Mictlantecuhtli, Lord of the Dead, and his female companion, Mictlancihuatl (Mictecacihuatl). Mictlantecuhtli is often represented as a plain skull or one with an obsidian knife stabbed through his nose.

To reach Mictlan, the dead were required to undertake a long journey filled with treacherous natural obstacles to be overcome in nine separate phases. In the first stage the dead had to cross a river called Apanohuaya. At the moment they reached the shore, they required the assistance of the Techichi dog, which had been buried with them, to swim across the river. After emerging from the river completely naked, the next barrier was to pass between Tepetl Monamictia, a pair of fierce mountains that constantly crashed against each other. From there, the dead climbed a mountain called Itztepetl, whose surface was a mantle of razor-sharp obsidian pieces. The next trial led the dead to cross eight gorges (Cehuecayan) where freezing temperatures facilitated a never-ending snowfall and eight valleys (Itzehecayan) where brutal winds cut through them like a knife. After surpassing this, they walked down a path that exposed them to a flurry of innumerable arrows (Temiminaloyan), only to discover that a jaguar had eaten their hearts. The next obstruction consisted of crossing a mysterious place called "where the flags wave" where the dead would find a type of lizard or crocodile called Xochitonatl. The lizard was the symbol for the Earth and also the last day of the year, which signaled to the dead that they were reaching the end of this ordeal and returning to Earth.

At this point in the odyssey, the dead were compelled to cross Chiconahuapan (the nine rivers), again with the aid of the Techichi dog, to finally reach Chiconamictlan (the ninth hell), where they were received by Mictlantecuhtli. This long and difficult journey was thought to take four years to complete. It is at this moment that the dead lost their attachment to their physical and earthly embodiment and he disintegrated and disappeared forever into darkness and nothingness. Seemingly, there was no possibility of eternal life or other existence for those destined to Mictlan. Immortality was reserved only for those chosen to inhabit the other three realms.

One existing interpretation to explain the necessity for such challenges in death contends that the soul's crossing into the realm of Mictlan with its nine trials, symbolized a reverse journey into a mother's womb. Much like a womb, the interior of Mictlan is described as a very dark place, without any windows or light. The practice of burying the deceased in a fetal position so as to return to the Earth in the same position in which he or she was born seems to support this. In addition, the specific number of obstacles—nine—might represent the nine missed menstrual cycles during pregnancy, and the difficulty might represent the risks, pain, and transformation of birth.

The passing of time, death, and the afterlife were fixations of the Aztec nation. They lived with the constant knowledge that every 52 years their world was vulnerable to destruction and that they had to renegotiate their continued existence with their gods. This extended to the realm of Mictlan and weighed upon those destined to the underworld—a majority of the Aztec population, regardless of social position. Upon reaching Mictlan after a journey of four years, a person's essence would be completely eliminated in a dramatic fashion from any conscious memory of the Aztec nation. The prospect of this demise brought feelings of hopelessness and despair to many Aztecs. Artists and thinkers contemplated and depicted death through philosophy and religion (see chapter 6), art (see chapter 8), and poetry (see chapter 10). As a result, the Aztec produced many renderings of the questions, doubts, and musings in regard to death and the afterlife that seemed to reflect a general sentiment of desolation.

BURIALS AND CREMATION

Funerary Ceremonies and Rituals

The passage of the body and soul from life to death required an intricate orchestration of rituals and mourning. Aztec preparations were meticulous, reverent, and expressive. Generally, funerary rites were performed in the same manner for all Aztecs. The funerals of rulers and nobility were more elaborate affairs that included the participation of nobility from other regions and a greater amount of preparation. Women who died in childbirth also required special treatment. In addition, the funerary destina-

tion also influenced the ceremonies, though to a lesser degree, as in the case of those who died by a cause related to water.

It is widely accepted that there were two forms of disposal of the dead available to the Aztec: burial and cremation. Burial was mostly reserved for Aztecs without rank, individuals from other territories, and those who assisted with the tasks of daily life—the young, the unmarried, women who died in childbirth, and those called by Tlaloc.

Cremation symbolized a transformation of the soul, which would ascend and live in the heaven of the Sun. It was reserved for rulers, great lords, and warriors who had been killed or whose blood had been.

Fire was an important medium of conversion for many elements of Aztec life. As in the creation myth of Teotihuacan, fire purified and transformed the gods that would emerge as the fifth sun. There were religious cults that worshipped the fire god Huehueteotl, whose double was Xiuhtecuhtli. He is depicted at the center position of the four directions, as a fire would be in the center of an Aztec home. Many ceremonies and sacrifices were held in honor of this god, including one that required that men be burned in his honor.

Fire played a particular role in death and the transition into the afterlife. By consuming the material and transforming it into the spiritual, fire allowed the deceased to take with them items that might help them, such as the Techichi dog, clothing, and other necessary implements. Furthermore, fire served as a conduit of power and communication between the living and the dead. Offerings, gifts, tears, and prayers were immediately transmitted to the dead via fire. The dead utilized these offerings to fortify themselves and receive necessary instructions to complete the journey into the afterlife.

The early Spanish chroniclers captured the burial practices of the Aztec through firsthand accounts and interviews with their informants. According to these narratives, the funeral rites occurred in five stages, which took place in five distinct rituals over the course of four years. The rituals began with a series of orations addressed to both the deceased and the mourner. It is unclear who the speakers were, but it can be inferred that they were probably priests or ritual specialists. The deceased was the first to be addressed, then the mourner or the heir. It was believed that the soul or essence of the person did not immediately leave the body, so the deceased was spoken to as if the individual might still be living.

FUNERALS OF NON-NOBLES

In general, when an Aztec of low (peasant) or medium status died, his or her eyes were carefully closed, and the highly revered masters of burial ceremonies were called. These officials cut up pieces of a paper made of tree bark (*amatl*), covered the body of the deceased with them, and then poured a vase of water on the person's head (a simulation of the amniotic fluid, because the dead is returning to the womb of Earth). They then dressed the body in accordance to his or her condition, fortune, or circumstances of death. For example, if the deceased had been a soldier, he was dressed like Huitzilopochtli, and those who died from indulgence in liquor were dressed with the emblems of Tezcatzoncatl, the god of wine.

A vessel of water was then placed near the dead person to satisfy his or her thirst during the journey to the other world, and the deceased was furnished with bits of *amatl* paper, whose usage was explained to him or her by the presiding funeral officials: One of them would be used to pass between the two contending mountains in safety; the second would allow the deceased to travel without danger on the road guarded by the great serpent; the third piece would allow the dead to cross the domain of the great crocodile, Xochitonatl, without being disturbed; the fourth was a passport to traverse the seven deserts; the fifth served for the eight hills; and the sixth, to defend him- or herself against the north wind. For this latter challenge, the Aztec burned the clothes and arms of the deceased, so that the warmth given out by their combustion might protect from the cold of this terrible wind.

One of the principal ceremonies consisted in killing a Techichi; this dog would then accompany the dead person on his or her posthumous journey. A cord was put around the animal's neck so that he would be able to cross the deep river of the Nine Waters. The dog was either buried or burned simultaneously with the deceased. The dog was usually yellow in color, not black, brown, or any other color combination.

The body was burned with a resinous pinewood effigy fully dressed in the clothes of the deceased. The corpse was usually put into a fetal position on the funerary pyre (as if returning to a mother's womb), and with it were also burned the tools of the person's trade. While the masters of ceremonies burned incense around the funerary pyre, the priests intoned a funeral hymn. When the body was consumed, its ashes were collected in an earthen vase, at the bottom of which a green jewel (*chalchihuitl*), of a value proportionate to the fortune of the deceased, was placed to serve the soul as a heart in the regions he or she was soon to inhabit. The vase was interred in a deep hole, which for four days was covered with offerings of bread and wine, a custom that continues among modern-day Nahuas in some villages.

If the body was buried rather than cremated, the actual burial ceremony occurred 80 days after death. The ritual of burning an effigy was repeated at this time and performed once a year for four years on the anniversary of a person's death, after which it was assumed that the individual's soul had arrived in Mictlan. Also after 80 days, the mourners of warriors could bathe and groom themselves for the first time since the person's death.

Another funerary ritual consisted of keeping the energy of the deceased close to family and relatives by cutting locks of hair from the top of the head (*teyolia*) before cremation and mixing these with locks from birth. These locks were kept in a vessel, which was stored in or near the home of the deceased's family.

ROYAL FUNERALS

Royal funerals were even more elaborate and magnificent. Royalty were buried with many of their possessions—rich textiles, jewels, fancy ceramic vessels, and other precious items. When this became known to Spanish conquerors, the tombs of rulers and nobles were increasingly subjected to pillaging.

When the *tlatoani* of Tenochtitlan fell sick, the face of the idols of Huitzilopochtli and Tezcatlipoca were covered with masks, which were not removed until the patient was either cured or dead. As soon as the king expired, the news was published with great pomp, and all the nobles of the kingdom were informed of the fact, in order that they might come to assist to the obsequies.

In the meantime the royal body was placed on costly mats (*petlatl*), and his servants mounted guard around him. On the fourth or fifth day, when the nobles, clothed in brilliant costumes, had come together, as well as the slaves who were to assist at the ceremony, the deceased was dressed in some 15 vestments of different colored cotton forming a mummy bundle, and the body was decked with jewels of gold, silver, and precious stones. A jade bead or an emerald was attached to his lower lip to serve him as a heart; his face was concealed under a mask; he was then decked with the insignia of the god of the temple in which his ashes were to be deposited. In addition, a part of his hair was cut off, which was placed with the locks kept since his youth. These relics were enclosed in a chest, upon which was placed a bust of stone or wood of the dead monarch to preserve his memory. Then the slave who had been accustomed to assist him in his devotions was

sacrificed so he could continue his service in the other world.

The royal corpse was carried away, escorted by relatives and nobles. The wives of the deceased figured in the cortege, filling the air with their lamentations. The nobles carried a large standard of *amatl* paper, the arms of the deceased, and the royal insignia. The priests chanted, but without any accompaniment of instruments.

The first step of the temple having been reached, the high priests and their acolytes came to receive the body; they placed it on a funeral pyre of resinous wood covered with incense. While flames consumed the royal body, a number of slaves who had belonged to the king, together with those offered by the nobles for this solemnity, were sacrificed. The priests also sacrificed some of the people with deformities whom the king customarily kept in his palace so that they might amuse their master in the other world. A number of his wives were also killed. The number of victims varied with the importance of the obsequies; according to generally accepted calculations, there were around 200 sacrifices, including the Techichi dog, without whom the deceased would not be able to cross the rivers or survive some of the dangers on his path to the other world.

On the following day the ashes and teeth of the deceased were collected, as was the jade or emerald that had been suspended from his lip; all these relics were placed, with his hair, in the chest, which became a coffin of sorts. For four days, offerings of meats were placed on the tomb; on the fifth day, other slaves were sacrificed, a ceremony that was repeated on the 20th, 60th, and 80th days. Dating from this moment, throughout the following year, nothing was offered to the dead but rabbits, butterflies, partridges, and other birds; after that came bread, wine, incense, flowers, and pieces of bamboo filled with aromatic substances. The anniversary of the death was celebrated for four years.

Mourning had two purposes: It facilitated the departure and subsequent journey of the deceased and eased the pain of the dead's survivors. According to scholars there were two modes of the mourning process. The first is referred to as lunar mourning, which fell under the custodianship of women. Women continued their lamentations and weeping for 80 days, or four calendar months, while ensuring

7.5 *Mummy bundle of an Aztec king, in the* Codex Magliabecchi (Drawing by Fonda Portales, after Alberto Beltrán)

that the community remained functional during bereavement. During this period the women were not allowed to wash their hair or change their clothing. At the end of the 80 days, priests called *cuauhuehuetqueh* collected the tears and dust on the women's faces and wrapped them in pieces of paper made specifically for this ritual. These small parcels were then incinerated, ending the first phase of mourning. In effect, grief had been transformed through this act, relieving survivors of their pain.

The second mode was called solar mourning. Practiced in accordance to the type of death of an individual, this period lasted four days each year for four years. Mourners conducted funerary rituals similar to those performed at the time of death. Mourning included offerings of songs, dances, and food, and weeping to an effigy of the individual constructed in accordance to the type of death and the corresponding destination.

FUNERALS OF MERCHANTS

According to the *Florentine Codex*, merchants were treated as special cases because of the long periods of time they spent traveling far from home on trade expeditions. They traveled in groups, and when they arrived at other cities, they assembled in one place and remained together in an improvised home. Their code of conduct was clear and stringent: No one was allowed to go anywhere alone. And, if they happened to abuse a woman, they were counseled, sentenced, and often slain.

If a merchant happened to fall ill or be killed, his burial began with the insertion of a feather object in his mouth. The hollows of his eyes were painted black and his mouth, red. His body was striped with white soil. His peers dressed him in a paper stole that stretched from one armpit to the other. After he had been properly attired, his body was tightly wrapped and bound onto a wooden frame of carrying racks, which the other merchants then took to the nearest hill or mountaintop. When they arrived there, they set the frame upright against elevated posts. The deceased's companions stood with him until the body was fully consumed by fire to ward off possible predators and prevent desecration of the body. It was a symbolic act meant to emulate the death of warriors, because merchants believed themselves to be disciples of the Sun whose destiny was to live the afterlife in Tonatiuh-Ilhuicac.

FUNERALS OF WOMEN WHO DIED IN CHILDBIRTH

Sahagún wrote that women who died in childbirth were held in the same honorable regard as warriors who died at war or on a sacrificial stone of the enemy. Their burials were treated with equal reverence. After a woman had died during labor, her body was cleaned, her head and hair were washed, and she was dressed in her best clothes. Her husband would then carry her on his back to the place were she would be interred. Her hair was left loose and untied. The midwives and the old women gathered to accompany the body; they carried shields and swords and made the same war cries of soldiers about to attack. Young men at the *telpochcalli* (*telpopochtin*) came out from the school to meet them and struggled with them, attempting to seize the woman's body from them.

These women were buried in the courtyard of the temple dedicated to the goddesses called the heavenly women or *cihuapipiltin* (princesses) at sunset. Her husband and his relatives or friends guarded the body for four nights in order to prevent anyone from stealing the body, because young warriors would keep vigil waiting for the opportunity to steal a corpse considered holy or divine. And, if by chance, in fighting with the midwives, they succeeded in seizing the body, then they immediately cut off the middle finger of the left hand while the other women watched. If they stole the corpse at night, they proceed to cut off this same finger and the hair and keep them as relics. The reason the bodies of these women were so highly coveted by warriors is that they believed them to have special powers; for example, if a warrior put the finger and hair of the woman in their shields while at war, they would blind their enemies and increase their bravery and strength.

These women were destined to inhabit the heaven of the Sun because of their courage in childbirth. Women killed in war or who died at childbirth were called *mociuaquetzque* (valiant women), and they were numbered among those who die in battle. They became the formidable deities of the twilight, and if on certain nights they were to appear at the crossroads, they struck those that met them with paralysis. They were identified both with the occidental goddesses of Tamoanchan, the western paradise, and with the monsters of the end of the world.

CEMETERIES

Cemeteries as they are today were not common to the Aztec. The ashes of the dead were buried near a temple, in the fields, or at the summit of mountains, where they were in the habit of offering sacrifices. The ashes of kings and nobles were deposited in the towers atop temples.

In Aztec codices, the dead are always represented bundled up in a fetal position, the legs drawn up in front of the trunk and the knees under the chin. According to the Anonymous Conqueror, bodies that were buried rather than cremated were placed in very deep trenches; the corpse was placed on a low chair, with the implements of his or her trade or position: Soldiers were interred with a shield and sword; women with a spindle, a broom, and culinary vessels; rich people with jewels and gold. For this reason Spaniards soon began to rifle the tombs, where they obtained great wealth.

Fray Diego Durán wrote that some people were buried in the fields; others, in the courtyards of their own homes; others were taken to shrines in the woods; others were cremated, and their ashes buried in the temples. No one was interred without being dressed in his mantles, loincloths, and fine stones. Women were dressed in a tunic. In sum, none of his or her possessions were left behind; and if the body was cremated, the jar that received the ashes was filled with the person's jewelry and stones, no matter how costly. Funeral hymns were chanted, and the dead were mourned with great ceremonies taking place in their honor. At these funerals people ate and drank; and if the deceased had been a person of quality, lengths of cloth were presented to those who had attended the funeral. The body was laid out in a room for four days, allowing time for mourners to arrive. Gifts were brought to the dead, and if the deceased was a king or chieftain of a town, slaves were killed in his honor to serve him in the afterlife. Funeral rites lasted 10 days and were filled with sorrowful, tearful chants.

Newborn and very small infants were buried in or close to the family corn bins. While the exact meaning of this custom is unclear, it can be surmised that the spirit and innocence of a small child was thereby mated to the store seed. This ensured a vigorous and early sprouting of corn after the next sowing.

Archaeologist Michael Smith points out that the placement of burials in and around the home provides insight into Aztec attitudes toward death. The dead were still considered part of the family, and they took their place within the household. It is likely that families conducted rituals or made offerings to their deceased members, much as modern Mesoamerican peoples do in the Day of the Dead ceremonies of early November.

As mentioned earlier, the bodies of the nobles were wrapped in compact bundles of *petlatl* (called *petates* in present-day Mexico) that were later incinerated. In modern Mexico, the verb *petatear* is used as a synonym of *morir* (to die). The word *petatear*, which clearly comes from the Nahuatl word *petlatl*, has its origins in the Aztec funeral rite of being wrapped in a *petate*.

SOULS

The rich spiritual life of the Aztec peoples and the meticulous study of Spanish friars allowed for a substantial investigation of their beliefs. It is difficult to assess the exact Aztec beliefs about souls because of conflicting accounts given by Spanish chroniclers; however, many theories have been explored and analyzed by such notable scholars as Alfredo López-Austin, who has contributed extensive research on this topic. Primarily, the Aztec believed the human body to be a receptacle of sacred energy as well as an earthly reflection of their cosmos. Whatever energy or power an individual might exude reflected a small-scale replica of the greater forces of their cosmos and gods at work.

The soul and its parts had indispensable functions in Aztec thought. According to some chroniclers, the soul had three manifestations, or animistic

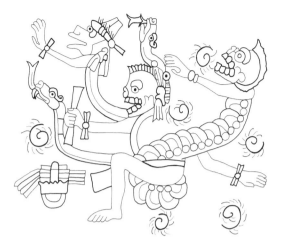

7.6 Various souls leaving the body of a dead person, in the Codex Vaticanus B *(Drawing by Fonda Portales)*

entities, in the physical body, which could be strengthened or weakened through the course of a person's life. All three had to function in harmony to maintain a person's balance and sanity. And if one of the entities was distressed, the others would be affected.

Like the body's transformation in death, the soul also experienced a conversion and separation, emphasizing, in yet another way, that the nature of life is transitory. Each of these experienced its own separation and journey at the time of death. An illustration in the *Codice Laud* depicts the distinct essence of each of the parts of the soul: The names of these entities are *tonalli* (head), *teyolia* (heart), and *ihiyotl* (liver or stomach).

The *Tonalli*

The *tonalli* (from *tona*, "to irradiate" or "make warm with sun") was a complex entity that resided in the head or brain, harbored by the human skull. It was the force of will and intelligence and perhaps the most transferable energy among the living. It is believed that the *tonalli* was derived from the supreme god of duality, Ometeotl, and that it reached human beings at the moment of concep-

tion through the actions of celestial beings sending essential energy into the womb, depositing the energy into the head of the embryo. This energy shaped a person's character and destiny. Young infants and children were placed near the fire and eventually in the sun to acquire more *tonalli*. It was also present in animals, plants, and other objects.

As evidenced in the creation myth, the Sun and its warmth influenced all aspects of life, and it was also the primary source of energy for the *tonalli*. The very nature of *tonalli* was shifting and fragmented. It could be gained or lost through almost any interaction, especially with people such as family members or others with whom one had intimate contact. Other areas of the body where this energy resided were the hair, especially that found near the front area of the head (*piochtli*), and the fingernails. The hair in particular was thought to be the recipient of power and that it protected and prevented *tonalli* from escaping the body. Warriors captured their enemies by the hair to take their *tonalli* and increase their own. There was no greater prize in battle than the decapitated head of the enemy. This idea was often depicted in Aztec art and drawings.

Some present-day indigenous groups believe that *tonalli* is vulnerable to shocks and that they can get a disease known in Spanish as a *susto* or *espanto* (fright). Even the simple act of a person snapping their photograph or a hit or being scared by a surprise can cause them to lose their *tonalli*. Modern markets are filled with a variety of herbal remedies, and local healers offer spiritual treatments for *susto* called *limpias* (cleansings), which are intended to bring back the lost *tonalli*.

The *tonalli* remained near the body for four days after death in an attempt to retrieve all of the pieces of itself on Earth. Its journey after death also consisted of wandering about collecting its scattered portions. It was believed that the ritual burning of effigies on the anniversary of death for four years offered the deceased yet another opportunity for the individual to attract and recover even more fragments of *tonalli* left on Earth. Survivors of the deceased were to keep a part of their deceased's *tonalli* in the vessel that held his or her ashes and the locks of hair from birth and death.

The *Teyolia*

The *teyolia* resided in the heart and was inseparable from the living body. It was considered the "divine fire" that animated humans, providing vigor and shape to a person's emotions and thought processes. It held a person's affections and vitality and represented their social nature. It was believed that a person could increase the quantity of this energy by performing extraordinary acts in war, art, government, and/or other social expressions. Priests, artists, and the men and women who impersonated deities during festivals were considered to be living transmitters of *teyolia*, a gift of good energy to the community.

It is also interesting to note that the *teyolia* was also believed to reside in any place that was perceived to have a "heart center," such as cities, mountains, lakes, plants, people, and any objects that held power. The power of the *teyolia* was such that if the head of a household took ill and was near death, the grain seeds of the house were removed so that they would not die with him.

Upon death, the *teyolia* did not immediately leave the body. Like the *tonalli*, it lingered for four days, suggesting that the center of a person's consciousness remained near the cadaver. During this time, it was possible for priests or relatives to communicate with the deceased. The *teyolia* remained for another four days before it began its journey to Mictlan or traveled to the "sky of the Sun," where it was transformed into birds. This corresponded with the belief that in offering human hearts through sacrifices, the Aztec increased the supply of energy procured to the sun gods.

The *Ihiyotl*

This soul was the part of the person caught between two worlds. It represented the air in the body and occupied the area of the liver or stomach. The power of the *ihiyotl* was found in bodily air, both that which one breathes and that which it expels as gas. It signified both the control over one's emotions and the final gasp of life's last breath. The *ihiyotl* held passion, luminous gas, and aggression.

The *ihiyotl* was thought to be a forceful, invisible energy source that could cast spells and attract other human beings. Transmitted through a person's breath or by the air produced by waving their hand, the *ihiyotl* had the power to enchant and bring health or cause damage to human life, plants, animals, and events.

The sum of these three souls gave the human body extraordinary value, vulnerability, and power and demonstrated in great detail how human beings held within them the celestial forces of the gods that created and ruled them. This was a principle of Aztec cosmology. The body was a sacred receptacle filled with the powers of gods.

Despite the separation caused by death, the Aztec believed that demise was not the ultimate experience of a soul. In fact, it is more probable that much like the cosmos and plant life, the soul, and therefore life, regenerates. However, it is conceivable that early Spanish chroniclers recorded and interpreted Aztec rituals and texts in a manner that conformed to Christian dogmas in order to facilitate the process of evangelization.

HUMAN SACRIFICE

Perhaps considered the most gruesome and violent aspect of the Aztec civilization, and certainly one of the most misinterpreted aspects, ritual human sacrifice had a place of honor and duty in Aztec cosmovision. It was a payment of debt (*tlaxtlaualiztli*) long ago owed to their astral rulers, a blood sacrifice (*nextlaualli*). Most indigenous cultures practiced a way of life that was efficient, not wasteful. Similarly, human sacrifice, in the vision of the Aztec people, was not a gratuitous act of killing; it was purposeful to the degree that they believed it to sustain their very existence.

Understanding the Aztec myth of creation in Aztec cosmology explains the prominence of human sacrifice in Aztec culture, because it emphasizes the indebtedness and interdependence that the Aztec felt toward their gods—a fundamental doctrine. According to Aztec beliefs, human sacrifice was not a frivolous act of cruelty, nor did it stem from a narcissistic need to exert power over other peoples (although captives were often those sacrificed). It was, in fact, a ritual of survival that ensured their existence by nourishing their gods in acknowledgement of the sacrifices made by the gods themselves. As the gods had sacrificed themselves to create the world and human beings, then humans needed to give thanks to them with the most precious substance they had, their own blood (the essence of life).

Scholars caution that analyzing human sacrifice requires bearing in mind some of the concepts discussed in describing the soul, primarily that the human body contained the natural and sacred forces of the world and that the heart held cosmic power renewable through nature. Aztec existence and religion were results of the work of the gods, both creative and destructive, and the Aztec lived in debt to them for their existence. Finally, this notion of reciprocity made it necessary to seek out potential sources of *chalchiuatl* (the precious water) through *xochimiquiztli*, meaning "flowery death."

An underlying fear that everything would cease to exist—the Sun would stop shining and moving across the sky, and life would come to a halting end—if the gods did not receive an adequate amount of human blood impelled the Aztec to war. Blood nourished and fortified the gods and, in particular, the Sun. It was the ultimate sacrifice to the gods. Great warriors met this fate with honor despite being offered clemency and the opportunity to live with great riches and power. It was understood to be their honorable destiny, and living otherwise would be cowardly, as was recorded by early chroniclers Sahagún and Durán. The need to pay this debt was also a main reason for war (see chapter 6).

A variety of sources indicate a fundamental Aztec belief that envisioned a shared cosmic energy between all living things—plants, animals, humans, and gods—that need to be exchanged regularly. This energy was transported from humans to the gods through various forms of sacrifice, human and otherwise. The gods returned it in the form of light and warmth (from the Sun), water, and food, especially maize. The Sun was the supreme recipient in this exchange of energy, for the Sun provided the key elements to the sustenance of life.

Sacrifice was also seen as a primary means of atonement for moral transgressions. Sacrificial cere-monies were complex affairs that required methodical preparation of the participants and specialized priests that were highly regarded by the Aztec. Those sacrificed included warriors, captives, slaves, children (sacrificed to Tlaloc), noblewomen, and certain criminals. Most sacrifices were conducted on a sacrificial stone called a *techcatl* at a temple or other sacred place with an obsidian knife, or *tecpatl*, used to remove the heart. Before the sacrifice took place, a series of rituals were performed.

The preceding rituals began with an overnight vigil. Next, hair was cut from the crown of the head, where the *tonalli* was found. The sacrificial priests were thereby taking away a person's power by cutting off his or her hair. The individuals were then bathed and dressed in the traditional attire of the god or goddess in whose name they were going to be sacrificed. In the next phase, the victims were treated as if they were the gods themselves and lived in a manner befitting this god for a period of time that could be as long as a year. The following step included painting those to be sacrificed in white. In the next to last rite, all of their personal belongings were burned. Finally, ritual dances were performed.

The sacrifice could include first the roasting of some victims followed by a ritual battle. Ritual death by sacrifice occurred in the following forms: extraction of the heart (*tlacamictiliztli*), decapitation, riddling with arrows (*tlacacaliztli*), rolling off the apex of a pyramid, by an arrow to the throat, being put in a cave and buried alive, drowning, gladiatorial sacrifice (*tlahuahuanaliztli*), and being flayed (see figure 6.7).

The sacrifice ended with another sequence of rituals. First, an effigy was offered nourishment, then the bodies of the victims were thrown down a stairway. Next, the heads of *ixiptla* (god impersonators) were cut off and placed on the *tzompantli* (skull racks). Some victims were then skinned and used to dress *xixipeme* (warriors who wore their captives' skins, emulating the god Xipe Totec). After this, the bodies were offered to the ritual priests.

Bodies of the sacrificed were prepared and cooked under very strict procedures and shared in a banquet. This cannibalistic event was a deeply religious and spiritual occasion where family and relatives were invited and honored. It was a time for socializing with distinguished members of the community and for increasing one's prestige. In fact, a family's entire harvest or earnings could be spent at this celebration. This was done with the belief that it was actually the gods partaking of the sacrificial victim through their human manifestations and was therefore an opportunity to commune with the gods. A theory regarding Aztec human sacrifice and cannibalism had argued that the Aztec diet lacked sufficient sources of protein; however, it has been long since refuted that cannibalism in Aztec ritual was primarily viewed as a necessity for feeding the gods to renew their energy, not a gastronomic requirement of humans. The Aztec in fact had an abundance of sources of protein in their diet. In other words, Aztec participation in human sacrifice and cannibalism was a rite practiced to commune with gods, families, and fellow citizens. It interestingly had certain parallels with the symbolic ingestion of the flesh and blood of Jesus Christ that Catholics practice in their Communion ritual.

In some cases, sacrificial offerings required the performance of ritual dances with the skulls of the sacrificed captives. And finally, some of the bodies were buried.

When captured warriors or effigies of the gods or their human representatives (*ixiptla*), usually slaves, were sacrificed, the process began with a ritual bath intended to cleanse and purify the individual. The *ixiptla* was a key aspect of human sacrifice. Those chosen to impersonate a god were prepared for as long as a year in advance. For the entire period leading up to the sacrifice, the *ixiptla* lived as a god would, with all the luxury and perks of a supreme being. Most *ixiptla* were enemy warriors captured in battle. When fighting, all warriors made an effort to kill as few opposing warriors as possible so as to return with a number of captives for sacrificial ceremonies.

It was believed that sacrificed individuals became the gods, only to be reborn stronger and revitalized. Death by sacrifice was also believed to be another way to exist after death by living in the house of the Sun.

Sacrifices were conducted through most of the year during the festival cycles designated in the sun calendar and the 260-day calendar. These often commemorated the anniversaries of the gods. The ninth month in the Aztec calendar was dedicated to Miccailhuitontli, or "little feast of the dead." The 10th month was the celebration of Huey Miccailhuitl, or "great feast of the dead."

There were other purposes for sacrifices as well. Some were performed to sustain the strength of important structures such as pyramids or other spiritual buildings. A dignitary's or nobleman's slaves or other servants were sacrificed to accompany and assist them in the underworld, as they did in the living world. Finally, there also were messengers who were sacrificed to send messages to the citizens of the underworld that were either relatives or gods.

Another common form of sacrifice was autosacrifice. This involved the use of a maguey thorn or another sharp instrument to pierce one's earlobes, thighs, arm, tongue, or genitals in order to offer blood to the gods. Some, such as priests, practiced this ritual daily.

Sacrifice, and the blood that poured from it, ensured that the Aztec would continue to have access to the necessary elements—sun, water, earth, and air—and all the fruits resulting from these. It was another expression of the idea that life energy was dynamic and mutable. It was in constant motion, traveling between the gods and the living—people, animals, and plants.

Conclusion

The vast landscape of the Aztec world is vibrant and dynamic. In an attempt to understand the world they were privileged to inhabit, they contemplated the purpose of death obsessively. What they concluded was based on cosmic principles of duality and reciprocal energy. The creators and gods provided them energy sources for life, and the Aztec people reciprocated with nourishment in the form of blood sacrifice.

Death was inevitable and necessary although painful and daunting. Through it, the Aztec found a way to guarantee that they would survive as a people for generations to come. Life and death were in fact two facets of the same energy and inextricably linked to their survival. It was experienced most dramatically with the rise of the Sun every morning and its setting every evening and in their yearly harvests both at the point of sowing seeds and at the time of reaping crops.

The Aztec also pondered deeply thoughts about the afterlife. Aztec understanding of death was not linear or one dimensional. Death was in the purview of all living things, and each level had its distinct purpose and relationship with the gods.

Historian Alfredo López Austin captures best Aztec views about death: "The living and the dead labored on different sides of the same field, some visible and others invisible" (1988: 315–336). The energy that created human beings did not obliterate them entirely from Earth; it just changed their form and allowed them to exist in another manifestation, equally alive.

READING

Creation Myths and Concepts about Death

Aguilar-Moreno, 2002, Caso 1982, Carrasco 1998, Soustelle 1979, León-Portilla 1970: creation mythology.

Funerary Places of Destination

Aguilar-Moreno 1996, 2002, Brundage 1985, Carrasco 1998, Clendinnen, 1991, Johansson 2003, Read 2002, Sahagún 1975, Smith 2003, Soustelle 1979: death/afterlife.

Burials and Cremation

Biart 1887, Sahagún 1975, Quiñones-Keber 2002: burials.

Souls

Carrasco 1998, López-Austin 1988: souls.

Human Sacrifice

Durán 1994, González Torres 1991: ritual festivals (calendar); Carrasco 1998, González Torres 2003, Graulich 2003: human sacrifice; Quiñones-Keber 2002, León-Portilla 1963: philosophy.

8

AZTEC ART

A primary function of Aztec art was to express religious and mythical concepts that would legitimize the power of the state. This artistic language spoke predominantly through the form of iconographic symbols and metaphors. The image of the eagle symbolized the warrior and the Sun at its zenith. Images of serpents were linked to the gods Tlaloc and Huitzilopochtli, and thus these gods were represented as water or fire serpents, respectively. Representations of frogs as aquatic beings were also reminiscent of Tlaloc. The conch shell was related to fertility, life, and creation. As indicated by anthropologist Doris Heyden and architect Luis Francisco Villaseñor, sculpture served as communication through visual metaphors, which were realized with a purity of techniques that allowed for refinement of detail.

It is unwise and misleading for modern Western scholars to label most forms of Aztec expression as fine art. Archaeologist George Vaillant points out that the Aztec, like many ancient non-Western civilizations, did not have a word to describe fine art, did not argue over questions of aesthetics, and did not create objects to be observed for their own sake. Instead, they created objects intended to serve a well-defined function—to indoctrinate standard religious, political, and military imperatives. Understanding the artistic principles of the pre-Hispanic indigenous past is difficult given our own cultural biases and our own definitions of an artistic world. But it is easy to recognize that the Mexica appreciated beauty in terms of their own culturally dictated standards.

AZTEC ARTISTS AND CRAFTSMEN

Though historians and European chroniclers found reasons to document information describing the daily life of emperors, members of the imperial family, and warriors, there is little information about the day-to-day life of Aztec artisans and craftsmen, despite the fact that artists at Tenochtitlan and other Aztec cities constituted a large sector with its own quarters and organizations. In the Aztec hierarchy, artisans were *macehualtin* who were immediately below the *pochtecah* (long-distance merchants), although in some respects they were affiliated to the *pipiltin*. Not so much is known about the guilds of the quarrymen or salters, who are sometimes mentioned in ethnohistorical sources without much detail. The only groups of artisans that were much taken into account were those associated with the decorative arts: the goldsmiths, the jewelers, and the *amanteca* (feather workers). They used various tools of stone, copper, and wood and wet sand for the abrasion of jade and crystal. Ethnohistorian Jacques Soustelle states that gold (*teocuitlatl*), silver, amber, crystal, pearl, and amethyst were popular materials for creating rich jewel, and vibrantly dyed feathers decorated fine clothing.

According to Soustelle, these craftspeople were named *tolteca* after the Toltec civilization to which the origins of their artwork was traditionally ascribed. The Aztec venerated the Toltec as their forefathers over the centuries.

Tolteca

Initially, the Aztec were a nomadic tribe, the Mexica, with no craftsmen or artists that arrived in the Valley of Mexico in the year 1325. Over time they came to dominate the citizens of small settlements, such as Colhuacan and Xochimilco, that preserved the ancient art traditions of Tula after the fall of the Toltec capital, along with its language and customs. According to Bernardino de Sahagún, the Toltec had been very skilled artisans, so to be referred to as a *tolteca*, or Toltec, was an honor for Aztec artisans and served as a reminder that as craftsmen they were members of the artistic traditions of a golden era. Aztec craftsmen were inspired by their Toltec ancestors, who created magnificent feather mosaics, worked gold and other precious metals, and carved stone to create monumental sculptures for their kings and gods.

SOCIAL STATUS AND WORK CONDITIONS

As Aztec rulers expanded the political boundaries under their control, reaching even the remote tropical regions, wealth began to accumulate rapidly, and artisans grew in social status as they became more in demand. The *tolteca* enjoyed certain privileges that other commoners did not have; however, most artisans did not rise from their own stations to any positions of considerable power, and so they maintained peaceful relationships with the ruling class. Presumably artists, given their unique talents, preferred to stay in their positions where they were respected and admired for their abilities.

Artisans who worked directly for an Aztec ruler performed their jobs either inside the palace or in their own homes, where raw materials such as stones, feathers, or precious metals could be sent. But they did not work alone. Interestingly, the artist's workshop witnessed the entire family's participation. Each family member worked in prescribed roles to complete pieces: For example, the wife of an artist might weave blankets of rabbit hair, dye feathers, or embroider clothing, depending on the particular art created by her husband. Children in such households would learn and inherit the artistic traditions of their parents.

Accounts regarding an artist's salary are rare. One account reveals that artisans were well paid for their work. For a stone sculpture of Motecuhzoma II executed by 14 sculptors, each artist was paid an advance of clothing for his wife and himself, cotton, 10 loads of calabashes, and maize. After the work was completed, they were each given two servants, cocoa, crockery, salt, and more clothing. Although artists may have been given good compensation, they were also taxed; however, they were not required to give personal service or any agricultural labor. And if legal disputes arose, the *tolteca* had chiefs who represented them before the authority of the law.

MONUMENTAL STONE SCULPTURE

Aztec sculpture was not the result of random inspiration but a monumental synthesis of religious and cultural concepts. An important characteristic of Aztec sculpture is the abstraction of whole images that retain realistic, concrete details. Sculptures represented their myths, dreams, and illusions of life and death. Monumentality was another important trend in Aztec sculpting. However, monumental art was not just the representation of something massive and enormous; it was the visual symbol of force of an idea, simply executed and manifested in the relationship between dimensions. Aztec monumentality awed and frightened the spectator and imposed a manipulated impression of power that the state invested in all Aztec art.

Ocelotl-Cuauhxicalli

The *cuauhxicalli* was used to store the hearts of sacrificed victims; some of these vessels were sculpted in the form of animals, such as the jaguar (*ocelotl*). On the inside bottom of the colossal Ocelotl-Cuauhxicalli, two figures with striped bodies and skeletal jaws are piercing their ears with sharp bones (see figure 8.1). The rim of the vessel is composed of concentric circles conveying jades with eagle feathers. In a general sense, the Ocelotl-Cuauhxicalli is a monument dedicated to the underworld, the Earth, and the deified kings of the past.

According to art historian Esther Pasztory, the great power of the jaguar is shown in this vessel, yet without its grace and swiftness, creating a somber version of an otherwise vivacious animal (1983: 172). As a vessel related to the act of sacrifice and death, the jaguar represents the god of the Earth, where the corpse would be buried, and the underworld, where the soul of the dead would travel. The image of the *ocelotl*, or jaguar, stands for the Earth receiving sacrificial offerings. Jaguars were also icons of royalty and status symbols. Rulers wore jaguar skins and were associated with the feline. Artists might have witnessed the jaguar firsthand in the zoos of Motecuhzoma II and prior *tlatoque*.

The two skeletal figures inside the vessel probably indicate the importance of ancestry to the Mexica people. They are shown with the smoking mirror foot of Tezcatlipoca, god of the many forms and protector of warriors, who possibly represents dead kings of past civilizations disguised as deities. They also extract blood from their ears utilizing bloodletting implements similar to the ones used in the penitential rituals performed by the Aztec kings,

8.1 The Ocelotl-Cuauhxicalli was a jaguar-shaped receptacle for hearts of the sacrificed, Museum of Anthropology, Mexico City. (Fernando González y González)

another sign that they are symbols of ancestry. As Pasztory points out, ultimately, the vessel, commissioned by Motecuhzoma II, links his own reign with the gods of the past (1983: 172).

Cuauhtli-Cuauhxicalli

The Cuauhtli-Cuauhxicalli, like the Ocelotl-Cuauhxicalli, was sculpted in the form of an animal—the eagle (*cuauhtli*). The circular hole in the back of the figure indicates that it served as a *cuauhxicalli*. According to Eduardo Matos Moctezuma and Felipe Solís Olguín, the Cuauhtli-Cuauhxicalli stored the hearts and blood of the sacrificed victims so that the deities, descending from the heavens, could feed themselves on the offerings (2002: 462).

Under the Aztec, the *cuauhtli* symbolized both the Sun and a strong warrior who fought the powers of the night under the direction of his patron deity Huitzilopochtli, the god of war. The eagle was responsible for feeding the Sun with the hearts and blood of the sacrificed victims, which gave the Sun its energy to make its daily journey across the sky. This vessel points to a vital belief encompassed in the Aztec worldview—that life and death are joined. Death must occur so that life can exist, making human sacrifice a necessary component in ensuring the survival of both the Sun and the universe, and consequently, human life.

This offering vessel is a magnificent example of the fine artistry of the Aztec sculptor. Sculpted as if the artist wanted to imitate in stone the real bird, the eagle eye is surrounded by delicate feathers while

8.2 The Cuauhtli-Cuauhxicalli was an eagle-shaped receptacle for hearts of the sacrificed, Museum of Anthropology, Mexico City. (Fernando González y González)

the tail is made of longer feathers that fall vertically. The details of the vessel are rich in texture and form.

The Sun Stone

Carved in the late Postclassic period, in 1479, or the year 13 Acatl during the reign of Axayacatl, this very elaborate monument to the Sun in its many manifestations is also known as the Calendar Stone and the Aztec Calendar, although in reality it was never used as a calendar. The stone represents human sacrifice related to the cult of Tonatiuh, the sun god (see chapter 6).

At the center of the Sun Stone, the wrinkled face of a blond-haired Tonatiuh is depicted with his tongue ravenously hanging from his mouth in the shape of an obsidian sacrificial knife (*tecpatl*). (Some scholars think that the deity is actually Tlaltecuhtli, the night sun of the underworld.) His wrinkles indicate his old age, and his blond hair (as described in indigenous chronicles) associates him with the golden Sun. But it is his tongue that so graphically links him to human sacrifice and blood.

Tonatiuh is surrounded by the symbol Nahui Ollin (4 Movement), the date on which the current sun of motion (the fifth sun) was created in Teotihuacan (see

chapter 6). In the four flanges of the Ollin sign appear the names of the four previous creations: 4 Jaguar, 4 Wind, 4 Rain, and 4 Water. Adjacent to the flanges, the four directions or cardinal points of the universe are represented like a cosmological map. The north is a warrior's headdress, which symbolizes the military power of the Mexica and their growing empire. The south is a monkey and represents a part of one of the previous suns or ages in the myth of creation. The east is a *tecpatl*, representing human sacrifice. The west is Tlalocan, the house of the rain god Tlaloc, and symbolizes water, essential for human survival.

In the next outer circle are shown the 20 days of the month. The solar calendar was composed of 18 periods of 20 days, plus five days called *nemontemi* (useless and nameless). Starting from the position of the symbol of the north and heading clockwise, the Nahuatl names of the months correspond to the figure carved in each box that form the circle. In order, they are Cipactli (crocodile), Ehecatl (wind), Calli (house), Cuetzpallin (lizard), Coatl (serpent), Miquiztli (death), Mazatl (deer), Tochtli (rabbit), Atl (water), Itzcuitli (dog), Ozomatli (monkey), Malinalli (plant, grass), Acatl (reed), Ocelotl (jaguar), Cuauhtli (eagle), Cozcacuauhtli (vulture), Ollin (movement), Tecpatl (flint or obsidian), Quiahuitl (rain), and Xochitl (flower). Out of this circle, eight

8.3 The Sun Stone (Aztec Calendar) represented the creation of the fifth sun, or the sun of movement, Museum of Anthropology, Mexico City. (Fernando González y González)

arrowheads symbolizing the Sun's rays scattering throughout the universe point in all directions.

The outermost circle depicts the bodies of two fire serpents that encompass the Sun Stone. These serpents symbolize the connection between the upper and lower worlds and work like an *axis mundi* (the crosspoint) uniting the two opposite worlds. Their opened mouths at the bottom represent the underworld. Two heads emerge from their opened mouths: Quetzalcoatl, personified as Tonatiuh (the Sun) on the right, and Tezcatlipoca, personified as Xiuhtecuhtli (the night) on the left. These two gods have their tongues out touching each other, representing the continuity of time. This interaction symbolizes the everyday struggle of the gods for supremacy on Earth and in the heavens with the rising and setting of the sun, which are always in contact (see also chapter 11).

The Sun Stone symbolizes the creation of the fifth sun and acts as a celebration for the creation of the world where the forces of creation and destruction play equal roles. The iconography also suggests that the Sun Stone is a testament to Aztec victory; for example, the glyph above 1 Flint states the day on which the Aztec began their migration from their original homeland of Aztlan (see chapter 2). According to Pasztory, this date was historically important; in that year, 1428, the Aztec defeated the Tepanec and became the new rulers of the Valley of Mexico. In that context, the Sun Stone supports the belief that the reign of the Aztec Empire was to be a new era in Mesoamerica.

The Stone of Tizoc

The Stone of Tizoc depicts the victories of Tizoc, the emperor during 1481–86, and is a masterpiece of intricate stone carving. Pasztory states that the monumental Stone of Tizoc is the first of its kind that was dated and associated to a known Aztec king. In 1988, a similar stone dedicated to King Motecuhzoma I was discovered. These stones, called *temalacatl*, were very probably used for gladiatorial sacrifices of important captured warriors (see chapters 6 and 7). The cavities that they each have in the middle of a solar disc suggest that they were also used as *cuauhxicalli*, vessels where the hearts of the sacrificed victims were deposited.

8.4 *The Stone of Tizoc was a* temalacatl-cuauhxicalli, *a monumental stone that commemorated Aztec conquests and was used for gladiatorial sacrifices, Museum of Anthropology, Mexico City.* (Fernando González y González)

8.5 A temalacatl-cuauhxicalli *dedicated to the emperor Motecuhzoma I and showing him in the capture of enemies, Museum of Anthropology, Mexico City*
(Fernando González y González)

In the Stone of Tizoc, the king, portrayed here in the guise of the god Tezcatlipoca, and his conquests are glorified in stone. He is identified by his glyph, the symbol for "leg." At the top of the cylinder is a sun disk with eight rays. Next to the cylinder, a sky border decorates the upper part, and a register conveying the maw of the earth monster borders the bottom. The frieze between the two borders portrays 15 Aztec warriors holding captive victims by the hair. Each of the 15 conquering warriors wears a smoking mirror in his headdress, the symbol of Tezcatlipoca, the god of shape-shifting and protector of warriors.

Only one of the 15 warriors is identified as Tizoc; he is the only warrior wearing the hummingbird helmet of the god Huitzilopochtli. The rest might have been captains under his rule. Pasztory states that the Aztec had 15 lords of 15 city districts, referred to as the *calpulli*, and the number 15 possibly symbolizes the Mexica's political and military divisions led by Tizoc (1983: 147–151). The captives represent their rulers since they combine human and divine attributes by dressing as their city's principal deities. Two female figures present are associated with the female patron deities of Colhuacan and Xochimilco. It was a tradition of the Aztec to take some of the local idols of a conquered city and bring them to a special temple in Tenochitlan. The stone suggests that these events take place in the human realm and the divine realm, in which historical emperors conquer specific towns while the deities ensure success or failure.

According to Pasztory, some of the conquests that appear on the sculpture are attributed not to Tizoc, but to his forefathers (1983: 150). The glyphs associated with the captured towns suggest that they stand for major Aztec conquests up to the time of Tizoc, or they might belong to some ethnic groups rather than cities. The *Codex Mendoza* attributes 14 conquests to Tizoc, but the monument probably commemorates the conquests of the Aztec expansion embodied by the *tlatoani* Tizoc.

The Stone of Tizoc was inspired by Mixtec-Puebla manuscript painting, as evidenced by the similarity of the sun disk border and the earth monster border to images in Mixtec-Puebla documents. In addition, each of the captives is identified by his own glyphs, which indicates that each is identified in the tradition of the Mixtec-Puebla historical codices. The stone also shows that the Aztec were deliberately imitating Toltec models by making their own imperial art. Reference to Toltec models is limited only to clothing details of the warriors, who wear a butterfly chest ornament like those worn by the Atlantes of Tula (see chapter 1). However, the use of a historical image in a cosmic setting to decorate a ritual object is especially Aztec in origin, and the patron gods of the Aztec are more emphasized in the stone.

The stone as a whole represents the Aztec Empire, originated by conquest, and the commemoration of Tizoc's reign. It is interesting to notice that the glyph next to Tizoc's prisoner is that of his first campaign, Matlatlan (see chapter 5). Ironically,

8.6 Detail of the Stone of Tizoc, showing him capturing warriors, Museum of Anthropology, Mexico City
(Fernando González y González)

Tizoc was militarily the most unsuccessful Mexica leader, and his very first campaign in Matlatlan was a total disaster; the monument amounts to political propaganda to glorify Aztec power. Tizoc is better known for his major contributions to architecture, not war. The stone was probably going to belong to his new monumental architectural project that implicated the rebuilding of many of the temples of the Sacred Precinct of Tenochtitlan (see chapter 9).

Dedication Stone

This skillfully carved greenstone plaque was made in commemoration of the completion of the Temple of Huitzilopochtli at Tenochtlan in the year 8 Reed, or 1487. Where this panel was located originally is still unknown, but relief panels with dates, such as this one, were usually set into architecture such as stairways and pyramid platforms. Very similar stones have been found in the Great Temple of Tenochtitlan, and this plaque was probably a part of those.

In the lower half of the stone, the glyph 8 Reed is carved in an abstract design with double outlines. The upper half of the stone is similar to the carvings in the Bench Relief (see next page) and the Stone of Tizoc. In the plaque, the rulers Ahuitzotl and Tizoc are dressed up as priests. They hold incense bags and are piercing their ears with a bone. Tizoc was in power between 1481 and 1486, and his brother Ahuitzotl succeeded him and ruled from 1486 to 1502 (see chapter 4). Blood is flowing from their heads into an incense burner and is represented as a serpent into the maw of the earth monster border. Between the two emperors, there is a grass ball of sacrifice, or *zacatapayolli*, with the bone piercers or maguey thorns used for autosacrifice stuck in it. Also, streams of blood are flowing from the wounds in each of their legs. Both *tlatoque* are identified by their own glyphs: Tizoc by his "bleeding leg" glyph and Ahuitzotl by the water being with a curly tail. The two kings appear in profile, with their heads and legs pointing sideways, while their torsos appear in a full frontal view. They are barefoot, which is a symbol of divinity. Above the two men, the date 7 Reed appears, the meaning of which is unclear.

This stone depicts an act of devotion. According to Matos Moctezuma and Solís Olguín, the Aztec

8.7 A dedication stone of Emperors Tizoc and Ahuitzotl relating to an expansion of the Great Temple (Lluvia Arras)

believed that humans could achieve immortality by their good actions, such as devotion acts performed for the gods. Expanding the Great Temple of Tenochtitlan, dedicated to the patron Mexica gods Huitzilopochtli and Tlaloc, was the duty of every *tlatoani*. This plaque reveals the same sentiment. Tizoc began expanding the Great Temple, and his brother Ahuitzotl finished the project. Also, both emperors are performing an act of sacrifice, which involves the offering of maguey thorns or bone piercers covered with their own blood and inserted in a *zacatapayolli* to Mother Earth.

Stone of the Warriors

Discovered in 1897 near the main square in Mexico City, the Stone of the Warriors is full of reliefs of warriors in procession, holding their weapons. As

Aztec Empire's mighty power and strength (1983: 146–147).

On top of the sculpture, the earth monster image (either Tlaltecuhtli or Itzpapalotl) is carved, symbolizing the devourer of human blood and hearts. The Earth covers the physical bodies of the dead and feeds on them, and it requires the sacred liquid of blood to be in balance with the universe.

The Stone of the Warriors probably served at one time as an altar or a throne. The depression in the center was made during the colonial period.

8.8 Stone of the Warriors, Museum of Anthropology, Mexico City (Fernando González y González)

described by Pasztory, the soldiers approach a symbol of sacrifice fully armed for battle, each wearing a different headdress; they approach the grass ball, or *zacatapayolli.* It is possible that a ruler at one time stood next to the grass ball, but time has abraded the stone, making it unclear. These 14 carved warriors may represent the city of Tenochtitlan and even the

Bench Relief

Until an early Chacmool sculpture was found, the Bench Relief was thought to be one of the earliest Aztec sculptures ever found. According to Pasztory, the Bench Relief is composed of 52 panels that were taken away and used to reconstruct buildings in Tenochtitlan (1983: 144–146). There is the important emblem depicted in the central stones of the monument, which show the grass ball of sacrifice stuck with

8.9 The Bench Relief, inspired by Toltec prototypes, shows a zacatapayolli *(ball of grass for inserting sacrificial piercers) and two high-ranking warriors, Museum of Anthropology, Mexico City.* (Fernando González y González)

thorns and human bones used to draw blood. Two warriors surround the *zacatapayolli*. These warriors belong to a high rank in Aztec society, as suggested by their clothing and headdresses, one with the turquoise diadem of a chief, another of feathers associated with a lord, and a two-feather headdress. The warriors are also carrying such weapons as spear-throwers (atlatls), spears, and shields.

All the images represent humans, except for the one on the left, which has a leg ending with a puff of smoke. According to Pasztory, the figure with the smoke leg is mixing human and divine features (1983: 165–168). The person with divine features is disguised as the god Tezcatlipoca, with the smoking mirror on his hair, and he is leading the other Aztec noble warriors to battle. The nose bar, as well as his turquoise diadem headdress, are symbols of royalty. The figure on the left might represent a king of Tenochtitlan, possibly Motecuhzoma I, who is praying, as suggested by the curled flower design in front of his face. If this is so, then the monument's date ranges between 1440 and 1469.

There are only a few traces of the stucco paint used to decorate the Bench Relief. The Aztec may have made an imitation, in this relief, of a Toltec bench relief, since it is closely similar to Toltec prototypes. The Toltec bench relief in the Burnt Palace in Tula also depicts a procession of warriors with feathered serpent borders. An Aztec trend in this relief is the grass ball of sacrifice in the center, serving as a penitential symbol and an emphasis on the image of the Aztec ruler.

Temple Stone

The Temple Stone, or the Teocalli (temple) of the Sacred War, as archaeologist Alfonso Caso calls it, is a commemoration to the New Fire ceremony of 1507, the sacred war, and the imperial power of the Mexica. It is composed of 16 images and six glyphs on both of its sides and forms the shape of an Aztec temple. A scene of a natural world with an eagle and a cactus on the back of the sculpture alludes to the founding of Tenochtitlan. According to the migration legend, the patron god Huitzilopochtli told them to build a settlement in the place where they would see an eagle landing on a cactus growing on a

lake (see chapters 2 and 6). When the Mexica saw the vision, they founded Tenochtitlan on Lake Tetzcoco.

On top of this colossal monument there is the date 2 House (1325), indicating that this was the date of the founding of the Aztec capital. The entire monument symbolizes the Aztec capital of Tenochtitlan rising from Lake Tetzcoco, and the monument itself mixes elements of a royal throne, a temple, and a year bundle (52-year period commemorating a New Fire ceremony). For the Aztec, the main temple of a city was its symbol, and in manuscripts, a burning temple represents that a city has been conquered. In Mesoamerica, temples were shaped in the form of pyramids symbolizing the mountains, where fertility and creation happens and where the wombs of creation are kept, which are the caves themselves. The Nahuatl word for "city" is *altepetl*, which literally means "water-mountain."

Some scholars suggest that the Temple Stone was in fact a royal throne of iconographical meaning. This monument was found in 1831 where Motecuhzoma II's palace had once stood, and it may have served as his symbolic or actual throne. The sculpture also is related to year bundles representing the 52 years of an Aztec "century." The year 2 Reed (glyph of the New Fire ceremony), 1 Flint, and 1 Death are represented in the stone sculpture. According to Pasztory, during important feasts, the year bundles were used as seats for the nobility, thus making the Temple Stone a royal throne, a symbol of the Aztec capital Tenochtitlan as a mountain pyramid, and the 52-year cycle in one (1983: 165). At the top of the stone there is a sun disk showing the glyph 4 Movement. The disk is flanked by a god or a priest dressed as the god Huitzilopochtli on the left and by Motecuhzoma II on the right. The sun disk symbolizes the Aztec dedication to a solar cult and a new era of their rule. Both god and human king carry sacrificial knives and bones for drawing blood. A *zacatapayolli* full of thorns to draw blood appears on top of the solar disk. In a sense, the Temple Stone is itself being crowned by an Aztec emperor and a patron deity, who are drawing sacrificial blood as a solar symbol for light, life, and time.

Opposing this image of life is the representation of death below the sun disk on top of the seat. Below the sun disk, lies the earth monster Tlaltecuhtli with a skull belt symbolizing the voracious power of the

Pasztory, when someone such as Motecuhzoma II sat in this royal throne, in a symbolical way he might have been resting on top of the Earth and the underworld, and on his back, he carried the Sun and the ancient past of the ancestors (1983: 168). Also, the glyph representing 1 Flint, next to Huitzilopochtli, is the mythical date in which the Aztec began their migration from Aztlan. Motecuhzoma II is glorifying his heritage and his ancestors by wearing a headdress of plumes tied to sticks. This was the headdress worn by the nomadic Chichimec ancestors of the Mexica. The Temple Stone embodies the concept of unbreakable continuity of Aztec and Toltec dominations, and the right of the Aztec to supersede the Toltec civilization by conquest, sacrificial death, and the divine guidance of Huitzilopochtli.

Portrait of Motecuhzoma II

Commissioned in the year 1519, when the *huey tlatoani* was 52 years old, this monumental portrait of Motecuhzoma II was carved in a cliff of Chapultepec

8.10 The Temple Stone, Museum of Anthropology, Mexico City (Fernando González y González)

Earth. Furthermore, the Tlaltecuhtli is flanked on the sides by weaponry such as shields, spears, and war banners, all of them representing emblems of war. The *cuauhxicalli* vessels, which are the earliest representation in a royal monument, are adorned with eagle feathers and jaguar spots, thus making them symbols of the Aztec warrior orders of the eagle and the jaguar. So, the sculpture is a monument to the sacred war in which the Mexica are conquering the Earth.

On two sides of the stone sculpture is a pair of seated images with skeletal jaws wearing triangular loincloths and feather headdresses, typical of Aztec warrior regalia. They may represent the ancestors of the Aztec, the ancient rulers prior to the Mexica conquest, or the Aztec deities, since the image on the left has the mustache and goggle eyes attributed to the rain god Tlaloc. Another figure has a royal diadem, and he is either a ruler or the fire god Xiuhtecuhtli. The Aztec associated Tlaloc and Xiuhtecuhtli with older civilizations, especially with the Toltec; they believed that Tlaloc was the patron god of the Toltec. The Aztec understood the importance of honoring their ancestors and sought to find their spiritual support for the empire. According to

8.11 Portrait of Emperor Motecuhzoma II carved in a stone on a cliff of Chapultepec in Mexico City (Fernando González y González)

(hill of the grasshopper), a sacred mountain shrine valued for its many freshwater springs. Chapultepec was important to the Aztec because it was the place where they first settled, chose their very first king, and made the first human sacrifice to bring blood and hearts to the deities. The Aztec emperors utilized this hill to make portraits of themselves carved in the rock.

According to Pasztory, the Aztec rulers wanted to erect portraits that would last longer than the images erected for the Toltec emperors (1983: 127–128). Perhaps in observance of the prophesies of his downfall, Motecuhzoma II wanted a permanent image of himself at a time close to the first news about the arrival of the Spanish explorers. Chapultepec was also a place that represented the royal Aztec ancestry, and it is said that the last Toltec ruler Huemac disappeared with all of his treasures into a cave in the hill. According to the postconquest Aztec chronicler Chimalpahin, Motecuhzoma was looking for Huemac's advice in dealing with the foreigners and a way to escape from them.

The monument was finished apparently in 30 days by 14 sculptors. Although the image is heavily damaged, it is clear that Motecuhzoma II is dressed in military costume shaped like Xipe Totec, the god of agriculture and fertility and the patron deity of the workers of precious metals (see chapter 6). At one time, the figure was life-size and very realistic, which was a characteristic in the sculpture court of Motecuhzoma II. He is identified by his glyph, the nose plug and royal headdress, and several dates refer to his reign: 2 Reed (1507) represents the New Fire ceremony, 1 Crocodile probably indicates the date of his coronation, and 1 Reed (1519) marks when the Europeans arrived in what was to become New Spain.

The Caracol

The Caracol, a spiral shell, was found in the Great Temple of Tenochtitlan. The sculpture shows the skill of the artists of the late Postclassic period

8.12 The Caracol, Museum of the Templo Mayor, Mexico City (Fernando González y González)

8.13 Tlaltecuhtli, the earth god, Museum of Anthropology, Mexico City (Manuel Aguilar-Moreno)

(1250–1521) in creating naturalistic figures related to symbolic metaphors. It was probably used as a musical instrument (*tecciztli*) in festivities and to announce the coming of a war. The spiral shell in general also became an emblem of the wind when it was cut transversally (*ehecailacacozcatl*). Surprisingly, the Caracol still shows the remains of the original stucco and blue paint that connect it to the Tlaloc shrine.

According to Matos Moctezuma and Solís Olguín, in the Aztec cosmovision, the universe was a layer of water that existed under the Earth, and the water was inhabited by fantastic animals such as the *cipactli*, or alligator. As an aspect of this watery domain, the conch shell was an important element in Aztec iconography as a symbol of fertility, life, and creation. In Mesoamerica, shells were associated with the god Tlaloc, the bringer of water and rain.

Spiral shell have been found next to altars, which indicates that shells might have been important for religious rituals, amulets, and offerings to Tlaloc.

Tlaltecuhtli

The external face of the base of this *cuauhxicalli* represents the earth monster Tlaltecuhtli. In this case, the earth god is depicted as a god diving into the soil with a fleshless mouth; two *chalchihuitl* (precious stones) decorate his cheeks, and a flint stone forms his ornamented knife-tongue. On his back he wears a skull. This monument represents the devouring power of the Earth, which needs the sacrifice of humans in order to maintain its life and to continue to provide fertility.

Tlaltecuhtli del Metro

According to Matos Moctezuma and Solís Olguín, this sculpture was found during the construction of a subway (*metro*) line in Mexico City, and because of its similarities to the statue of Coatlicue, it was initially thought to represent the goddess herself. Recent research, however, reveals the true identity of the sculpture: It is the earliest known depiction of Tlaltecuhtli, or Earth Lord, sculpted in the round (a sculpture given a three-dimensional shape that audiences can view by walking around the sculpture).

Tlaltecuhtli poses, crossed-legged with clawlike hands, as a devourer of human remains. He wears a necklace strung with human hearts and hands and an ornament at the back with a skull, a necklace similar to that of Coatlicue. His face is also similar to that in the center of the Sun Stone, which symbolizes a connection with Tlachi-Tonatiuh, or the Underground Sun. The Underground Sun was the nocturnal of the Sun's journey as it traveled around the world.

Matos Moctezuma and Solís Olguín suggest that this god represents the embodiment of Earth, which is the final place where the human remains rest (2002: 206). As such, this figure is also a monument for death and sacrifice, which are necessary to sustain life and persuade the gods to balance the world. According to Pasztory, the figure is an embodiment of the voracious force of the Earth that needs to be fed with sacrificial human victims (1983: 160–161).

Tlaltecuhtli del Metro shows the great skill achieved at carving in three dimensions during the reigns of Ahuitzotl and Motecuhzoma II.

Coatlicue

The masterpiece of Mesoamerican and Aztec stone sculpture is the spectacular representation of the goddess Coatlicue. Coatlicue (She of the Serpent Skirt) is the goddess of the Earth, a mother goddess; she is at the same time a deity of fertility and destruction, uniting the duality of life and death in an overwhelming and crushing vision.

Her statue is a sublime testament to the main principle of Aztec sculpture: abstraction of the whole and realism in detail. The figure in total represents the idea of the cosmic force that provides life

8.14 *Coatlicue, the earth and mother goddess, Museum of Anthropology, Mexico City* (Fernando González y González)

and renews itself in death; she is the cosmic-religious conception of the earth goddess in her two roles of womb and tomb (see chapter 6). By contrast, the details of the sculpture are realistic: Two serpent heads meet nose to nose to create a single impressive monstrous head; her hands resemble snakes, symbolizing the renovation of nature; interwoven serpents form her skirt and justify her name; a necklace is strung with hands, hearts, and the skull of a sacrificed victim; two breasts of an old woman hang from her chest, weary from an eternity of feeding all creatures; a thick serpent hangs between her legs forming a symbolized penis; the eyes and fangs that appear in her feet are monstrous maws that symbolize the devouring power of the Earth. There are two snakes forming her face that symbolize rivers of blood emerging from her decapitated neck. She stands as a sacrificed victim.

According to Pasztory, the colossal statue of Coatlicue represents the dual mind of the Aztec

(1983: 157–160). At the center of the figure there is a great contrast of opposing forces, in which the breasts are seen behind a skull, symbols of life and death. The sculpture is at the same time passive and active, monster and victim. Her arms are raised in a fearful gesture, and she wears a necklace of hand and heart trophies with skull pendants at the front and back.

The carving on the bottom of the sculpture is that of the god Tlaloc, bringer of water, in the earth-monster crouching position. Coatlicue is Huitzilopochtli's mother, making her the earth mother that gave birth to the Aztec (see chapter 6). Another possible identification of this magnificent work of art is that of Cihuacoatl, or Snake Woman, a goddess that embodies the voracious side of Earth. Cihuacoatl was the patron goddess of Colhuacan, a Toltec-related ruling dynastic community from which the emperors of Tenochtitlan claimed descent. Coatlicue is therefore the Aztec variant of Cihuacoatl, or the Toltec earth mother of the Mexica.

This colossal sculpture, one of the greatest surrealistic monuments in the world, should not be judged by traditional European artistic canons; its monstrous solemnity expresses the dramatic and dynamic energy of the cosmovision of a culture tragically destroyed. It can be said that the statue of Coatlicue is neither cruel nor good but simply the artistic manifestation of the Aztec reality of life and death, expressed in a monumental way. An almost identical sculpture known as Yollotlicue, because she wears a skirt of hearts instead of intertwined snakes, also exists.

8.15 *The Coatlicue of Coxcatlan, Museum of Anthropology, Mexico City* (Fernando González y González)

Coatlicue of Coxcatlan

This is another monument to Coatlicue, the mother of Huitzilopochtli. It was found in the town of Coxcatlan, in Puebla State. According to Matos Moctezuma and Solís Olguín, Coatlicue's serpent skirt, for which she is named, is a representation of the surface of the Earth, which the Mexica believed was composed of a network of serpents (2002: 463). Coatlicue represents the cycle of life and death. In this image, she is shown with clawlike hands raised in an aggressive position and with a skull-like head, claiming the bodies of human beings. She is the mother goddess of humankind and feeds the Sun

and the Moon; in reciprocity, she therefore needs human sacrifice. Her turquoise ornaments and inlays are still visible. The holes on her head were probably used to insert human hair, making the sculpture lifelike.

Cihuacoatl

This figure is a representation of Cihuacoatl, a powerful earth goddess who also represents fertility by giving life and keeping the souls of the dead (see chapter 6). Cihuacoatl means "woman serpent," which makes her a half-human, half-serpent deity. The divine being is shown as emerging from the maw of a snake with a long forked tongue that comes out of her mouth. Cihuacoatl is also related to Xochiquetzal, the goddess of flowers, and they are associated with the fertility of the feminine aspect of the cosmos.

The goddess Cihuacoatl also had a political significance, and her name was borrowed for the title of the official (prime minister) next in command after the *huey tlatoani*, the supreme Aztec ruler. The *cihua-coatl*'s job was primarily concerned with domestic affairs, while the *tlatoani* focused on war and foreign relations. Rulership was thus divided into two offices, with the *tlatoani* in the guise of the Mexica sun god Huitzilopochtli and the *cihuacoatl* in the guise of the Toltec earth mother. Pasztory suggests that this situation symbolizes a dual relationship that brings together opposing forces such as the old and the new, war and fertility, life and death, Mexica and Toltec, and conqueror and conquered (1983: 158).

Xiuhtecuhtli-Huitzilopochtli

The god represented in this monument is shown as a young man in ritual garb. His hands were probably made to hold weapons or banners; this figure is therefore also known as the Standard-Bearer. According to Matos Moctezuma and Solís Olguín, the figure is wearing the standard warrior clothing described as having a rectangular striped loincloth with a triangular cloth on top of it. He is also connected to the Sun, as represented by his sandals ornamented in the heels with solar rays and by a cape in the form of a tail of the *xiuhcoatl*, or "fire serpent." He is presented as a warrior ready for battle. His calendrical name, Nahui Cipactli (4 Alligator), is located on the back of his head. Also, his head is full of small holes for the insertion of hair to make the figure seem more realistic, and his eyes and teeth still have their original shell and obsidian inlays. It was found in Coxcatlan, in Puebla State.

Coyolxauhqui Relief

This great oval stone, once painted in bright colors, is an impressive example of the artistic heights reached by Mexica-Aztec artisans (see figure 8.18). It has a flat upper surface with the image of a dismembered goddess carved in low relief. She has been identified as the moon goddess Coyolxauhqui because of the symbols on her head: hair adorned with feathers, earplugs in the form of the fire god, and golden bells on her cheeks. Her face bears the band and rattles that identify her as Coyolxauhqui, or She of the Bells on the Cheeks. The goddess is depicted naked with large lactating breasts hanging out and folds in her belly. Her torso is surrounded by a rope belt threaded through a skull. Her behead-

8.16 Cihuacoatl, Snake Woman, a powerful earth and fertility goddess, Museum of Anthropology, Mexico City (Fernando González y González)

Some forms in the sculpture stand out for their realism, such as the modeled creases of the palms of the hands. Surprisingly, there are no glyphs made for this statue. Coyolxauhqui seems to be in a dynamic, almost running pose as if sculpted in the instant of her tumbling down Mt. Coatepec beheaded and dismembered.

The location where it was found offers another aspect of its meaning. The monument was placed at the base of the Great Temple in front of the shrine of Huitzilopochtli, with the head facing toward the stairway. It has been suggested that the sculpture might mark the conceptual center of Tenochtitlan, a point marked by sacrifice and conquest. This also may be the first image making reference to the myth of Huitzilopochtli as the main deity of the Aztec and his triumph on Coatepec, where he killed his sister Coyolxauhqui (see chapters 6 and 9). This relief monument must have been a frightening reminder to any visitor to Tenochtitlan of the sacrificial death awaiting those who were considered enemies of Huitzilopochtli and his people, the Aztec. Human sacrifice performed at the summit of the Great Temple was a ritual repetition of the execution of Coyolxauhqui, an eternal confirmation of Huitzilopochtli's power. In this way, art and architecture provided a setting for the reenactment of mythical-historical events.

8.17 Composite statue of the god Xiuhtecuhtli-Huitzilopochtli represented as a noble young man, Museum of Anthropology, Mexico City (Fernando González y González)

ing and dismembering confirms her role as goddess of the Moon, because those events are connected to femininity and the "mutilations" of the phases of the Moon.

The severed limbs arranged in a pinwheel manner indicate that she is dead. Her head is in profile and her body in a frontal view. This was an artistic device designed to show the entire body of the figure. Joints at her knees and elbows as well as her sandal heels have fanged monstrous masks. Such masks were usually related to earth monster figures.

8.18 Coyolxauhqui stone relief, showing the moon goddess dying at Mt. Coatepec, Museum of the Templo Mayor, Mexico City (Fernando González y González)

Head of Coyolxauhqui

This colossal head of Coyolxauhqui, goddess of the Moon, was the largest sculpture ever made using diorite, precious stone used in Mesoamerica. Figures of bells are carved on each of her cheeks, identifying her as Coyolxauhqui. The cross with four dots indicates that the bells are made of gold. According to Pasztory, the ornaments in her nose represent a day symbol, which is typical of the fire gods (1983: 152–153). The shells on top of her head are balls of down, which symbolize the sacrificial victims.

The head of the goddess is a complete work in itself; it is not a fragment of another statue. Underneath, it is carved with a relief of serpents intertwined in a river of water and fire (*atl-tlachinolli*), symbol of war, and a rope with plumes. As the goddess is decapitated, her head pours streams of blood represented by those serpents. This probably refers to a necessity to feed the gods with human sacrifices provided by warfare.

According to the legend, Coyolxauhqui was decapitated by her brother Huitzilopochtli for trying to kill Coatlicue, their mother (see chapter 6). The sculpture represents the death of the goddess and the founding of the Aztec capital Tenochtitlan under the

8.20 Xochipilli, the god of flowers and diversion, Museum of Anthropology, Mexico City (Fernando González y González)

guidance of Huitzilopochtli; the date 1 Reed is depicted in the figure, which is the date of the mythical creation of the world. This head was probably made for the dedication of the Great Temple in 1487; it is recorded that the king Ahuitzotl commissioned a figure of Coyolxauhqui for the temple.

8.19 Head of Coyolxauhqui, Museum of Anthropology, Mexico City (Fernando González y González)

Xochipilli

The picturesque town of Tlalmanalco, once part of the province of Chalco, is situated at the foot of the volcano Iztaccihuatl in the Valley of Mexico and was an important pre-Columbian religious center and a region famous for its artists. This sculpture suggests that the Chalco style had a high ornamental quality. According to the Spanish chronicler Fray Diego Durán, this region was a replica of Tlalocan, the exuberant paradise of Tlaloc at the lower slopes of the volcano Iztaccihuatl, which was considered the mountain of sustenance. Here was found a sculpture of Xochipilli, the Aztec god of flowers, music, dance, and feasting. Whether the statue depicts a priest wearing the mask of Xochipilli or the god himself is unclear.

The shallow and intricate floral reliefs on the body of Xochipilli show a pre-Columbian technique of flat and beveled carving. The flower ornaments that decorate the entire body of the figure determine the god's identification. On all sides of the pedestal of the monument are blossoming flowers with a butterfly drinking the nectar in the center, representing the blossoming of the universe.

The god is sitting with his legs crossed at the ankles in a tense position, but the organic and cylindrical form of the god's muscles makes him seem more alive and dynamic. The posture of Xochipilli suggests a shaman in a hypnotic trance of hallucinogenic ecstasy. He sits in shamanic flight to Tlalocan. The carvings on his knees and the pedestal bear the *teonanacatl*, a sacred hallucinogenic mushroom. In diverse parts of his body are representations of other hallucinogenic flowers.

Feathered Serpent

This sculpture portrays a snake in a coiled position with its jaw fully opened to reveal the sharpness of its teeth. It represents Quetzalcoatl, the Feathered Serpent, one of the most important gods in the Aztec pantheon. On top of the figure appears the date 1 Acatl, which is the year Quetzalcoatl promised to return to Earth before disappearing in the east. The Feathered Serpent gave humans the knowledge of agriculture and of art, fundamental for their survival and the development of their soul, and this piece pays homage to his role in fertility, renewal, and transformation.

Tlaltecuhtli, the god who devours human remains, is depicted at the bottom of the sculpture. His figure juxtaposed with the Feathered Serpent

8.21 *A coiled feathered serpent with the calendrical sign 1 Acatl, indicating the god Quetzalcoatl, Museum of Anthropology, Mexico City* (Fernando González y González)

signifies the green surface of the Earth covering the voracious underworld, making this a sculpture that celebrated the duality inherent in human endeavor: Fertility stands in contrast to the sacrificial death required to sustain life.

Xiuhcoatl

The colossal Xiuhcoatl with a daunting open jaw of fangs was found near the Ocelotl-Cuauhxicalli (see figure 8.22). Its size and modeling are similar to those of the jaguar vessel, and so the Xiuhcoatl sculpture is attributed to the reign of Motecuhzoma II, who held a New Fire ceremony in 1507. According to the myth of the birth of Huitzilopochtli, the Aztec patron god used the *xiuhcoatl* (plural, *xiuhcocoah*), which means "fire serpent," as a weapon to decapitate his sister Coyolxauhqui. The *xiuhcoatl* consequently became a national and political emblem.

According to Pasztory, through the serpent's fangs and open mouth curving back toward the top of the head, the sky was connected to the Earth, and the heavenly bodies traveled through the body of the creature (1983: 172–73). The *xiuhcocoah* carry the Sun in its daily cycle and represent its rays; understandably, they appear on the Sun Stone. They also symbolize the dry season in opposition to

important temple. This *chacmool* may represent one of the earliest examples of Aztec sculpture. According to Matos Moctezuma, the date of the figure may be 1375–1427 (1988: 38).

Besides being of importance for the Tlaloc temple, this figure is the first instance of an Aztec copy from the Toltec monumental arts. Pasztory asserts that the Aztec *chacmool* was influenced by Toltec art and represented Toltec ancestry, since Tlaloc is also associated with the Toltec *chacmool* (1983: 144). In some historical accounts, the rain god Tlaloc even gave approval to the Aztec to settle at Tenochtitlan. The Chacmool of the Tlaloc shrine is not as realistic as later Aztec carvings; it is angular and crudely finished, like its Toltec prototypes. Details were evidently painted rather than carved. The statue still preserves its original paint, including red, blue, white, black, and yellow.

The facial aspect of this statue is weathered by time, but it does not seem to represent a deity but rather, as in Toltec art, a dressed man holding a dish on his stomach. He is reclining in an uncomfortable position with raised knees while his head turns away from the temple by 90 degrees and looks over his shoulder to the horizon. It still is not known what this posture signified in either Toltec or Aztec art. A fan at the back of his neck symbolizes a fertility god.

8.22 Xiuhcoatl, Huitzilopochtli's "fire snake," Museum of Anthropology, Mexico City (Fernando González y González)

the Feathered Serpent (Quetzalcoatl), which represents the rainy, fertile season.

The Chacmool of the Tlaloc Shrine

The *chacmool*, a type of sculptural figure, has been found in various places of Mesoamerica, especially in the Toltec capital of Tula and the Maya city of Chichén Itzá. Mexica versions of the *chacmool* reproduce Toltec features, including the reclining posture and a receptacle, or vessel, on top of the stomach for offerings. *Chacmool*s are thought to be mediators between humans and the divine.

This monument displaying a reclining male figure was discovered during the 1979 excavations of the Great Temple of Tenochtitlan on the floor of the temple dedicated to Tlaloc. As in Chichén Itzá, this *chacmool* was set on the floor at the entrance of an

8.23 An early Aztec chacmool *found in the Tlaloc Shrine of the Great Temple* (Fernando González y González)

8.24 The Tlaloc-Chacmool, with attributes of the rain god, Museum of Anthropology, Mexico City (Fernando González y González)

Its location in the temple and the vessel it holds may suggest that the monument served as a sacrificial stone or a place to store offerings.

Tlaloc-Chacmool

This sculpture represents a reclining man wearing necklaces, a large feather headdress, bangles, and bracelets of jade, with gold and copper bells as attachments. According to Matos Moctezuma and Solís Olguín, it is also characterized by a mask over the mouth and the eyes, which connects the figure to Tlaloc (2002: 457). There are many indicators of a late date for this *chacmool*, such as its complex iconography, the three dimensionality of its carving, and the well-modeled hands and arms.

The *cuauhxicalli* (vessel for hearts) that rests on the stomach of the figure is surrounded by a relief of human hearts, and the god is in the pose of the earth god Tlaltecuhtli. The hearts and the god are surrounded by snails, symbol of fertility and life, and water creatures, which associate the figure with the sacred liquids of the universe—blood and underground water. Water was very important for the Mesoamerican people, whose main source of sustenance was agriculture.

This figure was probably associated with Tlaloc temples because it presents the deity himself. Although the Aztec built the next great empire after the Toltec, they worshipped them and their gods as their ancestors. This is a dual relationship in which a culture is supplanted and venerated at the same time. Pasztory states that this *chacmool* is a Mexica reinterpretation of a Toltec art form to honor and venerate the main Toltec deity and their Toltec forefathers (1983: 173–175).

Chicomecoatl

This sculpture represents the goddess Chicomecoatl (Seven Serpent). She was a fertility goddess responsible for the growth of maize. She wears the *amacalli,*

8.25 Chicomecoatl, the fertility and corn goddess, wearing the amacalli, *or temple headdress, Museum of Anthropology, Mexico City* (Fernando González y González)

a square headdress adorned with two or more rosettes, which is also known as the "temple headdress." As indicated by Matos Moctezuma and Solís Olguín, she wears the typical female costume: an ankle-length skirt (*cueitl*) and a triangular ritual cape that falls on her chest and back (*quechquemitl*). In each hand she holds a *cinmaitl*, which is a pair of corncobs decorated with strips of paper. Chicomecoatl is associated with Xilonen, the goddess of young maize, who is represented with a more simple cotton headdress and ears of corn. Xilonen represents the ripe ear of corn, and at the beginning of each harvest, the corn was collected and offered to her so that more prosperous harvests would come.

As maize was the fundamental food for the sustenance of the Aztec, there are strong conceptual and iconographic connections between Chicomecoatl and other fertility deities, such as Xochiquetzal (goddess of love and flowers), Cinteotl (young male maize god), Teteoinnan (old earth and mother goddess), and Chalchiuhtlicue (goddess of terrestrial water).

8.26 *Huehueteotl, the old god of fire, with attributes of the rain god Tlaloc, Museum of the Templo Mayor, Mexico City* (Fernando González y González)

Huehueteotl

This monument is dedicated to Huehueteotl, the old fire god, one of the most ancient deities of Mesoamerica. He is always portrayed as a seated god with his hands on his knees, the right hand open, and the left hand closed in a fist. His face is wrinkled, and his mouth is toothless, just like an old man's. He sits with a heavy brazier over his shoulders. This monument still preserves ancient Mesoamerican features, but with a few new elements. His face is almost hidden by a mask and his mouth has fangs. He has a great necklace with a large pendant that adorns the chest. He also has big ear flares.

The glyph 2 Reed is on the back of the figure, and the carvings of two shells surrounded by water and whirlpools are placed on top of the brazier. Because of this, the figure shows a relationship or association between the gods of fire and water, two opposites. Huehueteotl symbolizes the old god that governed the center of the universe while maintaining the equilibrium of the cosmos.

This statue was probably a synthesis of more than one god because it holds a number of icons representing fire, water, and death. Huehueteotl is another representation of Xiuhtecuhtli, the fire god of central Mexico, who was also known as Turquoise Lord or Lord of the Year. The stone figure has goggle eyes, a mustache-like feature, and fangs, which are characteristic traits of masks depicting Tlaloc. Also, masks with sharp teeth on his elbows and knees are similar to those that adorn Coyolxauhqui and Tlaltecuhtli, which might symbolize a passage to the underworld. The origins of the god Huehueteotl can be traced to earlier civilizations such as Cuicuilco and Teotihuacan. This Aztec version of the old god was found in Mexico City, north of the Great Temple, near the Red Temple, which also has features of Teotihuacan; as such, the stone god shows the Mexica appropriation of the Teotihuacan past.

Cihuateotl

Found in a temple dedicated to women who died giving birth, this Cihuateotl, meaning "deified woman," has the face of the living dead. The hands of this macabre figure have jaguar claws that are raised aggressively, as if to grab someone, and she has the tangled hair of a corpse. These deified women, who made up the Cihuateteo, were considered to be the female counterparts of the male warriors in the Mexica society. For the Aztec, women who died in childbirth were given the highest honor of accompanying the Sun from its midday zenith to its setting in the west, just like the warriors who gave their lives in battles and accompanied the Sun from its rising to noon.

It was believed that the Cihuateteo lived in the western horizon, or Cihuatlampa (place of women). They were admired, especially by young warriors (see chapter 5), but at the same time feared because they were considered evil spirits. It was thought that they haunted crossroads at night and were dangerous to young children, since they had been deprived of being mothers themselves. This is probably the origin of the modern legend of La Llorona (the crying woman), who wanders by night the towns of Mexico looking for her lost children.

8.28 Altar of the planet Venus, Museum of Anthropology, Mexico City (Manuel Aguilar-Moreno)

Altar of the Planet Venus

This altar of Venus depicts a three-lobed figure, a symbol used to identify this planet in other reliefs and codices. The Aztec believed that the 13 celestial realms that formed the universe served as a field of action of heavenly bodies. As Matos Moctezuma and Solís Olguín emphasize, the Aztec attributed a special significance to the planet Venus because of its year cycle of 584 days, which has two phases when it is invisible and another two phases when it is the last star to disappear in the morning and the first one to appear at dusk. This altar is like a prism with four sides. The upper register, or band, is a sequence of spheres that represent the canopy of stars. In the lower band Venus is shown with half-closed eyes, in her nocturnal nature, with monstrous jaws. Four *tecpatl* (flint knives) with faces jut from the personified star. There are two additional flint knives that commemorate the sacrifice of Venus, when it was pierced by the Sun with an arrow.

8.27 Cihuateotl, a deified woman who had died in childbirth, Museum of Anthropology, Mexico City (Fernando González y González)

Altar of Itzpapalotl

In contrast with relief carving, platforms or altars have sides that are also composed of carvings. This altar shows Itzpapalotl, a big butterfly with wings decorated with obsidian knives, which hold bleeding

8.29 *Altar of Itzpapalotl (Obsidian Butterfly), Museum of Anthropology, Mexico City* (Fernando González y González)

human hearts in its human hands. The monument probably represents the importance of sacrificial death to maintain a balance in life and the *tzitzimime* (female monsters of destruction). These creatures were among the most feared of all supernatural beings. They were considered to be stars that transformed themselves into "demons" that descended from the sky to devour human beings during certain calendrical and celestial events (such as solar eclipses). Itzpapalotl was primary among these deities and was associated with springtime and sacrifice.

Ahuitzotl Box

This box features three-dimensional carving and relief decorations similar to the works executed under the reign of Motecuhzoma II. The water monster that appears in three dimensions on the top and in relief inside of the box represents the king Ahuitzotl, who as a ruler-priest was expected to perform penitential rites involving the drawing of blood. There is a figure of the water god Tlaloc, who is pouring this sacred liquid and ears of corn from a jade vessel. There is a river of the fertilizing water surrounding the animal image of the king, probably representing his connection to lineage fertility and sustenance. This box was most likely used as a container for bloodletting implements because it is full of sacrificial symbolism. The box was a container to protect the sacred blood of the ruler.

The box was possibly made in the year 1499, as the date 7 Reed appears inside the stone lid.

Tepetlacalli with Figure Drawing Blood and *Zacatapayolli*

The *tepetlacalli*, a stone box, may have been inspired by utilitarian wooden or mat boxes since this type of sculpture is unique to Aztec art. These boxes have many functions, such as containers for carrying elite dead ashes or thorns used in bloodletting rituals and for storing assorted offerings. Alonso de Molina's 1571 Nahuatl dictionary defined the *tepetlacalli* as coffins or caskets, and this ethnohistorical source serves as evidence that these boxes were used to keep the ashes of cremated individuals. On the base of every stone box, including this one, always appears a carving of the earth monster as the voracious power of the Earth hungry for human remains. This particular box is full of images associated with penitential rites, such as an individual drawing blood from his ear with a thorn and a fire serpent in the background. Also present is a *zacatapayolli*, the grass ball used to keep the sacrificial bones.

8.30 *A* tepetlacalli *(stone box) with sacrificial elements such as a* zacatapayolli *and a bloodletting figure in its carvings, Museum of Anthropology, Mexico City* (Fernando González y González)

8.31 Stone box of Motecuhzoma II, Museum of Anthropology, Mexico City (Fernando González y González)

Stone Box of Motecuhzoma II

Stone boxes with calendrical symbols served in special rites for certain deities and/or in the households of the emperor and nobility. The ruler's name, in this case Motecuhzoma II's, usually appears on the box along with significant dates of his reign. This box has eight *quincunces* (cosmic diagram with five points) on the outside, which symbolize the Aztec universe. According to Matos Moctezuma and Solís Olguín, some scholars believe that the box stored the remains of Motecuhzoma II, since the carvings inside the lid depict his name glyph, the speaking *xihuitzolli o copilli* (royal headdress), and a design showing his hair, a nose ornament made of turquoise, and a decorated speech scroll, which was an emblem of *tlatoani* (meaning "he who speaks") (2002: 449–450). Also depicted on the lid is the date 11 Flint (1516), the year in which Nezahualpilli, the ruler of Tetzcoco, died. According to art historians Emily Umberger and Cecilia Klein, this date may indicate that this stone box was rather a present given by Motecuh-

zoma II at the death of the Tetzcocan lord, who was a close friend (1993: 295–330).

Head of an Eagle Warrior

In the Aztec army's higher ranks, there were two orders: the eagle and the jaguar warriors. Usually only members of the nobility could belong to these two orders. The *cuauhtli* (eagle) knights were associated with the Sun and with daytime battles. For the Mexica, the eagle symbolized the Sun at its zenith as well as the warrior. These warriors' job was to nourish the Sun by sacrificing their own blood, thus making them resistant to pain and capable of risking their own life unconditionally.

This statue presents the head of a young warrior with an eagle helmet, which in pre-Columbian times would have been covered with real eagle feathers and made out of wood. The sculpture shows the Aztec ideal in facial features seen in many stone works of heads and masks. The eyes may have been inlaid with shells, and dog's teeth perhaps were inserted into the holes in his mouth. The dog's fangs were probably used to intimidate others and show the warrior's ferocity and strength. The sculpture is also linked to the fire god Xiuhtecuhtli by the paper bow on the neck, which is also a mark indicating the appropriate lineage for an eagle or jaguar warrior.

Jaguar Warrior

This man with a jaguar helmet is believed to be a warrior of the Aztec jaguar order (see figure 8.32). This warrior wears a folded paper fan on the back of his head, connecting him to the fertility and nature deities. He also has a collar imitating jade jewelry like those of the Tlaloc-Chacmool. According to Pasztory, this feline helmet is associated with deities such as Tepeyollotl, who is the jaguar form of the god Tezcatlipoca (1983: 175–176). Tepeyollotl, meaning "heart of the mountain," is a deity related to Earth and nature, which connects him to the gods of the ancient past. Also, the jaguar symbolizes caves and the interior of the Earth, which associates the feline with fertility,

8.32 *Stone statue of a jaguar warrior, Museum of Anthropology, Mexico City* (Fernando González y González)

since the caves are the wombs of the mountains where creation happened. The jewelry is significant in this sculpture; greenstones were found in caves and guarded by ancient deified Toltec kings and rain gods.

Atlantean Warriors

A group of five colossal sculptures, the Atlantean Warriors represent the Aztec vision of the universe, inspired by the famous Atlantes of Tula (see figure 1.3 and chapters 9 and 11). Their military character is suggested by their spears, spear-throwers, and clay nose bars. They are warriors ready for battle and eager to feed the gods with human blood so that the universe stays in a constant balance. According to Matos Moctezuma and Solís Olguín, the sculptures represent warriors who support the creations of the gods by military actions. Four of the sculptures that

were found in Tenochtitlan are male; the fifth is female. One of the warriors is bearded and is supposed to guard the center of the cosmos. The other three males mark the north, east, and south. The female warrior belongs to the west, where the *cihuat-lampa* (place of women) is located. Together they create a *quincunx*, the four cardinal points that were the four directions of the universe, plus a center.

These possibly deified warriors who guard the Sun in its celestial realm resemble Toltec models such as the Atlantes of Tula. They have in the center of their bodies, as well as their helmets, the butterfly pectoral of Toltec warriors.

Feathered Coyote

This monument is the depiction of a sitting coyote covered in a fur of feathers that symbolize motion and movement. The coyote, which was not usually carved

8.33 *The Feathered Coyote was a symbol of sexual power, Museum of Anthropology, Mexico City.* (Fernando González y González)

in sculpture in the round, was a patron of the Aztec elite knight orders, since like the jaguar and eagle, the coyote was a powerful predator. According to Matos Moctezuma and Solís Olguín, the coyote was connected to Tezcatlipoca, who was the god of masculinity and war, thus making the animal a symbol of sexual male potency and fertility (2002: 416).

Acolman Cross

The most astonishing *tequitqui* (Indian-Christian) monument in the town of Acolman is the atrial cross (a monumental stone cross located in the center of the plaza in front of the church) (see figure 14.5). The Acolman Cross features at its top the INRI (Jesus of Nazareth King of the Jews) inscription, under which lies the Augustinian emblem of the arrow-pierced heart, an impressive realistic head of Christ in bulk at the intersection of the arms and the shaft, a chalice, pliers, a ladder, the spear, a palm leaf, a human bone, and a skull. The arms of the cross are decorated with plant motifs such as flowers, vines, and leaves. Each arm ends with a stylized fleur-de-lis. The base that supports the cross intends to emphasize the theme of Calvary (Golgotha, where Christ died), showing a crude image of the Virgin of the Sorrows surrounded by indigenous iconography.

Although there are precedents in Europe for open-air stone crosses along roads or in town squares, the Mexican crosses have a different iconography and an indigenous aesthetic. Dating to 1550, only 29 years after the fall of the Aztec Empire, the Acolman Cross provides, like all atrial crosses in general, a dual system of meanings: the Christian and the pagan. The cross is the central symbol of Christianity and represents the death of Christ, who with his resurrection made possible the redemption of human beings. The cross reflected the new doctrine taught by the friars to the Mexican native peoples, but their very rooted idolatry induced the Indians to bury images of their gods underneath the atrial crosses and continue the practice of old rituals. In time, these would become syncretized with the new religion.

At the same time, the Indians understood the Christian cross at the center of the *atrio*, or ritual plaza that served as an open-air place of worship, as

a representation of the World Tree, or Tree of Life. It was the *axis mundi* that connected the gods of the upperworld and underworld with the human beings on the surface of the Earth. The cosmogram was completed with the four *posa* chapels located at the corners of the *atrio* and which were interpreted to represent the four corners of the universe.

In the Mesoamerican vision of the world, the cycle of planting and harvesting of maize was sacred because it was the main source of sustenance for human beings. At the same time the cycle of the maize was a metaphor for the death and rebirth of humankind. When a maize seed was planted in the soil, it died, but from it a living plant emerged. It implied that from death life will come, a process that was energized by the Earth that lies in the underworld. In the same way, the people would die in order to rise again exactly like the maize god Cinteotl. This agricultural and cosmological belief was somewhat compatible with the Christian idea that God came to the world incarnated as Jesus Christ, suffered greatly, and died as a human man. Three days later, he was resurrected, and the blood of his sacrifice on the Cross redeemed and granted eternal paradise to believing human beings.

For the Aztec sculptor in the midst of conversion, Christ was the maize god, and the Cross was the maize plant. The fleurs-de-lis at the end of the arms of the Acolman Cross were the sprouts of the maize plant that represented the endless rebirth of fertility and life. The carved flowers, vines, and leaves that decorate the cross's arms were the vines of beans and squash that the peasants grew together with the maize stalks in the *milpas* (cornfields). The cross rising from Calvary, the hill where Christ defeated death, reflects also the maize plant (foliated cross) rising from the earth monster, where death is transformed to life.

At the foot of the Acolman Cross lies a crude image of the Virgin of the Sorrows that clearly incorporates Christian elements, such as the crossed hands and shrouded head. The style in which she is carved, however, distinctly resembles a typical Indian idol so that she becomes a Christianized Coatlicue or Teteoinnan, and the disk on her chest recalls the Aztec practice of insetting a jade or obsidian stone over the hearts of their idols as a symbol of their vital energy. From a Christian viewpoint the disk could be a wafer that together with the small chalice that appears under her hands are symbols of the Eucharist. The idea of communion with God through the partaking of his flesh and blood had some parallel with the Aztec practice of ritual cannibalism and human sacrifice. In both cases there was communion with the divinity, but in the Christian rite it is symbolic, while in the Aztec one it was a physical performance.

To the left of the virgin there is a skull that makes reference to her presence in Golgotha (place of the skull), the Hebrew name for Calvary. At the feet of the virgin there is a terrestrial sphere and a serpent, two symbols linked to the Immaculate Conception. For the Augustinian friars who built the monastery in Acolman, this apocalyptic association with pre-Hispanic elements probably was intended to remind the Indians that the new religion destroyed the old one of Quetzalcoatl (the Feathered Serpent) and would reign over the Earth. The very same message was sent to the Indians through the miraculous apparition of the Virgin of Guadalupe to the convert Juan Diego (see chapter 14). According to the historian Ignacio M. Altamirano, the Virgin Mary's words to Juan Diego were *Maria tecoatlaxopeuh*, meaning "Mary, the one who will destroy the stone serpent" (1974: 397), which through mangling of the Nahuatl language became *María de Guadalupe*. This action of destroying the serpent was a common image of the Immaculate Conception in Europe, while in the indigenous world it referred to the destruction of Quetzalcoatl and the triumph of the Christian religion over what was considered to be idolatry.

TERRA-COTTA SCULPTURE

For most cultures in Mesoamerica, terra-cotta sculpture was one of the principal forms of art during the Preclassic and Classic periods. The Aztec, however, were infatuated with the permanence of stone and so worked less often in clay than most of their neighbors. Except for a few larger, hollow fig-

urines, most Aztec terra-cotta sculptures are small, solid, mold-made figurines. According to Pasztory, terra-cotta sculptures are essential to identifying the cult practices and gods of the Aztec commoners in cities and remote areas (1983: 281–282). Their main subjects are the deities of nature and fertility and mothers with children; less frequently death may be the subject of a piece. Death and sacrifice seem to be the focus of noble terra-cotta works.

Eagle Warrior

This ceramic figure was found inside of the House of Eagles, a building constructed in a neo-Toltec style, north of the Great Temple in Tenochtitlan. He wears an eagle helmet, his arms are covered with

8.34 *A terra-cotta eagle warrior found in the House of the Eagles, Museum of the Templo Mayor, Mexico City* (Fernando González y González)

wings, and his legs are adorned with claws. Some remaining stucco paint reveals that the feathers on his clothes were painted in white.

Besides representing the mighty eagle warriors, this figure along with another figurine found in the same place are believed to symbolize the Sun at dawn. This sculpture was on top of a multicolored bench with the figures of warriors marching toward a *zacatapayolli* (a ball of grass in which the bloodletting instruments were inserted). The House of Eagles served as a place dedicated to prayer ceremonies, self-sacrifice, and spiritual rituals (see chapter 9).

Mictlantecuhtli

This figure was also found in the House of Eagles on top of benches, and it represents Mictlantecuhtli, god of the dead. Mictlantecuhtli lived in a damp and cold place known as Mictlan, which was the underworld, or lower part of the cosmos—a universal womb where human remains were kept (see chapters 6 and 7).

The god is shown wearing a loincloth and small holes in his scalp indicate that at one time, curly human hair decorated his head, typical of earth and death god figurines. His clawlike hands are poised as if ready to attack someone. Most dramatically, he is represented with his flesh wide-open below his chest. According to Matos Moctezuma and Solís Olguín, out of the opened flesh in the stomach, a great liver appears, the organ where the *ihiyotl* soul dwells (see chapter 7); the liver was connected to Mictlan, the underworld (2002: 458). The *ihiyotl* is one of the three mystical elements that inhabit the human body; the *tonalli*, the determinant of one's fate, is located in the head, and the *teyolia*, the house of consciousness, resides in the heart. In this sculpture the deity is showing where one of those three mystical elements rests in the human body until death.

Xipe Totec

Xipe Totec was worshipped by Mesoamericans since the Classic Period. Xipe Totec was the god of vegetation and agricultural renewal and was one of the

8.35 A terra-cotta statue of the death god Mictlantecuhtli, Museum of the Templo Mayor, Mexico City
(Fernando González y González)

patron gods associated with the 13-day periods in the divinatory calendar. He was also the patron of the festival Tlacaxipehualiztli, held before the coming of the rains, in which captives were sacrificed. After the sacrificed bodies were flayed, priests wore the skins for 20 days (see chapters 6 and 11).

Xipe Totec is depicted in one surviving sculpture as a man with a flayed skin. A rope, sculpted in detail, ties the skin at the back, head, and chest. This piece forms part of a series of great images created by pre-Columbian artists, who expressed their deeply held belief that only through death can life exist. The difference between the tight skin layer and the animate form inside is represented in a simple manner, without the gruesome dramatization that is typical in the images of death gods and goddesses. Remarkably, the sculpture still retains its original paint; the flayed skin is yellow, and the skin of Xipe Totec is red.

CERAMICS

The Aztec made several functional and ceremonial objects out of clay: incense burners, dishes, ritual vessels, funerary urns, stamps, and spindle whorls. Large vase-shaped incense burners were sometimes more than three feet in height with a figure in high relief on one side or an ornament of projections and flanges. Redware goblets were often made for drinking pulque at feasts. Many of these clay objects had decorations but usually without the elaborate icono-graphic meaning that characterized monumental sculpture and manuscript painting.

The ceramics of the Valley of Mexico have been divided into nine different wares on the basis of clay, type, vessel shape, surface, and decoration. Orange- and redwares are the most common. Redware, generally associated with Tetzcoco, is usually highly burnished and painted with a red slip; its painted designs are in black, black and white, or black, white, and yellow, and they consist of simple lines and frets that often appear boldly applied. These vessels vary significantly in quality. Redware was sometimes completely covered with white slip,

8.36 Vessel with a mask of Tlaloc, Museum of the Templo Mayor, Mexico City (Fernando González y González)

then painted with black designs of skulls and crossed bones. In its controlled quality, the line and design suggest Mixteca-Puebla vessels.

Vessel with Mask of Tlaloc

According to Matos Moctezuma and Solís Olguín this vessel was part of an offering (number 56) discovered at the Great Temple of Tenochtitlan, facing north in the direction of the temple of Tlaloc (2002: 459). As part of an offering, the pot was put inside a box made out of volcanic rock containing remains of aquatic creatures and shells, symbols of water and fertility. The box also contained a *tecpatl* and two bowls of copal.

This vessel represents the rain god Tlaloc. On the outside of the vessel, Tlaloc features goggle-like eyes and two fans; a serpent surrounds his mouth forming what looks like a mustache. The god wears a white headdress, a reference to the mountains where the deity was believed to keep his waters, a place where fertility flourishes and water flows down the hills to nourish the soil. In general, the vessel symbolizes the uterus and the feminine powers of creation.

Funerary Urn with Image of Tezcatlipoca

This urn was found in the Great Temple, near the monolith of the great goddess Coyolxauhqui. Inside it were found the cremated bones of Aztec warriors who probably died in battle against the Tarascans of Michoacan during the reign of King Axayacatl. A necklace of beads, a spear point, and a bone perforator were also inside.

Within a rectangle carved on the outside wall of the urn lies the image of Tezcatlipoca (Smoking Mirror) surrounded by a feathered serpent with a forked tongue. Wearing a headdress full of eagle feathers, symbols connected to the Sun, the deity seems to be armed and ready for battle. He has a spear-thrower in one hand and two spears in the other. In the hand holding the two spears he wears a protector similar to the ones used in Toltec imagery. He wears a smoking mirror, his characteristic symbol, on one of his feet.

According to Matos Moctezuma and Solís Olguín, this urn represents a warrior that embodies the image of Tezcatlipoca, a creator god that inhabits the four horizontal directions and the three vertical levels of the cosmos (2002: 469). Tezcatlipoca is also the protector of warriors, kings, and sorcerers and the god of the cold who symbolized the dark night sky. He was considered invisible and mysterious (see chapter 6).

Flutes

In Aztec festivities, clay flutes were commonly played. The shape and decoration of these instruments varied according to the gods being worshipped at the time. According to Matos Moctezuma and Solís Olguín, at the feast of Toxcatl, the person chosen to personify the god Tezcatlipoca played a sad melody with a thin

8.37 Ceramic funerary urn with an image of Tezcatlipoca, Museum of the Templo Mayor, Mexico City (Fernando González y González)

flute with a flower shape at the end as he walked to the temple to be sacrificed. Depending on the occasion, the Aztec made flutes with different shapes, such as the image of the god Huehueteotl-Xiuhtecuhtli. The god is shown as an old man with a beard symbolizing wisdom. Another flute ends in the shape of an eagle, a symbol of divine fire, the Sun, and warriors. The eagle seems to be wearing a headdress. Some flutes have elegant ornaments, like the step-fret design used in Aztec-Mixtec gold rings. This flute shows the blending of the Aztec and Mixtec cultures and suggests that besides wars there was trade and exchange of cultural traditions.

WOOD ART

Wood was not just a substitute for stone. Many of the icons, or idols, in the major Aztec temples were made out of wood and dressed in beautiful clothes and jewelry. However, the symbolic significance of wood for the Aztec is unclear. Many Aztec texts refer to the superiority of stone figures to wooden ones because of their durability and endurance. But, in weight, flex-

ibility, and resonance, wood was the perfect material for such objects as drums, spear-throwers, shields, and masks. Some objects were also made of wood so that they could be burned symbolically as offerings.

Huehuetl of Malinalco

In the town of Malinalco was found a wooden *tlalpan-huehuetl*, war drum, still used in some ceremonies until 1894, when it was transferred to its present location in a museum in the city of Toluca. This *huehuetl* (vertical drum) contains the date Nahui Ollin (4 Movement). The *ollin* symbol was used to represent the movement of the Sun and the dynamic life of the world. From the word *ollin* derives *yollotl* (heart) and *yoliztli* (life). Inside this particular *ollin* symbol is a ray emanating from a solar eye and a *chalchihuitl* (precious stone). The Sun was considered to be the Shining One, the Precious Child, the Jade, and Xiuhpiltontli (Turquoise Child). The date Nahui Ollin alludes to Ollin-Tonatiuh, the Sun of Movement, the present world that will be destroyed by earthquakes, and to the festival of Nahui Ollin, described by Durán, in which the messenger of the Sun was sacrificed.

To the right of the date Nahui Ollin, the artist carved the outstanding figure of an *ocelotl* (jaguar)

8.38 Wooden huehuetl *(vertical drum) from Malinalco, Museum of Anthropology and History of Mexico State, Toluca* (Lluvia Arras)

and to the left a *cuauhtli* (eagle), both dancing. These images represent eagle and jaguar warriors, distinguished orders of the Aztec army. These warriors carry the flag of sacrifice (*pamitl*) and wear a headdress with heron feathers (*aztaxelli*), a symbol of hierarchy.

In the lower sections that support the Huehuetl of Malinalco, there are two more jaguar warriors and one eagle warrior. From the mouths and beaks of the warriors and around their paws and claws, appears the glyph Atl-Tlachinolli, or Teuatl-Tlachinolli, which means "divine water (blood)-fire"; it signals the call of war and is sometimes represented as a song and dance of war. Atl-Tlachinolli is expressed as a metaphor in sculpture, carvings, and the codices as two intertwined rivers, one of water and the other of fire. The stream of water ends with pearls and conches, while the stream of fire ends with the body of the *xiuhcoatl* (fire snake), which is emitting a flame.

All the warriors depicted on the Huehuetl have in one of their eyes the sign *atl* (water), which indicates that they are crying while they sing. This sign reveals the duality of feelings before the sacrifice. One of the jaguar warriors has behind a paw the sign *atl* combined with an *aztamecatl* (rope), indicating that he is a *uauantin* (captive striped in red) who will be sacrificed on the *temalacatl* stone. The eagle warriors have obsidian knives hanging among their feathers, symbols of human sacrifice.

A band divides the two parts of the Huehuetl and portrays shields (*chimalli*) with bundles of cotton and arrows (*tlacochtli*), sacrificial flags (*pamitl*), and a continuous stream of the glyph *atl-tlachinolli*. All of these are metaphors of war.

Interestingly, the Huehuetl represents a real event that took place in Malinalco: the festival of Nahui Ollin, which included eagle and jaguar warriors singing, dancing, and crying and ended with the dance of the messenger of the Sun who would be sacrificed. This event is presented through images of Cuauhtehuanitl (Rising Sun) and Cuauhtemoc (Setting Sun).

The Sun was considered a young warrior that every day at dawn fought in the heavens to defeat the darkness, stars, and Moon (*metztli*) using the *xiuhcoatl* as a weapon. In this way he ascends to the zenith, preceded by Tlahuizcalpantecuhtli, the morning star (Venus). At dusk, the Sun, preceded by Xolotl, the evening star (Venus), sets in Tlillan Tlapallan, the Land of the Black and Red, and descends to the underground transformed into a jaguar to illuminate the world of the dead. The next dawn, in an endless cycle, he will repeat his cosmic fight to bring a new day to humankind.

On the Huehuetl, Cuauhtehuanitl's face is emerging from the beak of the eagle, and he has a turquoise (*yacaxihuitl*) in his nose. Under his chin appears the sign *cuicatl*, which indicates that the deity ascends singing. The feathers of the eagle are stylized in a way that resembles the precious feathers of the quetzal. Cuauhtehuanitl is accompanied by fire snakes, who carry him during his daily cycle. They are also the embodiments of the solar rays. We can see the representation of the heads of the *xiuhcoatl* featuring open mouth with fangs, solar eye, and a horn. One of them has a realistic shape, while the other is portrayed with more abstraction but shows the same characteristic elements.

The quality of the Aztec sculpture and carving applied to this *huehuetl* is so precise and refined that it is comparable to the amazing and powerful expression of the codices. The images shown by this musical masterwork confirm and complement the discussion about the function and uses of the *cuauhcalli* temple of Malinalco presented in chapter 9.

Teponaztli of a Feline

The *teponaztli*, a horizontal drum still in use today, was another popular instrument used by the Aztec. The drum is a sort of double-tongued xylophone. The tongues are made out of slits positioned in a hollowed piece of wood that works as the sound box. Sticks with rubber tips served as hammers to hit the tongues, thereby producing the tones and melodies of the drum. A *teponaztli* from Malinalco is in the National Museum of Anthropology in Mexico City. After the Spanish conquest, the missionaries prohibited traditional indigenous ritual practices, and they often destroyed artifacts belonging to those rituals, so it is fortunate that this *teponaztli* survives.

The animal carved on this horizontal drum is either a crouching coyote or a type of jaguar with its tail next to its left side (see figure 8.39). It could represent the *nahualli* (soul or double) of a coyote or jaguar

8.39 Wooden teponaztli *in the shape of a coyote or jaguar, from Malinalco, Museum of Anthropology, Mexico City* (Fernando González y González)

warrior; however, the curls on the head of the animal have led some scholars to identify it as an *ahuitzotl,* or a "water-thorn-beast," possibly a water possum. Amazingly, this horizontal drum still has the original canine teeth and molars placed inside the mouth to make the animal look more realistic and ferocious.

Teponaztli with Effigy of a Warrior

The human effigy depicted on this *teponaztli* is a representation of a reclining Tlaxcalan warrior. Matos Moctezuma and Solís Olguín point out that the representation of this warrior is decorated with the unique military emblems of his Tlaxcalan culture (2002: 438). His weapons include the jaw of a sawfish and an axe with a copper blade. The eyes of the warrior still preserve their shell and obsidian inlays.

Tlaloc

This wood sculpture is an example of a work meant to be burned in honor of Tlaloc. Such figures were usually made out of resin and copal applied to sticks and burned after a prayer was offered to Tlaloc. The Aztec believed that the smoke rising from the burning resin and copal would make the clouds dark and cause them to liberate a fertilizing rain over the Earth. This particular image was found inside a cave in the Iztaccihuatl volcano.

The sculpture features the characteristics consistently attributed to the rain god Tlaloc: ear ornaments, goggle-like eyes, protruding fangs, and a headdress symbolizing the mountains where he kept water. This sculpture also features a folded paper bow behind Tlaloc's neck, which, according to Matos Moctezuma and Solís Olguín, represents the *tlaquechpanyotl,* the sign of the deity's noble ancestry (2002: 460).

FEATHER WORK

Among the large variety of media utilized by the Aztec artists, their feather work is perhaps the least known today. The Aztec became master feather crafters before the arrival of the Spaniards and had developed highly sophisticated methods of gathering feathers throughout their territories and incorporating them into objects of impressive visual impact and surprising durability. The artists in the village of Amatlan (a district of Tenochtitlan) were known for their exceptional feather work.

The *amanteca* (feather workers) either fixed their precious tropical feathers on light reed frameworks by tying each one onto the backing with cotton or fastened them on cloth or paper to form mosaics in which certain effects of color were obtained by exploiting their transparent qualities. Belonging exclusively to the Aztec, this artwork lingered in the form of little feather icons after the conquest and then disappeared almost entirely.

Only a handful of these original masterpieces have survived, and today only a few artists scattered in diverse cities of Mexico keep the art of feather work alive. While the Spanish did not consider feather works to be as valuable as gold or precious stones, nor a treasure worth preserving, they sent shiploads of it to Spain as curiosities from the New World. The many churches, monasteries, and individuals who received these precious gifts did not protect them from the natural process of decay, and out of hundreds of costumes, mantles, standards, and shields sent to Europe, only a few pieces are now known to exist. There are some surviving examples, such as Christian symbols, made in colonial times in a style similar to that of the Renaissance, that constitute the best of feather work.

Pasztory affirms that colorful tropical birds such as the scarlet macaw, various species of parrot, the red spoonbill, the blue cotinga, and the quetzal provided most of the vibrant feathers used in mosaic feather work (1983: 278–280). The most common colors used were red and yellow. The most precious colors used were blue and green, the colors of water and agriculture, fertility and creation. Green quetzal feathers were among the rarest and most sought after; in Nahuatl, *quetzal* means "precious." The two long green tail feathers of the male quetzal birds were collected for great headdresses and standards. Unfortunately, quetzal is today an endangered species. Almost as precious as the quetzal were hummingbird feathers; often greenish in color, hummingbird feathers become iridescent when lit from certain angles.

As pointed out by art historian Teresa Castelló Yturbide, feathers, together with stones such as jade and turquoise, were considered among the most valued objects of Mesoamerica (1993: 17–42). They were so highly venerated that statues of Aztecs deities were clothed in cloaks full of brilliant feathers and precious stones. Viewed in magical terms, feathers were considered icons of fertility, abundance, wealth, and power, and they connected the individual or statue wearing them with the divine. According to Fray Diego Durán, the Aztec believed that the feathers were shadows of the deities.

The Headdress of Motecuhzoma II

Assembled from 500 quetzal feathers taken from 250 birds, this feather headdress is one of the best examples that have survived to the modern day. Despite its name, it is still unclear if it was used or it belonged to this emperor. According to Pasztory, a model of a crown used by Motecuhzoma was depicted in the *Codex Mendoza*, and it was composed of turquoise, not feathers (1983: 280). The headdress probably derives its name from the traditional story that when Motecuhzoma met Cortés, he gave the conquistador luxurious items in a diplomatic gesture to please and salute Emperor Charles V. These gifts included headdresses, gold and silver objects, and clothes, among many other things. When Spanish king Charles V's brother Ferdinand married, he received the Headdress of Motecuhzoma II, which had been stored in the Ambras Castle in Tyrol, Austria. In time, the art collections of the Habsburg monarchy were placed in state museums, and now the famous headdress is housed in the Museum of Ethnology in Vienna, together with a feathered fan and the Ahuitzotl Shield.

This kind of feather headdress was probably used as a military insignia instead of a crown. The feather headdress would have been placed on a bamboo stick and positioned on a distinguished soldier's back. Pasztory has suggested that there is evidence that headdresses such as this piece were used by Aztec royalty for ritualistic purposes, especially to be worn when impersonating the god Quetzalcoatl (1983: 279).

Feathered Fan

In preconquest periods, fans were a symbol of nobility or of belonging to the *pochtecah* (professional traders) class. According to Matos Moctezuma and Solís Olguín, fans gave a fancy touch to the wardrobes of the *tlatoani* and his royal family, who always looked elegant and distinguished (2002: 449). The fans were eye-catching pieces constructed of wood and decorated with colorful feathers.

A fan found north of the Tlaloc temple, in a place considered to be part of the Sacred Precinct of the Aztec capital, was restored by a professional feather worker and is kept in the National Museum of Anthropology in Mexico City. The tip of this fan depicts the head of a warrior who is well dressed for war. Another beautiful example of a preserved fan can be found in the Museum of Ethnology in Vienna, Austria.

Ahuitzotl Shield

The *chimalli* (shield) of Ahuizotl was a gift from Hernán Cortés to Don Pedro de la Gasca, bishop of Palencia, Spain. It is an assemblage of different types of feathers, including from scarlet macaws, blue cotingas, rose spoonbills, and yellow orioles; tassels of feathers hang from the lower edge. Vegetable fibers hold together the base of reed splints that supports the colorfully arranged plumage. On the back, two loops are formed to allow the shield to be carried.

The Ahuizotl Shield portrays the figure of a coyote warrior in gold and feathers. The symbol of the sacred war, *atl-tlachinolli* (the water, the fire), comes out of his mouth, indicating that he is shouting a call or song of war. The figure depicted on the shield is not an *ahuitzotl* (fantastical water being) as had been traditionally identified. Water creatures are linked to the rain god Tlaloc. Rather, the animal represented may be a coyote associated with warfare and a military Aztec order.

The Ahuizotl Shield is housed in the Museum of Ethnology in Vienna, along with the Headdress of Motecuhzoma II and a feathered fan.

Chalice Cover

This object, found by historian Rafael García Granados, comes from the early transitional times of the campaign to convert all of the Mesoamerican indigenous populations to Catholicism. The blue creature

8.40 This chalice cover made of feathers is an example of tequitqui *art, Museum of Anthropology, Mexico City.* (Manuel Aguilar-Moreno)

adorning the cover may be related to the god Tlaloc, since it has gogglelike eyes and a mustache. If this is true, the cover may be associated with one of the most sacred liquids of the universe—water. According to Matos Moctezuma and Solís Olguín, the circular panel surrounding the creature in the center represents water in motion and in terms of Christian doctrine symbolizes the holy water communicating the message of God (2002: 482). God is shown as a stylized Aztec Tlaloc mask with fangs, which throws fire out of his mouth. In the context of Christianity, the fire represents the blood of the sacrificed Christ that cleanses the world of human sin; at the same time, the fire is an indigenous symbol of the primeval waters of the old Aztec deities. This piece expresses the complex process of transculturation that occurred during the 16th century in Mexico while two different cultures tried to establish a religious dialogue.

Christ the Savior

After the Spanish conquest, feather art was applied to ritual objects with the shape and iconography of the new religion. On this wooden panel, feathers of different colors are arranged to form the image of Christ the Savior, who blesses the world with his right hand. The orb that he is holds in his left hand is an icon of sovereignty, which was considered, during the Middle Ages, an emblem of divine power. An inscription surrounds the image of Christ, but it has not yet been translated successfully.

LAPIDARY ARTS

The Aztec had a very special interest in precious stones of all kinds. As their culture was primarily Neolithic (New Stone Age), tools were predominantly made of stone, though copper tools were also utilized. Obsidian and flint were used to make the ritually valued sacrificial knives; obsidian also served for scraping utensils and more domestic cutting implements.

The Mexica-Aztec were particularly skilled at carving hard stones of different colors and brilliant surfaces, such as greenstone, porphyry, obsidian,

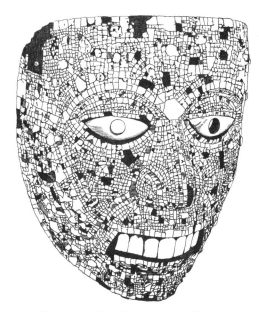

8.41 Turquoise and shell mask, British Museum, London (Lluvia Arras and Annelys Pérez)

Greenstone such as jade came from the province of Guerrero and was offered as tribute by the southern provinces. The most famous lapidary artists in the Valley of Mexico were the artisans of Chalco and Xochimilco.

Turquoise Mask

This beautiful blue mask is believed to represent Xiuhtecuhtli, the god of fire. Matos Moctezuma and Solís Olguín state that the deity's name Xiuhtecuhtli (Turquoise Lord) is a derivative of the Nahuatl word for year (*xihuitl*), which makes him also a deity of time (2002: 476). The turquoise pieces are affixed to a cedarwood base with a kind of resinous substance. Made out of pear oystershell, the eyes have a central hole suggesting that impersonators of divine beings in religious rituals wore the mask. His teeth are also made out of shells. This mask is one of the best surviving examples of its kind from the Postclassic period.

Double-Headed Serpent Pectoral

This pectoral features double-headed and intertwined serpents associated with the feathered serpent god, Quetzalcoatl. Their jaws are open, symbolizing the caves of Mictlan, gateways to the underworld. The whole piece is a wooden base covered with turquoise mosaic inlays making it look as blue as the sky. The noses, gums, and teeth of the reptiles are inlaid with white and red shells.

rock crystal, turquoise, and onyx. From these stones, they created a variety of sculptures, vessels, and jewelry. The Aztec made elaborate lapidary art pieces with rock crystal, amethyst, jade, turquoise, obsidian, and mother-of-pearl. Using instruments of reed, sand, and emery, they arranged small pieces of stone and minerals in brilliant mosaics on backgrounds of bone, stucco, and wood.

Lapidary artists were highly appreciated and respected in Aztec society. Their technique was called *toltecayotl* (matter of the Toltecs, or the Toltec thing) and was based on the Toltec artistic traditions that the Aztec so admired.

The greenstones, such as jadeite, diorite, and serpentine, were the most important precious stones in Mesoamerica. Jade beads were placed on a corpse's mouth as payment for the trip of the soul of the dead person through the underworld, a tradition also found in ancient China. The greenstone acted as an offering to protect the soul in its journey through the afterlife. Greenstones were also buried in the floor of the temples. Green was a symbol for water and plants, life and fertility. The word *chalchihuitl* (jade symbol) was an embodiment of preciousness.

8.42 Double-headed serpent pectoral, British Museum, London (Lluvia Arras and Annelys Pérez)

Double-headed intertwined serpents were icons in Mesoamerican art that represented the sky. The serpents were a symbol of renewal since they shed their skin. They are also metaphoric streams of blood. In this context, the pectoral is a work dedicated to life, which depends on death and the underworld in order to renew itself.

It is believed that a priest or noble wore this pectoral in rituals connected to the birth of the god Huitzilopochtli, the patron Aztec god who was born at Coatepec, the "snake mountain" (see chapter 6).

Sacrificial Knife

The *tecpatl*, or sacrificial knife, was an important feature of Aztec rituals. With the knife, priests cut open the chests of sacrificial victims to extract the heart that would feed the gods, hoping that such a gift would bring blessings to humankind. On the few surviving *tecpatl*, there are many representations of deities on the handles. One famous pre-Hispanic example is a *tecpatl* handle with the carved image of a figure wearing a circular ear ornament and a large feather associating the figure to Tonatiuh, the sun god. The arms of Tonatiuh seem to be supporting the blade. Matos Moctezuma and Solís Olguín state that the weapon of Huitzilopochtli, patron deity of war and the Sun, is referenced in the handle by the presence of the *xiuhcoatl* (fire serpent) (2002: 437). This particular knife emphasizes the importance of human sacrifice to the nourishment of the gods, especially the sun god, who illuminate the Earth and sustain life.

This handle, separated from its blade, was discovered in Mexico City; the blade, also pre-Hispanic, was attached later.

Knife with an Image of a Face

Found in excavations of the Great Temple of Tenochtitlan, this knife bears a face in profile that is presumed to represent the year-bearer *tecpatl*, a lesser deity, for which the sacrificial knives were named. Its teeth and eyes are accentuated by inlaid white flint and obsidian, a volcanic rock. Since this is a sacred sacrificial knife, it

8.43 Knife blade with an image of a face, Museum of the Templo Mayor, Mexico City (Fernando González y González)

is symbolically connected with Mictlan, the lower part of the universe where beings without flesh lived. Mictlan was associated with the color black and the sacrificial knife. According to Matos Moctezuma and Solís Olguín, this knife is associated with the Black Tezcatlipoca, who embodies an obsidian knife representing black wind (2002: 468). As a sacrificial knife, it is also associated with the north (the direction of death) and the flayed god Xipe Totec.

GOLD WORK

As time passed by, the once-nomadic Aztec became a hierarchical society. Wealth and power belonged to the *pipiltin* (nobles). Though gold was not as desirable as greenstone or torquoise, gold was a symbol of status, so Aztec metalworkers made expensive and beautiful objects of gold for the *pipiltin*. Tenochtitlan was the cosmopolitan center of Aztec art, and people of Mixtec origin were encouraged to settle there because they were famous for their gold work, which was distributed all over the city and the empire.

According to Matos Moctezuma and Solís Olguín, gold, combined with textiles and precious stones, was used to ornament the dress of both the gods and humans, as shown in various manuscripts (2002: 245–246). The Aztec nobility wore gold bells on their costumes. This clothing style was also depicted in monumental sculpture. After the Spanish conquest, figures of gold and other precious stones were taken to European countries and exhibited as exotic commodities. Hernán Cortés gave descriptions of such figures; for example, he saw a bird-shaped piece with green feathers and eyes, feet, and a beak made of gold.

A sense of mystery surrounded the *teocuitlahuaque* (goldsmiths). Though given the highly esteemed title of *tolteca*, goldsmiths were believed to be from a far, remote, and exotic nation. Xipe Totec was the patron deity of the *teocuitlahuaque*, and they worshipped him in a temple named Yopico (the Yopi ground). *Yopi* was the name of the people who lived in the western parts of the mountains reaching the Pacific Ocean in the present-day state of Guerrero. According to Sahagún, they did not speak Nahuatl, lived independent of the Aztec, and subsisted in very poor conditions. Even though they had their own customs and cultural traditions, they were embedded in the Aztec world and were considered rich due to their abilities to manipulate and work gold.

READING

Introduction

Aguilar-Moreno 1996, Vaillant 1938: explanation of Aztec art and its meanings.

Aztec Artists and Craftsmen

Soustelle 1979, Sahagún 1951–69: traditions of ancient Aztec art; Pasztory 1983, Soustelle 1979: taxation and income of Aztec artisans.

Monumental Stone Sculpture

Aguilar-Moreno 1996, Pasztory 1983, Alcina Franch 1983, Alcina Franch, León-Portilla, and Matos Moctezuma 1992, Matos Moctezuma and Solís Olguín 2002: the Ocelotl- and Cuauhtli-Cuauhxicallis and the Stone of Tizoc; Pasztory 1983, Alcina Franch, León-Portilla, and Matos Moctezuma 1992, Heyden and Gendrop 1975: the Sun Stone; Pasztory 1983, Alcina Franch, León-Portilla, and Matos Moctezuma 1992: Stone of the Warriors; Pasztory 1983: portrait of Motecuhzoma II; Aguilar-Moreno 1996, Matos Moctezuma and Solís Olguín 2002, Alcina Franch, León-Portilla, and Matos Moctezuma 1992: the Caracol; Aguilar-Moreno 1996, Pasztory 1983, Matos Moctezuma and Solís Olguín 2002, Alcina Franch, León-Portilla, and Matos Moctezuma 1992, Heyden and Gendrop 1975: Coatlicue; Matos Moctezuma and Solís Olguín 2002, Pasztory 1983: Coatlicue of Coxcatlan; Matos and Solís 2002, Pasztory 1983, Alcina Franch, León-Portilla, and Matos 1992: Cihuacoatl and Xiuhtecuhtli-Huitzilopochtli; Aguilar-Moreno 1996, Alcina Franch, León-Portilla, and Matos Moctezuma 1992, Pasztory 1983, Matos Moctezuma and Solís Olguín 2002: Coyolxauhqui; Matos Moctezuma and Solís Olguín 2002, Alcina Franch, León-Portilla, and Matos Moctezuma 1992, Pasztory 1983, Alcina Franch 1983: Head of Coyolxauhqui; Pasztory 1983, Alcina Franch, León-Portilla, and Matos Moctezuma 1992: the Ahuitzotl Box; Alcina Franch, León-Portilla, and Matos Moctezuma 1992, Matos Moctezuma and Solís Olguín 2002: altar of the planet Venus; Umberger and Klein 1993, Alcina Franch, León-Portilla, Matos Moctezuma 1992, Pasztory 1983: the Temple Stone (Teocalli of the Sacred War); Matos Moctezuma and Solís Olguín 2002, Pasztory 1983, Alcina Franch 1983: head of an eagle warrior; Pasztory 1983: statue of a jaguar warrior; Alcina Franch, León-Portilla, and Matos Moctezuma 1992, Pasztory 1983, Matos Moctezuma and Solís Olguín 2002: Xochipilli; Alcina Franch,

León-Portilla, and Matos Moctezuma 1992, Pasztory 1983, Alcina Franch 1983: *chacmool*; Pasztory 1983: Xilonen; Matos Moctezuma and Solís Olguín 2002: Huehueteotl; Alcina Franch, León-Portilla, and Matos Moctezuma 1992, Pasztory 1983: Tlaltecuhtli, the Bench Relief, the Feathered Coyote, and Cihuateotl; Pasztory 1983, Matos Moctezuma and Solís Olguín 2002: the Atlantean Warriors; Pasztory 1983: Altar of Itzpapalotl, Xiuhcoatl, and *tepetlacalli* with *zacatapayolli* and ruler drawing blood; Matos Moctezuma and Solís Olguín 2002, Alcina Franch, León-Portilla, and Matos Moctezuma 1992: Feathered Serpent; Matos Moctezuma and Solís Olguín 2002, Aguilar-Moreno 1999, Moreno Villa 1942: the Acolman Cross.

Terra-cotta Sculpture

Pasztory 1983: description of Aztec terra-cotta sculptures; Pasztory 1983, Matos Moctezuma and Solís Olguín 2002: eagle warrior and Mictlantecuhtli.

Ceramics

Alcina Franch, León-Portilla, and Matos Moctezuma 1992, Matos Moctezuma and Solís Olguín 2002: funerary urn; Broda 1970, Matos Moctezuma and Solís Olguín 2002: vessel with image of Tlaloc and Aztec flutes.

Wood Art

Pasztory 1983: description of Aztec wood art; Seler 1960, Romero Quiroz 1958 and 1980: Huehuetl of Malinalco; Alcina Franch, León-Portilla, and Matos Moctezuma 1992, Matos Moctezuma and Solís Olguín 2002: *teponaztli*s and sculpture of Tlaloc.

Feather Work

Pasztory 1983, Anders 1971, Broda 1970, Sahagún 1951–69, Castelló Yturbide 1993: history and function of Aztec feather work; Pasztory 1983, Alcina Franch, León-Portilla, Matos Moctezuma 1992, Matos Moctezuma and Solís Olguín 2002: Headdress of Motecuhzoma II and the Ahuitzotl Shield; Matos Moctezuma and Solís Olguín 2002: chalice cover and Christ the Savior; Pasztory 1983, Matos Moctezuma and Solís Olguín 2002: feathered fan.

Lapidary Arts

Sahagún 1951–69, Pasztory 1983: description of the Aztec lapidary arts; Matos Moctezuma and Solís Olguín 2002: turquoise mask; Pasztory 1983, Matos Moctezuma and Solís Olguín 2002: double-headed serpent pectoral; Alcina Franch, León-Portilla, and Matos Moctezuma 1992, Matos Moctezuma and Solís Olguín 2002: *tecpatl*s.

Gold Work

Pasztory 1983, Matos Moctezuma and Solí Olguín 2002: description and function of Aztec gold work.

9

AZTEC ARCHITECTURE

Aztec architecture reflects the values and civilization of an empire, and studying Aztec architecture is instrumental in understanding the history of the Aztec, including their migration across Mexico and their reenactment of religious rituals. Aztec architecture can be best described as monumental. Its purpose was to manifest power, while at the same time to adhere to strong religious beliefs. This is evident in the design of the temples, shrines, palaces, and everyday homes.

The capital city of the Aztec Empire was Tenochtitlan, the site of present-day Mexico City. Tenochtitlan was an overwhelming, monumental city built on top of small islands and marshlands. At the time, it was the third-largest city in the world, after Constantinople (Istanbul) and Paris, housing 200,000 inhabitants. Tenochtitlan was the city where the most impressive and monumental Aztec architecture was to be found. After the Spanish conquest, the city was looted and torn down, and its materials were used to build structures that still stand in Mexico City. From archaeological and various historical documents, such as the Spanish chronicles and codices written by friars, Indians, and historians, the extent and significance of the Aztec architecture can be deciphered.

Although Tenochtitlan was the most impressive of the Aztec cities, there are many archaeological sites that represent Aztec architecture, daily life, and ritual. The Chichimec peoples who became the Aztec had a long migration history, during which they split several times; however, the Mexica, the people who founded Tenochtitlan, remained united and devoted themselves to the worship of Huitzilopochtli, the sun and war god. Because the Aztec migrated for several hundred years and split several times, they adopted various gods, customs, architectural styles, and techniques. The final migratory split occurred at Mt. Coatepec (near Tula), where Huitzilopochtli, one of the most important Aztec deities, was born. Half of the Great Temple of Tenochtitlan was built in his honor and housed his history in sculpture.

The Great Temple was the sacred place where the Aztec worshipped Huitzilopochtli (as well as the rain god Tlaloc) and sacrificed human beings in order to appease him. To understand fully Aztec architecture, an extensive examination of Aztec cosmology, mythology, and culture is required because most Aztec structures were religiously charged. This is evident in the various temples and shrines that were built to worship the many Aztec deities and offer human sacrifices (see chapter 6).

Aztec architecture was heavily influenced by the Toltec of Colhuacan, the Tepanec of Atzcapotzalco, and the Acolhua of Tetzcoco. Because the Aztec Empire was built through conquest, the Aztec had to find ways to integrate the various dominated ethnic groups. Thus, the Aztec relied on their architecture and artwork to promote their worldview. The massive structures reflected the military might of the empire.

Aztec architecture, being similar to that of other Mesoamerican cultures, possessed an innate sense of order and symmetry. Geometric designs and sweeping lines were representations of religious tenets and the power of the state. In addition, the Aztec used bas-reliefs, walls, plazas, and platforms as media to represent their gods and ideals. During various periods of their empire, the Aztec added new techniques and materials to their structures. Examples of Aztec monumentality and grandeur are seen at the Great Temple, where 8,000 people could fit into its plaza, and the market of Tlatelolco, which accommodated 20,000 people on market days. Aztec architectural adaptation and ingenuity can be seen at Malinalco, where a temple was cut out of the rock and integrated into a mountain.

SYMBOLISM

Aztec architecture is deeply embedded with symbolism. The cardinal points are religious symbols for the four directions and corners of the Earth. They have divine patrons, colors, days, and year signs. For the Aztec, the north was represented by the color black and ruled by Tezcatlipoca, god of fate, destiny, and night; it was the region called Mictlampa, meaning the "place of death," and its associated symbol was a flint knife. The south was characterized by the color blue and ruled by Huitzilopochtli, the solar god and war deity; this was the region called Huitztlampa, the region of thorns, and its symbol was a rabbit. The east was associated with the color red and ruled by

Tonatiuh, the sun god; Xipe Totec, the god of fertility and vegetation; and Camaxtli-Mixcoatl, the god of hunting. It was the region called Tlapallan, meaning the "place of red color," and also Tlapcopa, the "place of light"; its symbol was a reed. The west was represented by the color white and ruled by Quetzalcoatl, the god of wind, Venus, and wisdom. The west, where the Sun goes down into the land of night and the dead, was the region called Cihuatlampa, meaning the "place of the women," where the Cihuateteo

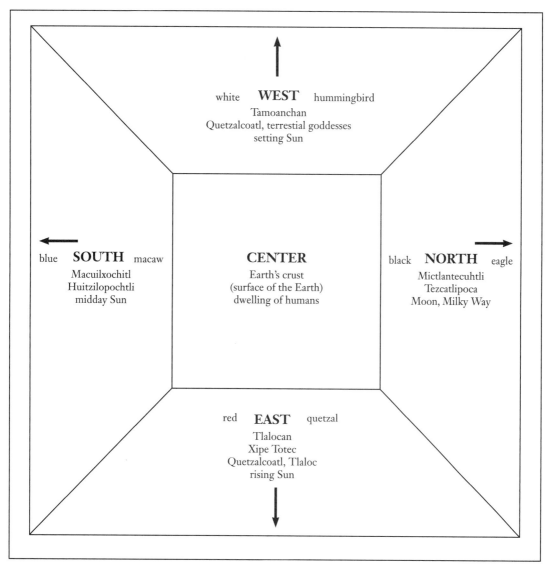

white **WEST** hummingbird
Tamoanchan
Quetzalcoatl, terrestial goddesses
setting Sun

blue **SOUTH** macaw
Macuilxochitl
Huitzilopochtli
midday Sun

CENTER
Earth's crust
(surface of the Earth)
dwelling of humans

black **NORTH** eagle
Mictlantecuhtli
Tezcatlipoca
Moon, Milky Way

red **EAST** quetzal
Tlalocan
Xipe Totec
Quetzalcoatl, Tlaloc
rising Sun

9.1 Diagram of the orientation of a pyramid-temple according to the four directions of the universe (Lluvia Arras, after Gendrop 1985) (deified women who have died in childbirth) escorted the Sun each evening after his journey across the sky; its symbol was a house. These gods of the four directions are responsible for fire, sunlight, water, earth, humans, the dead, and time. They maintain equilibrium on Earth (see chapter 11).

The city of Tenochtitlan and its structures, especially the Great Temple, followed those cosmological patterns. It is also clear in the *Codex Mendoza*, with the Sacred Precinct of Tenochtitlan at the center with four sectors emanating from it oriented to the four cardinal points. The Aztec wished to maintain equilibrium and appease their gods for fear that the Earth would collapse as it had during the previous suns (worlds). Thus, the city's orientation was a result of the belief that when the fifth (current) sun was created in Teotihuacan, the diverse gods faced different directions to see from which direction the new Sun would rise. According to the Legend of the Suns, the Great Temple faces west toward Cihuatlampa because the first god to see the Sun was Quetzalcoatl. Quetzalcoatl's temple, meanwhile, faces east toward Tlapallan, from which the Sun emerges every day (see chapter 6).

Other recurring symbols in Aztec architecture are the eagle, representing the Sun and the warriors; serpents, symbolizing water or fire serpents, linked to Tlaloc and Huitzilopochtli, respectively; and the conch shell, relating to fertility, life, and creation. Also prevalent are representations of frogs as aquatic creatures, reminiscent of Tlaloc symbols.

TYPES OF ARCHITECTURE

General Construction of Pyramid-Temples

Pyramid-temples (*teocalli*) were built to strengthen and impose the Aztec religion and worldview. Building pyramid-temples was one of the most important architectural duties for the Aztec because of their religious significance. They were government-sponsored public works designed to create a sense of religious piety and imperial power. They were believed to represent mountains, which were the sources of water and fertility and the home of the spirits of Aztec ancestors. Pyramid-temples, like mountains, also symbolized the concept of *altepetl*, or the heart of the city filled with fertilizing water. They also served as important sanctuaries where rituals were celebrated, and important people were sometimes buried within them. More important, they represented the celestial order where the cosmos was divided into 13 sections, each associated with a different superhuman phenomenon. For that reason, according to anthropologist Rudolf van Zantwijk, many of the pyramids that followed the blueprint of the Great Temple consisted of four platforms built, steplike, on top of each other, relating to the four cardinal directions. The three lower platforms consisted of 12 sections; the 13th section was the small top platform where the dual temples of Huitzilopochtli and Tlaloc were built (1985: 200).

Most pyramid-temples followed a general pattern that consisted of platforms and a long, broad, steep double staircase rising from the center, with balustrades along the sides of the steps. Sculpted stone blocks and skulls were used to decorate a platform and the end of the balustrades. Constructed with cosmology in mind, pyramid-temples always faced west and were situated on the eastern side of the town center/plaza border. The double staircase also faced west, where the Sun descended into the underworld. The tops of the pyramids had small flat plateaus where a temple or a sacrificial block was built.

Early Aztecs built pyramids in a style similar to the ones of Classic and earlier Postclassic Mesoamerican people. It is important to note, however, that there were some differences. Some of the most common features found in Aztec pyramid-temples are the 13 steps along the stairway; staircases with two balustrades with changing slopes at the top, almost becoming vertical; and representations of an eagle, which is the *nahualli* (disguise or form) of Huitzilopochtli-Tonatiuh. These elements can be seen on temples at Tepoztlan, the Temple of the Feathered Serpent in Xochicalco, the round temple of Cempoala, and the temple of Ehecatl in Calixtlahuaca.

Temples

A temple was usually found on the top of a pyramid, though there were exceptions. Temples consisted of a back room that contained the idol to whom the structure was dedicated and an antechamber for a priest. The inside walls of most temples were ornamented with either sculpture or paint. Temples were also decorated with geometrically carved blocks of stone.

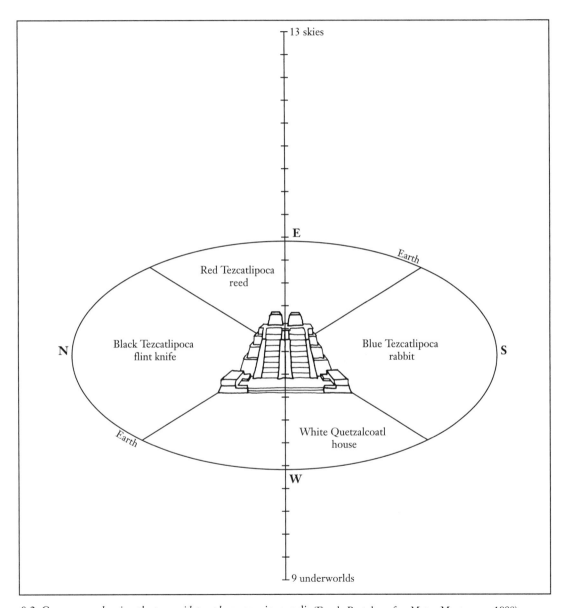

9.2 Cosmogram showing the pyramid-temple as an axis mundi *(Fonda Portales, after Matos Moctezuma 1988)*

Since many state-related ceremonies were held inside temples, politics and religion could not be separate. This union of politics and religion increased the emperor's authority and legitimized his respective god's power. Temples were provided with priests, adjoining residences, schools, and land (as seen with the Great Temple).

The empire's cosmological and religious ideals were manifested in temples. They were the center point for the four cardinal directions, the place where the vertical channel or axis led to heaven and the underworld, and where the supreme ruler interacted with the gods. Many of the ceremonies held at the temples followed seasonal and festival calendars. According to Aztec beliefs, it was essential to provide the gods with nourishment in order to prevent the end of the world. The nourishment of the gods was blood shed during human sacrifice.

Not all temples were built for human sacrifice. The Aztec were a polytheistic people who built various temples in honor of different gods. For that reason, the offerings or honors presented to different deities varied. In addition, temples were places for the renewal of the empire, altars of rebirth and hope. Temples, like pyramid-temples, were constructed in accordance with the four cardinal directions and faced west.

If a new temple (or pyramid) was to replace an already existing one, the older structure was not destroyed; rather, builders would add over the existing edifice. The result would be a new temple that was larger, more extravagant, and more detailed. Enlarging preexisting structures meant adding more stairs and making the sacrificial area more spacious. Layering a preexisting temple was acceptable because the gods had already blessed the original temple; in fact, building a more magnificent temple paid further tribute to the gods.

The appearance of most temples was similar: They resembled truncated pyramids. The outside of the temples had terraces and steps. Some of the most detailed and decorated parts of the temple were the staircases that pointed toward the heavens. Stone serpent heads were frequently placed at the end of the staircases. The serpent heads represented Coatepec, the birthplace of Huitzilopochtli. Also, it was believed that by using poisonous or dangerous animals for decor, evil spirits would be warded away.

Type of Pyramids

ROUND PYRAMIDS

Round pyramids are predominantly found in Calixtlahuaca, in the Toluca valley. They are dedicated to the god of the wind, Ehecatl, one of the forms of Quetzalcoatl. The structures were therefore constructed in a circular fashion to facilitate air flow. According to Aztec and other pre-Columbian beliefs, Ehecatl blew wind in the four cardinal directions so that the Earth would be cleansed, thus enabling Tlaloc to send rain. Gentle wind would be sent to the east, in the direction of Tlalocan (the paradise of god Tlaloc). Gales would be sent in the direction of Mictlan (the underworld), to the north. Gentle cold wind blew to the west, where the *cihuapipiltin* (noblewomen who died while giving birth) stayed; to the south, where the Huitznahua gods (the stars of the south) resided, were blown strong gusty winds.

TWIN STAIRS PYRAMIDS

An example of a twin stairs pyramid is the Great Temple of Tenochtitlan. It had a double staircase, and at its summit, it had two temples. The temple on the left side honored Tlaloc, the god responsible for providing a good rain season and an abundant harvest. If enough rain was not forthcoming, the result was famine. For that reason, Tlaloc was highly revered. His temple was decorated blue and white, the colors that symbolized water and moisture. The temple on the right side was dedicated to Huitzilopochtli. It was painted in red and white in honor of war and sacrifice. The Great Temple was very tall and steep, and the temples on top of the pyramid could not be seen unless a person stood elevated on a platform. Temples were typically tall because the gods lived in the sky and above the people. Being at the summit of a pyramid was the closest a person could be to the gods. Other examples of twin stairs pyramids are found in Tenayuca and Tlatelolco.

SHRINES

Aztec shrines were important religious structures. Each shrine honored one specific god, and the different shrines' appearances were relatively diverse.

Although shrines' exteriors varied, their internal structure was more uniform. The interior usually was circular, with a round table in the middle of the room that was used to hold the offerings to the shrine's god. Since the Aztecs were extremely devout and had many offerings, there usually was not enough room for all the offerings, and it was not uncommon for another building to be added. The adjoining structure consisted of a rectangular building that led to a smaller round room where there was a fire in the center to burn offerings. It was often the case that the second building would burn down because the roof was thatched of grass and straw. It is believed that the frequency of fires explains the large quantities of shrines that were built. These shrines played an integral part in the religious lives of Aztecs, who strongly believed that offerings were essential in pleasing the gods. Examples of these shrines are found on Mt. Tlaloc and Huixachtlan, or Hill of the Star (known today as Cerro de la Estrella) (see figure 11.3).

Early Capital Cities

The general layout and architecture of Aztec capital cities were formally planned around a center, with randomly situated homes on the outskirts of town. Buildings were cosmologically oriented. At the heart of the city, there was a rectangular public plaza with civic and religious buildings along its borders. Most

temples, shrines, and pyramid-temples were found in this area. Beyond the central area there were markets, dwellings, schools, and other buildings.

City-State Capitals

City-state capitals were cities that had control of provinces, and they were usually planned in a similar manner as the more local capital cities. Like the capital cities, city-state capitals were also cosmologically oriented. They had a central plaza with adjoining civic and religious structures. Pyramid-temples were on the eastern side of the plaza, facing west. Other important civic or religious buildings had a designated location according to the four cardinal directions. Since the Aztec Empire was large and dominated many cultures, most city-states had little or no contact with the imperial metropolis. As a result, the city-state capitals played a more important role in the daily lives of the people than did Tenochtitlan. City-state capitals were used by peasants to take care of personal, religious, and administrative obligations, like market days and other activities.

Ball Courts

Ball courts were used to play the famous Mesoamerican ball game, and they were generally constructed in

9.3 Ball court at Coatetelco, Morelos (Fernando González y González)

9.4 Remains of the aqueduct that carried freshwater from Chapultepec to Tenochtitlan (Fernando González y González)

the traditional I shape, though there were some variations (see figure 9.3). The ball court was called *tlachtli* or *tlachco*, and the game was called *ullamaliztli. Ullamaliztli* was an early Mesoamerican tradition handed down to the Aztec and is still played today in some parts of Mexico. For the Aztec, the ball game was the main sport, offering both recreation and religious ritual (see chapter 13). Whenever the Aztec settled a site, their first act was to build a shrine for Huitzilopochtli and a ball court next to it. Ball courts were associated with the myth of Huitzilopochtli and Coatepec, where he fought Coyolxauhqui and the Centzon Huiznahua, decapitated them, and ate their hearts at the center of a ball court. The myth of Coatepec reflects the daily cosmic fight between the Sun (light and life) and the nocturnal celestial bodies (death and darkness) and the Sun's victory, which allows the continuity of life in the universe. The movement of the ball was a metaphor for the drama of the moving Sun across the sky and was intended to reflect the celestial events on Earth.

Aqueducts and Dams

The major cities of Tenochtitlan and Tlatelolco were erected on tiny marshy islands on Lake Tetz-coco. Those swampy islands had a limited supply of drinking water, so an aqueduct was built to carry freshwater over the lake from springs at Chapulte-pec on the mainland. The Aztec also created long canals for irrigation of their fields, and in the times of King Motecuhzoma I, the Tetzcocan king Neza-hualcoyotl built a dyke that protected Tenochtitlan from floods, which were very destructive during heavy rainy seasons. These sophisticated hydraulic works were some of the most impressive accomplishments of Aztec technology.

Markets

All major cities had thriving markets located near or adjacent to the main temple at the center of the community. According to Spanish chroniclers, Aztec law required that one go to the market and bring supplies to town. Nothing could be sold on the way to the market for fear that the market god would punish the offender; this was enforced by strict penalties under the law. Markets were important not only for the economic prosperity of the city but also for gathering information such as rumors of rebellions or attacks by neighboring peoples, as was the case during the early years of the empire. Although markets and their respective plazas did not contain immense buildings, they are important to the architecture of the Aztec in terms of their location, layout, and cosmological implications (see chapter 12).

Gardens

Many Aztec gardens were modeled after the garden that once belonged to "the ancestors," discovered by Motecuhzoma I in Huaxtepec. The emperor decided to restore and rebuild the garden, and a variety of flora and fauna was brought from other regions. Thereafter, other gardens flourished, both in cities such as Tetzcotzingo, Iztapalapa, Tetzcoco, and Tlatelolco and in the palaces of future emperors. They were well organized and incorporated into the architectural plan of palaces.

Gardens were kept primarily for pleasure, but they also held medicinal plants. Most gardens were similar and can be compared to the one in the palace of Iztapalapa, which was described by Hernán Cortés as having many trees and sweet-scented flowers. There was a place for bathing in freshwater, providing the ruler a peaceful resting place. Well-constructed steps led the bather down to the bottom. There was also a large orchard tree near the house, overlooked by a high terrace with many beautiful corridors and rooms. Within the orchard was a great square pool of freshwater, very well constructed, with sides of handsome masonry, around which ran a walk with well-laid tiles, so wide that four people could walk abreast on it. On the other side of the promenade, toward the wall of the garden, were hedges of lattice work made of cane, behind which were all sorts of trees and aromatic herbs. The pool contained many fish and different kinds of waterfowl.

ley. In Tenochtitlan, however, the Aztec began to focus on the solidity of buildings constructed over the ever-sinking subsoil. *Tezontle*, a strong and light volcanic stone, became a popular alternative, and was used extensively. *Tezontle* was easy to cut, and its texture and color were appealing. It was used as filling in walls and roofing. The Aztec attributed the large quantities of *tezontle* stone available to the destruction of the world, as told in the Legend of the Suns, which explains that during the era of the third sun, there was a rain of fire that destroyed the world, leaving *tezontle* on the surface (see chapter 6). Another popular technique used to prevent the city from sinking was to use platforms as foundations or to drive wooden piles into the earth in close-packed formations. This has been revealed in excavations.

Hard metals like iron were unknown to the Aztec. Cords, wedges, or other objects would be used to cut stone; sand and water were common abrasives. Most building materials used by the Aztec were found in the region or acquired through trade. In Tenochtitlan swamp delicacies such as frogs, fish, and algae were traded for building materials such as rock and fill. Rock and fill were used to expand and stabilize the marshy *chinampas* (land plots used for agriculture). Rubble, plaster, adobe, and lime to make stucco were also commonly used. Loose stone and rubble was imported from coastal regions. Outside of Tenochtitlan, people used wood from uninhabited forests. Pine and oak were popular for making support beams and door jambs.

The Aztec were so adept in working and carving stone that in the colonial period, the Spaniards utilized Indian artists side by side with European artisans, who used metal tools in the construction of colonial edifices, resulting in the *tequitqui* art of Mexico.

BUILDING MATERIALS AND TECHNIQUES

The Aztec were adept builders and craftspeople who used chisels, hard stones, and obsidian blades as tools. Many of the materials used were the same as those used for about 2,000 years in the Mexica central val-

THE PRECINCT OF TENOCHTITLAN

Tenochtitlan was a monumental city that stood for power and endurance and was a living metaphor of

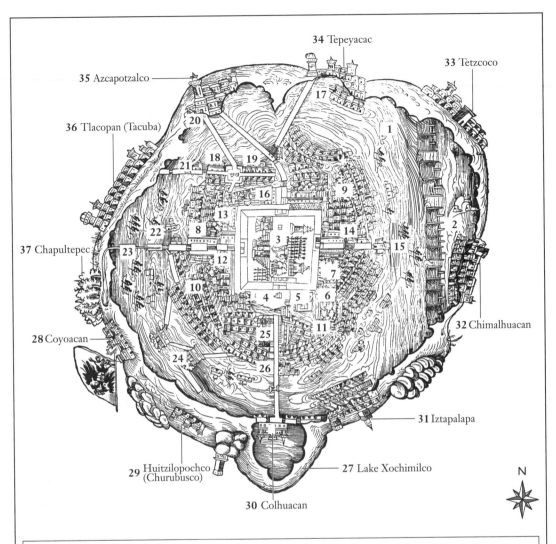

34 Tepeyacac

33 Tetzcoco

35 Azcapotzalco

36 Tlacopan (Tacuba)

37 Chapultepec

28 Coyoacan

32 Chimalhuacan

31 Iztapalapa

29 Huitzilopochco (Churubusco)

27 Lake Xochimilco

30 Colhuacan

N

1 Lake Tetzcoco	**15** Tetamazolco Dock	**24** Motecuhzoma's country houses
2 Nezahualcoyotl's Dike	**16** Tepeyacac Causeway	
3 Sacred Precinct with Great Temple	**17** Tepeyacac Causeway	**25** Causeway from Tenochtitlan to Iztapalapa
4 Plaza and market	**18** Tlatelolco's great temple	**26** Xoloc's fortress
5 Palace of Motecuhzoma II	**19** Tlatelolco's market	**27** Lake Xochimilco
6 Botanical garden	**20** Causeway and aqueduct from Azcapotzalco to Tlatelolco	**28** Coyoacan
7 Zoo		**29** Huitzilopochco (Churubusco)
8 Cuepopan District	**21** Causeway and aqueduct from Tlacopan to Tlatelolco	**30** Colhuacan
9 Atzacoalco District		**31** Iztapalapa
10 Moyotlan District	**22** Causeway from Tlacopan to Tenochtitlan	**32** Chimalhuacan
11 Zoquipan, or Teopan, District		**33** Tezcoco
12 Palace of Axayacatl	**23** Aqueduct from Chapultepec to Tenochtitlan lined up with Tlacopan causeway	**34** Tepeyacac
13 Palace of Cuauhtemoc		**35** Azcapotzalco
14 Causeway from Sacred Precinct to Tetamazolco Dock		**36** Tlacopan (Tacuba)
		37 Chapultepec

Map 7 City of Tenochtitlan, 1524, from a map included in the second letter of Hernán Cortés to Emperor Charles V

the Aztec story of migration and the supremacy of their sun god, Huitzilopochtli. It was an urban island settlement that housed approximately 200,000 inhabitants at the time of the Spanish conquest. Its name was derived from *tetl*, "rock"; *nochtli*, "cactus"; and *tlan*, a suffix signifying location. It is also believed that the city was named after Tenoch, a priest-king that ruled the Mexica when the city was founded in 1325 C.E. Tenoch had led his people through years of hardship in the Mexican central Valley, during which he devoutly followed Huitzilopochtli's signs that led to founding Tenochtitlan. Tenoch predicted that the land where the Mexica should settle would be found by searching for an eagle perched on a prickly pear cactus (nopal) and devouring a serpent, as well as for a white field, a white frog, and a white willow (some of the same foundational elements that appeared in previous cultural stories, such as those from Tula and Cholula). Finding the heart of Copil, nephew of Huitzilopochtli, would determine the exact location of where the city would be founded. Copil was the son of Malinalxochitl, a goddess sister of Huitzilopochtli's. Malinalxochitl was a mischievous sorceress who was abandoned by the Mexica in Malinalco due to her evil witchcraft activities. Malinalxochitl encouraged animosity between her son and her brother. When Copil and Huitzilopochtli fought, Copil was defeated, and his heart was thrown into Lake Tetzcoco. It landed on the island that would become Tenochtitlan (see chapter 6).

When the sacred city was founded, a temple in honor of Huitzilopochtli was immediately erected. The temple was constructed of reeds and straw with a foundation of swamp grass. According to Aztec history, that evening Huitzilopochtli spoke to a priest and advised him to divide the city into four *campan* (quarters) with a temple dedicated to him at the center. This nucleus became the ceremonial precinct of Tenochtitlan, with the Great Temple surrounded by other temples and shrines. The complex was enclosed by a wall and could be entered only through four gates oriented toward these cardinal directions, like the causeways that led out of the city (see map 3).

Initially, Tenochtitlan was structured in the same manner as other city-state capitals; it had a planned central area and an unorganized region on the outskirts of the ceremonial precinct. This layout changed, however, when Tenochtitlan's population began to grow exponentially. When it was determined that Tenochtitlan was the capital of a burgeoning empire, the city was renovated. The architects of Tenochtitlan borrowed many stylistic attributes (such as the urban grid) from Teotihuacan and Tula.

One of the defining features of Aztec architecture in Tenochtitlan was the monumental edifices. Since the structures were massive and built on top of a marshy, muddy island, they continuously sank. As a result, new layers were added to preexisting structures. This was particularly true of the Great Temple, in the central plaza. When the Spaniards came, they asserted their dominion by building present-day Mexico City over Tenochtitlan. These building suffer from sinking, too. In some parts of Mexico City, the Aztec structures underneath are now literally 26 feet (8 meters) below the city streets.

Tenochtitlan was said to have been a magnificent city, dubbed by some European observers to be the Venice of the New World. According to the Spanish chroniclers, it was the most impressive and beautiful city that they had seen outside of Europe. Shortly after the conquest, plans of the city showing the precinct of Tenochtitlan were drawn. One of them is known as the *Map of Mexico-Tenochtitlan of 1550* (Map of Uppsala), and the other was drawn up (or commissioned) by Hernán Cortés in his second letter to the emperor Charles V and published in Nuremberg in 1524. These plans as well as Spanish chronicles and archaeological data have been instrumental in documenting Aztec architecture and urbanization, despite the fact that between the conquistadores' systematic destruction and the missionaries' religious zeal, the precinct of Tenochtitlan no longer exists. Each source is usually consistent with the other, though there are some discrepancies.

Bernal Díaz del Castillo, a Spanish soldier who took part in the conquest, many years later wrote that the Spaniards were astounded by the sight of villages built in the water, which to them was an enchanted vision like the one written about in *Amadis of Gaul*, a Spanish romance of chivalry published in 1508. Believing the sight to be a dream, they were surprised when they found friendly lodging in the palace of Iztapalapa. The palaces were very spacious and built of magnificent stone, cedar, and wood of other sweet-smelling trees, with great rooms and courts, and all covered with an awning of woven cotton.

When describing the gardens, Díaz continued to recount the marvelous place. He never tired of noticing the diversity of trees and the various scents given off by each, the paths choked with roses and other flowers, the many local fruit trees and rose bushes, and the pond of freshwater. There were a variety of birds that came to the pond. Another remarkable thing he wrote about was that large canoes could come into the garden from the lake, through a cut channel.

When describing the Great Temple, Díaz added that to reach it, one had to pass through a series of large courts. These courts were surrounded by a double wall and paved, like the whole temple, with a smooth flagstone floor. Where these stones were absent, everything was whitened and polished. The temple was so clean that there was not a straw or a grain of dust to be found there. When Díaz del Castillo arrived at the Great Temple, he observed six priests and two chieftains walk down from the top of the temple, where they were making sacrifices; the Spanish climbed the 114 steps to the top of the temple, which formed an open square. There, on a platform, were the great stones where sacrifices took place. On that platform, Díaz also saw a massive image like a dragon and other "hideous" figures, as well as a great deal of blood.

From the top of the temple, one could see a great number of canoes, some coming with provisions and others going with cargo and merchandise. Díaz observed that no one could pass from one house to another in that great city or any other city built on water except by a wooden drawbridge or canoe. All the houses had flat roofs, and on the causeways were other small towers and shrines built like fortresses. The market swarmed of people buying and selling; some of the Spanish soldiers had been to many parts of the world—Constantinople, Rome, and all over Italy—and they proclaimed that they had never seen a market so well laid out, so large, so orderly, and so full of people.

Urbanism

The Aztec built their capital on a tiny island in Lake Tetzcoco, that was enlarged by filling in surrounding marshy areas. It was divided into four large *campan* (quarters), symbolizing the four cardinal directions, and a ceremonial center considered to be the heart, or the fifth direction in the *axis mundi* (Mesoamericans believed that the center, held the sky and Earth together). The quarters were then subdivided into smaller neighborhoods, called *calpultin*. Each *calpulli* had its own central plaza, shrines, patron deities, and administrative buildings but the major temples were in the ceremonial precinct of Tenochtitlan.

The city of Tenochtitlan was linked to the mainland by three main causeways, three other secondary causeways, and a double aqueduct that brought freshwater from Chapultepec because the lake was salty. To the north lay the road to Tepeyacac (Tepeyac), to the south lay Iztapalapa and Coyoacan, and to the west lay the road to Tlacopan (Tacuba) and Chapultepec. A network of canals that crossed each other at right angles divided the city into four quadrants, plus the center that was the Sacred Precinct. Each quadrant was further subdivided into the four directions, with a center and its own ceremonial center. The city followed Teotihuacan's grid system. The pyramids and plazas were metaphors for the surrounding mountains' volcanic shapes and the plateau of the lake.

Tenochtitlan had three types of streets: dirt roads for walking, deep-water canals traversed by canoe, and dual-laned dirt-water streets, which could be walked or canoed. Because the city was on top of a lake, many streets intersected with deep canals flanked by bridges made of wood beams.

The Aztec sought to acquire prestige by incorporating stylistic features of past great cultures, as seen in the Red Temples and in ceremonial banquettes (benches along the wall). The Red Temples were located on the north and south sides of the Great Temple proper. The temples were named after their color of decoration: dull-red murals. They were raised on low bases, and their styles were reminiscent of Teotihuacan. The ceremonial banquettes were identical to those constructed in the Charred Palace of Tula, illustrating a Toltec influence.

There were many sculptures, such as those of Coatlicue, systematically distributed in patios and temples. Many were destroyed during the conquest. The ones that remain are on display at museums in Mexico (see chapter 8).

Ceremonial Plaza

The central plaza was the religious and administrative center of Tenochtitlan. The core of the city was the Great Temple, which rose at the intersection of the three causeways. It was surrounded by a ceremonial center that formed a 400-meter (1,312-foot) square. It consisted of 78 religious structures, all painted in brilliant symbolic colors and surrounded by secondary complexes and rows of residencies (see map 6). This sacred area was bounded by the *coatepantli* (serpent wall) and was dedicated to the religious ceremonies celebrated throughout the year. The ceremonial center sat on a raised quadrangular platform, forming a square where ritual buildings were symmetrically arranged. The area consisted of recurring stairways, platforms, and houselike temples laid out in a hierarchy that faced the four directions on a prevalent east-west axis. The Sacred Precinct included diverse pyramid-sanctuaries, such as the Great Temple (Templo Mayor) dedicated to the gods Huitzilopochtli and Tlaloc, the circular Temple of Quetzalcoatl, the Temple of Tonatiuh, the temple-palaces of the eagle and jaguar warriors, as well as the ball court, a *temalacatl* (gladiatorial-sacrifice stone), the *calmecac* (school), libraries, the *tzompantli* (skull rack), ponds for ritual ablutions, and residences for priests. In the patio of the Yopico, the temple of Xipe Totec, there was an elevated platform that also had a *temalacatl*.

The ceremonial plaza was surrounded by the royal palace and the houses of nobles, which were located immediately outside the *coatepantli*. The homes of commoners (*macehualtin*) stood at the periphery of the precinct. The major market of Tenochtitlan was adjacent to the southern side of the main plaza. There were also small markets that served wards far from the precinct. Some sections of Tenochtitlan's outskirts consisted of cultivated *chinampa* plots that extended onto the lake. Crops were grown on these small, marshy floating islands. Their layout is illustrated in the *Plano en papel maguey*, an early colonial document (see chapter 12). The plans, monuments, and natural setting of Tenochtitlan thus functioned as expressions of the daily lives and religious beliefs of the people.

Tenochtitlan was a large city with multiple structures. These Aztec buildings lie immediately below Mexico City, but because the subsoil is fragile, excavations are limited. In addition, many of Mexico City's structures are from colonial times and thus are considered historic. For these reasons, there are limited areas designated for archaeological research. For example, some important Aztec structures are believed to be beneath the cathedral of Mexico City, but due to its historic and religious nature, the cathedral cannot be destroyed. Limited excavations are however taking place under the cathedral, allowing the rescue of interesting materials. For example, The Temple of Tezcatlipoca meanwhile lies beneath the present-day archbishop's headquarters. It is believed to have been 20 meters (65 1/2 feet) high, with an 80-step stairway. These now-buried Aztec edifices were once an integral part of the architecture and urbanization of Tenochtitlan.

On the west side of the Sacred Precinct was the *tozpalatl*, a structure surrounding the sacred spring used for ritual bathing. This area also contained the *teutlalpan*, a wooded hunting area enclosed by four walls. Also there was the tall pole, which was adorned during the Xocotl Huetzi (Falling of the Fruit) festival, when a sacrifice was performed in honor of the fire god Xiutecuhtli, and prisoners were thrown alive into the flames of a ceremonial fire.

The *coateocalli*, a temple where the gods and religious paraphernalia of conquered communities were housed, was located in the northwest part of the precinct. In that area were other buildings that functioned as lodgings for priests, as penance houses, and as "preparatory homes" for the youth in service of the temple.

The Temple of Quetzalcoatl was located directly in front of the Great Temple. Behind the Temple of Quetzalcoatl, on the western end of the ceremonial center, lay the ball court for the ritual ball game. The Temple of the Sun appears to have been located on the southwest corner of the precinct, and it faced the stone for gladiatorial sacrifices. Other temples in the ceremonial center were the Temple of Cihuacoatl; the House of Eagle Warriors, which formed one of the most important military orders (this was unearthed in the excavations of the Templo Mayor Project); the Temple of Chicomecoatl, the goddess of vegetation and corn; and the Temple of Xochiquetzal, the goddess of beauty and love associated with artisans and artists.

The Great Temple

The Great Temple was one of the finest testaments of Aztec monumental architecture and power. The temple's architectural layout, organization, location, and artwork represented the social, religious, and geographical center of the Aztec universe. According to Aztec thought, the central point where the temple stood was where the celestial and subterrestrial levels (vertical dimensions) intersected with the terrestrial realm (horizontal dimension). The celestial realm consisted of 13 heavens (where celestial bodies lay and gods lived), the terrestrial consisted of the four world directions, and the subterrestrial realms were made up of nine levels that the deceased had to pass through to get to the underworld. The temple was built on the conceptual spot where the vertical channel met with the horizontal; furthermore, it was built in a city surrounded by water, just as Aztlan, the Aztec homeland called Cemanahuac, meaning "the place in a circle of water," had been in the middle of a lake. Metaphorically, therefore, all shores and seas could be called Cemanahuac, according to the Aztec; thus, Cemanahuac or

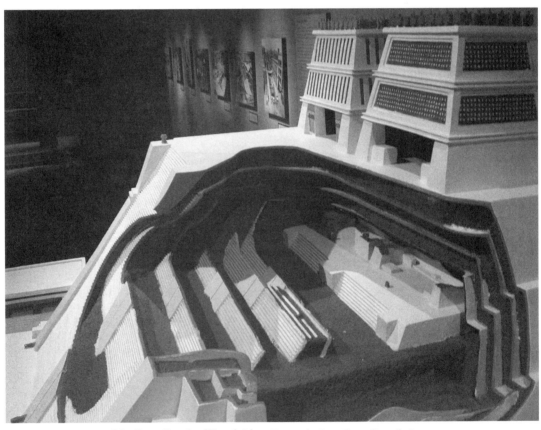

9.5 Superimpositions of the Great Temple of Tenochtitlan (Fernando González y González)

Anahuac was, by extension, the name that the Aztec used to refer to the Valley of Mexico and in general to the world. It had been prophesied that the god Huitzilopochtli would lead the Aztec to a place where they would have power and grandeur, and the Aztec claimed to be settled in the center of the universe as the chosen people.

The ceremonial center of Tenochtitlan developed around the temple of Huitzilopochtli. Over time, the temple followed the tradition of other Mesoamerican pyramids as it was rebuilt in enveloping layers. Thus, the original temple, with its offerings, sculptures, and related artifacts, was completely enclosed by subsequent superimposed structures, evolving from a humble dwelling to the monumental center of the Aztec universe.

During the excavations of the Great Temple, its architecture revealed some interesting facts. The growth of the temple during consecutive imperial reigns was a result of state patronage, in particular that of Motecuhzoma I Ilhuicamina and his son Axayacatl. Excavation also determined that the pyramid was organized as a symbolic human-made mountain and as a dual-purpose stage, where religious and mythological rites related to both the Tonacatepetl (the Mount of Sustenance associated with the rain god Tlaloc and his shrine on Mt. Tlaloc) and Mt. Coatepec (Snake Mountain, birthplace of Huitzilopolochtli) were reenacted.

The Great Temple was a microcosm for the Aztec worldview. According to archaeologist Eduardo Matos Moctezuma (1988: 129–135), the platform that supports the temple corresponds to the terrestrial level, as sculptures of serpents, earth symbols, are located there. There are two large braziers on each side of the serpent-head sculptures at the center of the north and south façades and on the east side, on the axis with the central line of the Tlaloc and Huitzilopochtli shrines. The braziers indicate that perishable offerings were given, further evidencing that the platform was the terrestrial level. Four slightly tapering tiers of the pyramid that rise to the summit of the two shrines of the chief gods represent the celestial level. The subterrestrial realm (underworld) lies beneath the earthly platform. Many offerings have been found below this floor. Nezahualpilli's words to Ahuitzotl, an Aztec emperor, during the commemoration of the comple-

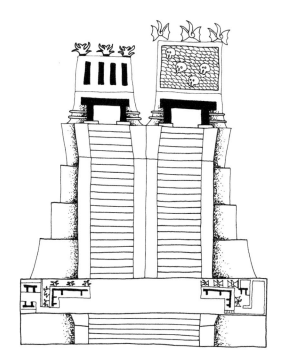

9.6 Frontal view of the Great Temple of Tenochtitlan, according to the Codex Ixtlilxochitl (Fonda Portales)

tion of one the temple's construction phases, affirmed the sacredness of this pyramid-temple. He stated that Tenochtitlan was a powerful kingdom— the root, navel, and heart of the entire world.

MYTHS SYMBOLIZED IN THE GREAT TEMPLE

The Great Temple is a dual pyramid with twin temples on its top platform, representing two sacred mountains: Coatepec on the south side and dedicated to Huitzilopochtli, and Tonacatepetl on the north side and dedicated to Tlaloc. The south side of the temple is an architectural representation of the myth of the birth of Huitzilopochtli on Mt. Coatepec, symbolizing the Aztec's rise to power. Coatepec is a Toltec site near Tula and was visited by the nomadic Mexica in 1163 C.E., during their long migration. It was at Coatepec that Huitzilopochtli, the child of a virginal conception, was born from the womb of Coatlicue and fought and killed his jealous sister Coyolxauhqui (the moon goddess) and his brothers, the Centzon Huiznahua (the 400 stars from the south) (see chapter 6).

Huitzilopochtli's temple is filled with sculptures of serpents, representations that are in accordance with the name Coatepec, which means "snake mountain." The myth of Coatepec probably had a historical foundation related to a conflict between two factions trying to gain control over the entire group and seeking to impose leadership during the migration. It is apparent that one group wanted to stay in Coatepec and the other group wanted to continue in pursuit of the promised land that Huitzilopochtli had offered to the Mexica. The myth was important because it represented the daily cosmic battle between the Sun (Huitzilopochtli) and the deities of the night (Moon and stars), and the Sun's triumph at dawn. It was also a theological justification for the Aztec's settling in the area of Lake Tetzcoco and for their practices of warfare and human sacrifice.

According to the myth, after his victory against Coyolxauhqui, Huitzilopochtli remained on the hill of Coatepec. His shrine on top of the Great Temple is a symbol of his reign. In the same myth Coyolxauhqui was decapitated by her brother, and her dismembered body rolled to the bottom of the hill. On the platform of the base of the pyramid, a large bas-relief sculpture representing the decapitated goddess was discovered, as were other Coyolxauhqui sculptures in several of the construction layers, illustrating the continuity of this myth. Some scholars believe that the sacrificial stone at the entrance to Huitzilopochtli's shrine indicates the immolation of his sister and that it was used in reenactment rites of human sacrifice (see chapter 6). There were decapitation rites that involved female victims during the festival of Ochpaniztli, and archaeologists have found female skulls placed as offerings at the Coyolxauhqui sculpture. In addition to excavation results, the Spanish chroniclers, through their descriptions of rites conducted during festivals, provide data suggesting that the temple was used to recreate the myth of the birth of Huitzilopochtli. During festivals, tribute was offered, and people were sacrificed at the top of a scaffold, thrown to the ground, beheaded, and rolled down the stairways that ended at the bottom of the pyramid. This ritual reenacted the mythic events at Coatepec.

The northern side of the Great Temple symbolizes the mountain Tonacatepetl (Mount of Sustenance) and is dedicated to Tlaloc, the god of fertility who provided food through his beneficial waters, which form rain clouds on mountain tops. This mountain is also related to the myth of the creation of the Aztec and of the discovery of maize. There are two interpretations concerning the association of this structure with Tlaloc. The first is that the temple represents Mt. Tlaloc, a hill located between the cities of Tetzcoco and Cholula, where nobles and rulers from central Mexico made offerings of jewels, valuables, and food to the deity so that he would provide the necessary rain for a good harvest season. The second, based on another myth, is that it represents the Hill of Sustenance, where Quetzalcoatl discovered maize and brought it to the gods so that they could give it to human beings as primordial foodstuff. Instead, the Tlaloques, rain deities and assistants to the god Tlaloc, seized the maize, and Tlaloc and the Tlaloques only provided the maize and other foods by fertilizing the earth and making the plants grow. This myth shows how the fertility of the earth is controlled by the power of water. Several Spanish chronicles describe the elaborate ceremonies conducted at Tlaloc's temple.

Archaeological and historical accounts show how the temple was the *axis mundi* of the Aztec and the place where some of their main myths came alive as they were reenacted through ritual. According to Matos Moctezuma, Tlaloc and Huitzilopochtli are joined together in architecture, myth, and ritual and represent water and war, life and death, and food and tribute—all fundamental to the very existence of the Aztec people (1988: 145). And so it is appropriate that they are connected to the Great Temple.

CONSTRUCTION STAGES FOUND IN THE ARCHAEOLOGICAL EXCAVATIONS

The Great Temple was enlarged at relatively short intervals, seven times completely and four times partially. Each subsequent superimposition was more grandiose because of a need to improve and to surpass the previous construction, as well as to project a

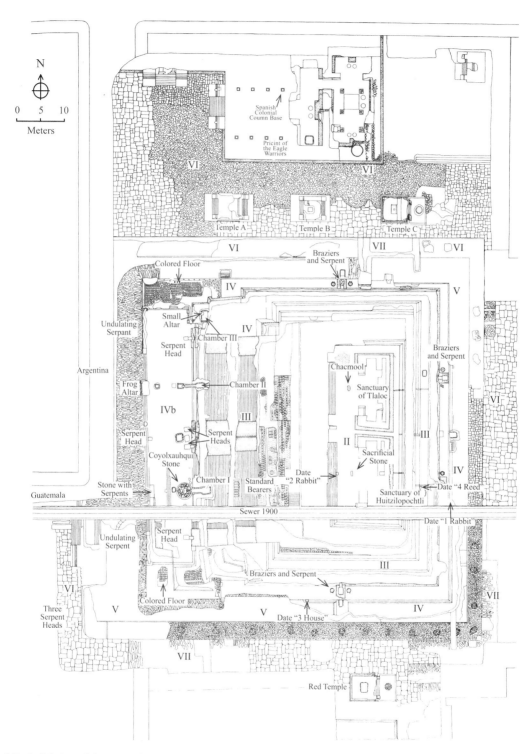

N

0 5 10
Meters

Spanish
Colonial
Coumn Base

Pricint of
the Eagle
Warriors

VI

VI

Temple A   Temple B   Temple C

VI   VII   VI

Colored Floor   Braziers
and Serpent

IV   V

Undulating
Serpent

Small
Altar
Chamber III

IV

Serpent
Head

Braziers
and Serpent

Chacmool

Sanctuary
of Tlaloc

Argentina

Frog
Altar   Chamber II

VI

IVb

III

Serpent
Head

Serpent
Heads

III

III

Coyolxauhqui
Stone

Chamber I

II

Sacrificial
Stone

IV

Stone with
Serpents

Standard
Bearers

Date
"2 Rabbit"

Date "4 Reed"

Guatemala

Sanctuary of
Huitzilopochtli

Sewer 1900

Date "1 Rabbit"

Undulating
Serpent

Serpent
Head

III

Braziers and Serpent

VI

V

Colored Floor

V

Date "3 House"

IV

VII

Three
Serpent
Heads

VII

Red Temple

9.7 *Aerial view of the seven phases of construction (superimpositions) of the Great Temple of Tenochtitlan* (Lluvia Arras, after Matos Moctezuma)

prestige and sense of power of the ruler in position. Each phase reflected the emperor's ambition and personality, which are also imprinted in the overwhelming monumentality of Aztec art in general to create a sense of imperial domination and religious transcendence.

Phase I Phase I is related to the first humble temple erected by the Aztec when they arrived in Tenochtitlan in 1325 C.E. This temple is known only from historical accounts because it is not possible to excavate below Phase II due to the fragile, watery subsoil.

Phase II The temple during this phase was very similar to historical accounts of the pyramid of Phase VII, which the Spaniards witnessed. At the summit, in front of the entrance to Huitzilopochtli's shrine, was a sacrificial stone (*techcatl*) similar to the one described by the chroniclers. Its building material was *tezontle* (volcanic stone). The entrance to the

Tlaloc shrine has a colorful *chacmool* used as a divine messenger that took sacrifices of children performed here and offerings from the priest to gods. Some interior murals of both shrines have survived. Representations and colors corresponded to the specific deity. Pine and other wood, used for pillars and door jambs, were also found. Archaeologists believe that Phase II corresponds to the period between 1325 and 1428, when the early emperors Acamapichtli, Huitzilihuitl, and Chimalpopoca reigned.

Phase III Not much has survived of Phase III except for the plain pyramidal base with the double stairways. Eight *tezontle* sculptures of life-size standard-bearers were found leaning near the base of the stairs that led to the Huitzilopochtli shrine. They perhaps represented the Centzon Huitznahua, Huitzilopochtli's 400 brothers. This phase, according to a date carved at the base of the temple, may correspond to 1431, during the reign of Itzcoatl.

9.8 Phase II of the Great Temple: the shrines of Tlaloc and Huitzilopochtli (Fernando González y González)

9.9 *Stairway and three statues perhaps representing the Centzon Huiznahua, from Phase III of the Great Temple* (Fernando González y González)

Phase IV Phase IV of construction is considered to be one of the most spectacular because considerable material and data have been found. During this phase, the pyramidal base was enlarged and adorned with braziers and serpent heads on all four sides. Oversized braziers at the rear of the Tlaloc side bear his visage, and the braziers on Huitzilopochtli's side have a large bow, a symbol of the sun deity. Traces of offerings have been found. Phase IV also included an additional partial enlargement. The west side of the main facade was amplified and adorned.

The temple lay on a vast platform with a single stairway. There were large, undulating serpent bodies around the corners. Each serpent had an individualized face on which archaeologists have found traces of paint. The stairway was broken by a little altar near the base of Tlaloc's shrine that had two frogs (symbols of water). In addition, the middle of the stairway on the platform side of Huitzilopochtli's

shrine had a two-meter- (6½ -foot-) long tablet that formed part of a fourth stair and had a serpent engraved on the rise. The base of the platform formed the stairs. Four serpent heads marked the place where the two structures dedicated to Tlaloc and Huitzilopochtli met. At the foot of the stairway, in the middle of Huitzilopochtli's side, the famous Coyolxauhqui stone showing the dismembered body of the moon goddess was found; it is a magnificent carving in low relief. Many offerings were found beneath this platform. It appears that this phase corresponds to the year 1454 and 1469 during the reigns of Motecuhzoma I and Axayacatl.

Phase V Little has survived of Phase V. Stucco plaster on the temple platform and part of the floor of the ceremonial precinct was found. This phase is linked to the reign of Tizoc (1481–86).

Phase VI The little that remains of Phase VI includes the great platform underlying the entire temple structure. Part of the stairway is still visible. The principal facade was adorned by three serpent heads and a balustrade. Three small temples designated as A, B (a *tzompantli*), and C (one of the Red Temples), as well as the precinct of the eagle warriors, belong to this phase. In the latter, once occupied by those brave elite warriors, is the Eagle Patio, which is flanked by decorated stone banquettes reminiscent of Tula. This phase corresponds to the reign of Ahuitzotl (1486–1502).

9.10 *A general view of the Great Temple from the southwest showing the location of the Coyolxauhqui stone from Phase IV* (Fernando González y González)

9.11 Interior of the House of the Eagle Warriors, next to the Great Temple (Fernando González y González)

Phase VII Phase VII constitutes the last building stage and was the phase of construction seen by the Spaniards in the 16th century. The stone flooring of the ceremonial precinct and traces of where the Great Temple stood are all that remain. This phase was undertaken during the reign of Motecuhzoma II Xocoyotzin (1502–20).

Emperors' Palaces

The Palace of Motecuhzoma II was one of the most elaborate and grand buildings constructed in the Aztec Empire (see figure 4.2). It was located on the southern side of the Great Temple. Motecuhzoma's palace was two stories tall and had a large courtyard. It was a large complex that occupied an estimated 2.4 hectares (a little more than five acres) and housed 1,000 guards, servants, nobles, cooks, courtiers, and members of the king's harem. It was reported that approximately 600 nobles attended the king's palace at all times. The aristocracy's residences were either attached to the palace or located nearby. The palace was surrounded by a garden, other minor palaces, residences, military houses, and other structures for military orders and warrior groups. The temples of the precinct were surrounded by similar edifices as the emperor's palace.

The palace had many rooms with the largest on the first floor. Columns on the first floor supported the weight of the second floor. The staircase con-

necting the two levels was made of pure marble and was located directly in the center of the palace. Marble was a luxury in the Aztec Empire; only the richest people had access to this fine material. The wealth of the emperor was manifested in the numerous paintings, gold panels, carvings, and mosaics found throughout the palace. According to the Spanish soldier-chronicler Bernal Díaz del Castillo, Motecuhzoma's dining room had a low wooden throne (*icpalli*) and a low table covered with fine cloths. When the emperor ate, he was hidden by a golden-colored wood screen door so that he would not be seen by those in attendance. The emperor was served by numerous women and was entertained by dancers, singers, and musicians.

There were several main rooms on the first floor. The room in which the emperor received nobles, travelers, and other officials was known as the reception chamber. The largest room (three times the size of the reception chamber) in the palace served as the main meeting chamber. It was specially designed to make the emperor appear omnipotent and powerful; for example, the emperor was raised above the people who visited him by an elevated platform with stairs that led to the emperor's throne. This was the room where messengers provided the emperor with news about the empire. The other main room on the first floor was the tribute room/store, which was used to house the gifts the emperor received from his loyal citizens. The emperor received such large quantities of gifts, that there was usually not enough space in the tribute room for all his gifts/goods. Another important section of the palace was the emperor's personal apartments.

Not only was the palace exceedingly large, but it was also highly complex. The structure had multiple rooms that served specific functions. There was an armory, a tribute hall, special rooms for women who wove textiles for the royal household, artisan workshops, an aviary, a zoo, and a pond. The aviary housed various species of birds from nearby and tropical regions. The zoo contained animals such as snakes, foxes, and jaguars. The special pond contained aquatic birds.

Motecuhzoma II's gardens and baths were an integral part of the overall layout and architecture of his palace. They were modeled after the gardens at Tetzcoco. Because the gardens and baths no longer exist, Díaz del Castillo's account is very important. He described the gardens as being filled with fragrant flowers and trees, promenades, freshwater ponds, and canals. He also wrote that the trees were full of small birds bred on the premises, and the gardens were full of medicinal plants.

The palaces of previous emperors were also magnificent. Axayacatl's palace is believed to be located beneath present-day Tacuba and Monte de Piedad Streets (it was initially believed to have been below Guatemala and Correo Mayor Streets). The Palace of Motecuhzoma II is believed to be below the present-day National Palace, a colonial-era building. On the western side of Mexico City's main plaza, or Zócalo (where the Aztec market plaza was), lay the *petlacalco* (great warehouse), *calpixcalli* (house of the butlers), *pilcalli* (house of the noblemen), and *cuicacalli* (house of singing). Cuauhtemoc's residency, erected by his father, Ahuitzotl, is believed to be west of today's Plaza of Santo Domingo.

Homes of the City's Inhabitants

The royal palaces and the homes of the nobility were built near the main square of the Great Temple, and the houses of the city's potters, stonecutters, weavers, jewelers, farmers, and fishermen surrounded the city centers. For the Aztecs, the type of dwelling in which a person lived was an indication of status. The homes of commoners (*macehualtin*) and nobles (*pipiltin*) were similar in layout and pattern but different in size, decoration, and construction materials. The nobles' homes were made of stone and whitewashed plaster. Their interior walls were of stucco painted with colorful murals. The dwellings of the *macehualtin* were humbler. They lived in different *calpultin* (neighborhoods), and their homes were made of adobe bricks (mud mixed with straw or rushes), wood, and straw.

Aztec residences were typically one story high, consisted of two structures, and housed up to 12 people. The first structure was a single room with a perfectly level floor divided into four areas. The bed area was where the entire family slept. The kitchen area was where the meals were prepared. Most

kitchens had a *metlatl* (flat stone for grinding corn) and a *comalli* (clay dish for baking tortillas). Another area was designated for eating. There, the family would sit, eat, and discuss the events of the day. The last area was for the family shrine and contained figurines of gods. Aztec homes did not have doors because theft was not an issue.

The second adjoining structure was a *temazcal* (steam bath). According to Aztec doctors, steam baths were therapeutic, and all families were advised to have one. Next to the bath area a chimney and a stove were found. The hot walls of the stove maintained the room's heat. When a person wished to steam the room, water would be poured on the stove's wall. In order to maintain the stove's heat, the furnace had to be constantly burning. Although most Aztec homes contained a steam bath, they were predominantly used by the nobles because nobles had more leisure time than peasants did.

Chinampas

The swamps and gardens were on the outskirts of the city. *Chinampas*, known as floating gardens, were used for farming; houses were also built on them. These rectangular patches of earth were constructed on the swampy lakebed. Stakes were woven together to fence in enclosures of about 2.5 meters ($8^1/4$ feet) wide and 30 meters (100 feet) long, which were covered with decaying vegetation and mud. Plots were constructed parallel to each other, with water in between forming a canal. *Chinampas* were stabilized by planting slender willows around their perimeter. The willows' dense roots anchored the retaining walls. In order to irrigate the *chinampas*, a sophisticated drainage system of dams, sluice gates, and canals were installed. The *chinampas* allowed the Aztec to have productive planting areas on the lake (see chapter 12).

Ball Courts

The main ball court (*tlachtli*) of Tenochtitlan was located on the east-west axis of the ceremonial precinct's western end, aligned with the Great

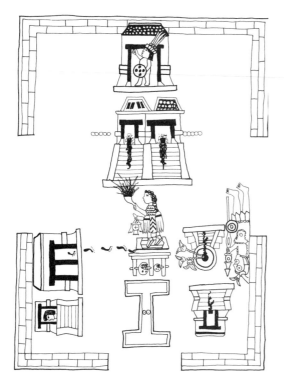

9.12 Plan of the Sacred Precinct of Tenochtitlan, including its central ball court, from Primeros memoriales *in* Códice matritense *(Fonda Portales)*

Temple and the Temple of Quetzalcoatl. The east-west axis of the ball court is meaningful in the context of sacred geography, because the ball game represents the daily cosmic battle between the day and night, Quetzalcoatl and Tezcatlipoca, and ultimately, Huitzilopochtli and Coyolxauhqui. In the architecture of the ball court, ancestral myths are brought to life.

The ball court was formed by an I-shaped area with two large sloping walls, tiers, porticos for dignitaries, and boxes for judges. The structure was adorned by skull racks, or *tzompantli*, which contained the heads of the decapitated captives from diverse rituals. In many cases the skulls were trophy heads from decapitation rituals linked to the ballgame. The skull racks consisted of a base with upright wooden posts. The skulls of the sacrificed were strung along bars held between the posts. It is

believed that the main skull rack of Tenochtitlan was located in an area that is now buried under the cathedral of Mexico City.

OTHER CITIES

The Aztec Empire was a large domain that extended from the Valley of Mexico to the Isthmus of Tehuantepec. Large portions of the empire were not occupied but governed. Other cities of the empire were occupied and were important for military, religious, or tribute purposes. Many places, such as Malinalco and Coatepec, held historical/mythical significance. In addition to Tenochtitlan, the more important cities of the Aztec world where archaeological remains can be visited are Tenayuca, Santa Cecilia Acatitlan, Teopanzolco, Tlatelolco, Tetzcotzinco, Tepoztlan, Huexotla, Calixtlahuaca, Coatetelco, and Malinalco.

Tenayuca

Tenayuca, meaning the "place where walls are made," was a Chichimec city founded in 1224 and was located northwest of Tenochtitlan. Tenayuca was an enclosed and fortified city founded by King Xolotl and was the capital of the Chichimecs until a later king, Quinatzin, moved to Tetzcoco. It had six major construction phases from 1224 to 1507. Mexica-Aztec influence was visible by 1325. Although its temple was built during the Postclassic Period, archaeological materials found inside the temple indicate that Tenayuca was inhabited long before. The early phases of pyramid construction began after the fall of Tula (1200) and before the founding of Tenochtitlan (1325). It is believed by some scholars that the Great Temple of Tenochtitlan was modeled after the great temple of Tenayuca. The city's double pyramid was four-tiered, faced the plaza, and was ornamented with rows of serpents surrounding all three sides of the base, forming a *coatepantli* inspired by the one in Tula. Since the snakes in the *coatepantli* have a spiral-like crest in their heads, they are identified as *xiuhcocoah*, or "fire serpents," the weapon of Huitzilopochtli. This symbol signified an association of Tenayuca with the sun god cult and fire renewal. The gods Huitzilopochtli, Tlaloc, Mixcoatl, Itzpapalotl, Chicomecoatl, and Coatlicue were worshipped there.

THE PYRAMID

Tenayuca's pyramid is composed of several superimposed layers. All layers follow the same system of construction, patterns of decoration, and layout. The earliest structure has carved stone slabs facing a rock core. Thereafter, the current pyramid would be used as a core for the next successive layering/construction phase. Slabs were coated with cement made from sand, lime, and crushed *tezontle*. Color would then be applied. Carved stone serpent heads, year glyphs, shields, knives, and other symbols were used for decoration. The low platform that projected from the pyramid was ornamented with bones and sculpted skulls.

WALL OF SERPENTS

The *coatepantli*, or wall of serpents, covers all three sides of the pyramid's platform. There are 43, 50, and 45 serpent heads on the north, east, and south walls, respectively. Greenish blue paint is visible on the snakes' bodies of the south side and half of the bodies on the east side. Their bodies' scales were outlined in black. The north wall's serpents were garnished in black with white ovals. Snakes' rattles were detailed by carving three stepped planes at the tip of their tails. It is believed that the color schemes used on the bodies were related to the symbolism of sun worship.

On the north and south ground level of the pyramid, coiled serpents were positioned. The heads of stone are ornamented with a spiral crest that identifies the serpent as a *xiuhcoatl*, which is associated with fire renewal, sun worship, and the 52-year calendar. The stone heads were decorated with bulging dots that are believed to symbolize stars.

The rocky stairway has visible engravings from the last structural addition. A year glyph, a linked

9.13 Pyramid of Tenayuca (Fernando González y González)

later occupied by the Mexica-Aztec and transformed into one of the numerous religious enclaves that surrounded the Tetzcoco lake region. Santa Cecilia Acatitlan has a double pyramid-temple that faces a cobblestone plaza that may have been used as a public arena during ceremonies. In that plaza, in front of the pyramid, there is a small church built in the late 16th century with stones taken from the pre-Columbian site.

THE PYRAMID

The pyramidal platform is composed of a double stairway that faces west and is separated by a balustrade that is twice as wide as the other two balustrades that form the extremes of the platform. On top of it are two temples. The North Temple was dedicated to Tlaloc. A *chacmool* (messenger of the gods who carries the human sacrifice offerings) accompanies Tlaloc inside his temple. The South Temple was dedicated to Huitzilopochtli. The roof of this temple was made out of inclining panels that were decorated with nail-like stones. The doorway of the shrine has a wood lintel.

The dual pyramid-temple of Santa Cecilia Acatitlan, with some variants, follows the traditional Aztec pattern of twin pyramids dedicated to Tlaloc and Huitzilopochtli.

9.14 The coatepantli *(serpent wall) of Tenayuca*
(Fernando González y González)

rectangle and triangle, banners, concentric circles, a knife, turquoise, *chimalli* (shields), and precious stones are still visible. The carvings do not appear to have a systematic order.

TOMB-ALTAR

Located in front of the pyramid, there is a combined tomb and altar with colored paintings of crossbones and skulls inside. The outside has carved stone reliefs illustrating skulls.

Santa Cecilia Acatitlan

Santa Cecilia Acatitlan is located north of modern-day Mexico City. Acatitlan, which means "between the canes or reeds," was originally a Chichimec city,

9.15 The dual pyramid of Santa Cecilia Acatitlan
(Fernando González y González)

9.16 The main pyramid of Teopanzolco (Fernando González y González)

Teopanzolco

Teopanzolco is located in the northeast part of the city of Cuernavaca and was originally under Tlahuica control and later taken over by Aztec imperial forces. This site, which contains early Aztec architecture, has a main pyramid believed to have served as a model for the Great Temple of Tenochtitlan, and a temple dedicated to Quetzalcoatl. The pyramid had double shrines: one dedicated to Huitzilopochtli and the other to Tlaloc. The Quetzalcoatl temple is circular in design, thus honoring the deity in his Ehecatl form.

THE PYRAMID

The pyramid displays similar attributes as the one located in Tenayuca. It has several superimpositions; two have been found. The only remains of the exterior walls' last layer are the sloping wall and a staircase flanked by balustrades that are divided in two parts by a central double one. The double balustrade forms the front of the pyramid, which faces west and has a rectangular base that is 50 by 32 meters (165 by 105^1/$_2$ feet). The substructure is better preserved than the most recent layer. It also faces west and measures 32 by 18 meters (105^1/$_2$ by 60 feet). Its stairway is limited by balustrades, and as in Tenayuca, they rise vertically in the upper section. This characteristic also occurs midway up the stairs, forming a type of pedestal.

The South Temple, dedicated to Huitzilopochtli and located on top of the pyramid, is rectangular, measuring 10 by 7 meters (33 by 23 feet). It has a wide entrance that is divided by a transversal wall with an opening leading to a room that has a bench. The North Temple, dedicated to Tlaloc, has a small rectangular room measuring 7 by 4 meters (23 by 13 feet) with an ample clearing and a bench at the end. There are also pillars presumed to have supported the wood that sustained the roof.

Tlatelolco

Tlatelolco was founded 12 years after Tenochtitlan by a group of dissident Aztec who moved northeast to Xaltelolco, meaning "on the hillrock of sand." Xaltelolco was one of the marshy islands located on

9.17 The twin pyramid of Tlatelolco, with a Spanish colonial church behind it (Fernando González y González)

Lake Tetzcoco. It had previously been inhabited by groups related to Teotihucan and the Tepanecs. Over time, this site came to be known as Tlatelolco. According to other scholars, its name is believed to have derived from the word *tlatelli*, which means a built-up mound of earth.

Tlatelolco and Tenochtitlan were contemporary cities that underwent parallel developments. They were rivals until Tenochtitlan attacked and defeated Tlatelolco during the reign of Axayacatl in 1473. Tlatelolco was then incorporated into Tenochtitlan.

The city originally covered an area of about 20 square miles. Tlatelolco today is a neighborhood of Mexico City and at its core is the so-called Plaza of the Three Cultures. The plaza has this name because Tlatelolco is a living testimony of the process of tran-

sculturation that created the mestizo nation of Mexico. Coexisting in this plaza are the remains of Aztec temples, a colonial church, and the convent of Santiago built by Fray Juan de Torquemada, surrounded by many modern Mexican constructions. Tlatelolco of Aztec times had a ceremonial complex that was dominated by a typical double pyramid similar to the Great Temple of Tenochtitlan and the largest market in Mesoamerica. There were also smaller pyramids, temples, and markets scattered throughout various districts.

One of the anomalies of Tlatelolco is that it did not appear to have the type of monumental architecture found at other Aztec sites. Tlatelolco was far from Coyoacan, the place where most of the Aztec monoliths were built, and it also was, for a long time, an independent city. In addition, Tlatelolco was incorporated into Tenochtitlan during the reign of Axayacatl, the emperor responsible for initiating the construction of large-scale projects. Prior to Axayacatl, Aztec architecture was not as massive. Another factor to consider is that at Tlatelolco the main building material used may have been wood, which disintegrates. Other perishable materials may also have been used, making it difficult to discern the architecture of the city prior to its incorporation into Tenochtitlan. Nonetheless, Tlatelolco was an integral part of the Aztec metropolis and continued to flourish after its annexation.

Similar to other towns of the empire, Tlatelolco had its share of shrines, temples, palaces, gardens, markets, and canals. One such shrine, located near the north door of the colonial church of Santiago, was built of human mandibles in a jewel-like manner. Similar altars were found throughout the ceremonial complex. Some other structures in Tlatelolco are reminiscent of Chichén Itzá and Teotihuacan. One of the edifices that displays Chichén Itzá–type qualities

has four staircases facing the cardinal directions. It is believed to have been situated in the middle of a plaza and to have been used for religious ceremonies, during which the priest would direct the smoke from his incense to the four cardinal points. For that reason this particular structure did not have an altar. Such influence is not surprising since Tlatelolco had been previously inhabited and had borrowed styles from other groups.

THE TEMPLE OF THE CALENDAR

The Temple of the Calendar is one of the most significant structures of Tlatelolco. It is a unique edifice whose decor deviates from the norm in that it is ornamented with elements of the *tonalpohualli* calendar. During Aztec times two calendars were used: the *tonalpohualli* and the *xiuhpohualli*. The *xiuhpohualli* was the civil calendar. It was used to determine festivities, record history, and date tribute collections. The *tonalpohualli* served as the ritual calendar. The *tonalpohualli* consisted of 260 days, and the

9.18 The Temple of the Calendar, Tlatelolco (Fernando González y González)

xiuhpohualli consisted of 360 days plus five "bad" days. The Temple of the Calendar is a quadrangular edifice with representations of 39 days; 13 on each wall painted in blues, reds, and whites. The base of the temple also has polychrome paintings with figures drawn similar to those found in the codices. These drawings correspond to early Tlatelolco and are intact on the front side of the temple due to a later superimposition. The temple was a very important religious structure because computing time—determining solstices, baptisms, rituals, festivals, commerce, tribute, and so on—was one of the primary duties of the priest. This is the only calendrical structure that has been found (see chapter 11).

TEMPLE OF EHECATL-QUETZALCOATL

This round temple was dedicated to Ehecatl-Quetzalcoatl, the wind deity. It consisted of a semi-circular base that wound into a conical roof, a staircase, and a quadrangular platform. In general, temples dedicated to Ehecatl were circular so as not to block the wind's trajectory. This temple's entrance resembles a snake's mouth, symbolizing Quetzalcoatl. This temple is similar to that in Calixtlahuaca and underwent two construction phases. Its construction dates back to the early times of Tlatelolco. In later times, other edifices were built over it. A rectangular enclosure decorated with polychrome paintings was found next to the temple. It is older than the temple itself.

PRIESTS' RESIDENCY

The priests' residency was located within the ceremonial precinct because they were responsible for the maintenance of the temples and shrines. Their residence was constructed of *tezontle* and wood. The structure consisted of an altar and two sections adjoined by a central corridor with a chimney-like area for burning wood. The structure also had wood wedges that supported lintels.

SACRED WELL

The sacred well is located next to the priests' residency. It is a small monument that resembles a staired swimming pool. The pool leads to the sacred well. The well is approximately three meters (10 feet) wide. Scholars believe that it may have been used for ablution practices by priests or as a sacred spring.

THE MARKETPLACE

Tlatelolco was best known for its immense and highly lucrative marketplace. Once Tlatelolco was incorporated into Tenochtitlan, its market became the principal market of the Aztec Empire. According to Spanish chroniclers, approximately 25,000 people came to market on a daily basis and 40,000 to 50,000 on special market days, held every fifth day. The market was directed, administered, and organized by merchants called *pochtecah*. The *pochtecah* were responsible for assigning each type of merchandise to a particular section of the plaza and for determining prices. The market was very orderly, well run, and very clean. The Spaniards were amazed at its organization and variety of goods. Spanish soldier-chronicler Bernal Díaz del Castillo described the market as an organized and well-managed space. Each type of merchandise was categorized and had its fixed place. The market was filled with luxury goods such as gold, silver, and precious stones, feathers, mantles, and embroidered goods, but it was also filled with the daily necessities and slaves, cloth, cotton, cacao. Every sort of merchandise that was to be found in the whole of the Aztec Empire was sold in this market, including the skins of tigers and lions, otters and jackals, deer, badgers, and mountain cats, some tanned and other untanned.

There were also buildings where three magistrates sat in judgment, and there were executive officers who inspected the merchandise. The great marketplace, with its surrounding arcades, was so crowded with people that one would not have been able to experience it all in one day (see chapter 12).

Tetzcotzinco

Tetzcotzinco is an important Aztec site perched on a hill and surrounded by agricultural terraces. It is located east of Tetzcoco in Mt. Tlaloc's foothills. It is associated with life-giving rain rites and agriculture. Although there has been little archaeological excavation at this site, survey plans, surface explorations, and aerial views demonstrate its layout. The architecture of this site combined landscape, sculpture, and ritual. Tetzcotzinco was a reenactment of the symbolic landscape of Mt. Tlaloc and was a place of worship since the time of the Chichimec.

After the famine of 1454, the *tlatoani* of Tetzcoco, Nezahualcoyotl, decided to build a new ceremonial center and to refurbish and reconstruct Tetzcotzinco. There, Nezahualcoyotl erected his personal palace, which included rock-cut baths known popularly as the "baths of Nezahualcoyotl,"

canals, aqueducts, gardens, and more than 300 rooms. Tetzcotzinco had a system of farming terraces extending northward from the hill, forming a huge natural amphitheater, and the hill and the neighboring towns, which still exist today, were supplied with water by aqueducts from springs high on Mt. Tlaloc. The hydraulic works of Tetzcotzinco are considered one of the major engineering accomplishments of pre-Columbian times. The aqueduct transported water over a distance of five miles from springs at the slopes of Mt. Tlaloc through the Metecatl hill to irrigate an extensive area of gardens, fountains, and baths carved in the

9.19 View of Tetzcotzinco and its aqueduct from Fountain System A, on Metecatl hill (Fernando González y González)

AZTEC ARCHITECTURE

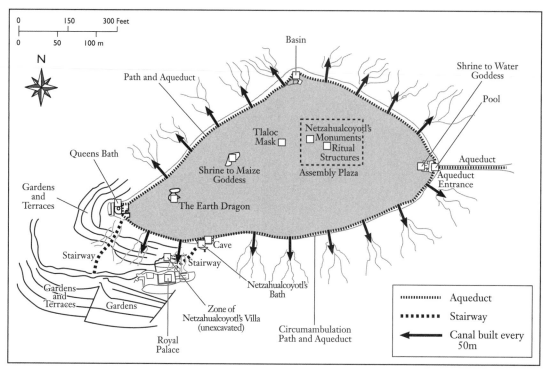

9.20 Plan of the site of Tetzcotzinco (after Townsend 2000)

rock of the Tetzcotzinco hill under the auspices of the great poet, engineer, and king Nezahualcoyotl.

Most of the monuments of Tetzcotzinco were destroyed by the Spanish in 1539; however, many pictorial manuscripts, texts, and related sculpture and architecture provide useful information to reconstruct what remains of the site. The archaeologist Richard Townsend mapped the area in 1979 and revealed that the upper hill was cosmologically designed. Approximately 55 meters (181 feet) below the summit, the ritual zone is demarcated by a walkway cut around the hill. On this path there are four baths, or shallow basins, oriented to the four cardinal directions. Their receptacles were manifestations of Chalchiuhtlicue's aquatic domain and were used for ritual purification. Their water was supplied by an aqueduct built in a circular path that served processional circumambulation and divided the upper sacred zone from the profane space below.

CIVIC MONUMENTS

Among the civil architectural features that can still be seen at Tetzcotzinco are the Reservoir System H and the Fountain System A, a group of water deposits built on the northern skirts of Metecatl hill with the intention to control the speed and flow of the water that descended to Tetzcotzinco; the Monolithic Room, a pool at the entrance of the hydraulic system that had a temple on top dedicated either to the wind god Ehecatl or to the sun god Tonatiuh; the aqueduct subsystem circuit, a series of channels every 50 meters to irrigate the gardens, farming terraces, and royal compounds; the so-called king's and queen's baths, a collection of rock-cut monolithic deposits of water positioned toward the magnificent view of the former gardens in the slopes of the hill and the Valley of Mexico; and the palace attributed to Nezahualcoyotl.

9.21 The "king's baths" in Tetzcotzinco (Fernando González y González)

SHRINES

Tetzcotzinco has a sequence of shrine stations along an east-west axis that follows the natural ridge of the hill. The alignment indicates the path of the Sun, leading scholars to believe that Tetzcotzinco had calendrical and astronomical functions determined by the solstice and equinox. At Tetzcotzinco's summit are remains of a temple. There is also a goggle-eyed mask of Tlaloc engraved on a bedrock boulder.

A sculpted cave that was an important shrine is located below the circumscribing path and near a system of lower terraces, where Nezahualcoyotl's palace and botanical gardens stood. Caves were associated with the heart of the Earth, with mountains, and with the womb. This cave was related to the ancestors and lineage of Nezahualcoyotl, recalling the genesis theme that people first emerged from the womb of the Earth through caves (Chicomoztoc). By placing his compounds next to the cave, Nezahualcoyotl legitimized himself and his legacy.

Another shrine is located high on the western axis, and it has two very damaged carved effigies on the living rock; they are of female divinities connected to the cycle of maize. The divinities are associated with the festivals of Huey Tozoztli, Huey Tecuilhuitl, and Ochpaniztli. Huey Tozoztli was dedicated to Chicomecoatl, the goddess of dried seed corn, and Cinteotl, the conflated male and female deity of the young corn, and was celebrated at the height of the dry season, when corn was consecrated for the coming planting. Huey Tecuilhuitl was dedicated to Xilonen, goddess of the mature corn, and it occurred during the middle of the rain season. Ochpaniztli was dedicated to the male and female earth and maize deities, and it was celebrated during the harvest to mark the start of the dry season.

The last shrines are Nezalhualcoyotl's personal commemorative monuments located on the eastern slope of the hill below the summit. There was an ample assembly plaza that was constructed facing an exposed rock face where the sculptures were carved. The monuments have been destroyed, but from the writings of chronicler Fernando de Alva Ixtlilxochitl, it is known that the first monument recorded the deeds of Nezahualcoyotl as a hero and founder of the Tetzcocan nation. Adjacent to this sculpture there was a seated stone coyote with Nezahualcoyotl's hieroglyphic name, which means "fasting coyote." The monuments faced east toward the rising Sun, associating Nezahualcoyotl with the daily appearance of light, heat, and the renewal of seasons.

Tepoztlan

Tepoztlan, whose name means "place of copper," is located south of Mexico City, near the city of Cuernavaca. Other meanings or names associated with the site are "place of split stones" or "place of axes." In some records the town is named Tepozteco after the spectacular and beautiful sierra of the same name that surrounds it. The city was founded in the late Postclassic period by the Tlahuica people. Its pyramidal complex was dedicated to Tepoztecatl, also known as Ometochtli, the god of pulque (alcoholic beverage made from the maguey plant). He was a legendary cultural hero who, after being a priest for the gods of pulque, was deified. Intoxication with pulque was an important religious practice that allowed the alteration of consciousness with the purpose of communication with the gods. According to the *Codex Mendoza*, Tepoztlan was conquered by Motecuhzoma I Ilhuicamina, becoming a tributary to Tenochtitlan.

THE PYRAMID-TEMPLE OF TEPOZTLAN

The pyramid was molded and cut into the rock on top of a mountain in the spectacular Tepozteco sierra. A platform 9.5 meters (31 feet) high was constructed there. The platform is accessed from the east side through stairs situated in the posterior part of the temple; there are other stairs in the southeast section of the edifice. On the back section of the platform is a raised base composed of two inclined sections separated by a passageway that has stairs on its west side leading to the temple.

The temple consists of two rooms bordered by two-meter- (6½-feet-) wide walls. The first room, a vestibule, is formed by the extension of two side walls and two pillars. The room is 6 by 5.2 meters (20 by 17 feet) and has lateral benches and a depression at the center similar to some of the temples in Malinalco. Archaeological remains suggest that the roof was made of *tezontle*; door jambs and benches were made of stone. The benches have small cornices whose ornamentation is believed to represent

9.22 View of the pyramid of Tepoztlan atop the Tepozteco hill (Fernando González y González)

the 20 day signs. In the lower part of the pyramid are
two plaques; one has the hieroglyph of King Ahuitzotl, indicating a date of 1500, and the other has the
date 10 Tochtli (Rabbit), which corresponds to the
last years of Ahuitzotl's reign. These plates indicate
that this monument was constructed sometime
between 1502 and 1520. The pyramid's 13 steps
symbolized the 13 levels of heaven.

As Ome Tochtli/Tepoztecatl, the patron deity of
Tepoztlan, was related to the earth goddess, festivals
at the temple were carried out after the crop season.
In addition, because he was the pulque god, when a
person died of alcohol intoxication, the town members would have a celebration in honor of the
deceased individual. At present, every December 8,
the day of the Nativity of the Virgin Mary, there is a
festival dedicated to the cultural hero Tepoztecatl,
and people still climb the mountain to place offerings to him.

Huexotla

Meaning "place of the willows," Huexotla is located
three miles south of the city of Tetzcoco. It was an
important city of the kingdom of Acolhuacan, whose
capital was the city of Tetzcoco. It consisted of an
urban center surrounded by suburbs and scattered
villages. Huexotla's formal qualities are those of a
military city suited for defense and attacks; it was
protected by a wall on the west side. Scholars believe
the main building of Huexotla is located directly
below the Franciscan convent and Church of San
Luis that was built in the 16th century. The great
churchyard (*atrio*) displays the unique characteristic
of being formed by two levels connected by a staircase due to an underlying pre-Columbian pyramid.
It shows the deliberate intention of the missionaries
to impose the Catholic religion physically and con-
ceptually.

THE WALL

The great wall around Huexotla was 650 meters
(2,130 feet) long and 6 meters (21 feet) wide. At present only part of the original wall remains. This
defense structure covered the space between two
gorges and completely enclosed the site. Evidence

9.23 The atrio *of the Church of San Luis was built on
top of the main pyramid of the site of Huexotla.*
(Fernando González y González)

suggests that what appears to have been the main
town area was accessed through several gates. Today,
two entrances remain: one in front of San Francisco
Street, which leads to La Estancia and La Comunidad buildings (see next page), and one in front of
the Church of San Luis.

The wall was made of the volcanic *tezontle*. Spikes
(stones cut into cones) were found on the first tier.
At present, only the round part remains visible; the
rest is embedded into the wall's core. Building the
wall was necessary because neighboring warring

9.24 *Ruins of the wall of Huexotla* (Fernando González y González)

groups sought to extend their territories. Other towns of the region, such as Tenayuca, were also built with bulwarks.

LA COMUNIDAD

La Comunidad (the community) is a staired structure that is superimposed on a previous building. It faces a different direction, and its function is unclear. It consists of two tiers and is believed to have been a palace with several rooms and a portico with four columns on top. In some of the rooms are *tlecuiles* (hearths). The floor has traces of red paint and is coated with plaster.

LA ESTANCIA

La Estancia (the hacienda) covers an older building. It consists of two tiers with a staircase in the front, connecting them. The front facade is a plaster-paved apron. Some of the original red paint is still visible.

SANTA MARÍA GROUP

The Santa María group consists of two structures. It is found past the San Bernardino Gorge over the colonial bridge. The first structure had two construction phases. The first was between 1150 and 1350. It consisted of a platform with a staircase on the west side. The second building phase (1350–1515) was very crude, suggesting that the site lost importance during this time. The second structure is located on the east side of the first structure. A section of the west wall can be seen from this building.

SAN MARCOS

Local people call this edifice the observatory, but its original function is unknown. This mound is a series of rooms with a small staircase that leads to a room plastered roughly with adobe. A stone structure rests on top.

SANTIAGO

The Santiago was a ceremonial platform in pre-Columbian times. Because 16th-century evangelizing Spanish friars had a chapel built over it, its only remains are the columns that held up the chapel's roof.

THE EHECATL-QUETZALCOATL BUILDING

This structure is located east of the other Huexotlan pre-Columbian structures. The structure was built on a circular platform that is 19 meters (62 feet) in diameter. The building was fashioned in the traditional circular form so that it would not act as a hindrance to the wind god's entrance (see figure 3.1). The front of the structure indicates that there are two impositions. The first building was erected with the small stones cut in a similar fashion as those from the Santa María building. The newest layer is the one that is presently visible.

Calixtlahuaca

Dating back to the early Postclassic period (900–1250), Calixtlahuaca was located in the Valley of Toluca, southwest of modern-day Mexico City. Calixtlahuaca, meaning "place of houses on the plain," was named by the Mexica-Aztec, who were impressed by the large quantity of towns that dotted the area of the Matlatzinca settlement. The city's overall architectural style is a combination of Toltec and Aztec motifs; however, when the Matlatzinca were in power, they developed a style reminiscent of Teotihuacan and built joined stone slabs covered with mud. The city was founded along the Tejalpa River, bordering the emerging Aztec Empire from the Valley of Mexico and the Tarascan domain to the west. This was a highly vulnerable position. For that reason, the Matlatzinca had fortifications and granaries placed in strategic areas in order to withstand a siege.

According to the writings of Fray Bernardino de Sahagún in the 16th century, the Matlatzinca were called the "net people" because of their innovative use of nets. Because Calixtlahuaca was in a region surrounded by lakes, the use of nets was common, and with nets they fished, thrashed corn, carried their children, trapped birds, and made sacrifices. The Matlatzinca were also referred to as *quaquatl*, a Nahuatl word alluding to use of slings for hunting small game. Slings were strapped to their heads.

Calixtlahuaca was conquered by the Aztec during the reign of Axayacatl (1469–81). It is believed that approximately 11,000 Calixtlahuacan prisoners were sacrificed in temple rituals at Tenochtitlan. Aztec families moved to Calixtlahuaca to solidify Aztec authority and to act as a buffer against the Tarascans. Major temples were added to the city. There are 17 visible mounds, with several of them lying on an artificially terraced hill. With the exception of the structures listed below, most of the monuments have not been excavated. It should be noted that a statue of Coatlicue was found at the top of the hill and is now at a Mexico City museum.

TEMPLE OF EHECATL-QUETZALCOATL

The temple was built in four separate stages. Each stage added a new layer, though the structure always maintained its circular form. The original temple was plain, without much decoration. The second layer was added during the Toltec dominion (900–1200). The third layer was erected at the time the Matlatzinca controlled the area (1200–1474). The final layer was added after the Mexica conquest. The temple also has a single stairway facing east with 13 steps, a symbol of the 13 heavens of the

9.25 Temple of Ehecatl-Quetzalcoatl in Calixtlahuaca
(Fernando González y González)

supernatural realm. Carved stones are embedded into the structure.

Next to the temple was found a stone image of the wind god Ehecatl wearing a *maxtlatl* (loincloth), sandals, and a mask with a beaklike mouth indicating he is an incarnation of Quetzalcoatl, the Feathered Serpent.

THE TLALOC CLUSTER

A group of three structures are clustered together around a small plaza in the middle of the hill. Archaeological findings associate them with Tlaloc. The *tzompantli* was erected in a cruciform fashion on the west side. The transverse part to the west is semicircular. The outside walls are covered with projecting skull-shaped carvings. Rows of skulls, possibly heads of prisoners of war, were found in this building. The other two structures in this plaza are rectangular platforms with a single staircase that face the plaza.

CALMECAC GROUP

The *calmecac* group is a series of clustered buildings around a courtyard on the lower part of the hill near the Tejalpa River. The word *calmecac* derives from the Nahuatl word *calli* for "house" and *mecactl* for "rope." The name is a reference to a building with long narrow corridors.

According to the Spanish chronicles, priests in charged of the education of the nobility's children lived in the *calmecac*. *Calmecac* were the elite schools

9.26 View of the Tlaloc Cluster, with the unique tzompantli (Fernando González y González)

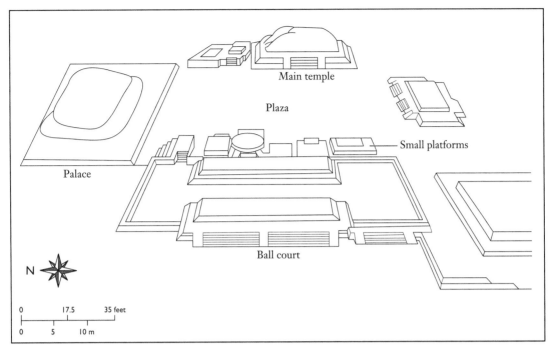

9.27 Plan of the site of Coatetelco (after Smith 2003)

where Quetzalcoatl was a patron god. Flowers, sugarcane, beverages, and food were offered to the god on the day Ce-Acatl, or 1 Cane, of their calendar. Trimmed snail shells, symbols of Quetzalcoatl, were found during the excavations of the rooms of the buildings.

BALL COURT

The site of Calixtlahuaca has a traditional ball court used to play the Mesoamerican ball game. The ball court has not been excavated.

Coatetelco

Coatetelco is an urban site of medium size built in the late Aztec period. The ceremonial center was excavated by the archaeologist Raúl Arana in the 1970s. It consists of a ball court, a small pyramid-temple, a building that seems to be a palace, and a few other edifices all clustered around a public plaza.

The ball court is one of the very few Aztec ball courts that have been excavated (see figure 9.3). Under the stairway of the western ball court platform, elite burials were found with a great amount of tomb artifacts, such as ceramic vessels; obsidian, jade, and copper-bronze objects; and a pile of manos (stone tools for grinding corn on a flat stone, called a metate). According to archaeologist Michael Smith, the residential areas of the site are buried today under the modern town of Coatetelco (2003: 177).

Coatetelco is important because it is one of the few surviving Aztec sites that was not destroyed deliberately by the Spanish conquest. Thus, its sacred precinct has been widely excavated and studied. There is a group of small platforms aligned in the plaza adjacent to the ball court. Besides being a unique feature in Aztec urban planning, they contained buried offerings that included long-handled incense burners similar to those shown in the codices and utilized by priests in diverse rituals. The provincial town of Coatetelco has an interesting architectural feature. Its main pyramid-temple is relatively modest, indicating that not all Aztec cities followed the pattern of building large, massive twin pyramids like those in Tenochtitlan, Teopanzolco, or Tenayuca. Excavations of the residential areas have not been conducted.

Malinalco

Malinalco is a city located in the east-central part of Mexico State, south of the modern city of Toluca. It is believed that the site was founded by the Matlatzinca and was taken by the Aztec in 1469–76, during the reign of King Axayacatl. Malinalco is best known for its rock-cut temples (similar to those of Ajanta and Ellora in India, the Longmen caves of China, the city of Petra in Jordan, and the temple of Abu Simbel in Egypt) and for being a fortress city of the Aztec. Called Cuauhtinchan (Eagle's Nest) by the Aztec, it served military-religious purposes and was the headquarters for the eagle and jaguar warriors, the prestigious Aztec military orders.

Malinalco's ceremonial center is located on a mountain cliff called the Cerro de los Ídolos (idols' mount), and it resembles an eagle's nest amid a mountainous region. Malinalco was a strategic location, allowing the Aztec to control the Valley of Toluca (Matlatzinca region), northern Guerrero, and the Tlahuica region. Its name means "place where Malinalxochitl [grass flower] is adored," or more simply, "place of the grass flower."

The temples of Malinalco are usually described as sculpture-temples or sculptural architecture. They were carved into a sloping hill, oriented southeast for

9.29 Temple I (the cuauhcalli) *of Malinalco* (Fernando González y González)

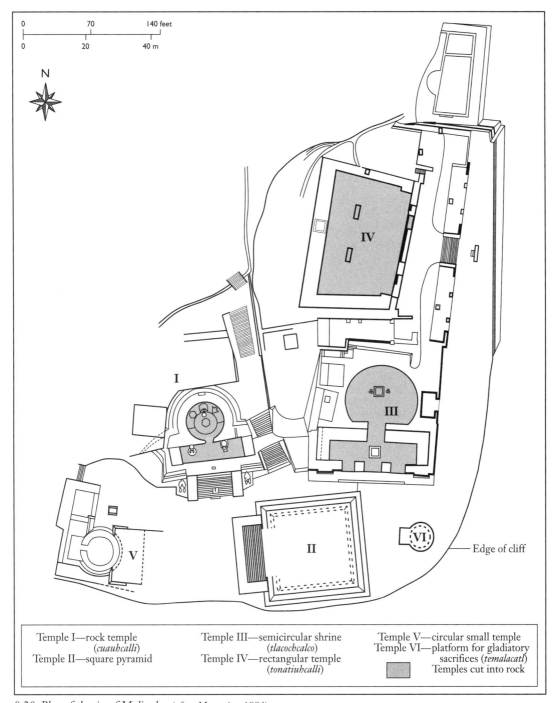

0   70   140 feet

0   20   40 m

N

IV

I

III

II

V

VI

Edge of cliff

Temple I—rock temple	Temple III—semicircular shrine	Temple V—circular small temple
(*cuauhcalli*)	(*tlacochcalco*)	Temple VI—platform for gladiatory
Temple II—square pyramid	Temple IV—rectangular temple	sacrifices (*temalacatl*)
	(*tonatiuhcalli*)	Temples cut into rock

9.28 Plan of the site of Malinalco (after Marquina 1984)

AZTEC ARCHITECTURE

255

9.30 Details of the facade of Temple I, Malinalco (Fernando González y González)

ritual purposes. According to the Aztec, Malinalco was one of the most important architectural sites because of its association with Aztec religious history and for its military nature. Malinalco is the place where the three levels of the cosmos unite: the sky, the Earth, and the underworld. It is well known for its shamanism and as the place where Copil, nephew of Huitzilopochtli and son of Malinalxochitl, fought Huitzilopochtli. Copil was defeated, and his heart was thrown over Lake Tetzcoco and landed on the island that would later become Tenochtitlan (see chapters 2, 5, and 6).

TEMPLE I (*CUAUHCALLI*)

The major structure of Malinalco is a temple called the *cuauhcalli*, meaning "house of the Eagles," by the archaeologist José García Payón (1974: 11–20). The circular *cuauhcalli* pyramidal base and balustraded

staircase is a rock-cut structure carved in the mountain side and is oriented south. It has two bodies in *talud*, or talus (sloping walls), with one superimposed on the other, with a height of four meters (13 feet).

The staircase, located on the front facade of the building, is two meters (6¹/₂ feet) wide and has 13 steps. The staircase has two balustrades with changing slopes at the top, each becoming almost vertical. On the left and right sides of the stairs, two squatting jaguars are found. On the fourth and seventh steps are remains of a damaged sculpture of a sitting standard-bearer (*pantli*) similar to ones that once stood on top of the balustrades of the Great Temple of Tenochtitlan.

At the top of the stairs is a low platform that functioned as an antechamber for the shrine of the temple. The platform floor has a rectangular perforation that is believed to have had an embedded *tech-catl* (sacrificial stone). Three-dimensional figures of a serpent head with an eagle warrior sitting on top (east side) and a *huehuetl* (vertical drum) covered with *ocelotl* (jaguar) skin surmounted with remains of a jaguar warrior on the west side flank the doorway. The doorway of the shrine is the open mouth of a serpent, with fangs on each side and a bifid tongue sculpted on the floor. García Payón believed that this architectural sculpture represented Tlaltecuhtli, the earth monster, but it is now more widely accepted that it is Coatlicue, the mother earth goddess. This characteristic suggests the *cuauhcalli* was rather a cave-temple, the entrance to the womb of the Earth.

The interior structure has a painted, raised ledge cut from rock that follows the circular contour of the wall and is almost six meters (19 feet) in diameter. The east and west sides have sculptures of flat eagles, and the north side has an extended jaguar. The sculptures were zoomorphic thrones. The extended jaguar was used by the king, and the eagles, by his imperial officers. In the center of the shrine there is sculpture of an eagle facing the doorway. Behind the eagle there is a circular hole, approximately 30 centimeters (12 inches) wide and 33 centimeters (13 inches) deep. It is believed that it was a *cuauhxicalli* (repository for the hearts of sacrificed victims) that held the offerings needed to maintain the movement of the Sun and human existence. The eagle is the *nahualli* (disguise)

9.31 Detail of the eagle representing Huitzilopochtli at the entrance of Temple I, Malinalco (Fernando González y González)

of the Sun and is the terrestrial form taken by the god Huitzilopochtli-Tonatiuh. The carved circular wall was completed with an extension of *tezontle* to support the thatched roof.

Like most Aztec architecture, the *cuauhcalli* represents in its construction historical and religious beliefs. As stated above, to some scholars it simply honors Tlaltecuhtli or Coatlicue, the earth monsters, through its function of a sanctuary that represents the Earth itself on which Aztec warriors struggled in warfare and perished fighting, offering their lives to the Sun. To other scholars, the temple represents, like the Great Temple of Tenochtitlan, Mt. Coatepec (Snake Mountain), which is a transitional place on the surface of the Earth (*tlalticpac*) connecting the middle world with the heavens and underworld. It is the mythical house of Coatlicue, represented by the serpent's mouth door.

Under this latter interpretation, when the interior chamber is entered, it leads to a cave, the womb of the Earth. It is a metaphor for the mythical creation place Tamoanchan-Aztlan-Chicomoztoc. Coatepec is the place where Huitzilopochtli was born from the womb of Coatlicue. There are physical elements referring to the myth of Coatepec in Temple I. The *cuauhtehuanitl* (ascending eagle), or rising Sun, is represented by the carved eagle in the center of the shrine that faces toward the portal of the Earth cave (Coatlicue). It symbolized Huitzilopochtli's victory over his siblings. The battle was reenacted every day for human beings: When the Sun rose from the east, it was carried to the zenith by warriors who had died in war or on sacrificial stones; when it set in the west, it was taken by the Cihuateteo, the deified women who had died in childbirth. It was believed by warriors that the hearts placed in the circular hole of the shrine's floor aided Huitzilopochtli in his nightly quests. In the exterior, next to the portal, on the southeast side, there is a *xiuhcoatl*, the weapon used by Huitzilopochtli when he traveled from east to west. The archaeoastronomical measurements of the historian Javier Romero-Quiroz and archaeoastronomer Jesús Galindo-Trejo confirm that the day of the winter solstice (December 21) at noon, the light of the Sun coming from a cleft in a mountain located in front of Temple I enters through the doorway, illuminating exactly the head of the eagle that is the embodiment of Huitzilopochtli, the Sun himself. Furthermore, we know through Fray

Bernardino de Sahagún that on this day, the Panquetzaliztli was celebrated, a festival dedicated to honor sacrifice because this was the day of the descent of Huitzilopochtli to the Earth. It means that the orientation of this temple was built with this solsticial effect in mind.

Flanking the door are images of the *Cuauhtli* and *Ocelotl* warriors who were the guardians of the temple and worshippers of the Sun. Archaeologist Richard Townsend points out that these warriors' ritual practices and ceremonies, such as initiation and graduation, were celebrated in this temple.

Although Temple I is circular, it is not associated with the cult of Quetzalcoatl (many circular structures in Mesoamerica honor the deity). This temple was erected in honor of the sun god Huitzilopochtli, as proven by the iconographic motifs.

TEMPLE II

Temple II is a truncated pyramid that is located a few feet southeast of Temple I. It has a square floor plan and a staircase on the west side of the facade. The balustrades were constructed with carved stones and were built with stucco plaster. Altar carvings and a platform were incorporated into the building. The building is consolidated, but it shows a state of deterioration.

TEMPLE III

Temple III was used to celebrate the funerals of warriors who died in war or captivity and were worthy of going to Tonatiuh-Ilhuicac (the paradise of the sun). The rock-cut structure holds two chambers, a circular and a rectangular one. The eastern portion of the building faces south and is part of a natural slope of the mountain. It is constructed of stone joined with soil and lime mortar. The temple's entrance consists of three doors that are separated by two columns.

The rectangular chamber has a fire pit in the middle of the room. The room contains a bench that runs through the east, west, and north sides. It is interrupted at the center of the north side and gives access to the circular chamber. The rectangular chamber originally had a mural that represented the *mimixcoua*, the deified eagle and jaguar warriors who lived in Tonatiuh-Ilhuicac. Unfortunately, this mural no longer exists.

9.32 Temples III, IV, and VI, Malinalco (Fernando González y González)

TEMPLE IV

Temple IV is partially carved into the living rock, faces east, and is considered to be a *tonatiuhcalli,* a sun temple. Half of the edifice is carved out of rock, while the other half, the front facade, is made of ashlars (masonry walls) of stone. The building is raised from a platform and has a central staircase. The interior consists of two rectangular pedestals that served as column bases supporting the roof. There is an altar carved out of the rock that lies along the main wall. Some scholars believe that an image of the Sun, similar to the Sun Stone of Tenochtitlan, is embedded in the main wall due to the fact that the temple wall was designed to receive the light rays of the rising Sun, illuminating every morning the face of the god.

TEMPLE V

This monument has a circular floor plan of two meters (6½ feet) in diameter and is built of stone ashlars over a platform. Even though it is dilapidated, its limited space and round form are similar to the kivas of the Southwest of the United States, an area located beyond the northern limits of Mesoamerica. The hole that this structure has in its center could have been used to hold the flag or banner of war.

TEMPLE VI

Temple VI was under construction at the time of the Spanish conquest and was never completed. Its platform is identified as that of a *temalacatl,* meaning "wheel of stone." The chroniclers and the codices show that on that particular type of stone, brave enemy captives were exposed to the gladiatorial sacrifice (*tlauauanaliztli*). Some *temalacatl* were also considered to be *cuauhxicalli* (vessels that contained the hearts of the sacrificial victims).

READING

Symbolism

Heyden and Villaseñor 1992, Matos Moctezuma 1988, Soustelle 1979, *Codex Chimalpopoca* 1986: symbolism.

Types of Architecture

Marquina 1964, Heyden and Villaseñor 1992, Kelly 1982, Bunson and Bunson 1996, Stierlin 1982, Townsend 2000, Heyden and Gendrop 1988, Wood 1992, Odijik 1989: general architecture, pyramids, and urbanization.

Building Materials and Techniques

Matos Moctezuma 1988, Heyden and Villaseñor 1992, Townsend 2000: building materials.

The Precinct of Tenochtitlan

Sahagún 1951–69, Díaz del Castillo 1963, Matos Moctezuma 1988, Heyden and Villaseñor 1992, Townsend 2000, Marquina 1964, Heyden and Gendrop 1975: the Great Temple; Marquina 1964, Heyden and Villaseñor 1992, Bunson and Bunson 1996, Stierlin 1982, Townsend 2000, Heyden and Gendrop 1988: city of Tenochtitlan; Townsend 2000, Velasco Lozano 2002: gardens; Townsend 2000, Marquina 1964: *chinampas;* Kubler 1990, Aguilar-Moreno 2002–2003: ball game; Heyden and Gendrop 1975, Marquina 1964, Townsend 2000: palaces; Díaz del Castillo 1963, Stierlin 1982, Townsend 2000: markets.

Other Cities

Townsend 2000, García Chavez 2002: Tetzcotzinco; Marquina 1964: Tepoztlan; Marquina 1964, Smith 2003: Teopanzolco; Zúñiga Bárcena 1991, Kelly 1982, Marquina 1964: Calixtlahuaca; Zúñiga Bárcena 1991, Kelly 1982, Marquina 1964: Tenayuca; Zúñiga Bárcena 1992, Kelly 1982, Alva Ixtlilxochitl 1975–77: Huexotla; García Moll 1993: Santa Cecilia Acatitlan; García Payón 1974, Kelly 1982, Townsend 1982 and 2000, Hernández Rivero 1984, Schroeder Cordero 1985, Galindo Trejo 1989, Romero Quiroz 1980: Malinalco; González Rul 1982: Tlatelolco; Smith 2003: Coatetelco.

10

NAHUATL LITERATURE

Tlacuilos and Their Techniques

Aztec people believed that artists were born, not made, and that artistic skills were intuitive. Nevertheless, artists were extensively trained. Generally, the skills of the *tlacuilo* (painter-scribe) were passed from father to son; the title of *tlacuiloque* (in Nahuatl), or *tlacuilo* (in Spanish), is believed by some scholars to have been hereditary. *Tlacuilos* were highly regarded in Aztec society; they had to become *yolteotl* (a heart rooted in god). They knew different kinds of Nahuatl writing as well as symbols of mythology and tradition, since they were responsible for painting and drawing the codices as well as murals on temple walls and administrative buildings. The outstanding paintings of the monastery of Malinalco, as well as the stone carvings of the open chapel of Tlalmanalco, confirm the surviving practice of using pre-Hispanic natural metaphors for categories of social hierarchy, supernatural beings, and afterlife destinies. The portrait of Fray Domingo de Betanzos was made by a *tlacuilo* on maguey paper in a chapel in Tepetlaoztoc (it is no longer extant). The amazing images of a pre-Columbian battle on the walls of the church of Ixmiquilpan and the many murals in the cloisters and *porterías* (archways) of the monasteries of the 16th century also display the talent of these artists.

Although *tlacuilos* painted and drew the codices, only priests and nobles were to interpret them. Nahuatl speakers called their divinatory books *tonalamatl*, the root word being *amatl* (paper). These books were read in various ways depending on what their function was or where they were created. Some were read from top to bottom and left to right, and others were read in a zigzag fashion or clockwise around each page.

The *tlacuilos'* work was intentionally left cryptic so that only people with formal training from special schools could read them. Furthermore, as artists, *tlacuilos* were not interested in drawing nature as they observed it. Theirs was a conceptual art, so an accurate, naturalistic portrayal of the world was not

vital. The goal of a scribe was not speed, legibility, or efficiency but rather ornateness and beauty. Creating an Aztec manuscript was a talent said to lie somewhere between writing and miniature painting. Some of these screen-folded books could be considered portable murals.

As representatives of the society they belonged to, *tlacuilos* did not sign their works; there are no signatures on any of the codices that remain. (Only on certain Mayan ceramics have signatures been found.)

Fray Bernardino de Sahagún worked with some Indian *tlacuilos* at Tlatelolco. He questioned elders and documented their responses, which were illustrated by the native artists, who were probably trained at their local *calmecac*. In the Franciscan schools, the friars taught Latin and Spanish to these native scribes in hopes of transcribing any remaining books, as well as to record what they learned about their education at the *calmecac* (priest school) (see chapters 4 and 13). At these schools they were taught how to interpret the sacred calendar, which guided the lives of the Aztec. This *tonalamatl* (book of the days) was used to understand various ceremonies and the variety of gods associated with them. It was a form of religious time count.

The Ladino Influence

The majority of painter-scribes were ladino, or bicultural. Ladino Indians were literate in both their indigenous culture and their newly acquired Spanish culture. They became bridges or mediators in the social and political exchange between the two groups. Knowing well the two legal and cultural systems, they had the power to defend their own indigenous communities utilizing the new Spanish legal system and at the same time use their bicultural knowledge to succeed individually in the colonial society.

It was the combination of both their preconquest teachings and their education at the Franciscan schools that made the *tlacuilos* extraordinary. While many ladino artists remained anonymous, some are known. Marcos Aquino (Cipac), for one, made the *retablo* of the open chapel of San José de los Naturales in 1554. Miguel Mauricio made the wood carving of Santiago "Mataindios" in the church of Tlatelolco in 1610. Juan Gerson made the outstanding cycle of paintings of the Apocalypse on *amatl* paper in the church of Tecamachalco in 1562.

Tequitqui Art

Tequitqui (Indian-Christian) art of the 16th century was a great example of the works created by ladino Indians. *Tequitqui* art was particularly essential for religious conversion. It is the combination of indigenous and European elements that makes this art style unique. This was the art that the conquered made for their conquerors. *Tequitqui* art is the interpretation of European architectural and decorative features according to the techniques and cosmovision of the Indians. Native artists decorated many parts of the convents with *tequitqui* art, including the facades, portals, cloisters, open chapels (*atrios*), *posa* chapels, baptismal and holy water fonts, atrial crosses, and mural paintings. They blended different historic European styles (Romanesque, Gothic, Mudejar, Plateresque, and Renaissance) with native aesthetics. The *tequitqui* style appears in almost all of the nearly 300 convents founded in New Spain during the 16th century. These are located mainly in the states of Hidalgo, Mexico, Michoacán, Morelos, Puebla, Tlaxcala, Guerrero, Oaxaca, Veracruz, Yucatán, and the Federal District (Mexico City metropolitan area).

Paper and Book—from Beginning to End

When bookmaking began in Aztec culture remains debated; however, books could not have been made without paper of some kind, and studying the beginning of paper is essential in determining when books began to be made in Mesoamerica. Paper was present in the early Preclassic period, and by the Postclassic period, stone bark beaters were already being used to smooth out pages of paper. Prior to the Postclassic, wood bark beaters were used, such as those still used today in Southeast Asia and Oceania.

Paper served an important role in Aztec civilization. Many religious ceremonies required the use of paper. Banners made of paper and decorated with ornamental bits of clothing often adorned festivals and rituals. Paper strips were daubed with blood, copal, or rubber as sacrificial offerings. Paper is often a popular motif in scenes related to death in Mesoamerican art. And tribute records for Tenochtitlan show that 24,000 packets of paper were paid in tribute annually.

In order to begin the process of creating a book, first the materials had to be gathered and prepared. The Aztec and the Maya both used *amatl* as their preferred writing surface; the Mixtec preferred to use deer and jaguar hide; cotton, cloth, and maguey were also for the purpose of creating books. The bark of the *amaquauitl* fig tree (*Ficus coinifolia, Ficus padifolina*) was used as the base for paper. The inner bark was macerated, and the fibers were separated from the pulp by soaking the bark in the river or in water with limestone. The separated fibers were next placed on a smooth surface and doubled over. They were then beaten with a stone that had a striated surface in order to mesh the fibers into a consistent surface.

After the fibers were well integrated, they were smoothed. Then gum of the *amatzauhtli* plant (papyrus gum) was coated on the smooth surface as an adhesive. When the adhesive was dry, a thin white plaster coating of lime gesso, starch, or calcium carbonate was spread on the surface to further smooth the surface and finally prepare it for painting; the same process is used today by painters who work on untreated canvas.

Only after the paper had a smooth glossy surface could it be written and painted upon. Both sides of the paper were used. The paints and dyes were created with animal, vegetable, or mineral materials. These colors were fixed onto the surface using vegetable gums. From natural sources only, these paints and dyes came in the colors of red, green, yellow, ochre, blue, gray, sepia, rose, orange, carmine, pale sienna, purple, white, and black. These colors have remained brilliant on the surviving codices, even after 500 years of storage and neglect. It should be noted that the murals on the walls have proven to retain their brilliant quality even 1,000 years after their creation.

Once the paint was dry, the book was either rolled up or folded into sheets of equal size in an accordion-style screenfold book (*tira*). It was bound on the front and back by gluing thin slabs of wood or skin slightly larger than the book itself to each end of the book; sometimes leather was used to protect the pages of the book. This wood was then adorned with colorful stones such as agate and jade and painted figures. The figures were drawn with an outline in black paint and then filled in with color, or vice versa. The pages were then divided into sections by red or black lines that worked much like periods at the end of a sentence.

CODICES

A codex is any rare manuscript. Some of the world's better known codices are those of Mesoamerican creation. Notably, Mesoamerica has been the only region in the New World where any books have been found. Serving as ethnohistorical sources, Aztec codices, as well as *lienzos* (histories painted on cloth), *hojas* (*amate* paper sheets), and panels, are particularly important in that they serve to reconstruct a nearly extinct way of life. They were an encyclopedic wealth of information on various topics: ritual ceremonies and laws, the deeds of kings, the participation of gods, the tributes paid, regional landscapes, conquests, and wars. Books were also written on botany, zoology, medicine, poetry, and songs, but none of these have survived. There are 61 native screenfold books, or *tiras*, which have come to be known as the Mesoamerican codices.

Early Cartography

Some of these sources served the function of modern newspapers; King Motecuhzoma II knew of all Spanish activity prior to their arrival in Tenochtitlan through information painted on cloth. Some codices are actually collections of maps, all of which contained detailed information. Even the Spanish used these sources to maneuver their way around the landscape; Hernán Cortés used one of Motecuhzoma's maps to travel. The painters were so innumerable that there was no topic or surface they did not paint. The general subject of the paintings was ruler successions, movements and notable signs in the sky, and general social and political events.

Considering the existence of pre-Hispanic Nahua cartography, we must acknowledge that pre-conquest maps were much more than mere geographical instruments; they served as the symbolic appropriation of space. They maintained a mythical, social, political, and economic memory of the past. Examples of these maps can be seen in various codices. The fact that one or a couple of these maps could hold an equivalent amount of information as that found in book-length works is relevant.

After the conquest, colonial viceroys and their officers recognized the efficiency and accuracy of the sophisticated system of conventions provided by the Indian maps and glyphs. Between 1570 and 1600, due to the forced concentration of Indian populations and the massive grants of land given to the Spaniards, Indian painters were requested to draw hundreds of maps by the new authorities. In 1577, for example, King Philip II of Spain ordered a census of all his territories in America. This project was called *Las relaciones geográficas* and consisted of a description of each town based on a questionnaire sent from Spain. The description included maps of the town showing all its urban features.

Codex maps displayed various types of travel routes for trading. The various types of roads were drawn as well as important details about these roads, such as where rivers could be crossed by foot and where makeshift bridges made from fallen trees and bridges made of wood planks were located. *Techialoyan* (rest areas) were indicated on certain maps so that merchants knew where they could spend the night. These maps still retained many of the old symbols and glyphs, like those related to rivers, springs, mountains, paths, and habitats; however, they were full of new signs required by the colonial presence and exploitation. More specifically, the *tlacuilos* created new glyphs to indicate new things: churches with their *atrios* (front courtyards) and bells, grid plans (*dameros*) of Indian pueblos, new Spanish estates such as *estancias* and

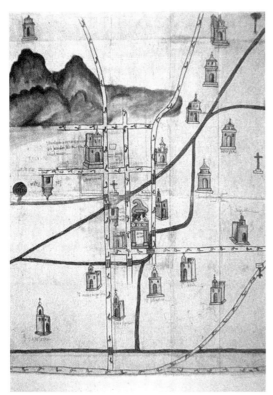

10.1 A map of Colhuacan, from Las relaciones geográficas del siglo XVI *(Manuel Aguilar-Moreno with permission of the Benson Latin American Collection, University of Texas at Austin)*

haciendas, corrals, water mills, covered carts drawn by teams of oxen, and so on. Circular yellow disks were drawn to represent gold coins, the new form of currency. European gold crowns were drawn to represent which areas were under the dominion of the Spanish king.

A common indigenous symbol that appears very often in these maps is the toponymic glyph *tepetl* (hill or mountain). It is used to identify sacred features of the landscape. This *tepetl* convention almost disappears entirely from maps after 1615. There is good reason to believe that missionaries in some parishes exercised direct or indirect censorship in regard to the *tepetl* glyph, probably feeling that the sacredness of salient points in the heathen landscape

would be located by readers of the map and thereby impeding the process of full conversion to the new faith. Like the idol buried under the house, the *tepetl* on the map was thought to be a dark force to be extirpated. It is reasonable to suspect that the phasing out of the *tepetl* as a convention, early in the 1600s, was indeed related to the complex process of indigenous conversion and reflected a more complete accommodation of the *tlacuilo* worldview to the new cosmology.

Bibliophiles and Burnings

While only a small percentage of Aztec society was literate, and although reading was a luxury enjoyed by the wealthy and educated, the Aztec treasured their books. When a Nahuatl student memorized and understood one of the ancient books, he claimed the honor of "singing" the pictures from the book and making the codices "speak." The fact that both Europeans and native Mexicans appreciated books is exemplified by an anecdote from Panama in 1514. When an Indian spotted a Spaniard named Corrales reading, he jumped with surprise. The Indian expected to see a book written in Mexican pictorial glyph, but Corrales was reading Latin script. Nevertheless, through an interpreter, he expressed his joy at meeting someone else who knew how to use books.

Because books were so highly valued in Aztec culture, burning books was considered sacrilegious and caused the Aztec great anguish; however, it was not unknown to burn books in Mesoamerica. King Itzcoatl burned all those books that did not legitimize the Mexica's ascent to power. Afterward he commissioned books to be written that emphasized King Itzcoatl's understanding of history. Yet, the Spaniards were infamous for destroying books. Bishop Juan Zumárraga threw thousands of Tetzcocan books into the fire. Bishop Diego de Landa did the same in the Yucatán area with Mayan literature. Though many of these books were casualties of war when certain buildings were burned down, most were later intentionally destroyed due to the fact that they were thought to contain superstitions and pagan lies.

The Holy Office of the Inquisition was responsible for further book burnings. House raids were not uncommon, and after some time, the native people themselves began to burn their own books lest they be charged for possession of them and be punished. Fortunately, in their religious zeal, some missionaries documented irreplaceable information. Priest Hernando Ruiz de Alarcón's antisorcery campaigns in the regions south and west of Mexico City led him to write down many native chants and prayers. In 1528, Fray Andrés de Olmos collected various orations and discourses that are now known as the *Huehuetlahtolli*. Motolinia, Fray Bernardino de Sahagún, Frey Gerónimo Mendieta, Diego Valadés, and Fray Juan de Torquemada were also priest-chroniclers whose works are valuable sources of information contained in destroyed Aztec literature. Colonal codices later became important documents in the litigation process, usually regarding land disputes.

Extant Aztec Codices

Existing codices are scattered worldwide; most pre-Hispanic codices are found in England, Spain, France, Germany, Austria, or Italy. Their names are derived from their location, discoverer, former owner, or place of origin. The interest in acquiring these works shifted from wealthy Europeans or Mexican scholars (Carlos de Sigüenza y Góngora, Lorenzo Boturini, Francisco Xavier Clavijero, Edward King [Lord Kingsborough], Joseph Aubin, Manuel Orozco y Berra, Alfredo Chavero, and Zelia Nuttall) to wealthy Americans and their institutions (such as universities in Chicago; Austin, Texas; and New York). The intense interpretation and study of codices has yielded many specialists such as Eduard Seler, Francisco del Paso y Troncoso, Alfonso Caso, Angel María Garibay, Eric Thompson, Donald Robertson, Yuri Knorossov, and Karl Nowotny. Contemporary specialists are even greater in number, among them Michael Smith, Elizabeth Hill-Boone, Eloise Quiñones-Keber, Barbara Mundy, Karl Butzer, John Pohl, Maarten Jansen, Miguel León-Portilla, Nelly Gutiérrez-Solana, Pablo Escalante, Joaquín Galarza, Eduardo Dou-

glas, Alfredo López Austin, Luis Reyes García, and Dana Leibsohn.

Although other pictorial works, such as *lienzos*, genealogies, cadastral (property) records, maps, and the Techialoyan-style (17th-century land records) documents are of equal importance to the study of Mesoamerican culture, only the foremost codices attributed to Aztec society are listed herein.

CODEX AUBIN

The *Codex Aubin* is a pictorial Nahuatl chronicle covering the years between 1168 and 1591 and 1595 and 1596, with an addendum for the years between 1597 and 1608. It begins with the Mexica departure from Aztlan and includes the dynastic history of Tenochtitlan and various colonial events. It is a codex made of European paper with 81 leaves that each measure 15 by 11 centimeters (approximately $5^7/_8$ by $4^3/_8$ inches). It was formerly known as the *Codex of 1576* and the *Histoire de la Nation Mexicaine depuis le depart d'Aztlan juscqu'a l'arrivée des Conquérants Espagnols*. This codex was once part of the Boturini, Aubin, and Desportes collections. It is currently housed at the British Museum in London.

TONALAMATL DE AUBIN

The *Tonalamatl de Aubin* is possibly a preconquest *tonalamatl* (divinatory almanac) painted in a pre-Columbian style. Each page depicts patron deities, 13 birds, 13 gods, and the Nine Lords of the Night associated with each 13-day period of the 260-day divinatory cycle. It is a screenfold text probably originating from Tlaxcala and made in the early 16th century on native (*amatl*) paper. It consists of 18 leaves that each measure 24 by 27 centimeters (about $9^1/_2$ by $10^5/_8$ inches). This manuscript is also known as *Kalendario ydolátrico y Códice Gama*. It once belonged to the Boturini, Nebel, Waldeck, and Aubin collections. It was housed at the Bibliothéque National de Paris until 1983, when a Mexican scholar who was studying the document took it with him back to Mexico and deposited it in the National Library of Anthropology. After a legal dispute of several years between the governments of France and Mexico, it was returned to Paris.

CODEX AZCATITLAN

The pages of the *Codex Azcatitlan* are annals of Mexican history commencing with the departure from Aztlan (Azcatitlan) and Colhuacan in 1168 and continuing with the migration and the beginnings of the dynastic history of Tenochtitlan through 1381. Following this are pages devoted to the individual rulers of Tenochtitlan, from Acamapichtli through Motecuhzoma II Xocoyotzin. The final pages present drawings of the Spanish conquest and of the early colonial period. It is a European-paper codex with 25 leaves that each measure 21 by 28 centimeters (approximately 8¹/₄ by 11 inches). It was formerly known as the *Histoire Mexicaine.* This codex was once part of the Boturini and Aubin collections. It is currently housed at the Bibliothèque Nationale de Paris.

CODEX BORBONICUS

The *Codex Borbonicus* is divided into four sections. The first section is a *tonalpohualli* (260-day divinatory almanac). The second section displays associations between the Nine Lords of the Night, with each assigned day for a period of 52 years. The third part is the festival calendar consisting of 18 months of 20 days each and their corresponding ceremonies. The fourth part has the 52-year cycle with its starting year date of 2 Cane and gives information about the next New Fire ceremony. The scholars Ernest Hamy, Aubin, José F. Ramírez, Seler, Caso, and George Vaillant all classify this codex as a preconquest original; Nowotny and Robertson claim it to be postconquest. It is a native-paper screenfold painted on only one side with 36 leaves that each measure 39 by 39.5 centimeters (about 15¹/₄ by 15¹/₂ inches). It was formerly known as the *Codex du Corps Legislatif, Codex Legislatif, Codex Hamy,* and the *Calendario de París.* This codex was originally found in a Mexican monastery and then sent to Spain. In 1826, it was discovered at the Bibliothèque du Palais Borbon. The first and last two pages were lost, possibly somewhere between Spain and France. The codex is currently housed at the Bibliothèque de l'Asemblée Nationale Française in Paris.

10.2 An image of the goddess Chalchiuhtlicue in the Codex Borbonicus (Manuel Aguilar-Moreno)

CODEX BOTURINI

The *Codex Boturini* is an early pictorial chronicle of the years between 1168 and 1355 in a native or slightly acculturated style. It is considered one of the most important documents regarding the Mexica migrations. It gives the history of the Tenochca-Mexica beginning with the emigration from Aztlan (see figure 2.1) through their arrival to Chapultepec to the period of their subjugation under Cocox, ruler of Colhuacan. The sole color is in the red lines that connect the dates. It was formerly known as the *Tira de la peregrinación* and the *Tira del museo.* This codex was discovered in a room of the National Anthropology Library of Mexico. The scholars Orozco y Berra, Ramírez, and Paul Radin all consider it to be a preconquest codex; Robert Barlow and Robertson consider it an early colonial work, and given its acculturated style, this is probably the case. It is an *amatl* paper screenfold painted on only one side with 21^1/$_2$ leaves that, when extended, measures 19.8 by 549 centimeters (approximately 7^3/$_4$ by 214 inches). It was once part of the Boturini collection. It is currently housed at the Museo Nacional de Antropología in Mexico City.

CODEX DE LA CRUZ-BADIANO

The *Codex de la Cruz-Badiano* contains 184 exquisitely rendered color drawings, some incorporating elements of native symbolism, by an Indian artist. It is a postconquest listing of Mexican plants and herbs from the native pharmacopoeia. These plants are drawn and named according to the native system of taxonomy, and their medicinal values are described. It is divided into 13 chapters. This codex was created in 1552 at the Colegio de Santa Cruz at Tlatelolco. The text is a translation into Latin by Juan Badiano (an Indian from Xochimilco, who was a scholar at the Colegio de Santa Cruz) of a Nahuatl text (not included in the codex) by Martín de la Cruz, a native physician at the same college. The text and glosses (definitions or descriptive text) give medical and pharmacological remedies for the treatment of diseases. It was dedicated to Francisco de Mendoza, son of the viceroy Antonio de Mendoza, and intended for presentation to King Charles V.

The *Codex de la Cruz-Badiano* is a European-paper codex with 63 leaves plus preliminary and end flyleaves that each measure 20.6 by 15.2 centimeters (approximately 8^1/$_8$ by 6 inches). It was formerly known as the *Libellus de Medicinalibus indorum herbis*, the *Badianus Manuscript*, the *Códice Badiano*, the *Badianus de la cruz herbal*, the *Codex Barberini*, and the *Codex Cruz*. It was once part of the Francisco Barberini and Diego de Cortavila collections. It was housed at the Vatican's Apostolic Library for a long time but was returned to Mexico by Pope John Paul II in 1992. At present it is kept at the Museo Nacional de Antropología in Mexico City.

CODEX EN CRUZ

The *Codex en cruz* is a chronicle cast in a unique framework of yearly events from 1402 through 1553, with additions through the year 1569. A later gloss refers to an event in 1603. The emphasis is on the dynastic successions at Tetzcoco, Tenochtitlan, Chiautla, and Tepetlaoztoc. It contains notices of famines, rains, war, and conquests. It is divided into three pages but was probably joined together at one point. Each page covers historical events of the native century (52 years). This "century" is divided into four periods of 13 years. The signs and numbers of the native years, reading from right to left, are drawn in horizontal and vertical rows that divide each page into quarters. After each quarter was read, then the manuscript was turned in a counterclockwise direction to read the next quarter.

The *Codex en cruz* is a native-paper *tira* (screenfold) with three leaves that, when extended, measures 57 by 166 centimeters (about 22^1/$_4$ by 64^3/$_4$ inches); it is missing its first page. It was formerly known as the *Codex en Croix*, *Annales de Cuauhtitlan*, *de Tetzcoco et de Mexico* and the *Anales de San Andrés Chiautla*. This codex was once part of the Boturini and Aubin collections. It is currently housed at the Bibliothéque Nationale de Paris.

FLORENTINE CODEX

The *Florentine Codex* is the final and complete manuscript of the 12 books of the *Historia general de las cosas de la Nueva España* written by Fray Bernardino de Sahagún and is inarguably the most important ethnohistorical source owing to its completeness. One of the oldest preliminary versions of this text is the *Primeros memoriales*, considered to be the record of Sahagún's informants. This is bound with the early manuscripts known as *Códices matritenses*. The *Florentine Codex* contains Nahuatl text and a parallel Spanish text that is part translation, part paraphrase. Those diverse manuscripts, which eventually formed the *Florentine Codex*, contain materials not in the others.

The *Florentine Codex* is illustrated by 1,846 drawings, which does not include the decorative tailpieces and ornamental designs. The content of the 12 books of the codex are as follows: Book 1 is about gods; Book 2 is about ceremonies of the 18 months; Book 3 is about the origins of the gods and the mythology; Book 4 is about the divinatory almanac and various customs; Book 5 is about omens; Book 6 is about moral philosophy (prayers to the gods, lords' discourses, moral exhortations, marriage and childbirth, adages, riddles, and metaphors); Book 7 is about natural philosophy and celestial phenomena (the Sun, the Moon, the stars, etc.) and the count and binding of the years; Book 8 is about the lords of Tenochtitlan, Tlatelolco, Tetzcoco, and Huexotla, and contains information about the education and customs of these lords (adornments, costumes, foods, government, and so on); Book 9 is about merchants and craftsmen; Book 10 is about the Aztec people and the nations of native Mexico (their vices, virtues, occupations, and illnesses); Book 11 is about natural history (animals, birds, trees, herbs, and so on); and Book 12 is about the conquest of Tenochtitlan-Tlatelolco.

This monumental codex, a pioneering example of excellent ethnographic work that established the standards for modern anthropological research, is also known today as the *Códice florentino* and the *Historia general de las cosas de la Nueva España*. It is a European-paper codex in three volumes. The first has 345 leaves, the second has 372, and the third has 493. It is currently housed at the Biblioteca Medicea Laurenziana in Florence.

CODEX HUAMANTLA

The nine fragments of the *Codex Huamantla* are part of a single, large painting; some of the fragments are believed to have been lost since it was first described by Boturini in the 18th century. Three of the remaining fragments fit together perfectly, and two others may also fit together, however imperfectly. The codex is drawn and painted in a distinctive style and its principal theme is warfare. Indians armed with bows, arrows, and *macanas* or *maquahuitl* (war clubs), and shields (with the *atl-tlachinolli* symbol for war between them) form a recurring motif. The taking of prisoners and their subsequent sacrifices are shown, as are clusters of native houses, place glyphs, and Indians. One scene depicts tribute being offered to a Spaniard; adjacent to this, two mounted Spaniards thrust lances into bleeding Indians.

Although there are both place and personal name glyphs, no native dates appear. Faded glosses in Nahuatl include place-names, some of which are at least homonymous with localities in the former districts of Juárez and Morelos in Tlaxcala. It is an *amatl* paper codex composed of nine sheets each measuring on average 154 by 90 centimeters (approximately 60 by 35 inches). This codex was once part of the Boturini and Humboldt collections. Seven fragments of it are currently housed at the Museo Nacional de Antropología in Mexico City. The other two are housed at the Deutsche Staatsbibliothek in Berlin, and are also known as Humboldt Fragments Nos. 3 and 4.

CODEX IXTLILXOCHITL

The *Codex Ixtlilxochitl* consists of three unrelated parts, two of which are pictorial. Of these two, Part 1 contains Spanish texts and drawings illustrative of the gods and ceremonies of 17 of the 18 months of the 365-day year, two drawings and texts of gods, and two drawings of funerary customs. This material is probably a copy of corresponding texts and drawings in the *Codex Magliabecchiano*. There are minor differences in the two texts, and the drawings in the *Codex Ixtlilxochitl* are more colonially acculturated. Some month names are given in Otomí and in an unidentified language, as well as in Nahuatl. Attributions of the codex to Fernando Alva Ixtlilxochitl or to Sigüenza y Góngora are speculative. This section of the codex was formerly known as the *Aubinschen Handschrift*, the *Códice geroglífico de Mr. Aubin*, and the *Códice Goupil*. It was once part of the Sigüenza y Góngora, Boturini, and Aubin collections.

Part 2 contains six drawings: four full-length portraits of Indians, including Nezahualcoyotl and Nezahualpilli, rulers of Tetzcoco; a similarly executed drawing of the god Tlaloc; and a drawing of the double pyramid-temple at Tetzcoco. The latter two have on their reverse sides descriptive texts, which are less corrupt versions of substantially identical passages in the *Relación de Tetzcoco* by Juan Bautista Pomar. The drawings may be leaves from a lost manuscript by Pomar or from a manuscript utilized by him. Attribution of the drawings and texts to Fernando Alva Ixtlilxochitl are unfounded.

Two further drawings now lost from the manuscript survive through copies. The copy of the drawing of the god Huitzilopochtli is in the *Codex Veytia*. A drawing of Nezahualpilli seated on a throne was copied by Gemelli Carreri in 1697 and published by him in 1700; in his publication, he misidentified Nezahualpilli as Motecuhzoma II. Another drawing published by Gemelli Carreri (*Soldato Mexicano*) may also derive from this manuscript. The Pomar *Relación* refers to at least six and possibly eight drawings, of which only three (of Huitzilopochtli, Tlaloc, and the Tetzcoco pyramid) may be identified securely with extant versions. This section of the codex was formerly known as the *Illustrations for the Relación de Tetzcoco* by Pomar. It was once part of the Sigüenza y Góngora, Boturini, and Aubin collections. These sections of the codex are made of European paper. Part 1 consists of 11 leaves, and Part 2 consists of six leaves, all of which measure 31 by 21 centimeters (approximately 12 by 8¼ inches). This codex is currently housed at the Bibliothéque Nationale de Paris.

CODEX KINGSBOROUGH

The *Codex Kingsborough* recounts a lawsuit held before the colonial Council of the Indies between Indians of Tepetlaoztoc and the *encomendero* (Spanish landlord) Juan Velásquez de Salazar. Part 1 contains two maps of the Tepetlaoztoc region and introductory material relating to preconquest history, tribute, genealogy, and social organization. Part 2 presents a yearly record of the tribute and other goods and services provided by the Indians to various *encomenderos* between the years 1522 and 1551. Part 3 contains a summary of selected items in Part 2 and a presentation of tribute and other matters between the years 1551 and 1554. Part 4 recapitulates the *servicio cotidiano* (daily service) part of the tribute for the years 1527 through 1551. Folio 72v has a textual conclusion to the document and a petition. The Spanish text is contemporary with the drawings. Discontinuities in two of the three foliations on the codex do not reflect missing pages.

It was formerly known as the *Memorial de los indios de Tepetlaoztoc* and the *Códice de Tepetlaoztoc*.

The *Codex Kingsborough* is a European-paper codex with 72 leaves that each measure 29.8 by 21.5 centimeters (about 11¾ by 8½ inches). This codex is currently housed at the British Museum in London.

CODEX MAGLIABECCHIANO

The *Codex Magliabecchiano* consists of native drawings facing Spanish texts, that depict and describe festival ceremonies of the 18 months, and a long section on diverse ceremonies related to the gods, funerals, sacrifices, and other customs. It was formerly known as the *Book of Life of the Ancient Mexicans* or the *Libro de la vida que los yndios antiguamente hazían y supersticiones y malos ritos que tenían y guardaban*. The *Codex Magliabecchiano* was once part of the Antonio Magliabecchiano collection. It is a European-paper codex with 92 leaves that each measure 15.5 by 21.5 centimeters (about 6⅛ by 8½ inches). It is currently housed at the Biblioteca Nazionale Centrale in Florence.

CODEX MENDOZA

The *Codex Mendoza* is believed to have been commissioned by the Viceroy Mendoza for presentation to Charles V and is said to have been seized by French pirates. It can possibly be attributed to the *tlacuilo* Francisco Gualpuyogualal and was translated by the *canónigo* (honorary ecclesiastical title) Juan González, a *nahuatlato* (translator) from the Cathedral of Mexico. It was in the possession of André Thevet, a French cosmographer, by 1553.

The *Codex Mendoza* contains 72 pages of drawings with Spanish glosses, 63 pages of Spanish commentary, one text figure, and seven blank pages. Its three sections, although drawn with a uniform style of drawing and annotation, have different subject matters and origins. The drawings of Part 1 present a history of the Tenochca-Mexica from the founding of Tenochtitlan (apparently given here as 1325) through 1521, focusing on the lengths of the reigns of the rulers and of the towns they conquered. The Spanish text adds some supplementary data. A version of the same text is given by Fray Gerónimo Mendieta.

Part 2 is a pictorial record of the tribute paid by the different provinces of the Aztec Empire with a Spanish interpretation. It closely resembles the *Matrícula de tributos;* the *Codex Mendoza,* in fact, has long been considered a copy of the *Matrícula de tributos* that preserves five pages now lost from the *Matrícula.* In a study of a third related source, *Información sobre los tributos que los indios pagaban a Moctezuma,* Woodrow Borah and Sherburne Cook advance reasons to indicate that Part 2 of the *Codex Mendoza* and the *Matrícula* derive from a common, lost prototype.

Part 3 is a graphic portrayal of Aztec life. It includes a year-to-year history of an Aztec individual from birth onward. Other pages depict warriors, priests, and other professions, the palace of Motecuhzoma, and the laws and punishments of the latter's rule.

The *Codex Mendoza* is an almost unique ethnographic account, comparable in its importance only to the later *Florentine Codex.* It was formerly known as the *Collection of Mendoza* and the *Códice mendocino.* This codex was once part of the André Thevet, Richard Hakluyt, Samuel Purchas, and John Selden collections. It is a European-paper codex with 71 numbered leaves plus an added title leaf that each measure 32.7 by 22.9 centimeters (approximately $12^3/4$ by 9 inches). It is currently housed at the Bodleian Library, in Oxford, England.

CODEX OF THE CHRIST OF MEXICALTZINGO

The *Codex of the Christ of Mexicaltzingo* contains seven fragments from three original Indian pictorial manuscripts, together with paintings and Nahuatl texts of Christian religious content; they were found within the structure of a cane sculpture of Christ in 1946. Most of the native pictorial fragments contain drawings of the heads of Indians with personal name glyphs, units of Spanish money, and various objects (including cattle and a spinning wheel) arranged in horizontal rows. The documents may be tribute registers accounting the payments for services performed by Indians. It is possibly a European-paper codex and has seven fragments of varying dimensions. It is currently housed at the Museo Nacional de Antropología in Mexico City.

CODEX MEXICANUS 1

The calendrical section of the *Codex Mexicanus 1* exhibits extensive and deliberate effacements of native symbols as well as palimpsests. They contain an incomplete Christian saint's calendar for 1570 based on dominical letters, a *tonalamatl* (each correlated with two or more native years), Christian and native calendar wheels, and various tables. One diagram relates illegible signs to parts of the body. A Nahuatl text inserted into the annals section deals with the zodiac. A genealogy of the descendants of Tezozomoc, Acamapichtli, Itzcoatl, and others takes up two pages. The bulk of the codex contains pictorial annals from 1168 through 1571, with some emphasis on the Tenochca-Mexica. These are continued by two different artists to 1590, but the last entry is for 1583. Christian scenes occupy page 88. This codex was once part of the Aubin collection. It is a native-paper codex with 51 leaves that each measure 10 by 20 centimeters (about 4 by $7^1/8$ inches). It is currently housed at the Bibliothéque Nationale de Paris.

CODEX MEXICANUS 2

This *tira* (screenfold) has native year dates, drawings of Indians and Spaniards, and Nahuatl glosses. Both preconquest and colonial events and persons are depicted. The *Codex Mexicanus 2* was once part of the Laine Villevigue and Aubin collections. It is a native-paper *tira* in two fragments that measure, when extended, 18 by 220 centimeters (about $7^1/8$ by $85^3/4$ inches). It is currently housed at the Bibliothéque Nationale de Paris.

CODEX OSUNA

The *Codex Osuna* consists of seven discrete documents forming part of an inquiry into the conduct of the Indian and Spanish governments of Mexico City by the *visitador* Gerónimo de Valderrama in 1565. It was painted between January and August of 1565. This manuscript was created by different painters. Document 1 concerns grievances over unpaid deliveries of lime used in construction by the colonial government; the services of Indian troops in the Florida Expedition; and personal grievances against the *oídor* (a Spanish political officer) Vasco de Puga.

Documents 2 through 4 concern unpaid accounts for services and fodder supplied to the viceroy and *oídores*. Document 5 presents unpaid accounts for service and food incurred by Puga. Document 6 is a listing of place glyphs of towns formerly tributary to Tacuba. Document 7 deals with various matters, including labor in public constructions. Documents 1 through 4 and 7 are from Mexico City and Tlatelolco, document 5 is from Tula, and document 6 is from Tacuba.

The *Codex Osuna* was formerly known as the *Pintura del gobernador, alcaldes y regidores de México*. It was once part of the Duke of Osuna collection. It is a European-paper codex with 40 leaves with undetermined dimensions. It is currently housed at the Biblioteca Nacional in Madrid.

CODEX RÍOS

The *Codex Ríos* and the *Codex Telleriano-Remensis* are currently believed to be copies of a common original, the lost *Codex Huitzilopochtli*. The *Codex Ríos* is believed to have been copied by a possible non-Indian artist in Italy, and its long Italian texts are believed to be based on a commentary by Friar Pedro de los Ríos. Its exact date of publication is uncertain. The date 1566 occurs in the text, but the paper appears to have been made in 1569–70; 1566 seems to serve as a reference to a past event.

The manuscript has seven major sections: 1) cosmogenic and mythological traditions with some emphasis on the four previous epochs, or suns, including notices about Quetzalcoatl and the Toltec; 2) a 260-day divinatory almanac; 3) calendrical tables without drawings for the years between 1558 and 1619; 4) an 18-month festival calendar with drawings of the gods of each period; 5) sacrificial and other customs, including portraits of Indian types; 6) pictorial annals for the years between 1195 and 1549, beginning with the migration from Chicomoztoc and covering later events in the Valley of Mexico; and 7) glyphs for the years between 1566 and 1562 without written or pictorial entries.

Most of the codex has a long written commentary in Italian, but only three pages of the historical section are annotated. The *Codex Ríos* was formerly known as *Codex Vaticanus A*, *Codex Vaticanus 3738*, and *Copia vaticana*. It is a European-paper codex with 101 leaves that each measure 46 by 29 centimeters (approximately 18 by 11 3/8 inches). It is currently housed at the Vatican's Apostolic Library.

CODEX SAN ANDRÉS

This is a fragmentary leaf with drawings of heads of Indians with numerical signs, items of tribute, and a place glyph interpreted to represent San Andrés (the preconquest town of Xaltocan). Glosses include Cuauhtitlan, San Andrés, Tenochtitlan, and a reference to a *calpixqui* (Aztec tax collector). Joaquín Galarza suggests that the document may be concerned with tribute or *repartimiento* forced labor. This codex was once part of the Louis Doutrelaine collection. It is made of native paper and measures 40 by 46.5 centimeters (about 15 1/2 by 18 inches). It is currently housed at the Musée de l'Homme in Paris.

CODEX SAVILLE

The *Codex Saville* is a vertical *tira* with pictorial annals of the years between 1407 and 1535, including succession of the rulers of Tenochtitlan from Huitzilihuitl through Motecuhzoma II Xocoyotzin and the Spanish conquest. A Christian cross, a saint, a Madonna, and a bell with Spanish monetary symbols are drawn opposite the years 1531 through 1535. Several final images in the codex are controversially interpreted by Mariano Cuevas to represent the apparition of the Virgin of Guadalupe. This codex was formerly known as the *Códice protohistórico*, the *Codex Tetlapalco*, and the *Codex Telapalco*. It is a native-paper screenfold measuring 145 by 26 centimeters (approximately 56 1/2 by 10 1/2 inches). It is currently housed at the Museum of the American Indian, Heye Foundation, in New York City.

CODEX TELLERIANO-REMENSIS

The *Codex Telleriano-Remensis* and the *Codex Ríos* are currently believed to be copies of a common original, the lost *Codex Huitzilopochtli*. *Codex Telleriano-Remensis*, glossed as "*Geroglíficos de que usavan lo . . .*" on the cover, has three major pictorial sections in several native styles. Each is annotated in Spanish, in several handwritings. One of the latter is believed to be of Fray Pedro de los Ríos. The first section is an

18-month calendar with drawings of the gods of each period and a symbol for the *nemontemi* (the extra five days in the solar calendar). The second is a *tonalpohualli* (260-day divinatory almanac). The third is a pictorial annal for the period 1198–1562, in two major styles. Two final pages contain historical notices in Spanish without drawings, for the years between 1519 and 1557. There are leaves missing from each pictorial section, but in every case they are preserved in the cognate *Codex Ríos*. The codex was formerly known as the *Codex Tellerianus* and the *Codex Le Tellier*. It was once part of the Charles-Maurice Le Tellier collection. It is made of European paper with 50 leaves, and it measures 32 by 22 centimeters (approximately $12^1/_2$ by $8^6/_8$ inches). It is currently housed at the Bibliothéque Nationale de Paris.

CODEX OF SAN JUAN TEOTIHUACAN

The *Codex of San Juan Teotihuacan* relates to a 1557 Indian revolt against the establishment of an Augustinian monastery in San Juan de Teotihuacan. The drawings, with occasional Nahuatl glosses, depict Indians tied together, an escape from a jail, friars, articles of tribute, and a map depicting Acolman, Tetzcoco, and presumably Teotihuacan. The five small fragments showing heads of Indians pertain to some otherwise unknown document. This codex was formerly known as the *Códice de San Juan* and the *Códice Tetzcoco-Acolman*. It was once part of the Boturini collection. It is made of *amatl* paper measuring 139 by 75 centimeters (about $54^1/_4$ by $29^1/_4$ inches), now mounted with five small, unrelated fragments. It is currently housed at the Museo Nacional de Antropología in Mexico City.

CODEX TEPECHPAN

The *Codex Tepechpan* is a screenfold chronicle, originally in 23 leaves, covering the years from 1298 to 1596. Portions of the initial and terminal leaves are missing; the extant portion spans the years from 1300 to 1590. The codex depicts the settlement at Chapultepec and the founding of Tepechpan, and continues with the dynasties of Tepechpan and Tenochtitlan. The colonial section is devoted to the occurence of plagues, the dates of viceroys, and

other events. The drawings appear above and below a line of native year glyphs that divides the *tira* into two horizontal divisions. This codex was formerly known as the *Mapa de Tepechpan, Histoire Synchronique et Seigneuriale de Tepechpan et de Mexico*, and the *Cronología mexicana, 1298–1596*. It was once part of the Lorenzo Boturini, José Antonio Pichardo, Jean-François Waldeck, and Joseph Aubin collections. It is made of native paper measuring 21 by 625 centimeters (about $8^1/_4$ by $243^3/_4$ inches). It is currently housed at the Bibliothéque Nationale de Paris.

CODICES OF SANTA CRUZ TLAMAPA

The *Codices of Santa Cruz Tlamapa* contain three separate pictorial manuscripts. The first codex is a vertical *tira* headed by drawings of a Christian church and place glyph. Below are eight horizontal rows of Indians identified by Nahuatl glosses as assistants of the church, officials of the town, and so on. It was once part of the Boturini, Jose Gómez de la Cortina (Conde de la Cortina), and Museo de Artillería, Madrid, collections. It is a native-paper screenfold measuring 74 by 17.5 centimeters (approximately $28^7/_8$ by $6^7/_8$ inches). It is currently housed at the Museo del Ejército in Madrid.

The second codex manuscript is now lost. No reproduction is known, but it may some day be identified on the basis of the descriptions in the Boturini collection inventories. It apparently concerned the tributes of Tlamapa and mentioned Bernardino del Castillo. It is a large screenfold made of European paper and was part of the Boturini collection.

The third codex is an incomplete vertical *tira* divided into 14 sections corresponding to the years between 1564 and 1577. In the first, or lowest, section is a Christian church surmounted by an Indian building, a place glyph, and a drawing of the *gobernador* (governor) and other officials. The remaining sections each contain a drawing of the *escribano* (town clerk or notary) and *mayordomo* (person in charge of the patron saint festival), moon symbols for the months of the Christian year, and numerical signs. The numerical signs may refer to tribute or to other financial expenses of the town. Names of town officers are given by Spanish glosses.

It is a European-paper *tira* measuring 383.5 by centimeters (approximately 149½ by 12 inches). It is currently housed at the Museo Nacional de Antropología in Mexico City.

CODEX TLATELOLCO

The *Codex Tlatelolco* is a pictorial chronicle of a period beginning some time before 1554 to after 1562, with notable drawings of colonial events and personages but without explicit chronological framework. Initial scenes refer to participation of Tenochtitlan and Tlatelolco in the Mixtón War of 1542. If this document is correctly identified as having been in the Boturini collection, then a long section at the beginning has been lost. The *Codex Tlatelolco* was formerly known as the *Manuscrito [Pintura] de Xochipilla*. It is made of *amatl* paper measuring 40 by 325 centimeters (about 15½ by 126¾ inches). It is currently housed at the Museo Nacional de Antropología in Mexico City.

HISTORIA TOLTECA-CHICHIMECA

The *Historia tolteca-chichimeca* exists in three parts. The first two contain 22 leaves of the original and copies made by Aubin. Modern editions combine the three parts, arrange the pages in logical sequence, and omit the redundant Aubin copies. The manuscript contains 37 pages of Nahuatl text; 35 pages of Nahuatl text with drawings; 25 full-page drawings, including six double-page maps; and seven blank pages. The manuscript is one of the major sources for the study of the early post-Toltec civilization and subsequent history of the Chichimec migrations from Chicomoztoc to the central Puebla region. It recounts the emigration of the Nonoalca and Toltec-Chichimec from Tula, the conquest of the Olmeca-Xicallanca at Cholula by the Toltec-Chichimec, emigration from Chicomoztoc, the founding of Cuauhtinchan, and the later history and wars of the inhabitants of Cuauhtinchan. The period embraced by this history is from 1116 through 1544. The drawings, none of which depict colonial events, are probably copies from the pictorial manuscript or manuscripts on which the Nahuatl text is based. This codex was formerly known as the *Historia tulteca, Anales de Quauhtinchan, Annales Tolteco-*

Chichimeques, and *Codex Gondra*. It was once part of the Boturini and Aubin collections.

It is made of European paper with 52 leaves that each measure 30 by 22 centimeters (about 11⅞ by 8⅝ inches). It is currently housed at the Bibliothéque Nationale de Paris.

ANALES DE TULA

The entire length of this *tira* is divided in half by drawings of the glyphs for the years 1361 through 1521. Above and below them are occasional simple drawings and short Nahuatl texts that refer to historical events in Tenochtitlan, Tetzcoco, Tula, and other localities. This codex was formerly known as the *Anales aztecas, Anales mexicanos del pueblo de Tezuntepec*, and the *Anales de Tezontepec*. The Anales de Tula or *Annals of Tula* is an *amatl*-paper screenfold that measures 17 by 487 centimeters (about 6¾ by 190 inches). It is currently housed in the Biblioteca Nacional de Antropología, Mexico.

CODEX XOLOTL

The *Codex Xolotl* is a detailed Tetzcocan history of events in the Valley of Mexico from the arrival of the Chichimecs of Xolotl in the year 5 Tecpatl (1224) through events leading up to the Tepanec War in 1427. It contains extensive genealogical information. Most of the relatively intact pages of the manuscript are also maps of part of the Valley of Mexico. The *Codex Xolotl* is essentially a postconquest pictorial manuscript annotated in Nahuatl. The importance of this codex is that it depicts the introduction of the art of manuscript painting from the Mixtec region. It was formerly known as the *Histoire Chichimeque* and was part of the Ixtlilxochitl, Boturini, Waldeck (one leaf), and Aubin collections. It is made of native paper with six leaves (of 10 painted pages), each measuring 42 by 48 centimeters (about 16⅜ by 18¾ inches), and fragments of a seventh leaf (with two fragmentary pages). It is currently housed at the Bibliothéque Nationale de Paris.

CODEX OF SANTA ANITA ZACATLALMANCO

The *Codex of Santa Anita Zacatlalmanco* consists of drawings of the Indian governors of Mexico City from about 1536 to 1602, the Viceroy Mendoza, and numerous lesser Indian officials with personal name glyphs. Cartographic detail includes a church within a rectangular plot interpreted as representing the *fondo legal* (jurisdiction) of Santa Anita, about 1535 to 1554. This is a European-paper codex measuring 41.5 by 56.5 centimeters (approximately 16¹/₈ by 22 inches). One part of the Pinart collection, it is currently housed at the Musee de l'Homme, Paris.

PICTOGRAPHIC-PHONETIC WRITING

To the Aztec, writing and all other forms of art were always associated with the Toltec—a name synonymous with artistic splendor. Mesoamerica is home to one of the world's original forms of writing. It can be compared in beauty to medieval illuminations, Chinese calligraphy, and the Islamic Koranic script.

The first appearance of writing is Mesoamerica is found in the inscriptions at the Olmec site of La Venta in Tabasco, dating to about 1000 B.C.E., and at San José Mogote in Oaxaca, dating to about 600 B.C.E. Writing fully developed by the Protoclassic Period in Veracruz and Oaxaca. The inscriptions found at La Mojarra display a very sophisticated arrangement of characters.

Linguistic Influences

By the first century B.C.E., this form of writing reached its most sophisticated peak with the Maya peoples. During the Classic Period, the Maya used a mixed script composed of both phonetic syllables and logographs (symbols that represent words). The word *balam* (jaguar) could either be drawn pictographically as the stylistic head of a jaguar, phonetically as the combination of the syllables *ba-la-ma* (with the final vowel silent), or a combination of both. By the time of the conquest, writing among the Aztecs was known as *tlilli tlapalli* (the black, the red). These colors were also associated with the Mayan codices since they are the primary colors used. In Nahuatl poetry, the legendary land of Tamoanchan (land of rain or mist, place of origin) is known by its Mayan name. It is clear that the Aztec trusted their Mayan counterparts when it came to mythology.

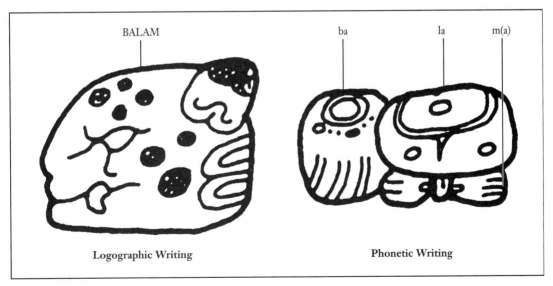

BALAM   ba   la   m(a)

Logographic Writing   **Phonetic Writing**

10.3 Writing of the word balam *as a symbol (left) or phonetically* (Drawing by Lluvia Arras, after Coe)

Tamoanchan is usually associated with the Olmec. The oldest known civilization in Mesoamerica was San Lorenzo, an Olmec site dating to 1800 B.C.E., and so it is commonly believed that the Olmec are the creators of all Mesoamerican writing. Another center is associated with the advancement of writing—Teotihuacan, cited in poetic verses as the ancient burial ground where the gods sacrificed themselves so that humans could exist in the world. It seems that there was a civilization transfer from the mythical Tamoanchan to Teotihuacan.

Writing Techniques

Tlacuilos used standardized signs known as glyphs to form messages, much like modern road signs use images to give directions. These signs functioned as simple pictographs of objects widely recognized by native people. In addition to pictographs, the Aztec used two principal kinds of writing: ideographs and a partially phonetic form of script. Pictographs are schematic representations of certain things; a drawing of a burning temple signifies a burning temple. Ideographs are symbolic representations of certain ideas; a burning temple signifies conquest and the attainment of sacrificial victims. Another example is the image of a footprint, used in other New World iconography; a footprint signifies travel. Phonetic forms are images drawn to represent particular pronounced sounds, mainly syllables. These were used phonetically in early

Acolhua pictorials more than in any other central Mexican records. The more developed use of phoneticism in late pre-Hispanic times and the Tetzcocan *tlacuilos'* rapid assimilation of European phonetic usage facilitated the use of the syllabic system. The techniques of Tetzcocan *tlacuilos* testify to such assimilation: renderings of field boundaries were drawn in black, the native ink, while glosses were written in a brown European ink. Another signal of assimilation in the codices is that the first names of natives were written in black ink; when they were given European surnames, these names were written in brown ink.

Nahuatl Words and Syllables—Prefixes and Suffixes

In order to understand the writing, the Nahuatl language must first be explored. Nahuatl words are formed by uniting syllables in the order of prefix + root + suffix. As a pictograph, a word is generally written as a small image of that item. If the word *xochitl* (flower) was to be drawn, then a small image of a flower is created. When two items are combined to make a new word, the suffix of the first word drops, and the second word is added. To write the word *xochimilli* (flower field), the combination of *xochitl* and *milli* must be made; the *-tl* drops from the first word and the combined word becomes

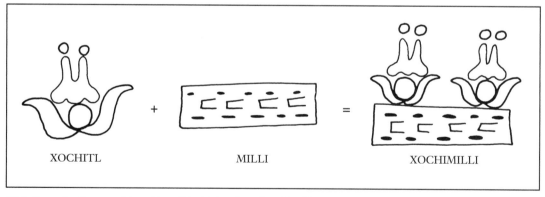

XOCHITL   +   MILLI   =   XOCHIMILLI

10.4 Example of pictographic writing of the Nahuatl word xochimilli (Drawings by Fonda Portales, after Galarza 1995)

xochimilli. It is written pictographically as two flowers (to show pluralism) atop one field. The suffixes *-tl* and *-li* denote common words.

To denote respect or reverence, the suffix *-tzin* is added to a person's name. To show pictographically that a common word is now being used as a name, a head is drawn with a line connecting to that word. With the name *Xochimiltzin*, both the *-tl* in *xochitl* and the *-li* in *milli* have been dropped, while a *-tzin* has been added as the suffix. This word would be drawn as a head of a person with a line connecting it (usually above) to the image of the two flowers atop the one field. The use of suffixes to expand the meaning of a common word can be see in modern Mexican Spanish, which has been Nahuatlized. The suffix *-ita* in the words *chiquitita* (very small) and *abuelita* (little grandmother) make the words diminutive in order to emphasize the word or to show more respect and affection, respectively, than the word would usually imply.

To denote plurality or singularity in common words in Nahuatl, the number of items precedes the word itself. If only one item, such as a flower, is to be written, then only one image of a flower is drawn. If more than one flower is to be written, then two dots are placed around the flower (see chapter 11). In Nahuatl, the colors of the items are pronounced prior to the word but combind as a prefix. *Iztaccihuatl* is the word for white (*iztac*) woman (*cihuatl*). It is drawn as a woman with a white painted face.

To denote a larger item, the prefix *huey-* is added to the word. A big house is written as *hueycalli*. To draw this word, one must simply increase the size of the original image enough to show it is bigger than other images in the text.

The symbol for *man* is the head of a man. To denote that the man is old, the image is drawn to look like a man's head with wrinkles. To say that there is one old man, the words *ce huehuetlacatl* are written. The word for a male child is *tlacapiltontli*, and the word for a female child is *cihuapiltontli*. To represent these words, a child's head (male or female) is drawn but drawn smaller than the head of an adult.

To indicate that a person is speaking, a speech scroll is placed in front of the mouth of the person's head image. The Nahuatl word *tlahtoa* means "to speak." To indicate that the speech is of a precious

10.5 Pictographic example of the phrase Ce huehuetlacatl xaltlahtoa (Drawing by Fonda Portales, after Galarza 1995)

nature (*xiuhtlahtoa*), the color turquoise is added to the image of the speech scroll. *Xiuh* was the word for precious, but it was often associated with the precious stone turquoise. To denote intense speech (*chichiltlahtoa*), the color red is used to fill the speech scroll image. Red is associated with intenseness because it is the color of chilies. When used as an adjective, red is written as *chiltic*. The repetition of the syllable *chi* was used to show the intensity of the speech. In modern Mexican Spanish, the prefix *ta-* is repeated to show degree. The word for great-grandfather is *bisabuelo*, but the word for great-great-grandfather is *tatarabuelo*, and the word for great-great-great-grandfather is *tatatarabuelo*. When showing that a person's speech is of a foreign origin (*xaltlahtoa*), a dotted speech scroll is used instead. The word *xalli* means "sand." To speak like sand is to not speak concretely enough to be understood. *Ce huehuetlacatl xaltlahtoa* is a Nahuatl sentence that means "the old man speaks a foreign language." This sentence is drawn as an old man's head, with a sandy speech scroll coming out of his mouth.

The Nahuatl word for smoke is *poca*. To denote much smoke, the word becomes *popoca*. To say that a house is burning, one simply says *popocalli*. This image is drawn as a house with smoke symbols above it. To say that one is near something, the word *-nahua* is added as a suffix and a white speech scroll is drawn coming out of a particular item. To say that a person is near a house, one would say *calnahua*.

Nahuatl Developments

Unlike the Mayan phonetic script, which was firmly in place by the time of the conquest, Nahuatl phonetics seem to have been a product of limitation and innovation. These types of writing are seen more often in postconquest documents. When writing the Nahuatl language, a pictographic image met the needs of the scribes. When forced to pronounce and draw Spanish words, native scribes were forced to adopt a more Mayan form of writing. Since there was no Nahuatl translation for Spanish names, phonetics was the best solution. Although basic phonetics was already used in Nahuatl writing, the introduction of many new words forced the use of nonpictographic writing. When reporting on the actions of Viceroy Mendoza, for example, *tlacuilos* combined the words *metl* (maguey) and *tuza* (feline-type animal). This word was written as a picture likeness of the Viceroy with a line joining him to the images for *metl* and *tuza*. The combination was pronounced *Metuza*—the closest possible pronunciation to *Mendoza*.

As with any innovation, there must be exceptions to the rules until all the quirks are worked out. Pedro Alvarado was a ruthless conquistador despised by many Aztecs and Mayas for his notorious cruelty. He was responsible for many massacres in Mesoamerica. He helped Cortés conquer the Mexica and then traveled to what is now Central America to destroy what was left of certain Maya leadership. One of Alvarado's main features was his golden blond hair, which became the nickname of Alvarado since his hair made him stand out from the rest of the conquistadores. His infamous status ensured that all native people knew of his nickname, Tonatiuh, the Nahuatl word for the Sun. Nahuatl scribes, rather than phonetically creating syllables to write Alvarado's name, drew a likeness of him and drew a line connecting it to a sun image. This is an example of the mixture of writing types used to record postconquest history.

Name Signs

Although the complexity of Nahuatl phonetics is uncertain due to lack of research, it is clear that it existed, although nowhere near as sophisticated as Mayan phonetics. It was by no means inferior, just more inventive and experimental as the research of scholars Alfonso Lacadena and Soeren Wichman shows. Lacadena has even proposed a Nahuatl syllabary. An excellent example of the use of phonetic syllables in the Nahuatl writing is found in the *Codex Santa María Asunción*. In a reference to the name San Francisco, a painter-scribe wrote it as *Xapasico*. The way the *tlacuilo* utilized the symbols was phonetic and not pictographic (*Xa-pa-si-co*). It can be seen in drawing: *Xa* (xalli = sand), *pa* (pantli = flag), *si* (silin = little conch shells), and *co* (comitl = pot). The individual meanings of the pictographs do not coincide with the idea of referring to the name of the Catholic saint San Francisco, so the indigenous writer used the syllabic value of the signs.

Aztec *tlacuilos* could join several pictographs to signify the elements comprising a proper name. Sixteenth-century cadastral manuscripts from Tepetlaoztoc and Tetzcoco display various examples of

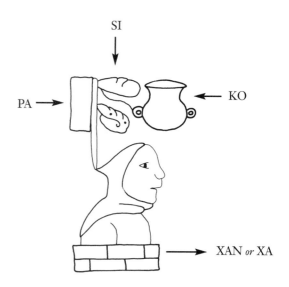

XA + PA + SI + KO = SAN FRANCISCO

10.6 Example of Nahuatl phoneticism in the name San Francisco *(Drawing by Fonda Portales, after* Codex Santa María Asunción*)*

NAHUATL SYLLABARY

	a	e	i	o
ch				
k				
kʷ				
m				
n				
p				
s				
t				
tl/l				
tz				
w				
x				
y				

(Alfonso Lacadena)

Note: A quesion mark (?) indicates that scholars are still looking to confirm the exact pictograph.

A blank field indicates that the pictograph has not yet been identified.

this. The name sign for Juan Xochimitl contains the pictographs for *xochitl* (flower) and *mitl* (arrow) symbolically forming *xochimitl*. The *xochitl* word is partially sounded, while *mitl* is voiced entirely. The name sign for Antonio Chalchiuhtemoc (one who descends like a precious greenstone) contains the pictographs for *chalchihuitl* (precious stone), *tetl* (stone), and *temo* (to descend), represented by a line of footprints directed downward. In this instance, *tetl* is a redundant phonetic indicator and a determinative. This is a pictograph that is not separately sounded but instead duplicates the initial sound represented by the entire sign, thereby minimizing ambiguity. This is proof of an Aztec use of phonetics because pictograph sound values are conveyed while meanings are not.

The name sign for Diego Tecolotl contains the pictograph for *tecolotl* (owl) and *tetl* (stone). The *tetl* pictograph guides the Nahua-speaking reader to deduce that the main pictograph stood for an animal that not only resembled an owl but had its name sounded by an initial *t* (from *tetl*) so that the reader would conclude that the main pictograph represented a *tecolotl*. *Tlacuilos* used redundant phonetic indicators to achieve even greater descriptive precision. The

name sign for Antonio Ayotl contains a pictograph for *atl* (water) and a pictograph for turtle. As there are two common words for turtle, *ayotl* and *chimalmichin* (depending on the species), then the *a* in *atl* helps the reader by providing the initial sound for the word. The name sign for Pablo Macuilcoatl is written nonphonetically by using the pictograph for *macuilli* (five) and *coatl* (snake). This name was found written once phonetically and twice nonphonetically in the same source. The word *macuilli* is still read nonphonetically, but *coatl* is no longer a stylized rendering of a snake. It is now written as a combination of the pictograph *comitl* (pot) and *atl* (water).

Unless otherwise noted, most name signs are read nonphonetically. The name sign for Cuauhtlehuanitzin (great ascending eagle) contains the pictographs for *cuauhtli* (eagle) and *tzintli* (anus or buttocks [herein represented by the lower half of a human body]). The word *tzintli* is used here phonetically as a homophone to convey the sound of a reverential suffix -*tzin*. In a different cadastral manuscript, it is a *quahuitl* (tree [here spelled *cuahuitl*]) pictograph drawn above and attached to the *cuauhtli* (eagle) pictograph that forms this name sign. The *cuahuitl* is not sounded separately because it is used as a redundant

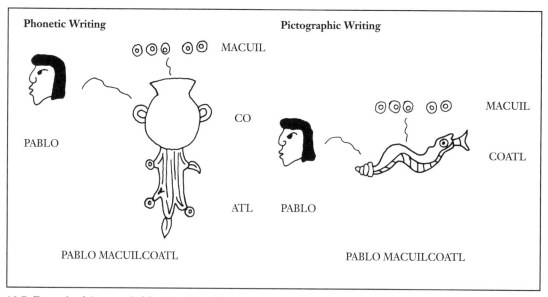

10.7 *Example of the name* Pablo Macuilcoatl *written both pictographically and phonetically* (Drawings by Fonda Portales, after *Codex Mendoza*)

phonetic indicator to reinforce the sign of a *cuauhtli*. When used this way, the tree pictograph directs the reader to interpret the sign that is represented by a bird as the eagle pictograph.

Cuauhtlehuanitzin was the name of a brother and a son (Moteixcahuia Cuauhtlehuanitzin) of the Tetzcocan *tlatoani* Nezahualcoyotl. The name sign for Ixhuitzcatocatzin (Great Illustrious One Who Laughs or Sneers) is represented by a laughing or sneering human profile face. The principal element of this word is *ixuetzca*, which is a verb that means "to smile or make gestures by laughing or sneering." This was the name of one of Nezahualcoyotl's brothers as well as one of his great grandsons (Don Alonso Ixhuitzcatocatzin). The name sign for Tzinpetlauhtocatzin (Great Illustrious One Who Shames Others) is represented by the pictograph for a *tzintli* (human posterior). In this case, the scribe intended the naked state of the pictograph to convey the concept of nudity. This signified *petlaua* (to be naked), which is the second part of the verb construction. Two phonic messages are conveyed by a single pictograph forming *tzinpetlaua* (to put to shame). The etymology of this suggests that the act of exposing an unclothed posterior to others was an expression of contempt. Since this sign functions as an ideograph and transmits semantic values, it was written nonphonetically.

The apostrophe was used by Indian and non-Indian colonial scribes to signify the omission of one or more letters from a word. The name sign for Temix'aziuaytzin is represented by a pictograph of a bundled cadaver pierced by an arrow. The name might have been *Temixhuaziuaytzin*, which would give the word a possessive aspect. It might also have been *Temixhuaciuaytzin*, which would have feminized the word. This name sign is not read as a pictograph for "bundled cadaver" but rather is an ideograph for *temicti* (killer) or *temictiliztli* (homicide).

Place Signs

As for the place signs in these cadastral manuscripts, unless otherwise noted, they are read nonphonetically. While all personal name signs are glossed, only one place sign is. Zoltepetl (hill of the quail) is represented pictorially by the head of a *zolin* (quail)

drawn atop a hill or mountain. Without the gloss, place-names must be derived from educated theory. The *tetl* (stone) pictograph is rendered alongside a sideway pyramid. Since this same sideway pyramid is written in another codex as *tenamitl*, this must be assumed for the present pictograph. The suffix -*co* (in, on, place of) is added to create the word Tetenanco. The sideway pyramid might also signify *momoztli* or *momoz* (altar) since it resembles one in another codex. The suffix -*tlan* (near, beside, by) is added to create the word Momoztitlan.

Another place sign displays the pictograph of a *maitl* (hand) joined with a *tetl* (stone). If constructed phonetically, then the name of this place would be Tema. A different codex uses this place sign to signify a place called Temacpalco or Temacpapalco. These might or might not be referring to the same place.

In another place sign, the *atl* (water) pictograph alone represents a place called Atlixcahuacan (place of those who possess groundwater). A *huexotl* (willow) pictograph is used for another place sign. In a different codex, this same place sign represents Huexotla (place of the willows). The pictograph of a *pantli* (flag) joined to a human skull might be resting atop a low platform. If the skull atop the platform represents a *tzompantli* (skull rack), then this toponym might be *Tzompanhuacan* (place of those who have a skullrack) or *Tzompanco* (at the skull rack). The pictograph of a *mazatl* (deer) atop an *atl* (water) image might represent the place Mazaapan (on the water of the deer). In other colonial works, this place is also Mazahuacan/Mazauacan (place of one who has deer).

Another place sign is formed by the pictograph *tlalli* (land), *calli* (house), and *pantli* (flag). As an ideograph read nonphonetically, this pictograph might represent the toponym Calpulalpan (on the land of the *calpulli* [neighborhood]). If the sign is read as a pictograph, then the place sign might denote Calpan or Callalpan (place of houses), which are listed in other codices. In a different codex, the pictograph of a *pilli* (child) holding a *xochitl* (flower) while sitting atop a hill or mountain represents the town of Xochipillan (now Juchipila). A last example of a toponym where a pictographic-phonetic combination is used is the name of a town composed by the pictograph, *tollin* (bundle of reeds) and *tzintli* (anus or buttocks). In this example, the drawing of the

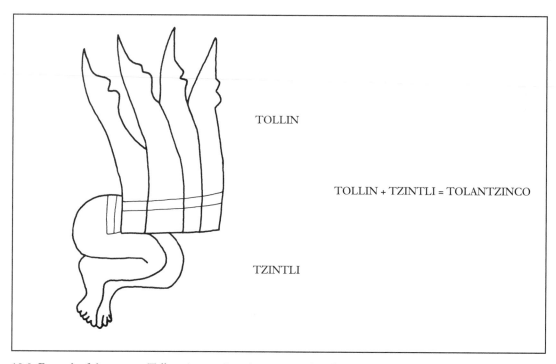

TOLLIN

TOLLIN + TZINTLI = TOLANTZINCO

TZINTLI

10.8 Example of the toponym Tollantzinco *written in a pictographic-phonetic combination* (Drawing by Fonda Portales, after *Codex Mendoza*)

lower half of a human body stands for *tzintli* and has the phonetic reading *tzin* because the town being represented is Tollantzinco, "the little place of the reeds" (now Tulancingo).

POETRY AND NARRATIVE

Through poetry, the Aztec recounted what was dear to them. All poems and songs dedicated to the gods were by far the most important to them. The patron god of poets was Xochipilli since he was considered the lord of flower and song. Aztec songs told of ancient traditions, remote deeds of clans, deities, wars, feats of famous warriors, hunt-

ing incidents, and natural phenomena, such as comets and earthquakes; they celebrated and mourned the dual nature of human life with such subjects as death and famine, love and humor, plagues and the afterlife.

Accompanying poetry and song, instruments were played to rouse the emotions of audiences and complement the orator/singer. The earliest musical instruments found in Mesoamerica are made of baked clay and bone. Early in the history of instrumentation, the drum became the foremost of all instruments. The drum was so vital to Aztec culture and festivity that parties could not begin until the drummer was there to initiate the celebration. During battle, a drummer gave directions to the warriors. In some Aztec celebrations, if the drummer threw off the beat and the dancers acting in accordance to the beat, then the whole event was canceled, because throwing off the beat was perceived to be a bad omen.

As ethnohistorian Jacques Soustelle says, the richness of the Nahuatl language allowed the piling up of near synonyms, separated from one another by faint shades of meaning, for the description of one deed. The language itself was full of metaphors in which one word could have several meanings. The word *coatl* translates literally as "snake," but other meanings of this word include "twin," "brother," and "friend." Context of the sentence was all that kept a brother from being a snake. An idea could be also be expressed with the juxtaposition of two words. *In xochitl in cuicatl* (flower and song) combines these two words to refer to poetry.

Most Aztec poetry was written with a philosophical-moral rhetoric. There were various men who crafted poetry using the exquisite language of Nahuatl. The most famous of all Aztec poets was King Nezahualcoyotl. It was said that as an artist paints a book, Nezahualcoyotl painted with flowers and songs (poetry). He was a scholar and a nobleman who had proven himself as a great warrior as well as a practical engineer. As a *tlamatinime* (he who knows something, a wise man), Nezahualcoyotl was the best individual to characterize what this priestly class of poets was about (see the appendix "Aztec Poems").

They were one of 30 distinct classes of priests. They stood out in particular because they were also scholars. The fact that they were astronomers, guardians of the codices and knowledge, and experts in calendars and chronology, added to their venerated status. An outstanding aspect of the priesthood was its freedom to express individual thoughts and emotions without fear of persecution. It was also these men that arduously defended the Aztec worldview and religion from the Catholic Church. They were known to reject Christianity openly, an act that led many to punishment. Nezahualcoyotl died prior to the European invasion. The topics he covered in his extant poetry give us an idea of the variety that must have existed. He reflected on change and time, the unavoidable death, the expression of truth, the afterlife, the place of the dead, and concepts about divinity.

There were also professional poets in the service of great men. These were men hired not merely to write poetry but also to perform it. The Nahuatl word for poet is *cuicani*, which also means "singer." A poem and a song were synonymous with each other. Poems were always sung or at least accompanied by musical instruments. As many Aztec poems honored certain people, places, or events, it can be said that the modern Mexican *corrido* is the descendant of this Aztec artform. Some poets taught singing and music in the *cuicalli* (house of song).

There were many types of poetry among the Aztec. Some were *teocuicatl* (holy songs or hymns), while others were more like sagas. Given that poetry was acted out at a type of recital, the verses were accompanied by a ritual or dance. The *tlaquetzaque* was the entertainer who read poems and recited legends. Not all of these poems/songs were comprehensible to the general masses. Religious poetry was often replete with esoteric allusions and metaphors that made it difficult for those not educated in the priesthood to understand it. The twin obsessions of Aztec poets were flowers and death. These motifs adorned all ancient Mexican lyric poetry with brilliance as well as shadows. The Nahuatl wise men reflected particularly in all the things that surrounded human beings, especially those that are good and beautiful: the flowers and songs, the feathers of a quetzal, the works of art, the golden cobs of maize, the faces and the hearts of friends, and even their ancient heritage. The descriptions of landscapes were truly vivid. It can be assumed that if there was something worth writing about, they did. The wind instruments that accompanied these poems were the conch, trumpet, flute, whistle, *huehuetl* (upright drum), and the *teponaztli* (two-toned horizontal drum).

Nahuatl poetry could be in prose or verse. Prose was used when referring to instructive treaties or mythological and historical narratives. Verse poems were for religious or profane topics.

Historical Poetry

Through the content of a poem can be seen what was in the heart of the writer. An appreciation for the shores of the Gulf of Mexico is felt when the author of one poem recalls the wisdom, the annals, the songs, and the flutes associated with the people from the Land of Black and Red Ink. The land being referred to was Tamoanchan, where the Olmec civilization evolved. The remnants of this civilization helped form the first great metropolis of the American continent, Teotihuacan. The respect for Teotihuacan is evident in a poem that mentions how the gods gathered and convened there long ago to create the fifth sun, the present world. Another poem marks the beauty of this city by using phrases such as "circles of jades," "quetzal plumes," and "flowery mist." The amount of poetry regarding this city and its history can only lead one to believe that it must have been an immensely important place.

Power transferred to Tollan (Tula), the Toltec capital after the fall of Teotihuacan. Although the power and influence of Tollan was great, it never matched its predecessor's immenseness. Tollan declined in power in 1100. There are also poems about its greatness. One poem reflects on the Toltec diaspora. To say that "truly a Toltec once lived there" is to lament the sophisticated ruins of this great civilization. It should be remembered that the Aztec used the word *tolteca* to refer back to a golden age of artistic creativity. The city's splendor came to an end, and the exile of the great Toltec leader Topiltzin-Quetzalcoatl is now legendary. His sadness is expressed in one poem that mentions that he sobbed like two torments of hail pounding down.

The replacement for this metropolis was Tenochtitlan, capital of the Aztec. In a poem about warfare, the author yearns for death on the battlefield. This displays the positive attitude that Aztec people had toward death as well as their eagerness to fight. The magnificence of Tenochtitlan is mentioned in various poems as well as in the writings of certain Spaniards. With a city of at least 350,000 people, *chinampas* expanding the island, and three defensive causeways, it truly must have been quite a sight. The self-restraint and humility that was expected of wealthy nobles and emperors is seen in one poem that alludes to their hearts as firm as stone, yet capable of understanding. An Otomí poet reflects on the situation of his people among the Aztec. They have become accustomed to being looked down upon but accepted their plight without bitterness and smiled the negatives away.

Pre-Columbian Poets

Sometimes the names of the poets are known. The uncertainty of the hereafter is expressed by the Tetzcocan *tlatoani* Nezahualcoyotl when he questions if one really lives on Earth since the time spent here is so short. Nezahualcoyotl has trouble finding satisfaction in earthly things in one of his more famous poems. In another, he boldly asserts that his flowers and songs will not come to an end (see the appendix "Aztec Poems"). Tochihuitzin Coyolchiuhqui of Tenochtitlan is one poet who wonders if life itself is not simply an illusion. A poet named Temilotzin of Tlatelolco reveals in a poem that even among the Aztec warriors, there were artists and wise men. In another poem, Prince Ayocuan Cuetzpalin of Tecamachalco wonders if flowers and songs survive into the great beyond. Tecayehuatzin of Huexotzinco overcomes this pessimistic attitude by explaining in one poem that only flowers and songs, art, and symbolism can overcome sadness because a man's riches are his joys on Earth. Cuauhtecoztli, a native philosopher-poet, questions the afterlife in one of his poems (see the appendix "Aztec Poems"). Axayacatl of Tenochtitlan, Nezahaualpilli of Tetzcoco, Tlatecazin of Cuauhchinanco, Cacamatzin of Tetzcoco, Macuilxochitzin of Tenochtitlan, Xayacamach of Tizatlan, Xicohtencatl el Viejo of Puebla-Tlaxcala, Chichicuepon of Chalco, Aquiauhtzin of Ayapanco, and Cuacuauhtzin of Tepechpan are other poets who contributed to the variety of ideas written by Aztecs.

There are many poems about the strength of the Aztec capital, but it is best expressed by one poet who questions if anything could destroy the foundation of heaven. The sorrows expressed in another poem about the fall of Tenochtitlan are felt with the usage of phrases such as "walls red with blood" and "water red as if dyed." Referring to this loss as a dead inheritance and lamenting that the warrior's shields could not save the city also displays the sorrow (see the appendix "Aztec Poems"). Chimalpahin best reflects the memory of Tenochtitlan when he writes that the fame and glory of this city will never perish. He could not have been more right.

Literature after the Conquest

When discussing postconquest writers or poets, it is customary to mention the school where those individuals learned their style and their teachers or mentors because this information helps to understand the "angle" taken on the subject. Other factors that defined each of these writers depended on their social status. There is a certain amount of confusion as to which indigenous or mestizo authors created books used today as primary sources.

TEACHING THE LITERARY ARTS

General education for the indigenous masses was disrupted by the conquest, and Spanish missionaries provided the only postconquest schools. In these schools, Christian doctrine was emphasized; for example, native students had to learn, in Nahuatl and Latin, the Pater Noster (Our Father), Ave Maria (Hail Mary), and Salve Regina. Also, the Creed, Ten Commandments, Seven Mortal Sins, Works of Mercy, and Cardinal/Theological Virtues were taught. Weekly attendance at mass, sermons, and adult catechism were required. Yearly confessions were also mandatory, but communion was only allowed at the priest's discretion, depending on a person's level of understanding of the faith. Men and women were also examined on their knowledge of doctrine before marriages were performed.

The sons of the nobility were given more intensive training. The people of the outlying communities received less attention because no friars were permanently set up there. The first of these missionary schools was opened in 1520. The Franciscan monk Pedro de Gante opened the famous school of San José de los Naturales in 1527. There, he took the sons of leaders and lords and instructed them in Latin, catechism, and arts and crafts. These students would then help educate their parents on the Catholic faith.

From the workshops of this school came young and adult men trained as painters, sculptors, goldsmiths, silversmiths, cabinetsmiths, carpenters, embroiderers, blacksmiths, and all other forthcoming guilds. The talent of these individuals was so great that they competed with the work of European artisans. Friar Motolinia observed that Spanish merchants accordingly had to lower their prices for certain goods as soon as the native peoples learned how to duplicate them. The quality of the replicas was equal if not superior to the European-made originals. The Colegio Imperial de Santa Cruz de Tlatelolco was later opened in 1536 as an institution of higher education. This was the equivalent of an Aztec *calmecac*. Both institutions were different in many aspects but similar in others. Asceticism, sobriety, and pedagogy were shared in their respective cultural contexts.

This Colegio de Tlatelolco counted among its faculty the most distinguished Franciscan scholars of the time. Bernardino de Sahagún, Andrés de Olmos, and Juan de Gaona were three of the more important ones. The brilliant students and teachers of the *colegio* were admired by the people of their time for their trilingual skills, having mastered Latin, Spanish, and Nahuatl. The most prominent Latinists and writers of this schools were Antonio Valeriano, Martín Jacobita, Diego Adriano, Juan Berardo, Francisco Bautista de Contreras, Esteban Bravo, Pedro de Gante (a name adopted after the great Franciscan), Agustín de la Fuente, Hernando de Ribas, Pablo Nazareno, Juan Badiano (who translated from Nahuatl to Latin the book written by the Aztec physician Martín de la Cruz), and Pedro Juan Antonio. This last individual was a specialist in the Classical authors. In 1568 he went to the University of Salamanca to study civil and canon law and in 1574 published in Barcelona a Latin grammar.

With infinite patience, friars and *ladino* Indian scribes undertook the task of illuminating manuscripts and translating complete volumes. Works turned out by them include *Doctrines and Vocabularies*, the *Florentine Codex*, the *Codex Mendoza*, the *Codex de la Cruz-Badiano*, and the *Map of Mexico-Tenochtitlan of 1550*. The Colegio de Tlatelolco was truly a center for Mexican studies in the 16th century. Archbishop Juan de Zumárraga opened eight schools for native girls (in Tetzcoco, Mexico, Coyoacan, Tlaxcala, Cholula, Huejotzingo, Otumba, and Tepeapulco) between 1534 and 1538. The College of the Holy Cross in Tlatelolco was built for the purpose of preparing young native men for the priesthood. The school had to be shut down in 1555 when the Council of Churches in Mexico decided that Indians, mestizos, and blacks were not fit to attend a seminary. This school later was reopened as a school for translators as well as an elementary school for children.

METHODS OF EDUCATION

In these boarding schools only the children of nobility or gifted commoners were educated. By being removed from their parental/traditional training, the loss of identity turned these students into conversional tools for the friars. Together with the friars, these youths often helped demolish pyramid-temples and disrupt native religious observations. In an extreme case in Tlaxcala they even stoned to death an indigenous priest, without friar supervision. This generation of Mexicans—ladino Indians—was not well liked by the majority of the native population. They were seen as spies and disrupters. Even their parents did not trust them. However, the education they received was intense. Within two to three years, most were fluent in Latin and Spanish, both in writing and in speech. Their education was the perfect tool to help evangelize the rest of the indigenous population. This was a different approach than the one that Diego de Landa used in Yucatán, when he organized the killing of priests and burning of books.

FRAY BERNARDINO DE SAHAGÚN AND LADINO INDIANS

Sahagún believed that in order to convert Mexico's native people, the church first had to understand them. He arrived in New Spain in 1529 and set out to salvage the remnants of the original native culture. Missionaries like himself (such as Diego Durán and Motolinia) are credited with being the first ethnographers of the New World. Sahagún, for example, is responsible for the *General History of the Things of New Spain*. At the time it was conceived and compiled, it was written not to detail preconquest life, but rather to tell how to recognize it and change it to Catholic European ways. He described how stubborn the natives were and instructed on clues to look for when dealing with

hidden heathen survivals. This collection of work would later become known as the *Florentine Codex*.

In the prologue he gave the names of the brilliant *indios ladinos* (Hispanicized Catholic natives) who participated actively in the great project as translators and researchers. The names of these students were Antonio Valeriano of Azcapotzalco, Alonso Vegerano and Pedro de San Buenaventura of Cuauhtitlan, and Martín Jacobita from Santa Ana (he was also the director of the *colegio*). The *escribanos* (writers) were Diego de Grado and Bonifacio Maximiliano of Tlatelolco and Mateo Severino of Xochimilco.

Sahagún also wrote *Postilla, Twenty-six Additions, Apendiz, Colloquios, Doctrina, Exercicio quotidiano, Manual del cristiano, Psalmodía cristiana, Sermones y santoral,* and *Primeros memoriales*. Books 4, 6, and 10 of Sahagún's *General History of the Things of New Spain* contained the sections that focused and reflected on the natives' *huehuetlahtolli* (the old men's words), which were written in the most correct and elegant language possible, as if addressing aristocrats. These were rhetorical orations in general: prayers, discourses, salutations, and congratulatory speeches. Traditional, religious, moral, and social concepts that were handed down from generation to generation were expressed in these. Through repetition, the students of preconquest schools were able to memorize the information given to them by their parents and elders.

THE *HUEHUETLAHTOLLI*

Fray Andrés de Olmos sought a way to use this learning technique against the native youths. By studying the *huehuetlahtolli* he was able to determine which aspects of the language to discontinue—such as the repetitions/parallelisms, metaphors (river, cliff, snare, stick, halter, and stone to represent getting into trouble), and *difrasismos* (the coupling of two images to suggest a third meaning)—as a means to speed up the process of evangelization. At the same time, the *huehuetlahtolli* helped the friars change their ineffective teaching styles, which must have seemed monotonous, repetitive, and uninventive compared to what the students were used to. Zumárraga, for example, would address the parents of the youths in the same manner as their elders had in pre-Hispanic times. Comparing Sahagún's works from the 1540s to the revisions in 1563, it is clear that he began to model his sermons after the *huehuetlahtolli*, too. In no way did he agree with every aspect of the "old" teachings. He denounced the way that parents would force small children to rise in the middle of night to perform devotional acts to win favors (with the gods) for them (the parents). However, in his sermons, Sahagún did not disagree with this practice if it was a protection prayer to the Christian God. As with the students at other boarding schools, these native youths were also used to help convert others. The only different between the two styles of outreach was that these students were used more as teacher to their communities than as snitches. Sahagún used no Spanish collaborators, only the trilingual students at the Franciscan schools.

POSTCONQUEST POETS AND WRITERS

Some of these individuals were true poets, while others were missionary informants with skill. Antonio Valeriano and Juan Bautista de Pomar were both poets and informants, but more the latter. They prided themselves in their use of the "old-style" Nahuatl verses, which were reminiscent of preconquest times. Valeriano is associated with Sahagún and is linked to the *Cantares mexicanos*. He was born in Azcapotzalco in 1531. He received a Franciscan education but was not from a noble family. Valeriano was one of Sahagún's closest consorts. Interestingly enough, Valeriano is often associated with the *Nican Mopohua*. This is the name given to the account of the events where the Virgin of Guadalupe appeared before a native man named Juan Diego. Just as with this religious account, there is no real proof that what is assumed is factual. Valeriano died in 1605.

Pomar is linked with *Romances de los Señores de Nueva España*. He was the son of an indigenous noblewoman from Tetzcoco and a conquistador. Through his mother's lineage he was actually the great-grandson of Nezahualcoyotl. While he took advantage of his father's privileges, he particularly esteemed his indigenous heritage. He sought to help recover some of the knowledge that had been lost when Cortés and the Tlaxcalans burned the royal palace and great library of Tetzcoco in 1520. His *Relación de Tetzcoco* was written in response to the 1577 questionnaire for geographic and census information. Pomar died in 1602.

Don Diego Muñoz Camargo (from Tlaxcala) is another mestizo writer who contributed to these works. His *Historia de Tlaxcala* covers the ancient migrations of the group, its dynastic history, and its role as allies of the Spanish in the conquest of Mexico. Fernando Alva Ixtlilxochitl (an Acolhua from Tetzcoco) and Hernando Alvarado Tezozomoc (of Mexica descent) were two indigenous historians. Alva Ixtlilxochitl left abundant accounts of Acolhuan history in his *Historia chichimeca* and various *Relaciones*, all of which he wrote in Spanish. Alvarado Tezozomoc also wrote the *Crónica Mexicayotl (Crónica mexicana)*. In this work, he left a major narrative account of the Mexica rise to power in the late 14th century up to the time of the Spanish conquest. Domingo Francisco de San Antón Muñón Chimalpahin Quauhtlehuanitzin is another individual who contributed to the collection of works that help reconstruct preconquest Aztec society. He is considered the most prolific historian of native descent.

These latter three men were of the Aztec noble class and thus were privileged enough to have had access to the ancient books. These writers represented themselves as lords or leaders of their respective groups, thereby claiming authority to speak on behalf of their people. Each was involved actively in legal petitioning for the restoration of rights, privileges, and properties. Their works were aimed at enhancing the prestige of the dynastic traditions they represented. They expressed directly only what was convenient to say, but their subtexts were equally informative.

Nahuatl Words in Modern Spanish

Many Nahuatl words are used regularly in modern Spanish (constituting Nahuatlisms) because they are integrated in the names of Mexican cities or states. *Oaxaca*, for example, comes from the Na-huatl word *Uaxacac*, which means "place where the *guaje* vegetables begin." *Toluca* comes from the word *Tollocan*, which means "where the head is bowed down." *Tlaxcala* comes from the word *Tlax-callan*, which means "where there is an abundance of *tlaxcallis* (tortillas)." *Mazatlan* translates as "place with an abundance of deer," and *Acapulco*, as "place near an abundance of thick reeds." *Chapulte-pec* means "hill/place of the grasshopper," *Michoa-can*, "place where they have many fish." *Jalisco* roughly translates as "place near an abundance of sand in the face." The word *Mexico* itself is said to come from "place near the maguey cactus navel" or "place of the god Mexitl (Huitzilopochtli)."

Some Nahuatl words with minor alterations of pronunciation are used in modern Mexican Span-ish because there were no existing European words for that object or simply persisted through constant use. Examples are *zoquete* (mud or a fool), *asquil* (a small ant), *mayate* (a green insect), *petaca* (a suit-case), *chiquito* (very small), *papalote* (kite and wind-mill), *mecate* (rope), *tocayo* (namesake), *malacate* (winch), *itacate* (bundle with food), *elote* (sweet corn), *olote* (corn cob), *popote* (drinking straw), *zen-zontle* (mocking bird), *guajolote* (turkey), *molcajete* (kitchen mortar), *petate* (woven mat), *jocoque* (yogurt), *cacle* (shoe), and *chante* (home).

Some Nahuatl words have even been carried over into English. *Chocolate* (from *chocolatl*) and *tomato* (from *tomatl*) are two such words. But it seems that only the easy Nahuatl words carried over into European languages, because none of the more complicated terms appear anywhere anymore other than in the old Nahuatl dictionaries. *Amama-chiotlacuiloltzaqua* is a word that means "to seal a letter." *Mitzmotzatzacuiltitimanizque* translates as "they will be at your sides, either left or right." *Techichiualtzitzquiliztli* is a somewhat vulgar word that refers to "the act of touching the breasts of a person." It is interesting to note that *chichi*, how-ever, is still used today as a colloquial word for breasts in Spanish. *Tlamiquiztlatzontequililli* trans-lates to "condemned to death."

Reading

Tlacuilos and Their Techniques

Anderson 1993: *huehuetlatolli* in Sahagún's ser-mons; Carmack, Gasco, and Gossen 1996: Mesoamerican history; Coe and Koontz 2002: indigenous history of Mexico.

Codices

Colston 1993: name signs from colonial Aztec manuscripts; Galarza 1995 and 1997, Mohar-Betancourt 1997, Glass 1975: Mexican codices study; León-Portilla 1963: Aztec thought and cul-ture; León-Portilla 1969: pre-Columbian litera-tures of Mexico; León-Portilla 1997: codices' history; Miller and Taube 1993: gods and symbols of Mexico; Peterson 1959: ancient Mexico.

Pictographic-Phonetic Writing

Reyes-García 1997: pictographic writings; Robertson 1959: colonial Mexican manuscripts; Robertson 1972: codices' study; Soustelle 1979: daily life of Aztec; Valle 1997: colonial codices; Vander-Meeren 1997: *amate* paper; Molina 1970: Nahuatl-Spanish dictio-nary; Karttunen 1983: Nahuatl-English dictionary; Barlow and MacAfee 1949: phonetic elements in the *Codex Mendoza*; Galarza 1995: Aztec codices' reading.

Poetry and Narrative

Aguilar-Moreno 1996, Garibay 1971, León-Portilla 1959, 1970, 1975, 1992 (*Fifteen Poets*), Sahagún 1951–69: Aztec poetry; Anderson 1993: *huehuetlatolli*; Alva Ixtlilxochitl 1975–77, Alvarado Tezozomoc 1975: Indian accounts.

11

THE CALENDAR,
ASTRONOMY, AND
MATHEMATICS

The Aztec were extraordinary time keepers and observers of the natural and supernatural phenomena that occurred around them. The structure of time and space within the universe and their comprehension of it were reflected in their calendrical systems, accurate mathematical computations, and sophisticated astronomical observation devices. Space and time made harmony possible among the gods. The celestial skies were like maps, compasses, and calendars that served to initiate the principal phases of Aztec life.

The specialists dedicated to finding order and meaning in the universe knew precisely when it was time to conduct harvesting, ceremonies, and other rituals. Astronomical knowledge gave the priests a solid base on which to predict natural phenomena, and these occurrences were seen as episodes in an essentially cyclical concept of time and history.

Since time governed all aspects of Aztec social, ritual, and economic life, hundreds of monuments were created with sacred space in mind. Buildings, temples, and city layouts were constructed with mathematical precision to align with the four quadrants of the universe and maintain the cosmic order.

THE CALENDAR SYSTEM

The calendar system was taught in the elite schools, the *calmecac*, whose attendees included sons of the upper nobility, some sons of lower nobles, and those who regardless of social class were destined for the priesthood. The Aztec calendar, *xiuhtlapohualli*, which existed in several forms, was based on multiple interlocking sets of cycles. It is speculated that the first calendar may have originated as far back as the Olmec period in the first millennium B.C.E. or even earlier, and that its methods were learned and redefined by cultures thereafter. Moreover, from this prior contact, the Aztec were able to create three types of calendars: the ritual calendar (*tonalpohualli*), the annual calendar (*xiuhpohualli*), and the 52-year calendar round (*xiuhmolpilli*).

The three calendars represented two methods of Aztec time-counting. The *tonalpohualli*, "counting of the days," was a 260-day cycle used for divination. The days were recorded in the *tonalamatl*, a sacred almanac widely used among Mesoamerican peoples long before the Aztec. Each page of this almanac pertained to a 13-day period in which one or two deities presided. The individual days and their companions were painted in rectangular compartments below and to the right of the patrons.

The second type of calendrical system was a 365-day solar count called the *xiuhpohualli*, "counting of the years," which was mainly used to organized the recurrent cycle of annual seasonal festivals. This calendar together with the *tonalpohualli* created a larger cycle of 52 years and functioned jointly as a calendar round of two engaged, rotating gears, in which the beginning day of the larger 365-day wheel would align with the beginning day of the smaller 260-day cycle every 52 years. This 52-year period constituted what could be interpreted as a Mesoamerican "century." The change from one 52-year period, or "bundle of years" (*xiuhmolpilli*), into the next was always the occasion of an important religious festival called the New Fire ceremony (see chapter 3).

The years, each named according to the *tonalpohualli* day on which it ended, contained one of the four signs (Rabbit, Reed, Flint, and House). Just as the *tonalpohualli* days progressed from sign to sign and from number to number, so did the years: 1 Rabbit preceded 2 Reed, 3 Flint, 4 House, 5 Rabbit, and so forth. Since some day names were also used as names for years, the Aztec solved the identification problem by enclosing the year name in a rectangular cartouche, that was almost always painted either blue or turquoise.

Each of the cycles—260 days and 365 days—was the result of a combination of still smaller cycles. One of these smaller cycles marked a "day" and was based on a series of numbers, starting at 1 and ending in 13. Each day number was also associated with one of the 13 Lords of the Day. The day numbers did not function in a mathematical fashion but only as a set of serial demarcations. Twenty day cycles made up a *metztli* or *metztlapohualiztli*, meaning "moon," comparable to a Western Calendar "month."

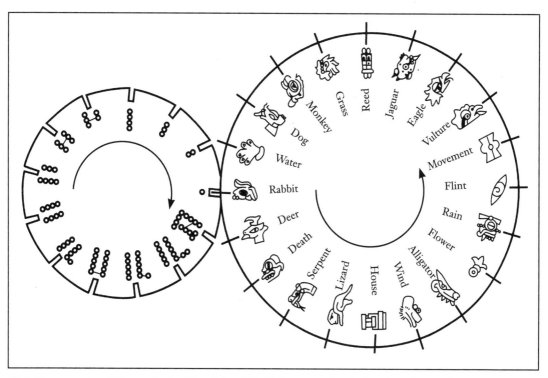

11.1 Representation of the tonalpohualli *cycle in which 20 day names interlock with 13 day numbers* (Lluvia Arras and Maria Ramos)

Aztec days were divided into four principal parts: from the birth of the Sun (sunrise) until midday, midday to sunset, sunset to midnight, and midnight to sunrise. The hours of mid-distance in each period—9:00 A.M., 3:00 P.M., 9:00 P.M., and 3:00 A.M.—were important for their symbolism. The beginning of the day (6 A.M.–12 P.M.) was called Iquiza-Tonatiuh; midday (12–6 P.M.), Nepantla-Tonatiuh; evening (6 P.M.–12 A.M.), Onaqui-Tonatiuh; and midnight (12–6 A.M.), Yohualnepantla.

The individual hours of the day did not have names. Observers would only refer to the position of the Sun in the sky. When they wanted to express the hour they would simply say, *"iz Teotl,"* meaning "here is the god" or "here is the sun." The hours of the night were regulated by the stars. The year count, the day sign, and the count of each 20-day period were said to have been created by the first human couple, Oxomoco and Cipactonal, who were later deified.

The *Tonalpohualli*

The 260-day *tonalpohualli* was a ritual and astronomical calendar used in casting horoscopes, interpreting the influences that affected people's lives, and recording the historical events of the world. The basic units of the *tonalpohualli* were the *trecena* (one group of 13 day numbers) and the *veintena* (one group of 20 name days or day symbols). The 13 day numbers combined with each of the 20 day symbols to generate the 260 days that constituted the *tonalpohualli* cycle (20 × 13 = 260). In this sense, this calendar can be defined by 13 groups of 20 days (13 *veintenas*) or 20 groups of 13 days (20 *trecenas*).

The former scheme was applied for astronomical purposes. The first *veintena* began with the number 1 and the day name that came up in the sequence of rotation. The second *veintena* started with the number 8, the third with the number 2, and so on, until

THE THIRTEEN *VEINTENAS* OF THE *TONALPOHUALLI*

	I	II	III	IV	V	VI	VII	VIII	IX	X	XI	XII	XIII
Cipactli	1	8	2	9	3	10	4	11	5	12	6	13	7
Ehecatl	2	9	3	10	4	11	5	12	6	13	7	1	8
Calli	3	10	4	11	5	12	6	13	7	1	8	2	9
Cuetzpallin	4	11	5	12	6	13	7	1	8	2	9	3	10
Coatl	5	12	6	13	7	1	8	2	9	3	10	4	11
Miquiztli	6	13	7	1	8	2	9	3	10	4	11	5	12
Mazatl	7	1	8	2	9	3	10	4	11	5	12	6	13
Tochtli	8	2	9	3	10	4	11	5	12	6	13	7	1
Atl	9	3	10	4	11	5	12	6	13	7	1	8	2
Itzcuintli	10	4	11	5	12	6	13	7	1	8	2	9	3
Ozomatli	11	5	12	6	13	7	1	8	2	9	3	10	4
Malinalli	12	6	13	7	1	8	2	9	3	10	4	11	5
Acatl	13	7	1	8	2	9	3	10	4	11	5	12	6
Ocelotl	1	8	2	9	3	10	4	11	5	12	6	13	7
Cuauhtli	2	9	3	10	4	11	5	12	6	13	7	1	8
Cozcacuauhtli	3	10	4	11	5	12	6	13	7	1	8	2	9
Ollin	4	11	5	12	6	13	7	1	8	2	9	3	10
Tecpatl	5	12	6	13	7	1	8	2	9	3	10	4	11
Quiahuitl	6	13	7	1	8	2	9	3	10	4	11	5	12
Xochitl	7	1	8	2	9	3	10	4	11	5	12	6	13

having completely repeated 13 times the 20 day symbols up to 260, as shown in the accompanying table. The calendar therefore began with the day signs 1 Alligator (Cipactli) and ended with 13 Flower (Xochitl). After 260 days, 1 Alligator would reappear.

The latter scheme of 20 *trecenas* was the foundation for an elaborate series of ritual associations. Each group of 13 days was a unit named by its first day (1 Cipactli), 1 Ocelotl, 1 Mazatl, etc.). These groups were thought to have special symbolic significance and were governed by a specific deity. This calendar also included 13 Lords of the Day, nine Lords of the Night, and one patron god for each of the 20 day names. Each unique number-name carried its own special fortune, either a good, bad, or indifferent one.

The *tonalpohualli* was recorded in an almanac called the *tonalamatl*, a book of days. Priests consulted the book when a newborn child was taken to them. The sacred book was referred to constantly for favorable and unfavorable days, for conducting commerce, going to war, sowing and reaping, traveling, and even in choosing mates. Offerings to the dead were made from May through August, the period between the two zenith passages when the Sun's shadow pointed north at noon, an important sign.

SACRED NUMBERS AND SIGNS

If a child was born on an unlucky day, the parents would wait to name him or her until an auspicious sign came in the following days, although they could wait no more than four days after the child's birth. The days that contained the numbers 3, 7, 10, 11, 12, and 13 were considered favorable, in general terms, and the numbers 4, 5, 6, 8, and 9 were generally unlucky. The number 13 was very important to the Aztec for it accounted for the 13 major gods and the 13 superimposed layers of the world and the sky. A list of the 20 *trecenas* and their fortunes follows:

1 Cipactli The sign of good omen. Those born in this *trecena* would be happy and fortunate.

1 Ocelotl An unlucky sign. Men born during this 13-day period would be immortal and would be taken as prisoners of war and finish their lives either sacrificed or as slaves. Women born during this period would be taken in adultery and as a consequence be put to death.

1 Mazatl A lucky period.

1 Xochitl Men born during this *trecena* were witty and fond of music. Women were inclined to be a little too liberal with their favors, a sign of promiscuity.

1 Acatl An unlucky period. Those born under this sign were liars, bearers of false witness, and scandalous.

1 Miquiztli This sign was neither lucky nor unlucky.

1 Quiauitl A disastrous period. Parents guarded their children against the malevolent spirits of the women who descended to the world to bring sickness to them (Cihuateteo).

1 Malinalli An unlucky sign.

1 Coatl A lucky 13-day period, especially for merchants and travelers.

1 Tecpatl During this sign, a great feast was conducted for the patron god Huitzilopochtli.

1 Ozomatli A fairly lucky period.

1 Quetzpalin An auspicious period. Men born in this *trecena* would be brave.

1 Ollin Neither a lucky nor an unlucky sign.

1 Izcuintli A very lucky period.

1 Calli During this period, the malevolent spirits of the Cihuateteo were active, spreading disease.

1 Cozcaquauhtli Those born in this *trecena* were to live a long and happy life.

1 Atl This period was a very bad omen.

1 Ehecatl Those born during these 13 days would turn out to be traitors, sorcerers, and witches.

1 Quauhtli An unlucky period.

1 Tochtli This last period was a lucky sign, except for those who would turn into drunkards.

A page from the *Codex Fejervary-Mayer* demonstrates one way in which the Aztec depicted their

11.2 *Cosmogram depicting the four cardinal directions and the center, presided by the god Xiuhtecuhtli in this case, and the 260-day calendar, from the* Codex Fejervay-Mayer (Manuel Aguilar-Moreno)

260-day cycle. In this schematic the calendar was organized as a floral symbol with two sets of four petals. The borders of the petals were marked with circles, totaling 260. Each petal of the Maltese-like cross design radiated toward a cardinal direction, representing the four regions of the universe, identified with a color and a distinctive tree and supported by the two gods associated with that direction. The center of the diagram where the god of fire and time, Xiuhtecuhtli, represents the center of the world and the zenith in the crossing of the Sun during its east-west journey. Since all the symbols were pictured at vertices of the double-cross design, the 260-day cycle was believed to have been made to contain all other astrological and calendrical matters.

This calendar can be used to calculate the ritual years of 260 days (*tonalpohualli*), the civil years of 365 days (*xihuitl*), or the count of years (*xiuhmolpilli*). To use it as a *tonalpohualli*, the ritual count starts with 1 Cipactli (Alligator), whose glyph is visible just above the upper right corner of the central square. Moving counterclockwise along the border, we count the days just as if we were following (downward) the sequence of the table on page 292. Once the *trecena* started by 1 Cipactli ends with 13 Acatl, the new *trecena* of 1 Ocelotl continues. The reader should notice that the day that starts the subsequent *trecenas*, 1 Mazatl, 1 Xochitl, etc., appears with its hyeroglyphic symbol to facilitate the counting. A full round along the diagram completes the ritual year of 260 days.

To use the calendar to count years of 365 days, it is used under the same principle, but it starts at 1 Acatl (chosen by Mesoamerican convention) located in the back of the bird in the upper-left intercardinal point. Moving counterclockwise 18 times the cycle of 20 days plus an additional five days completes a civil year of 365 days.

When counting the sequence of years on this calendar, all years of 365 days start in the name days Acatl, Tecpatl, Calli, and Tochtli, which are called the "year-bearers" or "New Year's days." So, starting in the year 1 Acatl, the count follows with 2 Tecpatl, 3 Calli, 4 Tochtli, 5 Acatl, 6 Tecpatl, 7 Calli, etc. After 13 Acatl continues 1 Tecpatl, 2 Calli, and so on. More details about the mechanisms of operation of the 365-day solar calendar are immediately below.

The *Xiuhpohualli*

This 365-day calendar was used for both practical and religious purposes. It functioned primarily to establish general planting and harvesting times and to organize the solar year into a series of feasts. Under this calendar, the year, *xihuitl*, was made up of 18 "months" of 20 days each plus five additional days—the unlucky *nemontemi*, or "leftover" days—in order to complete the solar year of 365 days. These extra days did not constitute a separate, shortened month nor did they fall within any of the 18 customary months; therefore, they bore no unit name in the 20-day cycle. Quarrels were especially to be avoided during the *nemontemi*, and only work that was indispensable to the community was to be conducted. Children who were born during these five unlucky days were given the name *Nemo-quichtli* (for males) or *Nencihuatl* (for females).

THE EIGHTEEN MONTHS OF THE *XIUHPOHUALLI*

1. Atlcahualo	Ceasing of water
(Cuahuitlehua)	(Raising of trees/poles)
(Xilomanaliztli)	(Spreading offering of green maize)
2. Tlacaxipehualiztli	Flaying of men
3. Tozoztontli	Short vigil
4. Huey Tozoztli	Long vigil
5. Toxcatl	Drought
6. Etzalcualiztli	Eating of grains
7. Tecuilhuitontli	Small festival of the lords
8. Huey Tecuilhuitl	Great festival of the lords
9. Miccailhuitontli	Small festival of the dead
(Tlaxochimaco)	(Birth of flowers)
10. Huey Miccailhuitl	Great festival of the dead
(Xocotl Huetzi)	(Falling of the fruit)
11. Ochpaniztli	Sweeping the way
12. Pachtontli	Small Spanish moss
(Teutleco)	(Arrival of the gods)
13. Huey Pachtli	Great Spanish moss
(Tepeilhuitl)	(Festival of the mountains)
14. Quecholli	Macaw
15. Panquetzalitztli	Raising of flags
16. Atemoztli	Descending of water
17. Tititl	Stretching
18. Izcalli	Sprout

Owing to the sensible demands of the vigesimal counting systems, 18 months of 20 days each was as close to numerological perfection as the solar year permitted. This calendar, like the *tonalamatl*, was not an Aztec innovation but part of the heritage shared by all Mesoamerican peoples. In actuality the solar year was closer to 365.25 days long, and earlier Mesoamerican peoples found a way to calculate its precise length. As indicated by Fray Bernardino de Sahagún, the Aztec has six *nemontemi* every four years, in order to make a calendrical adjustment in the same way the leap years make adjustments to the modern-day Gregorian calendar.

Each 20-day month was divided into four weeks of five days and had a symbol and feast dedicated to a specific god. This meant that the start of each new *xihuitl* advanced five days from the previous year in both the day-number and day-symbol counts, and in one form or another, it brought the count into approximate agreement with the solar cycle. The year names were based on the day symbol (*tonalli*) of the first day of the first month or the last day of the last month, a matter still under debate. Under the former scheme, if the first year began with Tochtli, that year would be 1 Tochtli, and the next year would be 2 Acatl, which is the day symbol of the first day of the second year, the day symbol moving by five because of the insertion of the *nemontemi* days. As the years continue, the next one began on 3 Tecpatl, 4 Calli, 5 Tochtli, and so on, through 13 Tochtli, when the 13-day number cycle would be repeated four times, generating 52 named years (the calendar round) in a cycle ($4 \times 13 = 52$) that could be divided into four quarters.

The Aztec celebrated their birth dates very differently from what we are accustomed. They would seize the individual whose birthday it was and toss the person into the water. When the celebrant came out of the water, he or she was bound and obliged to provide festivities for the day. If the person did not do so in that year, he or she would not be honored again, because it was said that he or she was still bound and there was no reason to celebrate his or her birthday anymore.

MONTHLY FESTIVALS

Solar phases and the culmination of a cycle of an astral body or constellation were celebrated with festivals in each of the 18 months of the *xiuhpohualli*. According to Aztec mythology, each astral body was incarnated in one of the major deities. The principal motives for conducting these festivals were to strengthen the forces of nature, such as those that created the rain, the fertility of the earth, and the movement of the Sun. Festivals held during the 18 months were as follows:

1. **Atlcahualo** (ceasing of water), or **Cuauhitlehua** (raising of trees)
   Correlation in the Christian calendar: February 14–March 5
   Symbolized by a "butterfly-motion" sign, which in Diego Duran's manuscript appeared underneath the Spanish inscription.

Deities honored: Tlaloc (related to the east as the god of rain and to the south as the god of rain of fire. East was the direction of Venus, the rising Sun, and the years that contained the *acatl* day sign), Chalchiuhtlicue (goddess of lakes and streams), Chicomecoatl (goddess of food and produce, especially maize), Xilonen (goddess of young maize), and Quetzalcoatl (the Feathered Serpent, one of the great gods, attributed to Venus)
   Rituals: Poles were erected and decorated with ritual banners in temples and homes. Offerings were made to maize deities. Children that were chosen to be sacrificed on mountains had to have been born under a lucky day sign. The tears from the children were said to be a good sign of rain to come. On the 17th day of this month the Feast of the Sun took place. This day fell on the day symbol called *ollin*, which means "motion."

2. **Tlacaxipehualiztli** (flaying of men)
   Correlation in the Christian calendar: March 6–25
   The constellation for this month has not been identified because the upper part of Durán's manuscript was cut and bound.
   Deity honored: Xipe Totec (god of vegetation and of the east and the rising Sun)
   Rituals: Gladiatorial sacrifice. Men who were sacrificed into honor of this god had their hearts taken out to offer to their most sacred astral body, the Sun. Once they had died, the priests would wear the victim's skins for 20 days, as would some of the young men. This act was analogous to the renewal of the earth's vegetation.

3. **Tozoztontli** (short vigil), or **Xochimanaloya** (offering of flowers)
   Correlation in the Christian calendar: March 26–April 14
   The constellation was represented in the form of a bird pierced with a bone.
   Deities honored: Tlaloc, Chalchiuhtlicue, Cinteotl (god of maize), Coatlicue (mother of the war god Huitzilopochtli), Coyolxauhqui (the moon goddess), and the Centzon Huiznahua (400 southerners or stars)

Rituals: Offering of flowers, first rituals in the fields, and ceremonial planting. The skins worn by priests in the previous festival were deposited in the symbolic cave of the earth-temple Yopico. In this month, many children were sacrificed so that the gods might send abundant rain.

4. **Huey Tozoztli** (long vigil, or great awakening)
Correlation in the Christian calendar: April 15–May 4
The constellation is the same as that of the previous month.
Deities honored: Cinteotl, Tlaloc, Chalchiuhtlicue, Chicomecoatl, Quetzalcoatl, and Xilonen
Rituals: Children were sacrificed on Mt. Tlaloc and at Pantitlan in Lake Tetzcoco. There was a procession of maidens carrying seed corn to be blessed by the maize goddess.

5. **Toxcatl** (drought)
Correlation in the Christian calendar: May 5–22
No constellation was visible.
Deities honored: Tezcatlipoca (god of the north and the night sky; also associated with Jupiter), Huitzilopochtli (god of war, associated with the Sun, the space of fire, of wind, of the meridian constellations, and the years dominated by the day sign *tochtli*), Mixcoatl (cloud serpent, associated with the Milky Way, the stars, the heavens; god of the north and nebulae that form in the night sky and the years dominated by the day sign *tecpatl*)
Rituals: For the Aztec this was the major renewal festival. A youth who had impersonated Tezcatlipoca during the previous year was sacrificed.

6. **Etzalcualiztli** (eating of grains)
Correlation in the Christian calendar: May 23–June 13
The constellation was represented by the figure of a man walking through water, carrying a cornstalk in one hand and a basket in the other and bearing a plumed device on his back.
Deities honored: Tlaloc, Chalchiuhtlicue, and Quetzalcoatl
Rituals: Offerings made to agricultural implements, marking the end of the dry season.

The lords danced with maize stalks, and the priests fasted for rain.

7. **Tecuilhuitontli** (small festival of the lords)
Correlation in the Christian calendar: June 14–July 13
Although this page of Durán's manuscript was mutilated, the remaining fragment of the constellation appeared to be the fringe of a sovereign's diadem.
Deities honored: Huixtocihuatl (salt goddess, oldest sister of the gods of rain) and Xochipilli (flower prince)
Rituals: Sacrifices to the deities. The ruler danced and distributed gifts. The lords hosted commoners at a feast.

8. **Huey Tecuilhuitl** (great festival of the lords)
Correlation in the Christian calendar: July 4–23
The three signs in the sky were royal diadems.
Deities honored: Xilonen and Cihuacoatl (one of the goddesses of the Earth and of midwives)
Rituals: The first tender maize festival commenced at sunrise and lasted until 9:00 P.M. The heart of a sacrificed woman was offered to the Sun. The ruler danced and distributed gifts. Lords again hosted commoners.

9. **Tlaxochimaco** (birth of flowers), or **Miccailhuitontli** (small festival of the dead)
Correlation in the Christian calendar: July 24–August 12
The symbol of a dead man in his shroud, reclining upon a seat with a banner (identical to the symbol for 20) protruding from his back was thought to have been seen in the heavens at that time of the year.
Deities honored: Huitzilopochtli, Tezcatlipoca, and the ancestors
Rituals: Offerings, feasts and dances in honor of the dead, sacrifice to Huitzilopochtli

10. **Xocotl Huetzi** (great fall of the *xocotl* fruit), or **Huey Miccailhuitl** (great festival of the dead)
Correlation in the Christian calendar: August 13–September 1
The constellation is the same for the previous month.
Deities honored: Xiuhtecuhtli (fire god), Huehueteotl (old god), Yacatecuhtli (god of the merchants), and the ancestors

Rituals: Human sacrifices by fire re-created the time of creation when the god Nanahuatzin threw himself into the fire so that the Sun would rise again. A pole-climbing (*xocotl* tree) competition was held among boys. Commemoration of ancestors

11. **Ochpaniztli** (sweeping the way)

Correlation in the Christian calendar: September 2–21

No constellation was shown for this month.

Deities honored: Toci ("grandmother," associated with the west, where the Sun sets and all that is old reside), Tlazolteotl (goddess of purification and also of filth), Teteoinnan (mother of the gods), Coatlicue, Cinteotl, and Chicomecoatl

Rituals: The major harvest season began. Ceremonies honored the earth goddesses, and general cleaning, sweeping, and repair was undertaken. The ripe corn deity was honored. The ruler gave insignia to warriors in preparation for the coming war season.

12. **Teotleco** (arrival of the gods)

Correlation in the Christian calendar: September 22–October 11

The constellation was represented by garlands of Spanish moss.

Deities honored: All the gods because it was the time when the gods arrived from their 20-day journeys

Rituals: General feasting, dancing, rejoicing, and offering of food

13. **Tepeilhuitl** (festival of the mountains)

Correlation in the Christian calendar: October 11–31

The constellation is the same as the previous month.

Deities honored: Tlaloc, Tlaloque, Tepictotan, and Octli (pulque deities), Xochiquetzal (epitomized young female sexual power, patroness of weaving and the arts), and the major rain mountains Popocatepetl, Iztacci-huatl, Mt. Tlaloc, and Matlalcueye

Rituals: Offerings conducted at shrines on mountains. For sacrifices and rituals amaranth-dough effigies and serpent-like branches covered with amaranth paste were used.

14. **Quecholli** (macaw, or precious feather)

Correlation in the Christian calendar: November 1–20

No constellation was shown.

Deities honored: Mixcoatl

Rituals: Commemoration of dead warriors. Ancient tribal hunting rites, communal hunts and prizes to the best hunter. Prisoners were bound like deer and sacrificed. Fasting of warriors. Manufacture of weapons for hunt and war

15. **Panquetzaliztli** (raising of flags)

Correlation in the Christian calendar: November 21–December 10

The month was symbolized by the figure of a man in a squatting position wearing a mantle and holding a feathered banner in his hands.

Deities honored: Huitzilopochtli and Tez-catlipoca

Rituals: Reenactment of Huitzilopocthli's victory over his sister at the Great Temple of Tenochtitlan. Large sacrifice of prisoners. Those who were to be sacrificed were taken to the ball court to be killed. Great procession from the Great Temple to Tlatelolco, Chapultepec, and Coyoacan and back to the pyramid

16. **Atemoztli** (descending of water)

Correlation in the Christian calendar: December 11–30

Symbolized a child dressed in a breechcloth and mantle.

Deities honored: Mountains of the rain gods because during this month thunder and light rain sometimes fell

Rituals: Rites to mountains

17. **Tititl** (stretching)

Correlation in the Christian calendar: December 31–January 19

Symbolized by two small boys dressed in mantles and breechcloths, tugging at each other. Durán compares this sign to Gemini.

Deities honored: Ilamatecuhtli (old mother goddess, also known by the names Tona or Cozcamiauh), Cihuacoatl, Tonantzin (earth goddess), Yacatecuhtli (god of merchants)

Rituals: Great feast with lords and priest dressed as deities. Merchants sacrificed slaves in traders' initiation rites. Weavers honor Ilamatecuhtli. Ritual dances in which the ruler participated.

18. **Izcalli** (growth or sprout), or **Huauhquiltamal-cualiztli** (eating of tamales stuffed with greens)

Correlation in the Christian calendar: January 20–February 8

This month was represented by two stellar signs. The first (on the top part of Durán's manuscript) shows a man dressed in mantle and breechcloth, wearing a band about his head, seated upon a stool of woven reeds. A bolt of lightning appears to be emerging from his back. The second sign (flower part) was symbolized with a tree, apparently symbolizing the forests of Matlalcueye (Mt. Malinche).

Deities honored: Xiuhtecuhtli, Tlaloc, Chalchiuhtlicue

Rituals: On the 10th day of this month, a new fire was lit at midnight. An amaranth-dough effigy of Xiuhtecuhtli was worshipped. Toasting of maize. The animals that had been hunted during these 10 days were sacrificed to fire and given to the people. Every four years, there was a special lordly dance, and children had their ears pierced and were assigned "godparents." Children were pulled by their necks to make them grow.

Nemontemi: The five useless and unlucky days

Correlation in the Christian calendar: February 9–13

Rituals: No rituals or business conducted. General abstinence.

The *Xiuhmolpilli*

The completion of a 52-year cycle was a time when life paused and had to begin anew. The Aztec understood that if this renewal did not occur, the world would be immersed into chaos causing the fifth sun to end. The renewal occurred at the onset of the year 2 Reed. Aztec scribes employed two different glyphs to indicate this cycle, one a bundle of reeds tied together with a cord, the other a drawing of the fire-drill and baseboard that the priest used to kindle the flames for the New Fire ceremony held at the end of every 52-year cycle. Special importance was placed on the completion of two cycles (104 years), called the *huehueliztli*, or an "old age," for at such times the *xiuhpohualli*, the *tonalpohualli*, the Venus count, and the 52-year cycle coincided.

A 52-year period was called a *xiuhmolpilli*, or *toxiuhmolpilli*, meaning a "bundle of years" or "tying up of the years." Every 52-year period was divided into four 13-year portions, each headed by a different year-bearer representing a given cardinal direction. An easy way to understand this cycle is from the following example. The year that Motecuhzoma II celebrated the last New Fire Ceremony (1507) in the Gregorian calendar was 2 Reed in Aztec terms. In other words, New Year's Day (day 1 of the new era in the solar year) fell on the day 2 Reed of the almanac year (*tonalpohualli*), a combination which would not recur until 52 years had passed. This is the reason why the Aztec "century" has 52 years, and the next New Fire ceremony would have been in 1559, but the Spanish conquest brought an end to Aztec time in 1521.

The New Fire Ceremony

The ending of the 52-year cycle brought on terror and crisis among the Aztec. The world had been destroyed four times upon the completion of cycles, and the Aztecs believed that their world was to suffer the same fate. The New Fire ceremony was a ritual carried out to ensure the rebirth of the Sun and the movement of the cosmos for another 52 years. The earliest date suggested by chronicles for the New Fire ceremony is 1195 C.E., or some similar date, as suggested in an image of the *Map of Cuauhtinchan No. 2*, where the New Fire ceremony is depicted in a cave during the Toltec-Chichimec migrations. In most Aztec historical chronicles, the first fire ceremony occurred in the year 2 Acatl and has an accompanying New Fire glyph.

The New Fire ceremony, or "Binding of the Years," symbolically tied together two important but very different ceremonial centers, the Great Temple of Tenochtitlan and the Hill of the Star (Huixachtlan). The first fire ceremony was said to have been celebrated on top of Mt. Coatepec, in the region of Tula, during the Aztec's migration to Tenochtitlan.

11.3 The Hill of the Star (Huixachtlan), where the New Fire ceremony took place every 52 years (Fernando González y González)

Every 52 years, that first ceremony was reenacted: People extinguished all fires and threw away most of their belongings. Women were closed up in granaries because if they remained in the open they could be transformed into fierce beasts who would eat men. Pregnant women wore masks of maguey leaves.

At nighttime, as the priests climbed to the summit of the hill of Huixachtlan, south of Tenochtitlan (known today as Cerro de la Estrella), they observed the progress of a star group known by the Aztec as Tianquiztli, or "marketplace"; today the cluster is called Pleiades. Those who had remained in the city went up on their roofs and watched the sky attentively, hoping that the stars would reach the meridian and that the Sun would rise again the following day. At the moment when the stars reached the center of the heavens, the priests sacrificed a man by cutting out his heart. A fire priest then made the "new fire" with a drill-board upon the chest cavity of the sacrificial victim and carried the flame to wood stacked high on the platform. Through the use of the fire drill, the fire was thought to descend from the sky to the earthly center and permeate the earthly landscape through the Sun's travels and ritual actions. In this case, if the fire flamed up, it was a sign that the universe would continue another 52 years. At this crucial moment during the ceremony, people cut their ears, even those of babies in their cradles. Then they would spatter their blood in the direction of the fire on the mountain. The priests then took the New Fire down the hill to the center of Tenochtitlan and the pyramid-temple of Huitzilopochtli, where it was placed in the fire holder of the statue of the god. The messengers, runners, and fire priests who had come from local regions took the fire back to the cities, where the rest of the common folk placed it in their homes after blistering themselves with the sacred fire.

According to the chronicler Fray Bernardino de Sahagún, this rite was performed for the last time in 1507, during the reign of Motecuhzoma II. In total,

11.4 The New Fire ceremony: Four high priests take 52 pieces of wood to be burned in the sacred fire. The pieces of wood represent four groups of 13 years in the 52-year cycle, from the Codex Borbonicus. *(Manuel Aguilar-Moreno)*

the New Fire ceremony ritual was celebrated seven times during Aztec rule. The eighth celebration would have occurred in the year 1559, but by then the Aztec Empire had already been conquered by the Spanish army.

CONCEPT OF THE UNIVERSE

The Five Suns

The Aztec believed that the universe was unstable, always threatened by death and destruction. The first human couple, Oxomoco and Cipactonal, knew that people had existed four times previously and that not until the fifth sun had the Earth and sky been established. The present world, the fifth sun, was said to have been created in 13 Reed, and it was

then that light came and all chaos was predicted to disappear.

The first sun, *nahui-ocelotl* (4 Jaguar), had been devoured by jaguars. The second sun, *nahui-ehecatl* (4 Wind), had been destroyed by the fierce winds that the god Quetzalcoatl had sent. The third sun, *nahui-quiauitl* (4 Rain), had been destroyed by a rain of fire, and the fourth sun, *nahui-atl* (4 Water), had been destroyed by a deluge that lasted 52 years. The fifth sun, designated as *nahui-ollin* (4 Movement), is calendrically condemned to be destroyed by a series of immense earthquakes.

According to ethnohistorian Miguel León-Portilla, the story of the five suns demonstrates the existence of five possible cosmological categories: 1) the concept of constant struggle for supremacy as a setting in which the occurrence of cosmic events can be understood, 2) the transcendence of the world into ages or cycles, 3) the idea of preexistent elements, 4) the division of space in the universe into quadrants or directions, and 5) the logical urgency for a universal base (1963: 48). Thus the myth of the five suns involves the cycles of the Sun in the creation of life on the earthly plane by the life force that lies at the heart of the universal order.

Stone of the Fifth Sun

In many religious systems, the Sun has been worshipped as more than an astral body. For many cultures, it represents the duality between sky and earth, good and bad, and light and darkness. In Aztec culture, it was considered to be the supreme god or the principal fountain of subsistence and life, the maximum force of peoples' souls, their *tonalli*. As a deity, the Sun took many forms and names, according to its many stages, and was depicted both symbolically and anthropomorphically, as demonstrated in one of the most famous and studied monuments of the Aztec civilization, the Sun Stone (Aztec Calendar).

The colossal monument was discovered on December 17, 1790, when workers were leveling and repaving the central plaza of Mexico City. For many years it was placed against the west tower of the Metropolitan Cathedral, until in 1885 the president of Mexico, Porfirio Díaz, ordered its transfer to the National Museum. The disk was more than 3.5 meters (11^1/$_2$ feet) in diameter and 25 tons in weight. Even though the stone's outer edges are not complete, it is evident that its original shape was not circular. Chroniclers document that the ruler Axayacatl commissioned the stone; thus, it is believed that the date on it of 13 Acatl, equivalent to 1479 C.E., is the date of its carving. Ethnohistorian Alfredo Chavero suggested that the colossal monument was originally set horizontally, not vertically as it now stands in the National Museum of Anthropology in Mexico City, and that it could not have served as a calendar for it lacked the required elements to compute time (1901: 552).

DESCRIPTION OF THE STONE

The original colors of the stone were blue, red, green, and yellow. Since some remnants of the colors were still visible in the 19th century, Dionisio Abadiano and some other historians and scholars believe that it could not have been used as a sacrificial monument, for the colors would have faded completely.

In the inner circle, the face of the sun god Tonatiuh is carved, although some scholars identify it as Tlaltecuhtli, the earth god; the matter is still subject to debate. The Aztec believed that the Sun was the star that gave light and warmth to the Earth, and to express that light, they painted it with its tongue sticking out, resembling a solar ray. Around his face is formed the symbol of Ollin with four dots, which can be read as the date 4 Movements, symbolizing our present era. He wears the sign *ome-acatl* on his forehead, which refers to the beginning count of the year after the New Fire ceremony. The tongue that emerges from his open mouth appears as an animated sacrificial knife, as depicted on many Aztec monuments. Tonatiuh wears as a necklace the six counts of the holy cycle, also considered as his beginning. Tonatiuh is surrounded by another, giant Ollin sign consisting of four calendrical glyphs and the cardinal points for the four previous suns, or worlds. The Sun, in the middle of these, is left soaring in the zenith, and that is why below him are the dates 1 Rain and 7 Monkey, days in which the Sun passed through the meridian in Mexico. Rain was the calen-

drical name of one of the divine women who died in labor and of the ancient goddess Ilamatecuhtli. Monkey was associated with the evening, and all the deities that carried this sign were also associated to the evening. Here the monkey represented Xochipilli, god of flowers, the sun in the evening.

The smaller rays surrounding this central circle are solar rays, and the larger ones are symbols for the four cardinal directions. Beside the middle ray on top of Tonatiuh's head are two glyphs: On the right is *tecpatl*, or flint, and on the left is *tletl*, corresponding to June 26, the day on which the Aztecs celebrated the summer solstice. On the next circle are carved the glyphs of the 20 names of the days of the *tonalpohualli* (260-day ritual calendar). On the outer circle are two fire serpents, *xiuhcocoah*, linked to Huitzilopochtli and sacred warfare. Over the serpents' nose are adornments that contain stars that are believed to represent the constellation *xonecuilli*. If this is true, then its symbolism would connect aspects of the year, fire, the sky, and the stars. From the faces of the snakes emerge two heads: Quetzalcoatl, personified as Tonatiuh, on the right, and Tezcatlipoca, personified as Xiuhtecuhtli, on the left. Allegorically, this is the daily struggle of the gods for supremacy on earth and in the heavens (day vs. night). The two gods have their tongues out, touching each other, signifying the continuity of time— the rising and setting suns, always in contact. A more recent interpretation of this iconography is offered by anthropologist Karl Taube, who suggests that they are not fire serpents but giant caterpillars representing the transformation and rebirth of the warrior as the Sun, emerging in the center of the image in the shape of a great butterfly (Carrasco 1998: 174). The glyph at the top, between the two tails, is 13 Acatl (1479) and refers in one sense to the date of the birth of the Sun and in another sense to the date of the carving of the monument.

In this monument the Sun appears as the god that makes the days and their smaller and larger components: morning, midday, evening, the years, and the five ages of the world. Thus the stone is important not only for its aesthetic value but because it symbolizes the Aztec cosmos. What makes it an extraordinary work of art is its rich and intricate composition, full of symbolism and myth (see chapter 8).

The Four Cardinal Directions

The Aztec world was thought of as a grand horizontal disk intersected by a vast vertical shaft. The vertical shaft was conceived of as a series of layers of heaven, Earth, and the underworld joined together by the *axis mundi*, or navel of the world. Each of these layers was divided into two opposing pairs, representing the crucial idea of duality that permeated all elements of Aztec life. The horizontal disk was believed to be surrounded by seawaters and raised up on its outer edges to form the walls that held up the sky. This disk, sometimes pictured as a rectangle, was organized into five major sections (the quincunx), with four quarters.

This quincunx design came from the idea that the universe had the form of a cross. The cross was the symbol of the world in its totality, and the Spanish were surprised to find many figures and temples that contained it. If the quincunx is rotated in a northerly direction on its east-west axis by 90 degrees so that it lies flat on the Earth rather than being perpendicular to it, the terminal points become east, north, west, and south, and lines run-

ning from the center to each of these points would have divided the surface of the Earth into four quadrants. The fifth cardinal point, the center, was attributed to the god of fire, Huehueteotl.

Each of the four cardinal directions dominated 65 days in the ritual calendar. Furthermore, each of the 20 days (*veintena*) in the calendar came under the influence of one of the four spatial directions through an indefinite rotation that took place.

East

Cipactli (Alligator)
Acatl (Reed)
Coatl (Serpent)
Ollin (Movement)
Atl (Water)

Called Tlapcopa, "the place of light"; Tlapallan, "the place of red color"; and Tonatiuh Yquiza-yampa, "where the Sun rises." Place of birth of the Sun (Tonatiuh) and Venus (Quetzalcoatl); region of Tonatiuh, Xipe Totec, the young gods of vegetation Mixcoatl-Camaxtli, the Tlalocan (paradise of the gods of rain), and the Tonatiuh-Ilhuicac (paradise of the dead warriors)

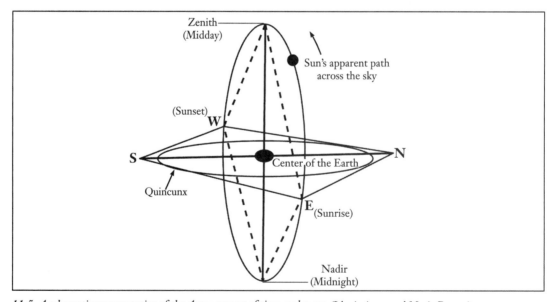

11.5 A schematic representation of the Aztec concept of time and space (Lluvia Arras and Maria Ramos)

North

Ocelotl (Jaguar)
Miquiztli (Death)
Tecpatl (Flint)
Itzcuintli (Dog)
Ehecatl (Wind)

Called Mictlampa, "the place of Mictlan," the
underworld, residence of the death god Mictlantecuhtli; region of war and the god Tezcatlipoca, place of darkness; also region of
Mixcoatl, god of hunting

West

Mazatl (Deer)
Quiahuitl (Rain)
Ozomatli (Monkey)
Calli (House)
Cuauhtli (Eagle)

Called Cihuatlampa, "place of the women," where
the earth goddesses (Cihuateteo) lived; also
called Tonatiuh-Iaquian, "where the Sun dies."
Region of old age, the Tamoanchan (place of origin), and house of corn and sustenance, Cincalco;
presided over by god Quetzalcoatl

South

Xochitl (Flower)
Malinalli (Grass)
Cuetzpallin (Lizard)
Cozcacuauhtli (Vulture)
Tochtli (Rabbit)

Called Huitztlampa, "place of the spines," region
left of the Sun where god Huitzilopochtli resides.
Also another residence of the god of death, Mictlantecuhtli and Tlaloc, the rain god

Graphically, the east was on top, north to the left,
west below, and south to the right. Among other
important characteristics of the cardinal directions
were its colors. Each god was characterized by one
or more colors, transferring their color(s) as they
dominated a different space.

Black was attributed to the gods of the night. Red
was given to youth, vegetation, pleasure, love, the
Sun, and fire. Yellow was associated with the Sun,
fire, and ripe maize. Blue and green were given to
water, precious jade, and turquoise. White represented old age and the rays of light.

Cardinal points	Fundamental colors	Secondary colors
East	red	yellow, green
North	black	red, yellow
West	white	blue
South	blue	red, green

Research by historian Johanna Broda suggests
that the Aztec practice of cardinal orientation went
far beyond the ordering of urban space to include
the ordering of parts of the tribute systems that
sustained the entire Aztec population (1970:
115–174). The *Codex Mendoza* demonstrates that
the Aztec government also followed the quincunx,
with the *huey tlatoani* at the center of power assisted
by four counselors. Not only in the Aztec Empire
but also throughout all of Mesoamerica, this form
became the structure for calendars and the material
and administrative shape of cities, monumental
sculptures, and pyramids (see figure 9.2).

Levels of the Universe

The *tlamatinime* (wise men), particularly those dedicated to the observation of the sky and its movements,
devised an astronomical explanation for the universe.
They theorized that there were 13 heavens (some
sources name nine or 12) and nine levels of the underworld (see figure 7.3). Within them were a series of
passages in which the heavenly bodies moved.

THE HEAVENS

The lowest heaven was the place where the Moon
traveled and from which the clouds were suspended.
The second heaven was the place of the stars, which
were divided into two large groups: the 400 stars of
the north (Centzon Mimixcoa) and the 400 (countless) stars of the south (Centzon Huitznahua). The
heaven of the Sun was the third region. Tonatiuh
traveled over this heaven in his journey from the
region of light to his home in the west. The fourth
heaven was the place where Venus could be seen. In
the fifth heaven the comets or smoking stars, traveled.

In the sixth and seventh of the celestial levels only the colors green and blue could be seen, or according to another version, black and blue—the heavens of day and night. The eighth heaven was apparently the place of storms, and the three heavens above this—the white, yellow, and red—were reserved as dwelling places for the gods. Most important of the 13 levels were the last two, which constituted Omeyocan, the dwelling place of the dual supreme deity, generator, and founder of the universe.

THE TERRESTRIAL LEVELS AND THE UNDERWORLD

Under the celestial column of the gods, forces, colors, and dualities floated the four-quartered Earth in the sacred waters. Below the terrestrial level were the nine levels of the underworld, realms that the souls of the dead had to cross: the place for crossing the water, the place where the hills are found, the obsidian mountain, the place of the obsidian wind, the place where the banners are raised, the place where people are pierced with arrows, the place where people's hearts are devoured, the obsidian place of the dead, and finally, the place where smoke has no outlet (Mictlan).

In some cases a World Tree joined these three levels, and in other cases there were four giant ceiba trees that held up the sky at the four quarters. These trees were considered to be the main entry points of the gods and their influences from the upper and lower worlds onto the surface of the Earth and into the realm of humans.

ASTRONOMY

The Aztec, like all peoples of Mesoamerica, were avid astronomers who carefully tracked the stars and planets at night. The two most important ritual hours to observe the sky were at sunset and at midnight. The primary importance for observing the heavenly bodies was for economic reasons, since it marked phases in the agricultural cycle and other activities related to the seasons.

Most observations and calculations were made by priests and nobles. The priest-astronomers kept track of the length of the solar year, the lunar month, the period of revolution of the planet Venus, and other celestial cycles. They were also able to chart the annual movement of the sunrise and sunset along the horizon, which resulted in the equinoxes and solstices, noting the regular coming and going of the two instances of the Sun's zenith passage each year. Aztec astronomers also used the sky to structure their history.

They gave special attention to eclipses that fell in particular years of their 52-year time cycle. They associated these with the recurrence of events, such as conquests and accessions. Throughout pre-Columbian Mesoamerica, solar and lunar eclipses were disastrous portents signaling destruction, possibly even the end of the world. During a lunar eclipse, the most affected were pregnant women. They thought the eclipse could bring about miscarriage; they also believed that the eclipse could turn the fetus into a mouse or deformed child. To avoid its impact, they would insert a piece of obsidian in their mouth or abdomen. All over the city, men, women, and children would organize themselves, make loud cries, and cut themselves on their legs and ears. The emphasis on the regularity of the solar and lunar cycles in the understanding of the cosmic unity would seem to indicate a need to deal with the phenomena of eclipses since they were clearly disruptions of those all-important cycles. Even today, in rural Mexico, some believe that eclipses affect fertility.

Insofar as the thinkers of Mesoamerica were interested in other celestial bodies, they were almost exclusively interested in those whose cyclical movements were apparently related to the Sun.

Methods of Sky Watching

The development of archaeoastronomy has proven to be one of the most important disciplines in the study of the Mesoamerican concept of the universe. With this new field, scholars have been able to better understand the methods and techniques for ancient sky watching. Such observations describe how the alignments between celestial events and human society were created and maintained. For most

esta zpintura es
ojos significa
la noche

alfaqui mapa 16 esta de no
se mirando las estre
llas enel cielo quberes
la cosa que es/que He
re zqur fof°2 comyo/.

11.6 *A chief priest makes an astronomical observation in the night sky. The inverted hemisphere above him is studded with stars, symbolized by the half-shut eyes.* (Maria Ramos)

11.7 *The Tetzcocan ruler Nezahualpilli observes the comet that was believed to announce the destruction of the Aztec Empire.* (Maria Ramos)

Mesoamerican cultures, astronomical observations were a constant necessity because so much of their belief systems was closely tied to celestial phenomena. The Aztec knew how to keep track of the solstices and equinoxes by a simple method of observation. They were aware that the Sun did not rise and set at the same points in the horizon. From its apparent deviation north and south, they would calculate the amount of time it took to make its route from one point to the next, comparing these movements to the fixed objects of the Earth located on the horizon.

Sky watching was a common occupation among the nobility. The rulers, along with their advisers-astronomers, frequently observed the heavenly skies to calculate and chart celestial events. Father Diego Durán documented that the Aztec emperor Motecuhzoma II went to Nezahualpilli, a well-known ruler and astrologer, to seek meaning of the comet he had been observing for quite some time. The king of Tetzcoco was baffled by the incompetence of Motecuhzoma's astrologers, since they could not interpret what they had seen. So it was

that Nezahualpilli informed the *huey tlatoani* that this great comet would bring disaster to his empire. Due to his knowledge of astronomy, the astrologer-king obviously was engaged in some sort of celestial measurement apart from basic stargazing.

One way of ensuring the position of a given star was to take a visual bearing on another object, such as a mountain peak or distant temple tower. If the exact bearing of this point was taken, it was quite easy to mark the movement of the stars through the sky. To calculate the synodical revolution (or year) of a particular planet, the observer had only to count the days until it reappeared in its original position

11.8 *Methods of sky watching using cross-stick devices, in the* Codices Bodley, Selden *and* Muro (Lluvia Arras and Maria Ramos)

THE CALENDAR, ASTRONOMY, AND MATHEMATICS

on the horizon. In all of Mesoamerica, hills, mountains, and pyramid-temples were very sacred because they had been aligned with the appearances of stars along the horizon.

The celestial cycles and their key points demarcated by direct observation seem to have been sufficient for marking the passage of time. In many codices, drawings suggest that certain temples, in particular their doorways, were used as sighting stations to observe astronomical events on the local horizon. It is still not quite clear whether a wide V-shaped symbol drawn in the entranceway of these temples (see figure 11.8) represented an actual measuring device capable of giving angular measurements of the separation of a pair of celestial bodies, or whether it was intended simply to guide the observer in performing a ritual operation in connection with the objects in question. However, in using a pair of cross-sticks, one as a foresight and the other as a backsight, an observer could have determined the position of an object near the horizon with great accuracy. It has been speculated that Nahua astronomers also used their hands in the manner of sextants to measure the movements of the stars.

Constellations and Celestial Orbs

All the celestial bodies and the constellations were divine to the Aztec. The changing position of stars in the night sky was important for their astrology—the practice of consulting celestial bodies for divination. The stars were divided into constellations, and those we know about appear to have been roughly the same as the constellations

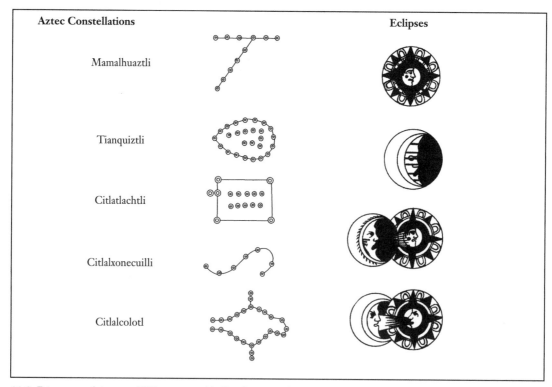

11.9 Diagrams of Aztec and Western astral bodies depicting the most important of the constellations that the Aztec

adopted in the European astrological tradition. According to anthropologist Hermann Beyer, the first 13 signs of the 20 day names in the calendar corresponded to one constellation called Ozomatli (monkey).

Many of the star groups had deities associated with them. Foremost among the star groups accorded a place of prominence throughout Mesoamerica were the Pleiades (Tianquiztli), or Seven Sisters of the classical world. This star group appears to have figured in

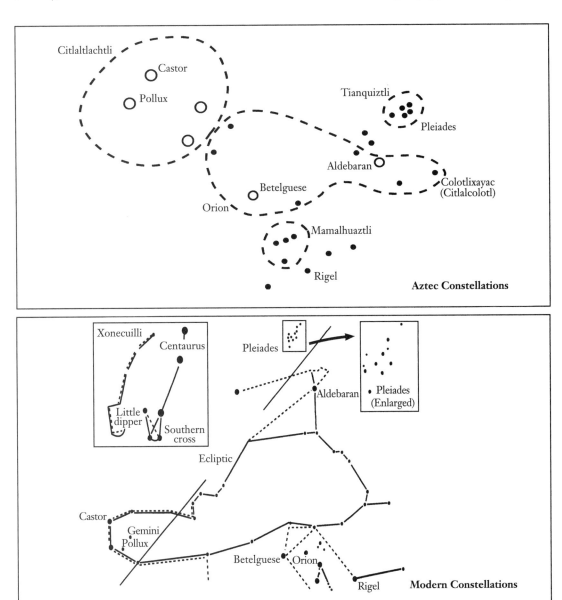

astronomers observed (Drawings by Lluvia Arras and Maria Ramos, after González Torres 1979)

King Motecuhzoma's inauguration ceremony. On the night of his ascent to the throne, he was advised to arise at midnight and look at the stars that precisely marked the four cardinal points of the sky. These were Yohualitqui Mamalhuaztli (Orion's Belt; Mamalhuaztli was also the name given to fire sticks such as those used in the New Fire ceremony, which resembled the growing stars), Citlaltlachtli (a celestial ball court, possibly identified with Gemini and other stars to the right), Colotl Ixayac (the Scorpion, which may be the same as that of Western astrology), and Tianquiztli. When these stars appeared, after the festival of the Sun, they were venerated in a special manner, and all the men would receive three burns on their wrist in honor of these constellations.

The Aztec called the comets *citlallin popoca*, meaning "smoking star." The comets and stars were said to have emerged from the fifth sun. Comets were portents of bad things to come: the death of a ruler, war, and other tragedies. The people feared that if the light from the comet shone on a living thing, that being would turn into a worm. Lightning and thunder were given many names, but they were attributed to the Tlaloque, the gods who made thunder and lightning.

Fray Bernardino de Sahagún noted that they had particular admiration for and made special sacrifices to the constellations Castor and Pollux (Citlaltlachtli), which move near the Pleiades. The stars that are in the Little Bear, or Little Dipper, were called Xitlalxonecuilli. The Aztec represented this constellation by drawing seven stars and arranging them in the shape of a backward S. The Big Bear, or Big Dipper, was called Tezcatlipoca, meaning "tiger."

Venus

Various visible planets were well known to the Aztec, and some of their synodic periods—the periods between their appearance at the same place among the stars and in alignment with the Earth—were included in the codices as numerical calculations. While they all represented gods, none was as important as Venus, the planet most carefully observed and studied by Aztec astronomers. Venus was the celestial equivalent to a warrior, a valiant champion whose challenges to the Sun were constant. Aside from Mercury, it was the only bright planet that appeared closely attached to and obviously influenced physically by the Sun, and that is one of the reasons that it obtained the name the Great Star Citlalpol. Other Nahuatl names for Venus were Totonametl, the "fiery arrow," and Tlahuizcalpantecuhtli, Lord of the House of Dawn.

Venus had two very important aspects, one as the Morning Star (Quetzalcoatl), and the other as the Evening Star (Xolotl). During two periods in its cycle, Venus was invisible; one was a short period of eight days, and the other was a longer period of 50 days. At those times it was thought that Quetzalcoatl was in the underworld, engaged in some sort of struggle with Mictlantecuhtli. Between these periods, Venus appeared for 263 days as the Morning Star and then as the Evening Star. As far as the common people were concerned, it was dangerous to go out at night when the Evening Star was shining, for fear that his rays would send darts of illness or even death. To be seen by Venus as the Morning Star, however, was a matter of good fortune.

The apparition of Venus from the west was always carefully studied. The astronomers knew in what sign it would appear and when it would shine, because the moment when Venus emerged from the underworld was considered a bad sign. People would close their windows and doors so that the light would not penetrate.

Not only was Venus tied visually to the Sun, but there were numerical relationships as well that fascinated the Mesoamericans. It was known that the synodic period of Venus was 584 days, the nearest whole number to its actual average value, 583.92 days, and that $5 \times 584 = 8 \times 365$; thus five synodic periods of Venus corresponded exactly to eight solar years. Sixty-five Venusian years were the equivalent of 104 years of the Sun, or two *xiuhmolpilli*, or one long period called a *huehueliztli*, meaning an "old age." This planet was so venerated by the Aztec masses that symbols associated to it ornamented many of their monuments and buildings.

Mercury

Venus and Mercury closely orbit the Sun and have similar cycles; they each disappear for a few days and then return, without passing a certain height above the Earth's horizon. Mercury is a planet that is less visible, and its elevation over the horizon line does not surpass 20 degrees. For the most part it is hidden, which explains why the Mexica-Aztec related it to the place of the dead and as the deity that guided the underworld. The planet Mercury was called Piltzintecuhtli (prince or princely lord), a young god whose hair was golden like the Sun.

The Moon

The Moon has a recurrent cycle of birth, growth, plenitude, decay, and death. For this reason it was considered to be a mysterious celestial body, and it was associated with natural phenomena and events: rain, vegetation, menstruation, fertility, and reproduction.

Unlike the planet Venus, the Moon was considered to be a replica of the Sun and something of a coward. Its name was *Metzli*, and all other words associated with lunar phenomena carried that root: *metztunalli* (clarity of the Moon), *metzliqualoca* (eclipse of the Moon), and *metzlimiquiz* (death of the Moon), for example. Generally the Moon was represented in the codices over a frame, and its interior was usually the figure of a rabbit, a flint, or in some circumstances, a small snail shell. Sometimes the Moon contained rays like those of the Sun, but with different colors. The manifestation of the Moon was rarely invoked; however when it was worshipped, it was represented either as Coyolxauhqui, Lady of the Golden Bells, sister of the solar deity Huitzilopochtli, or as the goddess Tlazolteotl, the Eater of Filth, a more magical aspect of this heavenly body.

The Aztec observed that in a lapse of 24 hours the Moon had two periods: the first called *sueño* (sleep) in which she was invisible or metaphorically she was sleeping. This period coincides with the cycle of the Sun (day-light). The second period was called *desvelo* (sleeplessness), when the Moon was awake by night. The Aztec's lunar calculations also served as a meteorological indicator, as it is still used today.

Red Moon: sign of heat
Bright red: dry temperature
White Moon: cold temperature; snow or hail; windy
Yellow or golden: water
North: when the tips of the crescent Moon point to the north it is an indication of rain
South: heat

11.10 Drawings of the Moon from diverse codices (Maria Ramos)

White ring: bad omen
Many-colored ring: good faith; births of animals and people; good time for commencing activities

Astronomy and Architecture

Important astronomical alignments and orientations were recorded and used by surveyors and architects to lay out cities and buildings. One of the most convincing examples of an astronomically oriented city plan is the Aztec capital, Tenochtitlan. There is specific evidence in the early postconquest literature hinting at an astronomical motif underlying the orientation of its most important building, the Great Temple. This pyramid-temple was the *axis-mundi*, the point of intersection of all the world's paths, both terrestrial and celestial. As such, builders laid out the temple at 7 degrees south of east to incorporate the equinoctial alignment as an enduring principle into the three-dimensional enclosed environment of their ceremonial space. This special placement ensured that the Sun could be seen as it rose between the temples on the equinox. When Anthony Aveni and Sharon Gibbs conducted excavations at the modern-day site, they confirmed that the building deviated 7 degrees and 6 minutes to the south of a true east-west line. The skew of 7 degrees south of east was necessary because

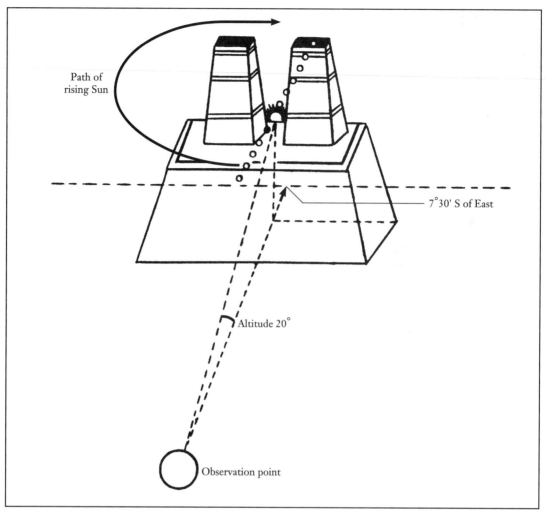

Path of
rising Sun

7°30' S of East

Altitude 20°

Observation point

11.11 Diagram showing the path of the Sun on the equinox at the Great Temple in Tenochtitlan (Drawing by Maria Ramos, after Carrasco and Matos 1992)

the Sun moved toward the southeast on a slanted path to an altitude of about 20 degrees above the astronomical horizon, before it could actually be seen in the notch of the day of the equinox.

The ancient small island of Tepetzinco held an astronomical significance closely related to that of the Great Temple. It was sited at 7 degrees south of east from Tenochtitlan's temple, at a radial distance of five kilometers (three miles). This marked the place where the Sun rose 20 days after the vernal equinox

and 20 days before the autumnal equinox. Meanwhile, the hills of the Tlalocan, the home of the rain god, were located 7 degrees north of east and marked the course of the rising Sun during the 20-day month before the vernal equinox, as viewed from the temple.

The great ceremonial centers constructed by Mesoamerican cultures served as focal points in rituals. They interacted with the natural and supernatural forces of the cosmos and were, from the earliest times, laid out on the basis of horizon sightings of solar positions. Structures were intentionally designed or oriented to make precise solar and other astronomical observations for ritual purposes.

MATHEMATICS

The Aztec devised what was the most advanced mathematics in the world at the time, one that used a notational system with place value and the concept of zero. Using only small sets of numbers and symbols, they were able to make calculations of amounts possible in modern times with electronic technology.

Methods of Computing

The rope was used to develop one of the first methods of computation, regardless of the system used. To mark a certain space, the rope was divided with knots, each knot representing a known measurement. A

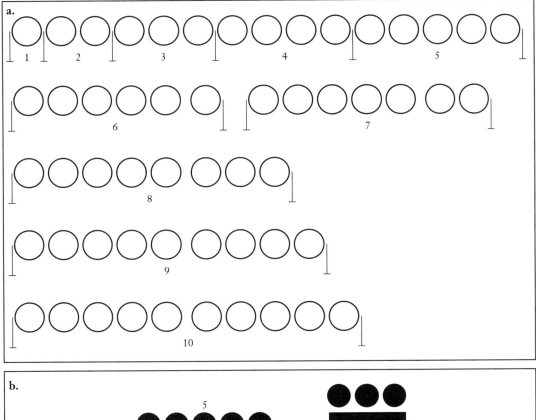

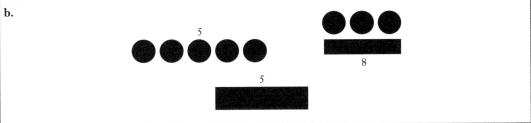

11.12 Methods used by the Aztec for counting: a) dots representing units put together in groups of five to facilitate counting; b) dots representing the number 1 and bars representing the number 5

small stone or ball, usually a precious gem such as jade or turquoise, was used as another marker for this counting method. A small hole was made at one of the ends to insert thread. The most common use of this ball was for counting lunar periods. For that purpose, rows of 28 counts (one lunar cycle) were framed by a rectangular ditch reed.

The cane was another instrument used for counting. Generally, this stick had a conical shape at one end. Using this point, the Aztec would make round marks in the dirt. This circular mark represented the Sun, just as the Moon was represented by the balls mentioned above. These marks were then grouped into five. After five, a new group would begin, until it had another set of five.

To count items rather than cycles, the Aztec used a different formula. They employed symbols to represent the day, year, and century. The pierced balls were once again used, by this time they were strung on much finer string. For amounts of things such as tribute quantities, they drew upon a slightly larger order of signs.

The numeric system of the Aztec was based on 20, which they designated as *cempoalli*, meaning precisely "one count." They used their 10 fingers and 10 toes to count, resulting in 20. The first four numbers had simple names. The numbers after that contained roots from other words. With the four main roots, *cem, pohualli, tzontli, xiquipilli*, plus *matlactli*, all quantities thereafter were more easily expressed:

1. *ce* or *cem*	11. *matlactlionce*
2. *ome*	12. *matlactliomome*
3. *yei*	13. *matlactliomei*
4. *nahui*	14. *matlactlionnahui*
5. *macuilli*	15. *caxtolli*
6. *chicuace*	16. *caxtollionce*
7. *chicome*	17. *caxtolliomome*
8. *chicuei*	18. *caxtolliomei*
9. *chiconahui*	19. *caxtollionnahui*
10. *matlactli*	

From numbers 20 to 80 they added the suffix -*pohualli*, which served as both a multiplier and a series.

20. *cempohualli*
21. *cempohuallionce*

29. *cempohualli onchiconahui*
30. *cempohualli onmatlactli*
39. *cempohualli oncaxtolli onnahui*
40. *ompohualli*
60. *yeipohualli*
80. *nauhpohualli*

Continuing in this manner, they formed numbers up to 399. At 400, a new suffix, -*tzontli* (hair), was introduced.

401. *centzontli once*
405. *centzontli onmacuilli*

At 500, the root -*ipan*, meaning "more," was introduced.

500. *centzontli ipan macuilpohualli*

The series after that was a mixture of the roots and suffixes.

800. *omzontli* (400 × 2)
1,200. *yetzontli* (400 × 3)
4,000. *matlactzontli* (400 × 10)

Then, at the number 8,000, a new suffix was introduced, -*xiquipilli* (bag).

8,000. *cemxiquipilli*
16,000. *omxiquipilli* (2 × 8,000)
24,000. *yexiquipilli* (3 × 8,000)
80,000. *matlacxiquipilli* (10 × 8,000)
3,200,000. *centzonxiquipilli* (400 × 8,000)

This continued until the number 64,000,000, a sufficient count to respond to the needs of the Aztec.

To count several items, such as chickens, eggs, cacao, fruit, books, or rounded items, they used a different suffix, -*tetl*.

1. *centetl*	20. *cempohualtetl*
2. *ontetl*	40. *ompohualtetl*
10. *matlactetl*	100. *macuilpohualtetl*
11. *matlactetlonce*	

For counting lines, walls, rows of people, or things in order by lines, they used the suffix -*pantli*.

1. *cempantli*
2. *ompantli*

3. *yepantli*
4. *nappantli*
5. *macuilpantli*
40. *ompohualpantli*

For counting items such as shoes, paper, or folded things, they used the suffix *-mantli*.

1. *centlamantli*   15. *caxtollamantli*
2. *ontlalmantil*   80. *nappohuallamantli*

3. *yetlalmantli*   100. *macuilpohuallamantli*

Shawls, meanwhile, were only counted by groups of 20: 20, *cemquimilli*; 40, *omquimilli*; 60, *yequimilli*, and so on.

The order of the terms followed a rigorous, logical, and scientific progression. With the roots and many suffixes, the Aztec could express an indefinite series of quantities. In cases where they had to count larger amounts, they probably did not use this

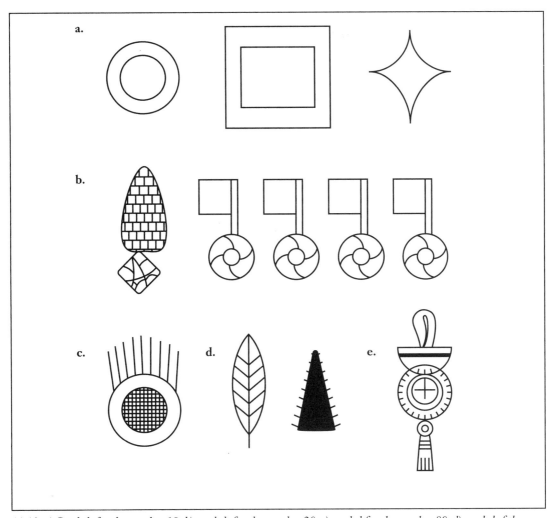

11.13 a) Symbols for the number 10; b) symbols for the number 20; c) symbol for the number 80; d) symbol of the number 400; e) symbol for the number 8,000 (Maria Ramos)

THE CALENDAR, ASTRONOMY, AND MATHEMATICS

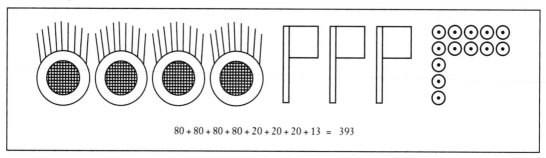

$$80 + 80 + 80 + 80 + 20 + 20 + 20 + 13 = 393$$

11.14 Symbolic notation for the number 393 (Lluvia Arras and Maria Ramos)

numeration form. It was then that they started to add symbols together in order to create large amounts. This was done by uniting one symbol with the other, either on the side or inside. When a symbol was placed on top of another, this would double the given amount. This method made it easy for the Aztec to compute, especially when they were dealing with matters involving tribute pay.

Symbols Used for Computation

In a very mysterious, yet ingenious manner, the Aztec devised symbolic number formations using a sole combination of numbers 1 to 4. Some of the combinations they could achieve with just four numbers, and their corresponding symbols, follow:

1 + 1 = 2	Omeyocan (place of the duality)
4	four stars, four suns, four initial signs
1 + 4 = 5	five days of the marketplace, five worlds/ages, the *axis mundi* (four directions of the universe, plus the center)
1 + 4 + 4 = 9	nine Lords of Day and Night, nine months (half a year)
1 + 4 + 4 + 4 = 13	thirteen day numbers (*trecena*) of the calendar, thirteen levels of the universe
1 + 4 = 5 × 4 = 20	twenty days (one month)

Units of one were represented by points, circles, disks, or the tips of the fingers (one dot = 1). Each unit of five was represented by a bar, dots, or an open hand. The number 10 was drawn as a square within a square or as a circle within a circle or in the shape of an angular diamond. Each unit of 20 was represented by a flag and strung together by a banner to reach higher multiples. In what seems to be a local variation of this, the painters of such Tetzcocan manuscripts as the *Codex Xolotl* replaced the flag with something very much like a corncob. The number 80 was depicted as a bundle of reeds or as a turquoise gem adorned with herbs. Often, to abbreviate, the numbers 5, 10, and 15 were represented by one-third or one-fourth of the flag.

The number 400 was represented by a tree or feather, which glyptically represented a number as bountiful as the hairs on the head, and 8,000 by a bag of incense. As in the case of the flag, three-quarters, one-half, or one-fourth of the feather served to indicate 300, 200, or 100, respectively. To represent the numbers 2,000, 4,000 or 6,000, the same method was used with the incense symbol.

Basic Math

Addition was pretty basic for the Aztec: They placed symbols on top of others, similar to the system we use, to produce sums of things. To form a subtraction problem, they would change the root of their written numbers to produce a new name; for example, 10 minus 1 became *in matlactli ce*, which was literally read as "minus 10 1," and 15 minus 1 became *in caxtolli ce*.

This method was used only if the number being subtracted was smaller. When the number being subtracted was larger (for example, 6 minus 12), they would break it down with the appropriate symbols for that number.

In multiplication, the Aztec used either numbers or symbols:

1 × 1   *ceppace* (*ceppa* = "one time," *ce* = "one," it means "one times one")
4 × 4   *nappanahui* (four times four)
9 × 9   *chicunappachiconahui* (nine times nine)
10 × 10 *matlacpa matlactli* (ten times ten)

1 flag (20) × 1 flag (20) = 1 feather (400)
1 flag (20) × 1 feather (400) = 1 bag (8,000)
1 feather (400) × 1 feather (400) = 20 bags (160,000)

There is not enough concrete evidence of divisional operations to explain its use. The scholars who have written about mathematics in Aztec culture have stated that division was a very complicated form of computation, and its method is still vaguely understood.

Apparently fractions were not commonly used, as Aztec mathematicians preferred to deal in whole numbers, except in cases where they would divide the numerical symbols into quarters and thirds. Occasionally in the historical codices, the painters wanted to indicate the passage of a quantifiable amount of time, although they did not necessarily want to give beginning and ending dates. In these instances they used the symbols for "day" and "year" and repeated them, employing the conventions for amounts, or some combination of the two, to yield amounts.

Summary

The Aztec were very careful observers of nature. The astronomical observations conducted by the priests and nobles were indispensable for creating calendar systems that would regulate the social and religious activities of their community. That the Nahuatl astronomers not only observed but also measured the stars, planets, lunar, and solar cycles is proved by the exact mathematical calculations involved in the calendar. They devised methods to calculate time by observing the forces of nature and the movement of the heavenly bodies, which were always full of energy and motion. The 260-day ritual calendar and the 365-day solar calendar dealt with human fate and the fate of all life. The numbers and signs of the Aztec calendars were much more than artistic combinations.

They controlled the social, ritual, and economic lives of the Mexica-Aztec, foretold the future, and identified the major gods. Most important, they gave balance to an otherwise unstable universe.

The methods used for ancient Aztec sky watching and computation are still being evaluated; however, the modern field of archaeoastronomy has generated a greater understanding of astronomical observations in Mesoamerican cultures. Through this specialization, understanding of the *Nahua* concept of horizontal space and sacred time has become more comprehensive. The central Mexican codices are also an aid in illuminating our understanding of the techniques and objectives of practical astronomy in Mesoamerica.

READING

Origins of the Calendar

Abadiano 1889, Boone 1994 and 2000, Carrasco and Matos Moctezuma 1992, Caso 1981, Chavero 1887, Clavijero 1978, *Codex Chimalpopoca* 1986, Davies 1982, Day 1992, Durán 1967 and 1971, Fagan 1997, Hassig 2001, León-Portilla 1963 and 1970, Matos Moctezuma 1988, Motolinia 1971, Orozco y Berra 1960, Sahagún 2000, Smith 2003, Soustelle 1982, Townsend 2000, Von Hagen 1978: general aspects of the Aztec calendar; Broda Carrasco and Matos Moctezuma 1987, Berdan 1989, Clavijero 1978, Hassig 2001, Horcasitas 1979, León-Portilla 1970, Smith 2003: the *tonalpohualli*; Aveni 2001, Burland and Forman 1967, Soustelle 1992, Townsend 2000: sacred numbers and signs; Boone 1994, Bray 1991, Hassig 2001, León-Portilla 1963, Markman and Markman 1989, Motolinia 1971, Smith 2003, Thompson 1933: the *xiuhpohualli*; Durán 1971, Ibarra García 1995, Miller and Taube 1993, Sahagún 2000, Soustelle 1982, Townsend 2000: the month festivals; Alcina Franch, León-Portilla, and Matos Moctezuma 1992, Berdan 1989, Bray 1991, Boone 1994, Burland and Forman 1967, Caso 1981, Carrasco 1998, Davies 1982, Day 1992, Durán 1994, Fagan 1997: the *xiuhmolpilli*; Berdan 1989, Bray 1991, Carrasco 1998 and

1999; Carrasco and Matos Moctezuma 1992, Durán 1967, Hassig 2001, Sahagún 2000, Soustelle 1992, Townsend 2000: New Fire ceremony.

Conception of the Universe

Codex Chimalpopoca 1986, León-Portilla 1963, Markman and Markman 1989, Orozco y Berra 1960, Soustelle 1992 and 1982: five Aztec suns; Abadiano 1889, Alcina Franch, León-Portilla, and Matos Moctezuma 1992, Carrasco 1998, Chavero 1887 and 1901, Clavijero 1978, León y Gama 1833, González Torres 1979, Matos Moctezuma 1992, Smith 2003: the Sun Stone; Carrasco 1998, Carrasco and Matos Moctezuma 1992, Clendinnen 1991, León-Portilla 1963, Markman and Markman 1989, Soustelle 1982: four cardinal directions; Carrasco 1998 and 1999, *Codex Ixtlilxochitl* 1996, León-Portilla 1963, Orozco y Berra 1960: levels of the universe.

Astronomy

Aveni 2001, Broda, Iwaniszewski, and Maupome 1991, González Torres 1979, Markman and Mark-man 1989, Orozco y Berra 1960, Smith 2003: general aspects of Aztec astronomy; Bray 1991, Carrasco 1999, *Codex Mendoza* 1988, Durán 1967, González Torres 1979: methods of sky watching; Aveni 2001, Burland and Forman 1967, Carrasco and Matos Moctezuma 1992, González Torres 1979, León-Portilla 1963, Orozco y Berra 1960, Sahagún 2000: constellations and planets: Burland and Forman 1967, Brundage 1979, González Torres 1979, León-Portilla 1963, Markman and Markman 1989, Orozco y Berra 1960, Spence 1995: Venus and Mercury; González Torres 1979: the Moon; Aveni 2001, Broda, Carrasco, and Matos Moctezuma 1987, Matos Moctezuma 1992: astronomy and architecture.

Mathematics

Aveni 2001, Boone 2000, Chavero 1887, Esparza Hidalgo 1975, León-Portilla 1963, Markman and Markman 1989, Orozco y Berra 1960: numerical symbols, methods of computing, basic math.

12

ECONOMY, INDUSTRY, AND TRADE

Aztec civilization flourished using extremely innovative technology that was applied to agricultural production. Their economy was founded primarily on agriculture. Agriculture usually produced enough food for the millions of Aztec living in the Valley of Mexico. Their economy was also partially reliant on crafts, valuable trade goods, industrial dyes, and many other essential items. The Aztec method of exchange was primarily through tribute and trade, though currency existed. Regional and long-distance trade were especially necessary, since they allowed the exchange of both utilitarian products and luxury items, which gave additional prestige to members of the elite class and to the sacred cities themselves.

The Aztec had an extensive knowledge of their flora and fauna; they classified them and knew their properties. They were also vastly knowledgeable about the minerals of their country. They extracted lead and tin from Taxco and copper from Zacatollan; both tin and copper substituted for iron, which the Aztec had no knowledge of. Gold and silver were used to make jewelry and adorn beautiful vases. Another mineral popularly used by the Aztec was *itztli* (obsidian), a transparent, almost-indestructible volcanic glass used to produce knives for sacrifices, daggers, jackknives, and saws. *Itztli* was so durable that the Aztec used it to carve stones for the construction of their important buildings.

MODES OF PRODUCTION

Distribution of Labor and Natural Resources

The Aztec performed separate jobs according to their class and status in society. As the majority worked in agriculture, labor was divided between what people could do in the fields and during the harvest. Men were responsible for collecting the harvest; women were responsible for the planting and cleaning harvested grains. Although some women were involved in harvesting, this was not typical. When a piece of land was exhausted, farmers left it to rest and recover its natural fertility. When land was ready for cultivation, farmers cut across their land with an innovative water pipeline system. With this system, the Aztec cultivated cacao, banana, and vanilla bean. However, their main agricultural product was maize. Kernels for grinding were separated from the cobs, and honey was extracted from the stalks. The maguey plant was also a staple crop; its leaves were pulped for paper, and its sap was required to make pulque. The Aztec also used its fibers to weave clothing and impenetrable armor to be worn during battle.

Land

Agriculture served as the foundation for the Aztec Empire, as it had for earlier Mesoamerican civilizations. Some agricultural products were produced throughout the empire: maize, beans, *chia* (a desert plant whose seeds were used), amaranth, chilies, and squash, each with regional varieties. Other food and nonfood crops were adapted. Tropical regions outside of the valley, where drought and seasonal frosts were infrequent, were especially conducive for growing fruit, cacao, and cotton. Unfortunately, drought was not an unknown phenomenon to the Aztec. From 1450 to 1454, drought caused starvation throughout central Mexico. The drought was so severe that it forced some Mexica to sell their own family members into servitude in exchange for maize grown successfully in fertile areas outside the Valley of Mexico. Anthropologist Frances Berdan mentions that families sold their sons and daughters to merchants and rulers who could support them. Parents would trade a child for a small basket of maize, and the child's new owner was obliged to raise and support the infant as long as the starvation lasted (1982: n.p.).

Farmers and horticulturists formed the primary workforce in Aztec agriculture. Farmers were described as general fieldworkers in charge of preparing the soil, weeding, hoeing (with a *coa*, or digging stick), planting, and irrigating, as well as

12.1 In this mural inspired by the Florentine Codex, *Diego Rivera depicted Aztec farmers using a* coa *(digging stick) to cultivate maize, National Palace, Mexico City.* (Fernando González y González)

harvesting and storing grains. Horticulturists were more specialized, with a knowledge of seeds and of planting and transplanting trees. The success of crops depended heavily on the insight of the horticulturists, since they knew the crop sequences and the rotations necessary to ensure substantial levels of production. Horticulturists also served as managers and supervisors of farms, and they were expected to read the *tonalamatl* (book of the days) to determine the best times for planting and harvesting (see chapter 11).

The Aztec held communal land divided among individual families. In the Valley of Mexico, as the old tribal clans, or *calpultin*, increased in size and number, they became closely identified with specific locations. When Tenochtitlan was founded, according to ancient custom, each *calpulli* was assigned its own place, with its own temple and local cult, within the four-quarter plan of the city. These *calpultin* territories were owned commu-

nally. As agricultural *chinampas* (raised fields in the lakes) were developed, individual families were assigned hereditary farming rights to particular areas (see chapter 3). These families paid a form of tax or tribute in exchange for their farming privileges, but the land could be reassigned if it was neglected or if the user died without an heir. At the time when new *chinampa* zones were established, a considerable number of farmers were not *calpultin* members, so tenants tied to the land of estates paid rent to owners residing in Tenochtitlan. These tenants were essentially indentured to the state and were supervised by state-appointed administrators.

By the middle of the 15th century, Tenochtitlan had a population estimated between 150,000 and 200,000, five times larger than Tetzcoco (with a population of 20,000 to 30,000). Tenochtitlan was growing, and production was becoming increasingly insufficient. Yet, it lacked a *chinampa* zone immediately attached to the city; therefore it was extremely important for its inhabitants to acquire new land. Tenochtitlan's *tlatoani*, Itzcoatl, reacting to the dire situation, led the conquest of the *chinampa* district around the southern lakes. Archaeological surveys suggest also that during the 13th and 14th centuries, *chinampa* zones were restricted to islands formed in the lake bed and shores of the lake. Motecuhzoma I resolved this problem, and by the 15th century, older *chinampa* zones had been incorporated in larger drainage and water-control systems that included large-scale construction of new *chinampa* fields.

Arts and Crafts Materials

OBSIDIAN

Obsidian, a strong volcanic glass, was found in large natural deposits in several places in the central highlands, where mines were established in antiquity. Teotihuacan controlled and exploited this valuable material and traded it as far south as Guatemala. Obsidian was utilized in an assortment of cutting and puncturing instruments, a technology that was essentially developed in Upper Paleolithic times. It was also used to make fine items such as polished mirrors, delicately thin ear plugs, and whole vessels.

TEXTILES

Textiles were another major part of Aztec production and trade. The beginning of textile production in Mesoamerica is unclear due to climatic conditions that rarely permit the survival of ancient clothing. Fortunately, early Spanish descriptions in codices reveal the intricacy and variety of cloth made throughout the empire. According to these sources, each region had its own unique motifs, which were woven, embroidered, dyed, or painted on basic garments in order to display the individual's social status. Among these colorful motifs were geometric designs and patterns reflecting local flora and fauna of the valley. Mineral sources, such as blue clay and yellow ocher, and vegetable dyes extracted from a multitude of plants gave an array of vibrant colors. Red was obtained from cochineal insects raised in nopal cactus groves; violet was obtained by dyeing cotton thread with a secretion from coastal mollusks.

FEATHERS

Feathers were gathered by professional hunters who trapped birds in the tropical forests; they were also obtained from birds raised in captivity. Feather garments were made by specially trained weavers called *amanteca*, and they were worn by the nobility and the highest-ranking officials (see also chapter 8).

CLAY

Ceramics were another important Aztec craft. The origins of pottery began in ancient Mexico when village agricultural life appeared, and like others before them, the Aztec had their own styles. In the 15th century, Aztec pottery was characterized by thin walls, fine proportions, and cream or red slipped (mixed pigment and fine clay) ware decorated with fine-line geometric designs and calligraphy.

The potter's wheel was not used on the American continent until it was introduced by the Spaniards, so Aztec clay vessels and figures were made entirely by hand. Several techniques were utilized: strips of clay were coiled and stacked and then scraped and paddled to thin the walls; slats were joined together; and molded sections were assembled to create a whole piece. Neither the Aztec nor their predecessors had developed the technology of vitreous glazes or of high-fired stoneware and porcelain.

METALS

The jewelry and metallurgy of the Aztec were greatly influenced by the Mixtec, who were noteworthy goldsmiths, and by cultures in South America known for gilding copper. Gold was cast using the lost-wax method; copper was mixed with gold to produce an alloy known as *tumbaga*. Jewelers working in Tenochtitlan combined cast and filigree gold work with other materials such as crystal, turquoise, and jade. Though most Aztec metalwork was lost to the Spanish melting pots after the conquest, pieces do survive in museums, and they testify to the Aztec achievement of a new and distinctive style, and a quality of work that equals the finest gold work in ancient America.

AGRICULTURE AND *CHINAMPAS*

Types of Soil

Pre-Columbian agricultural practices were highly developed, and the peoples were keenly aware of variations in soil, rainfall, cultivation techniques, and crops. According to anthropologist Ross Hassig, the Aztec possessed a rather sophisticated system of soil classification (1985: 14):

Atoctli	Fertile alluvial soil
Cuauhtlalli	Humus or soil enriched by decayed trees
Tlalcoztli	Fine, fertile reddish-yellow soil
Xalatoctli	Sandy alluvial soil
Tlahzollalli	Soil enriched by decayed matter
Xallalli	Infertile sandy soil
Tezoquitl	Firm, clayey dark soil

The basic Aztec classification system divided soils into one of the three types of earth material—rock, rocklike, and nonrock, determined by whether the soil could be held in the hands, crushed, and clumped. They also distinguished land by utility. Furthermore, the *Badianus Manuscript* and Aztec pictorial documents, distinguished soil by which plants could suitably flourish in it. Following is the Aztec land utility classifications, according to Hassig (1985: 15):

Tlalcohualli	Land that is bought or sold
Tlalmantli	Flatland, land that is neither hilly nor hollowed
Tlalhuitectli	Land that is worked down, packed
Tlalahuiac	Land to which fertilizer is added
Atlallic	Land that is irrigated

GEOGRAPHIC AND CLIMACTIC INFLUENCES ON SOIL

Agriculture was wholly dependent on geographical and climactic determinants. At the heart of Aztec agriculture was maize. Maize was grown ubiqui-tously; it was grown successfully from the tropical lowlands to the high plateaus due to the fact that throughout Mesoamerica, the rains were seasonal, occurring during the summer (May–September), and this provided optimal conditions for the maturity of maize. At lower elevations, two crops a year were often possible, but at the higher elevations, such as the Valley of Mexico, only one crop per year was normal, and even its success was precarious as droughts or early frosts were familiar devastations. In the maize cycle, timing was all important. It was critical that the summer rains began in May or June so that the maize could be planted early and mature for harvesting before the arrival of frosts, which often appeared as early as November. In the more temperate and tropical zones outside the valley, threats of drought or frosts were minimal.

Agricultural Methods

Based on planting practices, agricultural systems ranged from slash-and-burn and short-fallow cultivation to intensive-irrigation agriculture. Slash and burn was practiced primarily in the *tierra caliente* (hot land, i.e., the coast and tropical rain forest) and in the humid regions of the *tierra templada* (tempered or cool land). Short-fallow cultivation was primary in the arid and subhumid regions of the *tierra templada* and in the *tierra fría* (cold land, i.e., coniferous forests, high plateaus, and mountains).

Slash and burn, also known as swidden cultivation, involved clearing a section of land and burning the brush. The soil was then seeded with a digging stick, or *coa*, and periodically weeded. The field was usually abandoned after two years because the crops would no longer be plentiful. Fallowing, or infield-outfield, also began by clearing and burning the land. The planted field, or *milpa*, was cultivated in a manner similar to that used for slash-and-burn fields; the *milpa* was left fallow for short periods to allow for cleaning the plot.

Agricultural systems varied according to population numbers. When populations were low, farmers employed a long-fallow swidden system of extensive cultivation, since the yield per unit of labor was the greatest. But when the population increased and land became more scarce, cultivators practiced swidden, a more labor-intensive system.

CULTIVATING THE VALLEY OF MEXICO

The valley's native vegetation was easy to clear, and its fertile soils were easily cultivated with simple hoes and digging sticks. But the Valley of Mexico suffered a peculiar predicament. Since the prehistoric farmer often used sloping ground, he had a constant erosion-textured soil. Fertility was maintained by simple restoration techniques: using animal-vegetable fertilizers, rotting crops, and leaving exhausted fields to rest for a number of years. Rain and frost set serious limits for basin agriculture. The rainfall, early frosts, and frequent droughts made maize a relatively high-risk crop. If the farmer waited for the rains to start, and they were late, then planting was late, and fall frosts could ruin germinating seeds. The new plants also required plenty of moisture while the ears were forming on the stalk. According to anthropologist Brian Fagan, at elevations above 9,000 feet, 15 percent of the basin surface has a long frost season (1997: 8–9). Needless to say, farming in the valley was difficult, further complicated because rains in the valley were so localized that it was possible for drought to affect one area, while leaving region only a few miles away fertile and abundant.

THE TERRACING SYSTEM

The diverse methods of cultivation in the basin required very different labor inputs. Crop yields varied sharply from location to location. Several regions in the basin—the plains and the foothill slopes—depended on rainfall alone owing to the impracticability of irrigation. The Aztec used dry agriculture whenever they could, building huge terrace systems to protect steeper slopes against soil erosion. Carefully designed terrace systems covered most of the central and northern slopes in the 15th century. As long as these systems were maintained properly, they yielded bountiful crops. Such maintenance was possible because farmers built their houses close to their terrace systems, living among

their fields so that they could protect and cultivate very productive crops.

IRRIGATION

Another agricultural method system the Aztecs used was irrigation. Irrigation, which is watering the land by artificial means, provided a solution to the problems of frost and the intermittent rainfall. The simplest systems acquired the runoff water from higher elevations; these methods flourished in the central and northern valley, where soils had an incredible rate of water retention. Farmers organized their irrigation systems so that mountain runoff watered their lands at progressively higher altitudes as the threat of annual frost fell back. Fagan writes that Fray Bernardino de Sahagún mentions farmers watering between January and March, planting the maize in April or early May, and waiting for normal rainfall to sustain the growing crops (1997: 77–79). But planting dates varied from location to location, depending on rainfall and temperature.

Along with these simple irrigation techniques, the Aztec often used stone-wall terraces or equally conducive constructions made of hardened subsoil or another durable material. The terrace technique helped to retain moisture, to prevent soil erosion, and to allow channels filled by floodwater and permanent irrigation canals to keep the soil moist for longer durations. Villagers on the plains built drainage ditches near natural waterways to allow surplus water to be drained during the rainy season. Perhaps the same channels—a few serving a single village or an elaborate complex linking several communities—also brought irrigation waters into the crops. Floodwaters systems depended on storing local rainfall on the slopes, then releasing it by opening wooden floodgates. The success of irrigation systems like these depended not only on cooperation among individual farmers but also among families and often several villages or towns; such systems reveal much about how communities worked together to survive.

The farmers also retained moisture in the soil by planting maguey to control erosion. The Mexica developed their most impressive drainage and irrigation system—the *chinampas*—in the valley lakes, especially Lakes Chalco and Xochimilco.

12.2 Maguey farmers (tlachiqueros), *in a mural by Diego Rivera, National Palace, Mexico City* (Fernando González y González)

AGRICULTURAL TOOLS

The Aztec used a variety of fairly simple indigenous tools, most of them hand-held. The *huitzoctli* was a digging stick made of hardwood, its tip further hardened by fire. It was used predominantly for making seed holes and suspending soil. Another tool was the *tlaltepoztli*, probably a hoe or spadelike tool with a metal base, which was more valuable to them then the *huitzoctli*. The *tepozhuictli* was a digging stick with a metal tip or blade. Simple knives were also used to prune and harvest crops.

Chinampa Agriculture

The most intensive form of irrigation was the *chinampa* agricultural system. *Chinampas* were highly productive plots of land claimed from the shallow beds of freshwater lakes. Mistakenly described as "floating gardens," *chinampas* are still cultivated in and around Xochimilco, and today are a popular tourist attraction. According to Fagan, recent surveys have revealed that the *chinampa* system existed as early as 100 B.C.E. but expanded to its full extent

12.3 View of a canal and chinampa *(Fernando González y González)*

during the 15th century as the Mexica were reaching their climax in power (1997: 86–88). Extensive *chinampas* once flourished east of Lake Tetzcoco, along much of the Cuautitlan River, north of Lake Xaltocan, and east to Lake Chalco.

CONSTRUCTION OF THE *CHINAMPA*

To build a *chinampa*, which in Nahuatl means "on the square made of canes or stakes" or on the "fence of reeds," posts were driven into the shallow lake bottom. Between the posts, vines, and branches were interwoven to form an enclosure. Soil was placed inside. The structure was eventually anchored more securely by the roots of water willow (*ahuexotl*) trees, which were planted at the corners and along the perimeter. The entire plot thus served as a deep foundation filled with dark organic soils for continuous cultivation. It was bordered by canals and walk-

ways, and irrigation was provided by an adjacent canal. *Chinampas* were generally rectangular, but of varying sizes, on average 300 feet by 15 to 30 feet (100 meters by 5 to 6 meters). Construction of a *chinampa* 200 by 8 meters required eight days and a group of four to six men.

Chinampa agriculture was essentially a form of drainage cultivation that made use of swamps and heavy soils with water tables so high that they retained moisture for much of the year; the high water table also protected the crops against frost. Once such areas could be drained and the water table lowered, both agriculture and irrigation were possible provided that the farmers were prepared to put in the necessary intensive labor. The anthropologists Roberto West and Pedro Armillas surveyed the *chinampa* areas and have shown that the lake bottoms were shaped like saucers and were so shallow that the water depth probably never exceeded 3 to 7 feet (1–2.25 meters) (1950: 165–182). West and Armillas state that the drainage ditches used with *chinampas* first centered on offshore islands and mainland peninsulas, then rapidly spread over the lake. Moreover, the main drainage canals also served as principal passages of travel and communication among them. The whole system was so regularly laid out that it could only have been planned and executed under strong, centralized administrative control.

WORKING THE *CHINAMPA*

The *chinampero* (*chinampa* worker) planted seeds in small seedbeds, allowed them to germinate, and then transplanted them throughout the *chinampa*. This reduced the intervals between cropping because while one crop was about to be harvested, another was germinating in the seedbeds; maize was the only crop that could forgo the transplanting stage. Apparently, seven different crops were possible on any *chinampa* annually, and approximately 500 square meters (5,382 square feet) of *chinampa* land would be necessary to support a single individual. In the city of Tenochtitlan, *chinampas* ranged in size from 100 to 850 square meters (1,076–9,149 square feet) and were occupied by two to 30 people (with an average of 10–15 persons per *chinampa*). Once crops were harvested, the farmers simply loaded the har-

12.4 Model of a chinampa, *Museum of Anthropology, Mexico City* (Fernando González y González)

vest into their canoes and took the produce straight to the markets in Tenochtitlan and other centers.

FERTILIZATION

Using the simplest cultivation techniques, the Aztec fertilized the soil carefully. They knew that intercropping and interplanting of maize and beans sustained soil fertility. Having no animals to feed on the stalks, the farmers probably removed only the maize ears and bean pods at harvest time, digging the rest of the plant back under the soil. They left gardens fallow after two or three years and allowed them to rest for at least that length of time before cultivating them again. They also used a good variety of natural fertilizers, such as rotten leaves and human excrement. The latter was sold in the great markets of

Tenochtitlan and is said to have been used for the manufacture of salt and the curing of skins. Special huts were built near city streets and alleys for people to relieve themselves. This urban sanitation system yielded a good amount of human fertilizer for the fields.

CHINAMPA CROPS

A *chinampero* cultivated his plot year-round, providing much of the food for Tenochtitlan and much of its floral supplies as well. When conditions were right to successfully cultivate food surpluses, farmers diverted their energies to growing crops that were not food producing; this led to a great deal of specialized agriculture. The Mexica seemed to have used their diverse environment to the fullest. When flower production was advantageous to a particular region, the local people specialized in cultivating flowers; when maguey farming was most advantageous, as it was in drier regions, the local people farmed maguey, selling its many by-products in urban markets.

In those markets, crops such as maize, beans, and cotton were often differentiated according to the area they came from. Fray Bernardino de Sahagún states that cotton from irrigated lands was the most valuable, followed by the cotton from the tropical lowlands. Even chilies were classified by their place of origin. The great markets of Tenochtitlan, Tlatelolco, Tetzcoco, and other cities contained foodstuffs from every corner of Mexico. There were sellers of kidney beans and sage and other vegetables and herbs. The harvesting and marketing of agriculture was an organized tradition that the Aztec developed to nearly perfection.

CHINAMPA OWNERSHIP

The *chinampa* lands were owned not by the individual farmer or his immediate family, but by the *calpulli*. On the one hand, the farmer and his family who worked the local *chinampa* could enlarge their holding if for instance, the family increased in size and the *calpulli* owned vacant ground. On the other hand, failure to cultivate land under a farmer's control resulted, after two years, in a warning that one more year of neglect would mean loss of that land. These farmers paid taxes in the form of foodstuffs, flowers, and cloth woven by women. These taxes went to support local temples, schools, governors, ministers, the military, and especially the nobles.

Religious Rites Related to Agriculture and Fertility

As the rainy season drew closer, the Aztec performed rites carried out to summon life-giving water. At this time the seasonal drought was broken, fallow fields turned green again, and a new program of temple building began. In the Tetzcocan heartland, Nezahualcoyotl reconstructed several temples; the hill of Tetzcotzingo was especially important. Among the most important cults celebrated at Tetzcotzingo were those of Tlaloc, the god of rain; Chalchiuhtlicue, the goddess of groundwater; Tonan, the earth-mother; and Cinteotl and Chicomecoatl, the young maize god and maize-seed goddess, respectively (see chapters 3 and 9).

Mt. Tlaloc was another important site associated with agriculture. The chronicler Fray Diego Durán describes the temple on top of Mt. Tlaloc; the quadrangle originally contained a finely made temple of impermanent materials. Mt. Tlaloc was the destination of an annual royal pilgrimage made by the *tlatoque* of Tenochtitlan, Tetzcoco, Tlacopan, and Xochimilco. The rulers, acting as priestly rainmakers, traveled in April or May, at the height of the dry season, to perform a ceremony to summon rain from within the mountains. This was a seasonal rite of rebirth involving idols and prayers to the principal deity, Tlaloc.

USE OF WATER IN THE VALLEY OF MEXICO

Since the most remote times, people from diverse cultures have considered water to be one of the four fundamental elements of nature; water, fire, air, and earth constituted the primary forces that supported life. The Aztec believed that their origin was associated with water. According to their accounts, they came from Aztlan, which means the place of whiteness or of herons. Historical sources describe it as an island in the center of a lake, with a surplus of vegetation and aquatic life. The temporal location and space of Aztlan is unknown, and whether it existed or is a mythological place is still a matter of debate. Some authors propose its possible geographical placement in the north of Mexico, in the Chichimeca region. Historian Wigberto Jiménez-Moreno identifies Aztlan with Mexcaltitan Island in the state of Nayarit (1953: n.p.). His hypothesis is reinforced because the island is divided into four sectors, as Tenochtitlan was, and during the rainy season, the island floods, forcing people to use boats on the streets.

The Role of Water in the Aztec Migration

According to the *Codex Boturini*, the Mexica departed from Aztlan around 1116 C.E. Later, the Mexica lived on Colhuacan (Twisted Mountain) where Chicomoztoc (the Seven Caves) lay. Chicomoztoc was the mythical homeland of the Toltec-Chichimec and the other *Nahuatl*-speaking peoples. The caves were associated mainly with earth and water cults and were places of communication with the underworld and the ancestors. They represented the dark and humid womb of the Earth that produces fertility and humankind.

From Chicomoztoc, the Mexica continued their journey to the Valley of Mexico. Near Tula, in Coatepec (Snake Mountain), birthplace of Huitzilopochtli, the Aztec dammed the river, causing the diverted water to create a beautiful lake, with birds and aquatic fauna surrounded by willows and *ahuehuetl* trees; such engineering was a feat of human ingenuity and a work of great political magnitude, which is expressed in the myth of the fight between Huitzilopochtli and his sister Coyolxauhqui. According to the account, the *huiztnahuas*, a dissident group, refused to continue the migration after being able to reproduce the ecological environment of Aztlan. These rebels, led by Coyolxauhqui, were defeated and sacrificed by the people of Huitzilopochtli, who by the order of their god destroyed the reservoir and then headed toward the central lakes.

Finally, around the year 1300, the Mexica arrived at the Valley of Mexico and settled in Chapultepec (hill of grasshoppers), where there were rich springs of water. They were there for 25 years until the neighboring towns, led by the Tepanec of Azcapotzalco, defeated the Mexica and expelled them. After a series of battles and further wandering, the Mexica settled on a small, rocky, uninhabited islands surrounded by trees in the middle of Lake Tetzcoco.

The islands proved to be a strategic position. Communication with other cities and transportation by canoe was carried out with a minimum of effort. In the year 2 Calli (1325), Tenochtitlan was founded. The Aztec had finally ended their search to settle on an island similar to their place of origin. Interestingly, the Nahuatl name for city was *altepetl*, which means "water-mountain." This name implies that towns were to be situated between water and hills in order to be practically habitable.

The Water Deities

TLALOC

Owing to water and rain being essential regulating forces and indispensable elements for the Mexica, the most important deities in Aztec culture were water deities. Tlaloc, their rain god and the farmers' patron deity, was one of the oldest and most important gods of Mesoamerica. Tlaloc is shown in the codices with goggles and a full mustache from which jaguar fangs hang. In one hand, he holds a jade ax, which symbolizes the serpentine movement of a stroke of lightning; sometimes, in the other hand, he carries a vessel from which he pours water. In the *Codex Borbonicus*, Tlaloc's body comes out of a water spurt that drags human beings, demonstrating the power of water to be destructive as well as generative. One of the dual temples that form the Great Temple of Tenochtitlan was dedicated to Tlaloc; the other sanctuary of the Great Temple was dedicated to Huitzilopochtli, Tlaloc's sacred equal, and imitated the sacred Mt. Coatepec. Tlaloc's collaborators, the Tlaloque, were in charge of sending the different types of rain that were stored in four vessels arranged at the four cardinal points of the universe.

CHALCHIUHTLICUE

Tlaloc's wife was Chalchiuhtlicue (the One of the Jade Skirt), whose name was a metaphor for the water that brings about lush greenness of the land. She was responsible for the waters of the rivers, lakes, and seas, and she had the capacity of making storms and whirlwinds. In the *Codex Borbonicus*, she is represented with her jade skirt and a dress with aquatic motifs, paper bonnet decorations, and quetzal feather designs. In one hand, she carries a shield with a painting of a water lily, and in the other, she carries a type of maraca (wooden rattle).

From her skirt emerges a water stream that drags human beings. In her relation to the watery nature of the maternal womb, she was associated with the naming rituals of childbirth, which were similar to Christian baptism ceremonies. This ritual consisted of a priest or midwife spraying drops of water over the newborn child to clean and purify him or her of any contamination from the parents.

Festivals Dedicated to Water

The Aztec divided the year into 18 months of 20 days each; in seven of these months, the water gods were venerated. In the first month, Atlcahualo, or Ceasing of Water (February 14–March 5), there was a ceremony dedicated to Tlaloc, Chalchiuhtlicue, and the Tlaloque, to whom the Aztec especially implored for rain. In certain mountains surrounding Tenochtitlan, children and captives were sacrificed in honor of these gods; flag posts and offerings were raised to the corn deities as well. In the third month, Tozoztontli, or Short Vigil (March 26–April 14), a festival was dedicated to Tlaloc and Chalchiuhtlicue, as well as the earth goddess Coatlicue. Again, infants were sacrificed on the mountains, and priests performed bloodletting and gave offerings of flowers.

The fourth month, Huey Tozoztli, or Long Vigil (April 15–May 4), was dedicated primarily to the maize gods Cinteotl and Chicomecoatl, and secondarily to the aquatic couple Tlaloc and Chalchiuhtlicue. Infant sacrifices took place on Mt. Tlaloc and in a place called Pantitlan, in Lake Tetzcoco. In the sixth month, Etzalcualiztli, or Eating of Grains (May 23–June 13), the Aztec celebrated Tlaloc, Chalchiuhtlicue, and Quetzalcoatl. These gods were represented with live images in which slaves or captives who embodied the gods were purified and then sacrificed at midnight in Tenochtitlan's temple of Tlaloc. This festival celebrated the end of the dry season and the beginning of the rainy season. The priests painted themselves blue and fasted to invoke the rain; the nobles danced carrying maize plants, containers of beans, and grains of maize. They brought reeds from the lake to adorn the temples.

In the 13th month, Tepeilhuitl or Huey Pachtli, the Festival of the Mountains or Great Spanish Moss (October 12–31), the Aztec celebrated the rainwater gods (Tlaloc and Tlaloques), pulque (Mayahuel and Ome Tochtli), the goddess of beauty and love (Xochiquetzal), and the sacred high mountains associated with the rain (Popocatepetl, Iztaccihuatl, Mt. Tlaloc, and Matlalcueye, or Mt. Malinche). They decorated effigies of the mountains with amaranth paste and placed them on altars on the top of the aforementioned mountains, and then sacrificed two maidens who were living images of the goddess Xochiquetzal. The 16th month, Atemoztli, or Descending of Water (December 11–30), was dedicated to Tlaloc, the Tlaloque, and the High Mountains, which met the clouds in the sky. The ritual consisted of fashioning images of the mountains with amaranth (*tepeme*) and then symbolically decapitating the mountain to let the water out.

In the 18th month, Izcalli, or Sprout (January 20–February 8), the Huauhquiltamalcualiztli, a meal composed of amaranth tamales, was dedicated to Tlaloc and to Xiuhtecuhtli, the fire god. Worshippers sculpted figures of this god with amaranth paste, sacrificed animals, and roasted maize. Children were pulled by their necks to make them grow as corn grows. Governors actively participated in the ceremonies, since Xiuhtecuhtli was their patron deity. Every four years, they sacrificed the living images of Xiuhtecuhtli and his wife, and they celebrated a solemn dance that was exclusively for the *tlatoani* and the principal lords.

FOOD SOURCES

Animal Food

The Aztec subsisted mainly on the grains and vegetables from the diverse regions in their empire. With meat in short supply, most protein came from beans, maize, and squash. Domesticated animals became more important as the game populations of the valley were overhunted. The white-tailed deer was the most important game eaten, and these account for more than 90 percent of the animal bones at many sites. The white-tailed deer populated the woody forests of the valley. Deer also flourished on the fallow agricultural lands near human settlements and may explain the prevalence of deer bones on archaeological sites.

Domesticated animals were few, but they were very important in the diet. Turkeys were raised for eggs and meat; dogs provided companionship and meat. Anthropologist Frances Berdan writes that dogs and turkeys were occasionally served together, as in the lavish merchant feasts, in which the host provided 80–100 turkeys and 20–40 dogs. Sometimes the two meats were served in the same dish. Dog meat was served at the bottom of the dish; turkey was served on top, implying that it was more highly esteemed as a food source (1982: n.p.).

Aquatic Food

In the lakes of the Valley of Mexico, there was a great variety of creatures that provided nutritional value to the Aztec diet. Mollusks such as the *acocil*, which is a freshwater crab, insects, fish, and waterfowl (ducks, *chichicuilotes*, and white egrets) all added variety to the staple diet of maize and beans (López Luján 1994: 11–25). The Aztec also ate *axayacatl*, a nutritious dough made with diverse aquatic insects; *ahuauhtli*, ground and boiled fly eggs; *ezcahuitl*, a species of worm; and *tecuitlatl*, an aquatic algae, which flourished in salt lakes such as Lake Tetzcoco. Collected in nets and then dried in the sun, the algae was cut into bricks that tasted like cheesey bread. This latter food had several important advantages: It could be stored easily, grew abundantly and rapidly, and had a high protein content.

Game

Hunting was a highly valued enterprise among the Aztec, going back to the early history of nomadic Chichimecs. Land and water animals were hunted primarily for food and skins, but some were also captured for the rulers' zoos and for domestication (notably monkeys). Of the land animals, deer, rabbits, hares, opossum, armadillos, pocket gophers, wild boars, and tapirs were all eaten; their meat, raw or cooked, was regularly available in the major marketplaces. The skins of jaguars and deer were highly prized; rabbit fur was tediously spun, dyed, and applied to expensive capes. Hunters used the bow and arrow to hunt larger animals, and their success depended greatly on the cleverness and ability of the individual hunter. Snares and traps were used to catch the smaller animals.

The Aztec ate 30 different types of birds. Ducks were especially abundant, but geese, cranes, pelicans, and a number of lesser varieties were all plentiful and popular as well. Anthropologist Brian Fagan mentions that the freshwater and saline lakes of the basin were along the fall migration routes of ducks flying south. Although fowling was carried on during the entire year, it reached a peak in the winter with the arrival of huge numbers of migratory ducks. When ducks appeared in great quantities, they were often the focus of communal hunt. Hunters set large nets on poles at intervals in the water, then roused the ducks at dusk with loud shouts and clattering sticks, gathering those that became entangled in the nets. The atlatl, or spear-thrower, was also used. Other wild birds were served on the tables of the nobility: quail, pheasants, partridges, and pigeons; commoners rarely enjoyed such luxurious meats. Birds were prized for their feathers; feather work was valued by the Aztec as one of their finest artistic skills (see chapter 8).

In estimating the absolute contribution of meat to the Aztec diet, Fagan suggests that archaeologists have little more information to rely on than bone counts, and bones are normally too fragmented to provide an adequate account. Anthropologist William Sanders has calculated that deer meat accounted for approximately 13 percent of the total calories consumed before the second millennium B.C.E., a figure that compares quite well with figures for modern hunter-gatherers in Botswana's Kalahari Desert. The shift to agriculture increased population densities per square mile, pushed consumption of game meat to new highs, and carried with it the threat of overhunting. After 1000 C.E., meat eating declined sharply, with consumption levels falling below 1 percent at the time when Teotihuacan was rapidly expanding (1979: Fagan 1997: 90). By this time, hunting was no longer important in the food quest.

Fish

The valley lakes were filled with both large and small fish that were taken with nets, spears, and lines. In spite of this abundance, fishing existed as an individual, relatively small-scale enterprise. The lakeside villagers took turtles, salamanders, frogs, mollusks, and crustaceans. Sahagún mentions that a fisherman would wait for a turtle to come out of the water. When it emerged, the fisherman quickly grabbed it and threw it on its back. Catching 15 to 20 turtles in one outing was not uncommon. Fish were an important source of protein, but shrimp and the larvae of water flies were also collected, and insect eggs were skimmed from the surface and eaten like caviar. Food of this sort was for the poor and a standby food supply in times of shortage, but some of the items were also regarded as delicacies. *Axolotl* (an aquatic salamander) with yellow peppers was a dish fit for the ruler's table.

Wild Vegetables

The gathering of wild vegetables has been vital to human life since the earliest ages, and it was once important in the valley, too. Fagan mentions that the natural vegetation of the valley could have supported 15,000 collectors and 1,000 hunters, or a population density of about 1.04 persons per square mile (1997: 91). The population of the valley in the late 15th century was at least a million people. In such an advanced agricultural economy, gathering was not as significant an activity as it had been previously, but it did play a role. The fruit, grasses, and tubers gathered ranged from figs to acacia nuts, foxtail grass, and reeds. Since foraging added a relatively insignificant contribution to the

diet, the Aztec relied on irrigated agriculture and an environment in which every hydraulic resource—floodwaters, springs, and humidity—was fully utilized.

Cultivated Vegetables

The basic subsistence crop for the Aztec was maize. They ate it in tortillas, called *tlaxcalli*, and in a thick meal known as *atolli*, which was served in many variations with honey, chili and honey, and yellow chili. There was also a thick white gruel with fish, amaranth seeds, and honey. The Aztec enjoyed a rich variety of tamale recipes, too, including white tamales made of maize flour with ground amaranth seed and cherries added for extra flavor.

There were two kinds of corn planted in the basin soils: a lower-yielding, faster-maturing corn that produced ears in three to four months, normally planted late in fields where irrigation was impracticable; and a slower-growing variety, planted in irrigated fields, that matured in six months and produced a much higher yield. The latter was more commonly used. By the time of the Spanish conquest, the Aztec controlled maize-growing territory in such a variety of ecological zones that they could get corn in nearly every month of the year. But despite these imports, sometimes there was much hunger; in the lean months of harvest, maize could become costly.

The earth was considered to be a divine entity, a great sprawling god, sometimes many different gods, who provided food for humans and also consumed humans after they died. The people not only grew crops, but they also believed that they were created by the spirits of the crops, especially the maize god. A general view of this human agricultural relationship appears in a passage from the Maya creation story in the *Popol Vuh*, in which their human ancestors, the first mother and father, were created. Yellow corn and white corn made up their bodies, which was also their only food source. Davíd Carrasco writes that one of the most significant and creative cultural events in the development of pre-Aztec life, and one that was essential to the daily existence of Aztec families, was the control of the food energy contained in plants (1998: n.p.).

The domestication of several agricultural plants began before 6500 B.C.E., in numerous areas within and beyond the Basin of Mexico. During this period, ancient Mesoamericans came to rely on three important crops: corn, beans, and squash. This important group of vegetables, when consumed together, provided native Mesoamericans with the proper combination of proteins necessary for a complete diet. But for several millennia prior to the emergence of the Aztec, the central crop of Mesoamerica had become (and continues to be) white, black, red, and yellow maize. Maize, however, was originally developed at altitudes lower than that of the basin and had little resistance to frost—creating a challenging problem for the Aztec. This meant that a late rainy season or early frost could disrupt the growing season and ruin the economic well-being of the Aztec. In fact, records tell us about devastating droughts and famines in the 1450s, during the reign of Motecuhzoma I Ilhuicamina. According to reports, some Aztec sold themselves to the Totonac for 400–500 cobs of maize. During these periods, some families had to sell their children into servitude. But during periods of regular harvests, the agricultural system was a model of order and productivity.

The festivals of the midsummer month Uey Tecuilhuitl honored the young maize plant. The ruler would provide an abundance of tamales for a week-long festival, then green corn tortillas to commemorate the newly ripening maize, which had its own goddess, Chicomecoatl (Seven Serpent). The Aztec said that she was their flesh and their livelihood, and they cried as they dedicated seed to a new growing season. Sahagún lists a complicated agricultural vocabulary for maize cultivation, defining different characteristics of corn, such as *xiutoctli*, "tender maize stalk," or *cimpala*, "rotten ear of maize." Maize was so closely identified with people that an honored person might be described as one who had reached the season of the green maize ear.

Maize was the basic crop for the survival of the Aztec, but a variety of other crops were important components in the diet. Beans were a vital source of protein. According to Fagan, the *Relaciones geográficas* of 1580 and other Spanish sources referred to many acres of *huauhtli* (amaranth) along with maize, these being the two major sources of caloric energy for the Aztec. Amaranth seeds were made into a gruel known as *pinole* and sometimes mixed with ground maize in tamales. The farmers also grew a grain called *chia* (salvia), several varieties of fruit trees, including the prickly pear, which yielded the popular fruit *nochtli*, and gourds for containers.

Several varieties of squash and fruit were eaten raw or cooked, as were flowers that provided valuable flavoring. Tomatoes flourished in the *chinampas*, and chili peppers were a universal accompaniment to meals.

Every inch of soil was used; the acres with the thinnest soil, in low rainfall areas, were used to cultivate the maguey cactus (agave), a crop often used as a field boundary and fermented in a special process to make the intoxicating beverage known as *octli*, or pulque. The maguey plant also yielded some medicinal preparations, fibers for cape manufacture, and thorns for sewing needles and for use in the rites of penitence. The maguey had its own goddess, the 400-breasted goddess, Mayahuel. She and her children, the Four Hundred Rabbits, inhabited the world of drink and drunkenness. The consumption of alcohol was strictly controlled and forbidden to most people until age 50 (some sources say 70). In practice, alcohol was widely consumed, often as a medicine for ailments such as the swelling of joints. Maguey leaf pulp and salt were used to dress open wounds.

Cacao and cotton were farmed in tropical lowlands and other outlying parts of the Aztec Empire. Cacao beans were a universal currency, and chocolate was the favorite drink of the nobility and a major item of tribute from lowland areas. The intricately decorated capes and regalia of the nobility were woven from cotton, and only the ruler himself could wear the finest grades of cotton garments. Historians Wilma Hays and Vernon Hays indicate that the Aztec also ate the common white potato, sweet potato, and peanuts. Peanuts were roasted or pounded into a brown paste like peanut butter. They extracted peanut oil by grinding the nut between stones, and they used the residue to make flat cakes. They also used cracked nuts in a candy made of boiled sugar or honey.

The Aztec had two uses for the pineapple plant other than as a food source. One of these was lethal, as the conquering Spaniards learned the hard way. The Indians of the New World used the juice of decaying pineapple to poison the tips of their arrows. The second use of the plant was harmless and in fact pleased the Spaniards so much, they adopted the custom of their own. The Aztec, if they were feeling friendly, hung the crowns of pineapple at the entrances to their thatched huts as an invitation for all to enter. The Spanish introduced the custom to Spain, and it soon spread all over Europe.

Other food widely used by the Aztec was the vanilla bean and avocado, a fruit that originally grew in the wild.

LABORERS AND ARTISANS

The Aztec constructed an urban society as grand as any European city. Carrasco asserts that there is significantly less information about the people who live on the bottom half of the social pyramid, but ethnohistorical sources make it possible to obtain descriptions of the farmers, stonecutters, carpenters, shopkeepers, clay workers, candle sellers, and weavers of this stratified community. The following section describes the importance of these groups and their work.

Farmers

The good farmer was energetic, physically strong, and devoted to his fields, seeds, soils, and landmarks. According to Carrasco, the good farmer was thin, a sign that he worked long hours, ate small amounts, and kept guard of his land. The bad farmer was described as noisy, decrepit, and gluttonous (1998: n.p.).

Farmers were people of the earth who were skilled at making rows and ridges, breaking up the soil, working particularly hard in summer at planting, watering, sprinkling, sowing, thinning the bad corn from the good, and timing the harvest so as to cultivate an abundant crop. Farmers were the corn people, and as keepers of the corn, they called on the corn gods to assist them in their labors.

Some farmers acted as horticulturists, or specialists in different types of seeds and trees. This type of farmer held a managerial position and was responsible for reading the day signs in the almanacs that dictated when to prepare the land and when to plant, irrigate, and harvest the crop. This farmer knew a good deal about the stars and had to synchronize the signs in the books with the weather and the passing of the seasons.

Carpenters

The carpenter was described as one who uses the plumb, a resourceful tool that straightened, evened, and polished edges. Clearly, carpenters were experts in fitting things into their proper place. Carrasco mentions that good carpenters were highly valued, especially by the nobles, whose patios and furniture demanded good woodwork. Bad carpenters, in contrast, were noisy and careless with materials (1998: n.p.).

Carpenters were especially valuable since they produced flat-bottomed vessels made from planks tied together with tightly drawn fibers. They also made dugout canoes from logs hollowed out by fire. Only noble residences possessed much wooden furniture, and carpenters furnished these houses with screens to surround sleeping mats and wooden chests. The ruler sometimes sat on a simple wooden throne, the *icpalli*. Unfortunately, none of these items survived the conquest. Some carpenters enjoyed a reputation as wood carvers. They fashioned cylindrical drums, often carved in the form of hunched houses and animals. They hollowed out the instrument with carefully regulated fire and then delicately chiseled the walls to achieve exactly the right tone. Carpenters also carved wooden masks, vital to public ceremonies in which priests reenacted the deeds of the gods.

Stonecutters

The term *stonecutter* identifies a group of powerful and energetic individuals with very skilled hands. They were responsible for quarrying stones, breaking them into large and small pieces, splitting them, and cutting them with great dexterity, turning them into everything from walkways to houses and monuments. Stonecutters needed to be excellent draftsmen as well; they would sketch a preliminary drawing of a house and draw up the plans. Some of the imperial stonecutters were responsible for erecting great religious monuments, such as the Sun Stone and other marvelous artistic structures. The stoneworkers also produce ceremonial stone boxes for storing human hearts. These vessels were made by carving out lumps of lava and decorating the inside and outside walls with reliefs depicting honors paid to the gods. Obsidian was another material favored by stonecutters. Obsidian was used to create mirrors, which when polished produced unnatural and misty reflections, and the sacrificial knives that carved open the chest cavity so that priests could tear out the victims' palpitating hearts for their sacrificial ceremonies. According to Fagan, obsidian blades are occasionally used by modern surgeons for delicate procedures such as eye surgery.

Among the many groups of stonecutter craftsmen, referred to as *tolteca*, meaning "artists," were the feather workers, gold workers, copper workers, and lapidaries.

Feather Workers

The feather workers were imaginative artists whose arrangements of feathers were highly valued, especially by noble rulers. Feather workers appear to have had a good eye for color arrangements. Feather mosaic was an art form perhaps

12.5 Feather working depicted in the Florentine Codex *(Fonda Portales)*

unique to the Aztec. They fashioned the feathered shields, capes, and headdresses of the warriors and the fine clothing worn by the nobles and by the family members of the ruler. In addition to their work for the ruling class, many *amanteca* (feather workers) produced items to sell in the marketplace.

MATERIALS

Often, the feathers of readily available local birds, such as ducks and turkeys, were dyed, but the most striking colors were provided by the natural feathers of lowland tropical birds, such as parrots, macaws, and the quetzal. The long tail feathers of the quetzal in particular were esteemed for their shimmering green color. Quetzal feathers also figured prominently in the painted and carved art of earlier Mesoamerican civilizations, such as the Classic Maya and Teotihuacan. According to archaeologist Michael Smith, the name of the god Quetzalcoatl (Feathered Serpent) is testimony to the importance of these feathers in ancient Mesoamerica.

CONSTRUCTION METHODS

Smith describes the process by which feather workers produced a feather mosaic. It began with the preparation of a stiff panel of cotton cloth and maguey fibers held together and given strength with several layers of glue. The design, carefully drawn on a paper and cotton stencil, was then transferred to the backing by attaching the feathers with maguey yarn and glue. The inexpensive local feathers were applied first and then covered with the more attractive, expensive exotic feathers. Finally, ornaments of gold and other materials were added (2003: 93–94).

THE FEATHER-WORKING COMMUNITY

Sahagún described a division of labor within the households of feather workers: The master artisan prepared the stenciled backing and applied the feathers; women of the household dyed and organized the feathers; and the children prepared the glue. Like many Aztec crafts, feather work was a hereditary occupation; sons of artisans learned the craft by serving as apprentices under their father. The artisans were not considered part of the noble class, and they could not wear their own products. If they became wealthy, they were prohibited from openly displaying their wealth in public places.

According to Smith, Aztec feather workers lived together in designated *calpultin* (neighborhoods) in the major cities such as Tenochtitlan, Tlatelolco, and Tetzcoco. The best known of these *calpultin*, located in Tlatelolco, was Amanthan, from which name feather workers became known as *amanteca*. Within each *calpulli*, the feather workers had their own temple and school where they joined together to sponsor and participate in public foundations for apprenticeship in the craft. Feather work was a restricted occupation, organized much like medieval European guilds.

COMMISSIONED WORK

According to Smith, most of the feather mosaics were produced for rulers and elite members who provided the raw materials and supported the artisans with food and other necessities. The nobles used items with feather work for a variety of purposes: for clothing, for gifts to other nobles, for palace decorations, and for adorning images of their gods. Therefore, feather work was one of the ultimate artistic achievements of the Aztec, bringing great economic profits. Unfortunately, only a few fragments of this unique artwork survived the ravages of the conquest, and we have to rely on codices for most of the details (for specific examples of feather work, see chapter 8).

Metalworkers

Gold and silver were widely used in ceremonial objects such as necklaces of fine beads, earplugs, human and animal masks, plaques, and other elegant ornaments that excited the conquistadores. Motolinia described the artistry of the metalsmiths in almost poetical terms in his *History of the Indians of New Spain*. He wrote about metal artifacts such as the design of a bird whose tongue, head, and wings could move and designs of monkeys or monsters whose head, tongue, hands, and feet also moved. The smith would cast little implements in the hands so that the movable figure seemed to be dancing with them. Even more remarkable, metalworkers fashioned pieces half in gold and half in silver; a fish could be cast with all its scales in alternating gold and silver pieces. Unfortunately, most gold artifacts were either lost during the conquest or melted down by the Spaniards.

The goldsmiths were organized in a manner similar to that of the feather workers. They lived in their own *calpultin* and participated in common rituals in honor of their patron god, Xipe Totec. Most of their work was done for the king and nobles as well. The ruler restricted the privilege of wearing gold and silver ornaments so carefully that many metalworkers enjoyed a special relationship with the palace.

THE RAW MATERIALS

Some of the gold, copper, and silver came from coastal rivers and streams, and some came from mines deep in the mountains. Copper and gold were collected in nugget form and were often traded as dust in feather containers. The smiths melted the gold in simple, charcoal-fire furnaces, and relays of workers blew on the flames through a tube. The Aztec also imported finished metalwork from other regions such as Oaxaca, whose ornate metal ornaments were highly esteemed.

THE PROCESS

According to Fagan and other scholars, metalworking arrived in Mexico during the reign of the Toltec, around the 11th century, having been developed in Panama or coastal Ecuador and Peru. Only a few relatively simple techniques spread north to Mexico.

Artisans utilized the lost-wax technique. The artist began by sculpting a mold of ground charcoal and clay in the likeness of the finished object. Next, melted beeswax, rolled into a fine skin, was smoothed carefully over the mold and covered with a thin layer of ground charcoal paste. The completed mold was then surrounded by a protective layer of more ground charcoal and clay and allowed to dry out slowly. Once dry, it was heated until the beeswax melted and flowed out of holes intentionally left. When this process was completed, molten gold was poured into the mold, replacing the melted beeswax and producing a fine duplicate of the wax prototype. Since each mold had to be destroyed in order to extract the finished product, each metal piece was unique.

Lapidaries

Aztec lapidary specialists used a variety of precious stones to make jewelry and other valuable objects. Their creations were lip pendants, lip plugs, earplugs made of rock crystal and amber, and necklaces and bracelets. Necklaces and bracelets of jade beads were among the most popular forms of jewelry. Moreover, obsidian earplugs were among the finest objects made by lapidaries. The able lapidary was a clever designer of mosaics as well. The most spectacular Aztec mosaics were human skulls covered partially or entirely with stone and shell tiles. Mosaics and inlays were also applied to jewelry, knife handles, stone sculptures, and a variety of other objects.

Great skill and patience were needed to grind the obsidian into the large, thin cylinders favored by Aztec nobles. The ear- and lip plugs of obsidian were the only Aztec luxury craft items whose manufacture has been thoroughly documented by archaeologists.

MATERIALS

Lapidary artists worked with jade, turquoise, amethyst, and shells. Jade was the single most valuable material to the Aztec, partly because of its vivid color; green symbolized water and fertility. Small tiles of turquoise were abundantly used with shell and obsidian tiles, providing color contrast. Fine cane was used to grind and polish the precious stones.

THE ARTISTS

According to Smith, ethnohistoric information reveals that the artists were organized similarly to feather workers and goldsmiths (2003: 96–100). Lapidary craftsmen probably lived in their own *calpultin*, worshipped their own gods, and had a system of apprenticeship and hereditary recruitment. Precious stone products were so important to the noble class that their artisans were able to influence the course of Aztec imperial expansion. Durán writes that lapidary workers convinced Motecuhzoma II to conquer certain towns in order to provide them with more secure sources of the special sands and abrasives they needed for grinding.

Carrasco describes the differences between the skilled and unskilled lapidary artists. Unlike the bad lapidary worker, the skilled lapidary would not pulverize, damage, or shatter the stones they worked with (1998: n.p.).

Weavers and Tailors

Tailors (men and women) and weavers (mainly women) were widely appreciated by all levels of society, since they made, repaired, and decorated the clothes worn for a variety of occasions by all people. The good tailor knew the art of sewing, stitching, turning hems, and measuring and fitting clothes and had an artistic ability with designs, ornamentation, and color. Talented spinners formed thread of even thickness, stretching it delicately. Weavers were valued for their steady, dexterous hand and their capacity for focusing their attention and careful eyes as they wove intricate patterns. Every Aztec woman was expected to become a competent weaver, and she started learning the craft during her childhood.

Fine embroiderers (also mainly women) were so highly prized that if an especially skilled slave woman was destined for sacrifice, a replacement would be found. The social importance of weaving was reflected in the regalia and symbols associated with various divinities. The fertility goddess Tlazolteotl often appeared with thread-filled spindles, and Xochiquetzal, the patroness of weaving, was frequently painted with looms, spindles, and textiles. Weaving and cloth production were a fundamental part of female gender identity and were considered prestigious and important.

TRIBUTARY ITEMS

Capes and other ceremonial dresses of rank were major tribute items. The wearing of such garments, and of all textiles, in fact, was subject to strict sumptuary laws. Noblewomen and priestesses wove the finest capes and cotton garments for the nobility, as well as clothing for their gods, temple hangings, and other religious offerings. Common women sewed and wove fine garments, maguey capes, and wrappings for mummy bundles and ordinary household items.

12.6 A backstrap loom and tools of the weaver, from the Codex Mendoza *(Fonda Portales)*

THE LOOM

The art of weaving involved the backstrap loom, a simple and highly effective device still widely used in Mexico today. The loom is tied to the weaver by a strap that passes around her hips. She sits or kneels on a mat so that she can open the sheds and beat down the weft of the cloth with a strong stick. The crossbeam for the finished cloth lies across her lap attached to the ends of the strap. An identical beam on the upper part of the loom is attached to a tree or post and holds the warp threads in place. The backloom has the advantage of simplicity and portability. Most weavers worked outside, where the light was brighter.

MATERIALS AND MOTIFS

Aztec clothing may have been made from simple patterns, but they were brightly decorated with intricate designs and motifs. The weavers used brocade motifs on their looms, as well as striped designs. Other workers applied designs to the cloth by stamping and by dyeing. Flower and vegetable dyes provided a variety of fade-resistant colors. The dyers also used bright hues from shellfish and the female cochineal insect. Expert embroiderers worked on the finest garments using threads made from delicate plant fibers and from the fine underbelly fur of rabbits.

Sculptors

Fagan writes that Aztec sculptors were part of an organized guild; they were mostly city dwellers who sometimes worked in teams according to familiar, almost-standardized ways (1997: 189–191). They worked closely with palace and temple authorities, sometimes carrying out elaborate commissions. Sculptors used stone tools, but their approach to their work shows evidence of a preliminary work in clay to plan their ideas before translating the images into stone.

The Aztec artists inherited most of their techniques and motifs from earlier cultures, creating both massive works nearly 10 feet (3 meters) high and tiny figurines only a few centimeters long (see chapter 8). Statues of gods such as Coatlicue were often of massive proportions, brightly painted, and adorned with gold, semiprecious stones, and amulets.

Whether they worked in relief or in the round, sculptors almost consistently depicted military or religious motifs, and they were as comfortable with naturalism as with symbolic representation. The Aztec crafted realistic snakes and symbolic snakes feathered in honor of Quetzalcoatl. They also crafted images of jaguars, rabbits, eagles, and a host of other familiar beasts, even grasshoppers and flies. They created models of pyramid-temple and ceremonial drums and carved realistic representations of commoners and warriors. Fine masks carved in obsidian, rock crystal, and other precious and semiprecious materials were often used in religious ceremonies and worn by priests enacting the transformation of sacrificial victims from mortals to gods.

Painter-Scribes

The *tlacuilo* was the artist closest to the gods. These painter-scribes, trained in the priestly schools, were profoundly knowledgeable about the mythology, genealogy, and history of the community. The *tlacuilo* was required to develop a keen understanding about the nature and intentions of the gods; he had to become *yolteotl*, a heart rooted in god. An artist who became *yolteotl* could then transpose the images and purpose of divine reality into the paintings, codices, and murals that were so important to the Aztec. Few examples of Aztec muralism have been discovered, but those that have survived reveal that naturalism, perspective, and color values were subordinated to the requirement that ceremonial criteria be met to the letter, as Esther Pasztory asserts (1983: 111).

CODICES

The pictorial manuscripts of the Aztec recorded calendars, festivals, mythology, history, wars, omens, astronomy, coronation ceremonies, and many other aspects of social life. Many codices served as promptbooks for orators and were so exceptionally painted that the color, fluidity of line, composition of pages, and the frozen drama of the stories painted on the pages are inspirations even to those who do not understand the messages being conveyed.

12.7 Tlacuilos *pictured at work in a mural by Diego Rivera, National Palace, Mexico City* (Fernando González y González)

THE MARKETPLACE

The marketplace, *tianquiztli*, was where buyers and sellers congregated to exchange goods and services. Markets of this type are still living institutions in modern Mesoamerica. Present-day markets in the cities tend to be held daily in permanent buildings; markets in smaller settlements usually are held only once a week, often in an open public plaza. In areas with a large population and a complex economy, individual markets are usually linked together into an integrated market system. Such was the case of the Aztec market system, which, according to Smith, surpassed most modern market systems in Mesoamerica in terms of efficiency and exchange. It is believed that in almost every Aztec settlement, from the imperial capital to the smallest villages, there was a marketplace that came alive weekly on market day. According to Smith, a vast volume of goods moved through Aztec markets, and the efficiency and success of the market system was so remarkable that the state was relieved of the need to manage the distribution and exchange of goods and services the market provided (2003: 107–109). Unlike some early civilizations, in which the central government maintained profound control over the economy, Aztec markets and trade were largely independent of state interference.

The Tlatelolco Market

The largest marketplace in the ancient Americas was located in Tlatelolco. Hernán Cortés, Bernal Díaz del Castillo, and other Spanish conquistadores were astounded by the great size of the market square, the number of people who visited the market, the variety of goods for sale, and the orderliness and organization of the market. According to Fagan, an anonymous 16th-century chronicler estimates that between 20,000 and 25,000 people used the Tlatelolco market daily, and as many as 40,000 to 50,000 visited on the special market day scheduled every fifth day (1997: 200). The market was orderly in terms of both

12.8 Diorama of the Tlatelolco market (Fernando González y González)

12.9 Detail of a section of the Tlatelolco market (Fernando González y González)

cleanliness and its layout. Types of merchandise were kept separate and were given their fixed places in the market, much like how the Middle Eastern souk was arranged.

Fagan writes that market organization was carefully regulated by the state. There was a large building, an audience hall of sorts, where 10 or 12 people always sat as judges in disputes. Moreover, officials continuously walked through the market observing what was being sold and how quantities were being measure; they had the authority to fine dishonest vendors.

The Aztec bought and sold goods using a standard pricing system based on currencies such as cacao beans, cotton cloths known as *quachtli*, and small T-shaped pieces of copper. The *quachtli* came in standard sizes and were of greater value than cacao beans. One cloth was worth between 65 and 300 beans, depending on the quality of both items. Cacao beans remained in use as a form of currency long after the conquest. There is an image of Christ in the cathedral of Mexico City known popularly as the Christ of Cacao; people brought offerings of cacao beans, which can still be seen at the feet of the image. Gold dust stored in the transparent stem of goose feathers was also a medium of exchange. Taxes were apparently assessed on every stall, but there are no details on how they were collected and in what quantity.

Commodities for Sale

Everything that was grown or made in the empire could be found in the marketplace, which was under control of the ruling class. Trade was entirely by barter, but certain items came to have generally agreed-upon values and were used almost as we use currency today. The best description of the market is that written by Cortés. He wrote that every possible kind of merchandise could be bought in the market from some 60,000 vendors: food and groceries, ornaments of gold and silver, bones, shells, snails, and feathers, just to mention a few items. Game, such as rabbit, deer, and animals raised for their meat, such as dog, were also sold. All manner of roots and medicinal plants was available, as well as cotton thread in various colors. Quality ceramics and paints of the purest shades were also available. After shopping, customers could visit a shop for a haircut. And once ready to leave, porters, for a fee, would carry packages for shoppers.

As can be implied by Cortés's description, the goods offered for sale in the marketplace included luxury items and utilitarian items, plus a wide variety of meats, produce, prepared foods and drinks, live animals, and services. The many stalls selling utilitarian craft goods were operated by the families of artisans. Other stalls were operated by full-time or part-time merchants of various sorts.

The Valley of Mexico Market System

The Tlatelolco market did not operate in isolation. It formed part of a larger regional system of markets that covered the entire Valley of Mexico. Nearly all cities and towns had marketplaces, but they were considerably smaller than the Tlatelolco market, and they did not excite much comment. An early Spanish writer, Fray Juan de Torquemada, stated that there were countless markets in central Mexico, but since he did not have enough space to describe them all, he limited his description to that of Tlatelolco. Although markets existed in the early Aztec period, their size and importance increased greatly in late Aztec times.

According to Smith, some clues regarding the nature of markets outside of Tlatelolco were provided by an early colonial register of the taxes paid by vendors in the market of Coyoacan, a city-state capital on the southern shores of basin's lakes (2003: 110–111). The local *tlatoani* collected the market tax in Spanish money, but in pre-Hispanic times, the tax would have been paid in cacao beans or cotton *quachtli*. Vendors included either the artisans who produced the goods, or merchants or sellers, whose

relationship to the producers was not known. Among the vendors offering utilitarian wares were specialized potters (both stewpot makers and griddle makers), basket makers, obsidian-blade knappers, maguey garment makers, broom sellers, lime sellers, medicine sellers, and lake scum sellers. Merchants selling luxury goods included feather sellers, small bell makers, and metalworkers.

Some Aztec markets specialized in particular types of goods. For example, markets in the towns of Azcapotzalco and Itzocan were widely known for the sale of slaves. The city of Cholula, in the Puebla valley, east of the Valley of Mexico, had a reputation as a center for trade in luxury items such as jewels, precious stones, and fine feather works. Also, according to Durán, the market in Acolman, a town in the Teotihuacan valley, was famous for the sale of dogs.

Only a few Aztec markets were specialized in this fashion. Smith writes that in the Valley of Mexico, markets had their own hierarchy. The huge Tlatelolco marketplace was the sole example of the top level. The second level consisted of a few cities whose markets were larger or more important than most. Tetzcoco, the second-largest city, was a second-level market center, as was Xochimilco. The third level comprised markets in city-state centers such as Otumba, Coyoacan, and Acolman. Finally, the lowest level was filled by the markets of the smaller towns and villages (2003: 110–111). The levels were distinguished by the numbers of people buying and selling (with a greater number attending the higher level markets), by the quantity and variety of goods and services offered, and by the frequency with which the markets were held. The highest-level markets met daily, the city-state markets met once a week, and the smallest markets met even less frequently.

Aztec markets were not just economic institutions; they also served an important social function. Durán described the social attraction of Aztec markets: "The markets were so inviting, pleasurable, appealing and gratifying to these people that great crowds attended, and still attend them today, especially during the big fairs, as is well known at all" (1971: 274–276). He jokingly wrote that the women would prefer, after death, to go first to the market and later to heaven. It seems that the excursion into town on market day was a social event that provided one of the few opportunities for people who lived in different towns or villages to meet one another. On market day they could learn about the latest news or gossip, talk with friends and colleagues, meet potential spouses, and generally keep up with social life of the community, while also taking care of purchases and viewing the latest goods and styles.

TRANSPORTATION

Before the arrival of the Europeans, Indian cultures lacked both wheeled vehicles and draft animals. Although wheels have been found on toys in the Gulf Coast region, they were not used for functioning vehicles, possible owing to the lack of domesticated animals large enough to serve as draft animals. *Tlamemehque*, porters who transported goods to other towns, were the most common form of transportation.

Tlamemehque

Porters carried goods on their backs in woven cane containers called *petlacalli*, which were set on carrying frames (*cacaxtli*) and supported by a tumpline. The *petlacalli* were covered with hides to protect the contents. There is little information concerning *tlamemehque* before the conquest, although they are depicted in pre-Columbian codices. The most complete information comes from the conquistadores' accounts.

The origin of the *tlamemehque* is unknown. Before the conquest they formed a separate, most likely hereditary occupational group trained from childhood to engage in lifelong labor much like that of the *pochtecah* (see below). Most of the Aztec codices depict the training of children as young as five years old to carry burdens with a tumpline, a sling with a strap hung across the forehead to bear a

load resting on the back. According to Berdan, the *tlamemehque* were considered a class of citizen, but they were not any more distinguished than other low-status workers who worked in an occupation of a predominantly hereditary nature. *Tlamemehque* belonged to an ambiguously honorable profession. For example, marriage was referred to as a large carrying frame, a great burden. Thus, carrying was considered an honest occupation. Yet carrying also had negative connotations. The tumpline was thought to have been provided by the deity Cihuacoatl, along with other burdens and undesirable things. People born in the 13-day series (*trecena*) beginning with 1 Ocelotl were doomed to slavery, the digging stick, or the tumpline.

Becoming a *tlameme* did not always depend on inheritance of the position. Some became *tlamemehque* as a form of tribute as a result of a political demand. Some also took the profession by force of poverty, particularly in cities, where there were large numbers of people who could not own land. The *tlamemehque* of Tenochtitlan were from a different ethnic group. Thus, rising out of the *tlameme* class was difficult due to the lack of viable alternatives; most professions in Aztec society were hereditary in nature. Moving into another class or profession without a father to lead the way was generally not possible. But becoming a *tlameme* proved to be an easier task due to the low status of people trying to become one and the increasing demand for the job; the road system facilitated *tlameme* portage, channeling the flow of commodities.

Roads

According to Fagan, roads were not fully developed beyond the borders of the major urban centers in central Mexico, although a classification of road types existed throughout the empire: An *ohtli*, was a regular road; an *ochpantli*, a wide, main road rough with holes, muddy sections, and curves; an *ohpitzactli*, a narrow, straight trail; and the *ixtlapalohtli*, a straight shortcut. Another important road was the *ichtacaohtli*, which was a secret road only few were aware of. The *icxiohtli* was a new road, the *ohcolli* was an old, popular road that everyone used, and the *ohquetzalli* was a royal highway linking the cities of the Valley of Mexico to other distant cities.

Local authorities cared for the roads; organization of labor for public works already had a long pre-Colombian tradition. Furthermore, Aztec messengers were stationed along the main roads at two-league intervals (1 league = 2.6 miles = 4.2 kilometers). On receiving messages, the runners carried them in relays, supposedly at a rate of four to five leagues per hour, or 100 leagues per day. According to Hassig, Motecuhzoma II Xocoyotzin ate fresh fish from the Gulf of Mexico every day, a distance of 80 leagues by the shortest route (1985: 104).

Loads and Distances

It seems that the actual terms of portage loads, distance, and pay were problematic. The conquistador Díaz del Castillo stated that each *tlameme* carried a load of two *arrobas* (1 *arroba* = 25.35 pounds = 11.5 kilograms) and traveled five leagues (13 miles, or 21 kilometers) to the next district before he was relieved.

Distance and load weight were inversely related. The heavier the load, the shorter the distance traveled; the longer the distance, the lighter the load. Loads were lighter and distances were shorter when weather or rain worsened; thus, more porters were required to cover the usual distance.

Litters and hammocks were employed to carry personages of high status, bearers being employed singly, in pairs, and in fours. Individuals were also carried on the backs of a *tlameme* without litters.

Tlameme Organization

Tlameme organization reflected Mesoamerican political organization. On a local level, Indian society was organized in small districts. The native rulers, *tlatoque*, resided in capital towns, called *cabeceras* by the Spaniards. In 16th-century usage, a *cabecera* was the capital town of a local Indian ruler who bore the title *tlatoani*. According to Díaz del Castillo, the *tlatoani*

hired *tlamemehque* to carry commodities to the next district, where they were relieved of their carrying burden; however, precisely how the *tlamemehque* were organized is not clear. They were paid for their labor, but there were exceptions. Portage was considered part of the tribute payment to the *cabecera* and was therefore unpaid labor. Hassig mentions that in the postconquest period, *tlamemehque* were paid for carrying tribute, although apparently at a lower wage than that for carrying other goods.

Moreover, *tlamemehque*, as well as other groups, had certain obligations to the nobility. *Principales*, as the Spanish called the indigenous nobles, exercised limited rights to the labor of *tlamemehque* that were clearly documented for the Hispanic period. According to Hassig, these rights presumably arose from preconquest practices (1985: 32–33). *Principales* could order *tlamemehque* to carry for the nobles' personal benefit. Despite their organization by districts, *tlamemehque* made journeys apparently from their home *cabecera* to the *cabecera* of the closest district rather than from border to border within their respective districts. *Cabecera*-to-*cabecera* portage allowed for a simpler, more centralized organization of *tlamemehque* within each district. If border-to-border portage had been the routine, *tlamemehque* would necessarily have been stationed at the borders on major routes, or they would have been stationed in or near the *cabecera*.

Hassig lists at least four exceptions to the practice of local portage. *Tlamemehque* were used for long-distance portage to carry tribute from the provincial centers to Tenochtitlan, to carry some war supplies, to assist in some *pochtecatl* (long-distance merchant) trade, and, apparently, to provide public service similar to that required by other segments of the population. Furthermore, customs regarding *tlamemehque* varied by province, most likely reflecting not only ecological variables but also a province's role in interregional trade, political assimilation, and so on. As a consequence of imperial expansion, *tlamemehque* within the Aztec Empire seemed to have enjoyed a greater area of political neutrality, reflecting the Aztec interest in establishing and maintaining interregional trade.

Although conditions leading to work as a *tlameme* were usually landlessness and exclusion from hereditary occupations, with the expansion of the Aztec Empire, demand for both market and labor increased and *tlameme* ranks rose, possibly by absorbing persons dispossessed by Aztec and other conquerors. They labored as organized, professional carriers with general standards for portage, probable periodic rate stops, and loads proportionate with distance and road conditions and carried not only elite goods such as cacao and gold but ordinary commodities such as maize and cotton. The unique relationship of *tlamemehque* to the political leaders gave porters a higher value to their kin, and so they were more likely to be given or sold to the profession.

LONG-DISTANCE TRADE

Long-distance trade was an integral aspect of Mesoamerican civilization for centuries before the arrival of the Europeans. Tropical feathers, obsidian tools, jade, and cacao were just a few of the items exchanged among distant regions. The Spanish conquest of Mexico expanded markets. Goods produced in Europe were introduced to the New World, and American goods were shipped to European consumers. While the conquest altered the Aztec basket of marketed goods, economic exchange itself was nothing new to the economy.

According to anthropologist Richard Townsend, there were seven merchant wards in Tlatelolco and Tenochtitlan, of which the most famous was named Pochtlan. The other wards with important long-distance trading communities were Tepetitlan, Tzonmolco, Atlauhco, Amachtlan, and Itztotolco. Significantly, these names appear widely dispersed in regions far beyond the Valley of Mexico, and it has been suggested that some of these sites may have been trading centers as far back as Toltec times. Moreover, other towns in the Valley of Mexico with notable trading communities were Tetzcoco, Azcapotzalco, Huitzilopochco, Huexotla, Cuauhtitlan, Coatlinchan, Chalco, Otumba, Xochimilco, and Mixcoac.

Long-Distance Trade Centers

The origins of long-distance trading in Tlatelolco and Tenochtitlan probably date to the year 1380. Sahagún mentions that at first the merchants of these two towns sold only red macaw feathers and blue and scarlet parrot feathers. But in the early 15th century, cotton garments, quetzal feathers, and turquoise and green *chalchihuite* stones were traded. By the 1470s the list of imports had grown to include luxury garments, a wider variety of precious feathers, stone jewelry, and cacao. The relationship between rulers and merchants remained strong after the absorption of Tlatelolco into Tenochtitlan.

By the time of the Spanish conquest, the *pochtecah* (long-distance merchants) were trading in regions beyond the limits of the Aztec Empire. Most of what is presently known about this trade concerns the southern Gulf of Mexico region, but it is also probable that Aztec merchants were operating in the northwest, in the ancient mining districts of Hidalgo and Queretaro, and even farther north, in Zacatecas and Durango. To the south the trade routes led from the central upland down to Tochtepec, where the road divided. One branch continued into Oaxaca, the Isthmus of Tehuantepec, and Soconusco. The other branch led to the Gulf coast at Coatzacoalco.

Townsend writes that inland from Coatzacoalco lay the powerful Nahuatl town of Cimatan, strategically located on the Grijalva River—a major trade route leading into the Sierra of Chiapas, which was a source of amber. To the east of Cimatan lay the populous, tropical region known as the Chontalapa, the location of some 25 towns where the Aztec traders kept warehouses and representatives. Moreover, Townsend mentions that the trading center of Xicallanco, located at the outlet of the Laguna de Términos, was almost certainly the headquarters for Aztec *pochtecah*. The rulers of Xicallanco spoke Nahuatl, although the population was Chontal Maya, so it is quite probable that Aztec traders ruled that important town. Xicallanco enjoyed access by trail and canoe to the forests of Acalan in Guatemala and across the Gulf of Honduras (2000: 197).

Principal Exports

According to Townsend, the principal commodities exported by the *pochtecah* of Tenochtitlan, Tlatelolco, Tetzcoco, and other highland cities were manufactured sumptuary items made from imported high-quality raw materials or materials acquired as tribute. These commodities were supplied to the *pochtecah* by the nobility or by the *pochtecatl* network itself. Other tradewares included obsidian, copper bells, ornaments, needles, obsidian ornaments, combs, red ocher, herbs, cochineal, alum, and rabbit-fur skins. Many such items were supplied by commoners who had purchased them in the marketplace of the major city. Finally, slaves were exported to Cimatan and the Acalan regions to meet needs for rowers in those aquatic environments and possibly to act as laborers in the cacao groves, which required year-round work. In return for these commodities, the *pochtecah* received feathers of various kinds, valuable stones, animal skins, cacao, gold, and related luxury goods. Cacao was carried by the *pochtecah* en route to the trading centers and was used probably for exchanges and to purchase supplies along the way.

Cochineal Trade

One of the most important items in the long-distance trade was cochineal dye, or *grana*, as it was known in colonial Mexico. For much of the colonial period, cochineal was, after silver, Mexico's most valuable export, a commodity so highly in demand in Europe that it virtually guaranteed its seller a good profit, at least according to one 17th-century Spanish merchant. Cochineal dye comes from the dried bodies of *Dactylopius cocus*, an insect indigenous to southern Mexico that grows in the pads of the prickly pear cactus (nopal). However, according to historian Jeremy Baskes, the practice of producing dye from insects was not unique to America; even prior to the conquest, Europeans had been producing red dye from the insect *Kermes ilices* for more than 1,000 years (2000: 18–19). Mexican cochineal, however, revolutionized the dye business, for it was far more potent and its color more brilliant than that of the red dyes previously known in Europe.

The production of *grana* was labor intensive. The cochineal needed to be protected from its many predators, which included chickens, turkeys, lizards, and a number of other insects. Large-scale *grana* production based on wage labor proved uncompetitive. While plantations did exist, they were few, and their total output was small.

In his chronicle of the Mexican conquest, Díaz del Castillo reported that cochineal was abundant in the marketplace of Tenochtitlan. Cochineal was also among the particles paid in tribute by conquered tribes to their Aztec rulers. Only after the Spanish conquest, however, did cochineal production become a large enterprise. Production expanded early in the colonial period, as Spanish merchants purchased *grana* to sell in the markets of Europe. By the late 1540s, many Tlaxcalan Indians were producing it for export, and several merchants had evidently grown wealthy. By the end of the 16th century, Mexican cochineal was already widely traded in Europe—so much so that in 1589 the Amsterdam commodities exchange began recording its price. The annual exports, according to Baskes, before the 1700s range from 5,000 to 14,000 *arrobas* of 25 pounds each, which equaled 125,000 to 350,000 pounds. In the 18th century, however, the cochineal industry reached maturity. By midcentury, annual production of *grana* surpassed 1 million pounds in some years; in 1774 more than 1.5 million pounds were produced (2000: 179–185).

Types of Merchants

There were many different types of merchants that can be roughly categorized as follows:

A) *Pochtecah* — Long-distance merchants
   Pochtecatlatoque — Principal merchants
   Tecuhnenenque — Traveling lords, passengers
   Oztomeca — Vanguard merchants
   Nahualoztomeca — Disguised merchants
   Teyahualouanimeca — Spying merchants
   Tecuanime — Slave dealers

Tealtianime	Slave bathers
Tlacocohualnamacaque	Peddlers
Tlanamacanimen	Peddlers
Tlamicaue	Traders-dealers
B) **Tlanecuilos**	Regional merchants

The Aztec state did not control commerce in a heavy-handed, direct way. Rather, the state molded trade by more subtle strictures. Political control was exercised over the economy in two fundamental ways. First, the time, place, and nature of markets were determined by the polity, and regulations requiring attendance while banning extra market sales reinforced their significance. Second, access to transportation was controlled by the government; unless the *pochtecah* procured *tlamemehque* (porters) through the local rulers, they would have no way to move their goods.

POCHTECAH

One of the consequences of Aztec conquest was expansion of long-distance trade. The *pochtecah* were hereditary merchants, organized in guild fashion and occupying separate *barrios*, or wards of the city, at least in Tenochtitlan and Tlatelolco. In the beginning of Tlatelolco's long-distance trade, during the reign of the Tlatelolcan king Cuacuauh Pitzauac (c. 1350–1409), the *pochtecah* dealt only in red macaw and blue and scarlet parrot feathers. However, during the reign of Tlacateotl (c. 1409–27), their wares grew to include small quetzal feathers, tropical feathers, turquoise, greenstones, and capes and breechcloths of fine cotton. During the reign of Cuauhtlahtoatzin (c. 1427–67), their merchandise also included gold lip and earplugs, necklaces with radiating pendants, fine turquoise, enormous greenstones, long quetzal feathers, wild animal skins, long tropical feathers, and blue and red spoonbill feathers. During the reign of the last independent sovereign of Tlatelolco, Moquihuitzin (c. 1467–73), costly red capes with the wind jewel design, white duck feather capes, capes with cup-shaped designs in feathers, embroidered breechcloths, long capes, embroidered shifts, shirts, and chocolate were added to their inventory as well. Their trading had

12.10 Pochtecah, *as depicted in the* Florentine Codex (Lluvia Arras)

become extensive and went beyond the boundaries of the empire. In this way they acquired goods from areas beyond their control.

Pochtecatl trade eventually reached as far south as Guatemala, and it is claimed as far as north of the Chaco Canyon area of New Mexico. Hassig points out, however, that detailed records of their routes are absent, except for those serving the wealthiest and most remote regions of Anahuac (the Aztec world). The roads used by the *pochtecah* were maintained, and lodging houses were kept along the routes. At Tochtepec, the *pochtecah* of each city maintained separate storehouses and rest routes.

It seems that the *pochtecah* engaged simultaneously in foreign trade and covert military reconnaissance. From intelligence gathered by the *pochtecah*, the Aztec army conquered cities and incorporated them into the tribute-paying empire, whereupon the *pochtecah* ceased trading there and went farther, beyond the empire's boundaries, to repeat the process.

OZTOMECA

The *oztomecatl*, or the vanguard merchant, was a merchant, a scout, a transporter of wares, and an explorer. The good *oztomecatl* was an observer and an astute person. He knew the roads, he always sought out places to rest, and he always searched for good places to eat and to sleep. He was watchful and careful with his rations so as not to be hungry during the trip. A bad *oztomecatl* was stubborn, impulsive, unobservant, and careless.

TLANECUILOS

The *tlanecuilo* was the regional merchant who worked in the markets. He traded a smaller range of products that were less luxurious than those of the *pochtecah* (mainly foodstuffs and utilitarian items). These included cacao, maize, amaranth, *chia*, chilies, tortillas, turkeys, fish, salt, sandals, cotton, gourd bowls, baskets, and wood. Many *tlanecuilos* specialized in a particular type of good.

THE *POCHTECAH*

Not all the wide variety of merchandise sold in the Aztec markets was available or produced locally. Much of it came from neighboring highlands basins, from the most distant borders of the empire, or even from exotic lands beyond. Most of these items found in the marketplace were brought by long-distance merchants known as *pochtecah*. There were many different type of *pochtecah* who together managed the long-distance trade on behalf of the Aztec nobility and as individuals were independent traders in their own right. The importance of the *pochtecah* lies in their role in the expansion policies of the Aztec state, their role within the religious system, their association with the nobility, and their journeys to distant ports of trade, according to Berdan (1982: 31–33).

The *pochtecah* were considered extraordinary for their hard work and long-distance trade was considered an institution apart. They traded beyond the borders and formed a distinct and respected social group, and only the members made appearances in markets. Both the organization of caravans and the negotiating of exchange in foreign countries formed part of this specialized occupation. Hassig argues that the *pochtecah* have been classified as exclusively long-distance traders of elite goods from foreign markets and that this classification is misleading. Typically, the

Aztec economy is described in such a way as to leave a considerable gap between local market exchange and long-distance elite trade. He argues that both long-distance and local trade show evidence of free exchange and a close coexistence (1985: 116–118).

Townsend mentions that the difference between the long-distance *pochtecatl* trade and the predominantly local character of regular market trade was reflected in the fact that regular markets continued to exist throughout the colonial period and up to the present, whereas long-distance trade disappeared within about five years of the Spanish conquest (2000: 194). The disappearance was apparently due to the fact that the trade network dealt primarily in the importing of luxury items, such as the feathers of tropical birds, greenstones, and exotic animal hides, which had high value for the Aztecs but not for the Spaniards.

It seems that the *pochtecah* enjoyed a privileged position with the nobility: Although they paid tribute to the rulers in the form of merchandise, they were not obliged to render personal services. Also, theirs was an occupation that could only be inherited, and they were organized as a *calpulli* kin unit, living on the land passed down through their lineage. Townsend indicates that the term *pochotl*, from which *pochtecatl* derives, was the Nahuatl name for the towering, sheltering ceiba tree of the tropical forest, which was traditionally regarded as a sacred tree of life. In a figurative sense, *pochotl* also means "parent" and "governor, chief, or protector" (2000: 195). These meanings of the ancient title is important because it suggests that the *pochtecah* occupied very high positions in Mesoamerican societies, even before the Aztec.

The *pochtecah* made up a hereditary occupational group, and with some exceptions, their members appear to have been appointed by royal permission. On the other hand, there were, in fact, various alternatives open to the *pochtecah*; rather than immediately engaging in long-distance foreign trade, the *pochtecah* could and did begin their careers by entering the system at a low level, which did not require a major capital investment. Many of them traded within the empire, circulating among the markets and competing with others and benefiting from price differences. The poorest *pochtecah* traded in salt, chili, and other inexpensive articles door to door and in the smaller markets. Indeed, selling seems to have been relatively open at the lower end of the trading spectrum and was a key way to rise in social status.

The *pochtecah* rewards were not those of the noble or commoner. They achieved wealth and status within their own guild by using their personal riches to acquired higher rank and prestige; as they rose in the hierarchy, so too did their access to wealth. It was a self-perpetuating system that exercised such subtle power in Aztec society that the *pochtecah* had to be careful not to offend the community and its rulers.

Types of *Pochtecah*

Sahagún specifies four types of *pochtecah*, each with specific duties and obligations. The highest officials were referred to as the *pochtecatlatoque*, "commanders of the *pochtecah*." They were appointed by the ruler and selected from the oldest and most prestigious *pochtecah*. These merchants were seasoned travelers who later in life stayed home to serve in an administrative capacity, advising and admonishing younger traders and also commissioning outgoing trading groups to exchange good in the distant centers. Upon the return of the expedition, the gains were shared by both parties. Another duty of the *pochtecatlatoque* was to sit in judgment and deliver the appropriate sentences to offending *pochtecah*. The merchants' courts were held separately from those of the state, and no state authorities had the right to intervene. These principal merchant rulers were also assigned the important task of administering the marketplace.

The second group of *pochtecah* that Sahagún mentions was known as the *tlaltlanime*, "bathers of slaves." According to Townsend, this title referred to the ritual bathing of slaves, which was required before their use as sacrificial victims (2000: 196). These slave traders were the richest merchants, and they were also accorded special privileges by the rulers. Moreover, the slave traders were considered very religious individuals, and they also played a central role in the annual Panquetzalitzli festival, devoted to their deified hero Huitzilopochtli.

The third group of merchants was specially commissioned by the rulers to carry out their special and personal trade. On occasion they also served as trib-

ute collectors. This group was the *tecuhnenenque*, "royal travelers" and "passengers." According to Townsend, these special administrative officials probably were particularly able or trustworthy *oztomeca*, "vanguard merchants," who carried out the bulk of long-distance trade (2000: 196).

The fourth group was the *nahualoztomeca*, or "disguised merchants." The development of the trader-spy at the service of the state forms a most interesting theme in Aztec trading. Townsend notes that the *nahualoztomeca* began as ordinary travelers who disguised themselves as natives when entering enemy territories in search of rare goods (2000: 196). Sahagún pointed out that "when they entered land under which they were at war and went among people who were far distant, they became like their enemies in their garments, their hair-dress, and their language, that they might mimic the natives. However, if they were discovered, then they were killed in ambush and served up with chili sauce. But if any, even one or two, escaped alive, he would go and inform Motecuhzoma of the enemy's plans (1951–69: 9, ch. 5)." The gossip of the marketplaces and the network of commercial contacts brought vital information to the merchant spies. As the empire evolved during the 15th century, the *nahualoztomeca* were regularly deployed by the state before the initiation of hostilities.

By the reign of Ahuitzotl (1486–1502), merchants had attained particular prominence in Aztec hierarchy. After the remarkable outcome of their actions in the conquest of the province of Soconusco, the *pochtecah* were publicly acclaimed by the ruler in Tenochtitlan, and they were awarded special capes and breechcloth. The *pochtecah* thus became increasingly involved in the work of the imperial state, new categories of *pochtecah* developed, and they in general were brought into close commercial association with the military elites.

Religious Functions of the *Pochtecah*

Not only did the long-distance trade merchants play an important role in the economy of their time, they also played a central role in the religious life of Tenochtitlan, especially during the annual Panquet-zaliztli (Raising of the Banners) festival dedicated to Huitzilopochtli. This was celebrated on the 15th *veintena* (20-day period, or "month") of the *xiuhpo-hualli* cycle. The priesthood began preparing for this most significant festival 40 days in advance, and the singing and dancing began on the second day of the *veintena*.

On the day of the festival, four slaves were led by young initiate traders in a procession to the war temple in Pochtlan, where a ceremony was conducted in honor of Yacatecuhtli, the traders' patron deity. At the end of the festival, the four slaves were sacrificed. The young traders were then officially initiated and allowed to store their ceremonial attire in boxes to be kept until the end of their lives, at which they would be cremated with their owners. Also, parts of the body of one of the sacrificed slaves were taken home to be cooked and ritually eaten with maize and salt as part of a sacramental offering. A great banquet followed with lavish distribution of gifts for guests.

These feasts were an exercise in displaying wealth and exploiting consumption. It has been written that in one festival, the participants consumed as many as 100 turkeys and 40 dogs, as well as 20 sacks of cacao beans. More than 400 decorated lion cloths and between 800 and 1,200 richly adorned capes were distributed; these were capes with plaited paper ornaments, carmine-colored flowers (made with eight blotches of blood), and orange flowers, and included netted capes, capes with whorl designs, and capes with spiral designs.

Pochtecatl Trade

The *pochtecatl* guilds had their own laws of conduct. They enforced these in their own courts, which were distinct from the regular legal system. The *pochtecah* organized large expeditions lasting many months to conduct their trade with distant areas. Each expedition would involve several merchants and apprentices, as well as a crew of professional carriers, or *tlamamehque*, to bear the loads of goods

on their backs. Sahagún noted that the merchants were trained soldiers and carried weapons for their own protection. The merchants planned their itinerary carefully, with stops at a succession of marketplaces, in order to obtain the best bargains possible. In Mesoamerica, merchants were permitted to traverse foreign borders, even those between hostile enemies. When *pochtecah* traded in markets outside the empire, they often served as spies for the Aztec, gathering information on resources, armies, and defenses.

A portion of their trade was conducted directly for the emperor. Ahuitzotl, for instance, gave the *pochtecah* 1,600 cotton cloths, which they traded for such luxury items as jade, shell, and feathers for the ruler. Among the goods traded by the *pochtecah* were elaborately decorated capes and skirts, colorful tropical bird feathers, numerous objects of gold, necklaces, spinning bowls, ear spools, obsidian blades and shells, knives, coral, needles, animal fur and skins, various herbs and dyes, slaves, and jewelry of jade, jadeite, and turquoise.

Trade in central Mexico was carried out virtually by anyone—from small-scale producers to large-scale professional merchants. The small-scale producers of goods, both agricultural products and crafts, constituted the vast majority of vendors in the marketplaces; their wares may have been of interest to nobles or to commoners. The professional merchants, on the other hand, dealt with relatively large lots of goods, emphasized the luxury commodities, which were the prerogative of the nobility alone, and conducted economic exchanges in both marketplaces and politically neutral ports of trade beyond the boundaries of the empire.

Among the Aztec, marks of social status included both access to and control over strategic resources and rights to specific luxury goods as outward displays of rank. In these terms, the merchants were neither nobles nor commoners but were somewhere in between. On the other hand, they paid taxes in goods only, and in everyday situations dressed as commoners; on the other, they were greatly esteemed by the ruler and allowed to sacrifice slaves, have their own land (*calpulli*), and wear certain symbols of noble status at special annual festivals.

Tribute

In central Mexico, exchange took three major forms: tribute and taxation, state-sponsored foreign trade, and marketplace transactions. Tribute refers specifically to revenue collected by a militarily dominant state from its conquered regions. The payment of tribute served symbolically to express the dominance of one political entity over another, to stimulate production of specified goods in conquered areas, to provide a good source of income for the dominant state, and to enforce certain contractual agreements, such as protection of the dominant region from invasion by other groups.

Warfare and military conquest were activities central to the Aztec way of life. With each successful conquest, the Aztec gained territory, subjects, and economic resources, and all of these were placed in the service of the conquerors through the institution of tribute. According to Berdan, by 1519, 38 such provinces gave up sizable amounts of their production to support the burgeoning empire of the Triple Alliance (1982: 35–41). Goods of all kinds were demanded in tribute: luxury and subsistence items, manufactured and raw materials.

Typically, the people of a province surrendered goods that were locally available to them and that the rulers of the Aztec state deemed necessary for the sustenance of the state. Provinces in close proximity to the Triple Alliance capitals (Tenochtitlan, Tetzcoco, and Tlacopan) primarily gave goods such as foodstuffs, warrior costumes, and a variety of textiles, wood, bowls, paper, and mats. More distant provinces, usually in ecological zones quite different from the Valley of Mexico, provided goods considered luxuries by the Aztec: precious feathers, jade, turquoise, gold, cacao, and cotton. And the exotic provinces, such as Tochtepec on the Gulf coast of present-day Mexico, provided decorated cloaks, women's tunics, warrior costumes and shields, gold shields, feather standards, gold diadems, gold headbands, strings of gold beads, and many other exotic items. All in all, the annual revenue of the Aztec state through tribute must have been extraordinary.

It can be seen in the annual tribute tally (the *Codex Matrícula de tributos*) that the allied cities received quantities such as the following: 214,400 cloaks, 647 warrior costumes, 100 bins of foodstuffs, 16,000 bales of cotton, 4,800 wooden beams and an equal number of planks and pillars, 32,000 smoking canes, 28,800 gourd bowls, 3,200 deerskins, 6,400 bunches of quetzal feathers, and 240 gold disks.

The Triple Alliance capitals gathered tribute annually, semiannually, or quarterly, depending on the types of goods and the distance of the province from the Valley of Mexico. Tribute collectors (*calpixque*) were stationed in each province to ensure proper and prompt tribute deliveries. A province that failed to meet its obligations or that deliberately defied imperial rule was severely punished when imperial control was reestablished. As a general rule, tribute assessments were doubled for rebellious provinces.

Once tribute goods were delivered to Tenochtitlan, they were distributed, in principle, among the Triple Alliance capitals. Tenochtitlan and Tetzcoco each received two-fifths of the total, and the lesser Tlacopan was awarded only one-fifth. In addition, each capital had its own subject communities nearby that supplied revenue exclusively to that city.

Reading

Modes of Production

Berdan 1982, Fagan 1997, Palerm 1973: land and *chinampas*; Carrasco 1998, Fagan 1997, Smith 2003: arts and crafts.

Agriculture and *Chinampas*

Hassig 1985, West and Armillas 1950: types of soil; Alcina Franch, León-Portilla, and Matos Moctezuma 1992, Carrasco 1998, Sahagún 1951–69, Fagan 1997: agricultural methods; Carrasco 1998,

West and Armillas 1950, Palerm 1973, Fagan 1997: *chinampa* agriculture; Durán 1994, Townsend 2000: agricultural rituals.

Use of Water in the Valley of Mexico

Codex Boturini 1944, Durán 1994, Sahagún 1951–69: water and migration; *códice borbónico* 1985, Sahagún 1951–69, Soustelle 1979: gods of water; Durán 1994, Sahagún 1951–69, Townsend 2000, Smith 2003: water and festivals.

Food Sources

López Luján 1994, García Quintana and Romero Galván 1978, Fagan 1997: terrestrial and aquatic food; Berdan 1982, Fagan 1997, Sanders, Parsons, and Santley 1979: hunting; Berdan 1982, Carrasco 1998, Fagan 1997, Hassig 1985, Sahagún 1951–69: crops.

Laborers and Artisans

Carrasco 1998, Soustelle 1979: farmers; Carrasco 1998, Sahagún 1951–69: carpenters; Fagan 1997, Smith 2003, Sahagún 1951–69: stonecutters and feather workers; Fagan 1997, Smith 2003, Soustelle 1979: metalworkers and lapidaries; Pasztory 1983, Sahagún 1951–69, Motolinia 1971, Fagan 1997, Carrasco 1998, Smith 2003, Townsend 2000: weavers, tailors, sculptors, and painters.

The Marketplace

Smith 2003: marketplaces; Cortés 1989, Díaz del Castillo 1963: Tlatelolco market; Fagan 1997, Smith 2003: items sold; Smith 2003, Townsend 2000, Sahagún 1951–69: Valley of Mexico market system.

Transportation

Fagan 1997, Berdan 1982: *tlamemehque*; Hassig 1985, Sahagún 1951–69: roads; Hassig 1985, Berdan 1982: loads and distances, and *tlameme* organization.

Long-Distance Trade

Townsend 2000: trading centers; Townsend 2000, Smith 2003, Sahagún 1951–69: principal exports; Baskes 2000: cochineal trade; Soustelle 1979, Hassig 1985, Sahagún 1951–69, Torquemada 1980: types of merchants.

The *Pochtecah*

Townsend 2000, Soustelle 1979, Smith 2000, Sahagún 1951–69, Hassig 1985: type of *pochtecah*; Durán 1994, Townsend 2000: religious functions of the *pochtecah*; Townsend 2000, Smith 2003, Hassig 1985, Sahagún 1951–69: *pochtecatl* trade; Berdan 1982, Soustelle 1979, *Codex Mendoza* 1988, *Codex matrícula de tributos* 1997, Smith 2003, Hassig 1985: tribute.

13

DAILY LIFE

FAMILY

In the patriarchal hierarchy of Aztec culture, the man was the head of the household. Common men possessed more freedom than noblemen in choosing, or rather requesting, a bride for marriage. The noble classes predominantly married for profit and alliance. When a man married, he earned the right to a piece of land in the *calpulli*. He usually married at the age of 20 or 22, after he had completed his education. Together with his parents, he asked his teachers for the right to leave school and marry, but of course, all had been decided before this grand ceremony occurred. This ritual was a matter of social etiquette and provided another occasion for the Aztec family members to gather, honor their neighbors, and make speeches.

To obtain a master's permission to leave the school and marry, the man's family prepared an evening of feasting, smoking, and conversing. After the meal, the groom's father and elders approached the son's teachers and offered them a polished stone ax. After eloquently assuring the teachers that the groom wanted to leave the school to marry, they asked the teachers to set him free. The masters accepted the stone ax and offered a speech of their own. They encouraged the groom to be a brave warrior and to make the school proud by being a good provider and father. Then they gave their permission for the groom to marry and left the gathering, ax in hand. Women also received permission from their masters to leave their education to marry. Their masters encouraged them to serve the gods and their husbands, and to be, above all, chaste.

After receiving their masters' permission, brides and grooms commenced the rite of marriage under the guidance of a *cihuatlanqui* (see next page). This rite also required a play of social etiquette, but when completed, a principal marriage, signifying the first marriage, was established. Sometimes, a couple married without permission and without the observance of the marriage ceremony. In such cases, the couple appeared penitently before their parents, apologized, asked forgiveness for marrying in secret, and assured the families that their marriage was principal, sacred, and true. At this time, couples

would perform their marriage rite. Today it is still common in rural areas of Mexico for brides and grooms to skip the ritual of asking for their parents' permission to marry. The groom "steals" the bride, and they return afterward to perform the official ceremony.

Aztec families could live in joint households or independently; no customary laws existed regarding how families could live. Newly married couples usually lived with either the groom's or the bride's parents, but flexibility in the social customs allowed the couple to move into their own household, too. According to anthropologist Frances Berdan most Aztec families lived in joint households, combining the families of two brothers, for example, which probably was done for economic stability. In the situation of two brothers sharing a household, the elder married brother functioned as head of household. Joint households, especially between couples and parents-in-law, could cause problems. Aztec society considered the meddling in-law to be inconsiderate and detrimental to family dynamics; the good in-law contributed to the needs of the household.

Aztecs, according to their means, lived polygamously. Only principal relationships observed the aforementioned marriage rites. However, men took as many wives as they could afford. Polygamy, therefore, was a luxury. Nezahualpilli, ruler of Tetzcoco, possessed 2,000 wives and sired 144 children, 11 of whom were legitimate (that is, born to his principal wife). A concubine, though not the principal wife, lived in an officially recognized position within the household. Often she dwelled under the protection of the principal wife. Ethnohistorian Jacques Soustelle (1979) writes that the principal wife was responsible for tending to the concubine's needs when she was to sleep with the husband. Though a subservient member of the family, ruled by the principal wife, the concubine held a position of honor and respect. Her children, likewise, were legally recognized. In noble families, children resulting from a principal marriage typically succeeded power, but this was not always the case. It should be noted that Itzcoatl, an Aztec emperor, was the child of a concubine. Issues of legitimacy and illegitimacy did not appear to be of significant concern for the Aztec.

The existence of polygamy raises some interesting questions about the Aztec family: Did adultery exist, and to what extent was it considered a problem? Despite the repressive social expectations of discretion and moderation in Aztec society, adultery did exist, and it resulted in grave punishments. Aztec law required that the accuser prove adultery. Those found to be guilty of adultery were killed with a crushing blow to the head; women were strangled first. The severity of this punishment reflects just how dangerous the Aztec believed adultery to be to the stability of the family unit.

Adultery was not the only difficulty to affect the Aztec family. Sometimes women did not become pregnant and therefore could not produce an heir. Sometimes men could not provide financially for their families. Under these circumstances, Aztec laws allowed divorce. A divorce could also be granted if a wife failed to maintain a suitable household or if a husband abused his wife. If either the man or woman abandoned the household, his or her absence essentially constituted a divorce. Divorced spouses were free to remarry.

CHILDREN

The birth of a child was a momentous occasion in the life of a family and was charged with dual emotions. The induction of a child into the family unit began with a woeful speech about the hardships of life. Elderly family members and grandparents warned the new infant of life's anguish. They also spoke about the family ancestors. Aztec children entered the world with an understanding of suffering and tears.

As they grew, children experienced suffering firsthand. They were admonished for the smallest infractions of proper conduct and were lectured about the ethics of living an upstanding life. Punishments in the Aztec family were severe; parents beat their children with maguey spines or forced them to inhale chili smoke.

These punishments may seem severe to modern readers, but parents committed themselves to the training of their children to be exemplary citizens. This included, especially among the noble families, prudence, modesty, discretion, stoicism, courage, and, above all, obedience.

WOMEN

Spanish friars documented the roles of women. Though they were observant and insightful, they were men who belonged to a European culture with the intention of converting the Nahuatl people to Christianity. Their determination and their worldview decidedly affected how they interpreted the lives of women.

Although Aztec culture has been widely considered to be patriarchal, women played very important and very respected roles in society. This is especially illustrated in the Aztec definition of a bad husband—one who mistreated, beat, or spoke poorly of his wife. The most important role a woman played in Aztec culture was that of mother, and vital to a woman becoming a mother were two people: the matchmaker and the midwife.

The Matchmaker

The matchmaker (*cihuatlanqui*) was responsible for uniting suitable brides and grooms. When a man was of marrying age, after he had completed his education and military training, his family requested that a *cihuatlanqui* contact the potential bride's family; often matchmakers worked cooperatively with one family. The matchmaker played a sensitive role and one that involved an intricate play of etiquette. She needed to assure the bride's family that the bride would be taken care of, physically and financially, and to convince the bride's family that they were giving away their daughter to a good man. She then negotiated the terms upon which the marriage would proceed.

Initially, the family of the future bride humbly refused the matchmaker's advances, according to custom. The *cihuatlanqui* left and returned the next day to a more amenable answer: The family promised to consider the proposal. On her third visit, the *cihuatlanqui* would finally receive her positive answer. The patience and skill necessary in this ritual demonstrates the indispensability of the wise and gracious *cihuatlanqui*.

13.1 Scenes from a marriage ceremony, in the Codex Mendoza (Fonda Portales)

When a match between a bride and groom was contracted, the *cihuatlanqui* consulted the soothsayer to set the wedding day. Weddings could only be performed on good day signs—Reed (Acatl), Monkey (Ozomatli), Crocodile (Cipactli), Eagle (Quauhtli), and House (Calli). These days were thought to be lucky and prosperous. It was the matchmaker's responsibility, together with the soothsayer, to make sure that the couple began their marriage on a fortunate day.

Before the day of the marriage a wedding feast was planned at the bride's home. Preparations for the feast could last approximately three days. The bride had a bath and washed her hair. She then sat near the fire on a dais covered with mats and the elders of the young man's family came to offer her advice. She was told to leave childishness and to be most considerate, to speak well and tend to the sweeping. The advice of an elder was strongly encouraged.

Once the marriage had been arranged, the matchmaker's duties did not cease. The wedding of the young bride began at night, when a procession of family, elderly women, and young unmarried girls carrying torches led her to the groom's house. The matchmaker who contracted the marriage carried the bride on her back. Sitting on a mat in front of the hearth, the bride wore a new *huipilli* (tunic), beside her lay a wedding skirt. The groom, sitting next to her, wore a new mantle; beside him lay a new loincloth. The *cihuatlanqui*, acting as priest of the wedding ceremony, tied the bride's *huipilli* and the groom's mantle together and led them to the bedchamber, where they would stay and pray for four days under her guardianship. The bride and groom left the bedchamber only to give offerings at the family altar twice a day—noon and midnight. At the end of the four days, the couple could consummate their marriage. In these capacities, the matchmaker established her significance.

The Midwife

Midwives were respected women who supervised and assisted a woman's pregnancy and delivery, and performed the ceremonial rituals associated with childbirth. Aztec society cherished these women for their expertise in delivering children. Particularly revealing of the midwife's position in Aztec society is the turquoise earplug (*xiuhnacochtli*) she wore. Turquoise was a stone reserved for the venerated and powerful.

During a woman's pregnancy, the midwife (*temixiuitiani, tietl,* or *tlamatqui*) performed an extensive array of duties. She offered emotional support as well as medical advice. Given the Aztec love of speech and linguistic ceremony, the midwife addressed the pregnant woman with long speeches on how to protect the unborn child. The midwife instructed the woman never to chew *tzictli* (chewing gum), since this would cause the child to form a swollen mouth and a weak palate, leaving it unable to breast-feed. She also warned the pregnant woman never to look at red objects, since this would cause the child to be born in the wrong position. Advice was not reserved for the mother alone; the father, too, received admonitions. He should not look at phantoms for fear that the child would develop heart disease.

The midwife alone managed the household while a woman was pregnant. She prepared meals and took charge of the household chores. She also prepared baths for the pregnant woman and massaged

13.2 Image of a midwife handling an infant after delivery, in the Codex Mendoza *(Drawing by Fonda Portales)*

her belly, readying the womb for labor. When a woman first became pregnant, she bathed initially with the midwife in the *temazcalli;* here the midwife gently shook the womb to inspect how the baby lay.

Given the complications of childbirth, the midwife needed to have a comprehensive knowledge of medicinal herbs and surgical methods. When the pregnant woman neared delivery, the midwife gave her *ciuapatli* (a medicinal plant) to cause contractions. If this prescription proved ineffective, the midwife administered a liquid mixture of water and opossum tail (*tlaquatzin*) to hurry contractions. This mixture brought an abrupt and even violent delivery. If the child died in the womb due to complications, the midwife dismembered the fetus and extracted the remains.

After a woman successfully delivered, the midwife gave a long speech to warn the infant of the dangers and sorrows in life. The midwife also cut the umbilical cord, washed the baby, performed the naming ceremony, and recited prayers for the new child. Cutting the umbilical cord required more than performing the incision. A midwife was in charge of protecting the umbilical cord from theft. If the child was a girl, the midwife placed the dried umbilical in the hearth and prayed that the girl grow to be a talented weaver and gifted cook; if the child was a boy, the midwife placed the dried umbilical cord on the battlefield and prayed that the young boy grow to be a valiant and successful warrior. Praying to Chalchiuhtlicue, the water goddess, the midwife dedicated the child to her care. Today, near the shrine of Chalma, this practice continues. Pil-

grims often travel great distances to hang the umbilical cords of their newborns as offerings to fertility on the huge *ahuehuete* tree (a thick cypress), from which water springs out of the roots.

During the naming ceremony, the midwife acted as priest and ritually bathed the child under the early morning's sunlight, making sure to bathe the child on a fortunate day. If the child was born on an unfortunate day, it was the midwife's responsibility to postpone the bathing ritual and naming ceremony. She performed four water rites, during which she warded off evil spirits and begged the gods to watch over the new infant. After these rites, observing children shouted out the new child's chosen name, and a great feast, according to the family's means, followed.

The Wife/Mother

The Aztec woman married around the age of 15, and sometimes as young as 10 or 12. Aztec society expected her to be clean, hardworking, talented in the kitchen, and proficient at housekeeping—persistent in sweeping and purifying her home of evil spirits. The wife's domestic role, however, did not make her a second-class citizen. She was vital to the economic condition of her family. A wife owned her own property. She wove materials to be sold at the market as well as to pay tribute to the government. She tended to the family's domestic animals, making sure the animals could be sold for fair prices. Attending to the needs of her family's health and well-being, she ground maize for five to six hours a day to cook delicious meals. And finally, attending to the needs of her community, she prepared meals for offerings at the temple that ultimately fed the priests, as well as meals for warriors as they fought in battle. The image of an Aztec woman sitting at her loom all day reflects only the upper-class nobility, who, because they could afford servants, had time for more relaxing activities.

A woman's most important role was that of mother. In giving birth, a woman achieved the recognition and respect of the warrior. Fray Bernardino de Sahagún recounts the festivities surrounding a woman giving birth. When a woman delivered a child, her family members gathered around her and praised her strength in enduring fatigue and pain in the arduous separation of the "jeweled necklace" or "quetzal feather" (affectionate nicknames for the newborn child) from her womb. They entered her domicile with ash on all parts of their bodies, especially on their joints and knees to prevent the newborn child from being lame. Even children in the cradle had their joints ashed for the occasion. For four days, a fire was kept constantly stoked; this symbolized the new child's importance in Aztec society.

A woman who died in childbirth was revered as a woman warrior. Her death for such a noble cause placed her among the deified, and rather than traveling to the underworld, she was carried to the palace of the Sun, where she was destined to become a goddess of the Cihuateteo. The husband carried his wife's corpse on his back to the temple of the *cihuapipiltin* (princesses) and guarded her body for four days before her burial at sunset. He, with the help of his friends and the midwife, kept watch for warriors who would potentially steal her body. Considered sacred, the middle finger of a dead woman's left hand was thought to bring luck for warriors in battle, and her stolen hair was thought to be a vestige of divinity. Soldiers believed that if they placed the hair or the finger in their shields, they would be brave and would blind their enemies (see chapter 5).

Widows could either remain unmarried or remarry. She could, for example, become a secondary wife to one of her husband's brothers, and it was not unknown for a widow to marry one of her husband's slaves and make him her steward.

When a woman turned 50, her domestic obligations ceased. She became an elderly woman respected for her advice and wisdom, allowed to make long speeches, and allowed to drink pulque until inebriated.

The Courtesan

Folio 63r of the *Codex Mendoza* illustrates a woman standing near a *telpochcalli* youth, and the glossing of the folio implies her promiscuity. She is plainly dressed, reflecting a commoner status. This illustration clearly indicates a sexual relationship between

13.3 Image of an auianime *(courtesan) in Diego Rivera's mural in the National Palace, Mexico City* (Fernando González y González)

the woman and the young warrior in training, regardless of the father's strong warning to his son to preserve his sexual energy for marriage.

Sahagún describes the courtesan (*auianime*) as a woman infatuated with her own beauty. According to him, the harlot paraded about the town wearing perfume, makeup, and ornate jewelry, and carried a mirror with her to check constantly her appearance. Casting incense around her as she walked, the *auianime* pretended to be jovial, waving and winking at passersby. Despite her merry disposition, she fell to ruin by her gaudy appearance and lascivious behavior, according to the Spanish friar. Interestingly, in spite of the conservatism of the Aztec society, which valued moderation and solemnity, the courtesan played a role in the community, as a socially accepted escape valve and a motivation for the arduous life of the warriors.

The Sacrificial Maiden

Folio 63r of the *Codex Mendoza* also illustrates a woman connected by a dotted line to a novice priest. (A dotted line between two images implies a conceptual connection, not necessarily a physical connection.) Students at the *calmecac* were to keep their eyes cast downward when women were near, upon pain of death, so the illustration of folio 63r is rare and confusing. Though the relationship between the two figures is unknown, it has been suggested that this woman provided female companionship for a deity impersonator preparing to be sacrificed. Women in this capacity served the deity impersonator by grooming him and entertaining him with jokes and conversation. It is also implied, by mentioning that she embraced and caressed the impersonator, that this woman gratified the young man sexually until his death in the ritual sacrifice. When the young man had been sacrificed, the sacrificial maiden gathered his valuable belongings and departed.

Since sacrificial rituals were performed ubiquitously, the sacrificial maiden played an important role: She was a companion to men close to their death. She, too, wears the earplug with the highly esteemed turquoise stone, and her clothing is more ornately designed, suggesting a more elevated position than the common courtesan.

The Priestess

When a baby girl was 20 to 40 days old, her mother dedicated her to the service of the tribal temple. As she grew older, the girl paid tributes of brooms, wood shavings, and copal (incense) to the temple every 20 days. Though still a maiden, a girl could give herself willingly to the temple. The elder priestesses performed a veiling ceremony, at which time the young priestess took up the ladle and incense of the initiated priestess.

The priestesses were called *cihuatlamacazque*, although they were free to marry and leave their religious duties if they so chose. The festival of goddess Toci was conducted by an older priestess, the *cluazvacuilli*, but the preparation of the ceremony, including the sweeping of the temple and the lighting of fires, was the responsibility of another priestess called the *iztaccihuatl* (the white woman). During the festival of Ochpaniztli, the young priestesses of the goddess of maize, Chicomecoatl, impersonated her, carrying seven ears of maize on their backs. They sang in a procession, and at sunset they threw maize and calabash seeds to the crowd because they were a symbol of wealth and abundance for the coming year.

EDUCATION

Before children entered the formal educational system of the *calmecac* or the *telpochcalli*, they first learned from their parents. Young boys, around the age of three, began to learn the chores of men—carrying wood and water to the house, traveling to the market for sundries with his father. Young girls, around the age of three, began to observe the weaving and spinning chores of their mothers. As children grew older, they took on more responsibility. Boys, at the age of seven, began to fish and supervise boats on the lake; girls handled the spindle, ground maize on a stone *metlatl*, and wove cloth on a backstrap loom.

The education of children was the responsibility of each community member. Not only did everyone in the neighborhood help to raise the children, the extended family was also obligated to contribute their knowledge in life experiences to help develop the children's proper social etiquette. Education often came in the form of severe punishments. Parents would scratch idle children with agave thorns or force them to breathe the fumes of a fire burning with red peppers.

According to the *Codex Mendoza*, boys and girls began their formal educations at the age of 15. Other sources say that they attended school much earlier; sometimes boys were sent to the *calmecac* as soon as they could walk. Generally, both boys and girls began their formal education between the ages of six and nine.

The educational system of the Aztec reveals much about the priorities of Aztec culture. The Aztec government required all citizens to be educated; attendance at either the *calmecac* or the *telpochcalli* was mandatory. At birth, children's educational fates rested in their parents' decision to send them to the *calmecac*, the priests' house and school attached to major temples, or to the *telpochcalli*, the warriors' house. The existence of these two specific schools reveals that religion and war played the most important roles in Aztec society. In general, the *calmecac* educated the children of the upper class to become priests and government administrators, and the *telpochcalli* educated the common children to become warriors. This was not, however, always the case. Common children were allowed to attend the religious *calmecac*, and those educated at the *telpochcalli* were allowed to rise through the ranks to become administrators and rulers. The Aztec educational system was flexible, though not completely egalitarian. According to Sahagún, when it was determined that a child would attend the *calmecac*, the child, if a boy, was scarified on the chest; girls were scarified on the hip. When it was determined that the child would attend the *telpochcalli*, the child's lip was pierced.

The *Calmecac*

A child's induction to the *calmecac* began at birth. With a lavish ceremony, parents gave their child to the tribal priests to learn science, folklore, the calendar, history, mythology, writing, and the law. This ceremony began when the parents invited the priests and neighbors to a feast of food and drink. The father offered his son or daughter as a quetzal feather (Quetzalcoatl was the patron deity of the *calmecac* and of the education of priests and noblemen), and asked the priests or priestesses to take his child under their protection and affection. The father praised the priests for their skills in raising children to be priests or priestesses, administrators, judges, and high officials, and promised the priests lavish gifts should they accept the charge. The priests then took the child and offered prayers to Quetzalcoatl, honoring the deity as the chief teacher

at the *calmecac*. Following these prayers, the party proceeded to the temple to give gifts of mantles (*tilmatli*), breechcloth (*maxtlatl*), precious stone neck bands, and feathers to Quetzalcoatl. If poor, the family took only paper, herbs, and incense to give as offerings. In the temple, the priests smeared the child's face with black soot and placed around his or her neck a necklace of birthwort, or cotton if the family was poor. Then they cut the child's ears and cast the blood before an image of an evildoer to ward off evil spirits. When the party left the temple, the family left the child's neckband in the temple for the priests to take at a later time, and the child became the responsibility of the priests.

Boys and girls studied at the *calmecac* to learn the ways of the priests and priestesses. Boys lived on the temple grounds with the priests, but girls are not known to have lived at the *calmecac*. Students learned to live by the values of Aztec society—moderation, hard work, obedience, and discretion. They also learned self-control. Parents tried to prepare their children for the arduous life at the *calmecac* by advising them that their education was to be one of sacrifice, humility, and punishment. Good students (both boys and girls) performed an assortment of chores including sweeping, cooking meals, gathering and carrying wood for the fire, preparing body paints for the priests, working the land, and building walls and fences. In keeping with a moderate lifestyle, good students avoided the pleasures of wine and promiscuity. They also participated in the rituals of the priests such as fasting and praying at midnight to do penance. This involved walking far from the *calmecac* and planting maguey spines after the act of autosacrifice, signaled by the blowing of a trumpet. Good students also learned etiquette and articulate speech. Older students learned the martial arts.

When students misbehaved, a variety of severe punishments ensued. For minor acts of disobedience, students could be forced to inhale the smoke of burning chili peppers. Students could also be burned, cut and bled at the ears, chest, thighs, or calves, or beaten with nettle switches. More serious, and fatal, punishments existed. If students engaged in drinking or premarital sex, they could be strangled or thrown into a fire and shot with arrows. Sons of noblemen always warranted more extreme punishments, since more was expected of them.

The *Telpochcalli*

The *telpochcalli* provided a more general alternative to the prestigious, religious curriculum of the *calmecac*. In every town, large city, and neighborhood, there existed a *telpochcalli*. Students at the *telpochcalli* lived a more independent life. Because male students of the *telpochcalli* prepared for a life of battle and war, they enjoyed more freedoms. Under the tutelage of state-employed instructors, the *telpochtlatoque* (male master of youth) or the *ichpochtlatoque* (female master of youth), students learned much of the curriculum of the *calmecac* but without the behavioral expectations. At sunset, when the day of training had ended, students attended the *cuicacalco*, the house of singing, and sang and danced late into the night. Boys began their education in service to more experienced warriors, carrying arms for battle and learning the martial arts. As they grew older, boys could participate in battle and capture their own prisoners for sacrifice.

The prevailing attitudes at each school system created rivalry. Alumni of the *calmecac* looked down on the students of the *telpochcalli*, believing them to be indiscreet and frivolous. Sahagún subscribed to this opinion when he described the *telpochalli* students as promiscuous, inarticulate, and proud. This rivalry exploded during the month of Atemoztli, when teams from each school system engaged in mock battles. This rivalry was further justified by the fact that the *calmecac* was dedicated to the patron deity Quetzalcoatl, and the *telpochcalli* was dedicated to Tezcatlipoca, the enemy of Quetzalcoatl.

SHAMANISM AND MEDICINE

The Aztec ascribed illnesses of all kinds to three primary causes: supernatural, magical, and natural. When afflicted by illness, Aztecs believed that they had lost their *tonalli*, the soul unique to each person. The *tonalli* made each individual unique and determined his or her destiny. To determine whether a patient's *tonalli* had been lost, the physician (*ticitl*) held a vessel filled with water under the patient's chin. If the patient's reflection seemed shadowed, the patient had indeed lost his or her *tonalli*.

Supernatural Causes

Gods wishing to punish individuals sent supernatural illnesses. The Tlaloque, the mountain gods, sent illnesses believed by the Aztec to be caused by cold weather, such as gout, palsy, and arthritis. Xochipilli, god of youth, music, and flowers, punished the promiscuous with venereal diseases. Ulcers, leprosy, and paralysis were attributed to the god Tlaloc, and eye diseases were attributed to Xipe Totec. Shamans cured these illnesses with religious offerings, feasts, sacrifices, and recitations of prayers to the gods. The goddess Ixtlilton healed children, Chiuacoatl, goddess of the steam bath, healed illnesses of carnal love, and the goddess Tzapotlatenan healed ulcers and hoarse throats.

It is naive to believe that the Aztec were merely superstitious in their beliefs about health and healing. The Aztec strongly believed in the duality of the universe and in a symmetrical cosmology; the earthly pains of humans often reflected the divine pains of the gods, and illnesses affected both the body and the moral spirit. For instance, when a patient broke or fractured a limb, healers recognized the obvious source of the break, but they also believed the break to be the result of a mythological quail that caused Quetzalcoatl to break the bones of his ancestors. Physical splints and casts to support the break accompanied a ritual prayer recited over the break. This prayer acknowledged the supernatural presence in the break and the shaman's power to heal the break. This example clearly shows the relationship of the divine and the physical in the medical practices of the Aztec healers.

Magical Causes

Magical illnesses were the curse of a malicious sorcerer, the *tlacatecolotl*, or "owl man," and were diagnosed through the process of ritual divination. Shamans threw kernels onto a cloth and identified the patient's disease. Hallucinogenic drugs such as *peyotl* and *ololiuhqui*, taken by the patient or by a relative, would also reveal the identity of the magic curse. Other forms of divination existed. The *mecatlapouhque*, "fortune-tellers by the strings," used strings to divine the origin of illnesses. The *ticitl* would cover his or her hands with tobacco and measure the patient's left arm with his or her right palm. The measurement revealed the origin of the disease. Shamans cured these magical illnesses through the use of precious stones and the prescription of peculiar concoctions, like those made of worms, skunk blood, and skunk spray.

Natural Causes

Natural maladies, such as headaches, stomachaches, and head wounds, were healed through medicinal prescriptions. The Aztec physician was an educated and experienced person in healing and prescribed hundreds of medicinal herbs, proven by recent scholarship to be effective, to salve and heal wounds, and to cure disease. Spanish conquerors, impressed by the effectiveness of Aztec medical practices to cure the chronic illnesses of Spanish inhabitants, dispatched Spanish doctors to New Spain to study Aztec medicine. Many of the Aztec medicinal herbs are still used today in rural Mexico.

Sahagún described the good physician as one who had empirical knowledge of herbs, stones, trees, and roots. He knew, through his own experiments, which herbs worked to cure which ailments. The extent of the physician's knowledge is remarkable when one reads through Sahagún's descriptions of 149 varieties of herbs, their effects, and how they could be prescribed to heal a variety of complaints, from the common headache and fever to digestive problems and epilepsy. For example, if a patient suffered from inflamed eyes, he used drops of *naui iuipil* or *tetzmitl* to squelch the burning. *Naui iuipil*, if consumed by drink, also cured the common cough. And the bitterly sour *miccaxoxocoyoli* with a heated chili served as a local anesthetic.

Some maladies, like a toothache, required more attention than a medicinal herb could give. If a toothache worsened, the physician could prick the gums of the infected tooth with an obsidian blade or a maguey spine and apply a *tlalaccauctl* mixture. If this did not work, the tooth would finally be extracted. Tooth infections could be prevented by rubbing powdered charcoal on the teeth and cleaning them with salt and urine.

Head wounds also required extensive procedures. An initial cleansing with urine prepared the skull for an application of maguey sap. If the head wound became septic, *chipuli* leaves and eggs whites could dry and heal the festering wound. Bandages wrapped around the head kept the wound safe from infection. The average headache, though relatively easy to cure, could lead to intrusive surgery. The patient distressed by a headache inhaled green tobacco. If the headache continued, the patient inhaled a powdered form of the medicinal flower *cocoyatic*. If the headache still continued, the physician would cut and bleed the patient with an obsidian point.

Less serious discomforts also afflicted patients. When an Aztec patient complained of dandruff, the physician washed his head with urine, scrubbed the scalp with the *axin* powder of avocado pits, and applied *yiamolli* leaves to the head. Black clay was then smeared through the hair to give color. Scabies also afflicted the Aztec scalp and was treated by shaving the head, washing the shorn scalp with urine, and applying a mixture of pinewood, cottonseed, and avocado powders. Other cosmetic ailments occurred. Physicians treated complaints of acne or a rough face with a hot urine wash and an application of powdered yellow chili. The patient then drank the sap of *tlatlauhqui*, and thereafter drank only cold water to relieve the pain.

Hallucinogenic herbs and mushrooms are often closely associated with the work of the shaman. Sahagún gives a vivid description of the hallucinogens and their effects in the *Florentine Codex*. For the purpose of anthropological study, he himself took several of the hallucinogens and experienced firsthand what he labeled as maddening and disturbing effects. Among these herbs and mushrooms he lists: *peyotl* (peyote), a greenish cactus that could be eaten or boiled to drink; *tlapatl*, a blue-green skinned herb with white blossoms that could be snorted or eaten; *mixitl*, a round green leaf that caused a paralytic state of fixation in which the user became mute and rigid; and *teonanacatl*, mushrooms that grew on the grassy plains, had small heads and long, slender stems, and, when eaten, burned the throat and caused vomiting. *Teonanacatl* mixed with honey in a drink digested more easily. Sahagún warns that many of the mushrooms caused rectal bleeding, paralysis, or death but, if they were used medicinally, could cure skin sores. *Atlepatli*, *quimichpatli*, and *aquiztli* all burned away festering sores (and killed mice in the household). Both *tlapatl* and *mixitl* also cured gout. *Amolli*, a white flower with small shoots known to cause baldness, could be eaten to kill a swallowed leech.

13.4 Patolli *game, in the* Codex Magliabecchi (Fonda Portales)

GAMES

Patolli

Patolli was a racing game played with beans marked with varying numbers of dots, a cross-shaped game board divided into 52 squares, and stone pebbles. An illustration in the *Codex Magliabecchi* shows how *patolli* was played. The god Macuilxochitl, tutelary deity of gambling, sits to the side of the entire game while four players, sitting on mats around the board, take turns throwing the beans as we would dice. According to the fall of the beans, which determined how many spaces each player could move around the board, players moved six small, colored stones. The first player to return to the initial squares won the game. If any player rolled a bean that stood on its side, a very difficult task, that player would take all the winnings, despite the other players' places in the game. *Patolli* tournaments captivated Aztec communities. Bets were wagered on who could handle the dice best and on which numbers would be thrown. For good luck, men would superstitiously turn the mortar and griddle in their homes upside down and place the pestle in a corner. Everyone played, regardless of gender, regardless of class.

    Patolli served a dual purpose. The 52 squares of the game board represented the number of years it took for the divinatory and solar cycles to align. The game board, often painted on mats with liquid rubber, also represented a symmetrical cosmology—a visible world that mirrored the invisible world.

Ullamaliztli

Passed down from antiquity, *ullamaliztli* (the Nahuatl name for the ancient Mesoamerican ball game) was an essential element in the life of a *calpulli*. The *tlachtli*, or *tlachco* (ball court), of Tenochtitlan lay at the western side of the Sacred Precinct, surrounded by the palace and temple. The games played on the *tlachtli* provided entertainment; hundreds of spectators came out to watch the game and make grand wagers of feathers, precious stones, even land and houses, on the outcome. The ball game also provided ritual reinforcement for its *calpulli* and reflected the symmetrical cosmology of the Aztec mythology.

    The *tlachtli* was an I-shaped ball court surrounded by gradual inclines and 2.5- to 3.5-meter- (8- to 11-feet) high walls. Divided by a central line, identified by Sahagún as the *tecotl* and by modern players as the *analco*, the ball court was approximately 30 to 65 meters (100 to 200 feet) long. The objective of the game was to score points by passing a rubber ball through one of two stone-carved rings

13.5 Image of a pre-Aztec ball court in Xochicalco, Morelos (Manuel Aguilar-Moreno)

sticking out from both walls at center court. The ball, or *ulli*, was hard and weighed about nine pounds (four kilograms). The rings were 14 centimeters (35 inches) in diameter and were often carved in the shapes of animals. Specially trained, the *ullamanime* (ball players), using only their hips and knees, battled to hit the ball through one of the rings to win the game. The rules were many and complicated. If a player hit the *ulli* with the calf, foot, arm, or hand, or failed to hit the ball across the center line, that player committed a foul. Should teams prove unable to pass the ball through the rings, or if the court did not have rings, points could be awarded for technically skillful maneuvers, such as hitting any of the six markers distributed along the sloping walls of the court. However, because passing the *ulli* through the ring was a difficult undertaking and a rare achievement, if a player scored, the game ended instantly.

Winning was always a reward, but sometimes political situations could affect the results of the game. In the *Historia de la nación chichimeca*, Alva Ixtlilxochitl recounts a ball game played between Axayacatl, who wagered the marketplace of Tenochtitlan, and the king of Xochimilco, who wagered his beautiful garden. The king of Xochimilco won the game and the marketplace in Mexico but lost his life when Axayacatl's soldiers visited to congratulate him. The soldiers strangled the king of Xochimilco with a leather thong hidden in the garland they placed around his neck in celebration.

Each *ullamani* wore protective gear made of deerskin. Chin, hip, and thigh guards, gloves, and a half mask to cover the cheeks shielded the player from the rough, stucco ball court surface. The nature of the game required players to throw themselves to the ground to keep the ball in the air as it passed the central line. Durán witnessed players who kept the ball in the air for over an hour. Despite the protective uniform, players left the ball court exhausted, bleeding, and bruised. Incisions in the player's thighs and buttocks relieved the pressure of their wounds and drained blood from their bruises. Death from a swift hit to the stomach was not uncommon.

One of the few organized sports in Aztec culture, the ball game, like *patolli*, reflected a complex mythology and conception of the cosmos. The ball court mirrored the celestial ball court, *citlaltlachtli*. The earth-bound court (*tlachtli*), lying on the western axis, symbolized the underworld, through which the Sun, represented by the ball, passed each night. The game symbolized the battle between the Sun and Moon, or the gods of youth and maturity, each vying for supremacy.

As well as reflecting a symmetrical cosmology, the *Ullamaliztli* symbolized the sacrificial rite. The *tlachtli* in Tenochtitlan lay in front of the Great Temple's bloodstained staircase. As shown by *Codex Magliabecchiano*, skulls marked the central line, and the rubber ball represented the severed head of the sacrificed prisoner. It was not uncommon that the court became a stage upon which losing players were executed.

Being a ritualized reenactment of the cosmos, the game was played at important events. On the night of a king's inauguration, he would wake at midnight and gaze at the stars. The next day, a grand game of *ullamaliztli* would be played in the city center. *Ullamaliztli* was also played during religious festivals and market days. The outcome of *ullamaliztli* games also provided ominous forecasts for priests trying to predict the future and settled wagers between contentious parties.

13.6 Aztec ball court (tlachtli), *in the* Codex Magliabecchi (Drawing by Fonda Portales)

A version of the ancient Mesoamerican, and particularly Aztec, game still survives today. *Ulama* is played in a very small number of towns in the northern state of Sinaloa, Mexico. Some unique characteristics of the modern game, such as attire, rules, and organization of the game, point to its pre-Columbian origins.

Gambling

Despite strict Aztec rules of behavior and societal conduct, gambling raised the issues of addiction and deviance. Durán witnessed gamblers avidly traveling through the streets of the city with *patolli* mats under their arms and with dice tied into small bundles of cloth. *Ullamaliztli* tournaments encouraged gamblers to wage large sums of money on the outcome: Homes, land, maguey plants (a valuable commodity), and even children were sometimes sold or lost to pay gambling debts. In the most dire situations, a gambler could pay off debts by submitting to slavery. Becoming a *tlacoti* was an arduous task. The gambler appeared before four venerated elders who would witness the ceremony. The gambler would then announce his desire (or need) to become a slave and be given, by someone who would later own him or her, the price of his or her servitude. This fee was generally 20 pieces of cloth—one load of *quachtli*—which provided the *tlacoti* the means to live independently for a year before servitude began. When the gambler spent the allotted income, the *tlacoti* would exchange his or her services for food, shelter, and clothing. Any community member had the option of becoming a slave; the most populous class was that of voluntary slaves. However, because the *tlacoti* position was a position of ill repute, it was chosen as a last resort for paying off debts.

Though Aztec culture punished and demeaned excessive behavior of all kinds, only warnings were given as to the effects of gambling, possibly to support the large number of voluntary slaves who could only benefit the nobility. Aztecs believed that a person born under the sign of Ce Calli (1 House) had the potential to be a great gambler and possibly lose everything.

Personal Appearance and Attire

Clothing

Aztec society was intensely stratified, which is revealed in secular and ceremonial clothing. A garment's material allowed people to determine an individual's class and rank. Sumptuary laws enforced a rigid classification of status and gender, and one could be punished for wearing clothing outside one's social class. The laws allowed commoners (*macehualtin*) to wear only items of clothing made from maguey, yucca, or palm fibers. Though these were rough fibers, Aztec women adeptly spun them into supple threads. Furthermore, the laws allowed only the nobility to wear cotton garments, a more luxurious and comfortable material.

Patricia Anawalt, a leading scholar in Aztec costume, and anthropologist Frances Berdan separate Aztec clothing into five simple divisions: draped garments, slip-on garments, open sewn garments, closed sewn garments, and limb-encasing garments. With so little variety of garment type and despite rigid laws, Aztec creativity nevertheless manifested itself in a large variety of styles, decorations, and purposes.

DRAPED GARMENTS

Draped garments were woven materials worn directly from the loom. They were not altered or fitted to the individual wearing the garment.

Maxtlatl The older *maxtlatl* (loincloth) is an example of a draped garment. A long, narrow piece of cloth, the *maxtlatl* was worn by boys and men as an undergarment to shield the genitalia. Wrapped around the lower torso and passed between the legs, the ends were then tied at the waist. Two different styles of tying the ends served different purposes. The ends could be tied in front with a distinctive knot; this served a daily, secular, and functional pur-

13.7 *Attire of Aztec men: (left to right) the* maxtlatl, tilmati, *hip cloth, and a netted* tilmati (Fonda Portales)

pose. The ends could also be tied so that one end fell in front, over the genitalia, and the other end fell in back, over the buttocks. This style was reserved for deities and ritual ceremonies and was probably the more archaic of the two styles.

Earning the right to wear the *maxtlatl* was a rite of passage for Aztec teenage boys. Aztec tradition did not expect boys under the age of 13 to wear the undergarment; younger boys wore a small cloak tied at the shoulder. But after the age of 12, boys wore the *maxtlatl*, the most important piece of the male wardrobe. All men regardless of class or rank wore the undergarment. According to Sahagún's informants, to be without a *maxtlatl* was to be considered uncivilized. While the *maxtlatl* was a fairly plain garment, it could be decorated with embroidered designs at the ends to show the owner's class.

Hip Cloth The hip cloth is another example of a draped garment, though its presence was not as prevalent as the *maxtlatl*'s. It consisted of a square piece of cloth, folded to make a triangular shape. Modern examples of the hip cloths worn by the Tarahumara Indians of Chihuahua, northern Mexico, lead scholars to speculate that the Aztec used the same dimensions—approximately 101 by 76 centimeter (40 by 30 inches). Traditionally tied at the right side of the waist, it was worn over the *maxtlatl*. While little is known about its functional purpose, it was worn by all men of all classes and probably functioned to further delineate the upper classes from the lower classes by the complexity of designed motifs.

Tilmatli* and *Quachtli The *tilmatli* was also a draped garment and allowed the Aztec male individual the most opportunity for displaying wealth, status, and rank. The *tilmatli* was a mantle that acted as a cape or cloak worn around the shoulders and the entire individual's figure; a large *tilmatli* was called a *quachtli* (usually made of cotton). In the winter, a duck-feathered mantle provided warmth.

As anthropologist Andrea Ludden points out, when the Aztec male sat on the ground, he pulled the *tilmatli* around his shoulders to cover his body and legs. Depending on the owner's class, it was tied either over the right shoulder (commoner) or in front so that the knot lay over the breastplate (noble). Typically, the *tilmatli* and the *quachtli* were worn as garments; however, during the winter, these garments covered beds in the household. Each commoner owned two or three; nobles probably owned many more. The importance of the *tilmatli* to the Aztec wardrobe proved so vital that this garment was traded as currency. Slaves could be bought for 30 *quachtli*; slaves who could sing and dance could be bought for 40 *quachtli*.

The Aztec government dictated rigid laws regarding how the *tilmatli* could be worn. Commoners could only wear the *tilmatli* to their knees; warriors could wear the *tilmatli* to their ankles only if they had wounded their legs in battle and needed to protect themselves from further harm. Otherwise, noblemen and rulers alone could wear the *tilmatli* to their ankles.

Ornamental Distinctions Sahagún writes of several different designs covering the mantles he saw: whirlpools, turkeys, small faces, twisted weaves, stepped frets, jaguars, hummingbirds, and shells. Each of the 12 great lords and (11 *tlatoque* and the *cihuacoatl*) each minor lord of the Aztec Empire wore distinguishing designs on their mantles. Only Motecuhzoma II, the *huey tlatoani*, could wear the *xiuhtilmatli*, or "turquoise cloak," for example. When the Spaniards conquered the Aztec, the artistry of the *tilmatli* so impressed them they sent examples of double-faced mantles to Spain. Soldiers were expected to earn the right to wear such beautiful *cihuacoatl* designs on their mantles. Accounts of Motecuhzoma II report that he rewarded a warrior's first capture in battle with an orange *tilmatli* with a striped border and scorpion design. A soldier with two captures was rewarded with an orange-bordered mantle. Three captures earned a soldier a *tilmatli* with an *ehecatl* design (sectioned conch shell), and four captures earned a soldier the coveted *nacazminqui* cloak. In Tlatelolco, only soldiers successful on the battlefield were allowed to buy the sumptuous cloaks in the market, and a popular punishment for a nobleman in this city was to be forced to wear the *tilmatli* of the commoner, the weak-hearted man, that was made of *ixtle* (maguey fiber). This punishment was possibly more humiliating than death.

Sahagún also describes the *tilmatli* being smeared with corn dough and allowed to dry, making the mantle stiff and inflexible. The *tilmatli* was then burnished to a high polish and worn. This type of *tilmatli* was not practical for daily life and probably served ceremonial purposes only.

Cueitl The last style of a draped garment is the *cueitl*, a skirt wrapped around the hips with one end

13.8 Attire of an Aztec noblewoman, consisting of cueitl *(skirt) and a* huipilli *(tunic).* (Fonda Portales)

overlapping the other and secured by a beltlike strap. All Aztec women wore the *cueitl*. Noblewomen wore the *cueitl* together with a *huipilli* (tunic). Again, color and design indicated class and rank. A lord's wife wore an opulently woven *cueitl* with feathers and striking designs such as birds' gizzards, hearts, spirals, and leaves. A priestess, young or old, wore a pristine white *cueitl*. The commoner or slave wore a *cueitl* of *maguey* fibers with very little design. A *cueitl* serving ritual purposes could be made of coyote pelts, snakeskin, or jaguar skins.

While the *cueitl* distinguished classes and ranks, it also indicated age. Girls 11 years and younger wore an unadorned *cueitl* and an unevenly hemmed *huipilli* of maguey cloth for the commoners and cotton for the noble girls. At 14, when a girl became a woman, she earned the right to wear the bordered and completely hemmed *cueitl* and, if noble, the *huipilli* of her female elders.

SLIP-ON GARMENTS

Slip-on garments slipped over the head through a neck hole and hung from the shoulders. Characteristically, these garments did not have underarm seams. There is only one extant example of the slip-on garment in Aztec attire.

Quechquemitl The *quechquemitl* was made from two pieces of rectangular material. The word *quechquemitl* is derivative of the words *quechtli*, which means "neck," and *quemi*, which means "to put on a mantle." The etymology of the word sheds light on the appearance of the garment. When the two rectangular pieces were joined at the middle and sewn together, they formed a V-shaped garment with a neck hole at the top, which slipped on over the *tilmatli*. When worn, the points of the *quechquemitl* turned to the front and back of the figure, and gave the garment a triangular shape.

In the codices, the *quechquemitl* is depicted only in ritual contexts and is therefore presumed to have had no secular uses. It is also seen in the codices in connection to three fertility goddesses: Chalchiuhtlicue, who wears the *quechquemitl* bordered by tassels; Mayahuel, who wears the *quechquemitl* over a calf-length *huipilli*; and Ixnextli, the earth-mother goddess of flowers, pleasure, and lust, who

wears the *quechquemitl* without a *huipilli*, to expose her fecund breasts. In each depiction, the *quechquemitl* carries overt connotations of fertility. Only one codex, the *Codex Borbonicus*, depicts a man wearing the slip-on garment. He is pictured at a harvest-festival ceremony. He wears the *quechquemitl* over a *cueitl* and the flayed skin of a sacrificed deity impersonator.

OPEN SEWN GARMENTS

Open sewn garments join together panels of material and, though sleeveless, include underarm seams. These garments were worn open or fastened. There are two examples of this kind of garment in the Aztec costume repertoire—the *ichcahuipilli* and the *xicolli*.

Ichcahuipilli The word *ichcahuipilli* derives from two words: *ichcatl*, meaning "cotton," and *huipilli*, a woman's closed sewn garment. Since it served a military purpose, the *ichcahuipilli* was worn exclusively by soldiers. Quilted and stuffed with feathers and cotton batting, the *ichcahuipilli* formed a jacketlike armor that could stop arrows from penetrating the wearer's torso (see figure 5.9). The illustrations in the *Codex Azcatitlan* depict cloth covering the shoulders of the figures wearing the *ichcahuipilli*; however, the garment was sleeveless, and wide cloth panels hung over the shoulder and upper arm rather than forming a sleeve enclosure. The illustrations in the *Codex Telleriano-Remensis* show that the *ichcahuipilli* fell to the upper thigh, allowing the *maxtlatl* to be seen, and fit closely to the waist and hips. The *ichcahuipilli* ended in a feathered skirt, but the jacket of armor was also known to be bordered in leather.

Xicolli The *xicolli* was also a sleeveless jacket and was decorated with fringes at the bottom, but it was a ceremonial garment connected with the tobacco pouch, the incense bag, and incense burner. Sahagún associated the *xicolli* with seven stations: idols, gods, deity impersonators, merchants and their sacrificial slaves, pole decorators, priests in the sacrificial ritual, and aristocrats. The *xicolli* was a godly jacket; nevertheless, commoners were allowed to wear the *xicolli* when in a position mandated by officials. For instance, the *achcacauhtin*, or executioners, wore a *xicolli* or a cord jacket made of agave fiber or yucca rope. It was not the luxurious jacket of the aristocracy, but it designated the wearer as one bound to the business of the aristocracy.

CLOSED SEWN GARMENTS

Closed sewn garments are similar to open sewn garments in that they join together panels of material and include underarm seams. Closed sewn garments, however, have no open front; hence, fasteners are not necessary.

Closed *Ichcahuipilli* The closed *ichcahuipilli* was another garment worn exclusively by the warrior for the purpose of protecting himself in battle. There were two styles of this garment: an undecorated one that fell to the top of the thigh and a decorated one that flared as it fell to the middle thigh. Each was quilted, a pattern depicted in the codices by hatchmarks. The strength of the closed *ichcahuipilli* to safeguard the warrior from impending arrows so impressed the Spanish conquerors that they adopted the garment for their own use. They recognized that the Aztec garment provided better protection than the metal mail of the Spaniards (see chapter 5).

Ehuatl The *ehuatl* was a tunic much like the *ichcahuipilli*, except that it was not padded (see figure 5.10). The *ehuatl* was worn as an overgarment, and Sahagún describes the *ehuatl* as a type of human skin; Molina describes the *ehuatl* as the peeling from a fruit. This covering was fashioned entirely with feathered material and ended in a feathered skirt or border; the colors of the feathers—blue, yellow, white, dark violet, and red—depended on the rank of the soldier, captain, or lord. Kings reserved the right to wear the red feathers of the spoonbill.

Huipilli A tunic of sorts, the *huipilli* fell to the space between the hips and upper thigh. It was used only by upper-class Aztec women; lower-class women left their breasts uncovered. The *huipilli* was such a practical style that it still exists in areas of Latin America today. All upper-class Aztec women wore the *huipilli*, and together with the *cueitl*, it provided a complementary staple to the feminine wardrobe. The *huipilli* was identified by the rectangular shapes at the back and on the front of the piece below the V-necked opening, each rectangle functioning to strengthen the neck aperture from ripping through repeated use. Women spun the underside fur of rabbit into fine, silky thread (*tochomitl*), with which they elaborately embroidered the *huipilli* with such common motifs as the duck, parrot feather, and flower.

LIMB-ENCASING GARMENTS

There was only one garment worn by the Aztec people that included sleeves and trouser legs. It was called the *tlahuiztli*.

Tlahuiztli The *tlahuiztli* is the only example of a limb-encasing garment in the Aztec wardrobe, and it was worn exclusively by warriors over the *ichcahuipilli* and under the *maxtlatl*. This piece of clothing reflected rank and status on the battlefield (see figure 5.9). Costumes could represent natural themes, such as the starry sky or the flames of a fire, or they could represent animals important to Aztec mythology, such as the coyote and the jaguar. Depending on rank and success, the costumes could also represent death demons or gods such as Xipe Totec, Teteoinnan, Xochiquetzal, Chantico (goddess of the hearth), and the pulque deities.

Like the *tilmatli*, soldiers could earn their *tlahuiztli* by capturing prisoners during battle. Two captured prisoners earned a soldier the Cuoctlan warrior costume; three prisoners earned the warrior a butterfly device and the Cuoctlan warrior costume. Both priests and soldiers could earn the coveted jaguar costume and the *tlahuiztli* costume with a feathered staff by capturing four and five prisoners, respectively.

The word *tlahuiztli* is understood by Berdan and Anawalt to include only the entirely feathered bodysuit. Other scholars understand the word *tlahuiztli* to include the bodysuit, the arms carried by the warrior, and the headdress complementing the feathered garment. For example, if the limb-encasing garment represented a jaguar, it was oftentimes accompanied by a headdress representing the jaguar's head, complete with jaws and facial features. Sometimes the limb-encasing garment was worn without a headdress but instead with a ladder-device insignia strapped to the back of the soldier (see chapter 5).

SHOES

Most of the Aztec population walked barefoot. The right to wear shoes was reserved for the upper class and successful warriors. The upper class wore sandals, *cactli*, with a heel piece and interlacing straps. The warrior's straps formed a crude greave (shin shield), or *cozehuatl*. Motecuhzoma II wore *cactli* decorated with jewels and precious stones. The Mexican Indians of today wear *huaraches*, which are a continuity of these Aztec sandals.

Personal Hygiene

Aztec women lived by an Aztec standard of beauty. Women were taught to wear makeup and face paint moderately. Some Mesoamerican women wore red paint around their mouths; only promiscuous women used makeup and face paint excessively. Aztec women were also taught to dress well and to wash themselves and their clothes every day, and by these gestures, they would earn their husband's love. Women got ready for the day by looking into their mirrors made of obsidian or pyrites, by cleaning their mouth, and by washing their face and hands. It is said that when they were done preparing themselves, they looked like flowers.

Cleanliness was one of the most cherished virtues of Aztec society for all citizens, not just women. The Aztec used the fruit of the *copalxocotl* (called the "soap tree" by the Spaniards) and the root of the *Saponaria americana* for soap. These soaps were used to wash the body and to clean the laundry. Most people bathed often, and some bathed every day. It has been documented that Motecuhzoma bathed twice a day. However, not all of the people were very clean all of the time. Certain priests did not wash their hair so that the blood of sacrifices stayed in their long matted hair. Also merchants vowed not to bathe until they returned from a long, dangerous expedition. During the month Atemoztli, as penance, people did not use soap.

Women wore their hair loosely. Only a few women had their teeth dyed red with cochineal. They used a yellow cream called *axin* on their faces. Then they applied perfume with an odoriferous censer.

Hairstyles

Hairstyles, like the garments the Aztec wore, identified the class, age, and status of the wearer. The average male commoner wore his hair short (to the middle of the neck), with short bangs. Distinguished men—priests, warriors, teachers—wore different hairstyles marking their professions and status. The priest, *teopixqui*, wore his hair long, tied back with a white ribbon, and covered in black soot. From the time novitiates entered the *calmecac*, they began to grow and soot their hair, which easily grew to their knees throughout their education.

Before young boys began their education at either the *calmecac* or the *telpochcalli*, they were completely shorn. At the age of 10, they were allowed to grow a tuft of hair at the nape of the neck. When the boys had proven themselves successful on the battlefield, they were allowed to cut away the tuft and wear the hairstyle of the warrior. Older boys who still wore a tuft at the back of their heads were endlessly teased by classmates and, worse still, by girls. All warriors aspired to be allowed to wear the Tequihua warrior hairstyle, the elite *temillotl*, which was also worn by the merchant deity Yacatecuhtli. This hairstyle left the frontal section of the scalp pulled up into a columnar shape. Male "masters of youth" (*telpochtlato*) wore their hair long and shaved at the temples, and wore the identifying forked, white heron feather in their hair.

Women had more diverse hairstyles. Mothers, for example, as mature female adults wore their hair divided at the nape of the neck, tied with a cord, and drawn up toward the crown of the head so that the bulk of the hair draped at the nape. The ends were secured to the top of the head in such a way that the ends created tufts peeking from the crown of the head. Sahagún specified that some women shaved their completely, while others dyed their hair with "a black mud or a green herb called *xiuhquílitl* that produced a purple shining in the hair" (1951–69: 8, ch. 15).

Accoutrements

In his first letters to the king of Spain, Hernán Cortés wrote much about the appearances of the Aztec. He described them as people of medium height and well-proportioned bodies and features. He thought their ornamentation to be strange and deforming and described their colorful clothing motifs to be garish gash marks. Cortés's description reveals a Spanish colonist's perspective rooted in the belief that the Aztec people lived uncivilized lives and needed to be converted to Catholicism. Nevertheless, Cortés's detailed descriptions give us a vivid image of how the Aztec chose to decorate their bodies.

PIERCINGS

Though each province differed in its customs, several ornamentations were common throughout the empire. Pierced ears ornamented with large circular disks and pierced nostrils decorated with precious, mirrorlike stones seemed to be popular methods of adorning the body. Cortés also mentioned that the Aztec incised the middle of the lower lip to the gumline and hung gold and stone objects from each part, which pulled the lip downward.

Archaeological and scholarly evidence supports the observations in Cortés's accounts of the Aztec. The earplug, *nocochtli*, a large disk that opened a space in the earlobe, was commonly worn by both men and women. Priests and rulers reserved the right to wear the lip plugs Cortés spoke of, and only powerful men, such as Motecuhzoma II, wore the nostril ring, or staff, which pierced and hung from the septum.

MAKEUP

Makeup, as well as facial piercings, ornamented the Aztec visage. Because women were expected to be clean and chaste, they generally wore little makeup. Otomí women stained their teeth black and tattooed their breasts and arms, but this does not seem to have been a popular accent for most Aztec women. Yellow clay called *tecozahuitl* and a yellow-tinted body makeup known as *axin* were used to cover the limbs and face of Aztec women. Illustrations in various codices show women painted with yellow ocher and bitumen. During the marriage ceremony, the Aztec woman wore makeup around her mouth. But only the courtesan regularly wore rouge and lipstain. She also stained her teeth red.

Priests and the male *telpochcalli* instructors wore black body paint from the soot of resinous wood. Priests were also distinguished by a smear of blood in front of the ear. This smear suggests that priests performed a ritual of autosacrifice, whereby they would cut themselves with maguey spines to draw blood. Masters of Youth also used another black body paint of lighter tones around their eyes, mouth, and nose. Together with this makeup, the *telpochtlato* could be identified by a snail-shell necklace and net cape, vestiges of Telpochtli, a divine aspect of Tezcatlipoca.

ROYAL COURT LIFE

The minutiae of wardrobe, hairstyle, jewelry, and education all served to distinguish one level from another in the Aztec hierarchy. The details of the Aztec home proved no different. While the majority of the Aztec population struggled to live well, the ruling class enjoyed a life of ease and opulence.

Furniture

Most Aztec families possessed the same commodities. The common Aztec home had sparse furnishings, such as mats to sleep on (often substituted by the poor with platforms of dirt) and a *petlacalli*, a chest to store clothes. Noble homes may have had a curtain surrounding the sleeping mat (*petlatl*), a wooden screen to deflect heat from the fire, and frescos or animal skins decorating the walls. But the simple fixtures of a home remained the same throughout society—with the exception of the emperor.

Chroniclers witnessed Motecuhzoma II sitting on an *icpalli*, a high-backed, cushioned wood chair without legs or feet (see figure 4.1). The *icpalli* was so cherished by the emperor that Cuauhtitlan, a town known for making these seats, paid 4,000 of them in tribute to the state every year. Chroniclers also noted that Motecuhzoma ate at a table covered with a white tablecloth and white napkins, a comfort most Aztec did not have. The presence of a dining table suggests that Motecuhzoma's palace contained a reserved dining room for meals. Most Aztec common homes contained no dining room, and the commoners ate anywhere they could.

The Royal Residence

Furnishings alone, however, did not separate the common class from the ruling class. As mandated by law, common houses could be only one story high; noble houses could be built with two stories. Also, common Aztec families inhabited homes possessing at most two or three rooms, including the room occupied by the hearth. These rooms revolved around a simple inner courtyard. The ruling class, conversely, owned homes possessing many rooms: King Nezahualcoyotl's home in Tetzcoco contained 300 rooms, some of which served as administrative accommodations and offices.

ROYAL GARDENS AND ZOOS

The grand-sized palaces characteristically integrated lush gardens with fountains, ponds, canals, and elaborate irrigation systems capable of sustaining the gardens' vibrancy. A planted forest of 2,000 pine trees adorned the palace grounds at Tetzcoco. Nezahualcoyotl's wealth also supported another palace in Tetzcotzinco, which is famous for the formidable aqueduct that carried water from the mountains down to the gardens growing flowers imported from several regions of the Empire. Cut-rock formations splashed the falling water into showering cascades that watered the gardens. Several other cut-rock formations creating pools for royal bathers (see chapter 9). Naturally, Motecuhzoma II built lavish gardens as well. In Oaxtepec, he opened a tropical garden. To make sure that the garden was well tended, he transplanted 40 families from the tropical regions and supported them while they nurtured his garden.

All Aztec people shared a love for fragrant flowers and singing birds, but the royal class enjoyed an especially privileged luxury—the zoo. Nezahualcoyotl's palace at Tetzcoco showcased an extensive zoo complete with the birds, reptiles, and animals of Mesoamerica. It also included an exhibition of fish from lakes, rivers, and the seas. This demonstrative display of wealth even showcased creatures found only beyond the reaches of Mesoamerica: These were represented in gold.

Motecuhzoma II also kept animals in his palaces. Informers witnessed large jars housing hissing snakes and recounted tales of roaring lions and tigers, howling wolves and foxes, and singing birds. Motecuhzoma and his administrators possessed the wealth to demonstrate Aztec pride in the landscape of Anahuac.

Royal palaces also provided great protection from invasion and thievery. Axayacatl's palace had false walls that acted as vaults for expensive belongings. Another security method involved labyrinthine mazes. Motecuhzoma II was known to bathe two and three times a day at the center of the maze in his palace at Tenochtitlan, careful to be seen by no one. Commoners, who also bathed on a daily basis, knew little or nothing about this kind of luxury and privacy.

ROYAL FEASTING

Meals in Motecuhzoma's palace were bountiful. Daily, servants served 300 dishes to Motecuhzoma alone. After he ate, another 1,000 dishes fed the palace lords, administrators, priests, servants, and visitors. Meat dishes that commoners could not afford were spread on his table, including partridge, pheasant, and wild boar. Motecuhzoma ate small portions of fruit, though lavish plates were placed before him, a further testament of his excessive wealth. After his meal, he enjoyed a cacao drink (chocolate) and a pipe with tobacco before he retired for the evening. Other rulers probably enjoyed the same comforts, though not to the same degree of excess. Sumptuous meals such as frogs in pimento sauce, newt (*axolotl*), white fish with red peppers and tomatoes, winged ants, crabs, and oysters were reserved for the noble class and constituted the average royal meal.

Banquets provided an exceptionally lavish form of royal entertainment. Banquets began at midnight, and as guests arrived, they consumed *teonanacatl* (food of the gods) and hallucinogenic mushrooms, and began to sing and dance and have nightmarish visions. Under this influence, guests would eat throughout the early morning. After dining, they would drink *cacao*, smoke elaborately decorated pipes made of reed or baked clay, and share their visions. Tobacco seems to have been an indulgence only affordable by the royals.

All Aztec people valued cleanliness, but Motecuhzoma was afforded the opportunity and resources to make cleanliness a luxury as well as a virtue. Before and after a meal, Motecuhzoma was known to wash his hands in small finger bowls, *xicalle*, served by four servants. Noble classes probably followed his example.

THE ROYAL HUNT

The nobility was afforded the luxury of time to hunt. Commoners resorted to hunting to feed their families; the noble and warrior class hunted exclusively for sport. Stories about Motecuhzoma tell of him and an entourage of nobles traveling to his palace in Atlacuihuayan to hunt. Alone in silence, Motecuhzoma would shoot birds in the palace gardens using the traditional blowpipe with baked-clay balls for ammunition.

Each year during Quecholli, the 14th month of the Aztec calendar, a grand expedition in honor of Mixcoatl, the god of hunting, and Huitzilopochtli, the god of war, diverted the attention of the warriors. Darts and arrows were ceremonially produced, and many slaves were sacrificed. On the 10th day of this month, all of the warriors from Tenochtitlan and Tlatelolco traveled to the forested hills of Zacatepetl for a night of camping. They prepared their shelter from the branches of nearby trees, and at dawn, they rose and arranged themselves in a line to drive hares and rabbits, deer and coyotes from the forest. Then the warriors would hunt the frightened animals with bows and arrows. The emperor showered those who killed deer or coyote with gifts, and in the evening, the warriors returned home shouldering the heads of the animals they killed as trophies.

FOOD AND DRINK

Aztec commoners ate only two meals—one in the mid-morning after working for a few hours, and one in the mid-afternoon, when the sun was hottest. The common Aztec ate only two or three tortillas and a serving of beans at each meal. One might also partake of a nighttime snack of amaranth gruel. Despite the meager commoner's diet, Aztec cuisine was varied for the noble. Accounts of the eclectic culinary dishes reveal a great amount of creativity and invention with scarce resources.

Maguey

The maguey plant refers to several closely related species of the genus *Agave*, which grows at 5,940 feet (1,800 meters) above sea level or higher in central Mexico. The maguey plant supplied the Aztec with both fiber for clothing and rope and the juice for popular drinks such as the fermented *octli*, today called pulque, and unfermented *aguamiel*. Though archaeologists to date have not found pulque workshops on archaeological sites, obsidian blades covered with sap resin have been found. These blades are extensively dispersed throughout Aztec sites and give insight into how Aztecs produced pulque, a drink still consumed by Mexican peasants today. Witnessed by the royal physician Francisco Hernández, pulque production was a laborious process that is performed today in the same fashion as that of Aztec predecessors.

Once the maguey had grown to maturity, a cavity was carved in the center of the plant and scraped with obsidian blades. Scraping the cavity stimulated the flow of sap, and for several weeks to six months, this action was performed two or three times daily. The sap gathered in the center cavity was harvested by the maguey farmer by sucking it into a gourd.

The sap was taken back to the pulque workshop, transferred to ceramic jars, and then left to ferment. Such hard work was not without significant benefit: One maguey plant could produce two to four liters (about two to four quarts) of sap daily.

ALCOHOL CONSUMPTION

Octli was the only alcoholic drink of the Aztec. The alcoholic content of the spirit was, and is still today, similar to that of beer and wine—3.2 to 5 percent. However, it was illegal for the Aztec citizen to consume the drink to drunkenness. This indulgence was granted only to the elderly as a reward for long life.

Pulque and drunkenness were associated with the House of Two Rabbit, and a drunk person was said to be like a rabbit. At the feast of Cuextecatl, a ceremonial five-fold pulque was served in observance of the fertility deity Ometochtli and the maguey goddess Mayahuel. This feast recalled the mythical origin of *octli*.

Pulque was by no means the only product of the versatile maguey plant. Hernández wrote that it also yielded honey, vinegar, and sugar.

Maize

Maize was the most important staple of the Aztec diet and was served at every meal in a variety of forms, including the *tlaxcalli*, or tortilla (flat maize bread); *tamalli*, or tamale (steamed corn dough stuffed with meat); *atolli*, or atole (fine maize-flour water flavored with chilies or fruits); *pozolli*, or pozole (stew containing large maize kernels); and *elotl*, or *elote* (corn on the cob). It claimed this seat of honor for diverse reasons. First, maize grew in many varieties. Second, maize adapted to many climates and soil types, and could grow almost anywhere within the Aztec's imperial boundaries. Finally, and most important, maize yielded one of the highest caloric crops and supplied among the highest amounts of protein of the world's major food crops. Maize was of such importance to the Aztec diet that the plant had its own deities—Cinteotl (male) and Chicomecoatl and Xilonen (female). The midsummer festival Huey Tecuilhuitl celebrated and honored the young maize plant. Maize was also

used as a metaphor, the favored literary device of the Aztec poet. Sahagún reports that to honor someone, speakers would say that that person had reached the year of the maize ear.

PREPARATION OF MAIZE RECIPES

Before maize could be processed into nutritionally sound foods, the kernels needed to be shorn from the cob and soaked in an alkaline solution of water, limestone, and a source of calcium hydrochloride called *nixtamal*. To make tortillas, Aztec women ground the kernels into a flour on a *metlatl*, or metate (grinding stone), and shaped the dough into flat, thin circular pieces of bread. These tortillas were then cooked on a *comalli*, or *comal* (clay griddle) and served fresh or stored for later meals.

The presence of the tortilla in several rituals testifies to its significance within Aztec culture. Durán recounts that unmarried girls dedicated to the temple carried offerings of tortillas in ceremonial bowls to the temple at dawn. He also describes a custom during the feast of Tlacaxipehualiztli consisting of people wearing twisted honey tortillas and dancing all day. Sahagún recounts that a tortilla replaced the sacrificial blade in simulation sacrifices. He also witnessed dancing priests wearing S-shaped tortillas. Even in superstition, the tortilla played a role; if a woman's tortilla folded on itself on the *comalli*, she would say that a visitor coming to see her had kicked it over to signal her arrival. The tortilla provided more than just physical sustenance.

A more ancient maize-based creation was the *tamalli*. A grainy dough, shaped into balls, formed the body of the tamale, which could also be formed into pointed, rolled, and adobe shapes. Stuffed with beans—second only to maize in the Aztec diet and served at every meal—or chilies, the dough was then wrapped in maize leaves and steamed in a large clay pot. Variations of the tamale included fillings of amaranth seeds, maize flowers, honey, beeswax, turkey eggs, and cherries. Both the tortilla and the tamale, in different variations, are still eaten today.

Like the tortilla, the tamale also played a significant cultural role in Aztec communities, and Aztec residents acknowledged its importance in the feast of Atamalcualiztli (Eating of Water Tamales). Every eight years, in this seven-day observance, Aztecs ate

13.9 Cultivation of maize and preparation of corn-based foods, including tortillas, in a mural by Diego Rivera, National Palace, Mexico City (Fernando González y González)

cheese in the markets of Tlatelolco and Tenochtitlan. But these were not the only aquatic goods consumed by the Aztec. Sahagún writes that tadpoles, frogs, and *tentnonmichin* (thick, large-mouthed fish) were also eaten. *Axolotl* newts and *acocilin* (shrimplike crustaceans) offered variety to the diet as well.

Cacao was a popular drink among the royal classes and was a valuable commodity; 100 cacao beans could buy a small mantle. To prepare the beans for drinking, first they would be ground and soaked while being filtered. A frothy head would form on the surface; later this would be discarded. Then water would be added to make a bitter drink. The chocolate drink was so bitter that an assortment of additives would be used to flavor it: flowers, vanilla, honey, and even chile tamed the bitterness of the cacao bean and changed the color of the chocolate drink from white to colors ranging from red and orange to black.

plain tamales steamed in water; lime, ash, flavoring, chilies, and peppers were not included in the recipe. This pure method of cooking the tamales ritually allowed the maize a moment of freedom from the tortures of being worked and seasoned.

Women also ground maize kernels to make *pinole*, or gruel, in a variety of recipes—gruel with honey, with honey and chilies, and with honey, fish, and amaranth seeds.

Culinary Sundries

Aztec commoners did not live by maize and beans alone. Tomatoes, avocados, and several varieties of squash presented more choices at a meal. Chili peppers were used to flavor foods and were so vital to the Aztec meal that fasting often meant forsaking chilies alone. Ants, grasshoppers, maguey worms, and *jumil* bugs, all available in large quantities, provided protein. Commoners gathered *tequitlatl* (blue-green spirulina algae) in large fine nets to provide large harvests of protein. Bernal Díaz del Castillo described the blue-green algae sold as little cakes that tasted like

Fruits

The *nopalli*, or nopal (prickly pear cactus), served as a popular vegetable in the Aztec diet, and Sahagún reported on 13 different varieties in his *Florentine Codex*. He described the nopal plant as having wide, green branches and a smooth, though thorny, surface that excreted a saplike liquid. The cactus's succulent fruit, the *nochtli*, or tuna, had a fine and flavorful texture. This fruit, which could be eaten cooked or raw, provided a filling for tamales and was often served as a dessert, though always in moderation. Because the nopal cactus grew throughout Mexico, all Aztec were able to take pleasure in the *nochtli* fruit; however, only the royal classes enjoyed the more exotic varieties of white, green, and orange *nochtli*. *Quahcamotli* and *camotli* (sweet potatoes); *cimatl*, a cylindrical or balllike twisted tree root that would cause vomiting and diarrhea if eaten raw; and *atzamatzamolli*, a bulbous sea plant with white blossoms, were also eaten as fruit.

Animal Foods

Though not a strictly vegetarian society, the Aztec ate mostly from plants that grew in their landscape.

Partly due to large population growth and partly due to the lack of many domesticated animals, animal foods were not in significant reserve. Among the domesticated animals were dogs, turkeys (*uexolotl*), which provided both eggs and meat, and the muscory duck. Archaeologists have found quantities of fish, white-tailed deer, cotton-tailed rabbit, iguana, dog, and turkey bones in trash deposits, although these finds were not in high, dense concentrations. The upper echelon's diet included more variety in animal foods. Rabbit, possum, deer, crane, goose, quail, and eagle meat added variety to the Aztec diet, but these were probably luxuries enjoyed predominantly by the upper class.

Nutrition

Throughout studies of Aztec culture, the question of nutrition has arisen. Was the Aztec diet nutritionally sufficient to sustain a population for hundreds of years, and if not, did malnutrition contribute to the mass destruction of the Aztec people by the Spanish colonists? It has long been a popular myth that the Aztec engaged in cannibalism in order to meet their dietary and nutritional needs. The truth is that cannibalism existed only in a very limited ritual context (see chapter 6). Since animal proteins were scarce and populations exceeded environmental supplies, cannibalism seemed a reasonable answer to a nutritionally deficient diet; however, modern scholarship reduces this theory of Aztec cannibalism to mere imaginations of savagery and bloodlust. In fact, the Aztec knew much more about nutrition than has been previously discussed and subsisted on foods that met their caloric and protein needs.

In order for a food to be of nutritional value, it must include all of the 11 essential amino acids. Perhaps by accident, the Aztec created an evolved diet to meet their nutritional needs. Maize, though high in protein, lacks lysine and tryptophan. When Aztec farmers harvested maize, they left it to dry in the fields. To soften the kernels later for grinding, the Aztec soaked the kernels in a water and limestone mixture (*nixtamal*). The alkaline combination freed the tryptophan and added calcium. It also

added a distinct flavor that became traditional, and without it, tortillas did not taste the way the Aztec expected them to. Beans, high in lysine, when eaten with maize soaked in the alkaline solution, made a nutritionally sound meal. These two foods provided the cultural staples of the Aztec diet, without animal proteins. Chilies provided iron, riboflavin, niacin, and vitamin A, and *chia* (salvia) provided calcium and phosphorous.

Without textual documentation, it is impossible to know whether the Aztec were knowledgeable about the biological minutiae of nutrition. However, because the Aztec diet gave visible results of healthiness, it easily became a cultural fixture.

The largest question regarding the issue of nutrition lies in how drought, weather conditions such as rainfall and frost, locust and rodent plagues, and population affected nutritional needs' being met. Famine occurred regularly throughout the year, especially in June and July, the season between the two harvests. Quickly, the Aztec population exceeded the agricultural supplies of central Mexico: The population in the basin in the late 15th century stood at 1 million people. Low rainfall and drought especially devastated the overpopulated civilization in 1450, when a four-year drought resulted in a disastrous famine. Famine, rather than malnutrition, proved to be fatal for Aztec populations.

MUSIC AND DANCE

Sacred Hymns

The Nahua repertoire of songs granted the Aztec people hope in a world of suffering and inspired them to live correctly in the face of death. In 1558, a group of Aztec presented Fray Bernardino de Sahagún with a compilation of 20 sacred hymns, the Teocuicatl. The sacred hymns were sung or recited in reverence to the most powerful and most popular deities—Ometeotl, Tlaloc, Huitzilopochtli, and Tezcatlipoca, the *ipalnemoani*

(Giver of Life). The sacred hymns also celebrated the mighty deeds of the rulers. In one of the most famous sacred hymns, the Giver of Life is praised for bringing song to Earth. Song bestows color, nature, and shade to those who live on Earth, making life a painting of flowers and protection. Song, in the same sacred hymn, is also attributed to destroying friendship and brotherhood. The Giver of Life, Tezcatlipoca, acted as both creator and destroyer (see #13 and #17 in the appendix "Aztec Poems").

Sung at ritual feasts, these sacred hymns, according to Miguel León-Portilla, offered Aztecs an opportunity to honor the gods, supplicate them for rain, corn, and success in battle, and express gratitude. These sacred hymns were so important that special care was taken to teach and learn them. Professional singers and dancers trained at the *calmecac*, the local temple school. The *tlarizcatzon*, a special temple caretaker, acted as teacher of the sacred hymns, and he protected the sacred hymns from those who might employ them to do harm.

Young children of every class status, both boys and girls between the ages of 12 and 15, attended school to learn the traditional songs. Elderly men and women taught the children in the house of song, the *cuicacalli* attached to every community's temple. Here, an hour before sunset, students gathered together for sessions of singing, dancing, and recitation to learn the proper songs and orations for every major ceremony in the Aztec calendar. By memorizing the traditional ceremonial songs, the young were indoctrinated with Aztec myths of the origin of the cosmos, the migrations of the ancestors, and the role of the mortals in the universe. Through their education, students learned about their place in the symbolic world and in their spiritual culture.

Cantares

Another popular genre of songs was that of the *cantares*, dubbed by linguist and folklorist John Bierhorst as the "ghost songs," written between 1520 and 1560. Found in the manuscript *Cantares mexicanos*, these 91 songs constituted the chief source of Aztec poetry. Sung at times of battle, the ghost songs served several purposes. First, they connected the living on Earth to their dead ancestors in the garden of paradise and emboldened warriors for battle. Second, they acted as ritual reenactments of battle, further bolstering the courage of warriors preparing to fight. And finally, within the context of the Spanish conquest, they unified the Mesoamerican Indians against their tormenters and enemies. Since drums, costumes, and dancing accompanied the performances of the ghost songs, they must have been intimidating to foreigners.

Fray Motolinia describes ghost song performances in his *Memoriales*. As he recounts, the ritual performances took place in the city plaza, the palace forecourt, or the inner courtyard of a noble's house, all of which were decorated with artificial flowers and trees. The performances began with costumed dancers in jaguar, eagle, monkey, dog, butterfly, and bird disguises emerging from hidden places and positioning themselves on a mat, which served as a stage. As drummers played, two song leaders started to sing. Within this musical throng, several Indians whistled and signaled the beginning of the dance. The performances lasted for hours; they were the presentations of celestial dances, reflecting a symmetrical cosmology.

The singer of these *cantares* played an important role in the ritual. According to Bierhorst, he metaphysically traveled to a paradisiacal realm under the influence of a shamanic trance and retrieved the songs from the grasp of divine control by weeping. Brought down on stage as fully armored ghosts, these "songs" represented personifications of the supreme spirit. The singer recognized in prayer the symbiotic relationship between himself and the spiritual realm and promised to give in reciprocity sacrificed prisoners of war and, if needed, his own sacrificed body. When payment had been received, when the heart of the sacrificed prisoner had been removed and taken home to be ritually eaten, the song returned to paradise. Crowded with literary devices such as metonymy (for example, a sword representing the warrior), metaphor (a warrior being called a turquoise bracelet), and stacked synonyms (a deity described as god-life-giver), the *cantares* are illustrative of the Aztec passion for literary device. The language of the songs is esoteric, and words such as *bird, flower, song, comrade, heart, hand*, and *prince*, combined with verbs expressing coming, descending, weeping, seeking, and departing, are deep spiritual and poetic metaphors set in the interrelated context of Earth and heaven.

The *cantares* repeatedly refer to themselves as intoxicating narcotics, and it is probable that singers induced a shamanic trance with the use of hallucinogenic drugs. This enabled the singer to weep the songs out of their celestial homes. Weeping suggested the singer's awareness of the brevity and duality of life.

Alva Ixtlilxochitl suggested that kings and rulers wrote the *cantares*, but Juan Bautista de Pomar, a 16th-century mestizo chronicler, wrote that nobles and commoners alike wrote the *cantares* to commemorate the deeds of great kings. But it is important to note that secular poets did not sing the ghost songs in secular circumstances. The performance of these songs necessitated a public or semipublic ritual performed by a required number of participants, instruments, and dancers.

One of the most famous of the ghost songs is the "Beginning of Songs," the "Cuicapeuhcayotl." It is the first song in the first book of the *Cantares mexicanos*. It begins with a singer looking for flowers, meant to symbolize song. He asks the quetzal hummingbirds where he can find the flowers, and they lead him to a valley abounding with flowers. The singer gathers them under his cloak. The song ends with the singer weeping, crying out that the Earth is a place of unhappiness and that goodness lies elsewhere (Bierhorst 1985: 134–137). The song is meant to be a reminder that singers of the ghost songs must be in connection with the supernatural world in order to bring about song.

As Berdan points out, Aztec music was not always somber, as suggested by the sacred hymns and the ghost songs. Songs of youthful, amorous affections balanced the serious nature of the ritual songs (1982: 157).

Musical Instruments

Songs provided an important transmission of cultural ideology; hence, a wide array of instruments existed to accompany the poetic renderings of sound. Instruments such as the flute (*huilacapitztli*) and whistle accompanied the performances of sacramental songs and dances. Instruments made from natural resources—the turtle drum, *ayotl*; the conch, *tecciztli*; the snail horn, *quihquiztli*; and the shell trumpet, *tecciztli*—also complemented the great anthology of musical rituals. A resounding percussion section tremored as musicians beat a variety of percussion instruments: the horizontal log drum, *teponaztli*; the central instrument, the upright skin drum, *huehuetl*; the gong, *tetzilacatl*; and rattles and rattle sticks, *ayacachtli* and *omichicahuaztli*. *Huehuetl* musicians beat the drum with their bare hands, distinguishing themselves from North American Indians, who beat the same drum with sticks. Drums, as well as accompanying ritual performances, led warriors into battle and urged them to fight courageously.

Warned that life is suffering, the Aztec found a variety of means by which to enjoy life: family relations, rituals and elaborate celebrations, and poetry and song. The daily life of the ordinary Aztec citizen was laborious and difficult but ultimately filled with meaning and purpose.

13.10 Group of Aztec musicians with typical instruments, in the Florentine Codex *(Fonda Portales)*

READING

Family

Soustelle 1979: adultery, polygamy, divorce; Sahagún 1951–69, Smith 2003, Soustelle 1979: marriage; Sahagún 1951–69, Soustelle 1979: pregnancy and childbirth.

Women

Soustelle 1979: matchmaker; Sahagún 1951–69, Soustelle 1979, Sullivan 1998: midwife; Sahagún 1951–69, Soustelle 1979: courtesans, women's roles.

Education

Anawalt 1981, Fagan 1997, Smith 2003, Soustelle 1979, Sahagún (1951–69): *calmecac* and *telpochcalli*.

Shamanism and Medicine

Sahagún 1951–69, Smith 2003, Soustelle 1979: shamanism; Sahagún 1951–69, Soustelle 1979: medicinal herbs, narcotics and hallucinogens.

Games

Fagan 1997, Soustelle 1979: *patolli*, gambling; Aguilar-Moreno 2002–03, Carrasco 1998, Dávila and Brady 2004, Fagan 1997, Smith 2003, Soustelle 1979: *ullamaliztli* and *tlachtli*.

Personal Appearance and Attire

Sahagún 1951–69, Anawalt 1981, Ludden 1997, Soustelle 1979: clothing; Anawalt 1981, Soustelle 1979: hairstyles, makeup; Cortés 1986, Anawalt 1981: jewelry.

Royal Court Life

Soustelle 1979: royal banquets, royal furnishings, hunting.

Food and Drink

Smith 2003: nutrition; Berdan and Anawalt 1997, Díaz del Castillo 1963, Fagan 1997, Sahagún 1951–69, Smith 2003, Soustelle 1979: food resources; Berdan and Anawalt 1997, Díaz del Castillo 1963, Smith 2003, Soustelle 1979: maguey plant; Soustelle 1979: tobacco.

Music and Dance

Bierhorst 1985, Nicholson 1959, Sahagún 1951–69: *cantares;* Bierhorst 1985, León-Portilla 1959, 1970, and 1992 (*Fifteen Poets*), Nicholson 1959: sacred hymns; Bierhorst 1985, Smith 2003: musical instruments.

14

THE AZTEC AFTER THE CONQUEST AND TODAY

The Conquest of Mexico

In 1492, Christopher Columbus and his crew, representing the Spanish Crown, first landed on the islands of the Caribbean Sea (West Indies) and established a presence on Hispaniola (now the Dominican Republic and Haiti) and Cuba. Spain later founded colonies on the coasts of Venezuela and Panama. During this time of exploration and colonization, the Spaniards would travel in ships from island to island and to part of what is today the American continent. It was during these navigations that the Indians and the Europeans first made contact and learned of each other's existence.

At the time, the Spanish thought that America, or what they knew to be America, was part of land or islands off the coasts of Asia. The governor of Cuba, Diego Velázquez, had heard of Indians traveling for five or six days by canoes to Cuba from the north and soon learned of additional islands that lay beyond the western end of Cuba. Velázquez became curious as to what lay beyond Cuba, and his curiosity led to a series of expeditions, one of which would change the face of the continent forever.

The First Expedition

In 1517, Francisco Hernández de Córdoba was chosen by Velázquez to head the first expedition. This expedition made contact with the eastern coasts of Mexico in present-day Yucatán as well as in the Campeche regions. Hernández thought that the Maya city of Tulum on the coast of the Yucatán Peninsula was as grand as Seville in Spain. Even though his expedition did not make it to the interior of Yucatán, and though he was fatally wounded in a coastal battle with the Maya, he brought back great treasures of gold and the discovery of rich lands.

Not long after the first expedition, Velázquez began arrangements for a second expedition, one that would be able to pierce into the interior of this newfound territory. The aim of this expedition was more about obtaining personal wealth and prestige than it was about spreading the Christian doctrine and converting the Indians to Catholicism. In this pursuit, Velázquez petitioned the Crown for the title of *adelantado* (pioneering explorer) in the forthcoming discoveries in Yucatán. Like most conquistadores, Velázquez had personal ambitions of becoming rich and prosperous, and although he asked for permission from both the Crown in Spain and the priors of Santo Domingo on Hispaniola, Velázquez began making plans for the expedition before obtaining proper permission.

The Second Expedition

Juan de Grijalva, a nephew of Velázquez's, was chosen to lead the second expedition in 1518. This expedition reached the island of Cozumel and moved up the Gulf of Mexico coast to Veracruz, ending at the mouth of the Pánuco River. It was on the coasts of Veracruz that Grijalva and his crew made contact with the Totonac Indians, the Aztec's main oppositional force. The Totonac were subjects of the Aztec Empire and as such supplied the Aztec with a great wealth of luxurious goods in the form of tribute. The Totonac, unlike the Maya of the Yucatán, greeted the conquistadores warmly and gave them gifts of gold. Certainly they hoped that these bearded strangers would assist them on their own quest against the Aztec.

It was during this time that Motecuhzoma II sent two emissaries to the coast to report back on a rumor he had received about mountains or towers seemingly floating on the sea. To his dismay, his informants returned with the news that the rumor was true; foreign ships had arrived. Motecuhzoma then began preparations to have his two representatives make contact with these strangers at sea and ordered luxurious gifts and food to be brought to them.

Two important events occurred at this point. The Spaniards learned of the great city of Tenochtitlan from the Totonac, and two of Motecuhzoma's representatives made contact with Grijalva and his crew. This was to be the first encounter between the Mexica of Tenochtitlan and the Spanish conquistadores.

The conquistadores, who eventually made their way back to Cuba, reported on the richness of the land, the surplus of gold, and the expanse of the great city of Tenochtitlan. Back in what would later be Mexico, Motecuhzoma waited a year before his next (and final) contact with these strangers.

Hernán Cortés and the Third Expedition

Upon hearing the news of the great empire and wealth, Velázquez began plans for a third expedition. Hernán Cortés, an individual of minor nobility from Extremadura in Spain, was chosen by Velázquez to lead the third and most important expedition to Mexico. Cortés was to explore the shores of Mexico, infiltrate the mainland, and found Spanish territories. In return, he was promised gold and fame.

The official purpose of this expedition was to convert the indigenous population to Catholicism and to bring forth riches for Spain. Cortés was instructed to take control of newfound territories, which were to be placed under the rule of the king of Spain, Charles V. He was to colonize in the name of the Crown of Castile.

CONFLICTS WITH VELÁZQUEZ

Shortly before the expedition was to set sail, the ambitious and powerful Velázquez tried to curtail Cortés's expedition, fearing that Cortés would betray him and become more commanding. Despite Velázquez's opposition, Cortés and his fleet departed; in 1519, they left Cuba for the coast off the Yucatán.

Cortés and his fleet followed the same path that his predecessors had. On his journey to the interior of Mexico, he arrived at Potonchan (today called Champotón), where he was not welcomed. A battle ensued between the Spanish and the Chontal Maya Indians on March 24, 1519, in which the Spanish were victorious and Indian warrior prisoners were integrated into Cortés's army. Numerous battles fol-

14.1 *Tomb of Hernán Cortés in the Church of Jesús, Mexico City* (Fernando González y González)

lowed in which the Spaniards' military might and their use of horses, a foreign creature to the Indians, devastated Indian communities.

THE CONTROVERSY OF MALINCHE

In Potonchan, Cortés met one of the most important assets to his expedition, a noble indigenous woman named Malinali or Malintzin, called Malinche by the Spaniards. She was to become his foremost translator, knowing both Chontal Maya and Nahuatl, the tongue of the Aztec Empire. Malintzin, paired with Gerónimo de Aguilar, a Spaniard who had been shipwrecked and in Maya captivity for eight years and spoke Chontal Maya, became the interpreters that Cortés needed. Thus began a three-way translation from Nahuatl to Chontal to Spanish. After three weeks, Cortés and his men left Potonchan and set sail.

Malinche became Cortés's mistress and was soon christened under the Spanish name of Marina. She quickly learned to speak Spanish with such fluency that Cortés discarded the help of Aguilar, and Malinche became Cortés's only translator. Malinche has been considered by some to be a traitor to the Aztec by siding with the Spaniards. But in aiding the Spaniards, Malinche was protecting her own life and fighting against the Aztec oppressors for the freedom of her own people, who were Veracruz coastal natives, possibly Totonacs or even Tabascans. Malinche had lived among the Chontal Maya as a slave.

THE POWER OF VERACRUZ

On April 22, 1519, Cortés landed on the Gulf coast. It is important to note that Cortés founded the first Spanish city in continental America, which was named Villa Rica de la Vera Cruz, and in a strategic move, he destroyed his ships; this action symbolized Cortés's commitment to the realization of conquering the territory and sent the message that he and his men were resolute to stay. Perhaps more important, the city council of Vera Cruz (today called Veracruz, the major port of Mexico) appointed Cortés as commander and captain general of the expeditionary Spanish forces on behalf of the Crown of Spain. By its decree, Cortés received legitimate power from the Spanish authorities of Vera Cruz without depending on the authority of the governor of Cuba, Diego Velázquez.

ALLIES

As the Spaniards progressed toward the interior, they imposed their Christian doctrine on the native populations, toppled their religious icons, and where possible, recruited and joined forces with Indian allies who were hostile subjects of the Aztec. Among these allies were the Cempoalans and, after a fierce battle, the Tlaxcalans. The Chalca and Tepanec later joined Cortés on his way to the center of the Aztec Empire.

MOTECUHZOMA'S WARNINGS

Motecuhzoma interpreted the coming of these foreign invaders as the possible return of the Feathered Serpent, the Aztec god Quetzalcoatl. The Aztec had a cyclical view of time that coincided with that of their gods. They believed that by observing and interpreting signs, they would be able to predict future events. These signs came in the form of climactic or environmental changes, dreams and visions, and natural phenomena. Extraordinary events in the years before Cortés's arrival filled Motecuhzoma, a priest and deeply religious man, with anxiety. He sought consolation from priests and soothsayers and asked their advice about what the significance of these phenomena could be.

These signs, coupled with the appearance of these foreigners, were interpreted by Motecuhzoma as the prophesied return of Quetzalcoatl, who was to come from the east to reclaim his throne at the ancient city of Tula, the great capital of the Toltec before the domination of the Aztec at Tenochtitlan. Quetzalcoatl was to banish the followers of Huitzilopochtli, the Aztec's main god, and restore his rule. With the advent of his return, history would come full circle, and the Aztec would be reduced to subservient status. No doubt this belief paralyzed Motecuhzoma and facilitated the Spaniards' eventual conquest of the Aztec Empire.

The Aztec

Cortés and his expedition came in contact with the grand civilization of the Aztec in late 1519. Under the banner of the Triple Alliance, the Aztec Empire dominated over the central and southern part of Mexico.

The ruler, Motecuhzoma II, had succeeded Ahuitzotl in 1502. Motecuhzoma loved power and asserted his authority and stronghold as soon as he began his reign. His power became absolute in the empire, and he soon began subjugating the unconquered peoples of the terrain. Further, he established a class-based hierarchy in which merchants and elites predominated, thereby replacing a quasi-egalitarian system that had existed before. Despite this centralist position and Motecuhzoma's conquests, local dynasties still enjoyed autonomy, and their leaders remained in place in return for tribute.

Tenochtitlan was the capital of the Aztec Empire and the greatest city in the whole of Mesoamerica. When Cortés first saw Tenochtitlan, he compared it to the grandeur of Granada, a city on the Iberian Peninsula long under Muslim control and only recently reconquered by the Spaniards. Indeed, Tenochtitlan was a city like no other Cortés had encountered in the Caribbean or the American continent. Even before Cortés had reached the great city of Tenochtitlan, he knew its inhabitants to be more advanced than the Indians of Hispaniola and

14.2 Meeting of Hernán Cortés and Motecuhzoma II
(Lluvia Arras)

Cortés (see chapters 2 and 4). Then, in a seemingly ungrateful move, Cortés ordered Motecuhzoma a hostage of his own empire. This capture, coupled with Motecuhzoma's lack of resistance, caused great concern among the Aztec elite.

The Noche Triste

The Aztec elite, not as willing to surrender to the Spanish as Motecuhzoma had, decided to launch an attack on a Spanish garrison. The Spaniards reacted by massacring thousands of indigenous people and aristocrats at a religious festival for Huitzilopochtli. Motecuhzoma was injured and later died from obscure causes (see chapters 2 and 4).

Under the brief reign of Motecuhzoma's successors, Cuitlahuac and Cuauhtemoc, the last Aztec emperor, the remaining prominent Aztec rose and attacked the invaders. The Spaniards fled from Tenochtitlan in fear on a dark night. The Aztec assaults proved to be devastating for the Spaniards. Hundreds of conquistadores and thousands of Indian allies died and many others were taken prisoners in this assault that has come to be known as the Noche Triste, or Night of Sorrows. The Spaniards sought refuge in Tlaxcala, where Cortés would plan his final offensive on the Mexica.

Cuba, an observation also made by Christopher Columbus years before from reports by natives. However, the Aztec rule over Tenochtitlan was not secure, since the domains of the Valley of Puebla and Tlaxcala challenged their authority. In addition, their establishment of rule had only been recently acquired, dating from 1504 to 1516. These were but two of several factors that greatly aided the Spaniards on their quest to conquer the Aztec.

The European and American People Meet

Despite efforts of Motecuhzoma's emissaries to stop the conquistadores at Tlaxcala from traveling further inland, Cortés was determined to continue. Together with thousands of Indian allies, Cortés was successful and made his way to the Valley of Mexico.

Startled and in awe at the sight of such a grand city, the conquistadores were now faced with their biggest challenge thus far. On November 8, 1519, Cortés and Motecuhzoma II finally met. They presented each other with lavish gifts; Motecuhzoma bestowed gifts of gold and precious stones upon

The Siege of Tenochtitlan

Once more, with the aid of discontented natives, the Spaniards were able to rally thousands of Indian allies who would assist the Spaniards in their final attack against the Aztec. In addition to attacking the Aztec with their military might, which included brigantines on the lake and heavy artillery, the Spaniards blockaded Tenochtitlan, denying the population freshwater and food.

With the citizens of Tenochtitlan now being disenfranchised and deprived, additional devastation was caused by an unsuspecting factor—the introduction of smallpox and other communicable diseases. The Indians had no resistance to these European infections, and millions died as a consequence.

These diseases were responsible for taking more native lives than those lost in battle.

On August 13, 1521, the great Aztec city fell at the Spaniards' feet. Tenochtitlan became the capital of New Spain and was governed by a foreign emperor, King Charles V. The Spaniards killed Cuauhtemoc, the last of the Aztec emperors, in 1524.

Cortés became the governor and captain general of Nueva España (New Spain). The surviving Mexican nobility, including the indigenous translator Doña Marina, who married one of Cortés's men, enjoyed a certain amount of recognition and autonomy. The rest of the population was forced to pledge allegiance to a new and foreign government whose seat of power was oceans away (see chapters 2 and 4).

COLONIAL MEXICO: THE PROCESS OF TRANSCULTURATION

Birth of New Spain

Mexico City, the capital of New Spain, was built on top of the rubble of the Aztec capital of Tenochtitlan. Spanish institutions replaced native ones; however, despite the imposition of Spanish institutions, laws, religion, and language, native culture was not completely eradicated. The demands of the new colonies often required the integration of both Spanish and indigenous cultures.

The Spanish Crown prevailed as the controlling power of Mexico, but Mexico's distance from Spain and the overwhelming size of the new settlement made it difficult for the Crown to exercise its full authority. As a consequence, government officials in the colonies wielded more power than their counterparts in Spain did. To mend this inbalance of power, two institutions were established to assist in the administration and implementation of

the sovereign Charles V: the Council of the Indies and the Casa de Contratación, or the Board of Colonial Trade.

The Council of the Indies

Founded in 1524, soon after the conquest of Tenochtitlan, the Council of the Indies presided over and governed the colony of Mexico and other Spanish territories in the Western Hemisphere. Located in Seville, the council members were responsible for both judicial and legislative matters, as well as ecclesiastical, financial, and military affairs. All overseas positions, including religious and military ones, were approved by the royal crown but were nominated by the council. The council was eradicated in 1834.

Casa de Contratación

The Casa de Contratación, also located in Seville, was responsible for trade, commerce, and immigration laws in the Indies. It presided over all trade issues, secured taxes paid to the Crown, and ensured that Spain maintained its trade monopoly in the colonies. In 1790, this agency was eradicated. Both the Council of the Indies and the Casa de Contratación were the foundation for the transfer of power to the Indies and facilitated the rule of Spain over Mexico.

Encomiendas

To further assist the Crown in managing its vast territories, New Spain was divided up into *encomiendas*. These were massive estates operated by Spanish *encomenderos*, or estate owners. Unpaid Indians provided the land labor. Although the *encomenderos* were responsible for the well-being of the natives who worked their land, including ensuring their conversion, most *encomenderos* exploited and abused their enslaved Indians. Furthermore, as most Spaniards lived in the city rather than on their rural estates, their land was usually managed by a *mayordomo* (supervisor). This served as a way for the Spaniards to distance themselves from those they were subjugating. In fact, laws were passed restricting the Indians from living in Spanish designated zones and vice versa. This system of spatial segregation was created to ensure visible and legislated divisions between the conquerors and the conquered. At the same time, Spanish missionaries, intent on establishing a utopian community of Indian Christians, took advantage of this legal regulation in hopes that they could prevent the Indians from being contaminated by the religious and social misbehaviors of Spaniards who set a bad example for new Indian converts.

Audiencias

In 1527, the first *audiencia* was appointed in Mexico. The *audiencias*, or administrative courts, were responsible for judicial and administrative matters under their jurisdictions.

The Viceroy

A viceroy was the Crown's representative in the colonies and served as ruler of the new territories. Cortés's authority in the new colonies was thus suspended, and under the mandate of the king, Antonio de Mendoza became the first viceroy to Mexico, in 1535.

Since the viceroy was the top executive in a colony, he was responsible for all administrative and military functions, as well as the collection of colonial taxes to be remitted to Spain. The viceroys were men mostly from noble Spanish families.

A viceroy's power was not absolute. Other high-ranking officials, including in the church and the *audiencias*, worked to prevent him from being all-powerful, often by reporting to the Council of the Indies. Although the council set down decrees about how the viceroy should govern, distance as well as a sense of alienation allowed for the viceroy not to

execute the orders as he should, thereby giving rise to the popular dictum *Obedezco pero no cumplo* (I obey but I do not comply).

Social Structure

PENINSULARES

The colonizers of New Spain established a rigidly hierarchical society, with those who were Spanish-born, the conquerors, being at the top of the social pyramid and the conquered at the bottom. These Spaniards, called *peninsulares*, were but 1 percent of the population. They were usually from distinguished Spanish families and held the highest governmental, religious, educational, and military positions of power.

CRIOLLOS

Second in the social pyramid were the criollos. Criollos were those who were born in Mexico but whose parents and ancestry were from Spain. The criollos enjoyed a certain amount of prestige. They held positions in professional and official fields such as secular clergy, teachers, merchants, and landowners. They enjoyed a life of little strife; Indians provided the labor for their lands, haciendas, and mines. However, because criollos were born on the American continent and not in Europe, they were considered to be inferior to the *peninsulares* and were second-class citizens, despite their direct European ancestry.

MESTIZOS

Since there was a shortage of women during the first part of the colonization of Mexico, many unions were formed between Spanish men and Indian women. Although many of these unions were matrimonial, many others produced illegitimate children. The mestizo (mixed-blood) children resulting from these unions gave rise to a new people and culture, as well as to a new social class. Mestizos were thought of as *gente de razón*, or "people of reason," and they made up the lower middle class of colonial society. Mestizos were considered inferior to both the *peninsulares* and the criollos; however, the mestizos quickly became a large socioeconomic class and constitute the vast majority of Mexicans today.

INDIANS

The native Indians, the majority population during the colonial era, were considered to be the wards of both the Spanish Crown and the Catholic Church and formed the peasantry class below the mestizos. Indian nobles were recognized by the Spanish conquerors, and many noblewomen were married to Spaniards, thereby incorporating the Aztec nobility into the colonial elite or aristocracy. But the vast majority of Indians were reduced socially to a life of perpetual servitude. Although the Catholic Church tried to protect them, they were for the most part exploited and oppressed.

The native population was devastated during the colonial period by the introduction of diseases by the Spaniards. Such diseases included smallpox, measles, tuberculosis, and typhus, to which the natives had no immunity. This drastically reduced the native population by the millions, resulting in labor shortage—and the opportunity to exploit this class of people.

AFRICAN SLAVES

The second viceroy to Mexico, Luis de Velasco, prohibited Indian slavery in the mid-16th century, and the labor shortage resulting from a drastically reduced native population, owing to disease and exploitation, led to the importation of African slaves to the West Indies. The African slaves proved to be a better labor force for the Spaniards, since they seemed to be able to withstand hard labor better than the Indians could. Many Africans were able to buy their freedom eventually, and others were eventually given their freedom by their masters.

Miscegenation resulted in mulattoes, the children of African and Spanish parents, as well as *zambos*, the children of African and Indian parents. These racial mixtures would constitute an important part of the cultural formation and history of Mexico through *mestizaje*.

A SYSTEM OF CASTES

The Mexican population was therefore borne out of the mixture of indigenous people, Spanish colonizers, and Africans who were brought to New Spain by the slave trade. The intercombination of these fundamental ethnic groups created a system of 53 *castas* (castes) with curiously individual names; they are often portrayed in paintings known as *pinturas de castas*. Following is a brief list of the principal *castas:*

Spaniard + Indian = mestizo
Spaniard + mestizo = *castizo*
Spaniard + *castizo* = *español* (Spaniard)
Indian + Black = *zambo*
Zambo + Black = *zambo prieto* (dark *zambo*)
Spaniard + Black = mulatto
Spaniard + mulatto = *morisco*
Spaniard + *morisco* = *albino*
Spaniard + *albino* = *salta para atrás* (jump backward)
Salta para atrás + Indian = *chino* (Chinese)
Chino + mulatto = *lobo* (wolf)
Lobo + mulatto = *jíbaro*
Jíbaro + Indian = *albarazado*
Albarazado + Black = *cambujo*
Albarazado + mulatto = *barcino*
Albarazado + Indian = *no te entiendo* (I do not understand you)
Barcino + mulatto = *coyote*
Coyote + Indian = *chamizo*
Indian + *cambujo* = *tente en el aire* (hold yourself in midair)

It is important to remember that there was such a diversity of racial combinations that the definitions in the caste system were unable to provide for all possible mixtures of people. This complex fusion of races and cultures is what ultimately formed the Mexican people, who would later be named by the noted Mexican philosopher José Vasconcelos as *la raza cósmica* (the cosmic race).

Despite the Spaniards' efforts to classify the population and create social divisions, ambiguities between the castes existed, and classification proved difficult. For example, members of lower castes often passed for members of a higher caste, usually because of skin color and a certain level of

14.3 *The first Franciscan missionaries in Mexico, depicted in a mural in the monastery of Huejotzingo, Puebla* (Richard Perry)

assimilation. Mestizos were often able to pass as criollos by assimilating and abandoning any indication of Indianness and thereby acculturating to or imitating the dominant culture. After a time, a sort of social climbing emerged, in which people belonging to a lower social strata could "buy" entry into a higher social strata. The caste system of colonial Mexico was more than a separation of the different races; it was also a class-based system in which certain privileges were denied to certain sectors of the community, while others enjoyed a certain amount of prestige and social services or benefits.

The Spiritual Conquest

Paramount to the colonization of Mexico was the evangelical effort by the Catholic Church, supported by the Spanish Crown. Together with *mestizaje*, the religious goals behind the conquest laid the foundation for the creation of a distinctively Mexican identity and consciousness.

THE TRANSCULTURATION PROCESS

In addition to the implementation of Spanish political institutions and social organizations in Mexico, the Spaniards imposed their religion upon the native population. However, the Spaniards understood that in order to transform indigenous society, they would have to incorporate indigenous belief systems into their teachings of Catholic dogma, or at least find parallels between the two. Theoretically, this would allow the friars' doctrine to be more palatable to the native peoples and ensure greater success in their evangelical efforts. The integration of indigenous and Spanish cultures through not only religion but also marriage and colonial society produced a lengthy process of *transculturation*, in which the emerging people (Mexicans) would retain some elements of each culture, eliminate others, and thereby create a new culture. The church was therefore instrumental in the acculturation of the native population into the Spanish world order.

ARRIVAL OF THE RELIGIOUS ORDERS

Papal grants during the late 15th and early 16th centuries gave authority to the Spanish Crown over the Catholic Church in Spanish territory. This resulted in deeply embedded ties between the church and state because the church functioned as a branch of the state. The pope allowed these grants, known as the *patronato real*, or royal patronage, in recognition of the Spaniards' triumph in the reconquest of Spain from the Moors (Reconquista).

Knowing the corruption that permeated the secular clergy of the Catholic Church in Spain, Cortés specifically asked Charles V for Franciscan missionaries to carry out the evangelical efforts in New Spain. Charles V sent the first wave of Franciscan missionaries between 1523 and 1524.

Fray Pedro de Gante arrived in New Spain in 1523 accompanied by two other Flemish Franciscan monks. In 1524, Fray Martín de Valencia arrived in the colonies with 12 Franciscan monks, dubbed the Twelve Apostles. The latter group's arrival was noteworthy to the Indians because these monks walked from the coast of Veracruz to Mexico City barefoot. Upon their arrival, Cortés knelt at their feet and kissed their worn and disheveled robes. This act of humbleness and servitude to the Franciscans on the part of the prevailing Cortés made quite an impact on the Indians; it symbolized the importance of the arrival of the friars and their divine affiliation. These Franciscan monks were the first to be confronted with the great task of converting the Indians in the new territories. These monks belonged to the Observants, a subgroup of the Franciscan order that adhered to the strict Franciscan codes of poverty and asceticism. In addition, they were millenarians, whose evangelical objectives were to create a Jerusalén indiana, or Indian Jerusalem, in Mexico to fulfill ancient apocalyptic prophecies. They had a utopian vision in which the Franciscan friars and the Indians, whom they perceived to be pure and untainted, coexisted in a worldly paradise, one that was free of corruption. What would follow would be nothing less than the Last Judgment, the second coming of Christ, and the creation of the Jerusalén indiana.

After the Franciscans, Dominican missionaries arrived in 1526, and later the Augustinians arrived, in 1533. The Jesuits were the last to arrive in Mexico, arriving much later, in 1572. Of these orders, the Franciscans and to some degree the Augustinians were the only ones working with a millenarian agenda.

FIRST CONVERSIONS

Strategically, the Indian nobles and political leaders were the first to be converted and baptized. Because these leaders had influence and venerable status in their communities, the Spaniards believed that they could most influence their people to do the same. Whether these nobles voluntarily converted and for what reasons they chose to convert is debated.

Even though the evangelization process was facilitated by the fact that it was customary for native cultures to abandon their religious beliefs and take on those of the conquering tribe, the conversion process proved to be no easy task. The missionaries were confronted with many obstacles in their evangelical efforts during the 16th century, including the fact that the religion they were hoping to replace was a complex, deeply rooted agricultural religion profoundly ingrained in the fabric of native life.

The missionaries were successful in establishing churches and missions—physical manifestations of Catholicism. During the three centuries of Spanish domination, they managed to build, with Indian labor, approximately 12,000 churches. Quantitatively, conversion efforts and strategies seemed successful; however, problems lay in the quality and extent of the conversion process. There were many parallels and similarities between the pagan belief system of the Indians and the Christian belief system of the Spaniards, and these similarities facilitated the Indians' understanding of Christian doctrine. But oftentimes, these parallels were combined, resulting in a unique blend (syncretism) of two spiritual beliefs. In many cases, this merge resulted in a state of confusion in which individuals lost their old beliefs while acquiring no new belief in the new faith, or only a superficial understanding of it.

The Spaniards were not particularly tolerant of the indigenous religious practices, and the destruction of native belief systems was systematic. Yet many of the indigenous practices and concepts were assimilated into the Catholic Church. For example, the Day of the Dead, a Mexican holiday that is still celebrated, rose from blending the Catholic All Souls' Day and the Aztec autumn festival, which was a celebration of dead ancestors.

On their quest to eradicate Mesoamerican culture, the Spaniards toppled indigenous sacred structures and built Catholic churches and other religious edifices over them. Oftentimes, rubble from the destroyed indigenous sites was used in the construction of colonial palaces and Catholic edifices such as the cathedral and many other churches in Mexico City. This not only sanctified the space and legitimized the Catholic Church but also sent the natives the message that the Catholic Church was indeed supreme to the heathen and "demonic" spirituality of the indigenous peoples.

THE VIRGIN OF GUADALUPE

The most important spiritual phenomenon that serves as a prime example of the syncretism that occurred in colonial Mexico is the appearance of the Virgin Mary to the Indian Juan Diego. As the legend narrates, in 1531 the recently baptized Juan Diego was walking on the hill of Tepeyac, a site considered to be sacred by the Aztec for it was there that they worshipped the earth goddess Coatlicue, also known as Tonantzin (Our Mother). The Virgin, who came to be known as Our Lady of Guadalupe, a dark-skinned Madonna, miraculously appeared before Juan Diego with a request that a church be built on the hill of Tepeyac in her honor. As proof of her appearance, she supplied him with a bushel of roses, a miracle in and of itself, for the hillside was barren. He gathered the roses in his *tilmatli*, or cloak, and went to Bishop Zumárraga with the Virgin's request and evidence of her appearance.

When Juan Diego unveiled the roses from his cloak to the bishop, they were both startled and amazed to see the image of the Virgin of Guadalupe emblazoned on his cotton cloak. This apparition was perceived as a miracle, and today is still considered a mystery.

A church was erected on that sacred site, and the union between Coatlicue-Tonantzin and the Virgin Mary is now embodied in the Virgin of Guadalupe. This is a prime example of the syncretism of Indian and Spanish culture and spirituality and the transculturation process that occurred. Today the Virgin of Guadalupe is considered to be the symbol of identity of the Mexican people, and she stands as the reigning patroness of the Americas.

THE CHURCH AS PROVIDER OF SOCIAL SERVICES

The role of the Catholic Church was greatly expanded in Mexico during the colonial period, extending beyond evangelization. In addition to converting the

14.4 Image of the Virgin of Guadalupe (Manuel Aguilar-Moreno)

Indians, the church served as the major catalyst for the cultural transformation in America. Moreover, its friars proved to be steadfast supporters of the Indians—the friars protected them from injustices committed by the Spanish. But their role in the colonization of Mexico is controversial; though they accompanied the conquistadores in an effort to overpower an autonomous people, they nonetheless objected to the violations and abuses the Indian population suffered at the hands of the Spanish.

Bartolomé de Las Casas, a Dominican friar, is a prime example of a cleric who became a protector and defender of the Indians. He was nicknamed "Father of the Indians" and became bishop of Chiapas (1544–47).

In addition to overseeing the construction of religious buildings such as cathedrals, churches, and monasteries, part of the clergy's expanded role in the new territories was the creation of schools and hospitals. They became responsible for educating the natives and their children. They were the first Spanish educators and providers of social services in New Spain.

Language

Language defines and unites a people's worldview; therefore, the conversion of the Indian languages to Spanish was an important factor in the colonization of Mexico. Although there were many indigenous languages in existence before the arrival of the Spaniards, the language of the Aztec, Nahuatl, was the lingua franca of their empire. Many Indian tribes whose primary language was not Nahuatl nonetheless understood it.

As with the political and religious transformation, the implementation of the Spanish language among the natives was one of combining, adapting, and accommodating the two languages. Since the friars were the ones responsible for the instruction of the Indians, many educated themselves in Nahuatl as a way to be more effective in the evangelization and teaching of the natives. Some clerics, such as Fray Andrés de Olmos, a celebrated Franciscan scholar and humanist, went on to learn additional Indian languages.

Consequently, a Mexican Spanish, or Nahuatlized Spanish, emerged that was as unique as it was representative of the new people and culture. In today's Mexican Spanish, many Nahuatl words persist, albeit in a modified state. Some examples are *petate* (mat), *paliacate* (handkerchief), *mecate* (rope), *aguacate* (avocado), and *chichi* (breast) (see chapter 10).

TEQUITQUI ART

Tequitqui is a style of art produced during the colonization of New Spain. It is the Indian redefinition and reinterpretation of European art and architec-

14.5 *The Acolman Cross is an example of* tequitqui *art of 16th-century Mexico, Monastery of Saint Augustine Acolman, Mexico State.* (Richard Perry)

ture. The term *tequitqui* was first coined by José Moreno Villa in 1942 to describe the distinctive Indian-Christian art that emerged in the 16th century as a result of the collision of these two worlds. It combines the European artistic tradition with the Indian aesthetic. European styles that were transferred and then transfigured in Latin America include Plateresque, Mudejar, Gothic, Romanesque, and Renaissance (Aguilar-Moreno 1999: 106–119).

Tequitqui is a Nahuatl word that means "tributary" or "one who pays tribute." Although *tequitqui* has been a contested term to describe the art that emerged in early colonial Mexico as well as the circumstances under which it was created, it is a precise term that defines the Indians' inventive participation in a unique, transcultural art that had its own aesthetic categories. The *tequitqui* style was expressed in facade reliefs, mural paintings, atrial crosses, and sculptures.

Tequitqui's origins lie in the talented indigenous artisans that the Spanish found in Tenochtitlan. From the outset, the Spanish were confronted with marvelous Aztec architecture, sculptures, and codices, all speaking to the great aptitude and virtuosity contained within the Indian community. There is no doubt that the outstanding craftsmanship that the Spaniards encountered in New Spain was rooted in a very ancient and rich artistic tradition, and thereafter it could never be fully suppressed. The friars, who made themselves responsible for the reconstruction of sacred spaces, therefore used Indian labor to build and adorn the churches and convents of the new Spanish colony. Under the instruction of the friars, the natives constructed hundreds of churches and convents in a relatively short time. The friars used engravings and illustrations from European books as a guide for the Indian artisans, but the Indian aesthetic persisted and found its way through these instructions.

Indian-Christian Art

The art of colonial Mexico was a combination of both Indian and European aesthetics and resulted in a unique art form that reflected the collision of cultures and ideologies. This new art emerged despite the attempted eradication of Aztec architecture, sculpture, and design. In other words, even though the Spaniards physically won the military conquest, Indian culture refused to be repressed; it persisted and infiltrated every aspect of colonial life to such an extent that a new culture complete with an artistic expression arose, one that was neither solely Spanish nor solely Indian. This situation raises the question: Who conquered whom? *Tequitqui* art clearly reflects this fused ethnicity as well as the crisis of cultural identity that occurred in 16th-century Mexico.

Following the transfer of European artistic traditions to the New World, regional styles became more varied as traditions were shared and acculturated. For example, the Plateresque style, also known as the Reyes Católicos (Catholic Kings) style, which bears a resemblance to the work of silversmiths, was combined with Gothic or Renaissance aesthetics in New Spain, thereby producing a completely new and multifaceted artistic expression that could be seen in many of the churches that were built during the colonial era. In addition, the flat reliefs produced indicate the inventiveness and creativeness present in pre-Columbian styles meshed with the techniques used by the medieval engravers. What resulted was a *tequitqui* bas-relief, or low-relief, with undulated angles, carvings, and beveled edges so severe as to produce a strong light-and-shadow effect. When these artistic devices intermingled with the play of natural light, they produced a truly splendid vision.

14.6 An example of tequitqui *art: a mural of the earthly paradise in the cloister of the monastery of Malinalco, Mexico State* (Fernando González y González)

In addition, because Aztec stone sculptures embodied the belief system and worldview of the Aztec civilization and played an instrumental role in the cultural life of the Aztec, their motifs persisted well into colonial times and blended with Spanish architecture, creating yet another expression of *tequitqui* art. Aztec motifs that persevered were the water serpent, representative of Tlaloc; the conch shell, associated with fertility and life; and the eagle, which symbolized the Sun at its highest point and the warrior, an important figure in Aztec culture. (The eagle is now a national symbol, as evidenced in its prominent display on the Mexican flag.) These Aztec motifs were morphed with Spanish images resulting in a new Indian-Christian iconography.

Most examples of *tequitqui* artistic expression can be found in the convents that were built during the 16th century in the states of Hidalgo, Puebla, Michoacan, Tlaxcala, Morelos, Guerrero, Veracruz, Oaxaca, Yucatán, and Mexico and in the capital city. Of course, there were variations in the quality of the artworks produced. They ranged from nearly exact replicas of European works to rather unsophisticated representations.

Folk Baroque

Baroque art flourished in Mexico during the 17th and 18th centuries. Fine examples of baroque architecture are the churches of Santa María Tonantzintla and San Francisco Acatepec in the state of Puebla, the church of Santa Cruz de las Flores in Jalisco, the mission churches of the Sierra Gorda in Querétaro, the church of Our Lady of Ocotlan and the cathedral in Zacatecas. Some argue that the *tequitqui* artistic style persisted into the baroque era in Mexico; others disagree, stating that the term *tequitqui* should be used in reference to the 16th-century artistic production of early colonial Mexico and that any *tequitqui* art in the 17th or 18th centuries should be considered folk baroque. Whether the art is folk baroque or *tequitqui* baroque, the persistence of Aztec forms of art and that of other Indian cultures continued to penetrate later art forms as a silent reminder of the once great Mesoamerican civilization.

MEXICO AND ITS MESTIZO IDENTITY

The Criollo Sentiment

Mexico gained its independence from Spain in 1821 after 11 years of civil war and social unrest. The criollos were the first to advocate an independent Mexico, one that was free of Spanish domination and would allow the criollos to lose their second-class status. Independence, however, was not gained overnight, and the journey was a long and painful one.

Eighteenth-century Mexico was a seemingly functional colonial society with a performing social hierarchy, a strong and talented workforce composed of Indians and mestizos, an established church, and a promising economy supported by a strong mining industry. However, it was a society full of contradiction and discontent borne of the social injustices it promulgated. A growing dissatisfaction was brewing, and would soon come to a boil; the incessant oppression of the majority of the population could not continue uninterrupted. What began as a desire for reform resulted in the eventual struggle for an independent nation. During the early part of the 19th century, there had been many changes in Europe that affected the Spanish colony of Mexico. These changes included Napoleon's rise to power in France and his successful overthrow and exile in 1808 of the king of Spain, Charles IV, and his son, Ferdinand VII. Napoleon's brother Joseph Bonaparte was declared king of Spain on July 6, 1808. The legitimacy of the Spanish throne in the Spanish colony was now called into question, and this lack of legitimacy and authority resulted in political instability in Mexico.

The escalating resentment between the *peninsulares* and the criollos surfaced under this climate of uncertainty, as did the contradictions that had come to define Mexican colonial society. The criollos saw this as an opportunity to assert themselves. Their discontent grew out of their frustrations of being second-class citizens in their own country. Under the *casta* system of the colonial order, they would always be subservient to the *peninsulares*. The highest-ranking positions of power and prestige were not open to the criollos—such positions could be held only by the *peninsulares*.

Even though a few criollos tried to buy titles of nobility, it was a superficial remedy that did not address the real issues; the fact remained that only Spanish born in Spain, not in Mexico, were the real nobility. In this elite worldview, the American continent would always be subordinate to the European continent. The Bourbon reforms (economic, political, and social changes passed by the Spanish monarchy to increase colonial profit) of the second half of the 18th century reinforced this colonial structure and even worsened the social situation for the criollos. As a result, these reforms further agitated the criollos and added fuel to the fire.

Due to the power struggles that resulted during this time of political uncertainty, Mexico had, in the span of two years, a total of four viceroys. The criollos, like the Spanish *peninsulares*, organized themselves into political bodies. Because the criollos had the support of the clergy, they seemed to have an advantage over the *peninsulares*, for the clergy had a long list of complaints against the Spanish government. In addition, the criollos adopted the miracle of the apparition of the Virgin of Guadalupe, the Indian Madonna, as a legitimizing tool. Her appearance sanctified New Spain and thus her children as well. The criollos believed themselves to be the children of New Spain. A Mexican identity was slowly forming, as was Mexican nationalism.

Mexican Independence

MIGUEL HIDALGO Y COSTILLA

The movement toward independence gained momentum under the progressive criollo priest, Miguel Hidalgo y Costilla. He became both the military leader and the spirit behind the fight for independence, which he called for on September 16, 1810. He gathered mestizo and Indian support by taking up the symbol of the Virgin of Guadalupe, under which he led several military insurrections.

Hidalgo was captured by the so-called Royalists (Spanish forces), and after a lengthy trial, he was executed on July 30, 1811.

His death was not in vain; he was the first expression of liberation for Mexico. Today he is considered to be the father of the Mexican nation. During his brief tenure, he abolished slavery and the tribute system that the Indians were subjected to. In addition, he supported the allocation of land to the Indians, an issue that would be revisited during the Mexican Revolution.

VICENTE GUERRERO

After the death of Hidalgo, the Mexican independence movement lost its initial momentum and declined into 11 years of civil war, finally ending under the leadership of Vicente Guerrero. Guerrero combined forces with the Royalist opposition leader Agustín de Iturbide, and together they presented the victorious Plan of Iguala. This plan was not extreme in its measures; its aim was to join the interests of both sides of the political scale. Principal to the plan were the "three guarantees": Mexican independence from Spain, maintenance of the Catholic religion, and equal rights for those of different races. The plan gained support from the military as well as from the majority of the Mexican people. Viceroy Apodaca resigned. With the implementation of the Plan of Iguala and the Treaty of Cordoba of 1821, Mexico was granted independence of the Spanish Crown, with Iturbide as head of a provisional government.

The Struggles of Independent Mexico

Mexico's independence was bittersweet. Though it was now free from colonial rule, it was also economically and politically devastated. In addition, the prestigious criollos and their liberal agenda now held the seat of power, and this would prove to have contradictory results. A new constitution was created for independent Mexico, one that was not vastly different from the Spanish Constitution of Cádiz of

1812. It denounced the Spanish caste system as well as forced tribute.

Despite independence, the creation of a new constitution and the formation of a new nation free from the chains of colonial dominion, the criollo desire to create a homogenous nation that would unite all the peoples of free Mexico had negative effects for the Indians. The indigenous peoples were seen to stand outside the national agenda and as an obstacle to the future of Mexico because they insisted on keeping many of their traditional cultural forms. Independent Mexico was hostile to the Indians and their traditions and tried to erase them from the Mexican landscape. The criollo agenda therefore included the belief that the Indians posed a threat to the new nation.

The Indians perceived the situation differently, and their struggle for land ownership would come to a climax during this time. During the colonial era, Indians were allowed the rights of communal land ownership. This tradition was eradicated by the criollos' desire to privatize all lands. Communal lands were taken from the Indians and divided between owners in the private sector. The Indians were displaced, and as the haciendas grew, so did unfair Indian labor practices. This created an insurgency of Indian uprisings and rebellions.

A NATION UNCHANGED

Overall, independent Mexico looked a lot like colonial Mexico. As Guillermo Bonfil Batalla notes in his book *México profundo*, Mexican independence did not bring a thorough social and political revolution. Rather, the colonial structure was maintained to such an extent that it continues to inform Mexican society in the present.

As a result, Iturbide presided as the first of several Mexican dictators, the last being Porfirio Díaz, who rose to power in 1876. Up to this point independent Mexico had endured many conflicts, including a war with the United States, in which it lost more than half of its territory (the present-day states of Texas, California, Nevada, Arizona, New Mexico, Colorado, Utah, and part of Wyoming). In addition, the French occupied Mexico from 1864 to 1867 with Prince Maximilian von Habsburg as emperor.

The Porfiriato

For all its faults, the coup d'état that resulted in Porfirio Díaz's dictatorship (the Porfiriato) brought much-needed stability and material progress to Mexico. The Porfiriato spanned from 1876 to 1911, one of the longest-lasting dictatorships in Latin American history to date. The Porfiriato was marked by many injustices and the repression of the majority of its population, which was composed of mestizos and Indians. It was a government consumed with its interpretation of progress, which was pursued at the cost of the masses, while the landed aristocracy, which included many foreigners, held 90 percent of the land. Díaz, a mestizo general turned politician, attempted to modernize and bring prestige to Mexico by encouraging foreign investment. He succeeded in bringing an influx of foreign industrialists and investors to Mexico, while he left the peasant class to live on the haciendas in a state of perpetual servitude to the landowners. The philosophical guiding force behind this fundamental time in the history of Mexico was the ideology of the *científicos*, or "scientific thinkers." Their banner was "order and progress," and this was upheld by marginalizing the landless mestizos and Indians.

A consciousness was emerging, however, and it was embodied in the creation of the Ateneo de la Juventud (the Athenaeum of Youth). The Ateneo, founded by a sector of the intellectual community in 1907, was a response to the *científicos* and their exultation of the white Mexican or foreigner and the Westernization of Mexico. Among the group's most important and influential members was José Vasconcelos, who played an integral role in the formation of the new mestizo Mexican identity, which the Mexican Revolution would help canonize.

This group of radical intellectuals was not alone in its criticism of the Díaz dictatorship—they were representative of the country's growing discontent. A man by the name of Francisco Madero emerged as the leading oppositional force to Díaz and served as a voice for the disillusioned masses. Porfirio Díaz was well aware of his declining power, and at the start of the armed conflict that became the Mexican Revolution, in 1910, he resigned as the president of Mexico, fleeing to Europe, where he lived in exile.

The Mexican Revolution

During the Mexican Revolution (1910–20), Mexico was once again thrown into a state of instability and chaos. All peoples with grievances, including the Indians, joined or supported the revolution. What transpired were battles among one another, resulting in infighting and many deaths at the hands of supposed allies.

A REVOLUTIONARY MARTYR

Emiliano Zapata was an important revolutionary figure who coined the battle cry "Land and Freedom," but his struggle was mired with contradictions due to killings between his own men. Nonetheless, Zapata was a fighter for the Indians' cause, and his cry for land reflected their grievances and addressed the injustices of the previous regimes.

Zapata emerged as the first real voice for the Indians. His Plan of Ayala called for agrarian reforms and land redistribution for the Indians as well as an exultation of Indian virtues and values. His movement resulted in the 1917 agrarian articles of the constitution, which displaced the old landowners' stronghold and set forth the redistribution of land. Over time, these reforms were not enforced and, with a few exceptions, have been increasingly ignored.

A MESTIZO REVOLUTION

In the face of the contradictions that came to define the Mexican Revolution, *indigenismo* and the rediscovery of the mestizo mind emerged. The mestizo would once again surface as an important political body; however, unlike the criollo vision during the War of Independence, the mestizo of the revolution did not ignore and suppress the Indian but rather sought to integrate him. *Indigenismo* was a conscious effort to recover appreciation of Mexico's indigenous heritage and bring social justice to the Indian people exploited and humiliated for centuries.

Crucial to this rediscovery was the art and the cultural awareness that resulted. Important artists such as José Guadalupe Posada, a strong advocate for social justice, represented the views of the intellectual and critical masses in his prolific engravings, which illustrated the course of the Mexican Revolution as well as the political climate of the time.

A PHILOSOPHICAL FOUNDATION

The Mexican Revolution was grounded in an intellectual milieu that defined the future course of Mexican politics, identity, and consciousness, and sought to replace the *científicos'* ideology. The Institutional Revolutionary Party (PRI) that ended up dominating 20th-century Mexican politics emanated from the revolution and managed to eradicate some of the problems, injustices, and prejudices that had prevailed in prerevolution Mexico—many of which were initiated by the Spanish colonizers in Mexico and had persisted through the Díaz dictatorship. Unfortunately, the PRI stayed in power for 71 years, becoming a dictatorship itself, and its self-corruption distorted its mission of social justice and led to its demise, in 2000.

In addition, for the first time, the Indian was elevated to a figure to be valorized, and many artists, such as Diego Rivera, and thinkers, such as Vasconcelos, were instrumental in the remaking of the new Mexican identity. One of Vasconcelos's main contributions was his effort in the restructuring of the Mexican education system. He became secretary of state for public education under President Álvaro Obregón in 1921. In his effort to empower the masses, he created a public program that for the first time would provide education to the illiterate peoples of Mexico, mainly indigenous and marginalized mestizos.

The mestizos were now beginning to take their rightful place in Mexican culture; although mestizos had long been the majority, the criollos had dominated the Mexican cultural scene up until this point. The essence or the definition of being Mexican was, after all, typified in the mestizo. However, the political and social residue left from the conquest included the subjugation of both the Indian and the mestizo, who were considered inferior to both the *peninsulares* and the criollos. The irony of this philosophy was that the Spaniards themselves were mestizos (their own *mestizaje* occurred during the Moorish occupation, which lasted hundreds of years). In addition to this ethnic mixing of Moorish and Spanish blood, which was, incidentally, evidenced in every aspect of Spanish culture and art, the Catholic Spaniards also came from interreligious blendings of Jewish and Islamic backgrounds. Therefore, it can be argued that the Spaniards were more mestizo than the Mexican mestizos they subjugated.

The only way that the Spanish could justify their conquest was to assert their racial superiority over the natives, and this was maintained by the blood-based caste system they created and propagated. Even the level of *mestizaje* today in certain sectors of the population speak to the unequal distribution of genetic traits, serving as an indicator of the limited contact between the varying caste members. Again, Bonfil Batalla points out that the lack of visible Indian features in the dominant classes of modern-day Mexico testifies to the inequality in the racial "democracy" so idealized.

Vasconcelos would concede, for he was the major proponent of the democratization process. His forward-thinking ideas were contained in the books he wrote, such as *La raza cósmica* (The cosmic race). In his formulation of *mestizaje*, Vasconcelos considers the mixing of races as a process leading toward a more enlightened and tolerant future.

Postrevolutionary and Modern Mexico

THE CONSTITUTION OF 1917

During the revolution and the presidency of Venustiano Carranza, Mexico fell into a deep abyss of corruption. In an effort to stabilize the country, a convention was held in which a new Mexican constitution would be drafted. The Constitution of 1917 was conceived in Querétaro in December 1916. It was designed to ensure that the goals of the revolution would be upheld. Although this new constitution was not unlike the Constitution of 1857, it did contain articles that served as a stronghold for the rights of the Mexican people in addition to providing a road map for the new state.

Included in these new provisions was the expropriation of privately owned land by the *hacendados* (landowners) and foreigners, both of which were cornerstones of the Porfiriato regime. The ownership of Mexican property by foreigners would be acceptable only if it served the needs of the Mexican people. Once this ceased to be the case, the property would be up for expropriation by the Mexican government. In addition, the new constitution allowed the Mexican working class to organize itself into a political body and to demand workers' benefits and acceptable financial compensation, rights that were formerly denied to them. Of great significance was the constitution's stance on religion and the clergy. Article 3 of the new constitution declared the secularization of the public school system and the severing of ties with the Catholic Church. The new constitution, in accordance with the goals of the revolution, attempted to unify Mexican society, including the Indians, peasant laborers, mestizos, and intellectuals, to create a united nation.

President Carranza's influence and support had been greatly diminished by this point; the new constitution's success depended on the leadership of Generals Alvaro Obregón and Francisco Mugica. Although the new constitution was widely embraced, it still generated much opposition, and it would be a hotly debated issue among the Mexican population for years to come.

PRESIDENCY OF OBREGÓN

After Carranza's presidency lapsed in 1920, Alvaro Obregón would rise to become the next president of Mexico, for he, unlike Carranza, embodied the revolution and its ideals. Obregón would prove to be a shrewd politician, adhering to the dictum of keeping your friends close and your enemies even closer. The Confederación Regional Obrera Mexicana, or CROM, the nation's first union, together with bureaucrats from the Porfiriato formed part of Obregón's new government. His was a left-wing, socialist administration, yet he was reasonable and relatively moderate in dealing with critical political issues. These traits would work to his advantage, especially when dealing with powerful oppositional forces, such as foreign investors and the United States of America.

NEW EDUCATIONAL SYSTEM

President Obregón appointed Vasconcelos to head Mexico's newly secularized educational system. Education was paramount in the formation of the new nation, and it was now available to all sectors of society, including those who had been previously deprived of it. Under the direction of Vasconcelos, Mexico's educational system was taken to new heights with his introduction of classic literature, art, Mexican indigenous identity, and social consciousness. This new system was also a unifying tool with the intention of integrating the Indian into the mestizo nation that Mexico was to become. To this end, Vasconcelos would revitalize the Indian by using native imagery and icons; unfortunately, his educational system was not set to preserve that which was Indian but rather to "redeem" him by placing him in a historical context. This is evidenced by his conscious omission of an Indian education and nonpreservation of the native languages, such as Nahuatl or Maya, in the predominately Indian areas of Mexico. Nevertheless, for the first time, the Mexican government recognized the importance of its indigenous history and the consequent reclaiming of their lost civilization instead of practicing historical amnesia.

All these reformations resulted in the Obregón government's being accused of Bolshevism by the United States, which did not recognize Mexico politically until August 23, 1923, three years after Obregón's election. These accusations, however, worked in favor of the Obregón government, for the Mexican people interpreted this as a show of resistance to the U.S. government and foreign investors. U.S. president Calvin Coolidge's recognition of the new Mexican administration came with Obregón's announcement that Article 27 of the new constitution, the article that restricted the purchase of Mexican land by foreigners or Mexican *hacendados*, was not retroactive. This declaration, which benefited foreign investors, was the result of the U.S. backing of Obregón's chosen successor, Plutarco Elías Calles.

The dominant role enjoyed by the United States over Mexico had a long and deep history that influenced and oftentimes helped shape Mexican politics and policies. The unbalanced relationship, with the United States holding considerable weight over its more vulnerable southern neighbor, would continue to influence the Mexican political scene and culture.

PRESIDENCY OF CALLES

Supported by the U.S. government, Calles was victorious and became the next president of Mexico,

serving from 1924 to 1928. Keeping in line with the Obregón agenda, Calles was devoted to securing the goals of the revolution. He endorsed the formation of the National Agrarian Party and supported the *ejido* system (use of communal land by peasants). However, there was resistance from the religious sector of society, which opposed Article 3 of the constitution, the anticlerical provisions, and this opposition manifested itself in peasant uprisings and numerous insurrections in the countryside. These series of revolts, which were an affront to the revolution and its party, would culminate in the Cristero war, which lasted from 1926 to 1929 and was a fight for religious freedom.

During this time of church and state division and quarrelling, the Constitution of 1917 was amended to extend the presidential term from four to six years and to allow a former president to seek a second, nonconsecutive term. This is how Obregón came to be reelected president in July of 1928. But shortly after his election, a religious zealot named José de León Toral assasinated him.

Affected by Obregón's assassination, President Calles, or El Jefe Máximo de la Revolución (First Chief of the Revolution) as he had come to be called, would continue to exert control over Mexican politics, although not serve as president. Instead, Emilio Portes Gil would become the interim president from 1928 to 1930, and the *Cristero* war would come to an end under his direction.

Calles, meanwhile, created the National Revolutionary Party, or the PNR, in 1929, and in 1938, under the presidency of Lázaro Cárdenas, its name was changed to the Mexican Revolutionary Party (PRM). In opposition to the PRM and President Cárdenas, a new proclerical party was formed in 1939, the National Action Party, or PAN.

PRESIDENCY OF LÁZARO CÁRDENAS

After a slew of short presidential terms, Lázaro Cárdenas served a full six-year term as president from 1934 to 1940. Even though Calles initially endorsed Cárdenas, it would not be long before Calles was organizing an oppositional force against him. Cárdenas replied by eliminating all *"callistas"* from government and by forcing Calles into exile in the United States, thus ending Calles's and his supporters' political stronghold.

Cárdenas ran on his Six-Year Plan platform, which promised both social and economic reform. Labeled as radical by many, the Six-Year Plan sought to defend and support the expansion of labor organizations as well as to redistribute land to peasants and farmers. As with Obregón's administration, Cárdenas was committed to actualizing the revolution's educational agenda and supporting civic works or public works of art such as mural projects, both of which were part of the Six-Year Plan and the 1917 constitution.

Cárdenas's crowning glory would be the nationalization of all oil companies in Mexican territory in 1938, an issue born out of a labor dispute. For this, Cárdenas would be regarded as Mexico's preeminent leader of the people, a leader who stood up to corporate and foreign bullies in the name of the Mexican working class. What was to follow this legislation's liberal and socialist leanings would be a conservative regime, headed by Manuel Ávila Camacho.

LEADERS OF WESTERNIZATION AND MASSACRE

After 1940, Mexico's priorities changed to reflect the post–World War II reality. Following the presidency of Ávila Camacho, Miguel Alemán would take Mexico in an entirely new direction, one that moved away from the goals of the revolution and closer to the goals of the industrialists and big business. In fact, the party of the revolution, the PRM, was recast and renamed the Institutional Revolutionary Party, or PRI. Post-1940 Mexico obliterated the ideologies of the revolution, climaxing in 1968 with the Tlatelolco massacre of protesters in the Plaza of the Three Cultures.

Mexico hosted the 1968 summer Olympics, and students, joined by political agitators, took this opportunity to gather in protest of the government and its policies. The response by the Mexican government was remarkable in its heavy handedness. This act of violence by the Mexican government against its own people served to jolt the masses and remind them of what Mexico had become in its attempt to be an industrialized, modern nation. Crucial to this bourgeoning was the participation of the United States throughout the 20th and into the 21st centuries in Mexican politics, during which

Mexico strayed from its foundational ideals. For the decades to come, Mexico's political scene was informed by corruption, continued attempts at modernization at the cost of its people and vitality, and an unstable economy.

A RECENT ROAD TO DEMOCRACY

The PRI and its earlier forms (PNR and PRM) held onto power for 71 years, until the election of Vicente Fox, the PAN presidential candidate, in December 2000. This historic event was proof of the Mexican people's desire for social and political change and an end to the corruption that had come to define Mexican politics. Unfortunately the first PAN government has been plagued by political errors and missteps and the undermining dirty play exercised by the PRI. For the presidential election of 2006, the hope is that the Mexican people will have the clarity and patience to realize that the processes of change take time and thereby keep their faith in the future without being tempted by the dark ghosts of the past.

THE INDIANS OF CENTRAL MEXICO TODAY

The Nahua population of the central valley was largely obliterated during the time of the conquest. Many were killed in battle with the Spanish conquistadores; others died by diseases brought to the American continent by the Spaniards. Those who survived were forced to abandon their native beliefs and culture and replace them with those of the conqueror's worldview and culture, thus bringing an end to the Aztec civilization. Some fled to remote regions of the empire in an attempt to escape colonization; therefore, the Nahuas who exist today are largely scattered and many have been integrated into the Mexican mainstream. Although census reporting has been problematic, especially as it relates to indigenous cultures, it is calculated that there are approximately 1 million Nahuas in Mexico today. Additionally, of the many Indian cultures alive in modern Mexico, the Nahuas are among the majority. It is estimated that 50 percent of today's Nahuas live in 28 of the 32 Mexican states.

As is the case with native populations across the American continent, the Indians of Mexico, including those residing in the central valley region, the location of the once grand Aztec capital of Tenochtitlan, live in poverty and are largely marginalized and disenfranchised. Despite independence and the Mexican Revolution, the Indians of Mexico have historically been viewed as obstacles to the unification of the nation. The revolution, for all its valorizing of the Indian and reclaiming of its rich indigenous past, never really sought to maintain and preserve indigenous values and lifestyle. Instead, it sought to integrate the Indian into the national mestizo fabric. This is what the government meant when it championed the term *indigenismo*—that the Indian should be relegated to the past. The Mexican government further believed that it was necessary that the Indian disappear altogether if Mexico was to become a modern and vital country; Indian assimilation and modernization have always been part of the Mexican government's agenda.

The Mexica, or the Aztec, as they are now referred to, founded one of the grandest and greatest civilizations in the American continent during the time of contact with the Spaniards. The namesake *Mexico* is a testimony to this great civilization and its people. However, today's Indians survive as relics and reminders of a distant past, a people who have for the past 500 years struggled to maintain their lifestyle. The most successful have been those who fled the Aztec capital and headed to remote regions. Others maintained some of their native traditions and combined them with traditions that were forced upon them by the Europeans. It is safe to say that the Nahuas have survived to the present time through native traditions that refused to be suppressed, such as the food that is now part of the Mexican diet, the language, which contains many Nahuatl words, and oral traditions. No matter how much the powerful seek to eliminate the Indians, the Indians survive. It is for this reason that many scholars have stated that there are two Mexicos, one

being the visible Mexico, composed of mostly *mestizos*, or assimilated Indians who seek to Westernize and modernize Mexico, and the other, less visible Mexico, composed of the nation's indigenous peoples, who still live according to more ancient beliefs and maintain a native lifestyle despite modernization and Westernization efforts by the Mexican government.

The fact that the Indian population still exists in Mexico today is a testament to their perseverance, endurance, and resoluteness, for every method has been used to eliminate these people and their ancient ways. It is amazing that today, in the outskirts of Mexico City, in towns like Mixquic and Milpa Alta, there are still people speaking Nahuatl, the language of the Aztec. They resiliently survive despite five centuries of systematic assaults on their culture by diverse governments and more recently by capitalism. They endure protected by their resilient culture.

This situation can be dramatically portrayed by a fragment of the poem "Speech for the Flowers" by the Mexican poet Carlos Pellicer. It expresses the deep contradiction embedded in what it means to be Mexican:

> The Mexican People have two obsessions:
> the pleasure for Death and the love for flowers.
> Before we had spoken Castilian
> there was a day of the month dedicated to
>   Death;
> there was a strange war they called flowery war
> and full of blood the altars were dripping good
>   luck.
> In blood and fire the Mexican People have lived.
> They live of blood and flower their Memory and
>   Oblivion.

READING

The Conquest of Mexico

Gruzinksi 1992, Thomas 1993: Motecuhzoma, Aztec civilization, and Cortés; Burkholder, 2001:

colonial Mexico; Miller 1985: Aztec civilization to modern era.

The Process of Transculturation

Aguilar 1999: evangelization of Indians and millenarianism; Bonfil Batalla 1996: Mexican identity; Burkholder 2001, Miller 1985: colonial rule, transfer of power; Miller 1985: Maximilian, enlightenment, and independence.

Tequitqui Art

Aguilar-Moreno 1999: colonial art and cathedrals; Mullen 1997: architecture; Bonfil Batalla 1996: artistic acculturation.

Mexico and Its Mestizo Identity

Bonfil Batalla 1996: Indian and mestizo; Joseph and Henderson 2002, Miller 1985: Porfiriato and revolution; Paz 1985, Vento 1998: colonized identity; Paz 1985, Vento 1998: Mexican identity theory and history; Simpson 1971: Mexican presidents and Mexican constitution.

The Indians of Central Mexico Today

Montgomery 1982, Suchlicki 1996, Merrell 2003: Mexico today; Benítez 1964, Smith 2003: Indians of today; Bonfil Batalla 1996: Indian discontent.

MAIN MUSEUMS CONTAINING AZTEC COLLECTIONS

AUCH, FRANCE
Musée des Jacobins

BASEL, SWITZERLAND
Museum der Kulturen Basel

BELFAST, NORTHERN IRELAND
Ulster Museum

BERLIN, GERMANY
Staatliche Museen zu Berlin: Preussischer Kulturbesitz, Ethnologisches Museum

BOLOGNA, ITALY
Biblioteca Universitaria di Bologna

BRUSSELS, BELGIUM
Musées Royaux d'Art et d'Histoire

CAMBRIDGE, MASSACHUSETTS
Peabody Museum of Archaeology and Ethnology, Harvard University

CHICAGO, ILLINOIS
Art Institute of Chicago Field Museum of Natural History

CLEVELAND, OHIO
Cleveland Museum of Art

COPENHAGEN, DENMARK
National Museum of Denmark

EL ESCORIAL, SPAIN
Monasterio de San Lorenzo de El Escorial

FLORENCE, ITALY
Biblioteca Medicea Laurenziana
Biblioteca Nazionale Centrale di Firenze
Museo degli Argenti

GLASGOW, SCOTLAND
Glasgow University Library

HAMBURG, GERMANY
Museum fur Völkerkunde Hamburg

JALAPA, VERACRUZ
Museo de Antropología de Jalapa

LIVERPOOL, ENGLAND
Liverpool Museum

LONDON, ENGLAND
British Museum
Victoria and Albert Museum

LOS ANGELES, CALIFORNIA
Los Angeles County Museum of Art
Fowler Museum of Cultural History, University of California, Los Angeles

MADRID, SPAIN
Biblioteca Nacional

MANNHEIM, GERMANY
Völkerkundlichen Sammlungen der Stadt Mannheim im Reiss-Museum

MEXICO CITY, MEXICO
Fundación Televisa

Museo Nacional de Antropología
Museo Templo Mayor
Museo Universitario de Ciencias y Artes,
    Universidad Nacional Autónoma de México

MUNICH, GERMANY
Schatzkammer der Residenz München
Staatliches Museum für Völkerkunde

NEW HAVEN, CONNECTICUT
Peabody Museum of Natural History, Yale
    University

NEW YORK, NEW YORK
American Museum of Natural History
Brooklyn Museum of Art
Metropolitan Museum of Art

NUREMBERG, GERMANY
Germanisches National Museum
Museen der Stadt Nürnberg

OAXACA, OAXACA
Museo de las Culturas de Oaxaca

OXFORD, ENGLAND
Bodleian Library

PARIS, FRANCE
Bibliothéque Nationale de France
Musée de l'Homme

PHILADELPHIA, PENNSYLVANIA
Philadelphia Museum of Art

PRINCETON, NEW JERSEY
Henry and Rose Pearlman Foundation,
    University Art Museum

PROVIDENCE, RHODE ISLAND
John Carter Brown Library, Brown University

PUEBLA, PUEBLA
Museo Regional de Antropología de Puebla

ROME, ITALY
Museo Nazionale Preistorico, ed Etnografico
    "Luigi Pigorini"

SAINT LOUIS, MISSOURI
Saint Louis Art Museum

SAINT PETERSBURG, RUSSIA
State Hermitage Museum

TEOTENANGO, ESTADO DE MÉXICO
Museo Arqueológico del Estado de México
    "Dr. Román Piña Chan"

TEOTIHUACAN, ESTADO DE MÉXICO
Museo de la Pintura Mural Teotihuacana

TEPOTZOTLAN, ESTADO DE MÉXICO
Museo Nacional del Virreinato

TLAXCALA, TLAXCALA
Museo Regional de Tlaxcala

TOLUCA, ESTADO DE MÉXICO
Instituto Mexiquense de Cultura: Museo
    de Antropología e Historia del Estado de
    México

TULA, HIDALGO
Museo de Sitio de Tula

TURIN, ITALY
Museo Civico d'Arte Antica e Palazzo
    Madama

VATICAN CITY
Biblioteca Apostolica Vaticana
Museo Missionario Etnografico

VERACRUZ, VERACRUZ
Museo Baluarte de Santiago

VIENNA, AUSTRIA
Museum fur Völkerkunde

VILLAHERMOSA, TABASCO
Museo Regional de Antropología "Carlos
    Pellicer"

WASHINGTON, D.C.
Dumbarton Oaks Pre-Columbian Collection

AZTEC POEMS

Translated from Spanish by Kim A. Eherenman

1. And they took with them,
   their black and red ink,
   their annals and their paintings;
   they took all the arts with them, their culture,
   the music of their flutes.

   —*Aztec priest*

2. Even though it was night,
   even though it was not day,
   even though there was no light
   they gathered,
   the gods convened,
   there at Teotihuacan.

   —*Aztec myth*

3. The city spreads out in circles of jade,
   and radiates flashes of light like quetzal plumes,
   Beside it the lords are carried in boats:
   a flowery mist envelopes them.

   —*Nahuatl poem*

4. Everywhere that meets the eye,
   everywhere you look you see
   the remains of their clay vessels,
   their cups, their carvings,
   their dolls, their figurines,
   their bracelets,
   their ruins are all around,
   truly the Toltecs once lived there.

   —*Nahuatl poem*

5. Then he fixes his eyes on Tula and in that
   moment he begins to weep:
   as he sobs it is as if two torrents of rain are

falling down:
His tears slide down his face;
his tears perforate the stones drop by drop.

   —*Aztec legend*

6. There is nothing like death in war,
   nothing like a flowery death
   so precious to Him Who Gives Us Life:
   I can see it far off. My heart yearns for it!

   —*Nahuatl song*

7. The mature man:
   a heart as firm as stone,
   a wise countenance,
   the owner of a face and a heart
   who is capable of understanding.

   —*Huehuetlatolli*

8. When I suffer,
   I make myself strong.
   If we are sad,
   if we go around weeping while on earth,
   it will truly be over in a single moment.

   —*Otomí song*

9. I, Nezahualcoyotl, pose the question:
   Do we really live on earth?
   We are not on earth forever,
   we are only here for a little while.
   Even if life were jade, it would fall apart,
   Even if life were gold, it would wear away,
   Even if life were made of quetzal feathers,
   it would be torn apart.
   We are not on Earth forever,
   we are only here for a little while.

   —*Nezahualcoyotl of Tetzcoco*

10. What have you been seeking?
    Where has your heart been wandering?
    If you give your heart to each little thing,
    you leave it without direction;
    you lose your heart.
    Can anything be found on Earth?

    —Nezahualcoyotl of Tetzcoco

11. My flowers will never end,
    my songs will never cease to be.
    I, the singer, raise them up;
    they scatter, they disperse.

    —Nezahualcoyotl of Tetzcoco

12. Oh, Lords,
    We are mortal,
    our mortality defines us.
    We all have to die,
    We all have to go away,
    four by four, all of us.
    Like a painting
    we gradually fade.
    Like a flower
    we gradually dry up
    here on Earth.
    Like the plumage of the *zacuán* bird,
    or that of the precious rubber-neck bird,
    we are consumed bit by bit.
    Think on this, oh Lords,
    eagle and jaguar warriors,
    even if you were made of jade,
    even if you were made of gold,
    you would go there too,
    to the Land of the Fleshless.
    We all must disappear,
    not a single one of us will remain.

    —Nezahualcoyotl of Tetzcoco

13. Oh, Giver of Life, you create
    all those who live on Earth out of flowers,
    you color them with song,
    you shade them with song.
    Then you destroy the eagle and jaguar warriors.
    We only exist in your picture book
    here on Earth.
    You blot out what is left of the brotherhood,
    the community, the nobility,

with black ink.
You shade all those who live on Earth.

—Nezahualcoyotl of Tetzcoco

14. The house of He Who Creates Himself can't be
    found anywhere
    but our lord, our god, is invoked everywhere,
    he is venerated everywhere.
    We look for his glory, his fame here on Earth.
    He is the one who creates all things,
    he is the one who made himself god.
    He is invoked everywhere,
    he is venerated everywhere.
    We look for his glory, his fame here on Earth.
    Not a single person,
    no one on this Earth,
    can be the Giver of Life's friend;
    he is only invoked.
    We live on Earth
    by his side,
    next to him.
    The one who finds him
    knows that this is so: he is invoked,
    and we live by his side,
    next to him, on Earth.
    No one is really
    your friend,
    oh Giver of Life!
    We, who live on Earth,
    can only look for you
    as if looking for someone
    hidden among flowers
    while we are by your side.
    Your heart grows weary of us,
    for we will only be
    next to you, by your side,
    for a short while.
    The Giver of Life drives us mad,
    and intoxicates us here on Earth.
    No one can truly be by his side,
    succeed in life, or rule on Earth.

    —Nezahualcoyotl of Tetzcoco

15. Thus spoke Tochihuitzin,
    thus spoke Coyolchiuhqui:
    We only rise from sleep,
    we only come to dream.
    It is not true, it is not true,

that we come to Earth to live.
Our nature
is that of an herb in springtime.
Our hearts give birth, they make
the flowers of our flesh sprout.
Some blossom
only to wither and die.
Thus spoke Tochihuitzin,
thus spoke Coyolchiuhqui:

—*Tochihuitzin-Coyolchiuhqui of Tenochtitlan*

16. I have arrived,
    I stand up,
    and I will now sing songs.
    I will make the songs spring forth
    for you, my friends.
    I am God's voice,
    I possess the flowers.
    I am Temilotzin,
    and I have come
    to make friends here.

—*Temilotzin of Tlatelolco*

17. We have arrived on Earth in vain,
    we have sprung forth in vain.
    Am I to go just like that,
    like the flowers that perish?
    Nothing will remain of my name?
    Nothing of my fame will stay here on Earth?
    At least there are flowers!
    At least there are songs!
    What could my heart possibly do?
    We have arrived on Earth,
    we have sprung forth in vain.
    Friends, let's enjoy ourselves,
    let's embrace each other.
    We all walk along the flowery Earth.
    No one here can do away with
    the flowers and the songs,
    they will endure
    in the house of the Giver of Life.
    Earth is the home
    of the fleeting moment.
    Is it also like that in the place
    where in some way one survives?
    Is one happy there?
    Is there friendship there?
    Or is it that we only

come to know who we truly are
here on Earth?

—*Ayocuan of Tecamachalco*

18. Now, oh friends,
    listen to the word, the true dream:
    Each spring gives us life,
    the golden ear of corn replenishes us,
    the young ear of corn becomes our necklace.
    We know the hearts of our friends are true!

—*Tecayehuatzin of Huexotzinco*

19. Perhaps one of us,
    perhaps not all of us,
    will delight, will please,
    the Inventor of Himself?
    The Tamoanchan of the eagle warriors,
    The House of Night of the jaguar warriors,
    are in Huexotzinco.
    That is where Tlacahuepan,
    the one they so admired,
    died.

—*Tecayehuatzin of Huexotzinco*

20. I only grieve and lament:
    Don't let me go
    to the Land of the Fleshless.
    My life is precious.
    I exist,
    I am a singer,
    my flowers are made of gold.
    I have to leave them behind.
    I look at my house,
    the flowers are all in a row.
    Perhaps valuable pieces of jade,
    fanned feather headdresses,
    would buy me my life?
    I still have to leave by myself,
    my fate is what it is.
    I am only leaving
    to lose myself forever
    Oh, my God.
    I will abandon even myself!
    I decree: Wrap me up
    as they wrap the dead.
    Wrap me, the singer, in that way.
    Perhaps someone could take over my heart?
    That's the only way I could leave,

with my heart covered in flowers.
The quetzal feathers,
the precious carved jades,
will be destroyed.
Their equal is not to be found
anywhere on this Earth!
Let it be so,
let it be nonviolent.

—Tlaltecatzin of Cuauhchinanco

21. I, Cuauhtencoztli, suffer.
What is truly real?
Will my song still be real tomorrow?
Do men truly exist?
What will survive?
We live here, we stay here,
but we are destitute, oh my friends!

—Cuauhtencoztli

22. The city of Mexico-Tenochtitlan
is proud of itself.
No one here is afraid to die in war.
This is our glory.
This is your command,
oh Giver of Life!
Keep this in mind, oh princes,
do not forget it.
Who could possibly conquer Tenochtitlan?
Who could possibly shake the foundation of
heaven?

—Aztec poem in Cantares mexicanos

23. The march to the Region of Mystery
goes in step to this song!
You are celebrated,
you composed sacred words,
but you have died!
That is why such sadness fills my heart
when I remember you, Itzcoatl.
Did you go because you were tired of life?
Or did our ruler just give up?
No one can defend himself
against the Giver of Life.

That is why the funeral procession continues:
It is everyone's march!

—anonymous Aztec poem

24. As long as the world endures,
the fame and glory of Mexico-Tenochtitlan
will never perish.

—Chimalpahin of Chalco

25. Broken spears lie in the roads;
we have torn our hair in our grief.
The houses are roofless now, and their walls
are red with blood.

Worms are swarming in the streets and plazas,
and the walls are splattered with gore.
The water has turned red, as if it were dyed,
and when we drink it,
it has the taste of brine.

We have pounded our hands in despair
against the adobe walls,
for our inheritance, our city, is lost and dead.
The shields of our warriors were its defense,
but they could not save it.

—Aztec lament

26. Nothing but flowers and songs of sorrow
are left in Mexico and Tlatelolco,
where once we saw warriors and wise men.
We wander here and there
in our desolate poverty.
We are mortal men.
We have seen bloodshed and pain
where once we saw beauty and valor.
We are crushed to the ground;
we lie in ruins.
There is nothing but grief and suffering
in Mexico and Tlatelolco,
where once we saw beauty and valor.
Have you grown weary of your servants?
Are you angry with your servants,
O Giver of Life?

—Aztec lament in Cantares mexicanos

BIBLIOGRAPHY

Abadiano, Dionisio. *Calendario o gran libro astronómico: Historia y cronología de los antiguos indios*. México: Imprenta de la Secretaría de Fomento, 1889.

Adams, Richard E. W. *Prehistoric Mesoamerica*. Norman: University of Oklahoma Press, 1991.

Aguilar, Manuel, and James Brady, eds. *Ulama*. Estudios jaliscienses no. 56. Guadalajara: Colegio de Jalisco, 2004.

Aguilar, Manuel, Miguel Medina Jaen, Tim Tucker, and James Brady. "Origin Caves and Cosmology: A Man-Made Chicomoztoc Complex at Acatzingo Viejo." In *In the Maw of the Earth Monster: Studies in Mesoamerican Ritual Cave Use*. Ed. James Brady and Keith Prufer. Austin: University of Texas Press, 2005.

Aguilar-Moreno, Manuel. "Cultural Encounters in Mexico: Identity and Religion." *Praesidium* introductory vol. (November 2002): 110–116.

———. "The Death in the Aztec Cosmovision." Paper prepared for an art history seminar, University of Texas at Austin, 1996.

———. "The Mesoamerican Ballgame as a Portal to the Underworld." *Pre-Columbian Art Research Institute (PARI) Journal* 3, nos. 2 and 3 (2002–2003): 4–9.

———. *La perfección del silencio—El panteón de Belén—El culto a la muerte en México (The Perfection of Silence)*. Bilingual ed. Guadalajara: Secretaría de Cultura Jalisco, 2003.

———. "Semblanza del ejército azteca." In *Proceedings of the First International Symposium of Military History of Mexico (2001)*. Ed. Clever A. Chávez Marín. Guadalajara: Asociación Internacional de Historia Militar, 2002.

———. "The Tequitqui Art of Sixteenth-Century Mexico: An Expression of Transculturation." Ph.D., University of Texas at Austin, 1999.

Alcina Franch, José. *Pre-Columbian Art*. New York: Harry M. Abrams, 1983.

Alcina Franch, José, Miguel León-Portilla, and Eduardo Matos Moctezuma. *Azteca-Mexica*. Barcelona: INAH-Lunwerg Editores, 1992.

Altamirano, Ignacio Manuel. *Paisajes y leyendas: Tradiciones y costumbres de México*. México: Editorial Porrúa, 1974.

Alva Ixtlilxochitl, Fernando de. *Historia de la nación chichimeca*. Madrid: Historia 16, 1985.

———. *Obras históricas*. 2 vols. Trans. Edmundo O'Gorman. México: UNAM, 1975–77.

Alvarado Tezozomoc, Hernando. *Crónica mexicana (Mexicayotl–1598)*. México: Editorial Porrúa, 1975.

Anawalt, Patricia Rieff. *Indian Clothing Before Cortés: Mesoamerican Costumes from the Codices*. Norman: University of Oklahoma Press, 1981.

———. "Understanding Aztec Human Sacrifice." *Archaeology* 35, no. 5 (1980): 38–45.

Anders, Ferdinand. "Las artes menores; Minor Arts." *Artes de México* no. 137, (1971): 4–66.

Anderson, Arthur J. O. "Old World–New World: *Huehuetlatolli* in Sahagún's Sermons." *Current Topics in Aztec Studies*, San Diego Museum of Man Papers 30 (1993): 85–92.

Angulo Villaseñor, Jorge. "Teopanzolco y Cuauh-nahuac, Morelos." In *Los señoríos y estados militaristas*. Ed. Román Piña Chan. México: INAH, 1976.

Arana Álvarez, Raúl. "El juego de pelota en Coatetelco, Morelos." In *Investigaciones recientes en el área maya, XVII Mesa Redonda, Sociedad Mexicana de Antropología*, vol. 9. México: Sociedad Mexicana de Antropología, 1984.

Arroyo Gaytán, Rubén. "El origen de los aztecas." Paper presented at LASA Conference in Guadalajara, Mexico, 1997.

Aveni, Anthony. *Skywatchers of Ancient Mexico*. Austin: University of Texas Press, 2001.

Aveni, Anthony, Edward Calnek, and Horst Hartung. "Myth, Environment and the Orientation of the Templo Mayor of Tenochtitlan." *American Antiquity* 53 (1988): 287–309.

Baquedano, Elizabeth. *Aztec Sculpture*. London: British Museum Publications, 1984.

Barlow, Robert, and Byron MacAfee. *Diccionario de elementos fonéticos en escritura jeroglífico (Codice mendocine)*. México: UNAM, 1949.

Baskes, Jeremy. *Indians, Merchants and Markets*. Stanford, Calif.: Stanford University Press, 2000.

Beekman, Christopher, and Alexander Christensen. "Controlling for Doubt and Uncertainty Through Multiple Lines of Evidence: A New Look at the Mesoamerican Nahua Migrations." *Journal of Archaeological Method and Theory* 10, no. 2 (June 2003):

Benítez, Fernando. *Los indios de México. Los hongos alucinantes*. Mexico: Ediciones Era, 1964.

Berdan, Frances. *The Aztecs*. New York and Philadelphia: Chelsea House Publishers, 1989.

———. *The Aztecs of Central Mexico: An Imperial Society*. New York: Dryden Press, Saunders College Publishing, 1982.

Berdan, Frances, and Patricia Rieff Anawalt. *Codex Mendoza*. 4 vols. Berkeley: University of California Press, 1993.

———. *The Essential Codex Mendoza*. Berkeley: University of California Press, 1997.

Bernal, Ignacio. *Tenochtitlan en una isla*. México: INAH, 1980.

Biart, Lucien. *The Aztecs: Their History, Manners and Customs*. Chicago: McClury and Co., 1887.

Bierhorst, John. *Cantares mexicanos: Songs of the Aztecs*. Stanford, Calif.: Stanford University Press, 1985.

Blythin, Evan. *Huei Tlatoani: The Mexican Speaker*. Lanham, Md.: University Press of America, 1990.

Boas, Franz. "El dialecto mexicano de Pochutla, Oaxaca." *International Journal of American Linguistics* 1, no. 1 (1917): 9–44.

Bonfil Batalla, Guillermo. *México profundo: Reclaiming a Civilization*. Trans. Philip A. Dennis. Austin: University of Texas Press, 1996.

Boone, Elizabeth Hill, ed. *The Aztec Templo Mayor*. Washington, D.C.: Dumbarton Oaks, 1987.

———. *The Aztec World*. Washington D.C.: Smithsonian Books, 1994.

———. *Stories in Red and Black*. Austin: University of Texas Press, 2000.

Borah, Woodrow, and Sherburne Cook. *The Aboriginal Populations of Central Mexico on the Eve of the Spanish Conquest*. Berkeley: University of California Press, 1963.

Braunfels, Wolfgang. *Urban Design in Western Europe: Regime and Architecture, 900–1900*. Trans. Kenneth J. Northcott. Chicago and London: University of Chicago Press, 1988.

Bray, Warwick. *Everyday Life of the Aztecs*. New York: Peter Bedrick Books, 1991.

Broda, Johanna. "El tributo en trajes guerreros y la estructura del sistema tributario mexica." In *Economía, política e ideología en el México prehispánico*. Ed. Pedro Carrasco and Johanna Broda. México: NAH, 1970, 115–714.

Broda, Johanna, David Carrasco, and Eduardo Matos Moctezuma. *The Great Temple of Tenochtitlan: Center and Periphery in the Aztec World*. Berkeley: University of California Press, 1987.

Broda, Johanna, Stanislav Iwaniszewski, and Lucrecia Maupome, eds. *Arqueoastronomía y etnoastronomía en Mesoamérica*. México: UNAM, 1991.

Brotherston, Gordon. *Painted Books from Mexico. Codices in UK Collections and the World They Represent*. London: British Museum Press, 1995.

Brundage, Burr Cartwright. *Fifth Sun, Aztec Gods, Aztec World*. Austin and London: University of Texas Press, 1979.

———. *The Jade Steps: A Ritual Life of the Aztecs*. Salt Lake City: University of Utah, 1985.

Bunson, Margaret, and Stephen Bunson. *Encyclopedia of Ancient Mesoamerica*. New York: Facts On File, 1996.

Burkhart, Louise. *The Slippery Earth: Nahua-Christian Moral Dialogue in Sixteenth-Century Mexico*. Tucson: University of Arizona Press, 1989.

Burkholder, A. Mark, and Lyman L. Johnson. *Colonial Latin America*. New York: Oxford University Press, 2001.

Burland, Cottie, and Werner Forman. *The Aztecs: Gods and Fate in Ancient Mexico*. New York: Galahad Books, 1967.

Calnek, Edward. "The Internal Structure of Tenochtitlan." In *The Valley of Mexico: Studies of Pre-Hispanic Ecology and Society*. Edited by Eric Wolf. Albuquerque: University of New Mexico Press, 1976.

Campbell, Lyle. *American Indian Languages: The Historical Linguistics of Native America*. New York: Oxford University Press, 1997.

———. *Historical Linguistics: An Introduction*. Cambridge, Mass.: MIT Press, 2001.

———. *The Pipil Language of El Salvador*. Berlin: Mouton de Gruyter, 1985.

Campbell, Lyle, and Ronald W. Langacker. "Proto-Aztecan Vowels: Part III." *International Journal of American Linguistics* 44, no. 4 (October 1978): 262–279.

Canger, Una. "Nahuatl Dialectology: A Survey and Some Suggestions." *Journal of American Linguistics* 54, no. 1 (1988): 28–72.

Carmack, Robert M., Janine Gasco, and Gary H. Gossen, eds. *The Legacy of Mesoamerica: History and Culture of a Native American Civilization*. Englewood Cliffs, N.J.: Prentice Hall, 1996.

Carrasco, Davíd. *City of Sacrifice: The Aztec Empire and the Role of Violence in Civilization*. Boston: Beacon Press, 1999.

———. *Daily Life of the Aztecs: People of the Sun and Earth*. Wesport, Conn.: Greenwood Press, 1998.

Carrasco, Davíd, and Eduardo Matos Moctezuma. *Moctezuma's Mexico: Visions of the Aztec World*. Niwot: University of Colorado Press, 1992.

Caso, Alfonso. *The Aztecs, People of the Sun*. Norman: University of Oklahoma Press, 1982.

———. "Pre-Spanish Art." In *Twenty Centuries of Mexican Art*. New York: Museum of Modern Art and the Mexican Government, 1940.

———. *El pueblo del sol*. México: Fondo de Cultura Económica, 1981.

Castelló Yturbide, Teresa, ed. *El arte plumaria en México*. México: Fomento Cultural Banamex, 1993.

Cervantes de Salazar, Francisco. *Crónica de la Nueva España (1558)*. Madrid: Ediciones Atlas, 1983.

Chavero, Alfredo. *Calendario o rueda del año de los antiguos indios*. México: Imprenta del Museo Nacional, 1901.

———. *México a través de los siglos*. Vol. 1. México: T. I. Ballescá y Cía., 1887.

Childe, Gordon. *The Bronze Age*. New York: Biblo and Tannen, 1963.

Chimalpahin Quauhtlehuanitzin, Domingo Francisco de San Antón Muñón. *Codex Chimalpahin: Annals of the History of Central Mexico (1285–1612)*. 2 vols. Ed. Arthur J. O. Anderson and Susan Schroeder. Norman: University of Oklahoma Press, 1997.

Clavijero, Francisco Xavier. *Historia antigua de México*. México: Editorial del Valle de México, 1978.

Clendinnen, Inga. *Aztecs, an Interpretation*. Cambridge: Cambridge University Press, 1991.

Cline, S. L. *The Book of Tributes: Early Sixteenth-Century Nahuatl Censuses from Morelos*. Los Angeles: Latin American Center Publications, University of California, Los Angeles, 1993.

———. *Colonial Culhuacan, 1580–1600. A Social History of an Aztec Town*. Albuquerque: University of New Mexico Press, 1986.

Codex Azcatitlan. Paris: Societé des Americanistes, 1949.

Codex Boturini: Tira de la peregrinación mexica. México: Librería Anticuaria, 1944.

Codex Chimalpopoca: Anales de Cuauhtitlan y leyenda de los soles. Trans. Primo Feliciano Velázquez. México: UNAM, 1986.

Codex Ixtlilxochitl. Ed. Geert Bustiaan Van Doesburg. Graz, Austria: Akademische Druck und Verlagsanstalt, 1996.

Codex Magliabecchi. Ed. and analytical study Ferdinand Anders. Graz, Austria: Akademische Druck und Verlagsanstalt, 1970.

Codex matrícula de tributos (Codex Moctezuma). Ed. Ferdinand Anders, Maarten Jansen, and Luis Reyes García. Graz, Austria, and México:

Akademische Druck und Verlagsantalt/Fondo de Cultura Económica, 1997.

Codex Mendoza. Ed. Frances Berdan and Patricia Rieff Anawalt. 4 vols. Berkeley: University of California Press, 1988.

———. Ed. Francisco del Paso y Troncoso. México: Editorial Cosmos, 1987.

Codex Telleriano-Remensis. Ed. Eloise Quiñones Keber. Austin: University of Texas Press, 1995.

Codex Vaticanus A (Codex Ríos). Ed. Akademische Druck. Graz, Austria: Akademische Druck und Verlagsanstalt, 1979.

Códice borbónico: Manuscrito mexicano de la Biblioteca del Palais de Bourbon: Libro adivinatorio y ritual ilustrado, publicado en facsimil. Ed. Francisco del Paso y Troncoso. México: Siglo Veintiuno, 1985.

Códice de Santa María Asunción: Households and Lands in 16th Century Tepetlaoztoc. Analytic study by Barbara J. Williams and H. R. Harvey. Salt Lake City: University of Utah Press, 1997.

Coe, Michael, and Rex Koontz. *Mexico: From the Olmecs to the Aztecs.* New York: Thames and Hudson, 2002.

Coe, Sophie, and Michael Coe. *The True History of Chocolate.* New York: Thames and Hudson, 1996.

Colston, Stephen A. "People, Places, and Pictures: Name Signs from a Corpus of Early Colonial Acolhua Cadastral Manuscripts." *Current Topics in Aztec Studies,* San Diego Museum of Man Papers 30, (1993): 85–92.

Conquistador Anónimo (Alonso de Ulloa?). *Relación de algunas cosas de la Nueva España y de la gran ciudad de Temestitlán México, escrita por un compañero de Hernán Cortés.* México: Editorial América, 1941.

Cortés, Hernán. *Letters from México (1521–1526).* Trans. and ed. Anthony Pagden. New Haven, Conn.: Yale University Press, 1986.

Covarrubias, Miguel. *Indian Art of Mexico and Central America.* New York: Alfred Knopf, 1957.

Cowgill, George L. "State and Society at Teotihuacan, Mexico." *Annual Review of Anthropology* 26 (1997): 129–161.

Crosby, Alfred. *The Columbian Exchange: Biological and Cultural Consequences of 1492.* Westport, Conn.: Greenwood Press, 1972.

Cruz, Martín de la. *Libellus de medicinalibus indorum herbis (Códice de la Cruz-Badiano) (1552).* Trans. Angel María Garibay. México: IMSS, 1990.

Cyphers, Ann. "Olmec Architecture in San Lorenzo." In *Olmec to Aztec: Settlement Patterns in the Ancient Gulf Lowlands.* Ed. B. L. Stark and P. J. Arnold III. Tucson: University of Arizona Press, 1997.

Davies, Nigel. *The Ancient Kingdoms of Mexico.* New York: Pelican Books, 1985.

———. *The Aztecs: A History.* Norman: University of Oklahoma Press, 1982.

———. *The Toltec Heritage: From the Fall of Tula to the Rise of Tenochtitlan.* Norman: University of Oklahoma Press, 1980.

Dávila, Mario, and James Brady. "La producción del hule en el juego de pelota." In *Ulama.* Ed. Manuel Aguilar and James Brady. Estudios Jaliscienses No. 56. Guadalajara: Colegio de Jalisco, 2004.

Day, Jane. *Aztec: The World of Moctezuma.* Niwot, Colo.: Denver Museum of Natural History and Roberts Rinehart Publishers, 1992.

Díaz del Castillo, Bernal. *The Conquest of New Spain.* Trans. J. M. Cohen. London: Penguin Books, 1963.

———. *La verdadera historia de la conquista de México (1568).* México: Editorial Porrúa, 1993.

Drucker, Philip, Robert Heizer, and Robert Squier. "Excavations at La Venta, Tabasco, 1955." Bulletin 170. Washington, D.C.: Bureau of American Ethnology, 1959.

Durán, Fray Diego. *Book of the Gods and Rites and the Ancient Calendar.* Trans. D. Heyden and F. Horcasitas. Norman: University of Oklahoma Press, 1971.

———. *Historia de las Indias de Nueva España y islas de tierra firme (1579–1581).* México: Editorial Porrúa, 1967.

———. *The History of the Indies of New Spain.* Trans. annotated, and with an introduction by Doris Heyden. Norman: University of Oklahoma Press, 1994.

Edmonson, Munro S. *Sixteenth-Century Mexico: The Work of Sahagún.* Albuquerque: University of New Mexico Press, 1974.

Escalante, Pablo. "Las obras hidráulicas en tiempos mexicas." In *Atlas histórico de Mesoamérica.* Ed.

Linda Manzanilla and Leonardo López Luján. México: Larousse, 2002, 163–167.

Esparza Hidalgo, David. *Cómputo azteca*. México: Editorial Diana, 1975.

Fagan, Brian. *The Adventure of Archaeology*. Washington, D.C.: National Geographic Society, 1985.

———. *The Aztecs*. New York: W. H. Freeman, 1997.

Florescano, Enrique. *Memory, Myth, and Time in Mexico: From the Aztecs to the Independence*. Austin: University of Texas Press, 1994.

———. "Sobre la naturaleza de los dioses de Mesoamerica." *Estudios de Cultura Nahuatl*. Vol. 27. México: UNAM, 1997.

Fowler, Catherine. "Some Lexical Clues to Aztec Prehistory." *International Journal of American Linguistics* 49, no. 3 (July 1983): 224–257.

Fuentes, Patricia de. *The Conquistadors*. New York: Orion Press, 1963.

Furst, Peter. "Spirulina." *Human Nature* 1 (1978): 60–65.

Galarza, Joaquín. "Los códices mexicanos." *Arqueología Mexicana* 4, no. 23 (1997): 6–15.

———. *Lectura de códices aztecas*. México: Editorial Amatl, 1995.

Galindo Trejo, Jesús. "Cuando Huitzilopochtli descendió en Malinalco." *México Desconocido* 152 (October 1989): 17–22.

García, Gregorio. *Origen de los indios del Nuevo Mundo (1607)*. México: Fondo de Cultura Económica, 1998.

García Chavez, Raúl. "Tetzcotzinco y alrededores, Estado de México." *Arqueología Mexicana* 10, no. 58 (November–December 2002): 70–77.

García G., María Teresa. *Tetzcotzinco, Estado de México: Mini-guía*. México: NAH, 2001.

García Moll, Roberto. *Santa Cecilia Acatitlan, Estado de México: Mini-guía*. México: INAH, 1993.

García Payón, José. *Los monumentos arqueológicos de Malinalco*. México: Biblioteca Enciclopédica del Estado de México, 1974.

García Quintana, Josefina, and José Rubén Romero Galván. *México-Tenochtitlan y su problemática lacustre*. México: UNAM, 1978.

Garibay, Angel María. *Historia de la literatura náhuatl*. México: Porrúa, 1971.

———. *Teogonía e historia de los mexicanos. Tres opúsculos del siglo XVI*. México: Editorial Porrúa, 1965.

Gates, William. *An Aztec Herbal—The Classic Code of 1552*. Mineola, N.Y.: Dover Publications, 2000.

Gendrop, Paul. *Historia del arte en Mesoamérica*. México: Trillas, 1988.

Gendrop, Paul, and Iñaki Díaz Balerdi. *Escultura azteca. Una aproximación a su estética*. México: Trillas, 1994.

Gibson, Charles. *The Aztecs Under Spanish Rule: A History of the Indians of the Valley of Mexico, 1519–1810*. Stanford, Calif.: Stanford University Press, 1964.

Gibson, Charles, and John B. Glass. "A Census of Middle American Prose Manuscripts in the Native Historical Tradition." In *Handbook of Middle American Indians*. Vol. 15: *Guide to Ethnohistorical Sources, Part Four*. Ed. H. F. Cline. London: University of Texas Press, 1975.

Gillespie, Susan. *Aztec Kings: The Construction of Rulership in Mexica History*. Tucson: University of Arizona Press, 1989.

Glass, John B. "A Census of Native Middle American Pictorial Manuscripts." In *Handbook of Middle American Indians*. Vol. 14: *Guide to Ethnohistorical Sources, Part Three*. Ed. H. F. Cline. London: University of Texas Press, 1975.

Godoy, Ricardo. "Franz Boas and His Plans for an International School of American Archaeology and Ethnography in Mexico." *Journal of the History of the Behavioral Sciences* 13 (1977): 228–242.

González Rul, Francisco. *Urbanismo y arquitectura en Tlatelolco*. México: INAH, 1982.

González Torres, Yolotl. *El culto de los astros entre los mexicas*. México: SEP, 1979.

———. *Diccionario de mitología y religión de Mesoamérica*. México: Larousse, 1991.

———. "Human Sacrifice." *Arqueología Mexicana* 11, no. 63 (September/October 2003): 40–45.

———. *El sacrificio humano entre los mexicas*. Sep. Setentas: 217. México: SEP, 1985.

Graulich, Michel. "Human Sacrifice in Mesoamerica." *Arqueología Mexicana* 11, no. 63 (September/October 2003): 18–21.

———. "La Piedra del Sol." In *Azteca-Mexica*. Ed. José Alcina Franch, Miguel León Portilla, and

Eduardo Matos Moctezuma. Madrid: INAH-Lunwerg Editores, 1992, 291–295.

Grove, David C. "The Formative Period and the Evolution of Complex Culture." In *Supplement to the Handbook of Middle American Indians.* Vol. 1: *Archaeology.* Ed. V. R. Bricker. Austin: University of Texas Press, 1981.

Gruzinski, Serge. *The Aztecs: Rise and Fall of an Empire.* New York: Abrams, 1992.

Gutiérrez Solana, Nelly. *Códices de México: Historia e interpretación de los grandes libros pintados prehispánicos.* México: Panorama Editorial, 1985.

Hammer, Olga, and Jeanne D'Andrea, eds. *Treasures of Mexico from the Mexican National Museums.* Los Angeles: Armand Hammer Foundation, 1978.

Harvey, Herbert, and Hanns Prem. *Exploitations in Ethnohistory: Indians of Central Mexico in the Sixteenth Century.* Albuquerque: University of New Mexico Press, 1984.

Hassig, Ross. *Aztec Warfare, Imperial Expansion and Political Control.* Norman: University of Oklahoma Press, 1988.

———. *Time, History, and Belief in Aztec and Colonial Mexico.* Austin: University of Texas Press, 2001.

———. *Trade, Tribute and Transportation: The Sixteenth Century Political Economy of the Valley of Mexico.* Norman: University of Oklahoma Press, 1985.

———. *War and Society in Ancient Mesoamerica.* Berkeley: University of California Press, 1992.

Hays, Wilma, and Vernon Hays. *Foods the Indians Gave Us.* New York: Ives Washburn, 1973.

Hernández, Francisco. *Historia natural de la Nueva España.* 4 vols. México: UNAM, 1959.

Hernández Rivero, José. *Ideología y práctica militar mexica. El cuauhcalli de Malinalco.* Toluca: Ayuntamiento de Malinalco, Estado de México, 1984.

Heyden, Doris, and Paul Gendrop. *Pre-Columbian Architecture of Mesoamerica.* New York: Harry N. Abrams, 1975.

Heyden, Doris, and Luis Francisco Villaseñor. *The Great Temple and the Aztec Gods.* México: Minutiae Mexicana, 1992.

Hinton, Thomas B. *Coras, huicholes y tepehuanes.* México: SEP-INI, 1972.

Historia de los mexicanos por sus pinturas. In *Teogonía e historia de los Mexicanos. Tres opúsculos del siglo XVI.* Ed. Angel María Garibay. México: Editorial Porrúa, 1965.

Historia tolteca-chichimeca. Ed. Paul Kirchhoff, Lina Odena Güemes, and Luis Reyes García. México: Fondo de Cultura Económica, CIESAS, Estado de Puebla, 1976.

Histoyre du Mechique. In *Teogonía e historia de los mexicanos. Tres opúsculos del siglo XVI.* Ed. Angel María Garibay. México: Editorial Porrúa, 1965.

Horcasitas, Fernando. *The Aztecs Then and Now.* México: Editorial Minutiae Mexicana, 1979.

Huehuetlatolli: Testimonios de la antigua palabra. Attributed to Fray Andrés de Olmos. Introductory study by Miguel León-Portilla. México: Fondo de Cultura Económica, 1991.

Ibarra García, Laura. *La visión del mundo de los antiguos mexicanos: Origen de sus conceptos de causalidad, tiempo y espacio.* Guadalajara: Universidad de Guadalajara, 1995.

Jackson, Robert. *Race, Caste, and Status: Indians in Colonial Spanish America.* Albuquerque: University of New Mexico, 1999.

Jiménez-Moreno, Wigberto. *Apuntes de historia antigua de México.* México: Sociedad de Alumnos de la Escuela Nacional de Antropología, 1953.

Johansson, Patrick. "Death in Mesoamerica." *Arqueología mexicana* 10, no. 60 (March/April 2003): 46–53.

———. *La palabra de los aztecas.* México: Trillas, 1993.

Joseph, Gilbert M., and Timothy J. Henderson, ed. *The Mexico Reader: History, Culture, Politics.* Durham, N.C.: Duke University Press, 2002.

Kampen, Michael E. "Classic Veracruz Grotesques and Sacrificial Iconography." *Man* 13 (1978): 116–126.

———. *The Sculptures of El Tajín, Veracruz, Mexico.* Gainesville: University of Florida Press, 1972.

Karttunen, Frances. *Analytical Dictionary of Nahuatl.* Norman: University of Oklahoma Press, 1983.

Kehoe, Alice B. *North American Indians: A Comprehensive Account.* 2d ed. Upper Saddle River, N.J.: Prentice Hall, 1992.

Kelly, Joyce. *The Complete Visitor's Guide to Mesoamerican Ruins.* Norman: University of Oklahoma Press, 1982.

Kirchhoff, Paul. *Escritos selectos: Estudios mesoamericanistas.* México: UNAM, 2002.

———. "Mesoamérica: Sus líimites geográficos, composición étnica, y caracteres culturales." *Acta Americana* 1 (1943): 92–107.

Klein, Cecilia. "The Identity of the Central Deity on the Aztec Calendar Stone." In *Pre-Columbian Art History: Selected Readings*. Ed. Alana Cordy-Collins and Jean Stern. Palo Alto, Calif.: Peek Publications, 1977.

Klor de Alva, Jorge, Henry B. Nicholson, and Eloise Quiñones-Keber, eds. *The Work of Bernardino de Sahagún: Pioneer Ethnographer of Sixteenth-Century Mexico*. Albany, N.Y.: Institute for Mesoamerican Studies, 1988.

Konieczna, Bárbara. *Coatetelco, Morelos: Mini-guía*. México: INAH, 1992.

———. *Teopanzolco, Morelos: Mini-guía*. México: INAH, 2003.

Kubler, George. *The Art and Architecture of Ancient Mesoamerica*. New Haven, Conn., and London: Yale University Press, 1990.

Langley, James. *Symbolic Notation of Teotihuacan: Elements of Writing in a Mesoamerican Culture of the Classic Period*. Oxford, England: B.A.R., 1986.

León-Portilla, Miguel. *Los antiguos mexicanos, a través de sus crónicas y cantares*. México: Fondo de Cultura Económica, 1970.

———. *Aztec Thought and Culture*. Norman: University of Oklahoma Press, 1963.

———. *The Broken Spears: The Aztec Account of the Conquest of Mexico*. Boston: Beacon Press, 1992.

———. *De Teotihuacan a los aztecas*. México: UNAM, 1971.

———. *Fifteen Poets of the Aztec World*. Norman: University of Oklahoma Press, 1992.

———. *La filosofía náhuatl estudiada en sus fuentes*. México: UNAM, 1959.

———. "Grandes momentos en la historia de los códices." *Arqueología Mexicana* 4, no. 23 (1997): 16–23.

———. *Pre-Columbian Literatures of Mexico*. Norman: University of Oklahoma Press, 1969.

———. "Testimonios nahuas sobre la conquista espiritual." *Estudios de Cultura Nahuatl* 11 (1974): 11–36.

———. *Trece poetas del mundo azteca*. México: UNAM, 1975.

———. *La visión de los vencidos*. Madrid: Historia 16, 1985.

León y Gama, Antonio de. *Descripción histórica y cronológica de las dos piedras*. México: Imprenta del ciudadano Alejandro Valdés, 1833.

Limón Olvera, Silvia. *Las cuevas y el mito de origen: los casos inca y mexica*. México: CONACULTA, 1990.

Lockhart, James. *The Nahuas after the Conquest: A Social and Cultural History of the Indians of Central Mexico, Sixteenth through Eighteenth Centuries*. Stanford, Calif.: Stanford University Press, 1992.

López Austin, Alfredo. *Cuerpo humano e ideología*. 2 vols. México: UNAM, 1980.

———. *The Human Body and Ideology*. 2 vols. Salt Lake City: University of Utah Press, 1988.

———. *Tamoanchan, Tlalocan: Places of Mist*. Niwot: University Press of Colorado, 1997.

López Luján, Leonardo. "La cuenca de México durante la época mexica." In *Atlas histórico de Mesoamérica*. Ed. Linda Manzanilla and Leonardo López Luján. México: Larousse, 2002.

———. *The Offerings of the Templo Mayor of Tenochtitlan*. Niwot: University Press of Colorado, 1994.

Lorenzo, José Luis. "Archaeology South of the Rio Grande." *World Archaeology* 13, no. 2 (October 1981): 190–208.

Lorenzo, José Luis, Lorena Mirambell, and Jaime Litvak King, eds. *La arqueología y México*. México: INAH, 1998.

Ludden, Andrea. "Aztec Garments from Birth to Fullfilment." Paper presented at LASA Conference, Guadalajara, México, 1997.

MacNeish, Richard S. "Mesoamerican Archaeology." *Biennial Review of Anthropology* 5 (1967): 306–331.

Mangelsdorf, P. C., Richard S. MacNeish, and Gordon R. Willey. "Origins of Agriculture in Middle America." In *Handbook of Middle American Indians*. Vol. 1: *Natural Environment and Early Cultures*. Ed. by R. Wauchope. Austin: University of Texas Press, 1964.

Manzanilla, Linda, and Leonardo López Luján. *Atlas histórico de Mesoamérica*. México: Larousse, 2002.

Marcus, Joyce. *Mesoamerican Writing Systems: Propaganda, Myth, and History in Four Ancient Civilizations*. Princeton, N.J.: Princeton University Press, 1992.

Markman, Roberta, and Peter Markman. *Masks of the Spirit: Images and Metaphor in Mesoamerica*.

Berkeley, Los Angeles, and Oxford: University of California Press, 1989.

Marquina, Ignacio. *Arquitectura prehispánica*. México: INAH, 1964.

Matos Moctezuma, Eduardo. "The Great Temple." *National Geographic* 58, no. 6 (December 1980): 766–775.

———. *The Great Temple of the Aztecs*. New York: Thames and Hudson, 1988.

———. *Life and Death in the Templo Mayor*. Niwot: University Press of Colorado, 1995.

———. *La Piedra del Sol: Calendario azteca*. México: Grupo Impresa, 1992.

———. *Vida y muerte en el Templo Mayor*. México: Océano, 1986.

Matos Moctezuma, Eduardo, and Felipe Solís Olguín, eds. *Aztecs*. London: Royal Academy of Arts, 2002.

McDowell, Bart. "The Aztecs." *National Geographic* 58, no. 6 (December 1980): 714–751.

Méndez Martínez, Enrique. *Cerro de la Estrella, Ciudad de Mexico: Mini-guía*. México: INAH, 1993.

Mendieta, Gerónimo. *Historia eclesiástica indiana (1547–96)*. Analytic study by Joaquín García Icazbalceta. México: Editorial Porrúa, 1971.

Merrell, Floyd. *The Mexicans: A Sense of Culture*. Cambridge, Mass.: Westview Press, 2003.

Metropolitan Museum of Art. *Mexico: Splendors of Thirty Centuries*. Introduction by Octavio Paz. New York: Bulfinch Press, 1990.

Miller, Mary Ellen, and Karl Taube. *An Illustrated Dictionary of the Gods and Symbols of Ancient Mexico and the Maya*. New York: Thames and Hudson, 1993.

Miller, Robert Ryal. *Mexico: A History*. Oklahoma City: University of Oklahoma, 1985.

Millon, René. "Teotihuacan: City, State and Civilization." In *Supplement to the Handbook of Middle American Indians*. Vol. 1: *Archaeology*. Ed. V. R. Bricker. Austin: University of Texas Press, 1981.

Mohar-Betancourt, Luz María. "Tres codices nahuas del México antiguo." *Arqueología Mexicana* 4, no. 23 (1997): 16–23.

Molina, Alonso de. *Vocabulario en lengua mexicana y castellana (1571)*. México: Porrúa, 1970.

Molina Montes, Augusto F. "The Building of Tenochtitlan." *National Geographic* 58, no. 6 (December 1980): 752–765.

Montgomery, Tommie Sue. *Mexico Today*. Philadelphia: Institute for the Study of Human Issues, 1982.

Moreno Villa, José. *La ecultura colonial mexicana*. México: El Colegio de México, 1942.

Motolinia (Fray Toribio de Benavente). *Memoriales o libro de las cosas de la Nueva España y de los naturales de ella*. Appendix by Edmundo O'Gorman. México: UNAM, 1971.

———. *History of the Indians of New Spain*. Trans. Elizabeth Andros Foster. Westport, Conn.: Greenwood Press, 1977.

Mullen, Robert J. *Architecture and Its Sculpture in Viceregal Mexico*. Austin: University of Texas Press, 1997.

Muñoz Camargo, Diego. *Descripción de la ciudad y provincia de Tlaxcala de las indias y del mar océano para el buen gobierno y ennoblecimiento dellas*. Analytic study by René Acuña. México: UNAM, 1981.

———. *Historia de Tlaxcala (fin del siglo XVI)*. Ed. Alfredo Chavero. México: Editorial Innovación, 1979.

Nelson, Ben E. "Chronology and Stratigraphy at La Quemada, Zacatecas, Mexico." *Journal of Field Archaeology* 24 (1997): 85–109.

Nicholson, H. B. "Religion in Pre-Hispanic Central Mexico." In *Handbook of Middle American Indians*. Vol. 10: *Archaeology of Northern Mesoamerica, Part One*. Ed. Gordon Eckholm and Ignacio Bernal. Austin and London: University of Texas Press, 1971.

———. *Topiltzin Quetzalcoatl: The Once and Future Lord of the Toltecs*. Boulder: University Press of Colorado, 2001.

Nicholson, Irene. *Fireflies in the Night: A Study of Ancient Mexican Poetry and Symbolism*. London: Faber and Faber, 1959.

Noll, Arthur H. "Tenochtitlan: Its Site Identified." *American Journal of Archaeology* 1, no. 6 (1897): 515–524.

O'Connor, J. J., and E. F. Robertson. "Carlos de Siguenza y Gongora." MacTutor History of Mathematics Archives. Available online. URL: http://www=history.mcs.st=andrews.ac.uk/Mathematicians/Siguenza.html. Accessed May 16, 2005.

Odijk, Pamela. *The Ancient World: The Aztec.* Englewood Cliffs, N.J.: Silver Burdett, 1989.

Offner, Jerome. *Law and Politics in Aztec Texcoco.* Cambridge: Cambridge University Press, 1983.

Orozco y Berra, Manuel. *Historia antigua y de la conquista de México.* 4 vols. México: Porrúa, 1960.

Palerm, Angel. *Agricultura y sociedad en Mesoamérica.* México: SEP, 1972.

———. *Obras hidráulicas prehispánicas en el sistema lacustre del Valle de México.* México: SEP-INAH, 1973.

Parsons, Jeffrey R. "The Development of a Prehistoric Complex Society: A Regional Perspective from the Valley of Mexico." *Journal of Field Archaeology* 1, nos. 1–2 (1974): 81–108.

Pasztory, Esther. *Aztec Art.* New York: Abrams, 1983.

Payne, Stanley, and Michael Closs. "A Survey of Aztec Numbers and Their Uses." In *Native American Mathematics.* Ed. Michael Closs. Austin: University of Texas Press, 1986.

Paz, Octavio. *The Labyrinth of Solitude.* New York: Grove Press, 1985.

Peñafiel, Antonio. *Nombres geográficos de México en náhuatl.* México: Secretaría de Fomento, 1885.

Perry, Richard. *Mexico's Fortress Monasteries.* Santa Barbara, Calif.: Espadaña Press, 1992.

Peterson, Frederick. *Ancient Mexico: An Introduction to the Pre-Hispanic Cultures.* New York: G. P. Putman's Sons, 1959.

Pohl, John M. D. *Aztec, Mixtec and Zapotec Armies.* Oxford: Osprey Publishing, 1991.

———. *Aztec Warrior AD 1325–1521.* Oxford: Osprey Publishing, 2001.

———. *Exploring Mesoamerica.* Oxford: Oxford University Press, 1999.

Pomar, Juan Bautista, de. *Poesía nahuatl.* Trans. and ed. Angel María Garibay. México: UNAM, 1964.

———. *Relación de Texcoco, instrucción y memoria, romances de los señores de la Nueva España, 1577–1582.* Benson Library Manuscripts Collection, University of Texas at Austin.

Prescott, William. *History of the Conquest of Mexico and History of the Conquest of Peru.* New York: Cooper Square Press, 2000.

———. *The World of the Aztec.* Geneva: Editions Minerva, 1970.

Quiñones-Keber, Eloise, ed. *Representing Aztec Ritual: Performance, Text, and Image in the Work of Sahagún.* Boulder: University Press of Colorado, 2002.

Raat, W. Dirk, and William H. Beezley, eds. *Twentieth-Century Mexico.* Lincoln: University of Nebraska Press, 1986.

Read, Kay A. "Death and the Tlatoani." In *Representing Aztec Ritual.* Ed. Eloise Quiñones-Keber. Boulder: University Press of Colorado, 2002.

Relaciones geográficas del siglo XVI. 10 vols. Ed. and analytical study René Acuña. México: UNAM, 1984–87.

Reyes-García, Luis. "Dioses y escritura pictográfica." *Arqueología Mexicana* 4, no. 23 (1997): 24–33.

Robelo, Cecilio. *Nombres geográficos indígenas del Estado de México.* Toluca: Gobierno del Estado de México, 1974.

Robertson, Donald. *Mexican Manuscripts Painting of the Early Colonial Period, the Metropolitan Schools.* New Haven, Conn.: Yale University Press, 1959.

———. "The *Pinturas* (Maps) of the *Relaciones geográficas*, with a Catalog." In *Handbook of Middle American Indians.* Vol. 12: *Guide to Ethnohistorical Sources, Part One.* Ed. H. F. Cline. London: University of Texas Press, 1972.

Romero Quiroz, Javier. *Historia de Malinalco.* Toluca: Gobierno del Estado de México, 1980.

———. *El Huéhuetl de Malinalco.* Toluca: UAEM, 1958.

———. *El Teponaztli de Malinalco.* Toluca: UAEM, 1964.

Sahagún, Fray Bernardino. *Florentine Codex: General History of the Things of New Spain.* 12 vols. Trans. Arthur J. O. Anderson and Charles E. Dibble. Santa Fe, N.Mex.: School for American Research and the University of Utah, 1951–69.

———. *Historia general de las cosas de la Nueva España (1540–1577).* Ed. Angel María Garibay. México: Editorial Porrúa, 1975.

———. *Historia general de las cosas de la Nueva España (1540–1577).* Ed. Alfredo López Austin y Josefina García Quintana. México: CONACULTA, 2000.

———. *Primeros memoriales.* 2 vols. Paleography of Nahuatl text and English translation by Thelma

Sullivan. Norman: University of Oklahoma Press, 1993–98.

Sanders, William T., and Deborah L. Nichols. "Ecological Theory and Cultural Evolution in the Valley of Oaxaca." *Current Anthropology* 29, no. 1 (1988): 33–80.

Sanders, William, Jeffrey Parsons, and Robert Santley. *The Basin of Mexico: Ecological Processes in the Evolution of a Civilization.* New York: Academic Press, 1979.

Scarborough, Vernon, and David Wilcox, eds. *The Mesoamerican Ballgame.* Tucson: University of Arizona Press, 1991.

Schroeder Cordero, Francisco. "La arquitectura monolítica en Tezcotzinco y Malinalco, Edo. de México." In *Cuadernos de Arquitectura Mesoamericana.* Vol. 4. México: UNAM, 1985.

Seler, Eduard. "Die holgeschnitzte Pauke von Malinalco und das Zeichen Atl-Tlachinolli (Timbal de madera de Malinalco y signo Atl-Tlachinolli)." In *Colección de disertaciones.* Vol. 3. México: Museo Nacional de Antropología e Historia, 1960.

Silver, Shirley, and Wick R. Miller. *American Indian Languages: Cultural and Social Contexts.* Tucson: University of Arizona Press, 1997.

Simpson, Lesley Byrd. *Many Mexicos.* Berkeley: University of California Press, 1971.

Smith, Michael E. *The Aztecs.* Malden, Mass.: Blackwell Publishers, 2003.

———. "The Aztlan Migrations of the Nahuatl Chronicles: Myth or History?" *Ethnohistory* 31 (1984): 153–186.

Solanes, María del Carmen, and Enrique Vela. *El Tepozteco, Morelos: Mini-guía.* México: INAH, 1991.

Soustelle, Jacques. *The Daily Life of the Aztecs on the Eve of the Spanish Conquest.* New York: Macmillan, 1979.

———. *El universo de los aztecas.* México: Fondo de Cultura Económica, 1982.

———. *La vida cotidiana de los aztecas en vísperas de la conquista.* México: Fondo de Cultura Económica, 1992.

Spence, Lewis. *México y Perú.* Madrid: Ibérica Gráfica, 1995.

Stark, Barbara L., and Philip J. Arnold III. *Olmec to Aztec.* Tucson: University of Arizona Press, 1997.

Stierlin, Henri. *Art of the Aztecs and Its Origins.* New York: Rizzoli, 1982.

Suchlicki, Jaime. *Mexico: From Montezuma to NAFTA, Chiapas, and Beyond.* Washington: Brassey's Inc., 1996.

Sullivan, Thelma. "Hiring of the Midwife." *Arqueología Mexicana* 5, no. 29 (1998): 44.

Taladoire, Eric. "El juego de pelota." *Arqueología Mexicana* 8, no. 44 (July–August 2000): 20–27.

Taube, Karl. *Aztec and Maya Myths.* Austin: University of Texas Press, 1994.

Tena, Rafael. *La religión mexica.* México: INAH, 1993.

Terrés, Elodia. *La Ciudad de México: Sus orígenes y desarrollo.* México: Editorial Porrúa, 1977.

Thomas, Hugh. *Conquest: Montezuma, Cortés and the Fall of Old Mexico.* New York: Simon and Schuster, 1993.

Thompson, Eric. *Mexico before Cortez.* New York, London: Charles Scribner's Sons, 1933.

Torquemada, Fray Juan de. *Monarquía indiana.* Ed. Miguel León Portilla. México: UNAM, 1980.

Townsend, Richard. *The Aztecs.* New York: Thames and Hudson, 2000.

———. "Malinalco and the Lords of Tenochtitlan." In *The Art and Iconography of Late Post-Classic Mexico.* Washington, D.C.: Dumbarton Oaks, 1982.

Tsouras, Peter. *Warlords of the Ancient Americas: Central America.* London: Arms and Armour, 1996.

Umberger, Emily, and Cecilia Klein. "Aztec Art and Imperial Expansion." In *Latin American Horizons.* Ed. Don Rice. Washington, D.C.: Dumbarton Oaks, 1993.

Vaillant, George C. *Aztecs of Mexico.* New York: Penguin Books, 1962.

———. "A Correlation of Archaeological and Historical Sequences in the Valley of Mexico." *American Anthropologist*, New Series, 40, no. 1, part 1 (1938): 535–573.

Valle, Perla. "Códices coloniales: Testimonios de una sociedad en conflicto." *Arqueología Mexicana* 4, no. 23 (1997): 64–69.

Vander-Meeren, Marie. "El papel amate, origen y supervivencia." *Arqueología Mexicana* 4, no. 23 (1997): 70–73.

Velasco Lozano, Ana María L. "El jardín de Itzta-palapa." *Arqueología Mexicana* 10, no. 57 (September–October 2002): 26–33.

Velasco Piña, Antonio. *Tlacaelel.* México: JUS, 2001.

Vento, Arnoldo Carlos. *Mestizo: The History, Culture and Politics of the Mexican and the Chicano.* Lanham, Md.: University Press of America, 1998.

Vivo Escoto, José Antonio. "Weather and Climate of Mexico and Central America." In *Handbook of Middle American Indians.* Vol. 1: *Natural Environment and Early Cultures.* Ed. R. Wauchope. Austin: University of Texas Press, 1964.

Von Clausewitz, Karl. *On War.* London: Penguin, 1982.

Von Hagen, Victor. *Los aztecas.* México: Editorial Diana, 1978.

Wasson, Gordon. *Teonanacatl, el hongo maravilloso.* México: Fondo de Cultura Económica, 1983.

Waters, Frank. *Book of the Hopi.* Drawings and source material Oswald White Bear Fredericks. New York: Penguin Books, 1973.

Weaver, Muriel Porter. *The Aztecs, Maya, and Their Predecessors: Archaeology of Mesoamerica.* 3d ed. San Diego, Calif.: Academic Press, 1993.

West, Roberto, and Pedro Armillas. "Las chinampas de México. Poesía y realidad de los 'jardínes flotantes.' " *Cuadernos Americanos* 50, no. 2 (March–April 1950): 165–182.

Willey, Gordon R. "Developments in the Archaeology of Nuclear America, 1935–60." *American Antiquity* 27, no. 1 (1961): 46–55.

———. *An Introduction to American Archaeology. Vol. 1:* North and Middle America. Englewood Cliffs, N.J.: Prentice-Hall, 1966.

Wood, Tim. *See Through History: The Aztecs.* New York: Viking, 1992.

Zantwijk, Rudolf van. *The Aztec Arrangement: The Social History of Pre-Spanish Mexico.* Norman: University of Oklahoma Press, 1985.

Zorita, Alonso de. *Relación de los señores de la Nueva España.* Prologue Joaquín García Icazbalceta. México: Salvador Chávez Hayhoe, 1941.

Zúñiga Bárcena, Beatriz. *Calixtlahuaca, Estado de México: Mini-guía.* México: INAH, 1991.

———. *Huexotla, Estado de México: Mini-guía.* México: INAH, 1992.

———. *Tenayuca, Estado de México: Mini-guía.* México: INAH, 1991.

INDEX

Page numbers in **boldface** indicate major treatment of a subject; those in *italics* refer to illustrations. Page numbers with suffix *m* refer to maps.

embroidery 336
emperor. *See huey tlatoani*
encomiendas (estates) **384–385**
English language, Nahuatl words in 288
Epiclassic period 14–16
equinox *310*
espionage
    nahualoztomeca (disguised mer-
        chants) 106, 347
    spies *(quimichtin)* 107
estates *(encomiendas)* **384–385**
ethnohistory 22
Etzalcualiztli (eating of grains) festival
    155, **296,** 328
etzhuahuancatl rank 103
Evening Star (Venus) 308
expansion, military. *See* warfare

F

face paint 111
Fagan, Brian
    on agriculture 322, 323–324
    on artisans 333, 335, 336
    on food 329, 330, 331
    on markets 338–339
    on roads 341
fallowing 321–322
family **352–353**
    children 353
    household relationships 94
famine 374
fan, feathered **211**
farmers *323,* **332**
farming. *See* agriculture and *chinampas*
fasting 91
feasting
    inauguration feast 78
    in royal residence 370–371
    weddings 354
Feathered Coyote *202,* **202–203**
Feathered Serpent. *See* Quetzalcoatl
feather work **210–212,** *333*
    armor and shields 115–116, *116,*
        117
        Ahuitzotl *chimalli* (shield)
            211–212
    chalice cover *212, 212*
    Christ the Savior icon 212
    commissioned work 334
    community of 334
    construction methods 334
    fan, feathered 211
    feathers as arts and crafts material
        320
    feather workers *(amanteca)*
        333–334
    headdress of Motecuhzoma II 211
    materials 333
fertility gods 146
fertility rites **326**
fertilization in *chinampa* agriculture
    325

festivals
    award ceremonies for warriors
        109–110
    maize festivals 55, 331
    monthly 295–298
    religious ceremonies and festivals
        153
    sacred landscapes honored in 55
    sacrifice and 155–156
    Toxcatl 48
    of water 328
fifth sun, creation of **140,** 161. *See also*
    Sun Stone
Filth Goddess (Tlazolteotl) **151**
fire 166. *See also* New Fire ceremony;
    Xiuhtecuhtli (Turquoise Lord; god of
    fire)
fire priests *(tlenamacac)* **89**
fish **330**
"Five Flower" (Macuilxochitl) **149**
flag, Mexican 144
floating gardens. *See chinampas*
Florentine Codex 24, **268–269,** 286
    feather work in *333*
    Huitzilopochtli in *148*
    nopal in *373*
    pochtecah in *345*
    pochtecah uniforms in *117*
    on priests 152
    on Sacred Precinct of Tenochtitlan
        153
    Xiuhtecuhtli in *152*
Flower Prince (Xochipilli) **152**
    as patron god of poets 282
    sculpture of 194–195, *195*
flowers as motif in poetry 283
flower wars *(xochiyaoyotl)* 46, **133–134**
flutes, clay **207–208**
food and drink **371–374.** *See also* agricul-
    ture and *chinampas*
    alcohol consumption 372
    Chicomecoatl as goddess of 147
    culinary sundries 373
    fruits 373
    maguey 371–372
    maize 372–373, *373*
    for military campaigns 129–130
    nutrition 374
    royal feasting 370–371
    sources of food 328–332
        animal food 328–329,
            373–374
        aquatic food 329
        fish 330
        game 329–330
        vegetables, cultivated
            330–332
        vegetables, wild 330
Formative period. *See* Preclassic (Forma-
    tive) period
fortifications **125,** 126
fortune-tellers *(tonalpouhque)* 153–154

Fountain System A (Tetzcotzinco) 246
Fowler, Catherine 68
Fox, Vicente 398
Franciscans *387,* 388
funerary beliefs and customs **159–175**
    burials and cremation 166–170
        cemeteries 170
        funerals of women who died
            in childbirth 169–170
        merchant funerals 169
        non-noble funerals 167
        royal funerals 167–169, *168*
    creation myths and death concepts
        160–162
    human sacrifice and 172–174
    mourning 108, 168–169
    places of destination 162–166, *164*
        Chichihuacuauhco *163,* 163
        Mictlan 165–166
        Tlalocan 164–165, *165*
        Tonatiuh-Ilhuicac 163–164
    souls 170–172, *171*
        ihiyotl 172
        teyolia 172
        tonalli 171
furniture 94, **369–370**

G

Galarza, Joaquín 272
Galindo-Trejo, Jesús 258
gambling **363**
game hunting 328–329, **329–330**
games 361–363
    gambling 363
    patolli 361, 361
    ullamaliztli (ball game) 361–363,
        362, 363
Gamio, Manuel **21**
Gante, Pedro de 285, 388
García Granados, Rafael 212
García Payón, José 256, 257
gardens. *See also* agriculture and *chinampas*
    in Archaic period 5–6
    architecture of 224–225
    Díaz del Castillo on 228
    in palaces 236–237, 370
Garibay, Angel María 90
garments. *See* clothing
Gasca, Don Pedro de la 211
gates to Sacred Precinct of Tenochtitlan
    63
General History of the Things of New Spain.
    See Historia general de las cosas de la
    Nueva España
geography of the Aztec world **51–72**
    city-states and neighboring peoples
        65–67
        Aztec Empire 66–67
        Chichimec 66
        Teotihuacan, heritage of 65
    linguistic history and distribution of
        Nahua peoples 67–71

Ochpaniztli (sweeping the way) festival (continued)
    sacrifice at 156
    at Tetzcotzinco 247
octli. See pulque
Olmec **7–10**
    iconography origins 10
    La Venta 8–9, 275
    Mother Culture of 10
    San Lorenzo 8, 276
    Tres Zapotes and origins of early
        writing 9–10
    writing of 275–276
Olmeca-Xicallanca 14, 16
Olmos, Fray Andrés de 266, 286, 390
omens 160
Ometeotl (God of Duality) **149**
    celestial plane and 138
    as supreme god 145
    tonalli soul and 171
Ometochtli (Two Rabbit) **149,**
    247–248
Omeyocan (13th sky) 138, 149
Opochtzin 39
Otomí 66
otontin order **103,** *104,* 122
Our Lady of Guadalupe basilica (Mexico
    City) 65
"owl man" (*tlacatecolotl,* sorcerer) 359–360
owls 160
Oxomoco 140, *141*
oztomeca (vanguard merchants) **345–346**

P
Pablo Macuilcoatl, name signs for 280,
    280
painter-scribes. *See tlacuilos*
palaces *86*
    architecture of 228, 236–237
    baths of Nezahualcoyotl 245,
        247
    gardens and zoos in 225, 370
    royal feasting in 370–371
    as royal residence 370–371
    of *tetcuhtin* 92
    of *tlatoque* of Tenochtitlan 84–86
PAN. *See* National Action Party
Panquetzaliztli (raising of flags) festival
    297
    merchants and 348
    sacrifice at 156
    at winter solstice 258
papal grants (*patronato real*) 387
Parsons, Jeffrey 23
Pasztory, Esther
    on Bench Relief 185, 186
    on Chacmool of the Tlaloc Shrine
        196
    on Coatlicue 190–191
    on featherwork 211
    on headdress of Motecuhzoma II
        211

on head of Coyolxauhqui 194
on jaguar warrior sculpture 201
on Ocelotl-Cuauhxicalli 179
on Sun Stone 182, 183
on Temple Stone 187, 188
on terra-cotta sculpture 204
on Tlaltecuhtli de Metro 190
on Xiuhcoatl 195
patolli (game) 76, *361,* **361**
patronato real (papal grants) 387
Patzcuaro **33**
peanuts 331
pectoral, double-headed serpent *213,*
    213–214
Pellicer, Carlos 399
peninsulares (Spanish-born Europeans in
    Mexico) **385,** 392–393
petlacalli (chests) 94
petlatl (mat) 94
pharmacopoeia 268
Philip II 264
physicians (*ticitl*) 359–360
pictographic-phonetic writing 275,
    275–282
    linguistic influences 275–276
    Nahuatl developments 278
    name signs *278,* 278–281, *280*
    place signs 281–282, *282*
    roots, prefixes, and suffixes 276,
        276–277, *277*
    syllabary *279*
    writing techniques 276
piercings **368**
pillalli (land belonging to nobles) 92
pilli/pipiltin (nobles) **74**
    gold and 214–215
    houses of 64, 237
    land of 92
    military ranks and 102
Piltzintecuhtli (Mercury) **308–309**
pineapple 332
Pintura del gobernador 272
Pipil Nahuatl language 69, 70
place signs **281–282,** *282*
Plan of Ayala 395
Plan of Iguala 393
plant domestication 331
Plateresque style 391
Plaza of Three Cultures (Mexico City)
    64, 242, 398
pleasure, gods of 146, 147
Pleiades (Tianquiztli) *307,* 307–308
PNR. *See* National Revolutionary Party
pochtecah (long-distance merchants) *345,*
    346, 346–348. *See also* merchants
    religious functions of 347–348
    trade and guilds 348
    types of 347
    uniforms of *117,* 118
pochtecatlatoque (commanders of the
    pochtecah) 347
Pochutla Nahuatl language 69, 70

poetry **282–288**
    Aztec poems in English translation
        403–406
    historical poetry 283–284
    postconquest poets 287, 399
    pre-Columbian poets 284
Pohl, John 111, 128
polygamy 74, 352–353
polytheism 144–145
Pomar, Juan Bautista 269, 270, 287,
    376
Popul Vuh 330
Porfiriato dictatorship (1876–1911) 21,
    394
porters (*tlamemehque*) **341**
    loads and distances 342
    organization of 342–343
    supply mobilization and 130
Portes Gil, Emilio 397
Posada, José Guadalupe 395
Postclassic period **16–19**
    Aztec 18–19
    Maya-Toltec 18
    Mixtec 18
    Toltec 16–17
    Zapotec 18
Potonchan 381
pottery. *See* ceramics
prayer 91
Preclassic (Formative) period **6–10**
    Chiapa de Corzo 7
    Olmec 7–10
prefixes **276–277**
pregnancy 354. *See also* childbirth
prehistoric period **5**
Prescott, William 19
PRI. *See* Institutional Revolutionary
    Party
priestesses (*cihuatlamacazqui*) **90, 357**
priests (*tlamacazqui*) **87–91**
    activities of 91
    becoming a priest 88
    residency at Tlatelolco 244
    structure of priesthood 87
    tlamatinime (poet-priests) 283
    types of *88,* 88–91
        cihuatlamacazqui (priestesses)
            90, 357
        Huitznahua Teohuatzin and
            Tecpan Teohuatzin 89
        Mexicatl Teohuatzin 89
        nahualli (sorcerers) 90
        oceloquacuilli (jaguar priests)
            90
        Quetzalcoatl (high priests)
            74, 88–89
        tetonalmacani 90–91
        tlamacaztequihuaque (Lords of
            the Sun) 90
        tlamatinime (teacher-priests)
            90, 283, 303
        tlenamacac (fire priests) 89